EXPLORING
World Cultures

EXPLORING
World Cultures

Esko E. Newhill

Umberto La Paglia

Ginn and Company

About the Authors

Esko E. Newhill is Professor Emeritus of Sociology at Indiana University of Pennsylvania in Indiana, Pennsylvania. He holds a Ph.D degree in sociology from Syracuse University. He has five years of social studies teaching experience in the New York high schools prior to becoming a university professor. He has traveled extensively in Europe, the Soviet Union, Mexico, South America, Africa. and India. He is a member of many professional organizations, including the American Sociological Association.

Umberto La Paglia has taught more than twenty years in the Philadelphia public schools. He is presently a social studies teacher at Northeast High School in Philadelphia. He holds an M.A. in history from Temple University and has served as an exchange teacher in a secondary school in England. His travels include Western Europe, India, Pakistan, Africa, China, Afghanistan, and Japan. He is a member of several professional organizations including the National Council for the Social Studies.

Authors and publisher gratefully acknowledge the assistance of Robert Dankoff, Stanlake Samkange, and James Goodsell in the preparation of this book.

© Copyright 1986, 1981, 1977, 1974, by Ginn and Company
All rights reserved.
Home office: Lexington, Massachusetts 02173
0-663-41737-6

Table of Contents

UNIT 1 EXPLORING CULTURE — 1

1 Introducing Culture — 2
What Is Culture?   2
Culture Has Structure   8

2 The Origin and Development of Culture — 11
The Development of Culture   11
Social and Cultural Changes Are Continuous   16

3 Cultural Uniformities and Variety — 21
Social Institutions   21
Political Activities   24
Economic Activities   25
Social Stratification   28

UNIT 2 EXPLORING THE MIDDLE EAST — 31

4 Crossroads of Three Continents — 34
Major Landforms of the Middle East   34
An Arid Climate   37

5 The Record of Historical Change — 43
The Ancient Middle East   43
Two Centuries of Foreign Invasion   54
The Period of Ottoman Domination   56
The Arab World Achieves Independence   58

6 Religion and Tradition Shape Muslim Society — 63
People of the Middle East   63
Family and Society: A Man's World   67
Islam: A Way of Life   70

v

7 Economic Life in the Middle East — 75
Agricultural Production Is Limited   75
Focus on Egypt   78
Rapid Population Growth Limits Economic Development   81
Industry Develops Slowly   82

8 Political Systems of the Middle East — 87
Nationalism Replaces Islam as a Political Philosophy   87
Politics and Government in the Middle East since World War II   90
Sources of Conflict in the Middle East   94

9 Cultural Contributions of Islamic Civilization — 97
Achievements in Mathematics and the Sciences   97
Developments in the Fine Art   103

UNIT 3 EXPLORING AFRICA — 107

10 The Varied African Landscape — 110
A Continent with Many Climates   110
Land Formations Kept Africa Isolated and Inaccessible   113
Africa's Mighty Rivers and Lakes   114
Peoples and Languages of Africa   116

11 The African Past — 120
Early Cultures of the Green Sahara   120
Ancient Kindgoms of Western Africa   122
Kingdoms of Central Africa   127
Ethiopa, a Coptic Kingdom, Becomes a Republic   129
The Coming of the Europeans   130
The Slave Trade   132
Europeans in South Africa   134
The Division of Africa   136

12 Family, Clan, Tribe, and Nation — 140
Tribal Loyalties Are Still Strong in Africa   140
Status Differences Exist within Societies and Families   142
The Extended Family Is Typical in Africa   144
Urbanization Brings Many Changes   146
African Religion   150

13 The Rural and Urban Economies of Africa — 155
Africans Are Mainly Rural Farmers   155
African Resources and Industries   160

14 African Political Systems — 164
- Colonial Division of Africa 164
- Government since Independence 168
- Challenges to African Independence 171
- African Foreign Relations 174

15 Africa's Rich Cultural Heritage — 176
- A Rich Literary Heritage 176
- African Sculpture 181
- African Music is Distinctive 183

UNIT 4 EXPLORING INDIA — 185

16 India: Land and People — 188
- Landforms of the Indian Subcontinent 188
- India's Climate Controlled by the Monsoons 189
- Indian Rivers 191
- Natural Resources 193

17 Exploring India's Past — 195
- Ancient Indian Civilization 195
- The Muslims Come to India 200
- European Expansion into India 202
- British Rule Brings Both Reform and Domination 204
- The Indian Nationalist Movement 207
- Gandhi and the Drive for Independence 210
- Independence Follows World War II 212

18 Changing India — 215
- The Caste System Affects All Aspects of Indian Life 215
- Traditional Indian Family Life 217
- Hinduism 221
- The Life and Teachings of the Buddha 224
- Indian Education and the British Influence 225
- Education in India Today 227

19 Working toward a Modern Economy — 230
- The Indian Economy under the British 230
- The Indian Ecomony Depends Heavily on Agriculture 232
- Central Planning in the Indian Economy 235

20 Monarchy, Colonialism, and Independence — 240
- British Government in India 240
- Indian Government Today 242
- Indian Political Parties 243
- Foreign Relations 246

vii

21 Indian Culture Shaped by Religion — 249
Buddhist Art 249
Hindu Art 250
Islamic Architecture 252
Indian Literature 253
Ancient Indian Science, Mathematics, and Medicine 255

UNIT 5 EXPLORING CHINA — 257

22 China: Regions of Contrast — 260
Climate and Terrain Divide China into Two Regions 260
China's Rivers Helped Shape Its History 265

23 The Old China Gives Way to the New — 268
Early Dynasties 268
European Traders and Missionaries Reach China 273
Western Nations Fight to Divide China 279
Revolutionary Parties Begin Drive for Change in Government 281
Nationalists and Communists Become Bitter Foes 283
The People's Republic of China 287

24 Tradition and Change — 289
Social Structure in Traditional China 289
The Traditional Family 291
Education in Traditional China 294
Chinese Religion and Philosophy 295
Chinese Family Life Today 298
Communists Build a New Society 301
Education under the Communists 302
A New Philosophy for China 303

25 The Chinese Economy — 306
Chinese Agriculture 306
Communist Farm Policy since 1949 308
Chinese Industry 310

26 China's National Polices and International Relations — 314
The Cultural Revolution 314
Political Organization 316
China's Foreign Relations 318

27 China's Contributions to Civilization — 321
Chinese as Early Scientists 321
Chinese Art 324
Chinese Painting 325
Chinese Literature 327

viii

UNIT 6   EXPLORING JAPAN   331

28   Japan: The Island Empire   334
Influence of Land and Climate on Japan   334

29   The Making of Modern Japan   338
Early Japanese Society   338
Feudalism and Early Contacts with Europe   339
The "Opening" of Japan   341
The Rise of Extreme Nationalism in Japan   344

30   Japan Adapts to a Changing World   349
Traditional Social Structure   349
Traditional Household   350
Social Structure Changes   354
Changes in Family Relationships   356
Education in Japan   357
Japanese Religion   361

31   The Economic Modernization of Japan   368
Meiji Modernization Took Many Directions   368
Rebuilding After the War   369
Factors Contributing to Economic Recovery   371
Japan's Economy Today   372

32   From Monarchy to Parliamentary Government   376
The Meiji Government   376
American Occupation Reforms   377
Good Foreign Relations Essential to Economic Growth   379

33   Japanese Cultural Contributions   382
Diversity of Japanese Art   382
Japanese Literature   386
Japanese Theater   388

UNIT 7   EXPLORING SOUTHEAST ASIA   391

34   The Variety of Southeast Asia   394
Southeast Asia Can Be Divided into Sections   394
Climate, Resources, and People   396

35 The Road to Nationhood — 400
- Ancient River Valley Kingdoms of the Peninsula   400
- Early History of Island Civilizations   402
- The Europeans Arrive   403
- European Influence in Continental Southeast Asia   406
- The Indochina War   409
- Peninsular Southeast Asia since World War II   411
- Independence for the Islands of Southeast Asia   413

36 Southeast Asia's Ethnic Diversity — 417
- Chinese and Indians in Southeast Asia   417
- The Traditional Family   417
- Southeast Asian Education   419
- Education in Present-day Southeast Asia   420
- Religion in Southeast Asia   422

37 The Economy of Southeast Asia — 426
- Agriculture in Southeast Asia   426
- Industry in Southeast Asia   432

38 Political Uncertainty in Southeast Asia — 435
- Political Instability in Continental Southeast Asia   435
- Some Island Governments Make Progress toward Democracy   439

39 Cultural Contributions of Southeast Asia — 443
- Buddhist Architecture in Southeast Asia   443
- Literature and Dance   445

UNIT 8 EXPLORING THE SOVIET UNION — 447

40 Land, Climate, and People of the Soviet Union — 450
- A Cold Country   450
- Four Major Vegetation Belts   451
- Land of Ethnic Diversity   454

41 The Path to the Russian Revolution — 457
- The Early Russian State   457
- A Russian State Develops   461
- Russia Becomes a Major Power   464
- First Signs of the Coming Revolution   466
- Russia in the Twentieth Century: A Vast Empire   469
- World War I and the Revolution   471
- World War II and the Postwar Period   474

42 Social Life in a Soviet Society — 478
- Tsarist Society Had Rigid Social Divisions   478
- The Traditional Russian Family   480
- Religion in Tsarist Russia   483
- Life in the Soviet Union   484
- Communists Are Hostile to Religion   488

43 A Planned Economy — 491
- Industrialization Begins with Peter the Great   491
- Soviet Agriculture Is Collectivized   492
- Soviet Industry Expands   495

44 Soviet Government at Home and Abroad — 503
- The New Government Is Organized   503
- Nationality Groups Struggle to Maintain Their Identity   505
- Soviet Union and the Western World   510

45 Russian Contributions to the Arts and Sciences — 515
- Science and Mathematics Receive Government Attention   515
- Development of Literature   517
- Development of Fine Arts   522

UNIT 9 EXPLORING LATIN AMERICA — 527

46 Challenges of a Varied Landscape — 530
- Physical Features Vary Greatly   530
- A Variety of Climate and Vegetation Zones   533

47 The Building of Latin America — 537
- Early Inhabitants of the Americas   537
- The First Americans   538
- Spain Creates and Loses Its Colonies   545
- Independence Movements Begin in 1808   548
- The New Republics Are Beset by Problems   550
- Revolutionary Movements and Changes   553

48 A Region Strong in Traditions — 558
- Social Stratification: Historical Roots   558
- Family Life Is Closed and Reserved   562
- Formal Education Is Limited   566
- Religion in Latin America   567

49 The Economic Life of Latin America — 572

Traditional Agriculture 572
A Variety of Agricultural Systems in
  Latin America Today 574
Changes in Land Ownership 576
Industry 577
Challenges to Economic Progress 581

50 Latin American Political Systems — 584

New Political Parties Emerge 584
International Relations 589
Relations with the United States 591

51 Cultural Contributions of Latin America — 595

Scientific Achievements 595
Development of Literature 596
Latin American Creativity in Music 598
Art and Architecture 600

Atlas 603
Index 615

Maps

World: Political	6-7
Development of Agriculture and Cradles of Civilization	14
Diffusion of Paper and the Plow	17
World: Major Religions	22
World: Major Economic Activities	26
The Fertile Crescent	35
The Middle East and North Africa: Physical	37
Ancient Egypt	45
Ancient Mesopotamia	45
The Land of the Ancient Hebrews	46
The Muslim World, 850, A.D.	53
Egypt: Land Use and Resources	79
The Middle East and North Africa: Land Use and Resources	83
The Middle East and North Africa: Political	88
Sub-Saharan Africa: Physical	111
Early Trade Routes and African Empires	123
West African States, Up to 1600	126
Sub-Saharan Africa: Land Use and Minerals	156
Sub-Saharan Africa: Political	165
The Indian Subcontinent: Physical	189
Monsoons of Southern Asia	191
Ancient India	197
The Maurya Empire	198
The Indian Subcontinent: Land Use and Resources	232
The Indian Subcontinent: Political	241
China: Physical	261
Ancient China	269
Trade Routes to China, 200 B.C.	272
China: Land Use	310
China: Political	318

Japan: Political and Physical	335
Japan: Land Use and Products	373
Japan: Industrial Regions	374
Southeast Asia: Physical	395
European and American Possessions in Asia and the Western Pacific, 1900	407
Southeast Asia: Land Use and Resources	427
Southeast Asia: Political	436
Indonesia: Political	441
Soviet Union: Political and Physical	451
Soviet Union: Resources	495
Latin America: Physical	531
Latin America: Climate Regions	534
Latin America: Vegetation	435
Pre-Columbian Civilizations	540
South America, 1800	549
South America, 1830	549
Latin America: Population	559
Latin America: Minerals	578
Latin America: Political	585

ATLAS

World: Climate Regions	604
World: Average Precipitation	605
World: Average January Temperatures	606
World: Average July Temperatures	607
World: Landforms	608
World: Land Use	609
World: Population Density	610
World: Natural Vegetation	611
World: Food Staple Production	612
World: Animal Resources	613
World: Gross National Product	614

xiii

Preface

This text is unique in its emphasis upon culture as the key to understanding people. Traditional world history courses have been Europe-oriented and have emphasized political history. We hope that our interdisciplinary approach will enable the student to gain a greater sense of the humanity of other peoples. We have tried to avoid interpreting the behavior and customs of other peoples in terms of *our* motives and norms. We have tried to view the culture of other societies in the light of *their* traditions and values. We seek to emphasize what sociolgists call *cultural relativism,* the principle that human behavior should be interpreted within the framework of standards prevailing in the society under study. We try to have the reader see customs as the people of that culture do.

The sequence of topics follows a logical pattern. The introductory unit provides some basic concepts to aid in understanding the culture regions taken up in subsequent units. Cultural differences are seen as a result of different learning experiences. The first unit provides the student with the proper intellectual tools for the study of world cultures. Each of the units that follow begins with a chapter on the geography of the area. Having located the people, we seek further understanding of them by delving briefly into their past history. Their present culture is to a large degree the end product of their historical experiences.

Having gained some understanding of the setting and origin of the culture region, we next turn to a study of the culture area in the world today. Family organization, religion, economic life, political trends, and relations with the rest of the world receive special attention. Each unit ends with a discussion of the cultural contributions of the people to the total human heritage. We hope that readers will become better informed about the non-Western world and gain the ability to accord respect for people whose ways of life are different from their own.

Our survival depends on our ability and wisdom to maintain a livable world. As our small planet becomes more crowded, the need to live as good neighbors becomes more pressing. It is our hope that this book will make a small contribution toward that end.

UNIT 1
Exploring Culture

Chapter 1

Introducing Culture

In order to gain some understanding of other cultures a student should be equipped with the proper tools. This is as necessary for an intellectual project as it is for some other task. Instead of hammers and saws, however, our tools are concepts that social scientists have developed in their studies of human behavior.

The most important discovery of the social sciences may be the concept of culture. It has been called a revolutionary discovery because it has forced people to abandon older explanations of human nature and provided new insights. Differences in life-styles are no longer explained on the basis of race or some other hereditary cause, but as a result of culture. Therefore, as preparation for the study of particular world regions, it is important that we first understand our chief intellectual tool for our project, the culture concept.

What Is Culture?

To most people the word "culture" means refinement or sophistication. A "cultured" person has good manners, knows what to do in all situations, and appreciates art, music, and literature. The social scientist uses the term in a different sense. The scientist sees culture as the entire way of life within a society. In other words, the ways a people think about the problems of living – the tools, houses, and customs they have adopted as their own – are part of the culture of a people.

Culture has been called "a blueprint for living." It suggests two important aspects of culture: *(1) It is a pattern of living that people are expected to follow. (2) Every person is born into an existing culture, which must be learned and which shapes one's life.*

Society and culture. The terms society and culture should not be confused. A society consists of people interacting in the many tasks necessary for survival. Usually they occupy a definite area of land to which they have a claim. Culture is the way of life a society creates to satisfy its basic needs.

There is no human society that does not have a culture. Societies without cultures exist among animals like bees, ants, and baboons. However, their members' behavior is determined mainly by instinct. Only human societies create cultures. A culture cannot exist apart from people.

Culture is a total pattern. In summary, culture refers to a people's total way of life. It includes everything an individual has learned as a member of a

A culture often expresses its uniqueness in the dress and ornamentation of its members. These women are from Kenya (top left), India (left), and Peru (above).

society and will pass on to future generations. It affects the system of government, economic system, art forms, music, literature, religion, customs, and all material objects of a society's technology.

Human personality and behavior are influenced by the culture in which a person is raised. Even such basic acts as eating, sleeping, and expressing anger or love are affected by culture. A hungry American's mouth will water when

> **Contrasts in Culture**
>
> As we browse through the field reports of cultural anthropologists — the social scientists who specialize in the study of the various patterns of existence, or cultures — we find the contrasts to be as many as they are striking. There are groups whose standards of beauty require the reshaping of portions of the body, such as elongating the head or flattening it, putting large discs into distended lips or earlobes, filing the teeth to sharp points, scarifying or tattooing the face or body. Members of some groups relish snails, grub worms, ant larvae, locusts, rotten bird's eggs, and broiled monkeys. What is more, in some groups a slain enemy is eaten. In some groups, certain infants are put to death; in others, the aged. There is also an incredible range of rituals, beliefs, practices, ideas, and outlooks on life.
>
> Some of these ways of life seem so strange — so "unnatural" — that, until recent times, it was difficult to conceive of any explanation other than that of biological difference. Just as birds, alligators, or elephants automatically developed their separate styles of life, so the differing patterns of human existence were assumed to be the expression of different biological heredities.
>
> Then came the almost unbelievable discovery, gradually worked out by the anthropologists, that these various ways are not transmitted through biological inheritance but are acquired and passed on through learning. People learn these ways of doing and thinking. This is the significance of the "culture concept," for culture includes all the ways so acquired.
>
> It is difficult to exaggerate the importance of this contribution of the social sciences. The insight that the essential human differences are a social product — socially developed and socially transmitted — is, in every sense of the word, a revolutionary discovery. It is changing and stretching man's thinking as much as did the findings of Copernicus and Galileo.
>
> From Robert L. Sutherland, Julian W. Woodward, and Milton A. Maxwell, *Introductory Sociology*, Fifth Edition (Philadelphia, Pa.: J. B. Lippincott Company, 1956), p. 16.

broiled steak is smelled. A hungry Hindu would be sickened and perhaps angered at the smell of cooking beef. In Hindu culture eating meat, especially that of a cow, is usually forbidden.

Emotions are not expressed in the same way in all cultures. When two Karankawa Indian friends meet after a long absence, they cry. On the island of Bali in Indonesia, people shout and sing at funerals. One's culture teaches a person the proper way to express feelings. The reactions are not due to biological differences but to differences in learning and training.

What is desirable and beautiful is largely determined for the individual by one's culture. In some areas of Africa, for example Benin, a girl is most attractive if she is fat. When she has reached the age of marriage, a young woman is fattened as much as possible. The heavier she is, the more beautiful she appears to suitors. The Western view that beauty requires thinness is a recent one. As paintings of earlier centuries reveal, stoutness was much admired.

Desirable life goals are culturally defined, and individual choices are influenced by these definitions. Because music was admired and rewarded in Germany as was art in Italy, these nations trained many great musicians and artists. Beautiful poetry is much loved in the Muslim world and in East Asia. As a result, the finest literature of these culture areas has been in this form. From a practical point of view, the values of a culture may not always serve the major needs of the people. Until the Chinese annexed Tibet, one-third of Tibet's young men became Buddhist monks. A greater choice of occupations might have served the needs of Tibetan society better. Likewise Indian and Latin American young people crowd the law profession but look down on engineering, for which there is greater need. Engineering is regarded as manual labor in these cultures and therefore scorned.

The norms of culture. People may express their culture in outward behavior readily observable by others. The Muslim facing the holy city of Mecca praying, the Chinese speaking their language, the Masai of East Africa spear throwing or the American playing baseball are all examples of outwardly expressed cultural behavior. Beliefs and values that influence our actions and affect our outward behavior are called *norms*.

Customs are a kind of norm that usually came about as solutions to human problems. They are classified into folkways and mores (pronounced *mor'*-ays).

Folkways are, as the word implies, the ways of the folk. They are the ordinary rules of daily behavior which are accepted by the members of a given society. Rules of dress, courtesy, food preferences, and many other customs of daily living are classified as folkways. Many cultural differences are the result of folkways. Whether one eats with a fork or chopsticks, sleeps on a bed or a hammock, or greets friends with a handshake or a bow, is determined by the folkways of the society.

Mores are customs which are believed to be necessary to the welfare of the society. If we fail to observe folkways, we may be mildly criticized or laughed at. However, mores are required behavior. If we do not observe them, we are punished. Stealing someone's property, eating human flesh, or having several husbands or wives at one time are all violations of mores in our society, as in many others. Yet some societies do not condemn these acts. In Muslim countries wearing shoes in a mosque or a woman's showing her face in public are violations of traditional mores.

Laws supplement norms. In addition to the folkways and mores, laws are often needed to regulate behavior. They are deliberately created and are enforced by appointed officials such as police. Unlike some folkways and mores, violation of laws carries definite penalties.

In rural or tribal societies the folkways and mores are often sufficient to regulate behavior. People obey customs because they share the same beliefs and because it is often not possible to do otherwise. Everyone knows what is the property of others, and, therefore, no thief could use stolen goods. Besides, the goodwill and cooperation of others is so necessary for the welfare of each person that few would risk losing it by disobeying customs.

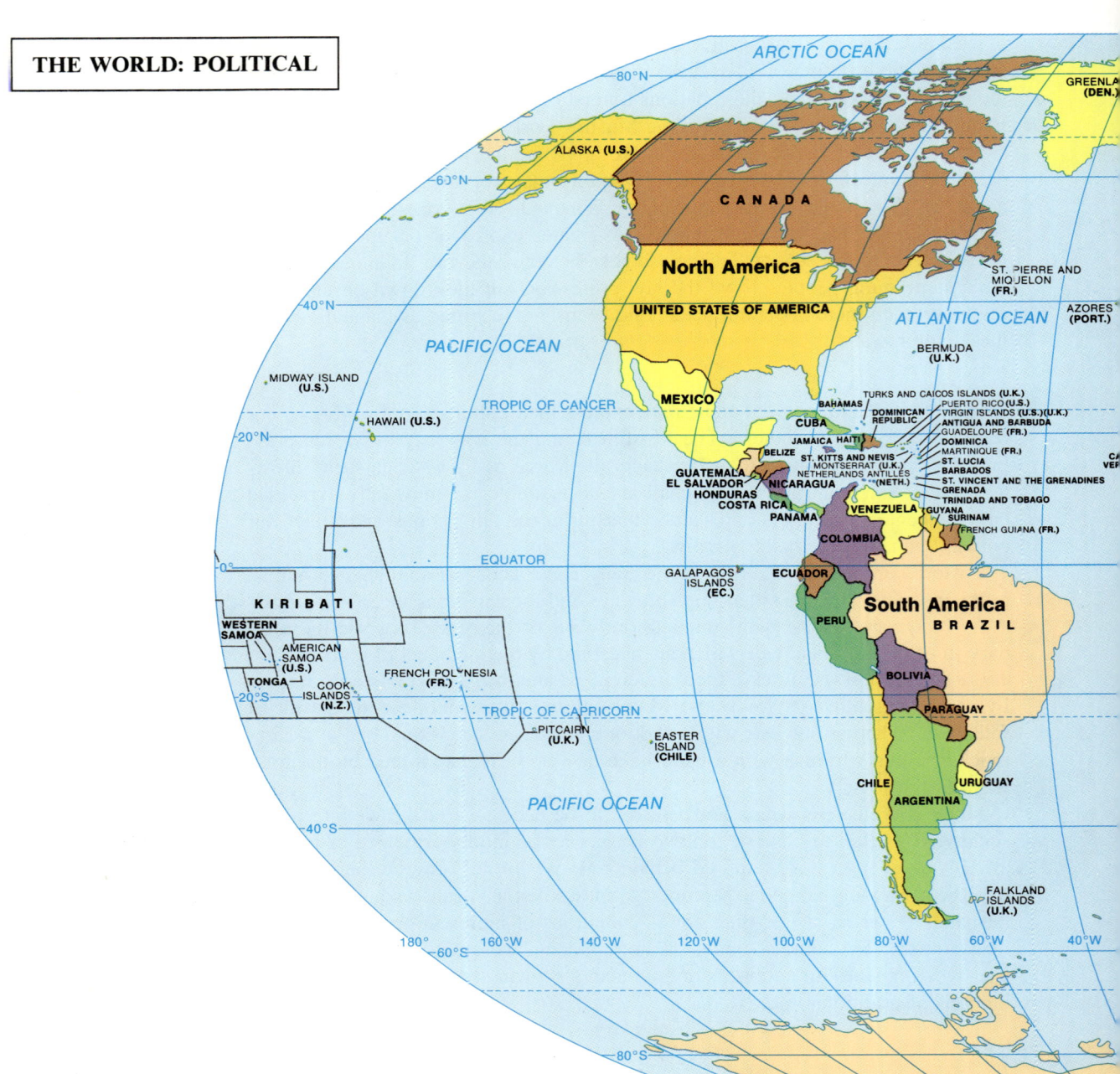

THE WORLD: POLITICAL

Abbreviations

AFG.	—AFGHANISTAN	E. GER.	—EAST GERMANY	NETH.	—NETHERLANDS
ALB.	—ALBANIA	HUN.	—HUNGARY	P.D.R. OF YEMEN	—PEOPLE'S DEMOCRATIC REPUBLIC OF YEMEN
AND.	—ANDORRA	ISR.	—ISRAEL	SWITZ.	—SWITZERLAND
AUST.	—AUSTRIA	LEB.	—LEBANON	U.A.E.	—UNITED ARAB EMIRATES
BEL.	—BELGIUM	LIECH.	—LIECHTENSTEIN	W. GER.	—WEST GERMANY
CZECH.	—CZECHOSLOVAKIA	LUX.	—LUXEMBOURG	YUG.	—YUGOSLAVIA

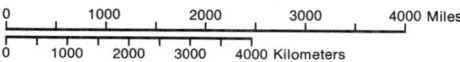

Most laws reflect norms and are intended to strengthen these traditional rules. Many people believe that unless laws are rooted in earlier customs they cannot be enforced. This is not necessarily true. Laws established by custom are accepted without much question because the rules are familiar. However, people can be educated to understand the need for new laws. Conservation laws in the United States, for example, are accepted because much has been said and written about the need for regulating the use of our natural resources.

Reviewing Your Reading

1. What is culture? Why has it been called "a blueprint for living"?
2. What is a society? How is it different from culture?
3. Define norms. Give an example of one.
4. Explain the terms "folkways" and "mores." Give an example of each.
5. How do laws supplement norms?

Culture Has Structure

No culture is a mass of unrelated parts like a scrap heap. Every culture has a *structure*. The seemingly separate parts fit together, somewhat like a jigsaw puzzle, to form a culture. Unlike the jigsaw puzzle, however, a culture does not fit together perfectly, and changes with time as new elements are introduced.

The fact that every culture has a structure permits orderly study. A Chinese village, for example, is not simply a concentration of people scurrying around haphazardly. It is an organized community of family units, economic groupings, and political establishments. There are orderly patterns of behavior, and the different groups relate to each other to form a total pattern of village life.

Importance of function. In studying a culture one tries to find out how the various parts interact with one another, or interrelate. The structure of a family, for instance, may affect patterns of childrearing, the use of time and space in the home, and other things.

Seen from the outside, patterns of behavior may be said to have social *functions*, or useful results. The social functions of the family, for example, include the care, training, and orientation of children. Seen from within, people sharing a culture have their own explanations, precedents, and reasons for behaving as they do. If one does not know what the parts of a culture mean to the people and what needs they satisfy, one does not really understand the culture. Foreign observers will then judge the behavior according to their own customs and values and may misinterpret what they see.

A few years ago a woman from the eastern United States visited a Navaho reservation in Arizona at festival time. As she watched the Indians do the rain dance, she ridiculed them for being so "ignorant and childish" as to believe that dancing could produce rain. Unfortunately she failed to understand the full purpose of the festival. More than a means of bringing rain, the dancing and festivities provided the occasion for a holiday. People everywhere enjoy festivals as a chance to escape the daily routine of work. How might someone from another culture interpret our Halloween? Do we really believe that witches ride broomsticks at midnight and ghosts rise from the grave? Perhaps a few people do, but such a general conclusion would miss completely the meaning of Halloween in our culture.

Ethnocentrism is common. Most people prefer their culture because it is familiar and comfortable. One's own customs seem so normal and sensible. However, it is well to remember that the people of another culture feel the same way about their way of life.

It is a common error to judge the customs of another society by one's own standards. When we make such judgments, we are guilty of *ethnocentrism.* Not only do ethnocentric people consider their society and culture superior to others, but they often regard outsiders with contempt.

Most people cannot avoid ethnocentrism to some extent. The members of other societies probably judge us ethnocentrically too. However, awareness of this tendency may help control it. Although we prefer our own way of life, we should be able to avoid looking down on other people because they are different.

Ignorance is an enormous aid to ethnocentrism. When it is possible to understand the customs of another people from their point of view, ethnocentrism decreases. In their life situation a given custom may be sensible even though it might not fit into our way of life. For example, polyandry, a custom in which one woman has several husbands, is practiced by some Tibetan people. Most Americans would condemn such a practice. When we understand that good land is very scarce in Tibet and that a group of brothers will share one wife in order to hold their tiny farm together, the practice becomes understandable. Knowing the facts, we can understand Tibetan society better.

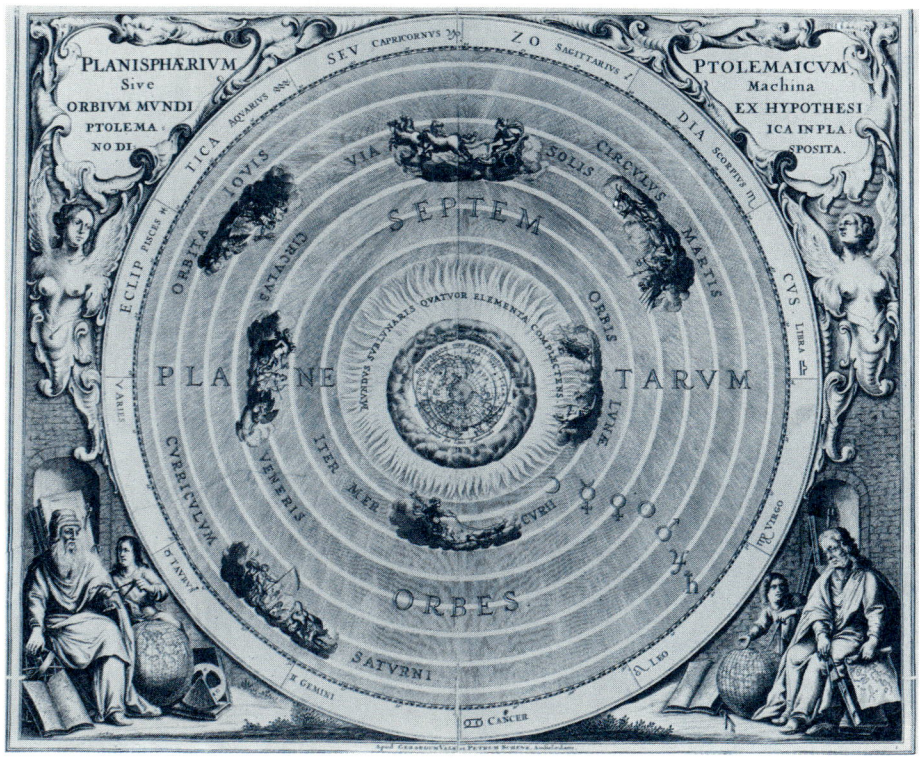

This map by the Alexandrian geographer Ptolemy shows the earth at the center of the universe, with the sun, moon, and planets revolving around it. Later scientists encountered strong resistance when they sought to disprove this geocentric view of the planets.

Racism: A world problem. *Racism* is an outgrowth of ethnocentric attitudes. It usually involves the belief that the races are not equally endowed and that some races are simply born superior to others. To a large extent racism is a modern problem. There is no evidence that ancient people believed in racial superiority. The Greeks were ethnocentric but not racist. To them all non-Greeks were barbarians. They regarded their culture as superior, but none of their writings suggest that they regarded themselves as racially superior to Africans or Asians with whom they had contact.

Ideas of racial superiority seem to have developed with the extension of European power to other parts of the world after the voyages of Columbus. It became a justification for the slave trade that expanded in the seventeenth and eighteenth centuries. Racism was an effort to make slavery respectable.

Racism is the most destructive form of ethnocentrism. Not only is it a major problem in the United States, but it is found in most areas of the world to some degree.

Summing up. People are cultural creatures with the characteristics peculiar to their culture. The first concern everywhere is to live. People apply intelligence to the problems of survival and gradually work out solutions. By such a process, a way of life – a culture – emerges.

People have traveled a long road from their beginnings to the present time. In the following chapter we will attempt to trace their journey, noting some of the major milestones along the way.

Reviewing Your Reading

1. Define the term "function." List a few customs in one society and tell what their functions are.
2. Define ethnocentrism. Why does it occur?

CHAPTER REVIEW

Recalling Names and Places

culture	function	racism
ethnocentrism	mores	society
folkways	norms	structure

Understanding This Chapter

1. People sometimes speak of "higher" and "lower" cultures. Can we make such distinctions? Why or why not?
2. All groups are regulated by some folkways and mores. List folkways of students in your school. What school rules would you list as mores?
3. Racism is a problem in many parts of the world. Name five countries outside the United States where people have suffered discrimination because of race.

Chapter 2

The Origin and Development of Culture

The full story of human cultural development will never be known. Yet much information has accumulated. One reason is the development of new techniques in archaeology that have led to more accurate dating of fossils and cultural remains. Thus many earlier beliefs about human origins and culture have been revised in the past quarter century.

The Development of Culture

Culture seems to have developed very slowly in early human societies. Changes in climate and other environmental conditions may have been the main causes of change in life-styles. Culture had to change when new adjustments became necessary. However, from very slow beginnings the rate of cultural change speeded up.

Discoveries of early humans in Africa. Recent evidence points to the first human beings living in Africa. In 1959 Dr. Mary Leakey, working with her husband Dr. Louis Leakey, discovered the skull of a humanlike creature that lived in Tanzania some 1.75 million years ago. They called this early human form *Zinjanthropus*. The Leakeys thought *Zinjanthropus* represented *Homo habilis* ("man with ability") who was believed to belong to the same genus as modern humans.

The discoveries of the Leakeys upset earlier theories about the age and development of modern humankind. But still further debate was touched off in 1972 when an expedition in Kenya, led by their son Richard Leakey, found a shattered 2.8-million-year-old-skull with a brain capacity much larger than that of *Zinjanthropus*. The brain capacity was also larger than that of Java Man and Peking Man, which date to around 500,000 years ago.

Richard Leakey believes that about 3 million years ago, three humanlike forms existed. Two died out and the remaining form, *Homo habilis*, evolved into *Homo erectus*, then *Homo sapiens*, modern humans.

At least some of these early species knew the use of fire and produced crude stone tools. About 100,000 years ago there appeared a species of human called Neanderthal Man. Although made to look rather brutish in pictures, these early humans possessed a brain as large as that of modern humans. It is believed that they had a language and were skillful hunters.

Louis and Mary Leakey found the skull of Zinjanthropus boisei *(also known as* Australopithecus boisei*) in Olduvai Gorge, Tanzania, in 1959. They determined that the creature had lived some 1.75 million years ago.*

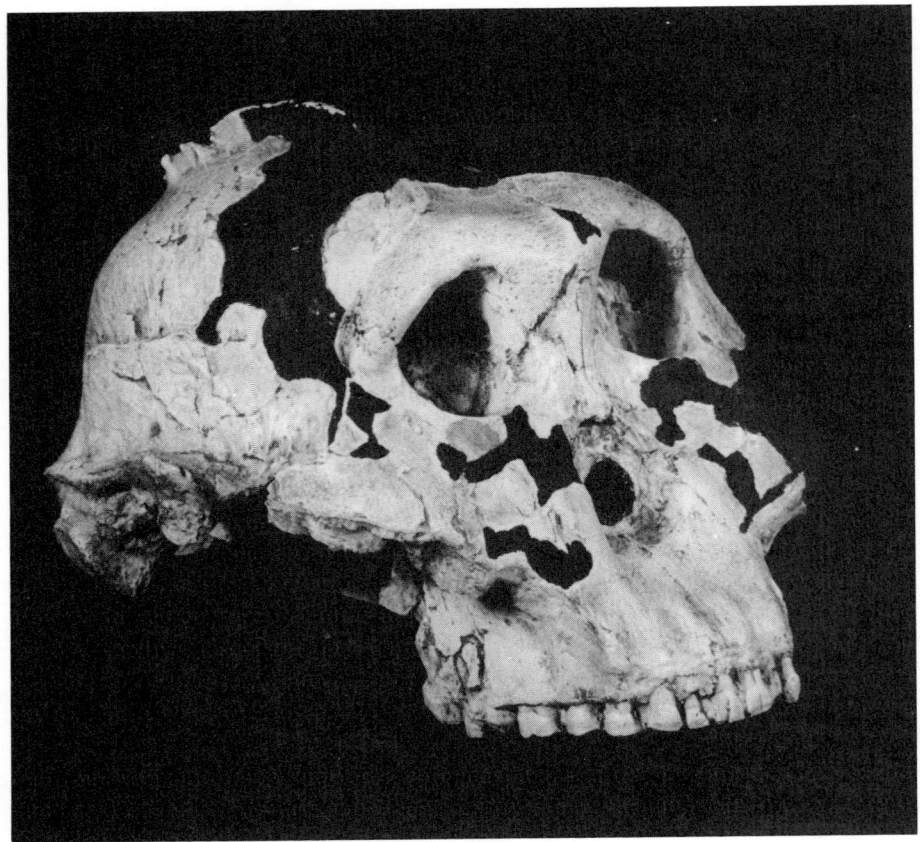

The direct ancestors of the modern human *(Homo sapiens)* appeared around 60,000 years ago, at the time the Neanderthal Man disappeared. Some think that *Homo sapiens* exterminated the Neanderthal. However, the two varieties of humans may have interbred until a single type remained.

Paleolithic culture. If we assume that the first true human being appeared 2 million years ago, this would mark the beginning of the *Paleolithic,* or Old Stone Age. The cultures of early people up to the invention of agriculture, around 10 thousand years ago, belong to this era. The era is so long that more than 99 percent of human existence falls into it. It was divided into three periods – *Lower, Middle, and Upper*. The Upper Paleolithic ended around 10,000 years ago in western Asia.

Many basic cultural achievements evolved slowly during this long time span. Speech, the earliest accomplishment, made humans truly unique among all creatures. This ability depended on sufficient development of the brain and nervous system. We do not know when this stage was reached. Until humans acquired language their cultural development was limited, since language is necessary for sharing most knowledge and skills.

Although humans probably learned to use many kinds of materials, only objects made from stone remain. Such cultural creations as the family, mores, religions, political systems, and economic institutions leave no traces. From artifacts archaeologists and anthropologists have learned that since humans lived by hunting and food gathering, they had to move about a great deal. Their mobility limited some types of cultural development.

Study of Paleolithic stone tools reveals a gradual improvement in skills. Lower Paleolithic tools are often called "pebble tools" because they consisted of pieces sharpened from large pebbles. Eventually humans learned to make a greater variety of better tools. In the Upper Paleolithic period they invented the bow and arrow, the boat, the harpoon, fish hook, and needle. We can assume that humans developed greater efficiency in other areas of their culture. There is evidence that they hunted more effectively, thereby increasing their food supply.

Paleolithic religion and art. Upper Paleolithic remains are more abundant than those of earlier periods. Discovered graves containing the dead had food, jewelry, and useful tools. Burying valuable objects with a body suggests that people had developed religious beliefs involving notions of life after death. The items were probably intended for the use of the deceased in the next life.

Upper Paleolithic people developed artistic talents. They skillfully carved small statues of human figures and painted many-colored pictures of deer, bison, mammoths, and other animals. Such pictures have been found in the famous caves of Altamira in Spain and Lascaux in France. Because many of the animals are shown wounded by spears and arrows, it is believed that one purpose of the paintings was magical. If an animal was pictured as wounded, that might weaken it in real life and make the hunt easier.

The Agricultural Revolution. About 10,000 years ago, in western Asia, human society began to undergo a drastic change. Humans discovered how to grow food and switched from being hunters, constantly on the move, to farmers settled in particular places. The earliest farming and animal husbandry began in those parts of the world where domesticable plants and animals lived. This change in life style is often called "the Neolithic Revolution." Neolithic means "New Stone Age" in contrast to the Paleolithic, which means "Old Stone Age." People living in areas lacking domesticable plants and animals did not experience an agricultural revolution. Such people include the Bushmen of the Kalahari Desert in southwest Africa, the native peoples of Australia, and some Eskimo tribes. They have retained their Paleolithic cultures until very recently.

Agriculture seems to have developed independently in three separate regions of the world – in the uplands of Mesopotamia (Iraq), in Southeast Asia (Thailand), and in Middle America (Mexico and Guatemala). Agriculture reached Europe and Africa from Mesopotamia. In the Mesopotamian highlands people relied on such wild seed grasses as wheat and barley for their food, because of the scarcity of game. About 10,000 years ago someone learned to control and increase the yield of this wild grain. This event opened the doors to a new way of life.

With the discovery of agriculture humans could give up their nomadic lifestyle to settle down and domesticate animals. As hunters they only had the dog as a domesticated companion. Following the discovery of agriculture, humans decided to tame other animals and use them as a source of food or for work.

Agriculture as a way of life soon spread in all directions. As the land lost its fertility, people sought other places for farming, gradually moving into Europe and Africa. Only in a few places, like the Tigris and Euphrates River valley and

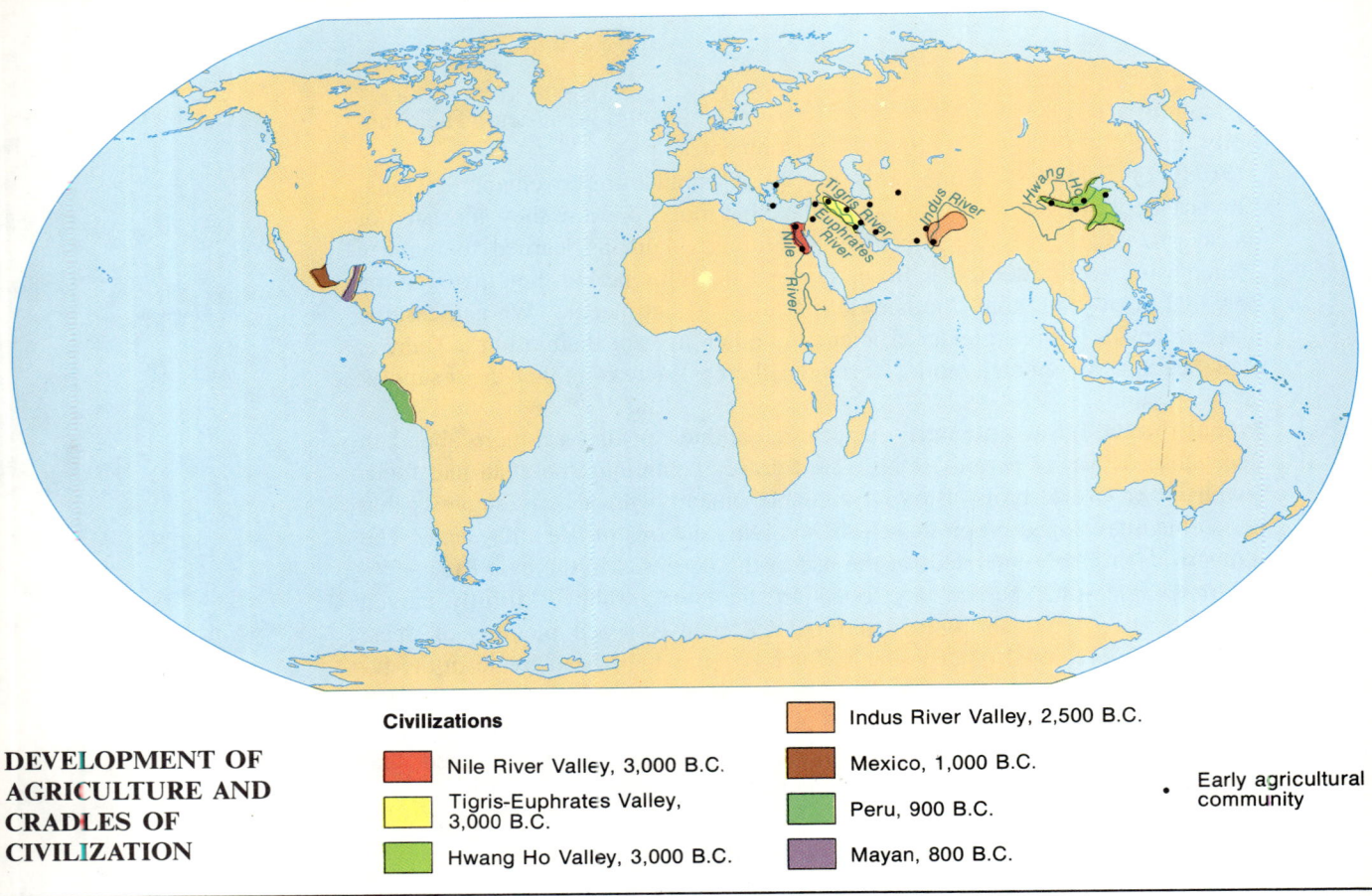

DEVELOPMENT OF AGRICULTURE AND CRADLES OF CIVILIZATION

Civilizations

- Nile River Valley, 3,000 B.C.
- Tigris-Euphrates Valley, 3,000 B.C.
- Hwang Ho Valley, 3,000 B.C.
- Indus River Valley, 2,500 B.C.
- Mexico, 1,000 B.C.
- Peru, 900 B.C.
- Mayan, 800 B.C.
- Early agricultural community

the Nile River valley, was the land always fertile. There the rivers flooded their banks regularly and deposited fresh layers of fertile soil on the surrounding areas.

The Urban Revolution. In the river valleys of Mesopotamia and Egypt, a surplus of crops enabled some people to engage in other activities, especially trade and manufacturing. About 6000 years ago a second revolution in human living took place in Mesopotamia. This was the Urban Revolution or the beginnings of city life. The city became possible when farmers produced a surplus that could be sold to the urban dwellers. It brought forth such major discoveries as writing, the wheel, metallurgy, the use of money, and more complex political

The First Farmers

Recent discoveries in Thailand may require some important changes in history books. For many years scholars believed that agriculture was first discovered in Mesopotamia. Recently, domesticated seeds of root plants, peas, and beans found in northern Thailand were proven to be 11,690 years old. Agriculture may have existed 2000 years earlier in Thailand than in Mesopotamia.

systems such as city-states and nations ruled by kings. These cultural developments caused major changes in living patterns.

After agriculture spread westward from Mesopotamia to the Mediterranean Sea region and eastward to the Indus River valley, many agricultural villages developed into cities. In the Indus valley a great civilization developed around the cities of Mohenjo Daro and Harappa. Present findings indicate that the culture of these cities had its origins in Mesopotamia.

The Industrial Revolution. The third great revolution in human culture began around 1750 and continues. This is known as the Industrial Revolution, which introduced machines to do work, changing people's relationship with their surroundings. Closely connected with this revolution in technology is a "knowledge explosion" that led to numerous cultural developments. Each new invention opened up still other possibilities, accelerating the rate of cultural growth. This knowledge explosion continues and, barring some great calamity like a nuclear war, will probably continue to transform human life.

The urban revolution began in the river valleys of ancient Mesopotamia about 6,000 years ago. Archaeologists' finds from that time include the ruins of a building in Nippur that had been used as a library (left) and a silver model of a boat that had been buried in a king's tomb in Ur (below). The boat is similar in construction to boats used by some of the people of southern Iraq today.

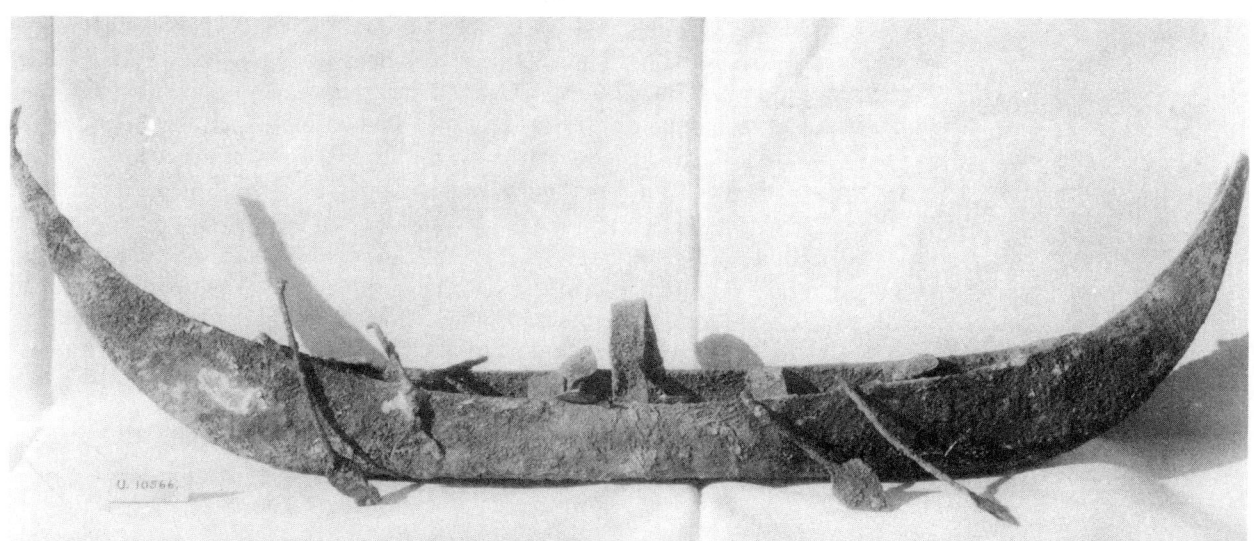

Reviewing Your Reading

1. What do we know about the first human beings?
2. Describe the Lower and Upper Paleolithic cultures.
3. How is Neolithic culture more advanced than Paleolithic culture?
4. What is meant by the term "Urban Revolution"?
5. How has the Industrial Revolution changed human culture?

Social and Cultural Changes Are Continuous

Societies and cultures are constantly changing. *Social* change refers to changes in human relationships and the organization of society. For example, in some societies men made all the important decisions, but now males and females make decisions as equals. *Cultural* change includes new technological developments like the automobile or television, as well as new religions, philosophies, and artistic styles.

It is hardly possible to have one form of change without the other, although people do not always realize this. Many Non-western nations, such as India, want to adopt Western technology but are determined that their traditional social system must remain unchanged. This is not possible. A major cultural change, like a new technology, will require new social arrangements to make it work, including changes in family living.

Four kinds of conscious or deliberate change can be seen in all cultures: invention or innovation, diffusion, acculturation, and revitalization. All of these forms have operated from early times, but never as commonly and universally as today. Let us consider each of these briefly.

Invention. We are so accustomed to thinking of inventions as mechanical devices or techniques that we often forget major social inventions exist. At first glance inventions may seem to be completely new. Actually an invention is only a new combination of elements, some of which may have existed for a very long time. The automobile, which was invented in the 1890s, was made up of parts, some of which had been around for thousands of years. The same holds true for social inventions. The Islamic religion, proclaimed by the prophet Muhammad, borrowed elements from the earlier religions of Judaism and Christianity.

In this steady accumulation of culture we may wonder whether anything is ever lost. This sometimes happens. Less efficient ways may be forgotten when better ways are introduced. Occasionally some great skills are lost, for example, the medieval technique of making beautiful stained glass and the early Chinese art of making fine porcelains. Earlier skills are lost for various reasons, but in many cases the need for a particular skill disappears.

Cultural change through diffusion. Another major source of cultural change is *diffusion*. This occurs when a custom or item of culture moves from one part of the world to another. Without inventions there would be no diffusion. However, without diffusion cultural change would be slower, since no society has ever invented more than a small fraction of its culture.

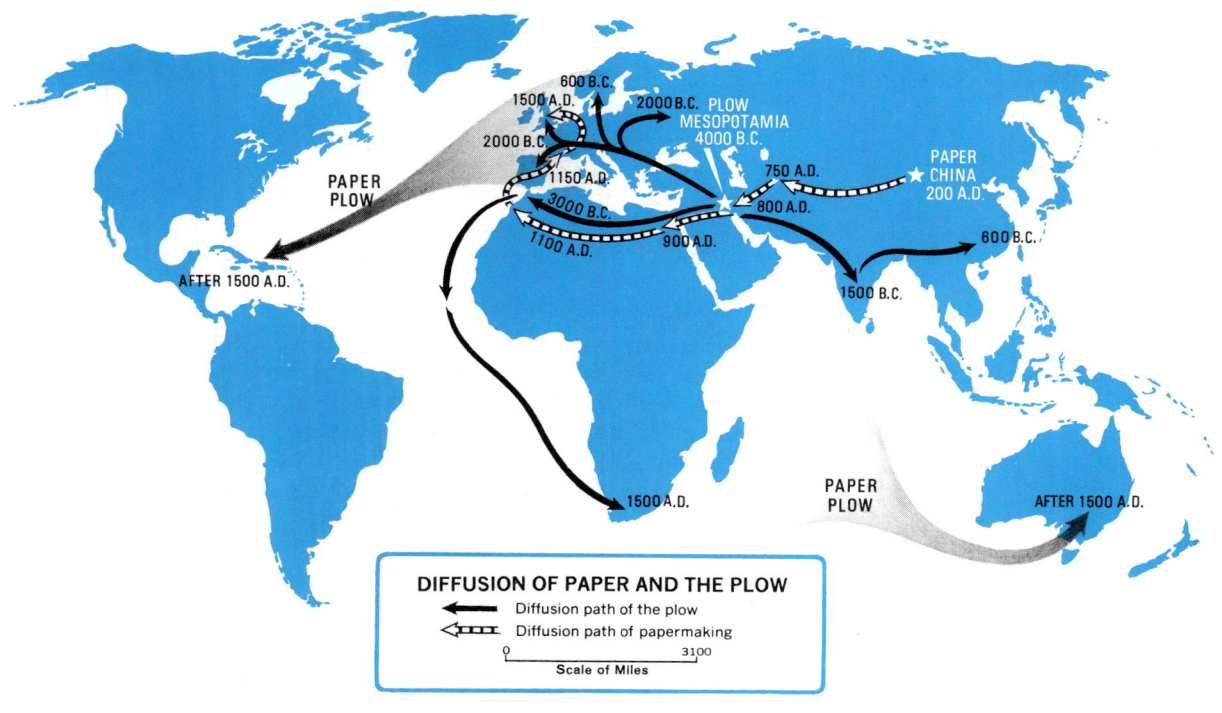

The inventions of one culture reach another culture and are adapted to its uses by a process of diffusion. These three men in the former British colony of Nigeria ride bicycles, an invention of the nineteenth-century Scots and British, down roads built in the 1960s with the help of the United Nations.

Culture by Diffusion

Ralph Linton, an anthropologist, has estimated that less than 10 percent of our culture has an American origin. Below he cites examples.

Our solid American citizen awakens in a bed built on a pattern that originated in the Near East but which was modified in Northern Europe before it was transmitted to America. He throws back the covers made from cotton, domesticated in India, or linen, domesticated in the Near East, or wool from sheep, also domesticated in the Near East, or silk, the use of which was discovered in China. All of these materials have been woven by processes invented in the Near East. He slips into his moccasins, invented by the Indians of the Eastern woodlands, and goes to the bathroom, whose fixtures are a mixture of European and American inventions, both of recent date. He takes off his pajamas, a garment invented in India, and washes with soap, invented by the ancient Gauls. He then shaves – a masochistic rite that seems to have been derived from either Sumer or ancient Egypt.

Returning to the bedroom, he removes his clothes from a chair of southern European type and proceeds to dress. He puts on garments whose form originally derived from the skin clothing of the nomads of the Asiatic steppes, puts on shoes made from skins tanned by a process invented in ancient Egypt and cut to a pattern derived from the classical civilizations of the Mediterranean, and ties around his neck a strip of bright-colored cloth that is a vestigial survival of the shoulder shawls worn by the seventeenth-century Croatians. Before going out for breakfast, he glances through the window, made of glass invented in Egypt, and, if it is raining, puts on overshoes made of rubber discovered by the Central American Indians and takes an umbrella, invented in Southeastern Asia. Upon his head he puts a hat made of felt, a material invented in the Asiatic steppes.

On his way to breakfast he stops to buy a paper, paying for it with coins, an ancient Lydian invention. At the restaurant a whole new series of borrowed elements confronts him. His plate is made of a form of pottery invented in China. His knife is of steel, an alloy first made in southern India; his fork, a medieval Italian invention; and his spoon a derivative of a Roman original. He begins breakfast with an orange from the eastern Mediterranean, a cantaloupe from Persia, or perhaps a piece of African watermelon. With this he has coffee, an Abyssinian plant, with cream and sugar. Both the domestication of cows and the idea of milking them originated in the Near East, while sugar was first made in India. After his fruit and first coffee he goes on to waffles, cakes made by a Scandinavian technique from wheat domesticated in Asia Minor. Over these he pours maple syrup, invented by the Indians of the Eastern woodlands. As a side dish, he may have the egg of a species of bird domesticated in Indo-China, or thin strips of the flesh of an animal domesticated in Eastern Asia that have been salted and smoked by a process developed in northern Europe.

When our friend has finished eating . . . he reads the news of the day, imprinted in characters invented by the ancient Semites upon a material invented in China by a process invented in Germany.

From: *The Study of Man: An Introduction,* by Ralph Linton. Copyright 1936 & 1964. By permission of Appleton-Century-Crofts, Educational Division, Meredith Corporation, pp. 326–327.

Diffusion is a very selective process, since people tend to select items that fit in with their existing culture. For example, Europeans found Chinese tea and ceramics to their liking, but did not adopt many other aspects of Chinese culture. Some cultural items have diffused to most parts of the world, like tobacco from the American Indians, coffee from Ethiopia, and cotton from India.

Military invasions and religious missions have often been active agents of diffusion. The new converts to Islam were filled with zeal to spread their new faith until it extended across North Africa and the Middle East, and eastward as far as the Philippines. Along with religion, other elements of culture, such as language, dress, tools, morality, and customs are diffused as well.

Cultural change through acculturation. Acculturation is change that affects relationships between people of different cultures who are in contact. When peoples of different cultures come into contact, several things can happen. One group may be assimilated into the way of life of the other group. In *assimilation*, cultural distinctions are eventually lost and both peoples come to share the same culture. Irish and German immigrants to the United States in the nineteenth century, for example, were rapidly assimilated. In another case, a group may be incorporated into another society but still live separately and practice its own customs. Many Chinese-Americans, for example, live in "Chinatowns" and retain their cultural distinctiveness. *Pluralism* is found in a society where people retain their distinctive cultures while at the same time sharing a territory and overall government. Often, however, contact between different peoples has resulted in the displacement or domination of one group by the other, or in one group's extinction. In the nineteenth century, for example, the U.S. government removed Indian tribes to reservations on unproductive lands. Some tribes, such as the Yuni of southern California, were hunted to extinction.

Cultural change through revitalization. Sweeping social changes within a society lead to *revitalization*. To revitalize means to bring back to life or infuse with new life. A society can be revitalized when new ideas are introduced or old, neglected values are reasserted. The result is a transformation of the people's way of life.

Revitalization often occurs in societies that are experiencing the stress of rapid cultural change. In the nineteenth century, for example, Japan underwent a revitalization that transformed it from a feudal society to a modern nation. Such movements may be sparked by gifted leaders who bring a message of hope for the future. New religions, such as Christianity in the first century and Islam in the seventh century; revolutions, such as the Russian Revolution of 1917; and social reform movements, such as the American civil rights movement of the 1960s, are examples of revitalization.

From slow beginnings the rate of cultural development has increased in tempo. This acceleration is due in part to the opportunities for innovations that a major invention often provides. The Neolithic invention of the wheel was first used for making pottery. In due time it was used for transportation, as a water wheel for irrigation, as a windmill for grinding grain, and for many other uses.

Developments in transportation and communication are bringing an end to geographic isolation for almost all the peoples of the world. Each of the culture areas we shall examine is affected by the diffusion of cultural elements from the rest of the world. Some of these influences are greatly changing patterns of living. While new opportunities are opening up for many, difficult problems may also result from such changes.

Reviewing Your Reading

1. Explain the difference between social change and cultural change. Give an example of each type of change.
2. How is a technical invention different from a social invention?
3. How does diffusion change a culture?
4. Explain how revitalization alters a culture.

CHAPTER REVIEW

Recalling Names and Places

acculturation	Industrial Revolution	revitalization
assimilation	Neanderthal Man	social invention
diffusion	Neolithic	urban revolution
Homo habilis	Paleolithic	Zinjanthropus
Homo sapiens	pluralism	

Understanding This Chapter

1. Many archeologists believe that the idea of agriculture was probably discovered by a woman rather than a man. Can you see why this was likely?
2. Recall the meanings of the terms "social change" and "cultural change". What changes of both kinds have occurred since your parents were your age? Since your grandparents were?
3. Can changes happen too rapidly and cause "culture shock"? Are there limits to human capacity to adjust to change? Discuss.
4. "Necessity is the mother of invention," says an old proverb. This is not entirely true, but necessity can be a stimulus to invention. Can you think of examples?

Chapter 3

Cultural Uniformities and Variety

People are sometimes so fascinated by the different customs, exotic foods, and unique beliefs of other societies that they overlook the many things they share in common. Because human beings belong to the same species, they have similar physical and psychological needs. All societies must take these needs into account in their cultural development. The culture of a people represents the best solutions available to that society.

Social Institutions

The people of every society have certain basic needs that must be met if they are to survive. Among these needs are (1) bearing and raising children; (2) providing all the material goods needed for survival; and (3) preserving the sacred values of its members. The arrangements that have been worked out over time to meet these basic needs are called *institutions*. They represent approved ways of fulfilling the requirements of living.

Once established, social institutions do not change easily. They are strongly interconnected with other institutions. The people may also regard their ancient institutions as sacred. New adaptations may then be difficult to bring about. For example, traditional family customs in sub-Saharan Africa require that a young man should aid needy relatives. A modern professional person in the city may be ruined economically if all his poor relatives expect him to provide for them. Changing times often call for new definitions of family obligations, but people often cling to old ways.

Cultural uniformities. George Murdock, an American anthropologist, compiled a list of activities that are found in every known society, past and present. These activities provide for each member's needs. After studying the ways of life of hundreds of societies, he listed more than seventy cultural behavior patterns that are universal. From this number a few examples are listed in the margin on the left.

Family structure. Of the three main classifications, the list of social activities is the most extensive. Hunting and gathering or tribal peoples, like the aborigines of Australia and the Indians of the Amazon Valley, have limited political and economic activities, but their societies have all those listed in the table. Numerous aspects of social organization in such societies are more complex than in our own society. For example, it took anthropologists more than twenty years to understand the complicated kinship system of an Australian tribe, considered among the most primitive people on earth.

SOME UNIVERSAL CULTURAL PATTERNS

- *Social*

    Family
    Language
    Medicine
    Education
    Athletics

- *Political*

    Community
     Organization
    Government
    Law
    Mythology
    Penal Sanctions

- *Economic*

    Cooperative Labor
    Housing
    Inheritance Rules
    Property Rights
    Trade

WORLD: MAJOR RELIGIONS

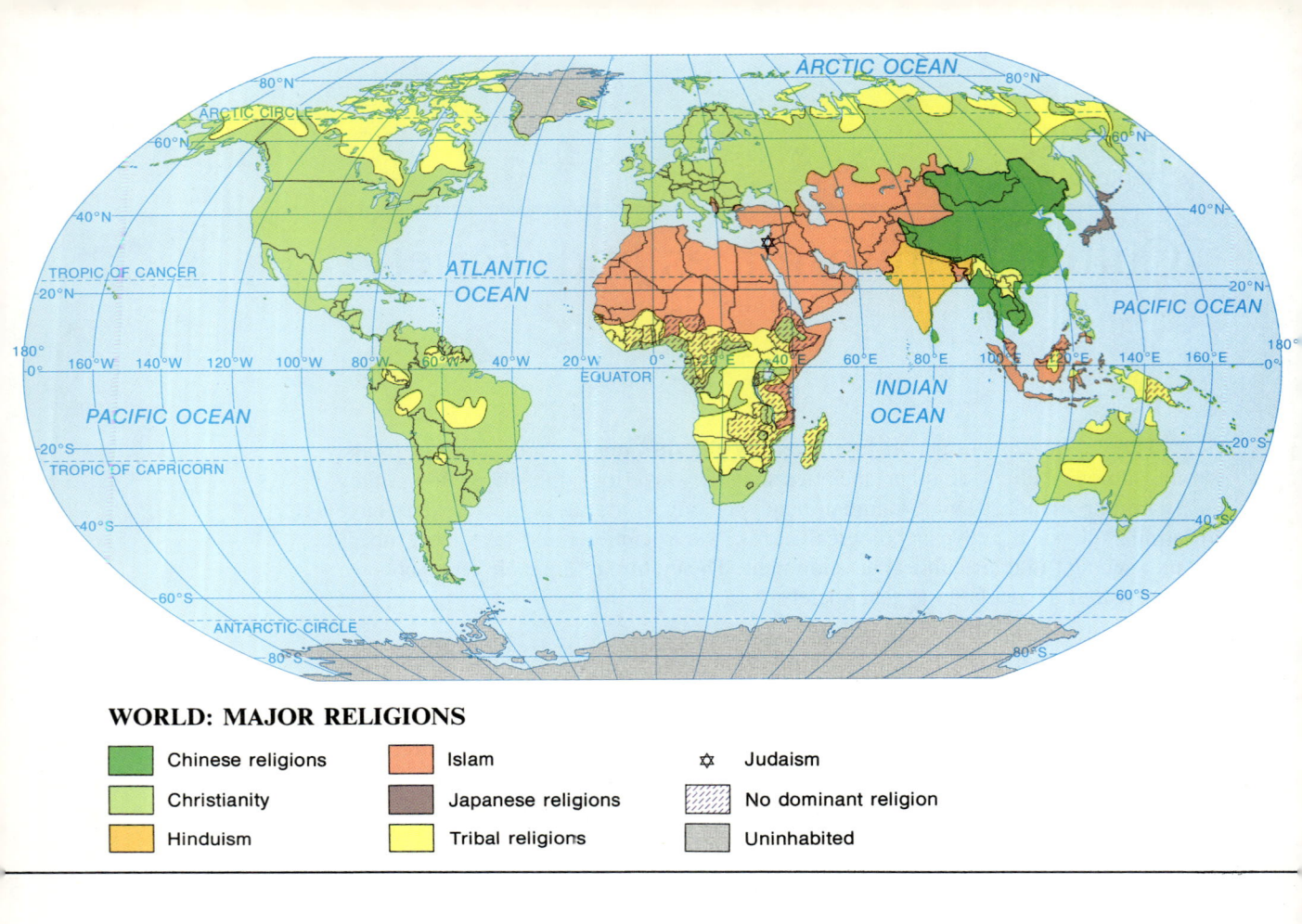

- Chinese religions
- Christianity
- Hinduism
- Islam
- Japanese religions
- Tribal religions
- Judaism
- No dominant religion
- Uninhabited

A *kinship system* consists of all the rules for determining who your relatives are, by blood and by marriage. These systems vary widely, but they all belong to one of eight types, depending on the classification of cousins. In our kinship system we use the term *cousin* for the children of our parents' brothers and sisters without distinction. In other societies a distinction is made between cross cousins and parallel cousins. The children of one's father's sisters or one's mother's brothers are *cross cousins*. The children of one's father's brothers and one's mother's sisters are *parallel cousins*. These distinctions are important because they may determine social relationships. In certain societies a person is supposed to marry one or the other type of cousin.

In American kinship, which is called *bilateral*, descent is reckoned through blood ties with both the mother's parents and the father's parents. Other kinship systems emphasize different lines of descent, and sometimes only one. In *patrilineal* kinship, for example, descent is reckoned only through the father's male ancestors. Kinship systems form the basis of larger social groupings, such as the *clan* and the *tribe*. The kin group formed by our system of bilateral descent is called a *kindred*.

Family organization. While the family is universal, the details of family organization vary enormously. The typical Western family, called a *nuclear* family, consists of the husband, wife, and children. However, in cultures like India, old China, Islamic nations, and Africa, grandparents and other relatives are also

This mexican woman prepares tortillas made of corn meal. Corn has long been a staple of the native American diet, so it is not surprising to find that many Indian languages have dozens of words for it. The Hopi, for example, distinguish ears of corn by such names as "hard blue corn," "yellow corn," and "purple corn."

members of the family. We call this an *extended* family. When siblings and their spouses live with their extended family we call this a *joint* family. Extended and joint families may be more common in the world than nuclear families.

Families vary in the number of marriage partners. When there is one wife and one husband, it is termed *monogamy*. *Polygamy* is a type of family in which several husbands or wives are permitted. Although polygamy exists in many societies, most families in the world are monogamous.

There are two forms of polygamy: polyandry and polygyny. *Polyandry* is a family type in which two or more brothers share a wife. This custom was practiced by the Todas of central India and some people in Tibet.

A more common form of polygamy is called *polygyny*. This type of family consists of a husband, two or more wives who are often sisters, children, and perhaps other relatives. Although many societies permit this type of family, including Islamic countries, Africa, and Oceania (Pacific islands), most families in these societies consist of only a husband and one wife.

Family authority. Families vary in regard to authority. Most are *patriarchal* with the husband or eldest male making the major decisions, as in China, Japan, India, and Muslim countries. A few are *matriarchal* with greater authority exercised by a woman. This type of family is found in some African and American Indian societies. Matriarchal families are less common than the patriarchal type.

In Western societies, including the United States, there is a strong trend toward the democratic family in which authority is shared by the husband and wife, and in which the children may share in the decision-making.

Language is universal. All people speak languages that have systems of grammar and rules of correct usage. Even an unwritten language can be a complex system of communication.

Every language creates words and forms with which to describe anything in its culture. Through language people classify reality as they experience it. The study of language, therefore, helps us to understand what is significant to people from their point of view. English has several thousand such words for the use and parts of the automobile. Arabic has about 6000 words for the camel and its characteristics. People always have plenty of words for what is familiar to them. When new cultural elements are introduced, people will either coin new words or borrow the necessary ones from another language.

Reviewing Your Reading

1. List the basic needs a society must fulfill in order to survive. How are these basic needs met?
2. Describe the term "cultural uniformities." Name some characteristics of our society that one can find in others.
3. What is a kinship system? Explain how some kinship systems are more complex than others.
4. Name and describe various family structures.
5. Explain how family authority varies.
6. How is language universal?

Political Activities

Political systems are structured to answer the following questions: Who has what power? When? To what end?

Universal political activities are fewer in number and less varied than social activities. Because people everywhere normally live in groups – in families that combine into clans, tribes, communities, towns, states, and nations – rules are necessary to regulate behavior and to make decisions affecting the group. People increase their chances for survival and a better life if they cooperate with their fellow humans. Occasionally cooperation breaks down and conflict occurs. People have suffered for it, as they still do today when war breaks out.

Families usually do not live far away from others, even in isolated regions. Neighbors can often help if illness, fires, or accidents occur. Moreover, people depend on each other not only in a time of need, but also for social companionship. Therefore, families and others group together to form communities, varying in size from a tiny village of less than one hundred people to a great city of many million inhabitants.

Government. Rights to land and the desire to provide for common needs, such as protection from attack, lead to the development of government. In some societies the elders may act as judges to decide what should be done. The final decision may be made by some person called a chief, a hetman, a hauptmann, or some other title. It is believed that quite early in history groups of families combined into tribes to meet these needs. In sub-Saharan Africa, and the more remote regions of Asia, Latin America, and Australia, such forms of government still exist.

Nomadic people who herd animals and people who live by hunting and food gathering have informal political systems. They are usually few in number, and their behavior is controlled largely by folkways and mores. However, agricultural societies develop more complex political systems. Growth of population and property increase the importance of government and laws. Development of urban life requires even more government and law. The culturally mixed population of cities cannot be sufficiently controlled by folkways and mores.

Most societies create an interlocking system of offices or positions to govern people. This type of bureaucracy, often called a state, is characteristic of modern nations. However, there are stateless societies. Some of the peoples of Africa and the Arabian Peninsula rely on elaborate kinship systems to maintain order. Conflicts are settled by councils of elders. In sub-Saharan Africa, societies of as many as a million people have been organized in this way.

Economic Activities

All of the economic activities listed on page 21 are found in every known culture. Everywhere people have discovered that some tasks can be best performed by working together. Because of the limits of an individual's strength, a team of workers can build a house or boat better and faster.

Political activity takes many forms. Here deputies of the Supreme Soviet of the USSR vote on a foreign policy resolution.

WORLD: MAJOR ECONOMIC ACTIVITIES

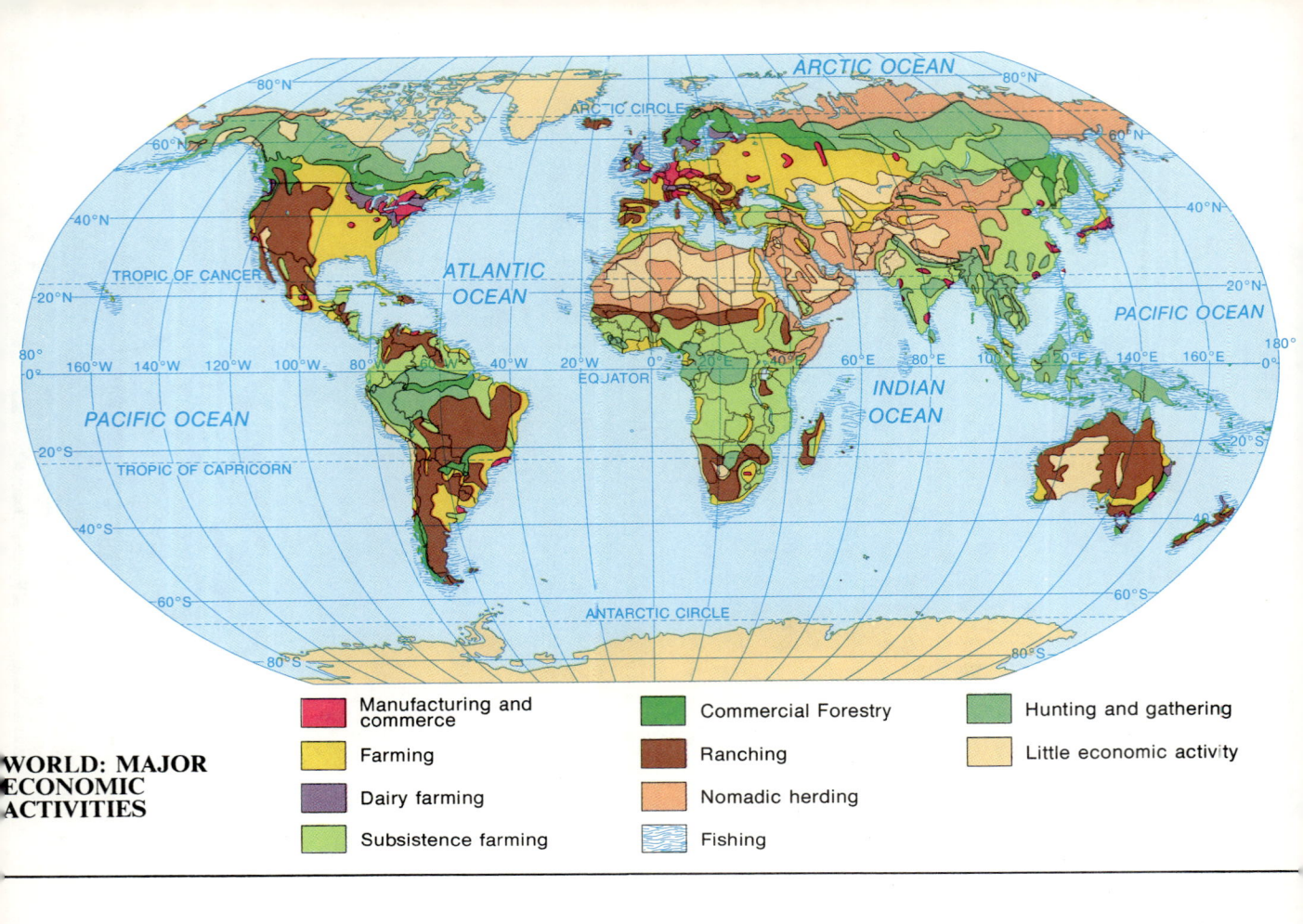

Legend:
- Manufacturing and commerce
- Farming
- Dairy farming
- Subsistence farming
- Commercial Forestry
- Ranching
- Nomadic herding
- Fishing
- Hunting and gathering
- Little economic activity

Cooperative labor. Some individuals have a knack for doing things better than others. Therefore some skills must be shared in order to perform a particular task efficiently. In every culture there is a division of labor by age and sex. However, the same divisions are not made everywhere. In our culture agricultural work is considered mainly a man's occupation, while in many African cultures these tasks are considered strictly women's work. We consider sewing and weaving a woman's job, but among many American Indian cultures this is men's work. A culture may not permit a man or woman with a special talent to practice it because it is not considered proper for that sex.

In spite of such restrictions all cultures recognize special talents, and from earliest times specialists have been welcomed. However, not until after the development of towns and cities were full-time nonagricultural occupations possible. The more complex the level of the culture, the greater the number of specialized occupations. The medicine man's job may be the oldest, but priesthood must be almost as old a profession.

Housing and inheritance. Everywhere people seem to need some kind of shelter. In the tropics, for example, some protection is needed when the sun is hot. Moreover, a house also provides protection from the rain, cold, insects, and animals that can make life uncomfortable.

More than shelter is involved in housing. Some buildings may have sacred or symbolic importance. A pagoda, a mosque, a church, and a synagogue are all sacred structures. Style of shelter may also reflect social class. A person of wealth or importance may demand housing that reflects high position in society.

All societies regulate the inheritance of property. In some the eldest son, often the firstborn, becomes the heir. This custom is called *primogeniture*. However, in a few places, for example Polynesia, the heir to the property is the oldest child, regardless of sex. A culture may also prescribe that some types of property must go to particular people. In the matriarchal Navaho society livestock is inherited by the father's sisters, but property of religious importance goes to a son.

Private property. The desire to own property seems to be a universal tendency in human beings. In certain societies, however, some enterprises, like forests, railroads, and factories, are owned by the government. In Communist countries most property is owned by the government.

Societies differ in the amount of importance they attach to the idea of private property. To some African tribes land and crops were generally not owned by individuals but by the tribe as a whole. European settlers could not understand African ideas of land ownership. When the Africans accepted money for land, they were not granting an exclusive use of the land but merely selling the right to share in its use. In general, smaller agricultural and pastoral economies tend to have community ownership of hunting lands, water areas for fishing, and the most fertile farmlands. More developed economies tend toward more private ownership of property.

The universality of trade. Economic systems solve the problem of getting and distributing food, goods, and services within a society. Hunting and gathering and tribal societies accomplish this through *reciprocity*, or reciprocal gift-giving among members of a kinship group. This complex network of social obligations became the basis of *barter*, which was the earliest form of trade between societies.

Trade is a universal feature of world cultures. Markets like this one in Tunis or their equivalents can be found in every part of the world.

Barter involves the direct exchange of one article for another without the use of money. In the African Congo the Bantu peoples and Pygmies depend on trade for their livelihood. The Pygmies trade meat, honey, fruit, and fibers for axes, knives, arrowheads, and other tools that the Bantu supply.

Certain societies are more enthusiastic traders than others but some trade exists everywhere. From earliest times the waterways of the world have been commercial highways, and the people who live along their shores have been the most active traders.

For any large-scale trading barter can be a clumsy process. Quite early in the development of civilization in Southwest Asia money came into use. It greatly simplified the job of determining the value of goods to be exchanged. Around 3000 B.C. metal currency came into use in Mesopotamia, while the use of coins seems to have originated in either Lydia or India somewhat later. Because of their beauty and scarcity, gold and silver became the favorite metals for money. In some parts of Africa, iron was also used for currency because it was considered valuable. An economy based on the buying and selling of goods and services is called a *market economy*.

A major outgrowth of trade between different peoples was the spread and exchange of ideas. This *cultural diffusion* has resulted in rapid cultural change for all peoples except the most isolated. By means of cultural diffusion many peoples have abandoned some of their traditional ways of living in order to share in the cultural achievements of the rest of the world. Modern transportation and communication have speeded this process of diffusion enormously.

Reviewing Your Reading

1. Why are political activities necessary?
2. Describe the term "cooperative labor" and give an example.
3. How may property be inherited?
4. How does trade affect people?

Social Stratification

Stratification means the ranking of people into higher and lower levels of prestige or status. Certain groups came to be regarded by the society as "better" than others, and therefore enjoyed more comforts, rewards, or power. Ownership of property or wealth in some form often determines one's status. For example, among some East African tribes ownership of many cattle gives one high social status.

In most societies occupation is an important factor in fixing one's status. The early professions of medicine man and priest usually had high status. Historically, in China the scholar had a very high status, while the actor was accorded a very lowly position. In our society successful actors are rewarded very handsomely. While we do not regard the scholars as lowly, we do not reward them nearly as well in money or status.

Class and caste. People could improve their social status in old China because Chinese society had a class system rather than a caste system. In a class system some advancement is possible.

In a *caste system* a change of status is extremely rare. Whether in a high or low caste, people must remain members of the caste into which they were born. India is generally given as the example of a society with a caste system. The Hindu view is that while it is not possible to change one's status in this life, one can improve one's status in future reincarnations, or rebirths, by living a good life.

An *open-class system* would be one in which a person's social position would be entirely determined by abilities, talents, and effort. This is the democratic ideal, but it really does not exist anywhere. Even in the most democratic society, family connections, racial and religious discrimination, and "pull" play a part.

Differences between cultures indicate the variety of ways in which people solve the same problems. We can observe great variations in dress, housing, mores, religion, government and so on. Religion can be defined as a system of beliefs, practices, and emotional attitudes that a group of people find helpful in dealing with the problems of life. No single element is found in every religion, not even a belief in a god or gods. Buddhism, a religion with over 150 million adherents, does not teach the existence of a Supreme Being. But most religions do share three characteristics: a belief in supernatural forces or beings, a moral code, and a system of rituals for controlling or invoking the supernatural forces.

Geographic influences on culture. An important reason for cultural differences is the geography of the area in which the people live. People who have to depend on what their immediate surroundings can provide have very limited

Fishermen from the West African city of Abidjan in the Ivory Coast (below left) make their living from the sea. Geography and climate are all-important to their economic prosperity. Andean Indians of South America (below) make the walls for a new house by ramming freshly dug earth into wooden forms. How have they adapted available technology to their uses? How might the introduction of more modern technology affect their lives?

29

choices. A natural resource, like the supply of water, can determine the crops grown, the size of the harvest, the necessity of developing irrigation systems, and the practicality of a nomadic way of life. However, geography *does not* determine the culture of the people who live in a specific area. Although geography may limit human choices, the way of life depends to a large extent on the culture of the people and the technology they develop.

Influence of knowledge on culture. The scientific knowledge available to a people is a major factor contributing to cultural differences. By applying scientific principles, people can develop new sources of power, better ways of producing goods, and more efficient means of transportation and communication. The Industrial Revolution not only changed the way most people earned a living, but also changed family life, education, government, and every other area of life. The rate of technological development increases rapidly, and it is bound to have a marked effect on living standards throughout the world.

Looking ahead. World cultures differ from one another in many details. However, interesting as these differences are, all cultures are very much alike. As all peoples become closer neighbors because of modern technology, it becomes more important to stress our common humanity.

Reviewing Your Reading

1. Define stratification. Name and explain two ways in which societies are often stratified.
2. Explain the difference between a class system and a caste system.

Chapter Review

Recalling Names and Places

bilateral descent	kinship system	polyandry
caste system	matriarchal	polygamy
clan	monogamy	polygyny
class system	nuclear family	primogeniture
extended family	patriarchal	reciprocity
kindred	patrilineal descent	stratification

Understanding This Chapter

1. Although many think of the American family as a nuclear family (husband, wife, and children) millions of American families do not fit this model. What other arrangements are common? Why?
2. Humans are social beings and join with others to form groups. Cities are great concentrations of people, and yet people are often lonelier there than in small villages. What happens often to social relationships with urbanization?
3. Cooperation, competition, and conflict are all universal forms of interaction between people. Any one of them may in some situations be constructive or destructive. Give positive and negative examples for each of the three forms of interaction from recent news stories.

UNIT 2
Exploring
The Middle East

| 3000 | 2500 | 2000 | 1500 | 1000 | 500 B.C. | 1 A.D. | 500 | 1000 | 1500 |

- SUMERIAN AND BABYLONIAN CIVILIZATIONS c. 3000–c. 1000
- DIASPORA 70–
- ISLAM FOUNDED 622
- OTTOMAN TURK EMPIRE 1453–1920
- EGYPTIAN NATION AND EMPIRE c. 3000–c. 1000
- SASSANIAN DYNASTY 200–650
- ABBASID CALIPHATE 750–1258
- PERSIAN EMPIRE 500–336
- BYZANTINE EMPIRE 312–1453
- MUSLIM EMPIRE 634–1258
- MAMLUK DYNASTY 1260–1517
- CRUSADES 1095–1229

THE MIDDLE EAST, INCLUDING NORTH Africa, is a vast culture region. It extends from the Atlantic Ocean to the foothills of the Himalaya Mountains. Lying in the middle between Europe, Africa, India, and Central Asia, it has long been a crossroads of trade and civilization. The earliest known civilizations – of Mesopotamia and of Egypt – arose along the two great river valleys of the ancient Middle East. The area between these two river valleys – ancient Palestine and Arabia – was the home of three of the great world religions: Judaism, Christianity, and Islam.

While Christianity prevailed in Europe, Islam, from the seventh century on, prevailed in the Middle East and in North Africa. A major theme of Middle Eastern history is continual interaction with Europe. This interaction includes the confrontation of religions, the exchange of ideas, trade and war, colonial domination and independence.

About one-ninth of the world's population, more than half a billion people, are Muslims. Of these only about 200 million live in the Middle East. Only one of the Middle Eastern states – Israel – does not have a Muslim majority. The dominant language of the Middle East is Arabic, which is the holy language for all Muslims. The Koran, the sacred book of Islam, is in Arabic. Throughout the Muslim world, even where Arabic is not the spoken language, the Koran is chanted in its original tongue. The Arabic call to prayer is heard five times a day in every Muslim town. The Koran, along with the sayings and actions of Muhammad, provide a strong cultural tie among all Muslims. They prescribe proper behavior in the family and in economic and political life.

Islam is the unifying element in the large and heterogeneous area that is the Middle East. However, as we have seen, Islam is not limited to this culture region. On the contrary, the majority of Muslims live east of this area – in India, Pakistan, Bangladesh, Indonesia, and Malaysia. There are also many Muslims in sub-Saharan Africa, in the Soviet Union, in China, in the Philippines, and elsewhere. But all of these countries belong to culture regions that are distinct from the one we are now studying. They will be taken up later in this book.

Timeline

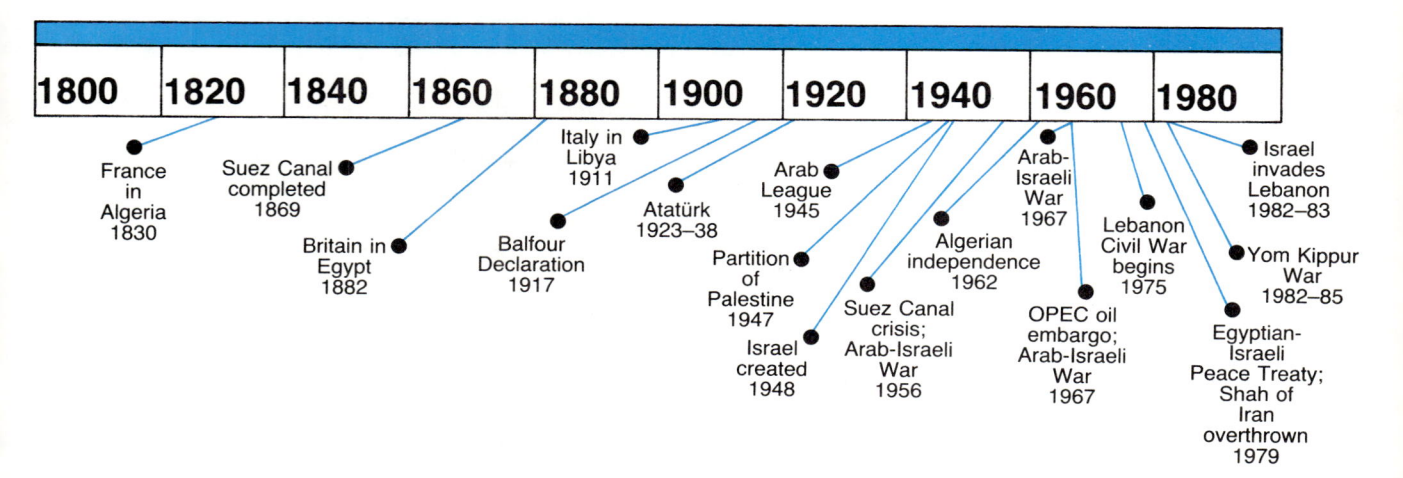

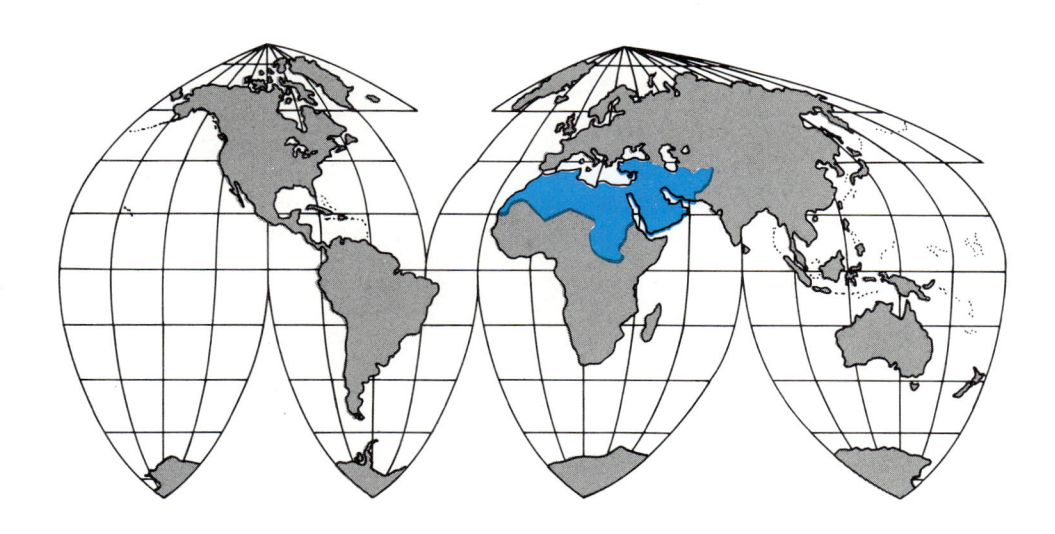

1830	France in Algeria
1869	Suez Canal completed
1882	Britain in Egypt
1911	Italy in Libya
1917	Balfour Declaration
1923–38	Atatürk
1945	Arab League
1947	Partition of Palestine
1948	Israel created
1956	Suez Canal crisis; Arab-Israeli War
1962	Algerian independence
1967	Arab-Israeli War
1967	OPEC oil embargo; Arab-Israeli War
1975	Lebanon Civil War begins
1979	Egyptian-Israeli Peace Treaty; Shah of Iran overthrown
1982–83	Israel invades Lebanon
1982–85	Yom Kippur War

The focus here is on the region where Islam first appeared and first flourished. It is the home of four great peoples – the Arabs, the Persians, the Turks, and the Jews. Its history is the story of the interaction of these peoples, and of their common interaction with the people of Europe, from the seventh to the twentieth centuries.

Chapter 4

Crossroads of Three Continents

Each unit in this book begins with a geographical description, for land and climate affect a culture in many important ways. Mountains and deserts may serve as barriers between different peoples and different languages. The presence or absence of water determines population densities and ways of living. Rivers and seacoasts offer opportunities for trade and for the development of civilization.

Major Landforms of the Middle East

The enormous region of the Middle East can be divided into four smaller areas. In the center are the five small countries of Syria, Lebanon, Jordan, Iraq, and Israel. The map on page 37 shows that this area is largely plateau. It contains some of the most fertile lands in the Middle East as well as stretches of barren desert.

To the north of these core countries are the larger, more mountainous nations of Turkey, Iran, and Afghanistan. South of this core lies the Arabian Peninsula, which is surrounded by the Persian Gulf, the Indian Ocean, and the Red Sea. This area is also plateau, consisting mainly of deserts.

West of the core area stretch the countries of northern Africa bordering the Mediterranean Sea. Although these are African nations, their language, history, and customs connect them with the Middle Eastern core and with the Arabian Peninsula. The Sahara, which extends east-west across the length of North Africa, has always hindered close connections between the northern and southern parts of this vast continent.

The center of the Middle East lies within the Fertile Crescent. The area between the Mediterranean Sea and the Persian Gulf is often known as the Fertile Crescent. This is because the area where the crops can be grown extends north along the Mediterranean coast, continues eastward in an arc, and follows the Tigris and Euphrates rivers southeast until they flow into the Persian Gulf. Bordering the crescent is the largely uninhabited Syrian Desert.

Melted winter snow and rains in the mountains of eastern Turkey bring flood waters down the Tigris and Euphrates rivers in May and June. This flooding brings much needed water to the otherwise dry land and makes agriculture possible. However, the amount of flooding within the Fertile Crescent is unpredictable. It is sometimes so heavy that houses are washed away. Iraq, whose ancient name was Mesopotamia, meaning "the land between the rivers," has been particulary troubled by the irregularity of its water supply from ancient times.

THE FERTILE CRESCENT

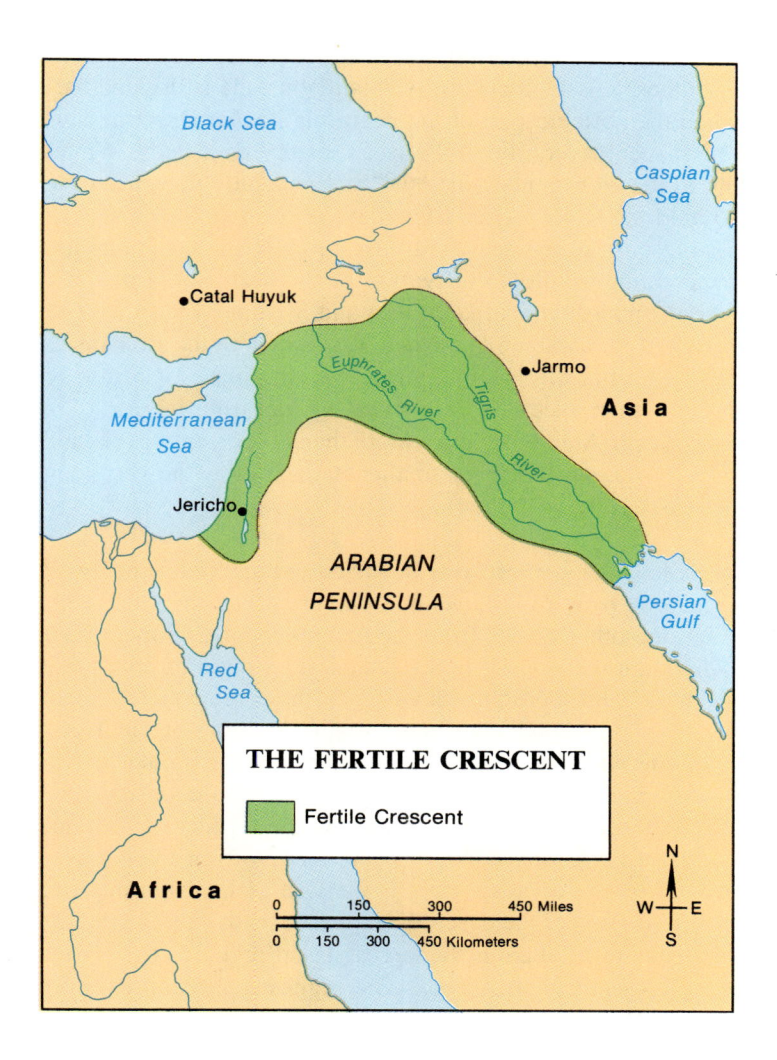

The great civilizations of Sumeria and Babylonia flourished in the eastern Fertile Crescent more than 3000 years ago. Here too, from the eighth to the thirteenth centuries, was the heartland of the Muslim world, with Baghdad as its capital.

The western part of the Fertile Crescent was the "Land of Milk and Honey," the "promised land" of the ancient Hebrews, or Jews. The great cities of Jerusalem, Damascus, and Aleppo are some of the oldest continually inhabited spots in the world. After the Romans completely conquered this area in the first century A.D., they renamed the land west of the Jordan River Palestine, after one of the enemies of the Jews, the Philistines. The Jews never forgot their attachment to this land, which they have always known as Israel.

The entire eastern Mediterranean coast was known to the Romans as "Syria." Today the eastern and central parts of the Fertile Crescent are occupied by the modern states of Iraq and Syria. Lebanon and Israel occupy the rest of the coastal strip. The country of Jordan, east of the Jordan River, is mainly a desert land.

35

The Arabian Peninsula is mostly desert. Except for some fertile regions on the mountainous southern coast, the entire Arabian Peninsula is dry and barren. The Romans called the northern part of the peninsula *Arabia Deserta*. This huge region has no permanent rivers, but only *wadis*. or dry river beds. Winter rains cause the wadis to run in torrents, since the land generally does not have enough vegetation to hold the water. After a few days everything is dry again.

Settled life is possible only in the scattered *oases,* where the ground water gathers in sufficient amounts to allow cultivation of the soil. Some of these oases are large enough to support cities, like Mecca and Medina in the west.

The southernmost part of the Arabian Peninsula was known to the Romans as *Arabia Felix,* meaning "Arabia the Happy." Here was the place of origin of frankincense, myrrh, and other spices, some coming by boat from India.

Today the country of Saudi Arabia occupies more than 80 percent of the land area of the Arabian Peninsula. A number of smaller states occupy the very long eastern and southern coasts.

North Africa. The Nile is the greatest river in Africa and the lifeline of Egypt and the Sudan. The map on page 111 shows that one branch of the Nile originates in Central Africa; the other comes from the mountains of Ethiopia. They meet at the city of Khartoum (car-*toom'*) in the Sudan. The water of both these sources originates in the annual monsoon rains. Since these rains are seasonal and regular, the Nile flooding is predictable, unlike the flooding of the Tigris and Euphrates in Iraq. The water rises in Egypt regularly every summer, overflowing its banks and watering the surrounding valley. It also deposits large amounts of silt in the delta region, gradually increasing the fertility of the soil. For this reason, the ancient Egyptians called their land the "Gift of the Nile."

To the west of the narrow Nile valley are the Western and Libyan deserts, both a part of the Sahara. Westward the desert extends thousands of miles, as far as the Atlantic Ocean. The great Sahara is the largest desert region in the world. *Sahara* means desert or wasteland in Arabic. The highest temperatures ever recorded have been in the Sahara. In the far west lie the towering Atlas Mountains. Between these mountains and the coast there is a fertile plain.

The northern African coast was an integral part of the Roman empire in ancient times. The Arabs, coming from Arabia, were familiar with the desert, and found North Africa easy to conquer. The Arab conquest in the seventh century broke the cultural ties of this area with the European lands along the Mediterranean and joined North Africa to the Middle East.

Turkey and Iran are plateaus ringed by mountains. Turkey is divided in two parts by the straits connecting the Mediterranean with the Black Sea. The smaller western part is in Europe. The larger eastern part is sometimes called Asia Minor, but a more common name for this area is Anatolia. Central Anatolia is a plateau consisting of dry grasslands. The Pontine Mountains in the north and the Taurus Mountains in the south separate the plateau from the coast. Turkey was the name Europeans gave this area after its conquest by the Muslim Turks, beginning in the eleventh century.

Iran, like Turkey, is also a large central plateau surrounded by mountains, notably the Elburz (el-*boarz'*) range in the north, and the Zagros (*zag'* rus) in the west. In southwestern Iran is the region known as *Fars*.

THE MIDDLE EAST AND NORTH AFRICA: PHYSICAL

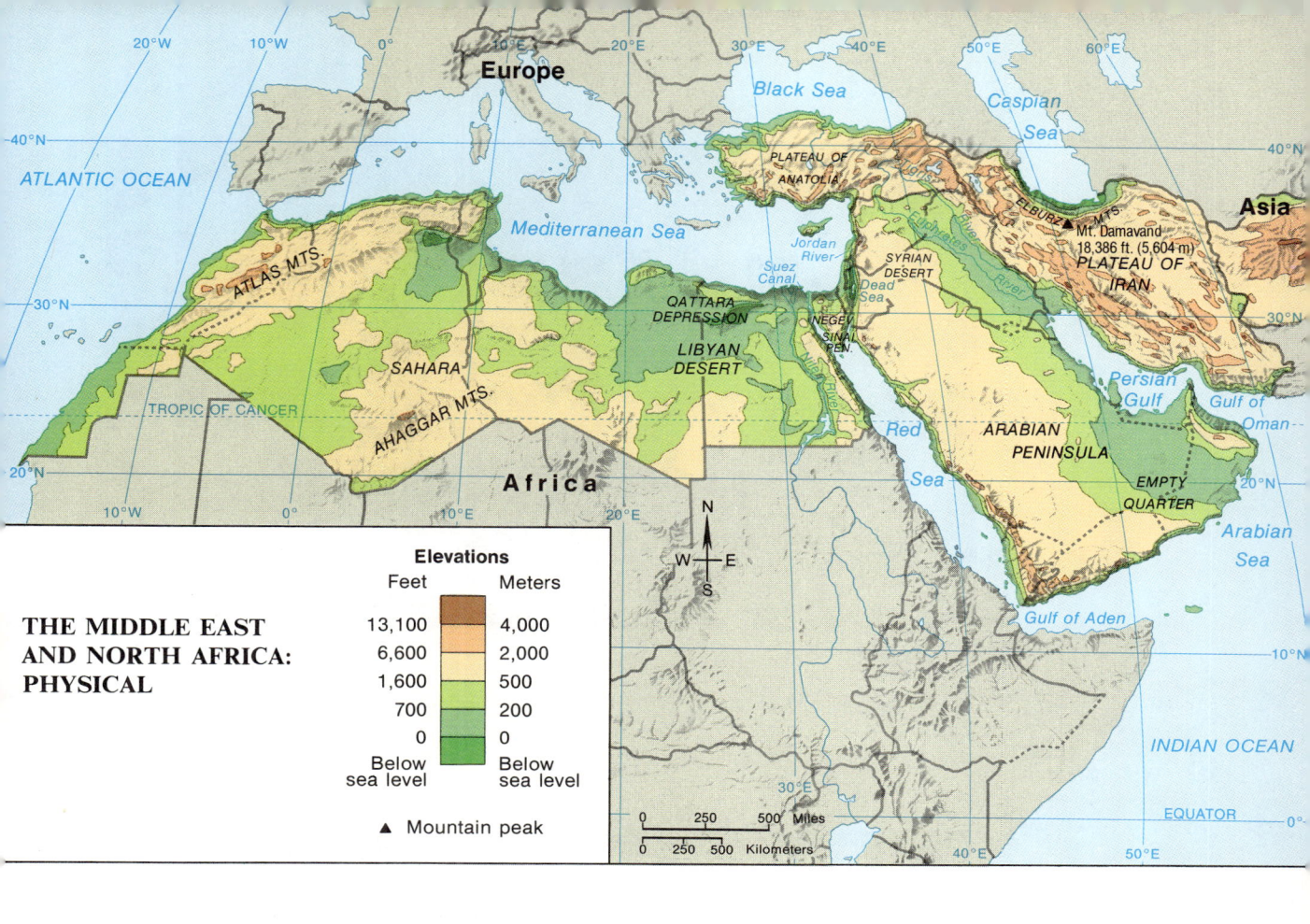

Armenia – between Iran and northern Turkey – has always been a battleground between the Persians and the rulers of Anatolia, first the Romans, then the Byzantines, and finally the Turks. The fate of the Armenians has been similar to that of the Jews in the Middle East. Both peoples were conquered, and both scattered throughout the Middle East as traders and craftsmen. But unlike the Jews, the Armenians have not regained their ancient homeland, although there is an Armenian republic in the Soviet Union.

Afghanistan connects the Middle East with India and Asia. The mountainous country of Afghanistan forms a bridge connecting the rest of the Middle East with India and Central Asia. Three major rivers find their headwaters in the mountains of Afghanistan. The Helmand, in the west, flows toward Iran. In the north rises the Amu Darya, which flows toward the Aral Sea. South of the Hindu Kush Mountains several tributaries of the Indus, the great river of Pakistan, gather.

An Arid Climate

The outstanding feature of the Middle Eastern landscape is its dryness. It is the driest of the world's culture regions.

More than 90 percent of North Africa and of the Arabian Peninsula is desert. These areas receive less than ten inches of rainfall annually. The occasional

Berber settlements like the one above are found throughout northwest Africa. Fez (below) is one of Morocco's larger commercial centers. Founded in the eighth century, it was once a major religious and political center of the Arab empire.

heavy rains can be destructive, causing flash flooding. Seasoned desert travelers never camp along a dry river bed or a land depression for fear they might drown during a rainfall.

Most of the deserts are rocky, with enough vegetation to support camels and grazing herds. A few are sandy, with large shifting dunes. One sandy desert is the Rub'al Khali *(roob' al kah' lee)*, or "Empty Quarter," in the Arabian Peninsula. Before the coming of the automobile this desert had seldom been crossed, even by the desert Arabs.

The dominant feature of the northern borderlands is the high grassland plateaus. The dusty plains of central Anatolia and central Iran may be considered extensions of the Central Asian steppes in the Soviet Union. In these northern lands the precipitation comes mostly in winter in the form of snow.

Mountains affect climate. The mountain ranges separating the coast from the inland regions account for the arid climate. The great Atlas Mountains of North Africa get in the way of moisture-filled clouds coming from the Atlantic. To get over these mountain barriers the clouds must rise to higher altitudes. As they rise, the cooler temperatures cause moisture in the clouds to condense and fall as rain on the mountain slopes. After passing over the peaks, the clouds contain little moisture.

Much of Syria is desert because of the north-south mountain ranges that follow the Mediterranean shore. By the time clouds from the west have crossed these mountains, little rain is left for the rest of the country. In Turkey and Iran similar conditions exist.

The coastlands receive more rain. The regions between the mountains and the coasts are well watered and therefore very fertile. Such areas are northwestern Morocco, the southern part of the Arabian Peninsula, the coastal plains of Lebanon, Israel, and Turkey, and the Caspian shore of Iran. The *Mediterranean climate* of these areas is characterized by hot, dry summers and cool, rainy winters. Olives, grapes, and citrus fruits flourish in this climate.

There is thus a dramatic contrast in many Middle Eastern lands between the dry, barren inland regions and the moist, fertile coastlands. There is a similar contrast in the life of the people. The dwellers of desert and plateau are mainly livestock herders. Those on the coastal plains are mainly farmers.

Climate affects population distribution. A striking result of the general dryness in the Middle East is a great imbalance in population from region to region. Population is concentrated along the narrow coast and river valleys. Fewer people live in the mountain and plateau areas, and population is very sparse in the vast deserts.

In Egypt 99 percent of the people live along the Nile valley and delta, which comprise only 3.5 percent of the land area. The population density in this area is 1700 people per square mile. Egypt as a whole has a population density of 78 people per square mile as compared with Libya's one person per square mile.

Although Turkey has about the same number of people as Egypt (around 50 million), its population is much more evenly distributed. About half the people live in villages, spread over the Anatolian plateau. The other half live in the larger cities, such as Ankara *(ang' kuh-ruh)*, Istanbul, Izmir, Adana, and Konya.

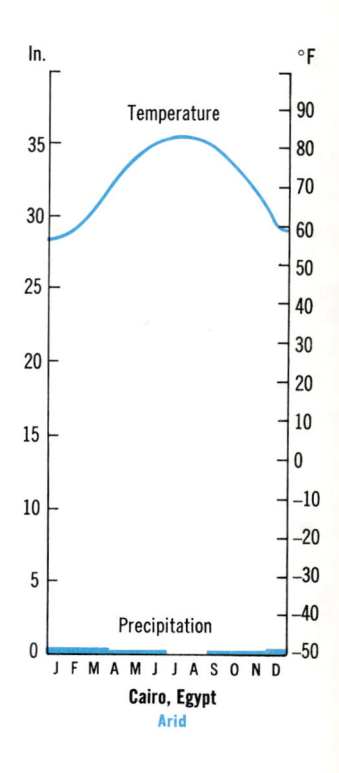

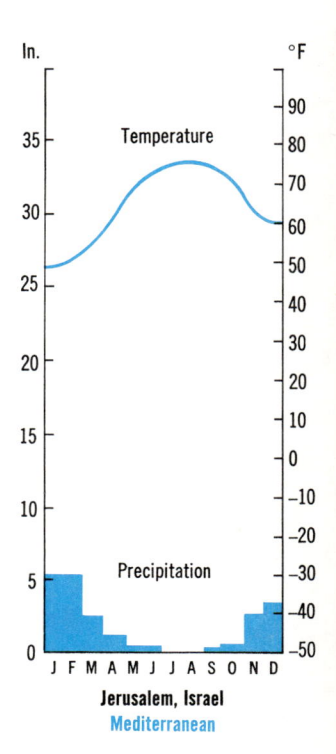

Cairo, Egypt
Arid

Jerusalem, Israel
Mediterranean

Turkey and Egypt have the largest populations in the Middle East. Next comes Iran with 44 million people. Morocco, Algeria, and the Sudan all have more than 20 million people. Iraq and Afgahanistan have about 15 million people each. Saudi Arabia's 11 million people make it the largest country of the Arabian peninsula both in area and in population. Oman, Bahrain, and Qatar have less than a million people each.

The small amount of arable land in the Middle East must support a large population that is increasing rapidly. The total population was close to 300 million in the mid-1980s. It is likely to grow to 600 million within twenty-five years at present growth rates. Deserts are expanding because of overgrazing and other poor land management practices.

Peoples of the Middle East

Over half of the 300 million people in the Middle East are Arabs. They form a majority in all of the North African and Arabian Peninsula countries and in all of the eastern Mediterranean countries except Israel. The other major groups are Persians, living mainly in Iran, and Turks, mainly in Turkey.

The Arabs spread their language, religion, and culture throughout the region. The original home of the Arabs was the Arabian Peninsula. For many centuries they were the carriers of trade between India and the lands bordering on the Mediterranean. With the rise of Islam the Arabs began to conquer the rest of the Middle East, spreading the message Muhammad had brought them. By the beginning of the eighth century the Arabs ruled all of North Africa, the eastern Mediterranean, Iran, and much of Central Asia. In the west they began to conquer Spain, and in the east, India.

Initially only a small proportion of the population outside the Arabian Peninsula itself was Arab. The Arabs were a ruling and aristocratic class. Gradually the peoples they conquered – Greeks, Copts, Syrians – learned Arabic and adopted many of the customs of their Arab rulers. There was also much intermarriage between the Arabs and the conquered peoples. The result was that the Arabic language became very widespread – from the Strait of Gibraltar to the mountains of Iran. Today every native speaker of Arabic is considered an Arab.

Many non-Muslim minorities live in the Arab world. Not all the peoples conquered by the Arabs gave up their language or their religion. Some of the Copts in Egypt, the Syrians in Syria, and the Maronites in Lebanon kept their own brands of Christianity. Although they learned Arabic, they retained their old languages – Coptic and Syriac – for their religious ceremonies.

Christian persecution between 425 and 630, followed by Arab insistence on the rule of the Muslim religion, resulted in a great decline in Jewish leadership in Palestine. The Jews, however, remained in the Middle East, kept Hebrew alive as a holy language, and continued to practice their religion. They learned Arabic for use in daily life and in their writings. In Palestine today, Hebrew is again the language of daily life. Since 1948, most Middle Eastern Jews have immigrated to Israel.

The Berbers of North Africa and the Kurds of Iraq each kept their own languages, Berber and Kurdish. But both groups became Muslims. Each of these groups was to play an important role in Islamic history, especially in the eleventh and twelfth centuries. However, they have remained minorities within the Arab countries, without states of their own. There are also large Kurdish communities in Turkey and Iran.

Muslim sects form another type of minority. The majority of Muslims are known as *Sunnis*. The *Shiites* (p. 72) are the largest minority. There are large Shiite communities in the eastern Mediterranean countries, especially Syria, Iraq, and Lebanon.

The Persians live mainly in Iran. Although the Persians were conquered by the Arabs, they retained their language and their ancient traditions of art and statecraft. Today most of them live in Iran, their ancestral homeland. Persian dynasties arose in Iran and elsewhere, and the Persian language rivaled Arabic in poetry and other forms of literature. Persian Muslims are predominantly Shiite. Today, Iran is the only Muslim state in which Shiite Islam is the official religion.

The Turks. Unlike the Arabs, whose original homeland was the Middle East, the Turks first appear in history in eastern Asia. In the sixth century A.D. they ruled a vast empire centered in what is now Mongolia. Then many of the Turkish tribes living north of Iran, in the area still known as Turkestan, became converted to Islam. Dynasties of Muslim Turks ruled in this area and led invasions into the Middle East. The most important of these were the Seljuk (sel-*jook'*) Turks. The Seljuks conquered Iran and the lands of the eastern Mediterranean, and eventually ruled over most of Anatolia.

Persian Muslims, like these girls from Tehran, Iran, are predominantly members of the Shiite group. Girls and women in Islamic countries often wear the traditional blanketlike chador.

41

Many Turkish tribes, with their herds of sheep and goats, followed the Seljuk warriors and began to settle in Anatolia. Like the Arabs before them, the Turks intermingled with the native peoples, who were mainly Greeks. Soon the entire land was predominantly Turkish and was known to Europeans as Turkey.

Many Turks live outside Turkey. Today, Turkey is the only country in which the Turks form a majority. There are also Turkish tribes living in Iran, Afghanistan, and western China. Many Turks also live in the Soviet Union. The area in the Soviet Union where they live is known collectively as Turkestan. All of these Turks are Sunni Muslims, like their cousins in the Middle East.

Armenians and Greeks. Until this century there were large Greek and Armenian minorities in Turkey, both Christian communities. Many Armenians were killed during the events leading up to World War I, and many others fled south. A sizeable Armenian minority live in Syria and Lebanon.

Most of the Greeks went to Greece in the 1920s. This was part of a population exchange in which many Turks who were living in Greece also came to Turkey.

CHAPTER REVIEW

Recalling Names and Places

Anatolia	Hindu Kush	Shiites
Arabian Peninsula	Mesopotamia	Sunnis
Arabs	Nile River	Syria
Armenia	oases	Tigris-Euphrates
Atlas Mountains	Palestine	Turks
Elburz	Persians	wadis
Fertile Crescent	Rub' al Khali	

Understanding This Chapter

1. Who are the three major peoples of the Middle East? Where are their original homelands? In what areas do they now form a majority? Who are the principal minorities in these areas?
2. Why is most of the Middle East so dry? What creates deserts?
3. What are the major rivers in the Middle East? Why are they important?
4. Most of the Middle East is desert, yet this region has been a cradle of civilization. What geographic factors might have aided the emergence of civilization?

Chapter 5

The Record of Historical Change

The drama of events in the Middle East goes back more than 4000 years. During this long period many different individuals and groups have occupied center stage. Much of the record of Middle Eastern history is a description of rule by various dynasties: their rise to power, their conflicts with one another, and their decline and fall. (A dynasty is a succession of rulers from the same family.)

At certain stages of history rulers have attempted to unify the entire Middle East, forming an empire. The Persian empire in the sixth century B.C. was the first of the great world empires. The Greeks, the Romans, the Arabs, and the Mongols each in turn dominated the area, and each eventually lost control. The last of the great Middle Eastern empires was that of the Ottoman Turks, which lasted from 1453 to 1920.

Conquest frequently brought hardships to the people of the Middle East, but it also encouraged the interchange of commodities and of ideas. This interchange continues today. Middle Easterners are assuming many Western innovations in government and technology, while trying to preserve their own religious and cultural heritage and way of life.

The Ancient Middle East

There is a Middle Eastern proverb, "When two elephants fight, the fly gets squashed in the middle." This was the fate of the Jews in ancient times.

Egypt and Mesopotamia, the great river valley civilizations. The two "elephants" of the ancient Middle East were the civilizations in the two great river valleys, the Nile in Egypt and the Tigris and Euphrates in Mesopotamia (Iraq). Both of them depended on the labor of a large agricultural population to support the priestly and ruling classes. In both places a powerful centralized government developed. Their leaders harnessed the energies of their people for public projects. In Mesopotamia this involved the building and maintenance of an immense system of canals and dikes, which directed the floodwaters of the two rivers toward irrigation channels. In Egypt, where the seasonal overflow of the Nile carried less danger of flooding, energies could be concentrated on building of the imperial tombs, the pyramids.

The Jews take possession of their homeland. The area between these two giants – the northern fertile Crescent and the eastern Mediterranean seaboard – was inhabited by a number of different peoples, most notably the Canaanites and the Philistines. The Bible tells the familiar story of how this area became the homeland of the Jews.

According to the biblical story, God promised the land of Canaan to His "chosen people," the Hebrews (also known as Israelites). Led by Moses, the Hebrews escaped from Egypt, where they were slaves. They conquered the "promised land" from the Canaanites and the Philistines and eventually created a state of their own. King Solomon (973–933 B.C.), son of King David, ruled a united kingdom of Israel from his capital in Jerusalem. There he built the Temple, the center of his people's religious life, devoted to the One God of Israel.

After Solomon the Israeli kingdom began to decline in power, never to recover its former splendor. The state split into two kingdoms, Israel in the north and Judah (from which come the words Jew and Judaism) in the south.

But more dangerous than this internal split were threats from the outside, for the "promised land" was on the crossroads between continents and between empires. Both the Egyptians and the peoples of Mesopotamia (first the Assyrians, then the Babylonians) attempted to gain control of this valuable region. The Mesopotamian peoples were more successful. The Assyrians conquered Israel; then the Babylonians conquered Judah. The Babylonians destroyed the Temple in Jerusalem in 586 B.C. and exiled many of the Jews. This was the beginning of the *diaspora* in Jewish history – the dispersion of the Jews from their ancient homeland of Israel to other parts of the world.

An Egyptian grave stele, or tombstone, from 2050 B.C. depicts a middle-class couple. They are drawn in the ancient Egyptian style — men dark, women light, with heads, arms, and legs in profile but shoulders in front view.

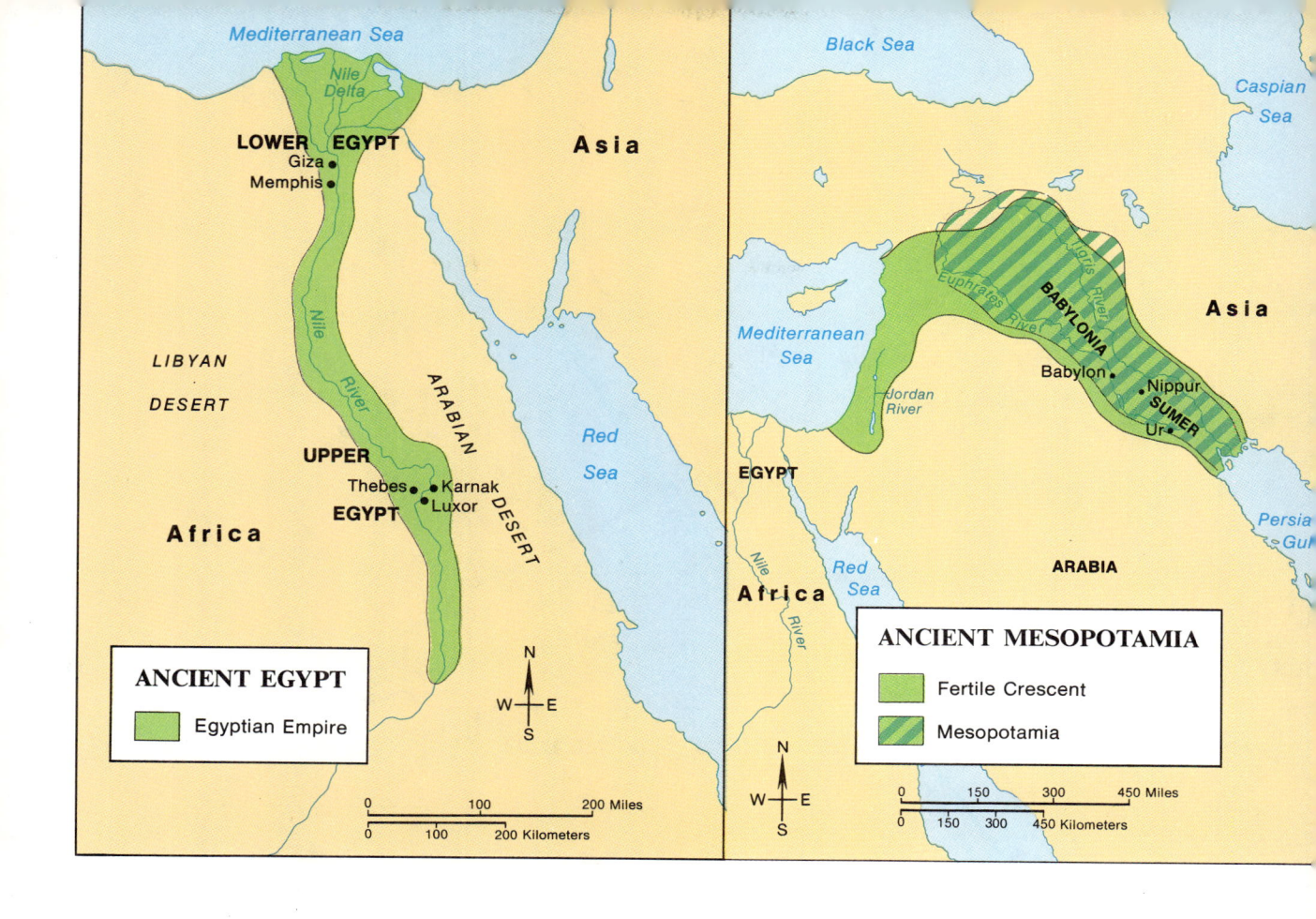

The Persians establish an empire. Before the end of the sixth century B.C. the Persians, living in Iran, had conquered the Babylonians. The Persians succeeded in creating the largest empire known until that time. It embraced Iran, the eastern Mediterranean lands, Egypt, and Anatolia. It was the policy of the Persians to allow their subject peoples some independence and self-government. They allowed the Jews to return to Israel, where they rebuilt the Temple in Jerusalem.

Alexander puts an end to the Persian empire. In hopes of expanding their empire, the Persians sent fleets into the eastern Mediterranean, where the Greeks had become powerful. They were unsuccessful in their efforts at conquest, and the Greeks drove the Persian armies out of Europe. In the next century Alexander the Great united the Greek city-states and began to march east. He conquered the Persians in 336 B.C. and created an empire that stretched from Greece to India.

Alexander hoped to establish Greek civilization throughout this huge area, but his attempts were only partially successful. Alexandria, in Egypt, became a center of Greek culture. But after Alexander's death in 323 B.C., his empire was divided into a number of smaller states. Egypt, Syria and Anatolia, and Iran were each under the control of different rulers, who were hostile to one another.

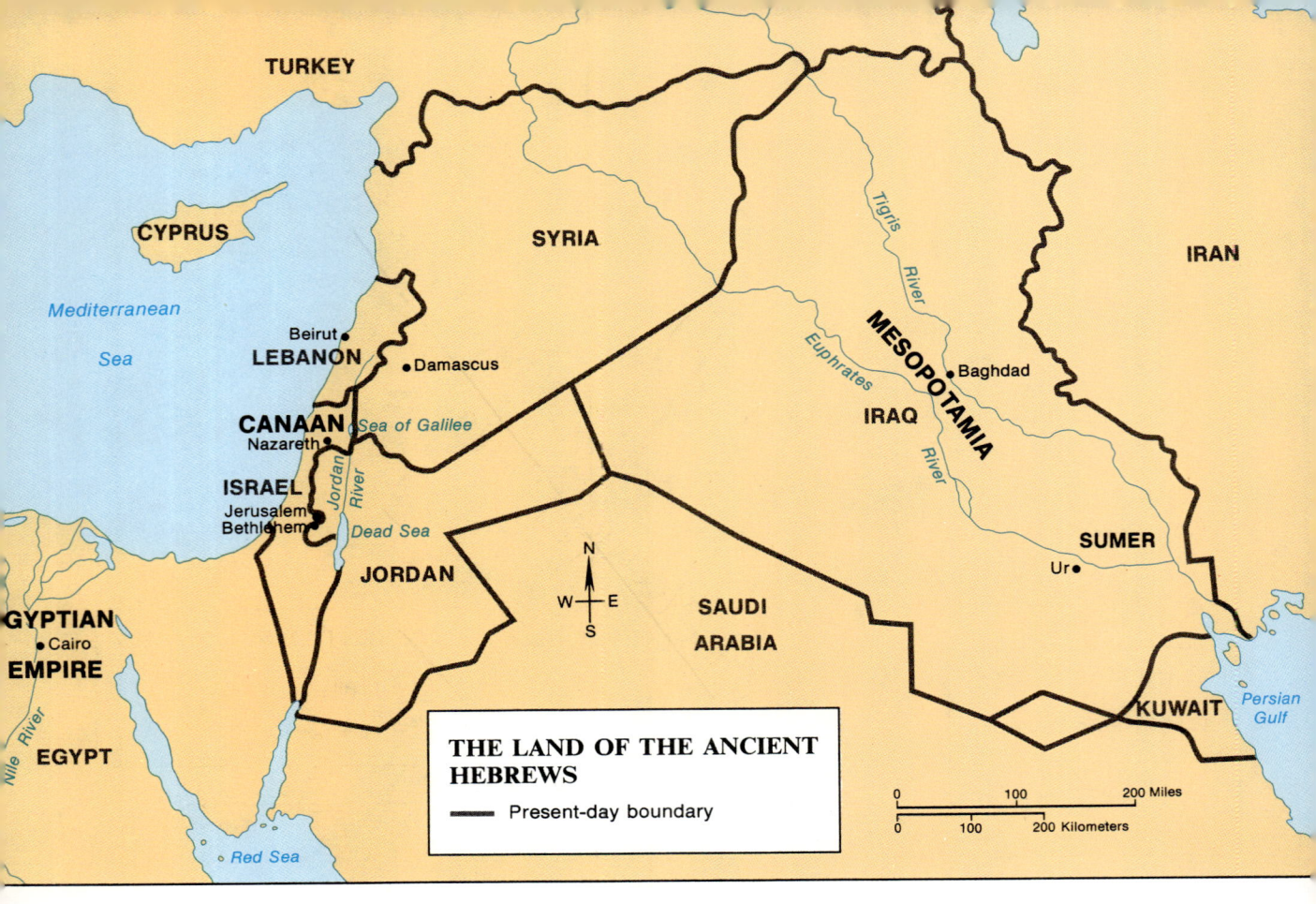

THE LAND OF THE ANCIENT HEBREWS
— Present-day boundary

Relief showing the combat of lions and bulls on the north stairs of the central palace of Persepolis in Iran.

Today Jews from all over the world come to Jerusalem to pray at the Western Wall, the remaining western section of the wall that enclosed the Second Temple, which was destroyed by the Romans in 70 A.D.

Romans conquer the Middle East and send the Jews into a second exile.
The Romans, invading from the west, were the next peoples to dominate the Middle East. They conquered all the lands west of the Euphrates.

In the year 70 A.D. the Romans destroyed the Second Temple in Jerusalem, putting the Jews to flight until the Jews returned in the twentieth century. For centuries the majority of Jews would live in the diaspora, scattered in various communities throughout the Middle East and Europe. While before they were an agricultural people, heavy taxation on their crop land and inadequate irrigation, especially under the Arabs, forced them to become mainly craftspeople and merchants.

Although the Romans conquered the Jews, it was a religion growing out of Judaism that finally "conquered" the Romans. The Roman emperor Constantine became a Christian in the year 312, adopting Christianity as the Roman state religion. Constantine recognized the growing importance of Middle Eastern political and religious life. He moved the capital of his empire from Rome to the city of Byzantium on the straits separating Europe and Anatolia. He renamed this "second Rome" Constantinople. The eastern Roman empire became known as the Byzantine empire, after the old name of the city, Byzantium. Today Constantinople is known by its Turkish name, Istanbul.

Reviewing Your Reading

1. When did the Jews first settle in their ancient homeland? What led to their first exile? the second exile?
2. Describe the role of the Persian, Greek, and Roman empires in ancient Middle Eastern history.
3. Why is Istanbul known by three different names?

The Rise of Islam

In the century before the rise of Islam, the Middle East was divided between two great empires. The Byzantines ruled over Anatolia, Syria, Palestine, and Egypt. The Sassanians, an Iranian dynasty that arose in the third century A.D., controlled Iraq, Iran, and Afghanistan. There were many contrasts between the two empires. The Byzantines spoke Greek and followed the Christian religion. The Sassanians practiced the Zoroastrian religion and promoted Persian culture.

Throughout the sixth century there were constant wars between these two great empires. Neither side won a decisive victory, and both were left weak and exhausted. They had spent their energies fighting each other. The result was a power vacuum in the Middle East in the early seventh century, waiting for any third power to step in and fill it. That third power was already in the making in the Arabian Peninsula.

The Arabs before Islam. The Arabs played only a minor role in the power politics of the ancient Middle East. Their desert lands, known as Arabia, were uninviting to the rulers of Egypt and the Fertile Crescent. These rulers were content to get the "perfumes of Arabia" – Arabian incense and Indian spices – at second hand, by boat or camel caravan.

Even in the large cities, such as Mecca and Medina in central Arabia, the Arabs were organized into rival tribal groupings. The tribes were constantly fighting each other. No tribal leader could control other tribes for long.

Mecca was a center of religious worship. In northern Arabia the tribes were mainly Christian, although Medina had some Jewish tribes. Mecca, however, was the center of the pagan Arab religion. Its followers worshiped a number of gods, the chief one named Allah. Religious rites included a yearly pilgrimage to a shrine in Mecca called the *Kaaba* (kah'uh-buh), which means "cube." The Kaaba was a cube-shaped building enclosing a black meteorite stone that the Arabs believed to be sacred. Once a year Arabs from the entire peninsula would gather in Mecca to perform the ceremony of circumambulation, or walking around the Kaaba.

The pilgrimage season coincided with the stopover of the caravan enroute between Syria and South Arabia. It was thus a season of commerce as well as religious observance. Whoever controlled the Kaaba also controlled this caravan trade. At the end of the sixth century the Quraysh (kuh-*rysh'*) tribe held this position. The Quraysh at that time were the most powerful tribe in the Arabian Peninsula.

The life of the prophet Muhammad. Muhammad (also spelled Mohammed), whom Muslims call "the Apostle of God," was born into the Quraysh tribe in 570. He was an orphan and was raised first by his grandfather, then by one of his uncles. As a young man he acquired a reputation for honesty and fairmindedness.

Muhammad was a merchant. He married a rich widow named Khadija, who had hired him to do business for her in Syria. Later on in his life, after Khadija died, he had other wives, but he was always devoted to Khadija's memory. He also had a number of children, but the boys all died young. His best-known daughter was Fatima, who married his cousin Ali.

> **Muhammad the Trustworthy**
>
> *In the biography of Muhammad by the Arab historian Ibn Ishaq, there is the following story: The tribes of Quraysh were rebuilding the Kaaba, but they disputed over which tribe should have the privilege of lifting the black stone into place. They prepared to do battle over the issue. The eldest man of Quraysh urged them to make the first man who entered the gate umpire in the matter. Everyone agreed, and the first to come in was Muhammad.*
>
> *When they saw him they said, "This is the trustworthy one. We are satisfied. This is Muhammad." When he came to them and they informed him of the matter he said, "Give me a cloak," and when it was brought to him he took the black stone and put it inside it and said that each tribe should take hold of an end of the cloak and they should lift it together. They did this so that when they got it into position he placed it with his own hand, and then building went on above it.*
>
> *The Life of Muhammad: A translation of Ishaq's Sirat Rasul Allah*, by A. Guillaume, (Oxford University Press, Pakistan, 1955) p. 86.

The call to Islam. When Muhammad was 40, he used to go into the hills surrounding Mecca to meditate. According to Islamic belief, one day the angel Gabriel appeared to him and announced: "You are the Apostle of God, and I am Gabriel." It is also Islamic belief that he revealed to Muhammad part of God's revelation, known as the *Koran*.

Muhammad was at first frightened by his experience. He told Khadija about it, and she comforted him. He subsequently had many revelations and came to believe that they were from God. They induced him to preach Islam, which means submission to the one God, Allah. Muhammad taught that the other gods the Arabs had worshiped along with Allah did not exist. Allah alone was "Lord of the Worlds."

Variations of the teachings of Islam – that God is one; that He reveals His will through His prophets in the form of a Book; that all men must submit to His commands or suffer punishment at death – are also found in Judaism and Christianity. In Muhammad's time, many Arabs had been exposed to Jewish or Christian ideas and had become dissatisfied with the religion of their fathers. Most at first denied that Muhammad was a prophet.

Conflicts with the Quraysh led Muhammad to emigrate to Medina. Khadija was the first to accept Islam. Other early converts were Ali, Muhammad's cousin and son-in-law, and Abu Bakr (uh-*boo' bek'* er) and Umar, two of his close friends.

Most of the Quraysh were violently opposed to these new ideas. They thought Muhammad was a madman, a soothsayer, or a poet. They were threatened by Muhammad's monotheism (belief in one God), fearing that if the Arabs gave up their old gods they would no longer come to Mecca during the pilgrimage season. The Quraysh would thus lose their monopoly of the caravan trade.

In the year 622 Muhammad decided to leave Mecca with his followers and establish Islam in a different community. The opportunity came when the people of Medina invited Muhammad to come to their city to settle disputes among its residents. They needed an outside person as an arbitrator, and they had heard of Muhammad's reputation for trustworthiness.

The emigration from Mecca to Medina is called the *hijra* (hidge'ruh). The people of Medina welcomed Muhammad into their city. With the exception of the Jewish tribes, most of the people converted to Islam, and the Koran was made the legal basis of the community. Because of this important event the Muslim calendar begins from the hijra, in 622 A.D. The time before the hijra is known to Muslims as "the time of ignorance."

The triumph of Islam. Within a very few years Muhammad made the Muslim community of Medina the strongest political and military force on the Arabian Peninsula. Tribes from all over came to Muhammad to become Muslims. In 630, two years before his death, Muhammad was able to return in triumph to Mecca. He was kind to his former opponents, once they accepted Islam. He incorporated into Islam the Meccan pilgrimage and the ancient ceremony of the circumambulation of the Kaaba. The only people who refused to accept Islam were the Jewish tribes of Medina. They were either exiled or killed.

Muhammad, through Islam, succeeded in uniting all the Arab tribes. All Muslims were brothers, and no Muslim was to fight another. Islam did urge them to fight non-Muslims, however, until Islam was victorious throughout the world. This was the principle of *jihad,* or "holy war."

The concept of jihad united the Arabs and directed them toward conquering the weakened empires to the north. The conquest began under the leadership of Abu Bakr, whom the Muslims chose as the Prophet's successor, or *caliph.* It was completed during the reign of the second caliph, Umar (634–644). In this short period the Arabs completely engulfed the Sassanian empire in Iraq and Iran and took Egypt, Palestine, and Syria from the Byzantines.

Invasion by invitation. The Arabs conquered this area without opposition from the peoples living there. Jews, Copts, and Syrian Christians were unhappy with Byzantine rule. They had suffered under corrupt governors and heavy tax burdens and were weary of armies constantly crossing their lands, interrupting trade and daily life. The Arabs did not force these older communities to accept Islam. On the contrary, with some local exceptions, they recognized Jews and Christians as "People of the Book" to be protected by Muslim rulers. Christians and Jews were required to accept Arabs as their worldly rulers, pay special taxes, and accept restrictions on their religious freedom. Pagans on the other hand were forced either to convert to Islam or be killed.

Reviewing Your Reading

1. Describe Muhammad's early life.
2. Who were the Quraysh? How did they influence Muhammad's life?
3. What was the significance of Muhammad's journey to Medina?
4. How was the Islamic faith spread?
5. Why was the Islamic conquest of the Middle East achieved so easily?

This sixteenth-century Iranian miniature shows Muhammad ascending to heaven. Frequently Muhammad is seen veiled because artists feared an inaccurate or sacrilegious depiction of his face. Another typical feature is the fiery halo surrounding his head.

Rise and Fall of the Arab Dynasties

Within thirty years of Muhammad's death great changes had occurred in the Muslim community. from being a dedicated group of warriors for the faith, the Arab tribesmen had become a wealthy and powerful aristocratic class. Their lands stretched from Egypt to Iran.

Conflicts arose within the Muslim community. The struggle revolved over who was the rightful caliph. Some Muslims thought that the caliphate belonged in the family of Muhammad. Only those who were related to the Prophet had the right to claim to be his successor. The group that supported Ali, the Prophet's nephew and son-in-law, were known as Shiites (*she'*-ites).

The Umayyads (661–750). In the year 661 Ali died, and the caliphate was assumed by the Umayyads (oo-*my'* yads), a noble Meccan family, but not close relatives of Muhammad. They established their capital in Syria, in the ancient city of Damascus.

Under the Umayyads the Arab conquests continued. By the beginning of the eighth century they had conquered all of North Africa, and began to conquer Spain. In the east the Arabs conquered Afghanistan, Central Asia, and the Indus valley in western India.

Toward the middle of the next century another dynasty known as the Abbasid (ab'uh-sid) gained control of the caliphate. They were descendents of Abbas, one of the Prophet's uncles. They were supported by the Shiites and many Persian converts who resented the domination of the aristocratic Umayyads. The Abbasids hoped to create a more democratic Muslim state in which Persians and Arabs would be equal as brothers in Islam.

The Abbasids rule from Baghdad. The Abbasids (750–1258) came to power in 750. They killed most of the remaining Umayyads and established their capital in Iraq. The second Abbasid caliph, Mansur (754–775), built a new capital called Baghdad. It was destined to become one of the greatest cities of the world.

Mansur carefully chose the site for his new capital on the Tigris River at a point where the Euphrates flows only a few miles away, and the two rivers are connected by canals. The Arab historian Ya'qubi speaks of Baghdad in the following enthusiastic words:

> It stretches out on the two banks of those two large rivers, the Tigris and the Euphrates, and watches commercial products and staples flow to it on land and on water. For it is with great ease that each commercial object is transported endlessly from East and West, from Moslem and non-Moslem regions. Indeed, merchandise is brought from India, Sind, China, Tibet, the land of the Turks, the Khazars, and the Abyssinians – from everywhere in short – to such a degree that it is found in greater profusion in Baghdad than in its country of origin.*

---

* From *Baghdad: Metropolis of the Abbasid Caliphate,* by Gaston Wiet. Copyright 1971 by the University of Oklahoma Press, p. 9.

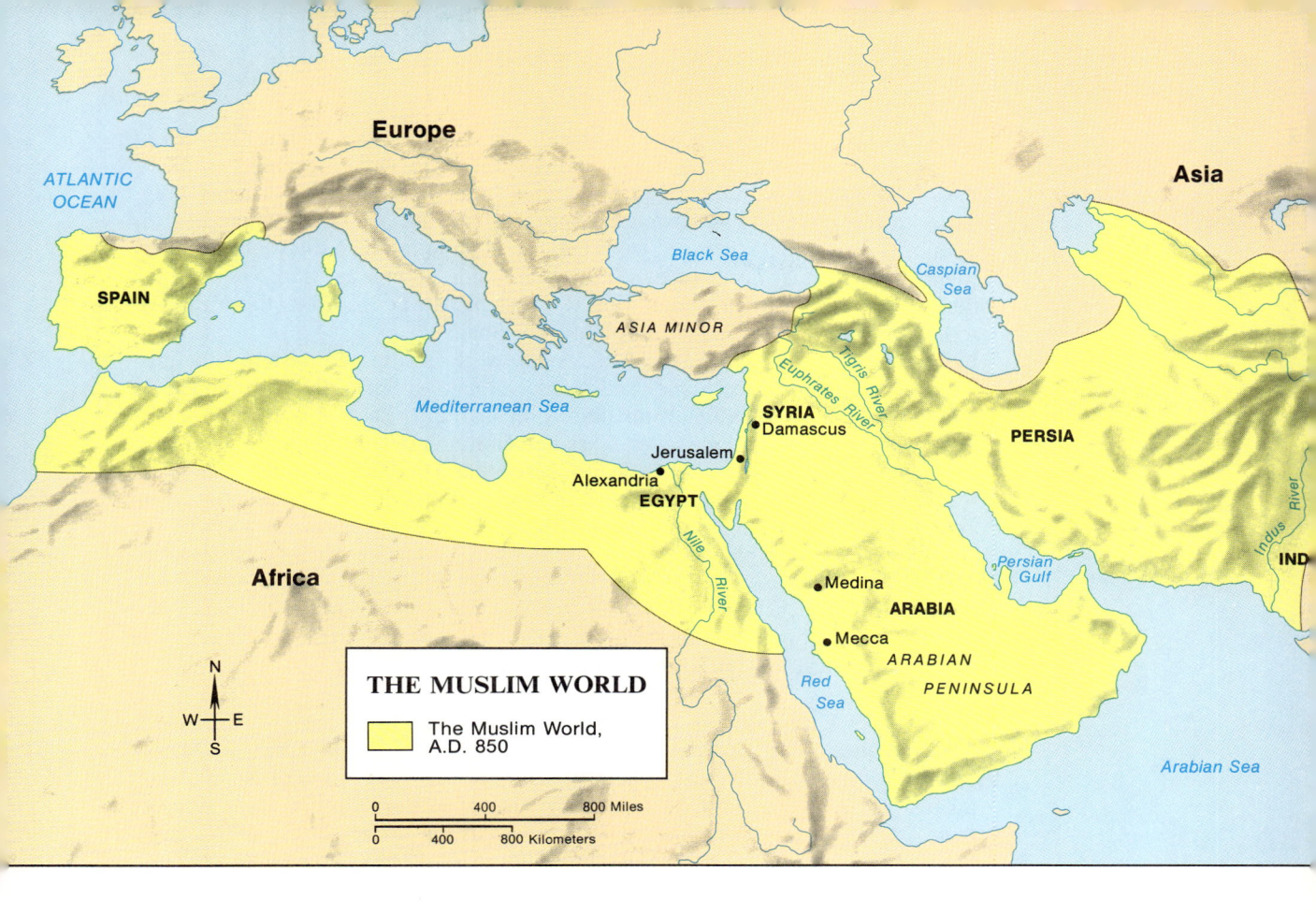

The Muslim empire declines. The Abbasid caliphate continued for 500 years, until the Mongol conquest in 1258. But much earlier the power of the Abbasids began to decline. Local dynasties assumed power first in the western and eastern extremities of the empire, then in the heartland.

Spain was the first to break away, in 756; then came Morocco, Tunisia, and Egypt. In the ninth century, Persian dynasties established themselves in Iran and Afghanistan. Some of these dynasties were Shiite and did not recognize the religious authority of the caliph in Baghdad. Political unrest was accompanied by social disturbances. A revolt of black slaves occurred in lower Iraq, and the caliph put it down only with great difficulty.

At the extremes of the Middle East — in Turkestan and in the western Sahara — Islam continued to advance, but more by peaceful propaganda than by conquest. Proselytizers would establish *ribats,* frontier convents, where they attracted new converts by preaching, by example, and by holy war when all other methods failed.

In this way Islam took hold among the Turks beyond the Amu Darya River on the Iranian frontier and among the Berber tribes in the Sahara south of the Atlas Mountains. In both cases, the newly converted tribes sought to spread Islam forcibly among other tribes living farther from the Islamic center.

The Almoravids bring harsh rule to Morocco and Spain. In the region of the Sahara that touches on the Niger River, in present-day Mauritania and Senegal, some proselytizers in the middle of the eleventh century established a ribat, that became a center of propaganda and reform. The leading families of this ribat were known as the Almoravids *(al' muh-rah' vids)* meaning "people of the ribat." In addition to converting tribes in Ghana and other African kingdoms, the Almoravids also wanted control of Muslim Morocco, where in their opinion the people had strayed from the true Islamic faith. In the year 1062 they founded a city just north of the Atlas Mountains known as Marrakesh, which they used as a base for conquering the rest of Morocco. From there the Almoravids went on to conquer all of Muslim Spain.

Ruling from Marrakesh, the Almoravids were fanatic and austere Muslims. They disapproved of the luxury and freedom found in Spain. They established a strict control over the Muslim institutions of learning. They also undertook persecutions of the large Jewish and Christian communities in Spain.

In the next century another Berber dynasty, the Almohad *(al' muh-hahd')*, defeated the Almoravids and established an even greater empire, embracing Spain and all of North Africa east of Libya. It gradually declined, however, and by the middle of the thirteenth century most of North Africa had again split up into separate states.

In Spain, the Christians drove out the Almohads. One Arab state remained — the small kingdom of Granada in the south. Granada flourished for two more centuries, until it too fell to the Christians in 1492.

The Turks enter the Middle East. At the same time that the Almoravids were conquering the far west of the Muslim world, the Seljuk Turks (p. 41) began to dominate in the east. The Seljuks were the champions of Sunni Islam against the Shiites. In 1055, when they succeeded in ousting a Shiite dynasty from Baghdad, many Muslims regarded them as the saviors of the caliphate.

The Seljuks also took up the jihad, or "holy war." They defeated the Byzantines at the battle of Manzikert, in 1071, and began to rule in Anatolia. Turkish tribesmen settled in this area where no Muslims had before.

Reviewing Your Reading

1. Describe the accomplishments of the Umayyad dynasty.
2. What groups supported the Abbasids in their efforts to take the caliphate from the Umayyads? Why?
3. Why was Baghdad chosen as the Abbasid capital?
4. What part did the ribats play in the expansion of the Muslim empire?
5. Describe the rule of the Almoravids. Where was their empire?
6. What impact did the conquests of the Seljuk Turks have on the Muslim empire?

Two Centuries of Foreign Invasion

In addition to the internal turmoil of the Middle East there were external threats by non-Muslim powers. The two centuries between 1100 and 1300 provided the most severe test for Muslim civilization. First the European Crusaders from the west, then the Mongols from the east successfully attacked the core lands of the Muslim world. The Crusaders were eventually defeated, and the Mongol rulers were converted to Islam. But both of these attacks left deep wounds that have not healed to the present day.

The Crusades. The Seljuk conquest of the eastern Mediterranean and of Anatolia was very disturbing to the Christian states, both Byzantine and European. They had seen Anatolia as a bulwark against an Islamic invasion of Europe. Now the Turks were there, threatening the Christian capital of Constantinople and cutting off the routes of pilgrimage to the Holy Land.

The call to crusade went up throughout Europe. It was answered by kings, knights, and common people. The Crusaders made their way across Anatolia, fighting off Turkish and Arab armies, toward the Holy Land in Palestine. In 1099 they conquered Jerusalem and massacred its Muslim and Jewish inhabitants. They established a series of Christian kingdoms along the coast of Palestine and in Syria.

The Crusaders were fortunate in the timing of their venture. The caliphate was at its weakest, and there was endless conflict within the Muslim community – Sunni against Shiite, Arab against Turk.

A strong Muslim leader put an end to the European invasion. Saladin, a Kurd by birth, became famous in Europe as both a fearsome Arab warrior and a noble and generous Muslim knight. Saladin's armies attacked the Crusaders, recovering Jerusalem for Islam in 1187. The Crusaders were able to hold a few cities along the Palestinian coast for another century, but neither Richard II of England nor Louis IX of France could revive the Christian kingdoms in the Holy Land.

The Crusades had a greater effect on Europe than on the Middle East. For Europeans they opened up a new world of trade and culture, and they were the first

This medieval print shows Crusaders attacking a Palestinian town. The Crusaders failed in their efforts to reunite the eastern and western branches of the Christian church under the Roman pope, but the West profited greatly from the Crusades. Medieval Europe was exposed to Eastern ideas, and the merchants of Europe found new markets for trade.

55

faltering steps in a movement of European expansion and world domination. To the Muslims, the Crusaders were primarily a foreign annoyance to be driven off as soon as possible.

The Mongols put an end to the Abbasid caliphate. A new power threatened in the east. The Mongols, a people related to the Turks, had created a large eastern empire under their leader Chingis Khan *(ching' gis kahn',* also spelled Genghis Khan). This empire already stretched from China to the borders of Iran by the time of Chingis Khan's death in 1227.

A Mongol general named Hulagu (who-lah'goo), Chingis Khan's grandson, struck into the heartlands of the Middle East. In the year 1258 Hulagu's armies conquered Baghdad itself. Hulagu killed the last Abbasid caliph and established his own rule.

This was a great disaster for the Muslims. The Mongols destroyed irrigation systems in Iraq, ruining much agricultural land. Cut off from trade with the Mediterranean area, Baghdad declined in prosperity and importance. The center of the Muslim world shifted to Cairo.

In 1260 a new Egyptian dynasty, the Mamluk (*mam'*luke), stopped the Mongol advance. Mamluk is the Arabic word for "white slave." Many of the Turkish dynasties in the Muslim world began when a Turkish slave, or mamluk, overthrew the ruler he was serving and put his own family in power. The Mamluks were one such dynasty. They had begun ruling in Egypt a few years before the Mongol conquest and were to remain as rulers of a flourishing Egyptian and Syrian state. Even after the Ottomans conquered them in 1517, the Mamluks continued to be the dominant military group in Egypt.

The Period of Ottoman Domination

With the exception of the Mamluk realm, the Mongols continued to rule the Middle East from their Iranian capital. Later Mongol rulers converted to Islam and adopted Turkish culture. They divided the empire into a number of smaller Muslim dynasties and became supporters of Persian and Turkish art and literature.

One of the Turko-Mongol princes in the late fourteenth century was Tamerlane. Tamerlane tried to revive the unified Mongol empire of his ancestors. From his capital at Samarkand in Turkestan he conquered northern India, Iran, and Iraq and threatened Syria and Anatolia. He even defeated the rising Turkish Ottoman dynasty at the battle of Ankara in 1402.

Tamerlane's empire, built on a wave of blood and terror, was shortlived. It died with him in 1405. The Middle East again split up into a number of warring Turkish states.

Establishment of the Ottoman empire. The Turkish Ottoman dynasty succeeded the Seljuks and Mongols in Anatolia. Their rulers had the title *sultan*. The Ottoman sultans continued the holy war against the Byzantines. By 1402, when Tamerlane defeated the Ottomans temporarily at the battle of Ankara, they had already conquered most of the Byzantine empire in southeastern Europe. All that remained was Constantinople, the capital.

In 1453 the Ottoman armies finally took Constantinople after a long seige. The city became the capital of the expanding Ottoman empire. From this time, Constantinople is also known by its Turkish name of Istanbul.

The Ottoman empire reached its peak in the sixteenth century. Sultan Selim I (seh-*leem'*, 1512–1520) conquered the Mamluks in Syria and Egypt and established Ottoman rule throughout the Arab lands. His harsh war tactics earned him the name of "Selim the Grim."

Under Selim's successor, Suleiman (soo-lay-*mahn'*, 1520–1566), the Ottomans completed their conquests in Europe, taking the Balkans and large parts of Hungary, Poland, and southern Russia. His armies reached the gates of Vienna. Under Suleiman's patronage Istanbul became one of the most splendid cities in the world, adorned with large and beautiful mosques and filled with treasures gathered from his huge empire.

"The Sick Man of Europe." After Suleiman, the Ottoman empire began to decline. The sultans were weakened by court luxury and intrigues. Their armies became unwieldy and old-fashioned compared to those of the new European nations. When expansion stopped, there were no new lands to tax. Many of the conquered lands were parcelled out to military commanders, who used them for personal gain. Bribery and corruption marked the civil service and the courts. Trade, always dominated by such non-Muslim groups as the Jews and Armenians, fell more and more into the hands of Europeans, who received special privileges from the sultans.

In 1683 the Turks made a final effort to conquer Vienna. When this effort failed, the Turkish armies began retreating. Throughout the eighteenth century the growing empires of Russia and of Austria-Hungary nibbled away at the Ottomans' European provinces, while Greek and Slavic national liberation movements succeeded in driving the Turks from most of Europe during the nineteenth century. By the beginning of the twentieth century Turkey was known as the "Sick Man of Europe."

Within the empire there were numerous attempts at reform. The army was reorganized, European battle techniques introduced, and innovations in the civil service and educational system undertaken. In 1876 liberal reformers pushed through a constitution. The constitution established a parliament and declared that all Ottoman subjects were equal. However, the reigning sultan, Abdul Hamid, soon suspended the constitution and dismissed the parliament. A group of young army officers then formed a revolutionary group called the Young Turks. They came to power in 1908, deposed Abdul Hamid, and forced the new sultan to restore the constitution.

Mustafa Kemal leads the nationalist movement in Turkey. When World War I came, the Turks fought with the Germans against the Allied powers — Russia, Britain, and France. By the end of the war in 1919, the British and French had divided up most of the Ottoman provinces in Arab lands and encouraged the Greeks to reclaim Anatolia. A Greek army landed at Izmir (Smyrna) on the Aegean coast and began to move eastward. A young Turkish army officer named Mustafa Kemal (moo-*stah'fah* keh-*mahl'*) revived the fighting spirit of the Turks and began a national movement to drive out the Greeks. This effort succeeded in 1922.

By this time Kemal was strong enough to abolish the sultanate. In 1923 he declared Turkey a republic and moved the capital to Ankara in the heart of Anatolia. The Ottoman empire was at an end. Mustafa Kemal became known as Atatürk (ah-tah-*turk'*), "father Turk."

Kemal Ataüturk (1881–1938) led Turkey to independence and served as the republic's first president until his death.

Reviewing Your Reading

1. What was the purpose of the Crusades? How successful were they?
2. How did the Mongols contribute to the decline of the Muslim empire?
3. Who were the Ottomans? Why did their empire become known as the "Sick Man of Europe?"
4. What part did Atatürk play in the creation of independent Turkey?

The Arab World Achieves Independence

At the same time that its European possessions were dwindling, the Ottoman empire also came under attack in its Arab provinces. Egypt in particular became the focus of rivalry between Britain and France over trade routes and markets to India.

Britain and France seek to dominate Egypt. In the second half of the eighteenth century the British East India Company defeated the French in India. Both France and Britain dreamed of dominating Egypt and of building a canal through the Suez isthmus to speed up passage to Asia and control the sea traffic between Asia and Europe.

The first push came from the French. In 1798 Napoleon invaded Egypt. The British responded by destroying the French fleet off the Egyptian coast and forcing Napoleon's army to withdraw in 1801. French influence, however, remained strong in Egypt.

Muhammad Ali begins the modernization of Egypt. In 1805 an Albanian soldier named Muhammad Ali (ah-*lee'*) took over Egypt and put an end to the Mamluks, who had remained powerful even after the Ottoman conquest in 1517. Muhammad Ali invited French soldiers, teachers, doctors, and engineers to train Egyptians in the latest European military and scientific techniques. He succeeded in improving Egyptian agriculture and industry, but he kept most of the profits.

The French build the Suez Canal, but the British get control. The period of French influence in Egypt reached its peak in 1869 with the completion of the Suez Canal. It was built by the French engineer Ferdinand de Lesseps, using Egyptian forced labor.

Muhammad Ali's grandson, Isma'il (iss-*mah'*eel), continued the policy of modernizing Egypt, but in such a way as to bring the country to bankruptcy. Isma'il improved communications systems, education, and shipping. The Civil

War in the United States temporarily interrupted the supply of United States cotton to Britain, and this led to a boom in Egyptian cotton. But the profits from this short-lived boom did not cover Isma'il's expenses on his army, new railroads and telegraphs, and other enterprises.

In 1875 Isma'il was forced to sell his controlling stock in the Suez Canal to Britain. Britain and France assumed joint control of Egyptian affairs. In 1882 the British occupied Egypt on a permanent basis. They were not to relinquish control of the Suez Canal until 1956, when it was nationalized by the Egyptian government.

Britain and France divide the crumbling Ottoman empire. Both the Turkish sultans and Egypt's Muhammad Ali attempted to replace the old Ottoman military system with modern national armies on the European model. However, neither of the reformed armies could resist the determined imperial conquests of the British and the French.

The British saw the Red Sea and Persian Gulf as links in the water "lifeline" between Gibraltar and Bombay. To secure this lifeline, Britain took Aden, the important south Arabian port, in 1839; occupied Egypt in 1882; and established dominance in the Persian Gulf area. By the end of World War I the British had secured control of the Persian and Iraqi oil fields and of the eastern Mediterranean approaches to the Suez Canal.

France, not to be outdone, gained influence among the Christian communities of Lebanon and Syria. The French conquest of North Africa began in Algeria in 1830. Algeria became a colony of France in 1848. France also occupied Tunisia (1881) and Morocco (1912) and secured a hold over the Sahara.

Other European countries also entered the struggle for land and influence in the Middle East. Russian advances in northern Iran and Afghanistan were countered by British pressure in the south, in defense of India. The Germans built the Berlin-to-Baghdad railway in the early 1900s, and began to influence the Ottoman military. Italy occupied Libya in 1911 and by the 1920s held parts of Somaliland and Ethiopia.

Nationalism becomes the main force in Middle Eastern politics. The presence of so many European powers in the Middle East stimulated nationalist movements. Nationalism is the desire of a people to throw off foreign rule and to become self-governing. In Egypt the reforms and innovations of Muhammad Ali, an Albanian by birth who was interested mainly in personal gain, paradoxically gave rise to Egyptian nationalism. A century later the slogan was heard: "Egypt for the Egyptians." In Turkey the Greek invasion following the humiliating defeat of the Ottomans in World War I sparked a national liberation movement, led by Mustafa Kemal. Similar events occurred in Iran and in the various Arab countries.

Independent rule in Saudi Arabia. During World War I, Britain supported an Arab national movement led by ibn-Ali Husein (1856–1931), the Sharif of Mecca. The British helped Husein (who-*sane'*) organize an Arab revolt against the Turks, their common enemy. In exchange for his aid, he was promised an independent Arab state after the war, to include northern Arabia, Iraq, and Syria.

Sharif Husein had a rival in the Arabian Peninsula itself: the bedouin prince Ibn Sa'ud (*ib'en sah-ood'*), who had the support of most of the Arabian tribes. Husein broke with the British after World War I, disappointed at their failure to keep their promise of Arab independence. The British then shifted their support to Ibn Sa'ud. Sa'ud now conquered Mecca and Medina, and he was recognized as an independent ruler in 1924. The area under his rule was named Saudi Arabia.

The Zionists lay the foundation for the state of Israel. Britain also supported a Jewish national movement – Zionism (named after Mount Zion in Jerusalem). Zionism was a movement among European Jews to recover the ancient Jewish homeland of Palestine.

Since their expulsion from Palestine in 70 A.D., Jews in the diaspora always hoped to return one day to Israel. In Europe during the nineteenth century many Jews had worked toward establishing a national home in Palestine. The Jews were spread in various communities, especially in Russia and Poland. As the peoples of eastern Europe began to stress their own national identities, the Jews more and more felt themselves a people apart, not belonging to any one of the European nations.

This feeling was strengthened by continual oppression. The Jews in Europe never enjoyed the protection of the rest of the community as they had in the Middle East. Islam recognized the Jews, along with the Christians, as "People of the Book." With very few exceptions (the Almoravids in Spain being the most notable) Muslims avoided persecution of the Jewish communities living in their midst. In Europe, on the contrary, anti-Semitism was a grave problem for the Jews. The Nazi extermination of six million Jews during World War II was the final act in the long and bitter tragedy of Jewish life in Europe.

In the early 1900s a number of Zionist communities established themselves in Palestine, buying land, engaging in agriculture and industry, and encouraging the British and other great powers to support their movement. In 1917, in the "Balfour Declaration," Britain declared:

> His Majesty's Government views with favour the establishment in Palestine of a national home for the Jewish people . . . it being clearly understood that nothing shall be done which may prejudice the civil and religious rights of existing non-Jewish communities in Palestine. . . .

The "existing non-Jewish communities" were Palestinian Arabs, who at that time far exceeded the Jewish population, and among whom a nationalist movement had already begun.

Mandates and independence. At the same time that they were supporting Arab and Jewish nationalist movements, the British made secret agreements with the French to retain control of the area once World War I ended. They kept this agreement, angering both Arab and Jewish nationalists.

In 1920 the British received the territories of Iraq and Palestine as "mandates." In 1922 they partitioned Palestine into two parts, Palestine and Transjordan. Although there had been Jewish settlements east of the Jordan before the mandate, Jews were now barred from the territory.

The founder of the Zionist movement, Theodore Herzl (1865–1904), became convinced of the need for a Jewish homeland after reporting on the Dreyfus trial. Dreyfus was a French Jew falsely accused of selling war secrets to the Germans.

60

The British allowed two sons of Sharif Husein – Faisal and Abdallah – to become kings of Iraq and of Transjordan respectively in 1921. Egypt, technically a British "protectorate," became independent in 1922, Iraq in 1932. But in both countries the British remained, in Egypt for the Suez Canal, in Iraq for oil. Transjordan did not become independent until 1946.

The French held their mandates even more tightly than the British. Syria and Lebanon did not achieve independence until the end of World War II, in 1945. Morocco and Tunisia, technically "protectorates" instead of "mandates," became independent in 1956. Algeria, which was a French colony, achieved independence only in 1962, after a long civil war.

The partition of Palestine results in war. In Palestine, meanwhile, the British maintained their mandate, trying to balance the rival national claims of the Palestinian Arabs and the Jewish Zionists. After much unrest and many unsuccessful attempts at settlement, a partition of Palestine was arranged by the United Nations in 1947. Although the Jews accepted the plan, the Arabs rejected it and attacked the Jewish settlers. The Zionists won and proclaimed the independent state of Israel in 1948. Transjordan, in support of the Palestinian

Yemenite Jews, a small and often persecuted minority, were transported in 1949 to the newly established state of Israel to settle. This program, known as Operation Magic Carpet, was set up and administered by an American Baptist minister. In Israel, the Yemenites joined Jews from all over Europe, the Middle East, Africa, and the Americas to create a Jewish homeland.

Arabs, had occupied much of the west bank of the Jordan River, which it now annexed. The name of the country was changed to Jordan in 1949.

Israel now became the target for Arab resentment of colonial domination. During the Suez crisis of 1956, and again in 1967, war broke out between Israel and the surrounding Arab states. In each case Israel emerged victorious. Many of the Palestinian Arabs had fled Israel in 1947, and most of them were left as refugees in Jordan, Egypt, and Lebanon. Palestinian Arabs along with Arab nationalists in other countries have continued to claim the territory occupied by Israel. The history of the Middle East will continue to be a troubled one until this dispute is settled.

Reviewing Your Reading

1. Why did European powers become interested in the Middle East?
2. How has the construction of the Suez Canal affected the history of the region?
3. Define nationalism. Why did nationalist feeling grow?
4. What were the goals of the Zionist movement? What part did it play in the establishment of the state of Israel?

CHAPTER REVIEW

Recalling Names and Places

Abbasids	Faisal	Muhammad
Almoravids	hijra	Muhammad Ali
Ataturk	Hulagu	ribats
Baghdad	Sharif Husein	Selim the Grim
Balfour Declaration	Ibn Sa'ud	Seljuks
Byzantines	Isma'il	Suleiman
caliphate	Kaaba	sultan
Constantine	Koran	Transjordan
diaspora	Mamluks	Umayyads

Understanding This Chapter

1. What was the diaspora in Jewish history? How were the Jewish people able to retain their identity as Jews?
2. What are the arguments for empires like the Persian and the Roman, which brought the Middle East under one rule? What are the arguments against such empires?
3. Vast empires, even though prosperous, are hard to hold together. The Islamic Empire and later the British Empire broke apart. Why do such breakups seem inevitable.

Chapter 6

Religion and Tradition Shape Muslim Society

People in the Middle East are peasant villagers, members of nomadic tribes, or city dwellers. New developments in technology, changing political systems, the growth of cities, and the continuing influence of the West are changing the lifestyles of each of these groups.

People of the Middle East

Less than half of the people are rural villagers. Agriculture was traditionally the mainstay of the Middle Eastern economy. Today, however, less than half of the people in the Middle East live in villages. The ratio has changed in favor of the cities, where the majority now live.

In the grassland plateaus of the north, agriculture is possible wherever a spring or stream can be diverted for irrigation. Villages cluster around the water sources. Most of the villagers till their fields of wheat and other grains, while others tend the herds in the surrounding pastures.

Along the coastal plains and river valleys where water is abundant, agriculture is more intense. The land tends to be overcrowded, and usually the farmer's plot is very small. In addition to grains, the farmers raise vegetables and fruit trees of all sorts.

In Egypt village peasants are known as *fellahin (fell' uh-heen')*. Most of them are very poor, usually living on what they can grow. Often the fellahin do not own their own land but must pay taxes to the landowners, who may live in the city. Land reforms, sponsored by national governments, have alleviated some of the poverty in the villages by breaking up large holdings and distributing land to the fellahin.

Only a small proportion of the population are nomads. Nomads are people who have no fixed home but move from place to place. They usually follow fixed seasonal routes, moving to another area as the vegetation becomes scarcer, then returning to where they started. They generally travel in tribes, held together by kinship ties.

There are two types of nomads, depending on whether they live in the mountains or the deserts. Mountain nomads are called pastoralists. They spend summers in the high upland pastures, where they find water and grass and where they can escape from the parched summer plains. When the upland pastures are

Berber dancers of Morocco perform at a coronation feast, with beautiful carpets spread on the ground beneath their feet.

covered with snow, they move to lowlands watered by mountain streams. The Berber tribes in the Atlas Mountains of North Africa, the Kurds in the Zagros Mountains of western Iran, and some of the Turkoman tribes of Afghanistan are pastoralists.

Nomads of the Arabian and Sahara deserts are called *bedouin,* an Arabic word meaning "desert dweller." There are also nomadic Berber tribes in the western Sahara, the most famous of which are the Tuaregs (*twah'regs*). Desert nomads are also found in southeastern Iran.

The bedouin usually spend the summer at a permanent water source, or oasis. During the rainy season, in winter, bedouin tribes are constantly on the move, driving their herds of sheep and goats to wherever a recent rainfall has brought grass from the desert floor. Along the way they might raid other tribes, since in the hard desert environment booty is an important additional source of income.

The staple food of the desert is dates, from the date-palm. The camel serves as a means of transportation and provides meat and milk, and wool for tents and clothing.

The bedouin way of life has hardly changed over the centuries. In the early 1900s, however, rich deposits of oil were discovered under the desert floor or in the offshore gulfs. For the powerful tribes who controlled these areas, Cadillacs have now begun to replace camels, and air-conditioned apartments are replacing the tribal tent.

Cities are centers of industry and trade. Towns and cities grow up around market centers, where farmers from the surrounding villages bring their produce, and nomads from the desert or mountains bring their animals for sale or trade. Both townspeople and nomads need the foodstuffs that villagers bring. City and farm people need the animals of the nomads for transporting their own goods and wares. The towns, in turn, provide villagers and nomads with manufactured goods – cloth, tools, and such processed foods as sugar and tea.

Cities are large towns, usually located along trade routes. They are gathering places of merchants and artisans and centers of culture and political life. Some

In central Turkey, farmers bring green peppers and other crops to be sold at a city bazaar (below). In Afghanistan, nomads on horseback relax by playing a game called boz *(right). In a market at Goulmimi, Morocco, bedouin meet to trade sheep for goats (bottom right).*

> **The Duty of Hospitality**
>
> The bedouin have become folk heroes to other Arabs, just as the cowboys of the old West are to many Americans. The bedouin represent the virtues of hospitality, bravery, and freedom. Among the bedouin, hospitality to strangers and the protection of fugitives are tribal obligations.
>
> Travelers would not be able to cross the desert unless they could count on help along the way. To the bedouin host, providing for strangers brings praise and improved standing within the tribe. The guest, in turn, brings news from outside and will carry abroad the host's good name.
>
> A fugitive from one tribe can find sanctuary in the tent of another tribe's leader. Pursuers may not seize the fugitive, who is safe for three days. Then the fugitive has to find protection elsewhere. During those three days the host can speak to the pursuers and try to settle their dispute without bloodshed.

of the most famous cities are along caravan routes where streams or oases support large numbers of people. Such are Mecca and Medina in the Arabian Peninsula, Damascus in Syria, Isfahan and Tehran in Iran, and Fez in Morocco. The largest cities are along water routes with good harbor facilities and a prosperous surrounding countryside. Such cities are Baghdad on the Tigris River and Cairo on the Nile; Istanbul on the strait linking the Black and Mediterranean seas; Beirut and Alexandria on the Mediterranean; and Casablanca on the Atlantic coast.

Social class divisions are important in the villages. Within the village, land ownership has been the chief basis of social class differences – people with more land have a higher status. However, education is becoming an equally important criterion.

In traditional villages older men are greatly respected for their accumulated wisdom; they know when to sow the crops and when to harvest them. They are consulted whenever a difficulty arises. A council of elders chooses the mayor or headman, who will represent the village in its dealings with the government or any outsiders. Usually they choose the one in the village who is wealthiest and enjoys the greatest prestige among the people of the village.

Social organization among nomads is more complex. The constant dangers and hardships of nomadic life require strong leadership and strict organization within the tribal camp. In each tribe there are several clans, or groups of families who are related to each other. They are organized like military battalions in an army. Among the bedouin, the leading family in each clan sends a representative to the tribal council. This council advises the *sheikh (shake)*, or tribal leader. The sheikh makes all the important decisions in the tribe, but he is careful to observe traditional rules. If he violates the customs of the tribe, the clans are likely to revolt and choose another leader.

The bedouin will obey a sheikh only if he comes from a very noble family. The noble families take great pride in their lineage, and there are different grades of nobility among various tribes and within each tribe, similar to the noble families of European aristocracy. The tribe as a whole is proud of its standing and has a fierce sense of independence from outside authority.

Social class differences are most prominent in the cities. Large landowners and industrialists enjoy the highest status, along with government officials and military leaders. The next highest class includes wealthy professional people – merchants, doctors, and lawyers – intellectual and religious leaders, and military officers. On the third level are middle professionals, such as teachers, government employees, and office workers. Skilled workers and shopkeepers are on the next level down. At the bottom, making up the vast majority of city people, are the laborers and service workers.

Reviewing Your Reading

1. How do most people in the Middle East earn a living?
2. Identify the two types of nomadic tribes. How do they differ?
3. In what ways are villagers, city dwellers, and nomads interdependent?
4. What are the bases of social class divisions in the cities? the villages? among the nomadic tribes?
5. How is the nomadic tribe governed?

Family and Society: A Man's World

The Koran says, "Men are dominant over women . . . and upright women are submissive." This is a keynote of society in the Middle East.

The traditional family is patriarchal. In the patriarchal family the father rules. The wife seldom acts without the approval of her husband. Children are expected to be completely obedient to their father. When he dies, a brother or an elder son assumes his role.

The man is the head of the household, and only men take part in community affairs. Women must care for the house and children. Veiling and the seclusion of women are practices mainly found in the city. The purpose of these customs is to prevent women from being seen by strangers. In the village and nomadic camp such seclusion is rare. Everyone is known to everyone else, and many are related by kinship. Also, much of the work – in the fields or among the animals – is women's responsibility.

The Koran allows a man to marry as many as four wives, but he is required to treat them all kindly and equally. In practice only the very rich – merchants, landowners, princes – could afford to maintain more than a single household. Islamic law also makes divorce a man's privilege. Women were traditionally not allowed to initiate divorce proceedings. Today, most Middle Eastern countries have laws requiring monogamy and giving women the same rights as men regarding divorce.

The patrilocal, extended family is typical among nomads and villagers. In the patrilocal family the sons bring their wives to live in their father's home. If there are many sons the total extended family is very large.

Marriage between parallel cousins is preferred. The child of one's paternal uncle or maternal aunt is a parallel cousin. Ideally a son would marry his father's brother's daughter.

Courtship is restricted. Young people do not enjoy much freedom after reaching adolescence. They must work for the family and assume adult responsibilities as early as possible. Teen-age girls and boys are not allowed to socialize together. An adolescent girl must not leave the house without her father or an older brother as an escort. Even among westernized families in the cities, dating is very limited, and parents still influence their children's choice of marriage partners.

In the villages, especially, marriage is regarded as a matter for the families to decide rather than as a free choice of young people. Girls belong first to their fathers, then to their husbands. The arrangement between the two families is often a type of economic transaction. The bride's father provides the dowry, and the groom's father provides the bride wealth, which goes to the bride's family. The dowry remains the bride's own property, and the husband cannot claim it in case of divorce. This gives the woman a measure of security and independence. She also has some other rights. For example, she can inherit property.

After the two fathers reach an agreement, the young couple are informed that they have been betrothed. Sometimes such agreements are reached when the children are still small. Other times the young man and woman might never have seen each other before the wedding day. The wedding itself is a time of rejoicing and festivity for the two families.

Although most countries have minimum-age laws for marriage, many villagers do not observe them. Egypt, for example, sets a minimum marriage age of sixteen for girls and eighteen for boys. However, many village girls still marry at the age of twelve or thirteen. Boys usually do not marry until they have fulfilled their military service, by which time they are eighteen or twenty.

Greater equality among urban families. Western influences on the family are much greater in the cities than in the countryside. Girls have more opportunities to get an education and to prepare for a career outside of the home. They are seeking more equality with men in marriage and jobs.

Among the small, educated middle class the nuclear family is emerging, consisting of the husband, wife, and their children. Limited housing in cities makes it difficult to preserve the traditional extended family typical of rural areas. The absence of relatives also makes it easier to break away from traditional patterns.

Traditional Muslim education. The birth of a child is an occasion for rejoicing, especially if it is a boy. Babies and young children are exclusively the mother's responsibility. At an early age they are given work to do. Boys assist their fathers and gradually learn the tasks of men. In the city they may be apprenticed to a craftsman or a merchant. Girls generally remain at home and learn the women's duties.

At one time all Muslim scholars memorized the Koran's 78,000 words. These students at a mosque in Isfahan, Iran, still receive strict religious instruction from their teacher.

Traditionally, education outside the home consisted of learning parts of the Koran by heart and memorizing the Muslim prayers. Boys apprenticed as shopkeepers or merchants also had to learn arithmetic and writing. Some boys would be singled out for a special education, which would take place in the religious colleges, or *madrasahs*. Every large town would have a madrasah giving instruction in Islamic law. The graduates of the madrasah would go on to become teachers, prayer-leaders, and judges.

Modern governments provide a nonreligious education. In most of the Middle Eastern countries today, the national government has assumed the responsibility for schooling. Most children go to public schools, where they learn to read and write, and may go on to courses in mathematics, history, science, or technical arts.

Although illiteracy is still a problem in the Middle East, schooling on all levels has increased greatly since World War II. About half of the children are attending primary schools, more in the cities than in the countryside. Few go on to secondary schools and universities, but enrollments are growing rapidly.

Social reform: Focus on Turkey. In the 1920s Turkey undertook a program of social reform at all levels, aimed at westernizing the country. The movement was led by Mustafa Kemal Atatürk, the first president of the Turkish Republic (1923–1938).

Some of Atatürk's reforms centered on external appearances. He outlawed the *fez*, the traditional male headgear, and required men to wear the European broad-brimmed hat. He also urged women not to wear veils. Today no fezes or veils can be seen in the streets of Turkish towns.

Other reforms affected more fundamental aspects of social life. Turkey adopted the Swiss civil code to replace Islamic law in the areas of family life and interpersonal relations. At one stroke women became the equals of men – at least on the law books. They were granted new property and divorce rights, the right to schooling and to employment, and the right to vote. The madrasahs were closed, and secular schools were founded to take their place. Atatürk called for strict separation of religion and politics. He felt that the conservatism of Islam would retard his efforts at reform.

Another radical reform was the adoption of the Roman alphabet. Up to this time Turkish was written with the Arabic script, which goes from right to left. Ataturk outlawed the use of Arabic script in all new books, roadsigns, and advertisements. In its place he instituted a Roman script, like that used for European languages. This made learning to read and write a much simpler process.

Other countries in the Middle East have instituted social reforms on the Turkish model. But none of them has gone so far as Turkey in breaking away from its Islamic heritage to adopt Western ways. And since 1979, Iran has led a trend back to Islamic fundamentalism.

Islam: A Way of Life

In the Middle East, religion is an integral part of everyday life. Islam is not simply a belief system or a set of rituals that come up one day a week or on special occasions. Rather, it is an entire way of life, influencing all the thoughts and actions of its followers.

Although Western and non-religious influences are steadily growing in this part of the world, the majority of Middle Easterners still order their lives according to Islamic customs and principles.

Five "pillars" are at the base of the Muslim faith. There are five fundamental Muslim obligations. These five "Pillars of Islam" are (1) believing in God and His Prophet, (2) praying five times a day, (3) giving alms to the poor, (4) fasting during the month of Ramadan, and (5) going on the pilgrimage to Mecca, if possible.

1. Witness. In order to be considered a Muslim a person must recite the formula of "witness," which is as follows:

> I bear witness that there is no god but God (Allah),
> I bear witness that Muhammad is the Apostle of God.

This is the Muslim creed. Muslims believe that God revealed His will to several prophets during the course of history, including Moses, Jesus, and Muhammad. Muhammad was the last of these prophets, and God's revelation to Muhammad, the Koran, is the most perfect revelation.

An Islamic prayer rug is usually large enough for just one person. Most, like this eighteenth-century Turkish rug, have a central panel that resembles the prayer niche in a mosque. Above this panel is a rectangle that worshipers touch with their foreheads while praying.

2. Prayer. Muslims are required to pray five times a day, facing Mecca. Prayers are said at dawn, noon, mid-afternoon, sunset, and early evening. Before praying, Muslims wash their hands, face, and feet as a ritual purification. In worshiping, there are a certain number of bowings and other movements, all fixed by tradition.

Muslims may pray wherever they happen to be, either alone or in a group. If they are in a group, one of the worshipers steps forward as prayer leader. The others stand behind him in a long straight line and follow his movements.

Every town has one or more houses of prayer, or mosques, where Muslims gather to pray at the appropriate times. Instead of bells, the Muslims have a call to prayer, which a caller recites from a high place, usually a minaret or tower near the mosque. The call to prayer includes the "Witness" formula; the phrases "God is most great," "Arise to prayer," "Arise to well-being"; and, at dawn, the phrase "Prayer is better than sleep."

One prayer during the week requires attendance at the mosque. This is the Friday noon prayer. It includes special prayers, and there is a sermon delivered by one of the religious leaders of the community. Friday is a special day for Muslims, but it is not a day of rest. Muslims work in the morning and afternoon on Friday, but leave their fields or close their shops for a few hours around noon in order to gather in the mosque for the community prayer.

3. Alms. Giving to the poor is a religious obligation, but it serves the social purpose of spreading the wealth. It lays the burden of supporting the needy upon the rich. Islamic law prescribes that one fortieth of a person's wealth is the proper amount to give as alms. This is not considered a gift, but the right due to those who cannot support themselves.

4. Fasting. The ninth month of the Muslim year is Ramadan *(ram' uhdon')*, the month of fasting. All Muslims above adolescence must not eat or drink between dawn and sunset each day during that month.

During Ramadan the days are spent in fasting, sleeping, and prayer. The nights are spent in eating and entertainment. The month ends with a festival day, during which there is much rejoicing and exchanging of gifts of sweets and other foods.

5. Pilgrimage. The twelfth month of the Muslim year is the month of pilgrimage. During this month Muslims from all over the world gather in Mecca to perform the pilgrimage rites. These consist of several ceremonies, the most famous of which is circumambulation, or walking around the Kaaba seven times. After performing all the ceremonies, the pilgrims sacrifice a sheep or other animal. On the same day throughout the Muslim world, believers sacrifice a sheep and distribute what they do not eat to the poor. This is the second great festival day in the Muslim calendar.

All Muslims who can afford it are required to perform the pilgrimage to Mecca at least once in their lives. The pilgrimage has been a great unifying force in the history of Islam. Each year pilgrims from all the Muslim countries in the Middle East, Africa, India, and Indonesia have arrived in Mecca to pray together and to exchange goods and ideas. Today, hundreds of thousands come every year by ship, bus, and airplane.

There is no priesthood or clergy in Islam. Islamic religious leaders are men with special training in Islamic law. They serve as judges in the religious courts, counselors on legal problems, teachers in the madrasahs, and prayer-leaders in the mosques.

Otherwise, they have no special religious function. They do not perform ceremonies on behalf of other believers. They do not hear confession or act as intermediaries between the believer and God. Each Muslim man or woman is required to observe the five "Pillars of Islam."

Koran and Sunnah Are the Bases of Islamic Law

Part of bearing witness to God and the Prophet is reciting and following the Koran. This sacred book is a guide to living. It contains prayers, stories, and laws. It is written in Arabic and must be recited in its original language. Most editions of the Koran are 300 to 400 pages in length. The book is divided into 114 chapters arranged according to length with the longest ones first. Muslims recite parts of the Koran during their ritual prayers and may study it alone or in groups.

For those areas of life that the Koran does not cover, Muslims rely on the acts and sayings of the Prophet Muhammad. The sum of these acts and sayings is called the *Sunnah,* meaning "Path." Followers of the Sunnah are called Sunni Muslims, from this word.

Another Muslim sect, concentrated in Iran, follows instead the way of Ali, Muhammad's cousin and son-in-law. This sect is called *Shi'a,* meaning the "Party" of Ali. These "partisans" are known as Shiite Muslims.

Strict religious observance has become more difficult. The Koran forbids pork, wine, gambling, and usury. In practice, only the first of these is avoided by everyone in the society. Many people drink wine and other liquors, although drunkenness is uncommon. Some countries have instituted state lotteries to raise funds for public needs. Since this is a type of gambling, religious leaders frown on it. The prohibition on usury meant that in the past banking was left to non-Muslims – Jews or Christians. Today there are national banks, and government loans at interest, all of which technically go against the Koran.

There are many other areas in which traditional values conflict with the needs of modern society. In some countries, religious reformers have begun to reinterpret Islamic laws and traditions in accordance with twentieth-century conditions. These leaders are attempting to incorporate traditional Islamic values into their

Prayers can be said at home or at work, but once a week — at noon on Friday — Muslims pray together. These men are gathered at the El Hassein Mosque in Amman, Jordan. They will be led by an imam, or prayer leader, and will hear a traditional Friday sermon.

modernizing efforts. Other countries, such as Iran, have responded to the pressures of modernization by attempting to follow Islamic law more closely. At some future time these two approaches to the problems of modernization may cause conflict within the Islamic world.

Summing up. Many Westerners criticize Middle Eastern society for its strong emphasis on tradition and religion. This emphasis supported an extreme change in Iran under the Ayatollah Ruhollah Khomeini, an Islamic religious leader. Rigid Islamic rule replaced an unpopular constitutional monarchy. This change illustrated the power of religion in the Middle East to profoundly influence political events.

Ayatollah Ruhollah Khomeini (1902–   ), while exiled in Paris, organized an emotional overthrow of the shah of Iran and his government in 1978 and 1979. In early 1979 Khomeini returned to Iran in triumph to head a new government based on the strict application of Islamic law.

Reviewing Your Reading

1. What is the place of women in traditional Middle Eastern society? What rights do they have? How is their position changing?
2. Describe typical village marriage customs.
3. Contrast traditional and modern educational practices.
4. List the social reforms undertaken by Atatürk.
5. Name and explain the five "Pillars of Islam."
6. What is the traditional Islamic view on charging interest on debts? relations between the sexes? religious observances? How have such practices been affected by changing times?

CHAPTER REVIEW

Recalling Names and Places

bedouin	parallel cousin	Ramadan
bride wealth	pastoralist	sheikh
fellahin	patrilocal	Shiite
madrasah	"Pillars of Islam"	Sunni

Understanding This Chapter

1. The Bedouin way of life is declining as more people move to cities. What do they gain by these changes? What do they lose?
2. Social class differences are important in both villages and cities. Why? How do class differences affect people's lives?
3. Islam requires daily religious observances of its faithful – for example; the Five Pillars. Of what importance is ceremony to religion?

Chapter 7

Economic Life in the Middle East

As we saw in the last chapter, there are three main groups of people in traditional Middle Eastern society – villagers, nomads and city dwellers. Each of these groups provides something necessary for the society as a whole. The villagers provide foodstuffs, especially in the form of grains. Nomads provide the camels, donkeys, and horses necessary for transporting goods and people from place to place. The city dwellers provide manufactured goods – processed foods, clothing and footwear, kitchen utensils, and tools of all sorts.

In the twentieth century one of these essential services – transport – has shifted its base from the tribal camp to the city. Engine vehicles – trucks, trains, airplanes – have, to a large degree, replaced the camel caravan. The technology needed to build and maintain these new vehicles is found only in the city. As a result nomadism as a way of life is declining, and the desert peoples are turning to farming.

However, some of the same areas that formerly provided transport animals now, luckily, provide the fuel needed for the new transport machines. Many of the bedouin who once made their living by raising camels now work on oil-drilling sites.

The main categories of production in the modern Middle East, then, are two: agriculture, located in the villages; and industry and commerce, located in the cities.

Agricultural Production Is Limited

Because of the dryness of the climate, less than one-tenth of the land in the Middle East is farmed. The most fertile land is along the great river valleys of Egypt and Iraq and in the coastal areas of the Mediterranean, Black, and Caspian seas. Elsewhere, lack of rainfall makes agriculture less profitable.

Lack of water makes farming difficult. The general dryness of the Middle East makes it hard to get enough water for the crops. Even in the large river valleys the farmers must rely heavily on irrigation. In the Nile and Tigris-Euphrates valleys hundreds of workers are employed to maintain the dikes and dams needed to control the floodwaters. Harnessing the smaller rivers and streams would help alleviate the water shortage, but it is also difficult. Poor management and political squabbling waste much of the region's water resources.

Overcrowding further reduces the land's productivity. Although less than a tenth of the total land area of this region is fertile, more than two-thirds of its people are farmers. In Egypt the land-population ratio is about a quarter acre of cultivated land per person. Over the centuries this overcrowding has led to the

> **Obstacles to Progress**
>
> *An American diplomat, Eric Johnston, wrote in 1958 about his attempt to get Jordan, Israel, Lebanon, and Syria to agree on a scheme to develop the resources of the Jordan River.*
>
> Between 1953 and 1955, at the request of President Eisenhower, I undertook to negotiate with these states a comprehensive Jordan Valley development plan that would have provided for the irrigation of some 225,000 acres. This is an area comparable in size and in climate to the Salt River irrigation project near Phoenix, Arizona, which produces crops valued at $326 per acre a year. After two years of discussion, technical experts of Israel, Jordan, Lebanon and Syria agreed upon every important detail of a unified Jordan plan.
>
> But in October, 1955, it was rejected for political reasons at a meeting of the Arab League. Syria objected to the project because it would benefit Israel as well as the Arab countries. Three years have passed and no agreement has yet been reached on developing the Jordan. Every year a billion cubic meters of precious water still roll down the ancient stream, wasted, to the Dead Sea.
>
> Eric Johnston, "A Key to the Future of the Middle East," *The New York Times Magazine*, October 19, 1958. Copyright © 1958 by The New York Times Company. Reprinted by permission.

subdivision of a farmer's land into smaller and smaller plots. This results in a reduction of agricultural efficiency and seldom provides the average farmer with enough land to make a decent living. In other countries conditions are somewhat better, but the fact remains that certain countries of the Middle East do not produce enough food to feed all their people.

The region as a whole imports more food than it exports. The main crops of the region are wheat and other grains – barley, rye, millet. Egypt and Iran have both had to buy grain abroad in recent years. Rice is also raised in irrigated areas. It is a luxury food, essential for the rice pilafs famous in Middle Eastern cuisine.

Foodstuffs that are exported are mainly tree crops, such as olives, oranges, and dates. Israel sends abroad Jaffa oranges, found in many United States markets in the winter. Turkey is a leading exporter of olives, nuts, and figs. Iraq produces most of the world's dates. Non-food crops, especially cotton and tobacco, are important in Egypt and Turkey.

Vegetation limits livestock. Domesticated animals are important for both nomads and farmers. The amount and type of vegetation in an area largely determine the kind of animals that can be raised.

Camels can live in areas too barren for other animals to survive. They eat dry, spiny plants and can go for days without water. Their numbers are declining, as other forms of transport take their place. Donkeys are commonly used for transportation and hauling burdens in the villages.

Cattle are not very numerous. They do not give much milk because fodder is limited, and scientific breeding has not been practiced until recently. Most farmers use cattle as draft animals to pull plows or wagons. On large farms the cattle-drawn vehicles are being replaced by tractors.

Irrigation projects have turned deserts into productive land like this almond grove in Egypt.

Workers process Jaffa oranges, one of Israel's most valuable exports, for shipment abroad.

Goats graze beside the Euphrates River near Sabkha, Syria.

The most numerous animals in the region are sheep, numbering in the tens of millions. Where vegetation is too sparse to support cattle, as on the grassland plateaus, these animals thrive. Sheep can eat blades of grass that are too close to the ground for cattle.

Herds of sheep always contain some goats, animals even hardier than sheep. Unfortunately, goats can ruin pastures, since they have sharp hooves and pull up grasses by their roots. They also eat seedlings of trees and shrubs and have been responsible for much deforestation in a region that greatly needs forests. Trees hold moisture in the ground and provide building material and fuel. Turkey and some other countries have set up government programs to decrease the goat population. However, herders often do not cooperate with these programs because goats provide meat and milk and can thrive in places where sheep cannot.

Focus on Egypt

Egypt was the granary of the ancient Mediterranean world. Today it is barely able to feed its own population. Two factors have contributed to its decline in prosperity: (1) its patterns of land ownership and (2) its reliance on a single-crop economy.

Patterns of land distribution. Over several centuries Egyptian villages gradually fell into the hands of absentee landowners and tax collectors. By the

EGYPT: LAND USE AND RESOURCES

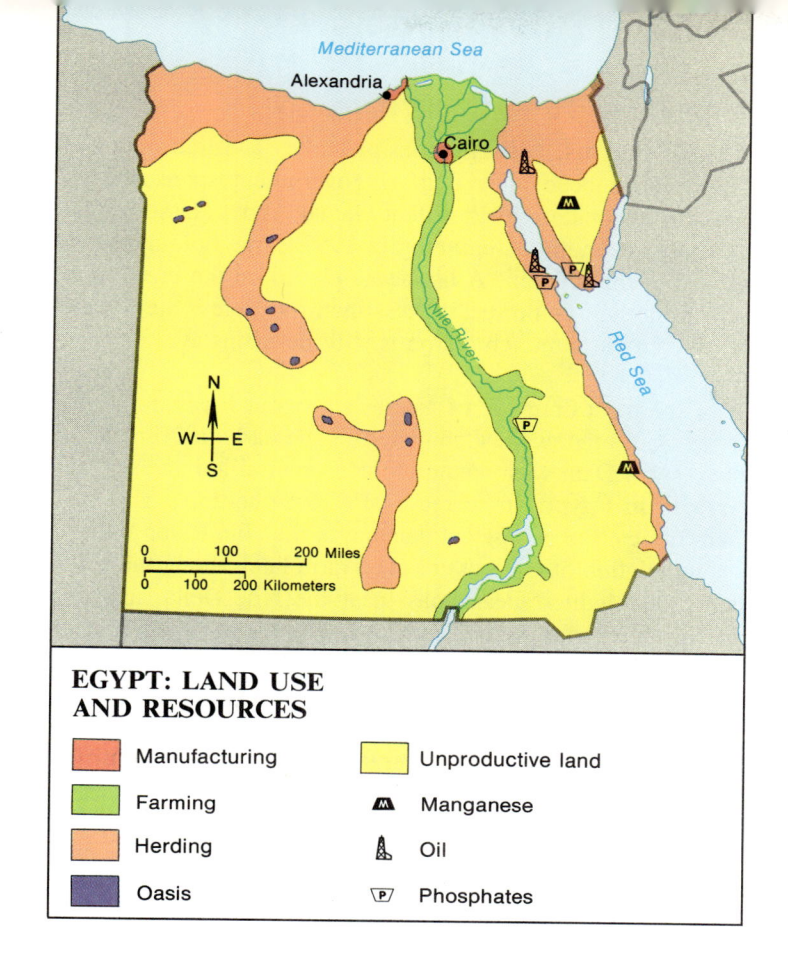

- Manufacturing
- Farming
- Herding
- Oasis
- Unproductive land
- Manganese
- Oil
- Phosphates

nineteenth century a third of Egypt's land was held by one percent of its people. Almost a third of the population held only three-quarters of an acre or less each.

The common method of inheritance in the Muslim world further reduced the size of the individual farmer's holdings. When a father dies, according to Islamic law, his property is divided among his children. Each son receives an equal share, and each daughter receives half a son's share. For sons of nomads or merchants, whose wealth is in animals or goods, this system works quite well. But for a farmer it can spell disaster, especially if the father's holding is small to begin with.

Dependence on a single crop. The British encouraged single-crop agriculture in Egypt. That crop was cotton, which Britain required for its textile mills. In the early 1800s Egypt shifted to this one-crop economy, buying other goods from the profits on cotton.

Since the value of a cash crop depends on world market conditions, single-crop farming is very risky. When the demand for cotton is high, the country prospers; when the demand is low, there is not enough income to support the population adequately. While the demand for cotton caused a boom in the Egyptian economy during the Civil War in the United States, the subsequent stabilization of world market conditions contributed to bringing the Egyptian government to bankruptcy.

Gamal Abdel Nasser (1918–1970) came to power in a 1952 military coup, and was president of Egypt from 1956 until his death.

The Aswan High Dam may have as many drawbacks as benefits. Floods no longer fertilize the lands below the dam or wash away the encroaching sea salt in the delta, and the new lakes above the dam are breeding grounds for diseases and insect pests.

Nasser undertakes land reforms. In Egypt, as in Turkey and Iran, many of the economic difficulties have been alleviated by government sponsored reforms. Land reform was a major item in President Gamal Abdel Nasser's program for building a socialist economy. Beginning in 1952, large holdings were broken up and distributed to the fellahin. A limit was placed on the breakup of inherited property, so that no heir could receive less than five acres. Steps were also taken to diversify the crops, although cotton is still the mainstay.

Aswan Dam. One of the most dramatic of Nasser's programs was the building of a new High Nile Dam at Aswan. Completed in the early 1970s mainly with Soviet funds, the Aswan Dam was planned to add one million acres to the land that could be farmed in Egypt, an increase of about one-third. Unfortunately, the Aswan Dam has caused ecological damage in the Nile River Valley. It has prevented the accumulation of silt that enriched farm lands along the Nile, increased erosion along the Mediterranean coast near the Nile Delta, and destroyed Egypt's formerly prosperous sardine industry. The dam's flood control has resulted in the increase of rodent infestation along the Nile, the clogging of sewage systems and a decrease in agricultural productivity of Egypt's richest farm land. To add to these problems, Egypt experienced a population growth that has more than counterbalanced any agricultural benefits that the dam may have provided.

The war with Israel in 1967 added to Egypt's economic problems. Besides heavy military losses, Egypt lost oil fields in the Sinai desert occupied by the Israeli army and also lost shipping revenues when the Suez Canal was blocked. By 1980, both the Sinai oil fields and Suez shipping revenues had been restored to Egypt, and by 1982 Israel had returned the remainder of the occupied Sinai lands.

Reviewing Your Reading

1. What is the traditional pattern of land ownership? How is it changing?
2. What factors have led to limited agricultural production in the Middle East?
3. How has vegetation limited livestock?
4. How has land reform in Egypt alleviated some traditional economic problems in the country?
5. What are the expected results of the completion of the Aswan Dam?

Rapid Population Growth Limits Economic Development

Birth rates are high in the largest Middle Eastern countries – Egypt, Syria, Lebanon, Jordan, Iraq, Iran, and Turkey – while death rates have fallen rapidly since World War II because of improvements in sanitation and medical care. The population of these countries is expanding at a rate of 2 percent per year – one of the highest growth rates in the world. A country like Egypt, with a growth rate of 2.7 percent per year, will double its population in 26 years. At this rate Egypt will have about 66 million people in the year 2000, while its present resources are scarcely enough to feed its 47 million people.

Cities are overcrowded. In the Middle East, cities are growing about twice as fast as the general population. Overpopulation of rural areas has forced many to become city dwellers. When there is no land available for young people, they go to the city seeking employment. The cities provide better economic and educational opportunities than the rural areas.

Industry and commerce are on the increase. Nevertheless, the rate of economic development in most countries is not rapid enough to provide all the jobs needed for the exploding population. The result is large-scale unemployment, or part-time employment, in many areas. Jobs are divided among people needing work, thus lessening efficiency and increasing labor costs. Wages are low. Shantytowns spring up around the cities.

The picture is not all bleak, however. In fact, for most Middle Easterners economic conditions have been improving. People are eating better, as a result of improvements in agriculture. Per capita incomes have been going up. Standards of living are on the rise. Transport and communications have grown, so that road and telegraph networks now cover most of the countryside, connecting city to city. The region has seen an increase in industrial productivity and the steady development of its natural resources, particularly its oil resources.

The construction of the Aswan Dam endangered many monuments of the ancient kingdom of Nubia. To save these treasures, Egyptian and United Nation forces cooperated to move the monuments to higher ground. Here the 18-ton head is lifted into place, completing reconstruction of the Great Temple of Ramses II at Abu Simel.

> **Population Growth Rates in the Middle East: Why So High?**
>
> Among factors that foster high fertility in [the Middle East] are the preference for male children, the low status or restriction of women in terms of work outside the home, and the Islamic divorce law. The failure to produce a sufficient number of sons may be cause enough for a man to consider a new wife. Accoding to Islamic law, a man is divorced after simply stating "I divorce you" three times to his wife. The oil-rich countries also see a need for larger populations for national defense and for an adequate supply of laborers for industrialization.
>
> "There's more to the Middle East than Oil," *Interchange: Population Education Newsletter,* November 1981. Courtesy of the Population Reference Bureau, Inc.

Industry Develops Slowly

The major industries in the Middle East are related to the three basic needs of food, clothing, and shelter. They are food and tobacco processing (including bottling of liquids), textiles and footwear, and construction materials. Minor industries include tool production plants.

In some countries oil production or processing is the dominant industry. Turkey has large coal deposits, and Turkey and Egypt have begun producing iron and steel. Morocco specializes in minerals and the tanning of leather. In Lebanon, trade and finance are the main "industry." Israel is the only country with a diversified industry and economy on a par with the Western countries.

Literacy and investment are important factors in industrialization. Large-scale industrialization has been slow. Illiteracy is one of the major handicaps. People unable to read instructions have trouble getting jobs in modern factories. Egypt, Iraq, and Iran have illiteracy rates between 50 and 60 percent. In Syria and Turkey they are somewhat lower. Israel's illiteracy rate is 8 percent, the lowest in the region.

Very few people have the money needed for investing in industrial development. Those with wealth are frequently the large landowners. They prefer to invest in land rather than risk their funds in industries, which generally do not begin to yield a profit for a few years.

In the cities there is only a small middle class of merchants, small business owners, and professional people. Few of them have enough money to establish large-scale businesses.

Government sponsored development. Since most people lack the means to build factories and plants, the government in many countries has taken the initiative in industrial development.

In Turkey during the 1920s, Atatürk founded a program known as *etatism* (statism). Under this program the government established industries throughout the country while at the same time encouraging private enterprise. Today, although more than half the economy is still government operated, industries are being transferred to private control.

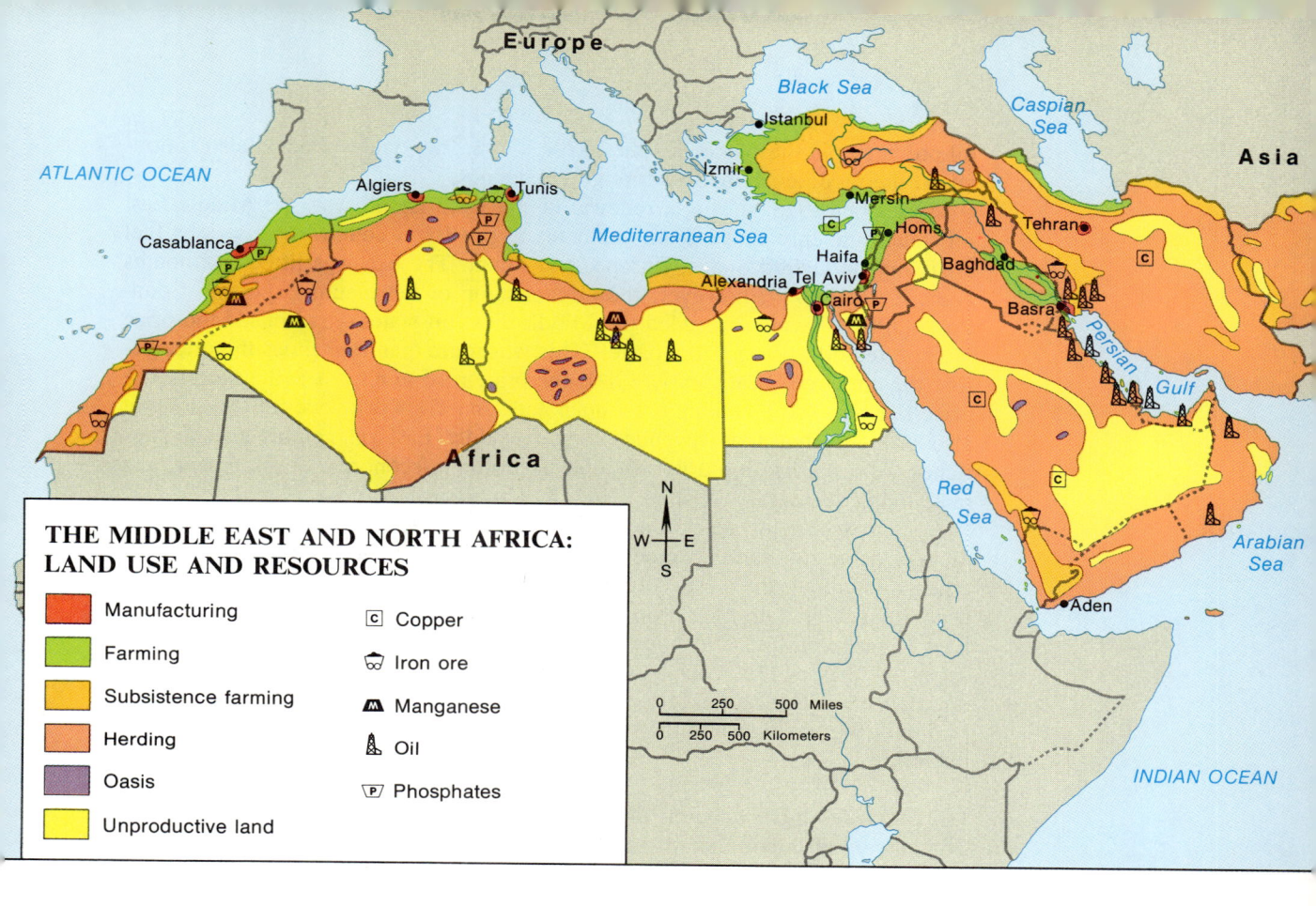

Iran under Shah Mohammed Reza Pahlevi had followed a course similar to Turkey's. Reforms introduced by the shah were aimed at improving the life of the poor villagers and nomadic tribes through such projects as land reform. In other countries the trend is toward more government control.

In Egypt, under Nasser and his successors, national plans were drawn up to diversify the economy. Prices are regulated, and the government tries to export more goods than it imports. The largest businesses have been nationalized and are now operated by the state bureaucracy. Such a system of economic regulation and ownership by the government is called socialism.

Iraq and Syria also have instituted socialist economies. In general, the change from private business to state ownership has not proved more efficient or productive for the industries involved.

Oil is now the major resource. Petroleum became an important commercial product with the invention of the internal combustion engine. The first commercial oil well in the Middle East was in Iran, developed by British companies after 1908. Subsequently oil was discovered in Iraq and the Arabian Peninsula and, more recently, in Libya and Algeria.

Oil revenues bring rapid changes. For years the foreign companies that developed the oil industry in the Middle East shared the profits about evenly with the producing countries. But the countries had long been seeking ownership or control of the properties and a bigger share of the profits. Iran took over foreign oil properties in the 1950s. By the 1970s Libya, Iraq, and Syria had also nationalized the facilities owned by foreign companies.

In October 1973, during a renewal of the Arab-Israeli war, the Middle East oil states suddenly shut off oil shipments to pro-Israel countries. A serious fuel crisis hit the United States, Europe, and Japan. The ban was lifted six months later. By late 1974, however, the Organization of Petroleum Exporting Countries (OPEC) – which included the Middle East oil states – had raised the price of exported oil to over $10 a barrel. This was more than four times the price before the embargo. In the early 1980s the price rose to almost $40 a barrel. The price rise hurt some nations very much and fanned a worldwide inflation. But it also brought enormous revenues to the Middle East oil countries. The new riches were used to build up armaments, promote economic development, and raise living standards.

Then a worldwide recession helped reduce the demand for oil and create a glut on the world market. Some OPEC nations chose to act independently of the others, lowering the price of their oil in hopes of boosting their lagging economies. Generally, the drop in prices did not hit oil producers in the Middle East as hard as it hit such nations as Nigeria, Mexico, and Indonesia. The global impact of these OPEC decisions on oil pricing was a reminder of the economic interdependence of nation. The increase in prices led to the reduction in demand by importing nations, and the reduction in demand had a strong impact on the exporting nations.

Oil revenues have created divisions among the Middle Eastern nations. The economic importance of oil has made Middle Easterners conscious of the unequal distribution of resources in the region. A division can be made between "have" and "have-not" countries, depending on the presence or absence of oil.

The chief "have" countries are Saudi Arabia, Iran, Iraq, Libya, and the small sheikhdoms of Kuwait, Bahrain, Qatar, and two of the United Arab Emirates: Abu Dhabi *(uh'boo duh' bee)* and Dubai. Except for Iran, these are all sparsely populated Arab lands. They are disproportionately wealthy compared to the rest of the Middle East. One country – Kuwait – had a per capita income of $19,870 in 1982, the second highest in the world.

Syria, Jordan, and Lebanon receive some revenues from the oil pipelines crossing their territories. Lebanon also has some oil refineries.

Egypt and Turkey, the two most populous states in the Middle East, produce very little oil, far less than they consume. Egypt is chief of the "have-not" countries. This partially explains the long-standing rivalry between Egypt and Saudi Arabia in Arab world politics.

Since the 1967 war with Israel, Egypt has also lost large revenues from the oil tankers that used to pass through the Suez Canal and pay tolls. In June 1975 the Canal was reopened. But during its long shutdown shipping companies had built huge tankers too large to pass through the canal. These tankers now transport oil economically from the Persian Gulf around Africa to Europe.

New deposits of oil have been discovered in Algeria and in areas outside the Middle East, which may reduce European dependence on the Persian Gulf area. There is also the possibility that new sources of energy will begin to replace oil in the future.

Foreign trade. In the Middle Ages, the Middle East was the center of world trade. After 1500 several European nations emerged as the dominant world

Most of the Middle East's oil is loaded onto tankers at terminals on the Persian Gulf, like this one, for export to oil consuming nations.

traders. In the nineteenth century commercial vessels using the Middle East as a passageway to other areas revived the area somewhat, especially after the Suez Canal was opened in 1869. But finances were mostly in the hands of foreigners. It was not until oil began to be exploited on a large scale, especially after 1940, that the region again became a world trade center.

The Middle East acquires new trading partners. Until recently Middle Eastern trade has been almost exclusively with Western Europe and the United States. Since 1955, as a result of strong Soviet support for the Arabs in their conflict with Israel, trade has increased greatly with the Eastern European nations and the Soviet Union. Japan also gets much of its oil from Middle Eastern countries.

Another important source of revenue in many countries is the pilgrim and tourist traffic. Visitors from abroad are attracted to the beaches along the eastern and southern Mediterranean coasts and to the magnificent remains of earlier civilizations in Egypt, Turkey, and Iraq. Pilgrims by the thousands each year visit the holy cities of Jerusalem, Mecca, and Medina.

Looking ahead. The Middle East as a region has enough resources to support itself and to modernize its society. But this will be possible only with mutual cooperation among the peoples of the area. As long as political fighting and social inequalities remain, hardships, waste, and poverty will continue.

Reviewing Your Reading

1. Why is the rate of population growth a problem?
2. What are some factors inhibiting the growth of industry in the Middle East? How have governments tried to increase industrial productivity?
3. How has development of oil resources changed the economy of the region?
4. What is the economic relationship between the Middle East and the United States? the Soviet Union?
5. In addition to its oil resources, what are other important sources of revenue for Middle Eastern nations?

CHAPTER REVIEW

Recalling Names and Places

Aswan Dam   deforestation   etatism

Understanding This Chapter

1. With little land and a rapidly growing population, how will the Middle East feed itself? What are some possible answers to these problems of survival?
2. Overgrazing by sheep and goats has turned millions of acres of grazing lands into deserts in the Middle East and Africa. Can you think of any solutions to this problem?
3. The Aswan Dam has resulted in both benefits and losses. List examples of both, and try to determine if one list outweighs the other.

Chapter 8

Political Systems of the Middle East

Traditionally, politics in the Middle East has involved clashes among opposing rulers or ruling families. The majority of the people were not involved in these struggles, except for an occasional revolt among villagers or city people when taxes or forced labor became too oppressive. With the growth of nationalism in the nineteenth century, more and more people supported new political concepts coming from the West – ideas of freedom, independence, national sovereignty, and social equality.

Today some Middle Eastern countries like Turkey are moving toward a Western-style democracy. Others, like Egypt, have developed a one-party government dedicated to social reform. Jordan and others have remained as monarchies.

All of these countries are trying, in different ways, to adjust their traditional societies to the modern world of space-age technology. Disagreements among the nations of this region, of which the Arab-Israeli conflict is the most dangerous and far-reaching, have diverted their energies and slowed their efforts at modernization.

Nationalism Replaces Islam as a Political Philosophy

Muslim religious teachers in the Middle East traditionally discouraged participation in government. The Islamic belief that whatever happens is the will of God led to extreme conservatism in government. However, religion and politics were never separate areas of life in the Middle East. On the contrary, every new religious movement took on a political coloring. The early Arab conquests, for example, were carried on in behalf of the new Islamic faith. The various Shiite dynasties and the reforming dynasties, like the Almoravids, sought political power in order to spread their religious beliefs.

The gradual expansion of Islam until the defeat of the Turks at Vienna in 1683 (p. 57) strengthened the Muslims in their faith that God was on their side. However, by the nineteenth century European nations held the reins of power both in India and throughout the Middle East. Many Muslims became disenchanted with the old ideas of government and sought new guiding ideas for their political life.

The victory of nationalism. As we saw in Chapter 5, nationalism became an important movement in the Middle East in the nineteenth century. By the beginning of the twentieth century, the call for "Turkey for the Turks" and "Egypt for the Egyptians" had become loud and clear. Supporters of the nationalist

THE MIDDLE EAST AND NORTH AFRICA: POLITICAL

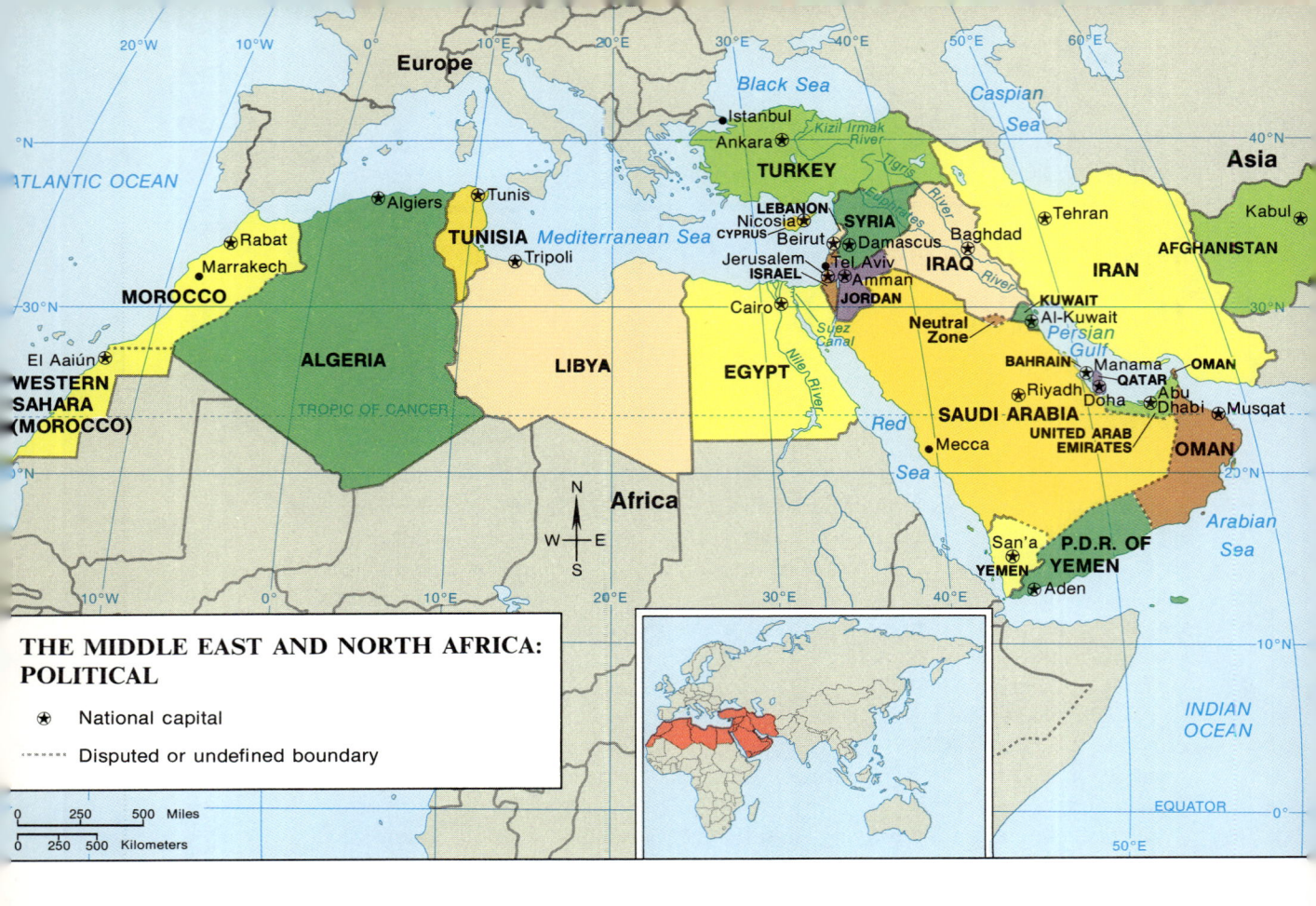

✪ National capital
------ Disputed or undefined boundary

movements were primarily educated people reacting against European domination. Although other political philosophies attracted supporters, no philosophy appealed to modern Middle Easterners so strongly as nationalism. It aroused and unified the people, especially the dominant groups within the society — the educated elite and the military.

Turkey's leaders reject Pan-Turkism. Pan-Turkism was a prominent ideology among some Turks in late Ottoman times. It was attractive to the Young Turks, who came to power in 1908. The Pan-Turkists hoped that all Turks, both in Turkey and elsewhere, would be united in a single Turkish nation. This was an unrealistic goal because the Turks are spread over thousands of miles between Europe and China and do not share a common language or history.

When Atatürk came to power he very wisely limited Turkish nationalism to the area of Anatolia and European Turkey, in which all the Turkish inhabitants share a common language and a common historical experience.

Pan-Arabism is a goal of Arab nationalism. To many Arab leaders, all the world's Arabs are considered to belong to a single "Arab nation." This concept is known as Pan-Arabism. Arabs from many different countries hope that someday the entire "Arab nation" will be united under a single government, rather than being fragmented and hostile to one another, as today. Such a union would bring together the economic resources of these countries and would be a major political force in world affairs.

The Arab countries have many things in common that together form the basis of the Pan-Arab concept. Most Arabs are Sunni Muslims and see themselves as belonging to a larger religious community. Although the spoken dialects vary widely, Arabs share a common written language and a common history. They are proud of the great civilization that was formed during the first centuries of Islam under Arab rule. They recall bitterly the centuries of subjection, first to the Turks and then to the Europeans, and the long struggle for independence. Their common hostility to Israel is a further source of unity.

Obstacles to Arab unity. On the other hand, there are strong local traditions in each of the Arab countries that work against Pan-Arabism. There are large groups in the Arab world who are either not Arabs – such as the Berbers in North Africa and the Kurds in Iraq – or not Sunni Muslims – such as the Shiite, Druze *(drooze')*, and Christian communities in Syria and Lebanon. Differences of wealth and of political philosophy also make it difficult for the Arab states to cooperate. Those with large oil resources are reluctant to join with poor ones. Conservative rulers, like the kings of Saudi Arabia have resisted giving up their thrones for a union with socialist republics like Egypt and Syria.

In 1980 a border dispute between Iraq and Iran turned into a full-scale war. For years, neither nation was strong enough militarily to defeat the other. It became a war of attrition, with heavy casualties on both sides. Other Arab nations sided with one country or the other, causing further divisions within the Arab world. In 1985, increasing attacks on cities by aircraft and heavy artillery resulted in many civilian casualties in both countries.

Another obstacle to Arab unity has been Egypt's decision to sign a peace treaty with Israel in 1979. Many Arab nations reacted angrily to this move, breaking off relations with the Egyptians. In 1981, in the midst of rising religious tensions, the Egyptian president who had negotiated the treaty, Anwar el-Sadat, was assassinated by Muslim extremists. Hosni Mubarak became the new president. He has continued the effort to solve Arab-Israeli differences. Egypt also began renewing relations with other Arab countries the following year.

The creation of the Arab League, in 1945, provided a forum where Arab leaders could voice their ideas. This organization now includes all the major Arab states. They have had some success in economic cooperation and in a boycott of Israel and nations trading with Israel. But efforts at political unity have failed. Pan-Arabism remains, for the most part, an unfulfilled dream.

Arab Socialism. Since World War II, socialism has become an important part of nationalism in much of the Middle East, especially in Egypt and some other Arab countries. Arab leaders feel that organization of the national economy along socialist lines will lead to more efficient government and greater satisfaction of human needs. A socialist philosophy also emphasizes the importance of citizen participation in the building of society.

There are strong incentives for Middle Easterners to turn to socialism. The emphasis on equality for all citizens has popular appeal. There are real economic disparities and injustices which governments in the Arab socialist countries are coming to grips with. Socialism also emphasizes mutual help, social justice, and charity, all of which are traditional Islamic values.

Nationalist leaders in the Arab countries and elsewhere in the Middle East associate Western capitalism with the colonialism they fought against. Communism, on the other hand, has made few converts. Most socialists in the Middle East oppose the anti-religious philosophy of the Communist Party, both the Soviet and the Chinese varieties.

Reviewing Your Reading

1. How has Islam influenced political life in the Middle East?
2. Why did nationalism attract so many followers in the nineteenth century?
3. Define Pan-Arabism. How did it differ from Pan-Turkism?
4. List factors which favor a Pan-Arab union. What factors make it unlikely?
5. What is Arab Socialism? Why do many nations favor this system?

Minorities and Oppression in the Middle East

Violations of human rights occur all over the world, and the Middle East is no exception. If we apply as a measure the United Nations Universal Declaration of Human Rights we find violations of these principles in all or almost all the nations of the Middle East.

Among current violations of human rights probably the most tragic victims are the members of the Baha'i faith in Iran, a nineteenth-century offshoot of the Shiite sect. From the time of their founding in 1845 they have suffered persecution, though they are a gentle, peaceful people. Their religion is not recognized as a religion in Iran and they are accused of treason, immorality, and many other evils. Of perhaps 3 million Baha'is in the world, between 150,000 and 350,000 are in Iran. They are viewed as heretics and can be attacked with impunity.

Since the 1979 revolution more than 170 Baha'is have been executed or have died under torture. More than 750 are in prison, many sentenced to death. Torture of these prisoners is common. All appeals on behalf of the Baha'is have failed.

A more complete survey of violations of human rights would have to include such minorities as the Kurds of Iran, the Copts in Egypt, the Palestinians in Israel, the Armenians in Turkey, and many groups in Lebanon, which has been called a nation of minorities. The largest group by far, however, are the women in many Muslim nations. In countries such as Saudi Arabia and Iran women are denied most of the freedoms enjoyed by men.

Politics and Government in the Middle East since World War II

Crosscurrents of many different ideas and ideologies have influenced Middle Eastern politics in the past century – Islamic tradition, nationalism, and socialism. Now let us turn to the actual political developments within the countries of the Middle East to judge the impact of these ideas.

The Arab monarchies. In 1946 the League of Nations mandate over Transjordan ended, and Transjordan became independent. Under King Abdullah portions of Arab Palestine were annexed in 1950, and the country was renamed Jordan. The nation is a constitutional monarchy. The king appoints the prime minister and Council of Ministers (the cabinet). The country's legislature is composed of an elected Chamber of Deputies and a Senate appointed by the king. There are no officially recognized political parties in the country.

In 1951 a Palestinian refugee assassinated King Abdullah for allegedly attempting to make peace with Israel. Since 1953, his son, King Hussein, has tried to keep the Palestinian refugees under control. However, more than half of the Palestinian Arab refugees in the Middle East live in Jordan, and they continue to be a dissatisfied element in the population. Civil war broke out in 1971 between Jordanian troops and Palestinian guerrillas. The Jordanian army stopped the guerrillas in bloody fighting, for which Hussein came under attack by other Arab leaders.

Saudi Arabi, one of the wealthiest countries in the world, is also among the most conservative politically and socially. The king is both the supreme governmental and religious leader. He may act as prime minister and foreign minister. King Faisal (1964–1975) deposed his brother Sa'ud during a period of instability and corrected some of the abuses of the conservative monarchy. The next king, Khalid, set up a kind of collective leadership to share the royal power. Kahlid's policies were continued by his successor, King Fahd.

Besides Jordan, Saudi Arabia, and the small sheikhdoms on the Arabian Peninsula, the only other monarchy in the Middle East is Morocco. Morocco has a constitutional government, and its king, Hassan, is a popular leader attempting to modernize his country.

In 1971 Iran celebrated its 2500th year as an established monarchy. It was a constitutional monarchy headed by a shah, who appointed the prime minister and the cabinet. The last shah, Mohammed Reza Pahlevi, made many efforts to modernize the country with the new wealth gained from oil. In 1979 he was overthrown by religious leaders who returned the country to Islamic rule.

Egypt's Nasser led the drive for Arab Socialism. In 1952 an Egyptian army revolt overthrew the British-supported monarch, King Farouk (1936–1952), and set up a republic. Among the leaders of this revolt was Gamal Abdel Nasser (1918–1970), the leading spokesman of Arab nationalism in modern times. Nasser controlled Egypt's single party from 1954 until his death in 1970. Following a program of Arab Socialism, he instituted land reforms, industrial development, and other improvements in the economic and social life of Egypt's majority, the village fellahin.

King Hussein of Jordan.

Anwar el-Sadat succeeded his long-time associate Nasser to the presidency of Egypt in 1970. He signed a 1979 peace treaty with Israel, which was widely denounced in the Arab world. In 1981 he was assassinated in the midst of rising religious tensions.

The nationalization of the Suez Canal in 1956 sparked a severe world crisis. French, British, and Israeli troops descended on Egypt, and only the joint intervention of the United States and the Soviet Union forced them to retire. Thereafter, a United Nations Emergency force kept peace at the Israeli-Egyptian border until 1967.

In 1958 Nasser spearheaded a movement to unify Egypt and Syria into a single state, called the United Arab Republic (UAR). This attempt at unification lasted three years before Syria broke away in 1961. The Syrians felt that the Egyptians were dominating the union. Both countries, however, kept the name Arab Republic in their official names: the *Arab Republic of* Egypt and the *Syrian Arab Republic*.

Iraq and Syria have experienced much political instability. The other major supporter of Arab Socialism is the Ba'ath (bah-*ahth'*) Party, which is strong in Syria and Iraq. An army-led revolt in 1958 killed King Faisal (1939-1958), ending 26 years of constitutional monarchy in Iraq. The king was replaced by a military government. In 1968 the leader of the Ba'ath Party assumed control of the government and has ruled through a fourteen-member Revolutionary Command Council. The Ba'ath Party came to power in Syria in 1963.

Israel and Turkey are the democracies of the Middle East. In Turkey, Mustafa Kemal Atatürk was chief of a one-party government from 1924 until his death in 1938. After World War II a multiparty system developed, with abuses and extremist movements kept in check by the military. In 1980 the Turkish armed forces overthrew the civilian government, suspended political parties, and

Beirut, Lebanon's capital, has become the battleground for the Middle East's historic conflicts. As different Lebanese groups fight for power and foreign countries assert their claims, the civilian population is subjected to battles, bombings, homelessness, and the constant threat of terror.

The Tragedy of Lebanon

The roots of Lebanon's problems reach far into the past. Following World War I, in 1920, the French established a mandate over the former Ottoman territories of Lebanon and Syria. To make Lebanon a more viable state the French transferred the northern area around Tripoli, the southern region around Sidon, and the eastern Bekaa Valley from Syria to Lebanon. These actions added large numbers of Shiite and Sunni Muslims to the population of Lebanon, which had been dominated by Maronite Christians.

A casually conducted population census in 1932 concluded that the Maronites were the largest religious group, the Sunnis next in number, and the Shiites third. Smaller groups included Druse, Greek Orthodox, Greek Catholics, Protestants, and others. It was decided that there was a six-to-five ratio of Christians to Muslims, and that administrative posts would be allocated accordingly. When Lebanon became independent in 1943 the formula was preserved. It was also agreed that the president would be a Maronite, the Prime Minister a Sunni, and the speaker of the legislature a Shiite.

The creation of Israel in 1948 had two major consequences for Lebanon: economic prosperity following the shift of Arab trade from Haifa to Beirut, and an influx of hundreds of thousands of Palestinian refugees from the West Bank and Jordan. When the PLO established headquarters in southern Lebanon, military clashes with Israel increased and the internal stability of Lebanon was affected.

By the 1970s it was clear that Muslims had become the majority in Lebanon. The Shiites, with an estimated 1.5 million people, are the largest group, the Sunnis next, and the Maronites third. However, the Christians were determined to try to retain control it they could.

In April 1975 a Maronite military force attacked a busload of Palestinians and killed all the passengers. This event marked the beginning of a civil war that has continued for more than ten years. The conflict has involved many different groups within Lebanon, some receiving aid or encouragement from outside the nation. The years of conflict have seen great destruction of lives and property, reducing the nation to near anarchy.

It is the view of many observers that outsiders cannot solve Lebanon's problems. The Lebanese themselves must resolve their differences and reach agreements that all can live with. A desire for national unity based on mutual trust must somehow emerge if Lebanon is to survive.

---

began to draw up a new constitution. A National Security Council ruled the country until 1983. At that time, power was formally transferred to an elected parliament.

Aside from Turkey, the only other democratic republic in the Middle East is Israel. The executive power is held by the prime minister, while the office of president is largely a ceremonial one. The prime minister is appointed by the president and is usually the leader of the political party which has the strongest representation in the Israeli parliament, the Knesset (kuh-*ness'* et). The Knesset is a single-house legislature whose members are selected by popular vote.

David Ben-Gurion (above), Israel's first prime minister, and Golda Meir (below), prime minister from 1969 to 1974, were both pioneer settlers and founders of the state.

The constitution of Lebanon tried to provide a balance of power among the country's ethnic and religious groups. But from the mid-1970s on Muslims were fighting Christians for control. The bloody fighting led to near anarchy. For years Lebanon tried to avoid involvement in disputes among Arab nations. But Palestinian guerrillas, using Lebanon as a base to make raids on Israel, fanned the Muslim-Christian conflict and added to Lebanon's political instability. In 1982 an Israeli military incursion into southern Lebanon drove the Palestine Liberation Organization (PLO) forces from Beirut.

Sources of Conflict in the Middle East

Israel is the most prosperous and the most technologically advanced country in the Middle East. One reason for this is that many Israelis were immigrants who brought with them the skills and experience of centuries of European technological advancement and world leadership. Another reason is that Israel has received massive aid from abroad – German reparations for Jews killed by the Nazis, United States government aid, and monetary support from the world Jewish community, particularly in the United States.

Arguments in the Arab-Israeli disputes. To the surrounding Arab countries Israel has remained a source of tension and conflict. Arabs argue that Israel is a remainder from the colonial era in the Middle East. They say that the Zionists forced out the Palestinian Arab population, who had lived there peacefully for many centuries. They say that the Palestinian Arabs are being made to suffer for wrongs committed by Europeans against Jews.

Israelis reply that Palestine is the ancient Jewish homeland, to which they have a right to return. They say that the Palestinian refugees left of their own accord and that the fighting would never have started if the Arabs had accepted the United Nations partition plan in 1947. Israel and its neighbors have fought five times – in 1948, in 1956, in 1967, in 1973, and in 1982–1985.

The Palestine Liberation Organization (PLO), an umbrella organization of Palestine refugees and other sympathetic Arabs, has kept the Palestinian claims a focus of world attention. The PLO has as one of its aims the removal of "the Zionist presence from Palestine." The PLO has been denied diplomatic recognition by both Israel and the United States. The United States position has been that it would not recognize the PLO until the PLO recognized "Israel's right to exist." World leaders continue their attempts to deal with the question of a Palestinian homeland. Where such a homeland would be located and how it would be governed are the main issues in the debate.

The Arab-Israeli conflict has affected foreign relations of the region. The Arab-Israeli conflict has increased Arab hostility toward the west, especially the United States. American support of Israel has led the Arabs to regard the United States as the successors of Britain and France with colonial ambitions. With the signing of the Egyptian-Israeli Peace Treaty in 1979, Egypt became more allied with the interests of the United States in the area. Other Arab nations were highly critical of Egypt's actions and the peace treaty.

Russian interest in the Middle East goes back nearly 200 years, when the tsars extended Russian territory as far as the Black Sea and began to seek an outlet on the Mediterranean. Until July 1972, when Egyptian Premier Anwar Sadat asked them to withdraw, the Soviets provided military aid and advisers to Egypt. Their financing of the Aswan Dam in Egypt and military support put Egypt in their debt for many years.

In 1979, Russian troops occupied Afghanistan, causing concern among Middle Eastern countries and throughout the world. The Russian occupation placed new military pressures on Iran and Pakistan and raised questions about Russian military plans in the region. The Russian move met an unusually strong vote of disapproval in the United Nations General Assembly. Still, efforts to dislodge the Soviet forces have failed.

A Soviet soldier guards a road near Kabul, Afghanistan. After a sudden invasion in December 1979, the Soviets found themselves bogged down in a long war to put down the uprising against their client government in that mountainous country.

Looking ahead. After the closing of the Suez Canal in 1967, the other world powers learned that they could get along without it. The tapping of oil reserves elsewhere in the world – in Alaska, the European North Sea, Siberia, and the Asian Pacific coast – and the development of other sources of power may make the rest of the world less dependent upon Middle Eastern oil, and so less involved in the region as a whole. However, the period of thaw in the "cold war" between the United States and Soviet Russia seems to be giving way to a period of increasing tensions. The Middle East is even more volatile today than in the past. Until the issue of the Palestinian refugees is settled, it is likely to remain that way. Its importance as a focus of potential world conflict grows steadily.

Reviewing Your Reading

1. Describe the various forms of government in the Middle East and give an example of each.
2. State the sources of disagreement between the Arabs and Israelis.
3. Why has the Soviet Union gained influence in the Middle East?
4. How have changing trade patterns affected Middle Eastern foreign relations?

CHAPTER REVIEW

Recalling Names and Places

Arab League	King Hussein	Mohammed Reza Pahlevi
Arab Socialism	Gamal Abdel Nasser	Anwar el-Sadat
Ba'ath Party	United Arab Republic	

Understanding This Chapter

1. Why did the influx of Europeans into the Middle East in the nineteenth century give rise to feelings of nationalism among the Middle Eastern peoples?
2. Pan-Arabism emphasizes the idea that all Arabs belong to one nation. So far all efforts at uniting Arab states under single governments have failed. Why are such unions difficult to achieve?
3. The Middle East seems to many to be in endless conflict. Some say the root causes are poverty and ignorance. Might education and economic improvement make the area more stable? Why?

Chapter 9

Cultural Contributions of Islamic Civilization

Great civilizations are the result of the contributions of many peoples. This was especially true of Islamic civilization during the Middle Ages when Muslim culture was a blending of Arabic, Persian, Turkish, Greek, Roman, Indian, Egyptian, Chinese, and many other elements.

The Arabs provided the foundation for this civilization in two ways. One was the Arabic language, which became the language of government and literature and was adopted by many non-Arabs. The other was the Islamic religion. This faith proved to be remarkably flexible and tolerant, at least during the first few centuries of its existence. Islam stimulated the search for knowledge and allowed creativity in literature and the arts.

Achievements in Mathematics and the Sciences

There is a traditional saying Muslims attribute to the Prophet Muhammad: "Seek knowledge, even in China." Scholars everywhere in the Muslim world studied past intellectual achievements, especially those of the Greeks, in science and philosophy. These achievements might have been lost to us if Muslim scholars had not translated Greek writings into Arabic.

Muslim scholars made numerous original contributions as well. The Muslims were outstanding scientists. They developed methods of careful, systematic study and observation.

Interest in science had a practical and religious basis. Scientific investigation was stimulated by practical religious needs. To compute shares of inheritance according to Muslim law, people had to be well versed in arithmetic. Geometry was important for surveying land, designing mosques, and making battle instruments for the jihad, or holy war. Algebra was useful in computing the division of estates. Astronomy was necessary for computing the times of the five daily prayers, the exact direction to Mecca during prayer, and the timing of the religious fast during Ramadan.

Other sciences were related to the welfare of the community. Muslims made important contributions in medicine, optics, mechanics, and hydraulics. Other intellectual areas they developed were history, geography, cosmography, sociology, and philosophy.

Developments in mathematics. Although our system of numbers originated in India, it was introduced to Europe by the Muslims. Hence we call our numerals "Arabic numerals," though the Arabs call them "Indian numerals." It is a simpler system than the cumbersome Roman numerals used in Europe during the Middle Ages. With only nine digits and a zero any number can be easily written. The Arabs also introduced decimals with this numbering system.

There were many great Muslim mathematicians. Perhaps the greatest was the Persian Al-Khwarizmi (780–850), the founder of modern algebra. Another Persian, Omar Khayyam, better known as a poet, added to Al-Khwarizmi's algebra and largely brought it to its modern form.

Muslim mathematicians translated Euclid and developed Euclidian geometry. They were also the inventors of trigonometry.

Achievements in medicine. The Muslims were interested in medicine, especially ophthalmology (the study of eye diseases). With interest in curing disease came the search for effective drugs and medicines. The earliest hospitals and pharmacies were established by Muslims; and pharmacists as well as doctors had to take examinations to prove their competence.

Muslim physicians were among the first to understand that diseases can be contagious. For a long time people in Europe and throughout the world thought that a disease either originated within the person or was caused by evil spirits.

The world of science owes Muslim scholars a large debt for their contributions to mathematics, medicine, and technology, and for their translations of Greek manuscripts in those fields. This illumination, entitled "Two Apothecaries," is taken from an ancient Mesopotamian manuscript.

> **A Cure for Melancholia**
>
> *Muslim physicians were among the first to recognize that many ills are psychosomatic, that is, psychological in origin. Diseases that ordinary medicines might not cure are often relieved by treating the patient's emotional state. Ibn Sina, the famous Baghdad physician, recognized this relationship of mind and body. The following anecdote is told about him:*
>
> A certain prince . . . was afflicted with melancholia and suffered from the delusion that he was a cow. Every day . . . he would low like a cow, causing annoyance to everyone, and crying, "Kill me, so that a good stew may be prepared from my flesh;" until matters reached a pass that he would eat nothing, while the physicians were unable to do him any good. Finally Avicenna . . . was persuaded to take the case in hand . . . First of all he sent a message to the patient bidding him be of good cheer because the butcher was coming to slaughter him, . . . the sick man rejoiced. Some time afterwards Avicenna, holding a knife in his hand, entered the sick-room, saying, "Where is this cow, that I may kill it?" The patient lowed like a cow to indicate where he was. By Avicenna's orders he was laid on the ground bound hand and foot. Avicenna then felt him all over and said, "He is too lean, and not ready to be killed; he must be fattened." Then they offered him suitable food . . . and gradually he gained strength, got rid of his delusion, and was completely cured.
>
> Browne, E.G. *Arabian Medicine,* (London: Cambridge University Press, 1921), pp. 82–89.

Understanding the nature of contagion was a giant step forward in the development of modern medicine.

The greatest Muslim physician was a Persian named Al-Razi (865–925). He wrote, in Arabic, over fifty books on medicine, including the earliest studies of smallpox and measles. He summed up the medical knowledge of the Greeks, Persians, and Hindus, and added much that was his own discovery. Al-Razi became known to medieval Europe as Rhazes. His books were translated into Latin and used for centuries in European medical schools.

Next to Al-Razi in importance was Ibn Sina (*ib'n see'* nah, 980–1037), known in Europe as Avicenna. Ibn Sina wrote nearly a hundred books, not only on medicine but also on philosophy, astronomy, mathematics, and other subjects. His encyclopedia of medical knowledge became a standard textbook in European medical schools during the Middle Ages.

Interest in geography. As citizens of a great empire many Muslims developed a love of travel, and some wrote of their experiences. Ibn Battuta (1304–1377) was perhaps the most widely traveled man of his time. Born in Tangier, Morocco, he voyaged to India and China and throughout Africa and the Middle East. Ibn Battuta wrote in great detail about the geography and customs of the places he visited.

The Rich Heritage of Muslim Literature

Muslim literature in the Middle East was written in three languages. Arabic, the language of the Koran, was used in many religious, scientific, and literary writings. Persian became important during the Abbasid dynasty and was especially promoted in the Seljuk and Mongol courts. Turkish became the language of government and of court literature during the period of Ottoman rule.

Each of these languages has produced an outstanding literature of its own in both poetry and prose. And each of them is alive and vigorous today, the language of daily newspapers and of popular and scholarly literature on all levels.

The Koran is the basis of Muslim religious literature. Since the time of Muhammad, for thirteen and a half centuries, the Koran has been the model for all Arabic literature. When people write in Arabic, they use the language of the Koran. For this reason, the Arabic literary language has not changed, even though the spoken language has changed a great deal.

Muslim religious literature grew out of studying the language of scripture and the Koranic allusions. People collected traditions about the sayings and deeds of Muhammad and of his companions, and wrote biographies and histories.

A copy of the Koran was often a masterpiece of Arabic calligraphy. This page, in the Arabic script known as Masahif, reads: "No bearer of burden shall bear the burden of another. Man gets only what he strives for, and the result of his striving will be seen; then he shall be rewarded for it fully. . . ."

> **Our Middle Eastern Vocabulary**
>
> *Whenever there is major cultural diffusion from one civilization to another, language is affected. In agriculture and industry, medicine and music, astronomy and mathematics, many items entered Europe from the Middle East and along with these items their Arabic or Persian names.*
>
> *All of the following English words derive from Arabic or Persian. Most of them came into English by way of other European languages, especially Spanish and French.*
>
> | | | | |
> |---|---|---|---|
> | alchemy | camphor | logarithm | sofa |
> | alcohol | cheque (check) | lute | sugar |
> | algebra | cipher | magazine | syrup |
> | alkali | coffee | mattress | taffeta |
> | almanac | cotton | orange | tambourine |
> | azimuth | damask (from Damascus) | rice | tariff |
> | bazaar | guitar | sherbet | zenith |
> | calibre | lemon | soda | |

Poetry was the favorite literary form. Even before Islam the Arabs were fond of poetry. Each tribe would have its poet, who put tribal feelings into words. His job was to praise the tribe and criticize others, to describe battles, eulogize dead warriors, and sing of the desert and its beauties.

The Arabs developed a rich oral literature. Poems were memorized and passed on from speaker to listener, not written down. Only after the rise of Islam, when the Arabs were dispersed throughout the Middle East and reading became popular were these poems collected into books. Study of this classical poetry became part of religious education. Since the poems were in the language of the Koran, they could be used to explain difficult Koranic passages.

During the Umayyad and Abbasid periods poetry continued to be the favorite literary form among the Arabs and indeed has remained so until the present day. But some poets developed new styles and subjects for the refined courtly life of a conquering and aristocratic people. The poets sang of love and flowers, praised the nobility and generosity of their patron princes, and expressed their own hopes, fears, and reflections.

The Persians developed new poetic forms. Beginning in the tenth century, Persian began to rival Arabic as a language of literature. The Persians borrowed some of the Arabic poetic forms, but also developed new ones of their own.

The finest form of Persian poetry is epic, or narrative, verse. And the greatest epic poem in a Muslim language is the *Shah-nameh* by Firdawsi, written about the year 1010. Firdawsi used as his source the stories of the pre-Islamic Persian kings and heroes. These stories formed part of the folklore of his people. Firdawsi rewrote them in verse, producing a long work known as the *Shah-nameh*, or "Book of Kings." Later poets found subject matter for narrative poems in biblical and Koranic stories about Joseph and other figures, and in Arabic and Persian love stories.

> ### Omar Khayyam, Poet and Scientist
>
> *The Persian poet who is best known to the English-speaking world is Omar Khayyam (1043–1123). The reason is not that he was a great poet, but that his poetry was translated by the great English poet, Edward Fitzgerald (1809–1883). Fitzgerald was attracted to the "eat-drink-and-be-merry" philosophy expressed in Omar Khayyam's* Rubaiyat. *His translation of these verses includes some of the most famous expressions in English verse of the inalterable passage of time.*
>
> Think, in this batter'd Caravanserai
> Whose Portals are alternate Night and Day,
> How Sultan after Sultan with his Pomp
> Abode his destined Hour, and went his way.
>
> * * *
>
> Come, fill the Cup, and in the Fire of Spring
> The Winter Garment of Repentence fling:
> The Bird of Time has but a little way
> To fly – and Lo! the Bird is on the Wing.
>
> *In his own day Omar Khayyam was less known as a poet than as an astronomer and mathematician. He was also famous as a philosopher and a physician and was much respected in both scholarly and government circles.*
>
> Browne, E.G., *Arabian Medicine*, (London: Cambridge University Press, 1921), pp. 88–89

Persian poets also distinguished themselves in mystical poetry, a type of religious verse in which the poet expressed his love of God in sensual terms. He compared his ecstatic religious experience with intoxication from wine or with love for a beautiful person.

Popular literature. Books on religious subjects were written in the mosques and madrasahs, and poetry was patronized in the courts of princes and kings. Popular stories and folk tales were enjoyed by all sectors of society. One famous collection of such stories, not written down in its present form until the fourteenth century, was *A Thousand and One Nights,* also known as *Arabian Nights*. The core of this work was a collection of Persian tales, many of them of Indian origin, told within the frame-story of Shahrazad, the beautiful princess who night after night put off her execution by entertaining the king with stories. To this core were added stories that were being told in Baghdad and set in the fabulous court of Harun al-Rashid, the great Abbasid caliph. Later more stories were added – Indian, Egyptian, Hebrew, and Greek – but all of them retold in Arabic and set into the original frame.

Many other literary forms were enjoyed by the Muslim peoples. To these were added, in the nineteenth century, certain Western literary forms, such as the novel, short story, and essay. Under the influence of European writers and of nationalism a new outburst of literature in all forms has occurred in the last hundred years.

The Dome of the Rock in Jerusalem is one of the holiest shrines in the Muslim world. According to Islamic belief, Muhammad ascended to heaven from the rock in the center of the mosque.

Developments in the Fine Arts

Islam was a stimulus to artistic creativity during the Middle Ages. The great monuments are the large mosques, built everywhere in the cities of the Middle East for the Friday community prayer. Much artistry was also expended on traditional crafts, such as weaving, ceramics, metalwork, and glass. Finally, music and painting, although not encouraged by Muslim religious leaders, still flourished, especially in the princely courts.

Architecture was a major art form. Two beautiful mosques that survive from the Umayyad period are the Dome of the Rock in Jerusalem (completed in 691) and the Great Mosque of Damascus. Many of the Abbasid monuments were destroyed when the Mongols took Baghdad in 1258.

When the Ottoman Turks conquered Istanbul in 1453, they converted the magnificent Byzantine cathedral of Saint Sophia into a mosque and began to beautify the city further with mosques and palaces. Especially famous are the Suleymaniya Mosque, built in 1557 during the reign of Suleiman the Magnificent (p. 57), and the Blue Mosque. Turkish mosques are noted for their slender, cylinder-shaped minarets, which rise high above the mosque's dome.

An illuminated Turkish manuscript, dated 1583, showing Noah's ark in the flood. Books decorated in this way were the prized possessions of the wealthy and noble in the Middle East of the day.

This Syrian enameled lamp of the fourteenth century once hung in a Muslim mosque. Its principal ornamentation is the swirling design in Arabic script.

Other splendid mosques are located in Cairo and in Shiraz and Isfahan in Iran. In addition to building religious structures, Muslim princes erected palaces and on the caravan routes between the large cities built caravanserais, or inns.

The favorite decorative technique for carpets, ceramics, and even buildings, was Arabic writing. The elegant Arabic script was used for decoration especially in the mosque, since Muslims are opposed to the portrayal of animal or human images in places of worship. Calligraphy, the art of writing, became a major religious art form in the Muslim world.

Music and painting developed in the courts. Religious teachers in the Muslim world disapproved of music, saying that it was frivolous and drew the mind away from God. They also disapproved of painting, saying that it was a blasphemous imitation of God's creative handiwork. Muslims knew the important role that both music and painting played in Christian religious worship. They felt that praying to icons and portraying God in pictures were forms of idol-worship.

For this reason, no musical instruments accompany Muslim prayer; and mosque decoration, though rich in calligraphy and abstract designs, contains no imagery of animals or human beings.

Art on a smaller scale. In the princely courts of Baghdad, Istanbul, and other cities, music and painting continued to flourish, away from public gaze and religious censure. The princes appreciated singing and dancing girls and instrumental music and generously supported talented musicians. They also desired to own decorated books of poetry, history, and other subjects. There thus developed the art of the miniature painting. Some of the most beautiful paintings in the world are found in books hand-copied and decorated for Middle Eastern princes and sultans. The Mongol and Persian courts of the thirteenth to sixteenth centuries especially patronized this art form. The most famous Islamic painter was Bihzad, who lived in Iran in the early 1500s.

Looking ahead. Muslim scholars in the Middle Ages preserved the scientific heritage of the ancient world and transmitted it to the West. Muslim poets and artists created works of great value to world culture. Middle Easterners today are justly proud of their intellectual and artistic heritage. Political independence and modern economic and social developments are all very recent in the Middle East. They may open doors to new creativity in the arts and sciences.

CHAPTER REVIEW

Recalling Names and Places

Al-Khwarizmi	Bihzad	Omar Khayyam
Al-Razi	Dome of the Rock	*Shah-nameh*
Arabian Nights	Ibn Battuta	Suleymaniya Mosque
"Arabic numerals"	Ibn Sina	

Understanding This Chapter

1. Why does the Arabic language occupy a unique place in Muslim culture?
2. How did the Islamic religion favor developments in mathematics, astronomy, geography, and architecture? What were the practical applications of mathematics and geography to the Muslim world?
3. What were some major Muslim contributions to mathematics? to medicine?
4. What are some themes of Persian and Arabic poetry?
5. Describe some popular forms of art and architecture in the Middle East.
6. Based on the list of words in the box above, what are some contributions of the Islamic Middle East to our own culture?

UNIT 3
Exploring
Africa

| 1 | 200 | 400 | 600 | 800 | 1000 | 1200 | 1400 | 1600 | 1800 |

- RISE OF ISLAM 639

CENTRAL AFRICAN KINGDOMS
BENIN, ASHANTI UNION, BANTU
1200–1967

- CHRISTIANITY IN NORTH AFRICA
c. 300

SLAVE TRADE
c.1440–c.1890

WEST AFRICAN KINGDOMS
GHANA, MALI, SONGHAI
c. 500–1600

EUROPEAN
COLONIALISM
1657–1951

INDEPENDENCE •
1951–

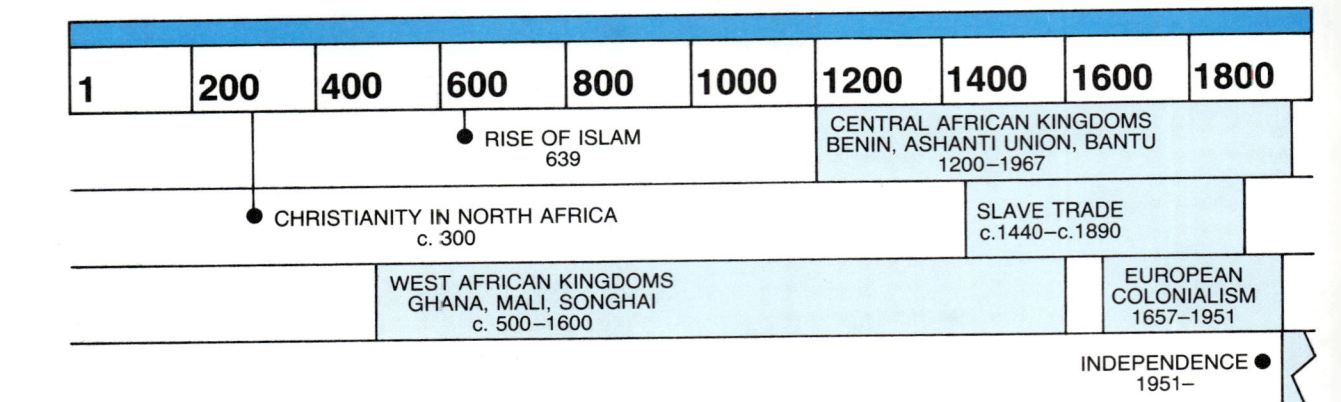

THE EMERGENCE OF AFRICA INTO WORLD affairs is one of the important events of the twentieth century. Known as the "Dark Continent," Africa was exploited for centuries by the Arabs, Europeans, and Americans. Fifty million Africans were victims of the trans-Atlantic slave trade from the fifteenth to the nineteenth century. For eighty years, until 1960, most of Africa was under colonial rule. Africa is at last emerging into the community of independent nations.

A huge continent, extending about equal distance north and south of the equator, Africa has been a fascinating land to the rest of the world for a long time. Because it was geographically rather inaccessible to the outside world until recently, fantastic tales were told about Africa in the past. Medieval Europe thought Africa was inhabited by grotesque people and monstrous animals. However, more accurate knowledge of Africa has not made this continent any less interesting to the outside world.

Although most of the new African nations are still poor, many of them have enormous natural resources for future development. With wise leadership and some assistance from the rest of the world, the Africans may achieve success as modern nations. More than forty independent nations are found in Africa. Some are very small and have limited resources. Joining with other African nations into larger federations might improve their prospects as modern nations. African leaders know this, and many are working for regional cooperation. A new awareness and pride in Africa's achievements has developed within the United States. This awareness is shown by the popularity of traditional African dress, interest in the study of Swahili, and the increase in African studies.

Research on Africa's past has been stimulated by the discovery of the remains of very early human species in Africa. A new awareness of Africa's ancient past has developed, resulting in a great increase recently in African literature. Africa has never been more interesting than today.

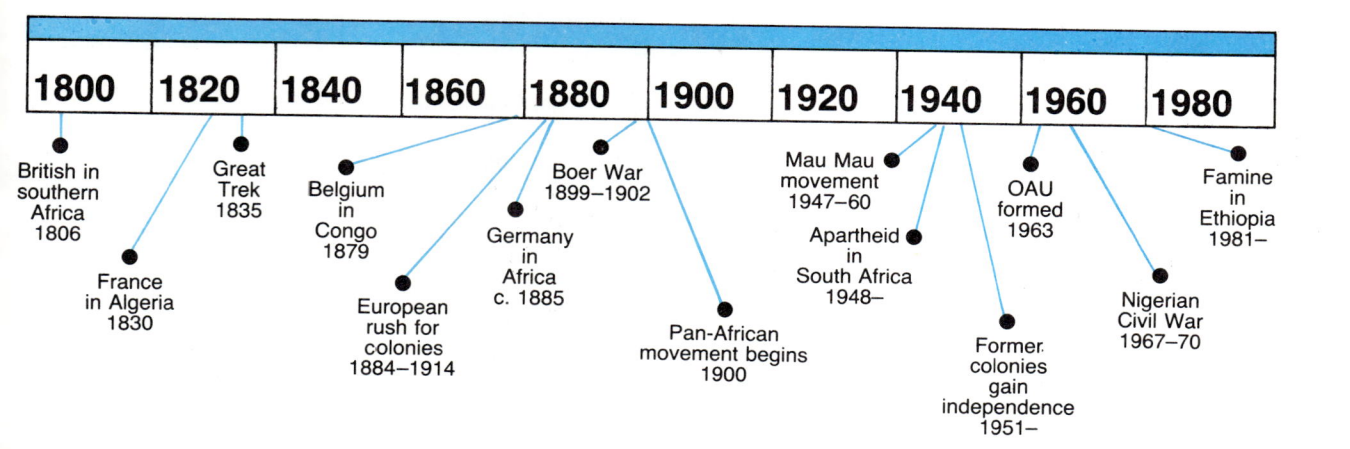

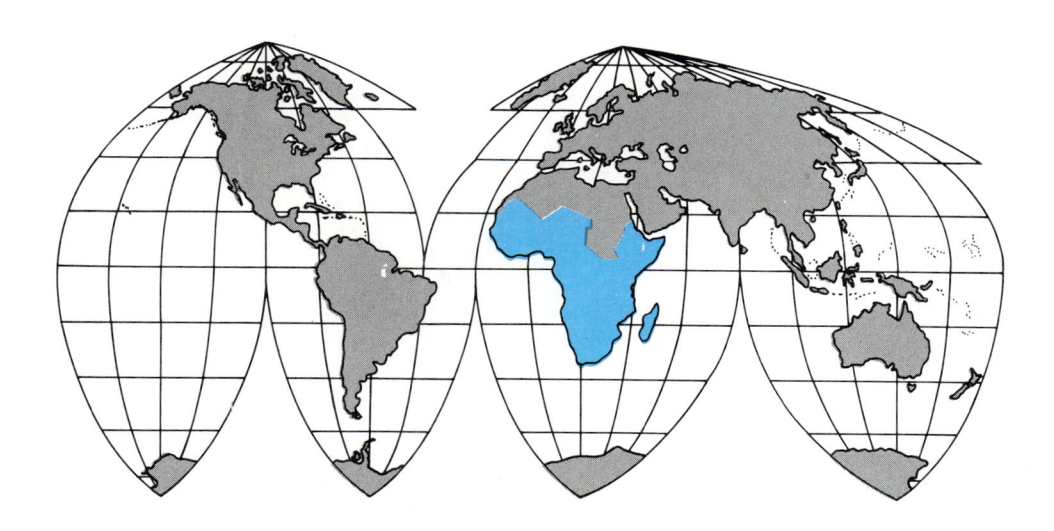

| 1800 | 1820 | 1840 | 1860 | 1880 | 1900 | 1920 | 1940 | 1960 | 1980 |

- British in southern Africa 1806
- France in Algeria 1830
- Great Trek 1835
- Belgium in Congo 1879
- European rush for colonies 1884–1914
- Germany in Africa c. 1885
- Boer War 1899–1902
- Pan-African movement begins 1900
- Mau Mau movement 1947–60
- Apartheid in South Africa 1948–
- Former colonies gain independence 1951–
- OAU formed 1963
- Nigerian Civil War 1967–70
- Famine in Ethiopia 1981–

We shall begin with a brief review of the geography of Africa. Then we will explore some aspects of the past and present of sub-Saharan Africa. Although on the same continent, North Africa is a part of the Mediterranean region. Since independence, sub-Saharan Africans are developing more ties with North Africa. Nevertheless the two parts of the continent are different cultural regions.

Chapter 10

The Varied African Landscape

If we include the island of Madagascar, the total area of Africa is nearly 11.7 million square miles. In size Africa is three times larger than the United States. The distance between the most northern and most southern points of the continent is nearly equal to the distance between New York City and Buenos Aires. The distance east to west at the widest point is almost as far as from New York City to Moscow.

A Continent with Many Climates

The equator crosses Africa almost at the midpoint between the northern and southern ends of the continent. Thus most of Africa lies within the tropics. Since most of Africa south of the Sahara is within the same latitude, one might think that all areas would have the same hot climate. However, differences in wind patterns and elevation cause some variation in climate. For example, highland areas of East Africa have cool winters and snowcapped mountains, because temperatures are cooler at high altitudes.

The arid climate regions. Perhaps one of the most impressive physical features of Africa is the Sahara. The Sahara, meaning desert or "wasteland" in Arabic, is larger than the continental United States. It extends across the northern third of Africa from the Atlantic Ocean to the Red Sea.

The Sahara created a barrier to human migration for many centuries. Great differences between peoples and cultures exist north and south of this desert. Nevertheless, the Sahara was not a complete barrier between the peoples living on either side. On the eastern side trade and cultural influences traveled along the Nile River and coastal waters. In the western Sahara caravan routes maintained contact between the north and south over many centuries. While the desert slowed down cultural exchange, it did not prevent cultures from taking ideas, inventions, and practices from each other.

In southern Africa another important desert, the Kalahari (kah-lah-*hah'* ree), extends from Namibia (South West Africa) in southern Africa to Botswana. Less dry than the Sahara, certain grasses and wild melons can grow in a few places on this otherwise barren land. Some cattle and such wild animals as gazelles and wild dogs live here.

Nearly 40 percent of Africa is desert. Rock, gravel, and sand cover the ground in desert areas. Water is scarce, with most areas receiving less than 10 inches of rainfall annually. Additional water may come from oases.

SUB-SAHARAN AFRICA: PHYSICAL

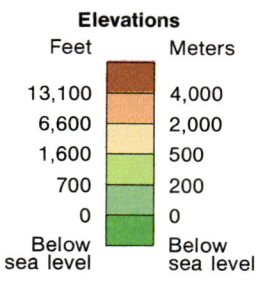

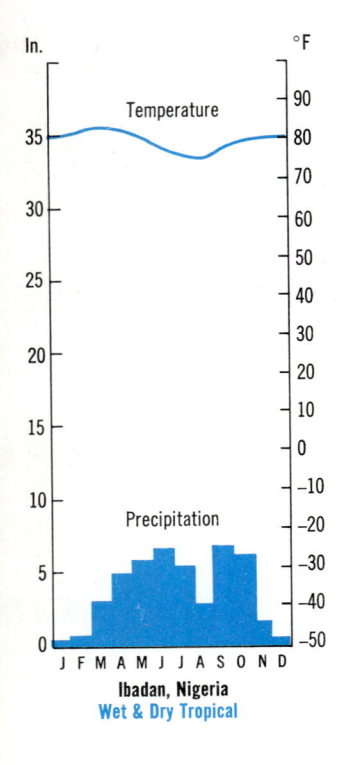

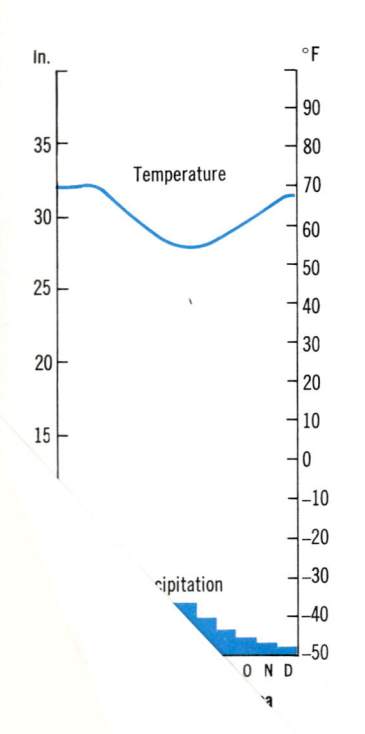

The savannah region. The savannah climate zone begins at the southern edge of the Sahara and the northern and eastern edges of the Kalahari. The savannah has both a wet and dry season. An area of greater rainfall than the desert, the savannah region has more vegetation. The vegetation varies somewhat, depending upon the amount of rainfall. Primarily it is a grasslands area, although trees dot the landscape when rainfall is adequate.

Near the arid desert areas rainfall is small, but as one continues southward from the Sahara or northward from the Kalahari, the amount of precipitation steadily increases. Two-fifths of the continent has this type of climate, and in this region zebras, antelope, giraffes, and lions roam. In East Africa cattle are raised on the savannah.

A limited tropical rain forest region. Tropical rain forests cover 8 percent of the continent. This climate region is found in Guinea *(gin' nee)* and the Ivory Coast of West Africa. It also extends from Nigeria southward into Zaire and continues eastward, reaching the highlands of East Africa. A third rain forest area exists in eastern Madagascar.

In the tropical rain forest region, rain falls almost every day. Temperatures remain around 80° throughout the year. Large trees grow close to one another, preventing sunlight from reaching the forest floor.

Tropical soils are noted for their lack of fertility, especially tropical rain forest soil. With constantly warm temperatures the humus formed by dead leaves and branches quickly decays. Warm rains dissolve and wash away minerals that would enrich the soil. This process is called leaching.

In cooler climates the cold season slows the leaching process and allows the humus to accumulate, providing a richer soil. The thick vegetation of the rain forest is very misleading. The plants are drawing nutrition from recently produced humus, since no accumulation from the past exists. If the forest is cleared away, the soil quickly becomes worthless.

Tropical rain forests are often incorrectly called jungles. Jungles are found along river banks. In jungle areas the trees grow far enough apart so that sunlight reaches the ground. As a result, plants grow so thickly that travel is difficult without a knife to cut a path. In rain forests, travel is easier.

A few areas with a pleasant Mediterranean climate. Some of the best farmlands are found at the extreme ends of Africa, north and south, where the climate is temperate. Such places as the coastal areas of Morocco, Algeria, and Tunisia in the north and the Cape Town region of South Africa have a climate often called Mediterranean because of the cool winters and warm summers. Here it is possible to raise olives, figs, grapes, and wheat.

Irregular rainfall makes large areas of Africa unsuitable for farming. As we have seen, large areas of Africa are desert, and in many other areas the soil of the rain forest is unsuitable for crops. In drier regions where the soil is richer, lack of rain is a major problem. For example, in East Africa the term "average rainfall" can be misleading. While official statistics may show that this area receives 40 inches of rainfall a year, this figure is an average. This amount does not necessarily fall annually. It may vary from 60 inches one year to 20 inches the next. A very typical problem is that one cannot depend on the rain coming when it is most needed. Some years ago in Kenya the rains did not come on schedule and countless animals died of thirst. A few months later the rains came, drowning many animals who survived the drought.

Tropical savannah regions like this one form transitional zones between jungles, where the rainy season lasts all year, and steppes and deserts, which have a dry season almost all year round.

Land Formations Kept Africa Isolated and Inaccessible

North Africa became part of the Mediterranean world early in history. Africa south of the Sahara was much more isolated from the rest of the world. The vast Sahara was a barrier to easy contact between the northern and southern portions of the continent. Caravans took many days to cross the Sahara.

Waterfalls and cataracts prevented interior navigation. While ships could travel along the coasts of Africa, few navigators were willing to face the risks of sailing up the rivers into the interior of the continent. Those who did faced a nearly impossible task. Sub-Saharan Africa has a large central plateau, slightly tipped in the east to form the highlands, which descend abruptly to the coastline from the edges of the plateau. This abrupt descent creates waterfalls and rapids that make river navigation impossible. The effect of this land formation was to cut off the interior from exploration by foreigners and to limit African contacts with the outside world.

However, once the many waterfalls and cataracts are passed, the rivers on the interior plateau are often navigable for long distances. The Congo River and its tributaries have 6000 miles of navigable waterways. The waterfalls also provide great opportunities for hydroelectric power. They may become a major source of energy in the future.

Eastern Africa has impressive land formations. The highest mountains in Africa are found in the eastern part of the continent. Millions of years ago violent disturbances caused the land to rise in some places and sink in others. Great volcanic eruptions produced Africa's highest mountain peaks, 19,340-foot-high Mount Kilimanjaro (kill-uh-mahn-*jah'* row) in Tanzania (tan-zah-*nee'uh*) and 17,040-foot-high Mount Kenya in Kenya. Much volcanic material was also deposited in the high plateaus of East Africa.

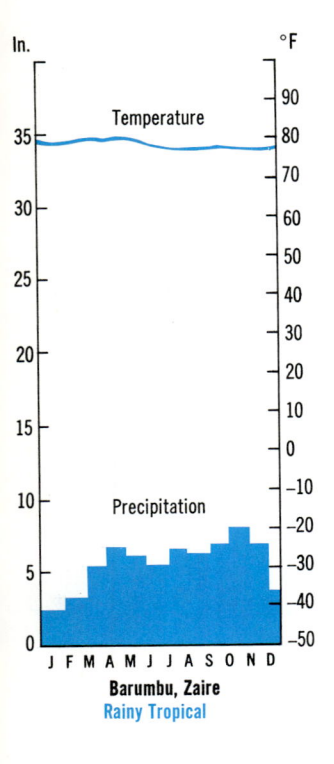

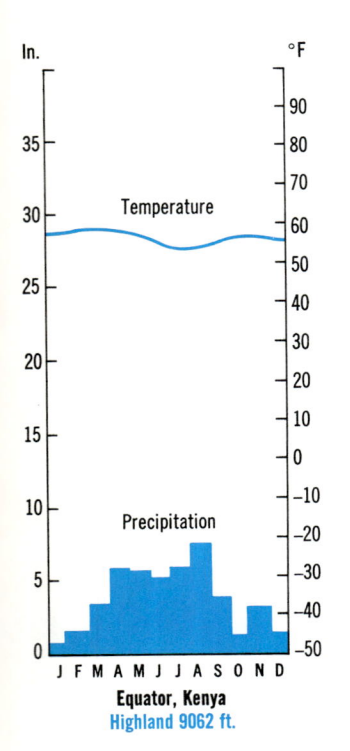

As the land sank, it produced the Great Rift Valley, a trough or canyon, thousands of miles long. The walls of this depression are often like cliffs, standing 15 to 100 miles apart to form the sides of a rift. The bottom of the valley varies in depth from a few hundred feet to almost a mile.

The valley begins near the mouth of the Zambezi River in Mozambique (moe-zam-*beak'*) and extends northward through Lake Malawi (mah lah'we). North of this lake it divides into two branches. The Western Rift, which includes lakes Tanganyika, Kivu, Edward, and Albert, runs in a northwesterly direction. It ends a short distance north of Lake Albert.

The Eastern Rift is much longer. It has a number of small lakes within its walls. It stretches through Tanzania, Kenya, and Ethiopia. Moving north, the Rift includes the Red Sea, the Gulf of Aqaba, and the Jordan Valley. It ends in Syria, covering in all a distance of 4000 miles.

Mineral resources. Africa is rich in mineral resources. Since ancient times gold has been mined in many parts of Africa—in Ghana, Zaire, and southern Africa. Iron ore is found in all parts of the continent, and Africans learned to smelt iron centuries ago.

Modern Africa's mineral resources are a major source of wealth. There are huge copper deposits in southeastern Zaire, Zimbabwe, and Zambia. More than 80 percent of the world's diamonds come from Africa. Although South Africa is the chief source, Ghana, Angola, and Sierra Leone (see-*air'* uh lee-*ohn'*) also have important deposits. Uranium, tungsten, bauxite, and other minerals have recently become important too.

Africa's Mighty Rivers and Lakes

Although Africa has a great many rivers, four are of major importance—the Nile, Congo, Niger, and Zambezi. Because of the variations in rainfall these rivers may vary dramatically in depth from one season to the next. During a rainless season many streams dry up entirely or become a series of pools. The Niger River, for example, may vary more than 20 feet in depth between the dry and the wet season. When the water level is low, rocks make travel difficult. During the rainy season, many rivers overflow their banks, causing flooding and breaking transportation and communication links. Rivers which do not change very much from season to season are usually more economically useful.

The Nile is Africa's most important river. Of all Africa's rivers, the Nile is probably first in importance, length, and fame. Although it is used chiefly by peoples of North Africa, it has its source south of the Sahara. Flooding annually, it deposits fresh topsoil along its banks making it possible to grow food for many thousands of people. Thus the Nile River Valley is among the most densely settled areas on the continent. The Nile is 4145 miles long—the longest river in the world.

The Zaire River is the longest river in Africa after the Nile. It is only navigable for short stretches, however. Several waterfalls prevent ships from traveling its entire course.

The Congo River, which is about 3000 miles long, drains a vast area of 1.4 million square miles. Ships can travel only about 85 miles to the port of Matadi (muh-*tah*'dee), Zaire, because of falls created by the central plateau. After the last waterfalls and cataracts, the Congo River is navigable.

The Niger and Zambezi are smaller but economically important rivers to the people living near them. The Niger flows in a broad arc through a very dry region of West Africa and provides water for irrigation. Without the Niger the ancient empires of Ghana, Mali (*mah*'lee), and Songhai (sahn *guy'*) probably would not have developed in western Africa. The Zambezi River flows through Zambia and empties into the Indian Ocean. At one point in its descent to the ocean, it tumbles over a cliff, forming the Victoria Falls. These falls are much broader and almost twice as high as Niagara Falls. Downstream from the Falls the Kariba Dam was built to regulate the water's flow and produce much-needed electrical power for the area. The dam created one of the world's largest artificial lakes, Lake Kariba.

Most lakes are in eastern Africa. Because of the deep depressions formed by the Great Rift Valley, most of Africa's lakes lie in the eastern part of the continent. Lake Victoria, located in this region, is the largest in Africa and one of the largest in the world. Other lakes in the Great Rift Valley are smaller but deeper than Victoria.

Lake Chad, between Niger, Chad, and Nigeria, is a large, very shallow lake just south of the Sahara. Fed by two rivers, it is five times larger in the wet season than in the dry. Although this makes planting crops near the shores difficult, Lake Chad is an important source of fish.

Peoples and Languages of Africa

Africa today has a greater variety of racial groups than any other continent. It has both the tallest and shortest people in the world. The Nilotics, a Negroid people of the upper Nile, are often seven feet tall. Pygmies of the Congo rain forest are about four and a half feet in height.

Bushmen and Hottentots were early African inhabitants. Among the people living in Africa today, the earliest inhabitants were probably the Bushmen, also known as the Khoisan *(koy' sahn)* peoples. They are a gentle people who once lived over a large part of the African continent but were later pushed out of most areas by other groups. There are only about 50,000 Bushmen, now confined largely to the Kalahari Desert and the number is declining.

Long ago Bushmen may have been artists, and their interesting rock paintings are found in many parts of Africa. Today they continue to live simply, hunting game with poisoned arrows and gathering roots, nuts, and edible plants.

This woman is a member of one of the San ("Bushman") tribes of the Kalahari Desert area in southern Africa. The San, a hunting and gathering people who believe in the communal ownership of property, have difficulty adjusting to the European-style laws of the ruling Bantu tribes in Botswana, which are all based on the private ownership of property.

> **From Where Did You See Me?**
>
> Along with the Hottentots, Bushmen, and Pygmies, Bantu legends describe the existence of a mysterious short people called *"Vana wandi wonerepi,"* meaning "from where did you see me." Children are warned that if they ever meet a strange, short man who asks, "from where did you see me?" they are to reply, "I saw you when you were far away, beyond those hills over there." The short man will then leave them alone and go on his way, pleased that he is a big man visible from a long distance away. For if they reply, "I saw you just now when you were right here," the short man would be displeased and might cause them harm.
>
> Stanlake Samkange, *African Saga* (Nashville, Tenn.: Abingdon Press, 1971), pp. 164–165.

The Hottentots also lived over a larger area of the continent before they were pushed into a small part of southwestern Africa. Their origins are unknown. Today they number no more than 24,000. Less primitive than the Bushmen, they are herders. Hottentots tend cattle and sheep and live in small huts that resemble beehives.

Most of the African population is Negroid racial stock. By far the largest proportion of the population of all countries of sub-Saharan Africa are the people of Negroid racial stock. Divided into hundreds of tribes and many nationalities, the population developed many different life styles. Superior in cultural development and in numbers, they have dominated the smaller Bushmen and Hottentot populations. From an original homeland in the region of Nigeria and Cameroon, people of Bantu (ban-*too'*) speech migrated to other parts of sub-Saharan Africa. Today they are the largest language group on the continent, numbering around 60 million.

People of the forest. The Pygmies of the Ituri (ee-*too'* re) Forest of eastern Zaire are the forest people of Africa. They range in height from four feet six inches to four feet eight inches. The Pygmies have lived in the tropical rain forest for thousands of years, and some anthropologists believe they are the oldest inhabitants of Africa. They live in small groups and are hunters and food gatherers.

Many fear that the Pygmies may become extinct. They seem to be unable to live outside the forest. When forced to do so, most Pygmies soon sicken and die, often from sunstroke. Living in the forests they are not exposed to the direct rays of the sun. As the forests shrink in size because of the need for more farmland, the Pygmies will lose their way of life.

Many Africans have come from other areas of the world. Some Europeans of Caucasian racial stock have lived in Africa since ancient times. In South Africa, where they number about 4.5 million, Europeans have lived since the seventeenth century. They also settled in the East African highlands of present-day Kenya and in smaller concentrations across the continent. About 800,000 Asians, mainly from Pakistan and India, have settled in South Africa.

Others settled along the East African coasts of Kenya and Tanzania. Many of the Asians are merchants and shopkeepers.

At least 1000 distinct languages are spoken in Africa. The differences are great enough to create serious communication problems. In Nigeria alone people speak over 100 different languages. Because of the large number of native languages, certain European languages used during the colonial period are used today. In such former British colonies as Ghana, Nigeria, and Sierra Leone, English has remained the official language. French is still the official language in the former French colonies of Ivory Coast, Guinea, and Mali. Portuguese is spoken in Angola and Mozambique. In the Republic of South Africa, English and a Dutch dialect, Afrikaans (af-rick-*ahnz'*), are the official languages.

Swahili is a non-European language that might be adopted by Africans as an official means of communication. It was a commercial language along the east coast of Africa for a long time. Swahili has already been adopted as the official language in Kenya and Tanzania. A blend of Bantu and Arabic, Swahili may find increasing acceptance in other African countries in the future.

African languages can be divided into four major groups. African languages are usually classified into language groups. Although not all the languages within a group can be understood by members of the group, they resemble each other. Not all scholars agree upon what languages belong in each group or what these groups should be called. However, the generally accepted four major groups are described here.

1. The largest grouping is the *Niger-Congo*. People speaking languages in this group live along the Gulf of Guinea, as well as inland and southward, including much of Africa south of the equator. In this group are the Bantu languages.
2. Eastern and Central Sudanic languages have been linked with Nilotic languages to form a second group which the linguist Joseph Greenberg has called *Nilo-Saharan*. All of these languages, spoken by people like the Masai (muh-*sigh'*) of Kenya and the Nuer of Sudan, are somewhat alike.
3. Over much of northern Africa people speak *Afro-Asian* languages. This group includes Hebrew, Arabic, Amharic (am-*har'* ick, spoken in Ethiopia), Somali, and other Semitic languages. Another spoken in this region is Berber in North Africa and Hausa in northeastern Nigeria.
4. The Bushmen and Hottentots of southern Africa speak *Khoisan* languages. These are sometimes called "Click" languages because clicking sounds are made while speaking them. These clicks sound somewhat like the sounds a farmer makes to a team of horses.

Dialect languages are commonly used. Afrikaans, mentioned earlier, is a Dutch dialect. The South Africans have changed the language so much that the Dutch would have difficulty understanding it. The English spoken in West Africa is equally difficult for people from England to understand.

Looking ahead. Africa is rich in mineral wealth and potential hydropower. The continent's leaders seek opportunities to develop industry and technology. Africans are hoping to find new ways of improving living conditions and eradicating poverty.

CHAPTER REVIEW

Recalling Names and Places

Bushmen	leaching	Sahara
Congo River	Mediterranean climate	savannah
Great Rift Valley	Niger River	tropical rain forest
Hottentots	Nile River	Zambezi River
Lake Victoria	oasis	

Understanding This Chapter

1. Why was the Sahara not a total barrier to trade and cultural diffusion?
2. What is the vegetation and climate of the savannah region? the rain forest?
3. What is the dominant feature of Africa's land surface? How has it affected Africa's development?
4. What are Africa's four major rivers? Where are they located?
5. Why are most African lakes found in the eastern part of the continent?
6. As need for farmland has increased there has been more clearing of tropical rain forests. Give reasons why this is bad policy.
7. How is a Mediterranean climate different from other climatic types in Africa?
8. Rainfall is unpredictable in many parts of Africa. That is also true in many areas of the United States. But when the rains don't come in Africa, it is more serious. Why?
9. Africa is at a disadvantage because so many languages are spoken. Would it be an advantage for Africa to adopt English as an official language? Why? Would another language be better? Why?
10. Africa has been very inaccessible to the outside would until recently. How has this affected African life and development?

Chapter 11

The African Past

Recent evidence seems to indicate that the earliest people lived in East Africa about three million years ago. We do not know how soon they began to migrate from Africa to Asia and Europe, but some very early remains have been found in China and on the island of Java in Indonesia. Nevertheless, Africa has been the chief human homeland for the greater part of our existence on earth.

Early Cultures of the Green Sahara

Eight thousand years ago the Sahara was green. Trees and grass grew, while rivers and lakes were filled with fish. Wildlife was abundant, and fairly large numbers of people could live in the region because food was plentiful. At the time of the Romans, two thousand years ago, people grew wheat where today it is too dry.

During the moist period, some of the region's inhabitants were highly artistic. In the west central Sahara is a high plateau called Tassili n' Ahaggar. On the rock walls are hundreds of paintings which were done between 6000 and 600 B.C.

The Tassili paintings, preserved by the desert air, tell us what life in the well-watered Sahara was like. Elephants, rhinoceroses, giraffes, gazelles, horses, and cattle are shown. Hunting scenes, cattle herding, dancing, and other activities were also painted. Certainly the Sahara was a region where for thousands of years large numbers of people and animals could live.

Population forced out. Around 6000 years ago the Sahara began drying up. As the lakes and rivers disappeared and the vegetation died, most people were forced to migrate elsewhere. They traveled in all directions. People moved north to the Mediterranean coast to become part of the Berber people. Others went east until they reached the Nile Valley. Some traveled south until they found watered areas.

We may never know much about these Sahara people, but some scholars believe the region might have been the nursery of African cultures. If so, it would help explain why ancient Egyptian customs and those of sub-Saharan Africa have so many similarities. The Egyptians believed that their king was a god. This belief, known as divine kingship, was also found among many African kingdoms south of the Sahara. Similarities also existed in other religious beliefs. For example, the ancient Egyptians believed that every person had a spiritual double called "ka." The Ashanti peoples of sub-Saharan Africa believed in a spirit named "kra."

In 1956 French ethnologist Henri Lhote began an extensive study of the rock paintings of Tassili n'Ahaggar, a barren plateau 900 miles southeast of Algiers. These pictures of the herders, hunters, animals, and vegetation of the green Sahara provide a vivid glimpse of prehistoric life. South of the Sahara, Ashanti merchants traded extensively with other Africans and Europeans. Their standard currency was gold dust, which was weighed in scales against fanciful brass weights like the ones below.

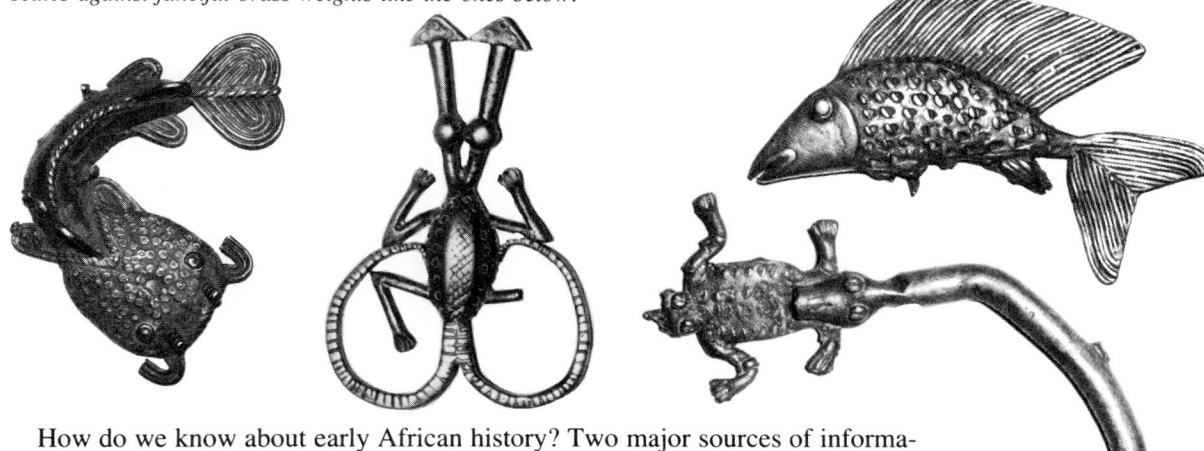

How do we know about early African history? Two major sources of information are archaeological findings and the African oral tradition – myths, legends, and histories passed by word of mouth from one generation to the next. Other sources are the chronicles of Arab traders who began trading in Africa in the eighth century. Although most Arab travelers were mainly interested in trade, a few were scholars who wrote in detail about African civilizations. For example, in the eighth century an Arab author, Al Fazari, was the first to write about the ancient kingdom of Ghana in the western Sudan. In the fourteenth century Ibn Battuta wrote a fascinating chronicle of the people of Mali. We shall look at the accounts of some of these Arab scholars in this chapter.

121

Ancient Kingdoms of Western Africa

In West Africa near the southern edge of the Sahara a number of great civilizations developed between 500 and 1600 A.D. With their economies based on trade and agriculture, these West African kingdoms became important centers of culture.

Muslim traders made the first contact with African kingdoms. As we saw in Chapter 5, Arab warriors swept across North Africa in the seventh century spreading the Islamic faith. Meeting little opposition, they moved with amazing speed. When they reached Algeria and Morocco, the Berbers, nomadic tribes of North Africa, opposed them. However, by the eighth century the Arabs and Berbers had joined forces, crossed into Spain, and conquered that country.

The Arab armies went southward as well. Missionaries and tradesmen went along, converting people to Islam and establishing trade relations. The tradesmen were primarily interested in obtaining gold and slaves. Since the Koran forbids enslaving Muslims, slaves had to be found in the non-Muslim south. The traders soon thought of West Africa as their major supplier for both gold and slaves. A prosperous trade developed between Muslim Northwest Africa and the African kingdoms along the western coast.

The kingdom of Ghana. Ghana was the earliest of several prosperous commercial kingdoms in West Africa. This ancient country was northwest of the present-day Republic of Ghana and located between the Senegal and Niger rivers. It became known to the rest of the world as a kingdom of fabulous wealth. Entertainers at the medieval courts of Europe told marvelous tales of the lavish banquets of the kings of Ghana.

Ghana was the title given to the king. It meant "war chief." The king and his kingdom became so inseparable in the minds of people that both were called by the same name. According to tradition, Ghana began around 300 A.D. However, it may have been 500 A.D. before it was an organized kingdom. This country lasted until 1200 A.D.

Two metals made Ghana a powerful and wealthy state. Iron and gold made Ghana prosperous. Skill in extracting iron from the earth came from tribes in what is northern Nigeria today. Somehow Ghana monopolized this skill for a long time. With iron weapons Ghana's rulers created an empire and held it together.

The exact source of the great gold supply is not known today. The gold fields were located in a remote area not easily reached except through Ghana. The kings successfully guarded them. The gold fields were probably in a region at the headwaters of the Senegal and Niger rivers in the present-day country of Guinea. Some gold has recently been found in this area.

Towns in Ghana became busy market centers. Gold was the main article of trade. Traders from the north brought salt along with cloth, horses, and other articles to exchange for gold and slaves.

Salt was the product most wanted by the people of Ghana. The human body needs salt for health, but this compound was scarce in Ghana. It was literally

EARLY TRADE ROUTES AND AFRICAN EMPIRES

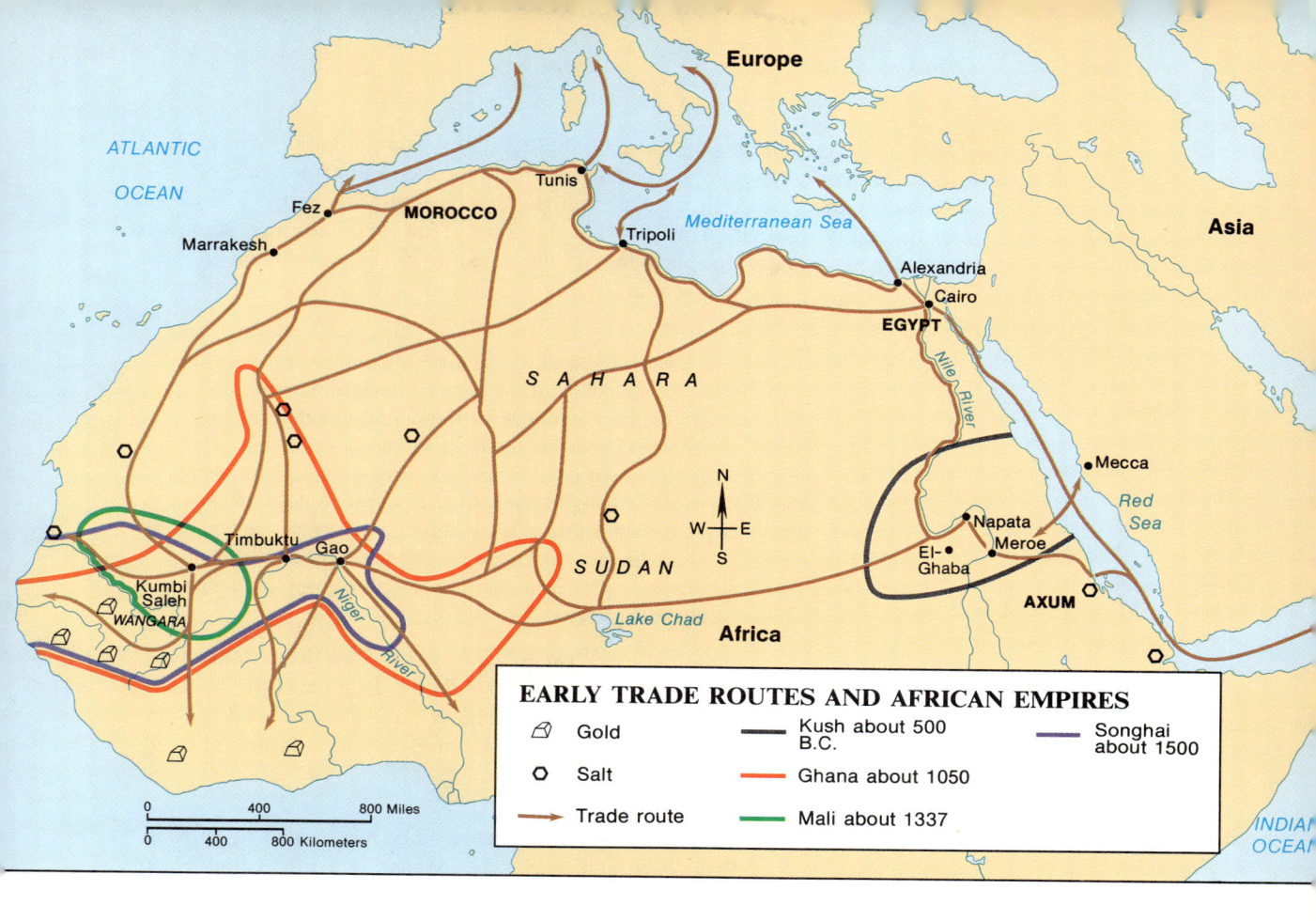

⛰ Gold	▬ Kush about 500 B.C.	▬ Songhai about 1500
○ Salt	▬ Ghana about 1050	
→ Trade route	▬ Mali about 1337	

worth its weight in gold. It is said that Ghana traded an equal weight in gold for the salt it received.

As a result of this trade, the nation became wealthy. Taxes on these traded items were an additional source of wealth. The king was responsible for tax collection and trade regulation.

Ghana fails to regain power after brief Muslim rule. In 1076 a fanatical Muslim group, the Almoravids, came south from present-day Mauritania and overran the kingdom. They converted the people to the Islamic faith. Although Almoravid control lasted only a short while, Ghana was unable to regain its former position of power. A long period of decline continued until finally, around 1230, Ghana disappeared. A new empire, Mali, developed and absorbed the kingdom.

The great empire of Mali. One of the peoples ruled by Ghana were the Mandingoes (man-*ding'* goz). They extended their control over neighboring peoples until they created a new and even greater empire. Called Mali, it became a much larger nation than Ghana had ever been.

Islam becomes chief religion in Mali. When the Almoravids arrived, the Mandingoes accepted the Islamic religion. From the beginning the Mali empire was securely Muslim. Sharing a common faith with North Africa not only added

123

to Mali's safety, but also encouraged mutual trade. The gold and slave trade resumed. Moreover, the empire became a prosperous agricultural region.

A widely traveled Arab scholar, Ibn Battuta, visited Mali in 1352–1353 and was favorably impressed with what he saw. However, he was somewhat shocked and perhaps disapproving of the freedom accorded women in Mali. Coming from a strictly patriarchal (father-dominated) Arabic society, he was not accustomed to equality between the sexes. He wrote:

> Their women are of surpassing beauty, and are shown more respect than the men. The state of affairs amongst these people is indeed extraordinary. Their men show no sign of jealousy whatever; no one claims descent from his father, but on the contrary from his mother's brother. A person's heirs are his sister's sons, not his own sons. This is a thing which I have seen nowhere in the world except among the Indians of Malabar. But the Indians were heathens, these people are Muslims, punctilious in observing the hours of prayer, studying books of law, and memorizing the Koran. Yet their women show no bashfulness before men and do not veil themselves though they are assiduous in attending prayers.*

It is interesting to notice that the West Africans did not wholeheartedly accept all aspects of Muslim culture. For example, while the Islamic faith diffused to West Africa from the Middle East, the patriarchal family system did not. In a later chapter we shall find that the matrilineal family system described by Ibn Battuta still exists in many parts of Africa.

Mali's most famous ruler was Mansa Musa. The most powerful of Mali's leaders was Mansa Musa *(man' sah moo' sah)*. Mansa is a title which means "emperor." As Mali's ruler, from 1307 until 1332, he led his nation to its golden age. Under Musa, Mali may well have been one of the most civilized countries of the world at that time. Here is how Ibn Battuta described it:

> The Negroes possess some admirable qualities. They are seldom unjust, and have a greater abhorrence of injustice than any other people. Their sultan shows no mercy to anyone who is guilty of the least act of it. There is complete security in their country. Neither traveller, nor inhabitants in it, has anything to fear from robbers or men of violence. They do not confiscate the property of any white man who dies in their country, even if it be uncounted wealth.**

Perhaps the only other society which could be described in such terms at that time was China. Ibn Battuta's description could not have applied to Europe during that era. Much of that continent was still politically disorganized, and people risked both life and property if they dared to travel.

Musa was a very devout Muslim and carefully followed the rules set down by the Koran. Since one rule was to make a pilgrimage to Mecca, Musa made the long journey of almost 3000 miles in 1324.

Musa traveled with an enormous caravan carrying several thousand pounds of gold. Tens of thousands of people accompanied him on the trip. When he

---

* Quoted by Stanlake Samkange in *African Saga*, pp. 127–128.

** Quoted from Roland Oliver: *The Dawn of African History* published by Oxford Univeristy Press (1961), p. 41.

124

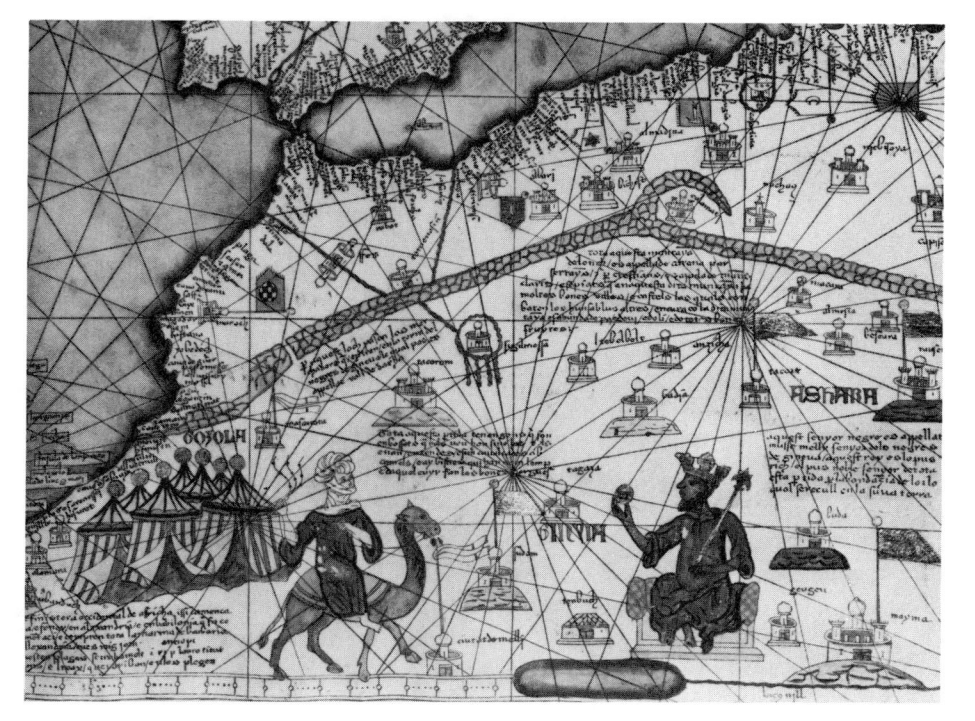

After Mansa Musa's journey to Mecca, tales of his enormous wealth spread throughout Europe. This fourteenth-century European map shows Musa holding a scepter in one hand and a large gold nugget in the other. The inscription reads: "This Negro Lord is called Mousse Melly [Musa of Mali], Lord of the Negroes. . . . So abundant is the gold found in his country that he is the richest king in all the land."

reached Cairo, Egypt, he gave much gold as gifts. Musa distributed so much gold that this precious metal's value dropped considerably. It remained low for years because of this sudden increase in supply. Musa's fame spread far and wide. In Europe he was called the "Lord of the Negroes," an emperor of fantastic wealth.

Maintaining this prosperity required an outstanding ruler. After Musa's death in 1332, those who followed him were men of lesser talent. Mali went into a long decline and finally disappeared in the seventeenth century. As early as the fifteenth century, a new empire appeared that was to surpass Mali in the western Sudan.

The mighty Songhai empire. The development of the Songhai state overlapped that of Mali. When Mali reached its height under the rule of Mansa Musa, Songhai had already begun to grow. When Mansa returned from his pilgrimage to Mecca, his military leaders proudly announced that they had captured Gao *(gah' oh)*, the Songhai capital, during his absence. Gao had long been an important trading center because of its location at the southern end of the trans-Saharan trade routes. Moreover, the people had already converted to the Muslim faith.

The Songhai empire became a prosperous nation whose wealth was based on successful trade and agriculture. Foreign visitors were impressed by the high level of culture of Songhai and the happiness of the people. Leo Africanus, a Moorish visitor to Songhai in 1513, wrote: "The inhabitants are people of gentle and cheerful disposition, and spend a great part of the night singing and dancing through all the streets of the city. . . ."

125

Sunni Ali makes Songhai into a great empire. When the most famous emperor of Songhai, Sunni Ali *(sue' knee ah' lee)*, ascended the throne in 1464, he set out to make his kingdom the largest in West Africa. Mali, as well as land as far east as Lake Chad, became part of Songhai. Frequently, Sunni Ali gained the new land through warfare. When he died in 1492, the year Columbus landed in America, it is said that he had never lost a battle.

Today about 600,000 Songhai people still live in the present-day republics of Mali and Niger. Although Sunni Ali lived nearly 500 years ago, the Songhai think of him as a hero.

Timbuktu is a dusty town in the Republic of Mali, but 500 years ago it was an important trading city on the Niger River. It was the location of a great Muslim university. Students and scholars came from afar to study, teach, and do research there. It was a prize for the growing empire.

Southwest of Timbuktu, in an area surrounded by rivers and swamps, is the town of Djenné *(jen-nay')*. In the days of Sunni Ali, Djenné rivaled Timbuktu as a trading and cultural center. Djenné's importance was due to its location. It was a main point for trade with regions to the south. Gold and slaves arrived first at Djenné and then were transported farther north. As a part of the Songhai empire, Djenné added much to its wealth.

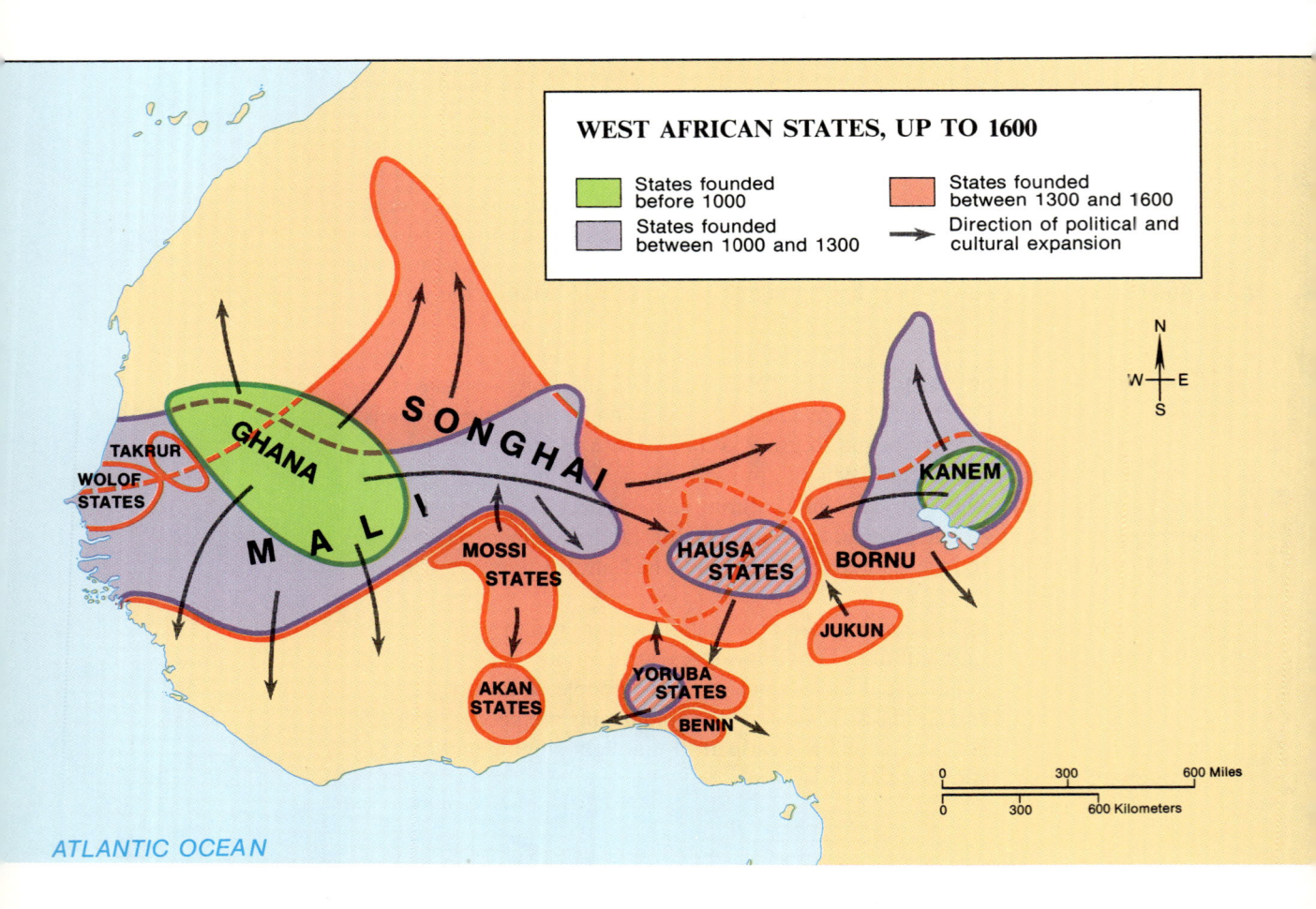

Askia Muhammad was Songhai's second greatest leader. About a year after Sunni Ali died, Askia *(ahs' key-uh)* Muhammad seized control of Songhai after his battle victory over the late ruler's son. Askia ruled for thirty-five years until he became blind. Called Askia the Great, he continued the great work of Sunni Ali. During his reign the Songhai empire became the mightiest political system in the western Sudan. He encouraged trade and supported education.

Askia was a devout Muslim, and he made a two-year pilgrimage to Mecca. Like Mansa Musa earlier, he went with a great caravan, and gave away vast amounts of gold on his journey. Still remembering Mansa Musa, the people in Egypt and Arabia were not surprised by Askia's great wealth.

Askia the Great's rule ended in 1528, although he lived for another ten years. Later rulers of Songhai did not stay on the throne long. There was much conflict in the empire. When a king named Dawud ruled, prosperous times returned until the end of his 33-year reign.

Songhai's warriors defeated by modern weapons. In 1589 the ruler of Morocco, Al Mansur (ahl-mahn-*soor'*), greedy for the famed wealth of Songhai, decided to invade the country. An army of 4000 men supported by 9000 transport animals was placed under the command of a young Spaniard named Judar. Moving such an army across the desert from Morocco to Songhai was a remarkable feat. It took six months, and only 1000 survived the trip. The Songhai king was informed of the coming invasion and met the enemy with 18,000 cavalry and 9000 infantry. However, the Moroccan soldiers were armed with a new weapon, the arquebus, an early type of gun. The Songhai fought bravely, but their spears and swords were no match for the guns of the Moroccans. They were defeated, and a great empire came to an end in 1591. Later, other African armies were to learn that simple weapons could not succeed against the guns of invaders.

Kingdoms of Central Africa

Because Arabs frequently traveled to Ethiopia and the Sudanese empires, many historians were able to write about these African nations. We did not have written records of central and southern Africa until European explorers and missionaries came. Their records are not as extensive, and our knowledge of this area is more limited.

From the writings of European travelers we know that many kingdoms and empires developed in the area of present-day Congo and Angola and in the great lakes region of East Africa. With the arrival of European traders, coastal kingdoms became disorganized. Those inland were less affected.

The forest kingdom of Benin. The culture of Benin has become known throughout the world since the discovery of the beautiful art works produced in this ancient kingdom. Heads and statues of bronze and brass were taken to Europe by the British in 1897 and were soon rated among the great art works of the world.

Benin was a Yoruba (*yoh'* rue-bah) kingdom located in the coastal region of modern Nigeria near the delta of the Niger diver. Benin, like other Yoruba kingdoms, built great walled cities as early as 1300 A.D. and cultivated fields outside the city walls. As time went on, trade became increasingly important. After the sixteenth century, Benin became an important trading center for Europeans. The wide streets, well-built houses, and luxurious palace of the king impressed the Europeans.

The growing slave trade carried on by the Europeans brought Benin into decline by the beginning of the eighteenth century. Slave raiding reduced the population and left the city and countryside in ruins.

The golden stool of the Ashanti. In West Africa near the coastal region of present-day Ghana, a prosperous kingdom emerged late in the seventeenth century. A number of smaller Akan-speaking states joined together to form the Ashanti Union of Akan States.

The kings of the various Akan people swore allegiance to a golden stool. According to sacred legend it had descended from a dark cloud onto the lap of Osei Tutu, one of the kings attending the conference at which the Ashanti federation was formed. The golden stool, it was said, came from God and therefore Osei Tutu was chosen by divine will to rule the nation. The golden stool became a sacred symbol of chieftainship carried in procession on important occasions.

Under the leadership of Osei Tutu and his successors the Ashanti nation expanded into a powerful empire. Ashanti prosperity was based on trade in gold and slaves. The nation became involved in conflicts with Europeans and was finally conquered by Great Britain in 1825.

Zimbabwe. When Ghana converted to Islam in the eleventh century, Arabic writing came into use. The surviving written records give us a good picture of the events that followed. In other parts of sub-Saharan Africa, however, writing did not come into use until the nineteenth century. As a result, large gaps in our knowledge of the region's early history exist. One of the most fascinating puzzles is Zimbabwe (zeem-*bah'* bway).

A conical tower rises to a height of 34 feet in the ruins of ancient Zimbabwe's Great Temple.

The ruins of Zimbabwe are in Rhodesia (now called Zimbabwe), but due to lack of written records we do not know when or why these stone temples and forts were built. Some people believe the stone walls and buildings were constructed in the thirteenth century, while other structures were built at a later time. When Europeans first saw these huge buildings in 1867, they revealed their prejudices by refusing to believe that blacks could have had the knowledge to build them. Now scientists agree that Zimbabwe was built by Africans.

The walls of Zimbabwe are as much as 16 feet thick and over 30 feet high. The stones were so carefully placed they required no mortar to hold them together. Building with stone in this style was common in a large part of southern Africa. Recently, walls and ruins built in the same fashion have been found in Angola.

Some think Zimbabwe was the center of a large empire in an area where gold was found. This gold was used for trade with India and China. Pieces of Chinese porcelain and Indian and Persian art have been found among African articles.

Enduring Bantu kingdoms. One kingdom that endured for many centuries was the kingdom of Buganda (boo-*gahn'* duh) on the northwest shores of Lake Victoria. The kingdom lasted for about three hundred years until 1967, when Buganda and the other Bantu states of the area became the Republic of Uganda. More than 10 percent of Uganda's people belong to the Baganda tribes. This is the largest tribal group in Uganda. Their kingdom was prosperous, since they could grow a variety of food. An extensive network of highways provided excellent transportation and communication throughout the country.

The Baganda resist Uganda's independence. When Uganda was preparing for independence in 1962, the Baganda tribes feared that they would lose their traditional position of leadership among the other tribal kingdoms of the area – the Bunyoro, Toro, and Ankole. Under British rule the Buganda kingdom had become more economically and socially advanced than other parts of the country. This political problem was temporarily solved in 1962 when Uganda gained independence. The federal government created a constitution that specified a special, semi-independent relationship between the Buganda kingdom and the national government. However, in 1967 under a new constitution Uganda became a republic, and the Buganda kingdom lost its special privileges.

Ethiopia, a Coptic Kingdom, Becomes a Republic

All but one nation in northeastern Africa became Muslim. Axum *(ahk' soom)*, the nucleus of present-day Ethiopia, was Christian. This kingdom became Christian around 300 A.D. Since its religious ties were with Alexandria, Egypt, this kingdom adopted Coptic Christianity as the official religion. The word "Coptic" is of Arabic origin and means "Egyptian." Followers of the form of Christianity practiced in ancient Egypt were known as Coptic Christians.

Not only is Ethiopia one of the oldest Christian nations in the world, but it is also the oldest independent nation of modern Africa. During Ethiopia's early history, it enjoyed friendly relations with the Egyptian Muslims. The Ethiopians were permitted to travel freely through Egypt on pilgrimages to the Holy Land. Non-Christian states to the south threatened its existence, and Ethiopia barely survived their invasion during the tenth century. Five centuries later, a Muslim

Haile Selassie, last emperor of Ethiopia, claimed descent from King Solomon and the Queen of Sheba. In honor of this biblical ancestry he was known as the "Lion of Judah."

state along the Red Sea acquired guns and prepared to invade Ethiopia. The Portuguese came to Ethiopia's assistance in time to save the kingdom.

Ethiopia had a long history of stable government. Emperor Haile Selassie ruled for forty-four years. In 1974 he was deposed by a group of dissatisfied army officers, and in 1975 the ruling military council abolished the monarchy. After the military takeover, the country was plagued by political unrest. Uprisings by tribal and political groups, aided by Somalia and Sudan, led the government to draw closer to the Soviet Union. The Organization of African Unity (OAU) has its permanent headquarters in Addis Ababa, the capital of Ethiopia.

By 1985 Ethiopia was in its fourth year of hunger. Africa's worst drought on record had caused more than 300,000 people to starve and millions more to suffer from hunger in Ethiopia alone. By late 1984 massive shipments of food were on the way from the United States and other countries, but hunger and famine continued to threaten large areas of Africa.

Reviewing Your Reading

1. How did Ghana get its name? Why was it a wealthy kingdom?
2. Describe Mansa Musa and the kingdom he ruled.
3. How was Mali's family system unique in the Muslim world?
4. Who was Sunni Ali? How did he expand the empire of Songhai? Why was the Songhai empire conquered?
5. Who was Askia the Great?
6. Where was Zimbabwe? Why is so little known about it?
7. Why was Buganda a prosperous kingdom?
8. Account for the fame of Benin.
9. Describe the legend of the golden stool.
10. Why was Ethiopia called a Coptic kingdom?

The Coming of the Europeans

Contact between North Africa and Europe began in ancient times. Crete carried on a profitable trade with Egypt as early as 2000 B.C. Similar relations between Europe and sub-Saharan Africa began about five hundred years ago. East Africa traded with India and China as early as the seventh century. The Europeans wanted African ties for economic reasons, although political and religious reasons also played a part.

The penetration of Africa by the Europeans was a slow process. As late as 1880 most areas of the African interior had not been visited by Europeans. As we noted earlier, the central plateau of the continent did not allow clear navigation from the sea. Therefore, pack animals and human carriers had to be used. There were almost no roads. However, perhaps the most serious barrier to exploration was disease. Europeans lacked means of preventing malaria, yellow fever, sleeping sickness, and other diseases of the tropics in the nineteenth century. Many died or were forced to return to Europe because of these illnesses. As Africans became more aware of European colonization plans, they began to resist these efforts. Hostile tribes were another barrier to exploration.

Portuguese sailors were the first Europeans to reach Africa. Portugal's nearness to Africa and its seafaring tradition led to early exploration of the African coast. By the middle of the fifteenth century Portuguese ships had worked their way down the continent's west coast. In less than fifty years the Portuguese had built forts along the Gulf of Guinea to keep out other Europeans. In 1488 Bartholomew Dias sailed around the southern tip of Africa, preparing the way for Vasco da Gama, who sailed around the continent to India in 1497. At many points along the African coast the Portuguese briefly explored and occasionally built bases or forts.

The Portuguese brought the slave trade to the Kongo. When Portuguese traders reached the mouth of the Congo River in 1482, they found the large kingdom of Kongo. The highly talented Bantu people of Kongo were skillful wood carvers and iron workers. At first the Portuguese were well received by the Kongolese. One of their leaders was converted to Catholicism by Portuguese missionaries and baptized "Affonso" in 1491. When he later became king, Affonso I wanted to make his kingdom as Christian and European as possible. However, Portuguese traders soon realized that the slave trade was more profitable than the creation of a Christian kingdom.

The West African city of Loango was once a busy commercial center. Its Bantu citizens were taken as slaves to the Americas, and the city declined in prosperity.

131

Affonso appealed to the Portuguese king, Manuel I, to aid him in his westernizing efforts and to curb the growing slave trade. The Portuguese king replied with the *regimento* of 1512. This instructed the Portuguese residing in the Kongo to act more properly and offered Affonso guidelines for making his court more European. In return for aid from the Portuguese in implementing these reforms, the king suggested that his citizens be paid in slaves, copper, or ivory.

The regimento failed to solve the Kongo's problems. Although willing to help the Kongo, the Portuguese were even more determined to exploit the country. The greed for wealth through slave trade was stronger than the impulse to do good. By 1530 about 5000 slaves were being taken annually, draining the youth of the Kongo.

The Slave Trade

Slavery was not a new concept to the Africans. Africans had been slaves in ancient Greece and Rome. While Islam forbade enslaving fellow Muslims, it did not prevent the use of non-Muslims as slaves. However, Muslim slavery in Africa involved far fewer people than did the European slave trade. The slave's life was harder in the Americas than in Africa or the Muslim world.

The Portuguese started European slavery, having slaves in their country in the 1440s. By 1492, some Portuguese provinces had more black slaves than white people.

Settlement of the Americas encouraged the slave trade. In the late fifteenth and the sixteenth centuries, Europeans wanted African gold, ivory, pepper, and slaves. In exchange they offered liquor, cloth, guns, and other manufactured goods. The settlement of the Americas increased the demand for slaves, as sugar plantation owners and cotton planters desired ever larger supplies of inexpensive labor. The Europeans lost interest in other African products, preferring the profitable slave trade.

Africans, too, became interested in one product more than any other – guns. These weapons were more and more needed to provide all the slaves the Europeans demanded. With enough guns a chief or king could successfully attack a neighboring tribe and take many captives. These people could then be sold to the slavers.

Slaves were secured by traders in a variety of ways. Often ships would anchor at a harbor and wait for sellers of slaves to arrive from the interior. To avoid a long wait for a full cargo, boats might be sent up river, and Africans kidnapped and brought to the ship. Slavers incited wars between villages, and sometimes Europeans would take part in hopes of increasing the number of captives.

A major evil of the trade was that it encouraged intertribal warfare and destroyed mutual trust among neighbors. It became easy to settle old feuds by seizing and delivering one's neighbor to a slave ship for money.

Effects of slavery on Africa. Slavery was destructive. Many whites became cruel and indifferent to the Africans' suffering. Some scholars estimate that Africa may have lost 50 million people between the sixteenth and nineteenth centuries. Many died in tribal warfare caused by the slave trade. Millions died in shipwrecks and from disease. Slave ships were usually the poorest boats afloat,

> **Ben Johnson Caught in His Own Trap**
>
> In the late eighteenth century an African named Ben Johnson became a famous kidnapper along the Guinea coast. A huge and powerful man, he kidnapped hundreds of people for the slavers. One day he seized a young girl and dragged her to a slave ship and sold her. The girl's brothers, missing their sister, set out to find her and discovered what had happened. They could not free her, but they ambushed Ben Johnson and delivered him, tied up, to the same slave ship. The captain knew Ben as an old supplier. Nevertheless, the kidnapper followed the steps of his countless victims.
>
> *Black Cargoes: A History of the Atlantic Slave Trade: 1518–1865* by D. P. Mannix and Malcolm Crowley (New York: The Viking Press, 1962), p. 92.

sinking in storms and drowning all aboard. Packed tightly into the ships, the slaves frequently became victims of such deadly diseases as smallpox. Some believe that only 15 million of the 50 million captives reached the Americas.

It is hard to imagine the monumental suffering which the slave trade inflicted on its captives. A British observer of the slave trade wrote the following account of it early in this century:

> The sufferings of the slaves were so appalling that they almost transcend belief. It would seem as though the inhuman traffic had created in Arabs, Negroes and white men a deliberate love of cruelty, amounting often to a neglect of commercial interests; for it would obviously have been more to the interest of the slave raider and the slave trader and transporter that the slaves should be landed at their ultimate destination in good condition – certainly with the least possible loss of life. Yet, as the present writer can testify from what he has himself seen in the eighties and nineties of the last century, a slave gang on its march to the coast was loaded with unnecessarily heavy collars or slave-sticks, with chains and irons that chafed and cut into the flesh, and caused virulent ulcers. The slaves were half-starved, overdriven, insufficiently provided with drinking water, and recklessly exposed to death from sunstroke. If they threw themselves down for a brief rest or collapsed from exhaustion, they were shot or speared or had their throats cut with fiendish brutality. . . . Children whom their mothers could not carry, and who could not keep with the caravan, had their brains dashed out. Many slaves (I again write from personal knowledge) committed suicide because they could not bear to be separated from their homes and children. They were branded and flogged, and, needless to say, received not the slightest medical treatment for the injuries resulting from this usage."*

Although the slave trade ended early in the nineteenth century, it left a long heritage of bitterness, suffering, and social problems. After the shipment of slaves ended, slavery continued for many decades in the United States and even longer in Brazil. The descendants of former slaves are still struggling for full equality.

---

*Sir Harry H. Johnston, *A History of Colonization of Africa by Alien Races* (London: Cambridge University Press, 1913), pp. 81–82.

Joseph Cinque, an African prince, was kidnapped from his home and sold into slavery in Havana, Cuba. Cinque and other captives were put aboard the Spanish ship Amistad *to be taken to a plantation in the West Indies. Two days out of port, Cinque led a mutiny of the slaves aboard the ship.*

The Amistad Mutiny

The nightmare of slave traders was that their captives would mutiny on the high seas. Usually careful precautions were taken to prevent such an event from happening. Nevertheless, they did occur.

One of the famous slave mutinies happened in 1839 on board the schooner *Amistad* off the coast of Cuba. Led by a young man named Cinque, fifty-two African slaves seized machetes that had been carelessly stored within reach. After killing the captain and the cook, they ordered the steersman to sail east for Africa. However, each night the steersman headed the ship west instead of east. Therefore, after seven weeks of sailing, the ship arrived at Long Island instead of the shores of Africa.

In the court case that followed, the Spanish government demanded that the mutineers be returned to Cuba, and many Americans agreed with that view. However, the courts decided that the mutineers had been taken to Cuba illegally and were freed to return to Africa.

It is reported that after Cinque, the leader of the mutineers, returned to Africa he used the knowledge he had gained to become a slave trader as well.

Europeans in South Africa

In 1652 the Dutch East India Company established a port on the southern tip of Africa. The long journey from the Netherlands around Africa to the Southeast Asian islands required a place where water and food could be obtained. The Company had not intended to establish a new colony, only a stop-over where its ships could take on fresh supplies. Nevertheless, this base gradually expanded into a colony. Today the republic of South Africa is about the size of Texas, Oklahoma, and New Mexico combined.

The Europeans were not the first settlers in this region, however. The Bushmen and Hottentots lived in the area of Cape Town, where the first base was established. Farther north and east lived the Bantu. For many decades after their arrival, the Europeans fought various African tribes to gain control of the land north of Cape Town.

The Boers were South Africa's first permanent settlers. The first group of European settlers were the Boers (borz). "Boer" means farmer in Dutch. They wanted a free source of labor to work on their farms and saw nothing wrong with using African slaves for this purpose. Relations between the Boer minority and the Africans steadily worsened as the Boers fought for control of fertile South African farmlands.

After the British seized control of the South African Cape in 1806, more white settlers arrived. Most of them were British, and they wanted a way of life and a system of laws similar to what they had had at home. They believed that slavery was wrong and disliked the Boers' harsh treatment of the blacks. The British government's efforts to protect the Africans angered the Boers.

Because of the disagreements between the two groups, the Boers began the "Great Trek" northward in 1835. Although they had been going north for some time, this was the final big migration from the Cape area. The Great Trek brought them into direct conflict with the Zulu nation, which claimed all the land between the Drakenburg Mountains and the sea. The Zulus were defeated and their power broken at the Battle of Bloody River in 1838. The Boers created several republics, the largest of which were the Transvaal (trans-*vahl'*) and the Orange Free State. Here they felt they would be free from British rule and could treat the Africans as they pleased.

The Boer War, 1899–1902. Diamonds were discovered near the western border of the Orange Free State in 1871, and vast gold fields were found in the Transvaal in 1886. These minerals increased British interest in the Boer republics. An Englishman, Cecil Rhodes, through clever maneuvering, gained extensive control of both the diamond and gold production. News of the discoveries spread, and many people rushed to the Boer republics.

Two great leaders lived in South Africa at this time. One was Cecil Rhodes, who not only had vast mining interests but was prime minister of the Cape Colony for many years. The other was Paul Kruger, the president of the Transvaal Republic. Rhodes wanted a South African federation of Englishmen and Boers. Kruger desired a white South Africa under Boer rule in which black Africans would have no power.

In addition to their differing opinions, other problems existed. Rhodes wanted to extend British control northward into Central Africa. If he had been successful, he would have boxed in the smaller Boer republics and prevented their growth. Impatience with the Boer leader finally caused Rhodes to plot Kruger's overthrow. His intrigue failed, ending Rhodes's political career.

Unable to find a peaceful solution for South Africa's complex problems, the British government turned to military force. The Boer War began in 1899. Outnumbered, the Boers carried on guerrilla warfare and were defeated in 1902. The Boer states became the British colonies of Orange Free State and Transvaal.

In fierce guerrilla warfare, the Boers held out against the British army for three years. Even after the British subdued them, the Afrikaaners gained political equality and eventually won political control of South Africa.

After the war Britain tried hard to restore good relations with the Boers. In 1910 the Union of South Africa was created giving the Boers equality with British settlers in a democratic system. With their higher birth rate, the Boers gained in numbers over the years. By 1948 they controlled the government and passed the laws they wanted.

The South African Republic is created. In 1961 South Africa ended its membership in the British Commonwealth of Nations and became an independent republic. The Boers, now called Afrikaaners (ahf-rick-*ahners'*), are the largest group of whites, and their policies prevail in government. Chief among these policies is apartheid (uh-*par'*tight), meaning "apartness." It is a system of segregation imposed on each racial group in the country by the whites. The Boers had always hoped to enforce this policy. In our later discussion of African politics (Chapter 14) we shall return to this topic.

The Division of Africa

In 1880 the Europeans controlled a very small portion of the African continent. The French had occupied the coastal region of Algeria since 1830, and the British had some influence in Egypt. Europeans in Africa remained in the trading ports, except in South Africa where they moved inland. Yet in less than twenty years they carved up Africa.

King Leopold of Belgium started the European rush to divide Africa. Leopold had been interested in Africa for many years. He pretended to set up an organization for scientific study of central Africa. This group was to protect missionaries and guard against the slave trade. The group's real purpose was to help the

EUROPEAN COLONIES IN AFRICA, 1900

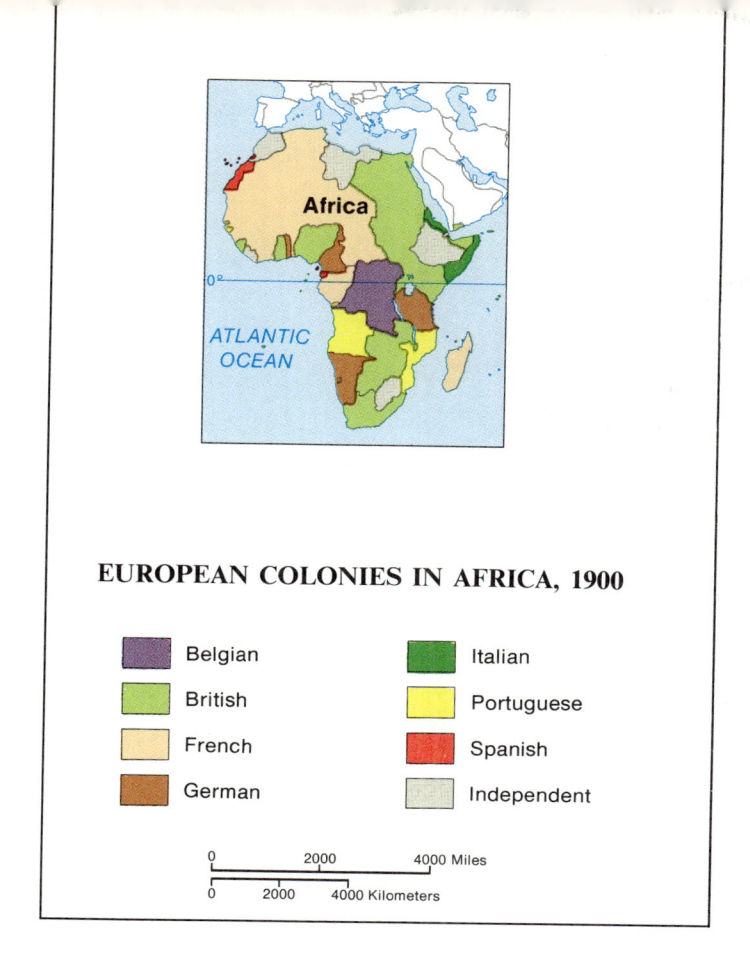

- Belgian
- British
- French
- German
- Italian
- Portuguese
- Spanish
- Independent

king gain control of as much land as possible. By 1879 Leopold decided to take control of the vast Congo River basin. The writer Henry Stanley, who met Livingstone in 1870, became associated with the king. In 1877 Stanley crossed the continent from Zanzibar by way of Lake Victoria and down the Congo River. After exploring much of the region for the king, he was rewarded by being named "Governor-General of the Congo Free State." However, Stanley held the position only briefly.

Stanley was a vulgar showman, eager for public acclaim. He deserves credit for carrying through a dangerous expedition down the Congo River. On the other hand he joined with King Leopold in a cruel exploitation of the Congolese people. Wealth and fame were his chief concern.

Soon after Leopold set up his organization, Germany moved into Africa, claiming control of four areas located on both the east and west coasts. After the Germans made their territorial claim in 1885, other European powers scrambled for colonies.

The rush to gain territories was aided by the decisions made at an international conference in 1884. At this meeting in Berlin, Leopold received formal recognition of his ownership of Congolese territory. The members of the Berlin Conference also made guidelines for creating colonies.

The African colonies. The European nations divided Africa through a series of agreements with one another. Most Africans were unaware that their homelands had become the territory of foreign powers. Since the Europeans sent few

137

In the Battle of Adowa (March 1, 1896), the forces of King Menlek fought the Italian army for control of Ethiopia. An African artist depicted the king viewing the battle, with the Bible in his hand open to the passage, "O Lord, hearken unto my prayer."

people into their recently claimed colonies, the Africans did not know what had happened for some time.

The Europeans had no immediate plans for their colonies. They claimed all the territory they could, hoping it might be useful in the future. Besides, patriots at home could take pride in all the African land their country owned. When the division of territory ended, only Ethiopia and Liberia remained independent.

The Europeans wanted the colonies to pay for themselves and were not eager to spend much money developing them. For many years people sent to the colonies received little money from home to carry on their work. Increases in administrators and funds came gradually.

When Africans realized what was happening, they began to organize against their rulers. Revolts against colonial rule occurred in some locations. Elsewhere Africans welcomed the Europeans as their allies in disputes with neighboring tribes.

After World War I, colonial rule began to change. Germany lost its African territory following defeat in the war. German colonies became mandates, territories controlled by the newly created League of Nations. Other European nations realized that it would become difficult to hold on to their colonies in the future. The British government decided to prepare its African colonies for eventual independence. The other colonial powers did not adopt this view. France, Portugal, and Belgium insisted that their colonies were part of the mother country. As a result, when the independence movement swept through Africa after World War II, only the former British colonies had any preparation in modern government.

Reviewing Your Reading

1. Who were the first Europeans to explore the African coast?
2. Describe the slave trade. What effects did it have upon Africa?
3. Who were the Boers? Why did they fight the English settlers?
4. How did King Leopold start European colonial rule of Africa?
5. What did the Europeans hope to gain from their colonies?

CHAPTER REVIEW

Recalling Names and Places

Askia the Great	Ghana	Songhai
Axum	King Leopold	Sunni Ali
Benin	Paul Kruger	Tassili n'Ahaggar
Boers	Mali	Timbuktu
Cecil Rhodes	Mansa Musa	Transvaal
Coptic	Orange Free State	Zimbabwe

Understanding This Chapter

1. How did the coming of the Muslims affect the West African kingdoms?
2. What sources of information describe the existence of civilizations in West Africa?
3. Why was slavery always regarded as the most profitable type of trade?
4. What were some lasting effects of the slave trade?
5. More Europeans have been attracted to South Africa than anywhere else on the continent. What have been the chief attractions?
6. Explain how Britain's policy toward its African colonies after World War I differed from that of other colonial powers.

Chapter 12

Family, Clan, Tribe, and Nation

Making generalizations about African society is difficult since social organizations and cultures vary throughout the continent. Geography, history, and climate have created regional customs. Moreover, as contact with others outside the region grows, African customs will change. Many African and European customs seem to have originated in the Jordan River Valley and in Mesopotamia. Thus the peoples of Europe and Africa have much in common.

Tribal Loyalties Are Still Strong in Africa

Many Africans are tribal members, and the tribe is the social organization that is most familiar to Africans. While the map of Africa shows the continent divided into various countries, to the majority of ordinary people the family, clan, and tribe are the groups they know best. Few have strong feelings of national pride for their country.

The nations of Africa are largely the result of boundaries drawn by European colonial rulers. These boundaries were drawn with little knowledge of the social and cultural divisions in Africa. Decisions were often made in European foreign offices by officials who had never been to Africa. European politics rather than African social life determined the boundaries in most cases. Many of the nations include tribes which are traditional enemies. A good example of the problems this division of Africa created can be seen in Nigeria. Between 1967 and 1970 a civil war was fought in Nigeria because the Ibo (*ee*'bow) tribe wanted a separate country called Biafra (bee-*ahf*'ruh). In Kenya tribal rivalries between the Kikuyu (keh-*coo*'you) and their traditional enemies, the Luo, resulted in the death of Tom Mboya, a brilliant young political leader, in 1969.

Land belongs to the tribe. The African's concept of land ownership differs from that of most Westerners. The tribe, rather than the individual, owns the land. One reason for the lack of private ownership has been the land itself. Since forested land is difficult to clear, men living in the community did it together. Consequently they felt that the land belonged to the entire clan or community.

Inability to work the land for more than a few seasons also discouraged the concept of private ownership. African farmers did not know how to restore the earth's fertility. After planting the same crop on the same land for several seasons, the soil became exhausted. The tribe would then move and clear new land for planting. Thus, the European idea of long-term land ownership did not usually develop.

Because of misunderstandings between European settlers and Africans over land ownership, conflicts often arose. For instance, European settlers in the highlands of Kenya claimed permanent ownership of the best land in the area. Although in some cases these settlers were willing to pay the Africans for the land they took, the tribes of the area were not familiar with the European idea of land transfer. The Mau-Mau *(mow'mow')* movement of 1947–1960 among the Kikuyu tribes of Kenya attempted to restore land and other rights to the native Africans. Usually their methods were terroristic. When Kenya became independent in 1960, the European settlers were forced to compensate Africans for land taken.

Tribes are composed of smaller clan groups. Related families often form a larger grouping called a clan. All members of a clan claim descent from a common ancestor. A tribe is usually a grouping of clans who are related to one another by a common language and customs.

The Kikuyu clans share a common account of their origin. The Kikuyu consists of nine clans: Wacheera, Wairimo, Waithera, Wamboi, Wangari, Wangoi, Wanjiko, Wanjiro, and Warigia. All Kikuyu clans believe that the supreme god, named Ngai, lived on Mount Kenya. Ngai created the first man of the tribe, named him Kikuyu, and gave him a wife, Mumbi.

This first couple had the nine daughters whose names are those of the nine clans. When the daughters were ready for marriage, Ngai performed a miracle, and nine handsome young men suddenly appeared. The daughters married the young men, and they became the parents of the nine clans. Today the Kikuyu still call themselves "The Children of the Nine Daughters."

Although the Kikuyu trace their origins to the nine daughters, their families today are patriarchal and patrilocal. The Kikuyu have an explanation. They say that women were once the rulers, but they became so cruel that the men gained control.

The clan performs important social functions. In Africa, as in many other culture areas, a person's clan membership is a very important part of life. It provides a sense of identity. In time of trouble one can turn to members of the clan, knowing that help will come.

Each clan has a chief as its head. The chief is often believed to be the reincarnation of the clan's founder. Members think that the spirit of the founder is in his body. As a result the chief plays an important part in the clan's religious activities.

The chief's position is usually hereditary. When the chief dies, his oldest son does not necessarily succeed him. The father decides which of his sons is most able, and that son becomes the next chief.

Each clan has special symbols and markings to distinguish it from others. Sometimes the members of a clan wear certain items of clothing. They may scar their bodies with special markings or symbols. Plants, animals, or other objects that have special importance to clans are called totems. Only under special conditions can totem animals be killed or eaten by clan members.

Initiation into age groups begins in adolescence. Another important grouping in African society is the age group. Children go through a series of

The rural villager and the city office worker above both have tribal scars on their left cheeks. These marks help tribe members identify one another even in unfamiliar surroundings.

ceremonies usually called puberty rites. Puberty refers to the beginning of adolescence, when youngsters reach sexual maturity. Boys and girls have separate ceremonies in which they are given instruction that will help to prepare them for adulthood. They may also undergo tests of strength and be asked to demonstrate their ability to withstand pain. At this time participants may also receive the special scarring of the tribe. Circumcision is an important part of male age-group ceremonies. All the boys who participate in the ceremonies at the same time become members of an age set or brotherhood. This age set may become an important bond for the rest of their lives.

Such male age groupings are especially important among the nomadic cattle herders of East Africa. The members of such a brotherhood may give military service as a unit and will aid each other throughout life. Elsewhere on the continent age groups are not as important. In Zaire and in Nigeria the formation of such groups is also associated with the ceremony of circumcision. However, the members of a group do not form as close a relationship as in East Africa. In some African societies age groupings may be formed without formal ceremonies.

As the members of an age group become older, their duties to one another change. They may help each other in arranging marriages, assist each other's children, or give economic aid. As older men they may share in political leadership of the tribe or nation. Such groups of elders are especially important among tribes of the Kasai region of Zaire.

Status Differences Exist within Societies and Families

Cultures throughout the world differ greatly in how strictly members divide their societies into classes. While by no means the most rigid in this regard, Africans draw definite class lines in their societies.

Kings, commoners, and slaves. Class differences are probably drawn most sharply in those parts of Africa where complex political systems have developed, for example, Ethiopia and Uganda. Traditionally there were three classes – royalty, commoners, and slaves. Slaves usually were well treated and had certain recognized rights.

Most slaves were part of the family group and were regarded almost as kinsmen. If they suffered abuse from outsiders, the slave owner would come to their aid. Although they usually worked hard, they would marry, and their families would become part of the household. African slavery was rarely as harsh and brutal as slavery in the Americas.

In some African kingdoms, such as Dahomey, a class of nobility existed between royalty and commoners. Sometimes when a commoner performed special services to the king, he would be granted property, a government position, and the status of a noble.

Emphasis on status continues to exist today within the family. Fathers are superior to their children, and husbands are superior to their wives. Male supremacy is typical in most African societies. However, the father does not have the same status in all African societies. In the West African matriarchal

This woman, a member of the devout Muslim Fulani peoples of northern Nigeria, is one of several wives of the same husband. In all likelihood she and the other wives are not-too-distant cousins of their husband.

families, like the Ashanti, the mother's brother is the adult with most authority over the child. Among the Lebou tribe of Gabon the child often resents his father. He spends most of his time with his mother and is jealous when his father visits. The father has very little authority over his children.

Among the Bunyoro tribe of Uganda the father is called the "master of the household." He is given much respect. Just as a king of a nation, he is regarded as the king of his home. The father is the owner of the family. Even the property of the married sons is his, and they are expected to address him as "master."

Among the Swazi of South Africa, the title of "father" also carries great respect. A child calls the brother of his father, as well as his own parent, "father." However, his parent is called "the father who bore me." His oldest paternal uncle is called "my big father" and the youngest uncle "my little father." In a similar fashion the mother's sisters are called "mothers." However, a father's sister is called "female father" and the mother's brother is called "male mother." Anyone called "father," including "female father," is accorded great respect.

The father's status is different in the cities. Among the educated people, parents give their children more freedom than do parents in rural areas. Fathers do not insist on titles of great respect. Often they behave in a spirit of equality toward their wives and children. Education and urban life usually make families more democratic. The Western idea of equality among family members is stronger in cities.

Reviewing Your Reading

1. Why is the tribe important to many Africans?
2. How is a tribe different from a clan?
3. What is an age group?
4. Describe class systems in Africa.

The Extended Family Is Typical in Africa

Most Africans live in rural areas where they belong to extended families. Each family consists of husband, wife, unmarried children, married children and their families, and perhaps grandparents as well. They may live in one home or in a group of houses close together. The extended family is less common in the cities than in rural areas.

Many African families might best be termed "joint families." In this system two or more nuclear families live in separate houses within a compound or enclosed area and share their property. The oldest male, perhaps a grandfather, is the leader. New households are established when a joint family becomes too large or when a son begins his own joint family.

Family patterns vary widely. Most African families are patriarchal (male-dominated), patrilineal (descent traced through males on the father's side), and patrilocal (living in the father's home). Societies in East Africa and in southern Africa usually follow this pattern, including the Kikuyu of Kenya, the Baganda of Uganda, and the Swazi of Swaziland. Frequently East Africans are Muslim, and their faith emphasizes male dominance.

Many peoples living in West Africa and the Congo region are members of matrilineal and matrilocal families. They are not generally matriarchal. The Ashanti tribes have a family organization typical of West African matrilineal societies. Children trace their descent through their mothers. A boy inherits property from his mother's brother rather than his father. He also lives with this uncle and takes his name. In the same way the father is responsible for *his* sister's children. As far as name, lineage, and inheritance are concerned, the family consists of brother, sister, and her children. If necessary, a child's uncle will defend him against the father.

The Ashanti believe that the child's blood comes entirely from the mother. From the father the child receives a certain "spiritual substance" that is not precisely defined. Therefore, the mother's brother (uncle) has a closer blood relationship to the child than the father.

Ashanti home life is similar to that in other African societies. The husband does the heavier work of clearing the forest, and the wife does the planting and harvesting. However, the wife enjoys a higher status in the family than the husband. Because she bears the children, the Ashanti believe she causes the land to be fertile. Since the mother is the central member of the Ashanti family, she owns the land and rules the home.

Polygyny is common in Africa. Almost all African societies permit polygyny. The Pygmies are one of the few exceptions. Most men have only one wife because they cannot afford to have more. Having several wives is evidence of a man's prosperity.

Some anthropologists say that polygyny is common because women outnumber men. Men have a higher mortality due to hunting, warfare, and other dangerous activities. Other scholars reject this explanation. They say that childbirth in Africa is as dangerous for women as the other activities are for men.

A surplus of females is not necessary for polygyny to exist. In Africa women marry very young, as early as fourteen or fifteen. Because men must earn the necessary bride wealth, they may be thirty years old or more before they marry. In some societies they must serve in the army before they can get married. As a result, many women become widows early and then later remarry.

Jealousy is not inevitable. We might suppose that a wife would object to her husband having other wives, but this does not seem to be the case. Women in Africa find this custom advantageous. They often work much harder than the men. In farming regions men clear the forest land, but the women not only raise and harvest the crops but also care for the home and raise the children. Wives, therefore, welcome each other's help. Usually the first wife supervises the other women.

Sharing a husband is not as likely to cause trouble between wives as sharing a kitchen. In the polygynous family the husband solves this problem by building a separate house for each wife. The greatest possibility of conflict comes from the treatment of the children. If a husband favors, or is thought to favor, the children of one wife more than the other children, a problem may develop. Treatment of children probably causes the most conflict in the polygynous family.

Bride wealth is customary. Before a couple is married, the groom or his family gives something valuable to his future wife's family. The contribution varies from one part of the continent to another. In the eastern Sudan where cattle herding is the main occupation, the bride wealth is a certain number of cattle. In West Africa payment might be in goats, pigs, or articles like cloth, tools, or metal goods.

Bride wealth is given as a payment for the loss of services and labor which the bride provided her family. Since women do most of the work in African society, when a daughter marries, she no longer helps her parents.

To some extent the payment is insurance for the bride that her husband will treat her well. If he is unkind or cruel, she may return to her parents, and he may lose what he paid. Still another function of the bride wealth is to make the marriage acceptable to the community. A large wealth shows that a bride is worthy of respect from both her husband and community members.

Most Africans permit divorce. African societies vary greatly in their attitude toward divorce. Among the Zulus of South Africa divorce is not permitted. In other tribes husbands and wives may separate by mutual consent. Most African societies fall between these two extremes.

If a divorce occurs, the bride wealth may have to be returned by the wife's father. Sometimes this is difficult to do. If the father has another daughter to marry off, the wealth paid for her may be given to the divorced husband.

When a divorce occurs in a patrilineal society, the children go to the father. Each child left to the father reduces the amount of the bride wealth he can demand.

Urbanization Brings Many Changes

African nations have some of the highest birth rates in the world. Better disease control is leading to a declining death rate. The result is an increasing rate of population growth. This has led to the rapid growth of cities. In rural areas the population is growing so rapidly that the land cannot support all the people. An increasing number of young people must leave their homes and go elsewhere. Most of them head for cities like Lagos (*lay'* gos), Kinshasa (kin-*shah'*suh), or Johannesburg. Others are attracted to the city because of dissatisfaction with the traditional way of life. They have heard exciting stories about the city, and they want to be a part of this new life.

Technology has changed the way many jobs are done in Africa. In Nigeria, a mechanical harvester is used in the corn harvest.

Illiteracy remains a problem. However, with the exception of the Republic of South Africa, industrial development is still limited. It is growing, but not fast enough to provide jobs for the people who are pouring into the cities daily. With great expectations for a better life, people come from rural areas with little formal education and few skills. They are shocked that the city often has no place for them. Usually the only homes they can find are in already overcrowded urban slums.

Often the city provides educational opportunities lacking in rural areas. However, even the most developed African nations, such as Ivory Coast, Ghana, and Kenya, have illiteracy rates of 60 percent or higher. Poverty and illiteracy form a vicious cycle, each causing the other. Africans know that education is necessary for economic success, but most families are too poor to pay the costs of schooling. Nevertheless, education is increasing rapidly. Cities with high schools and colleges are drawing young people in ever larger numbers.

The majority of African children are still educated in the traditional way. Most do not receive formal training in reading, writing, and arithmetic. In the daily life of the family and the village, they learn the culture of their people by living with adults and other children.

With the coming of adolescence, the young people usually receive special instruction in the secret rituals of the tribe as part of the puberty rites described earlier (p. 141). Sometimes a special ceremony is provided, called a "rebirth." Adolescents are reborn as full members of the tribe with all the traditional knowledge shared by others. Increasing numbers of African children are now receiving more formal education to fit them for the modern world as well.

Rural schools like this one in Botswana are bringing literacy and technological sophistication to the countryside. Graduates of such schools are often attracted by the excitement of the cities and choose not to remain in the villages, where they are needed.

City life in Africa's major cities shares features of life in many of the world's urban centers. This vast city market is in Abidjan, Ivory Coast.

City life means emotional readjustments. In addition to the inadequate housing and limited job opportunities, city dwellers lack the strong support of family and clan found in rural areas. In their villages they had many people with whom they shared a close relationship. Within this group each person felt he or she had a place. Life had specific goals. Although famines might come, the individual never starved unless the whole clan went hungry. All shared whatever there was to eat. When illness occurred, healthy members took care of the sick. To newcomers the city can be a lonely place where few are willing to help out.

The close kinship ties of rural life are weakened for those who move to the cities. Unless the city is very close to their native village, the typical urban dwellers do not see kinfolk often. Nevertheless ties remain strong.

When the children find jobs in the city, they are expected to send part of their earnings to the family. Most young Africans are very loyal to their families and send home a generous part of their earnings. They know that if they should become unemployed, their families would provide for them.

Can the extended family survive? As African countries become more urbanized and industrialized, perhaps the traditional family will break up. Some believe that able young people cannot succeed in a modern business if they must spend all they earn on endless numbers of relatives. Sometimes poor relatives, expecting room and board, descend on a successful young city dweller.

The crisis for the extended family may come when the children who are born in the city grow up. They do not have the memories of rural life, which their parents had and may not be willing to give assistance to their country cousins.

Most likely the extended family will continue in a modified form. Many urban Africans want to preserve their unique traditions and respect the ancient customs of their people. They do not want to substitute Western traditions for their heritage.

Social changes create new problems. As African life becomes more westernized, problems of choice arise. Africans want to become part of the modern

---

The Tragedy of the Marginal Man

Chinua Achebe of Nigeria is a noted African writer. His novels have been well received and have been translated into many languages. He writes movingly of the problems of the "marginal man" – the individual caught between two culture worlds, the culture of old Africa and the new modern Africa. In Achebe's stories tragedy is the usual result of this conflict.

The hero of the novel No Longer at Ease *is Obi, a young Ibo from eastern Nigeria. His village association, the Umuofia Progressive Union, paid Obi's costs of schooling in England. He was expected to pay back the loan so that the association could assist other young people of the village.*

Although the salary of the educated young Nigerian looked enormous by village standards, it was very small for life in the city. As debts piled up, he was tempted to accept a bribe but was caught in the crime. Although they disapproved of his actions, the members of the association will not abandon one of their own people. The author describes their loyalty:

In recent weeks the Union had met several times over Obi Okonkwo's case. At the first meeting, a handful of people had expressed the view that there was no reason why the union should worry itself over the troubles of a prodigal son who had shown great disrespect to it only a little while ago.

"We paid eight hundred pounds to train him in England," said one of them. "But instead of being grateful he insults us because of a useless girl. And now we are being called together again to find more money for him. What does he do with his big salary? My opinion is that we have already done too much for him."

This view, although accepted as largely true, was not taken very seriously. For, as the President pointed out, a kinsman in trouble had to be saved, not blamed; anger against a brother was felt in the flesh, not in the bone. And so the Union decided to pay for the services of a lawyer from their funds (to defend Obi in the bribery case). . . .

They had no illusions about Obi. He was, without doubt, a very foolish and self-willed young man. But this was not the time to go into that. . . .

From *No Longer at Ease,* © 1960 by Chinua Achebe. Reprinted by permission of Astor-Honor, Inc., Stamford, Conn., and William Heinemann Ltd., Publishers, London. pp. 4–5, 72.

world. They also want to remain distinctively African. Compromises are called for, and these are sometimes difficult to work out.

Family life is especially affected by this struggle to find a compromise between past traditions and modern needs. Educated wives often want greater equality than their husbands are willing to allow. On the other hand, an uneducated traditional wife may not be able to fit into the life of a modern African business or professional man. Such conflicts produce tensions.

Population growth is high. Africa's greatest need may be to reduce its birth rate. It is not a densely populated continent, but large areas are unproductive. In the productive agricultural regions, such as the Guinea Coast and the Eastern Highlands, the population is dense.

Reviewing Your Reading

1. Describe some of the family patterns existing in Africa.
2. Why does bride wealth exist?
3. How are children usually educated in the rural areas?
4. How do city dwellers retain their kinship ties?
5. Why is the high population growth a concern?

African Religion

Religion has an important place in African life. Although religious customs vary greatly from one tribe to the next, some basic ideas and beliefs exist throughout the continent. Africans have many religious beliefs similar to members of Western culture.

Africans believe in one supreme God, even though they may also have beliefs in lesser gods and ancestral spirits. They feel God created the universe and set it in motion. Some Africans think that God created everything and then withdrew to let the system run on its own. Other Africans believe that God continues to be involved in human affairs to varying degrees.

Most Africans follow tribal religions. However, there are about 150 million Muslims (including North Africa) and about 130 million Christians. About a million Asians, many of them Hindus, live in East and South Africa. Except in such places as Dahomey where a priesthood prescribes what people should believe, a great deal of variation in beliefs exists from tribe to tribe, and from one village to another.

Animism is common in many parts of Africa. Like hunters and food gatherers elsewhere in the world, many Africans have a faith which is sometimes called animism. This is a belief in the existence of spirits in both living and non-living things like mountains, lakes, forests, or sky. For example, the Pygmies of the Ituri forest in northeastern Zaire believe in a Supreme Being which they identify with the forest. Unlike other Africans they do not fear the forest, for they do not think of it as a dangerous place.

Ancestor worship. Everywhere in Africa, people respect their ancestral spirits, especially those belonging to the founder of the clan and their heroes. They think these ancestral spirits continue to have an active interest in their descendants and are able to do them either good or harm. They can harm by causing disease. Therefore, rituals, prayers, and sacrifices are important and are usually directed by the chief of the clan. Some Africans, like the Baganda of Uganda, believe that the soul comes back inside the children born to the clan. Worship of a particular spirit ends when it returns in a newborn child. Thus a spiritual link between the living, dead, and future tribal members is maintained.

The religion of herders. Since pastoral peoples love their cattle, cows are part of the religion of the herders in such countries as Sudan, Kenya, and Tanzania. Herders do not consider cows sacred in the way Hindus do, but they believe that their cattle are a gift from God. Since God sent cattle as a means of support, the herdsmen feel a sacred duty to protect the animals and pass them on to the next generation. (See poem, p. 157.) Some of the cattle people believe in a world of spirits and have developed rituals connected with these beliefs. When a boy is initiated into manhood among the Nuer of Sudan, his father presents him with an ox. The animal becomes a very special pet for the son. The ox also has religious meaning as a link between the boy and the spiritual world.

Religion among farming people. Religion is more complicated among farming people. Because they move less often, they establish more permanent institutions. Priests and other religious officials are important, and shrines are established. In Kenya there is a sacred tree and a deep hole nearby where Kikuyu, the first man of the tribe, was created. Other tribes have sacred rocks, streams, or mountains which are remembered for special religious reasons.

The medicine man. The medicine man is an important and highly honored person. He is usually very intelligent, having a great knowledge and understanding of his people. Sometimes he is also a diviner, a person who is believed to be able to see into the future or explain the unknown. When sickness strikes or some other disaster occurs, the victim or the victim's family may go to the diviner to find out why it happened. The diviner will explain the event and tell them what necessary prayers, rituals, or sacrifices should be made to correct the situation.

The medicine man's main duty is to help heal the sick. He may not have modern medical training, but he often has practical knowledge from his predecessors of numerous medicines. Moreover, the medicine man is usually a good practical psychologist who knows how to deal with people in trouble. When one adds to that the great respect and confidence the people have for him, his success as a healer is not surprising.

An important activity of the medicine man is making fetishes. A fetish is an object that has the supernatural power to bring good or evil for the person who possesses it. The material from which a fetish is made gives it power. Materials might be from plants or animals, and many of the most powerful fetishes contain human blood or bones.

Modern methods of healing exist alongside the traditions of the medicine man. Here a physician prepares to examine a mother and child.

Fetishes are made for different purposes. In Cameroon, people will buy a fetish to hang on a pole in the field. It is believed that the fetish will help produce a good harvest and protect the crop from thieves. Among the Baganda a fetish made of special herbs and pieces of the hearts of buffalo, crocodiles, and lions will give a soldier great strength and courage.

The power of the fetish is believed to come from the spirit that is in the object. The owner of the fetish will benefit from the power of this spirit. A medicine man believed able to make powerful fetishes is highly regarded.

Christianity and Islam in Africa. Christianity came to Africa soon after Christ's death. At the time of the Roman Empire, important centers of Christianity were established at Alexandria in Egypt and at Carthage in Tunisia. Carthage was the home of St. Augustine, one of the greatest early Christian leaders. Christianity in Ethiopia is the Coptic form (p. 129).

When the Arabs brought Islam to North Africa, people began converting to that faith. Although the Copts were rarely persecuted by the Arabs, their membership shrank. With the exception of Ethiopia, the Muslim religion replaced Christianity as the major religion throughout the northern portion of the continent.

Missionaries in Africa. Both Muslims and Christians have actively attempted to attract converts in Africa. Consequently most African nations are officially either one or the other. Many of the common people, however, still cling to their tribal religions.

Since many basic similarities between the African religions and the missionaries' teachings exist, such as the belief in a Supreme Being and a spiritual existence after death, blending the two has not been difficult. Africans are frequently able to accept the new beliefs and still hold on to most of their tribal religions.

Most African schools have been established, staffed, and supported by Christian missionaries. They laid the foundations of the educational systems in most African countries, and most of Africa's present leaders had part of their training in these schools. Without question the most lasting achievement of the missionaries was the establishment of school systems.

Countless self-sacrificing missionaries worked hard in Africa. Their founding of schools and hospitals as well as their service to others was in the finest Christian tradition. Unfortunately, many whites acted in unchristian ways toward Africans, destroying many of the missionaries' efforts.

Modern missionaries are more sensitive to the evils of prejudice and discrimination. There is far less racism in their attitudes than in the past. Though there is more emphasis on education and welfare than before, their behavior is actually more true to Christian ideals than in the earlier period.

Looking ahead. Africa is a continent undergoing rapid changes. As industry develops and people are drawn to cities, traditional customs will be changed.

From its beginnings in the Arabian peninsula, Islam spread throughout North and Central Africa. It also has a following in such West African countries as Senegal. Here a Dakar man studies the Koran.

Modern communication and swift access to other nations will speed diffusion of influences to Africa as well as spreading African influences abroad. Africans seem determined to preserve as much of their traditions as possible and yet modernize their nations in order to provide a higher standard of living for their people.

Reviewing Your Reading

1. Why are ancestors considered to be important?
2. What is animism?
3. Why is the medicine man an important member of the community?
4. What is the purpose of fetishes?
5. How has the Christian religion affected African life?

CHAPTER REVIEW

Recalling Names and Places

age groups	fetish	patrilineal
animism	joint family	puberty rites
bride wealth	matrilineal	tribe
clan	medicine man	

Understanding This Chapter

1. What methods might be used to develop loyalty to the nation despite family and tribal ties?
2. Special initiation ceremonies of "rites of passage" are common in Africa and elsewhere. Do American children and young people have any ceremonies of that kind?
3. What advantages does an extended family have over a nuclear family for the individual? What disadvantages?
4. Although loneliness and loss of family supports are the price of going to the city, African youths are leaving the rural areas in large numbers. What are some of their reasons?
5. It has been said that the religious beliefs of a people tend to reflect their way of life. Show how this is true of Africans.
6. As modern medical care becomes more general in Africa, are there any reasons Africans might want to preserve the services of medicine men?

Chapter 13

The Rural and Urban Economies of Africa

Most sub-Saharan countries are over 80 percent rural. In many of them, industrial growth has taken place since gaining independence. People in this region, like those in many other parts of the world, are flocking to the cities, in search of jobs and greater opportunities.

Africans Are Mainly Rural Farmers

Most Africans earn their living by subsistence farming. All family members work to provide enough food to feed themselves and rarely have any surplus for trade. In a few places like the Niger River and Lake Chad areas, rivers or lakes flood the land annually, leaving deposits of fresh, fertile soil. Such areas are farmed each year. Where farming and livestock raising are combined, permanent settlements exist.

Bush-fallowing is typical in most regions. Most rural Africans use the "bush-fallow" method of agriculture. Farmers cut down and burn bushes and small trees. Larger trees are left standing because they are harder to remove and do not interfere with farming. Farmers till the soil with digging sticks and hoes. Usually, after three or four crops, the land loses its fertility. It is abandoned, and a new area is cleared in the same fashion. The old land may be used again after lying fallow for some years.

Africans usually plant a mixture of seeds, often including beans, squash, and yams. The nature of the land determines the combination of crops. Since different plants take various nutrients from the soil, planting a mixture of seeds preserves soil fertility a little longer.

The time between planting and harvesting is often a period of hunger. The food supply from the previous harvest may not last until the next one. Insufficient rain may reduce the size of the crop. Tribes depending on wild game to supplement their crops may find fewer animals.

The typical unit of labor is the family. The tribe owns the land, and the village leader distributes a portion of it to every family. Each family has a right to use a fair share of the land.

Cattle culture. The savannah region, especially in East Africa, is cattle country, since this area is too dry for crops. Almost a third of Africa's people are herders, particularly in such countries as Chad, Sudan, and Kenya. However,

SUB-SAHARAN AFRICA: LAND USE AND MINERALS

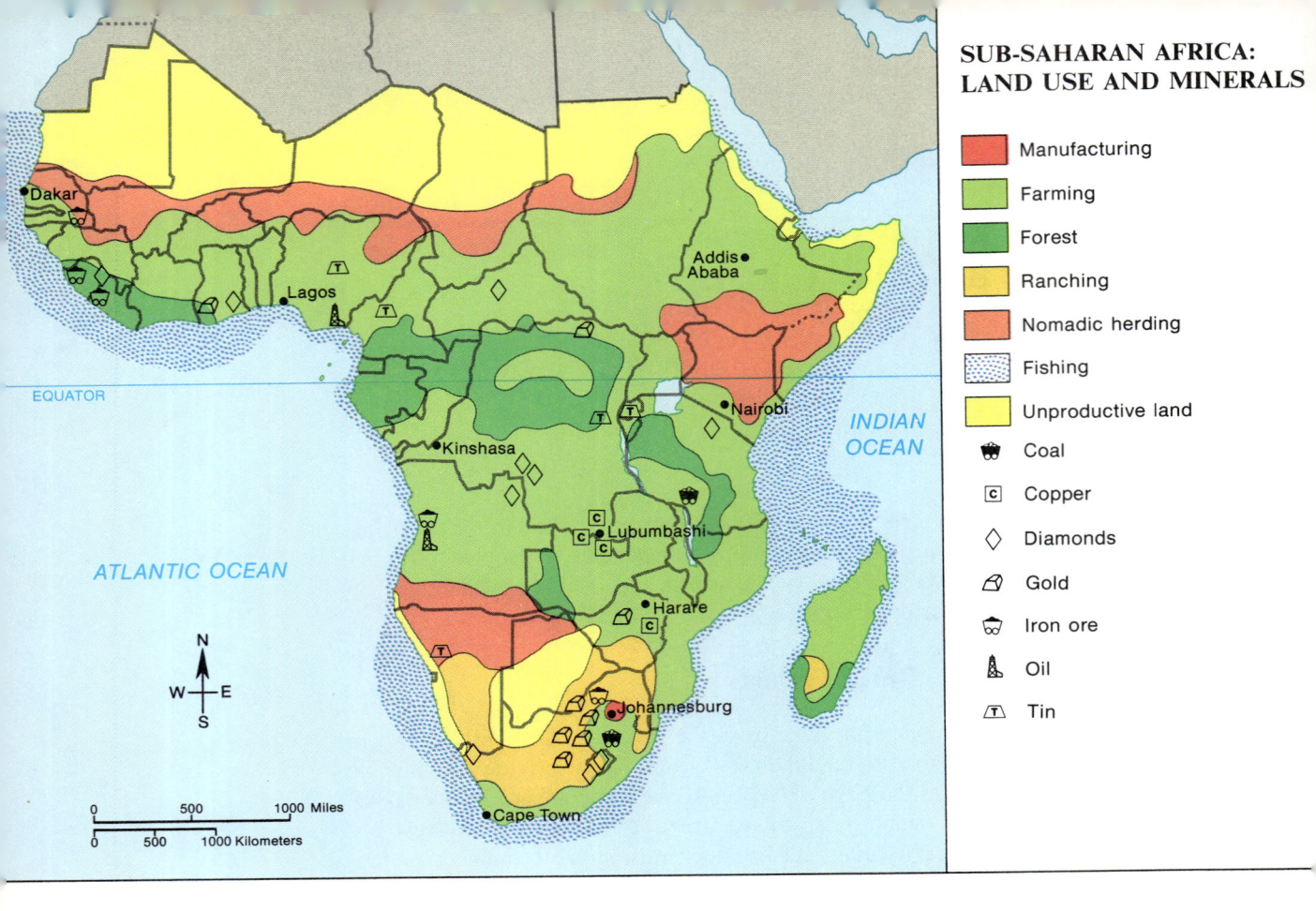

Legend:
- Manufacturing
- Farming
- Forest
- Ranching
- Nomadic herding
- Fishing
- Unproductive land
- Coal
- Copper
- Diamonds
- Gold
- Iron ore
- Oil
- Tin

The Blessing of Rain

Isak Dinesen, whose real name was Baroness Karen Blixen-Finecke, was a Danish noblewoman who owned a coffee plantation in Kenya. Here she describes the dependence of the African farmer on rain:

When in Africa in March the long rains begin after four months of hot, dry weather, the richness of growth and the freshness and fragrance everywhere are overwhelming.

But the farmer . . . dares not trust to the generosity of nature, he listens, dreading to hear a decrease in the roar of the falling rain. The water that the earth is now drinking in must bring the farm . . . through four rainless months to come.

It is a lovely sight when the roads of the farm have all been turned into streams of running water, and the farmer wades through the mud with a singing heart, out to the flowering and dripping coffee-fields. But it happens in the middle of the rainy season that in the evening the stars show themselves through the thinning clouds; then he stands outside his house and stares up, as if hanging himself on to the sky to milk down more rain. He cries to the sky: 'Give me enough and more than enough. . . .

Isak Dinesen, *Out of Africa* (New York: Random House, 1938), pp. 274–275.

> **Cattle Are All Important**
>
> *Cattle are very important to the herders. Even in their prayers, the cattle people refer to their beloved animals. A Didinga warrior, praying to a full moon, sees it as a cow of heaven:*
>
> White cow of heaven, you have fed in rich pastures
>   and you who were small have grown great.
> White cow of heaven, your horns have curved full
>   circle and are joined as one.
> White cow of heaven, we throw at you the dust which
>   your feet have trampled in our kraals [pens].
> White cow of heaven, give your blessing on the kraals
>   which you have overseen that the udders of our
>   cows may be heavy and that our women may rejoice.
>
> Melville J. Herskovits, *Cultural Anthropology* (New York,: Alfred A. Knopf, Inc., 1963), p. 407.

where there is enough moisture to grow some crops to add to their food supply, the African herders do so.

For pastoral people like the Nilotic tribes of the Sudan, the Masai of Kenya and Tanzania, and the Watutsi (wah-*toot*'see) of Rwanda (ruh-*wahn*' duh), cattle are more than a source of food and clothing. Owning many cattle gives a man high social status. Cattle are like money. If a man has many cattle, he can pay the bride wealth for several wives.

While women do most of the work in farming regions, the men tend the herds in the cattle culture. The cattle owners have an unusual love for their animals. They know each individual animal, and if one should die, they feel the loss deeply.

The men milk their cows every morning and evening. Often they bleed their animals. Using a small bow and arrow, they make a wound in the neck vein to draw a quart or two of blood. This operation does not seem too painful, and the wound is carefully closed.

Blood is a very nourishing addition to the milk. To supplement their diet, the cattle people also raise some crops if conditions permit. The land is often too dry to grow anything more than grass for the herds. Occasionally the herders raise corn, pumpkins, or peanuts to add to their meals.

The cattle people are proud of their way of life and look down on the farmers. Sometimes they have dominated the farming people because they are more skillful as warriors. For example, since about the seventeenth century Rwanda and Burundi (boo-*run*'dee) were ruled by an upper caste of the cattle-herding Tutsi. They had invaded the area from the north and conquered the agricultural Rundis. The rule of the Tutsi was ended in Rwanda in 1959 and in Burundi in 1966. Many Tutsi were killed by the Burundi during the change of government. In 1972 the Tutsi countered an attack by Burundi's major tribe, the Hutus, slaughtering thousands of them.

The pastoral people do not want to change their way of life. This refusal to adjust to change may mean the end of their nomadic life in the future. The new African states may insist on a more efficient cattle industry. If they do, change may be forced on these people, and their present way of life will come to an end.

Agriculture in Africa takes many forms. Nomadic herders of the Masai tribes water their cattle at Lake Amboseli (above left); the people of a Luo tribe chop their cassava by hand (left); and cash crops are grown in geometric plots like these in the Kikuyu highlands (above). All three of these scenes come from the same African country — Kenya.

Fishing grows in importance. Fish have not always been an important part of most Africans' diet. Many live far from fishing waters, and even where fish are available, many Africans do not regard them as proper food. For example, some Ibo tribes believe that their ancestors' souls live in fish.

However, such tribes as the Ga of Ghana or the Lokele of Zaire are skillful fishermen, using cleverly designed nets. Many of the ocean waters are teeming with tuna, sardines, and snoek (a type of pike), but Africans are handicapped by the lack of harbors and by dangerous currents. Some of the best fishing waters are off the coast of northwest and southeast Africa. Foreign vessels catch the fish, and Africans do not benefit from the supply.

Many changes must be made before commercial fishing becomes profitable in Africa. Transporting fish is difficult. The warm, humid climate spoils fresh fish quickly, unless they are salted or smoked. As refrigeration is adopted, it will be easier to ship fish to distant places. African prejudice against fish may also be weakening. Some people, like the Kikuyu, are beginning to eat fish as they see their neighbors doing so. To increase the amount of protein in African diets, many African governments encourage the use of more fish. Fish farming – raising fish in shallow water – is developing in Uganda, Zimbabwe, Zaire, and Nigeria.

Colonial rule changes agriculture. During the colonial period the British, Portuguese, and French hoped to make profits in Africa. Rapidly growing industries in Europe needed vast amounts of raw materials. To meet this demand, Europeans established plantations and used African labor to grow such products as cocoa, palm oil, and sisal for their factories back home. Such products grown for sale or export are called cash crops.

Plantations, the large farms used for growing cash crops, continue to be an important form of agriculture today. In Tanzania and Uganda, for example, the operation of cotton and coffee plantations is being transferred from European to African control. Elsewhere Africans are encouraged to grow certain cash crops in addition to those grown for home use.

The importance of cash crops has grown since World War II. The rapid rise in the standard of living in industrial nations has increased the demand for such goods as coffee and cocoa and for raw materials like sisal and cotton. The African nations are eager to meet this need. Although over fifty cash crops are raised in Africa, five products account for 80 percent of the output. They are cocoa, coffee, cotton, peanuts, and palm products (oil and kernels). Palm oil is used for making soap, and palm kernels for margarine. Other plantation crops include bananas, tea, and sisal for rope.

Improving agriculture is a major goal. Probably the backwardness of agriculture is Africa's most serious economic problem. Until farming becomes more efficient, other economic programs will be held back. According to United Nations' figures, the average African farmer produces only about a third as much as the average farmer elsewhere. There are several reasons for this. Africa's soils tend to be poor. More extensive use of fertilizer is needed to produce higher crop yields. The bush-fallow method (p. 155) is wasteful, producing low crop yields. Artificial fertilizers, better tools and seeds, and instruction in modern agricultural techniques need to be applied.

Declining productivity. Africa's total food production has declined since the 1960s while the population has accelerated during the same period. In 1970 Africa produced almost all the food it needed. Increasing amounts of food must now be imported.

Wars in countries like Ethiopia and Uganda have reduced food production. Traditional farming methods are not efficient, but there is resistance to change. Production is further reduced by erosion of the land.

Because 90 percent of the people still depend on wood for energy, forests are rapidly being cut down. Loss of forests contributes to the erosion problem and to the advance of deserts, especially in the Savannah region. Crop and animal wastes, once used as fertilizer, are now used for fuel.

Overgrazing is another cause of the advance of the deserts. The lands are held by the tribe, so there is little incentive to protect them. The United Nations Environment Program estimates that about 24,000 square miles of African land turn into desert each year. That is about the size of the state of West Virginia.

Traditional farming methods are no longer adequate to feed Africa's rapidly growing population. It will double in twenty-two years if the current growth rate continues. Moreover, the urban population is constantly increasing. The food surplus must be increased to feed the industrial workers in the cities. One temporary solution of the many independent nations has been to buy food abroad. Liberia, for example, sells rubber and iron ore to Europe and the United States and buys much of its flour, sugar, and meat abroad. Ghana also imports large quantities of canned goods, packaged cereals, and alcoholic beverages.

Reviewing Your Reading

1. What is the bush-fallow method of agriculture?
2. Describe the cattle culture of the savannah regions. How has it affected agricultural improvements in Africa?
3. What are some of the agricultural problems facing Africans today?

African Resources and Industries

The African continent possesses abundant mineral resources and potential hydroelectric power. Yet the development of these resources and the creation of new industries has been held back by the lack of adequate transportation and communication lines and the scarcity of skilled workers.

Africa is rich in mineral wealth. Africa has great mineral resources, and new discoveries occur yearly. Already Africa's present production of certain minerals is impressive—more than 95 percent of the world's diamonds, 80 percent of its cobalt, over 50 percent of the gold, over 30 percent of the phosphates, 25 percent of the chromium and manganese, and 20 percent of the copper.

A few countries possess most of Africa's mineral resources. South Africa, Zaire, Zambia, Angola, Cameroon, and Gabon have the largest shares. South Africa is the world's leading producer of gold. Zaire has enormous resources of copper, tin, manganese, and uranium. It is second only to South Africa in mineral wealth. In 1979, for example, cobalt, copper, and diamonds made up 89 percent of Zaire's exports.

All African nations seek mineral wealth. The discovery of minerals would aid industrial development throughout Africa, providing raw materials and finished products for export. While many mining companies are still under foreign control, African governments are buying them out as Zaire and Ghana have done with their Belgian and British investors.

Energy resources are limited. Energy resources are sources of power necessary to run machines. Since such sources of energy are needed to build industry, they are essential to the development of a modern economy.

Coal has been the most important source of power for the industrialized nations of the world to date. Unfortunately, few African countries have coal deposits, and those which do exist are often of low quality. South Africa, Zimbabwe, and Zaire have the best coal resources.

Nigeria, Gabon, and Angola have oil supplies. Nigeria, in fact, is the world's sixth leading oil producer. In 1982 oil represented 94 percent of its exports. However, most of the continent is built on a kind of bedrock in which oil is not found. Thus prospects for oil discoveries are poor in most sections.

Africa's greatest energy resource may be water power. Africa has 40 percent of the world's total water-power potential. Less than one half of one percent of this power has been developed, even though some large dams on the Zambezi, the Nile, and the Volta rivers have been built.

Money is a major problem. The Kariba Dam on the Zambezi River cost $215 million to build. Such sums are hard to find. Furthermore, a need for power and flood control must exist before such costs seem worthwhile. Planning for industries and hydroelectric centers usually has to be done for the same location at the same time.

Until the 1950s Zambia's copper belt consisted mainly of dense bush. Today such factories as the Rhokana mine in Kitwe are common.

Improved transportation is a major need. Mining and industry require transportation to carry heavy and bulky products, like iron ore, steel, and cement. Only South African railroads follow the Western pattern of connecting urban, agricultural, mining, and industrial centers with seaports. Elsewhere, railroads are a single track, stretching inland from a seaport to a certain economic center.

Rivers are usually the cheapest way to ship goods. Waterfalls and changes in depth of African rivers limit their economic value, however. The rivers present problems for road and railroad builders, too. Heavy rains cause flooding, washing out roads and bridges.

Heavy rains make the soil spongy, cracking pavements and sinking railroad beds. But the dry season also causes transportation problems. Dust wears out machinery, often reducing the lifespan of a truck or bus to a year or two. Vehicles also wear out more quickly since many of their drivers are unfamiliar with automobiles and fail to maintain them properly. For instance, a driver may not know how to change the oil.

Air travel is the most developed form of transportation in Africa. Ethiopia Airlines, Air Zaire, and Ghana Airways are among the many airlines that provide travel service between Africa and Europe. Airport construction has some of the same problems as road building. Dust and humidity reduce the life of engines. Tropical storms create terrific air currents that can destroy planes. The thin air of high-altitude airports limits the loads that can be lifted.

Adequate transportation is necessary for economic development. Like industry, it needs money for expansion and depends upon agricultural improvements for growth.

Subsistence economy is the rule. Many Africans are still largely on a subsistence economy. The average per capita income in many sub-Saharan countries is less than $100 per year. Many Africans use very little money, and barter is still common. For example, herding people, like the Masai, will trade milk or meat for grain or vegetables from farmers. Agricultural people in Zaire will trade their produce and tools for meat and honey provided by the Pygmies.

In the past, trading people used strings of cowrie shells for money in many parts of Africa. The Tiv in Nigeria used three-foot-long brass rods for currency. Contact with Europeans brought the use of modern money, and all African countries now have an official currency.

Probably few Africans are entirely outside of the money economy. In such countries as Ivory Coast, Ghana, Kenya, and Zambia the money economy is dominant. The need for money to pay taxes and buy manufactured goods has grown. Manufactured clothing, processed foods, bicycles, and other machines usually must be bought with money. As people's desire for money increases, many begin working for wages, particularly in the cities.

Asians in Africa. In the 1890s the British imported Indian and Pakistani laborers into East and Southeast Africa. Their descendants remained, working as merchants and shopkeepers. In the early 1960s about 350,000 South Asians lived in Uganda, Tanzania, and Kenya, but the Africans came to resent them. Many of the Asians were clannish, and the Africans felt that they limited economic opportunity for others.

Since the early 1960s several East African governments have demanded that the Asians become African citizens or leave. In 1972, under the dictator Idi Amin, Uganda ordered the expulsion of almost all 45,000 non-citizen Asians. Although Uganda belonged to the British Commonwealth, Britain did not welcome the expelled Asians. Some returned to South Asia. After Amin's fall in 1979 and the institution of a new government, Uganda offered to return property taken from Asians if they would become Ugandan citizens.

Following independence, many African nations encouraged Europeans to remain in important positions because of a shortage of trained people. As qualified Africans are trained, they will replace foreigners.

Africa's development needs are so great that these nations must have international assistance. They cannot do it alone. Foreign aid to Africa so far has been mainly in the form of military supplies. Africa has other needs that are far more urgent, especially improvement of agriculture and transportation.

The economies of the world are interrelated. If economic disaster befalls Africa, the rest of the world will be affected. A prosperous Africa would contribute to the stability and prosperity of all nations.

Reviewing Your Reading

1. How are Africa's mineral resources being developed?
2. What problems hinder the development of necessary transportation routes?
3. Describe a barter system.

CHAPTER REVIEW

Recalling Names and Places

barter   bush-fallow method   cash crops

Understanding This Chapter

1. The bush-fallow or slash-and-burn method of farming requires an abundance of land. As land becomes more scarce, are better methods available? What might be done?
2. If pastoral peoples shifted to fewer but better cattle, how would their way of life be changed?
3. Traditional African agriculture is not now able to produce the food Africa needs. Yet the population is increasing rapidly. Should the outside world help? How?
4. What factors are leading to an increased use of money in African economies?

Chapter 14

African Political Systems

Before the colonial period, many types of government existed in Africa. Hunters and food-gatherers had the simplest form, sometimes called "primitive democracy." Under this kind of political system, characteristic of Bushmen, Pygmies, and many small Negro tribes, decisions are reached by consensus. An elder or group of elders provides leadership and recommends action. The clan or tribe decides whether to follow the recommendations or not.

Among pastoral peoples the complexity of the political system depended on how frequently they moved to find pasture. Those who migrated constantly had political systems similar to the hunters. Others who had the same pasture through the year because of an adequate water supply developed more complex political systems. For example, the Shilluk tribe of Sudan protected its choice land through a centralized government ruled by a king.

Usually farming and trading people created the most complex political systems, which traditionally were kingdoms or empires. The rulers tended to be autocratic and often were considered divine. They ruled in lavish surroundings with much ritual and ceremony. Kingdoms in Nigeria, Uganda, and Ethiopia were highly organized politically.

Traditional political practices still continue in many regions of Africa, especially among the hunters, food gatherers, and pastoral people. As the influence of central governments extends to the remote regions, many traditional practices will probably change.

Colonial Division of Africa

When the Europeans partitioned Africa, the continent was already divided into thousands of tribal territories. Most tribes lived apart from each other much like separate countries. As they partitioned the continent to suit their interests, the Europeans paid no attention to these tribal divisions.

Colonial division creates conflicts. Present African boundaries largely resulted from the colonial period, causing many present political problems and conflicts. In some cases rival tribes live in the same territory. For example, many of the nearly 300 Nigerian tribes dislike each other. The Hausa (*how'*sah) hate the Yoruba; the Yoruba hate the Ibo; and the Ibo hate the Efik. A Nigerian civil war in the late 1960s showed how deeply the Ibos resent other tribes. Similar tribal hostilities exist elsewhere.

European boundaries also split many tribes. Today, members of the Hausa tribe live in Nigeria, Mali, Upper Volta, and Niger. The Bakongo are in

SUB-SAHARAN AFRICA: POLITICAL

✯ National capital

> **The Nigerian Civil War (1967–1970)**
>
> Nigeria, with more than 62 million people, has the largest population of any nation in Africa. A land rich in resources, including oil and an industrious people, Nigeria could become a dominant nation of Africa. Unfortunately, like many other African nations, Nigeria is divided into many tribes, the dominant ones being the Hausa in the north, the Yoruba in the west, and the Ibo in the east.
>
> Having more than half of the nation's population, the Hausas dominated the Nigerian government for several years following independence in 1960. The Ibos resented this domination, and in January 1966 the Ibo head of Nigeria's armed forces, General Ironsi, seized control of the government and became president. Rioting and killing of Ibos, especially by Hausas, followed. General Ironsi was murdered, and a Hausa leader, Major General Yakubu Gowon took control of the government. Later in 1966 new riots resulted in the killing of up to 30,000 Ibos.
>
> After seeking local autonomy without success, General Odumegwu Ojukwu declared the Ibo region of eastern Nigeria the independent Republic of Biafra. A bloody civil war followed. Lack of food supplies caused widespread starvation in Biafra, and in January 1970 the Ibos had to surrender. General Ojukwu went into exile to the Ivory Coast.
>
> Since the war Nigeria has made more rapid progress than expected. New discoveries of oil have helped restore prosperity to the nation.

Congo, Zaire, and Angola. Since there are thousands of tribes in Africa, it would not be practical to have each tribe a separate nation-state. On the other hand, tribes should not be split by boundaries nor should hostile tribes be forced to live together. Nationalist leaders are deeply concerned about tribal hostility and are seeking solutions to this problem.

Colonialism produced nationalism. Nationalism was a by-product of colonial rule. Prior to the colonial era, Africans felt loyalty only toward family, clan, and tribe. They felt what is usually called "tribalism," already described in Chapter 12. European rule tended to expand these feelings of loyalty to a concept of national allegiance. Nonetheless, feelings of nationalism were confined to the educated minority of Africans. This is still true, and political leaders are working to broaden nationalist feeling.

Nationalism was accompanied by greater racial pride. An important part of growing African nationalism is greater racial pride. Leopold Senghor, a philosopher, poet, and former president of Senegal, has called this pride *negritude*.

Negritude seeks to give blacks a sense of personal dignity, and the feeling that they are complete human beings. Some writers speak of the special talents and feelings black people have and others do not. Most of all, negritude is an effort to undo the damage that prejudice has done. It calls for active assertion of the pride and self-confidence blacks feel in their racial heritage and African history.

Pan-Africanism: Africa for the Africans. An important reaction to European colonialism was a movement called Pan-Africanism. Begun around 1900 its advocates' slogan was "Africa for the Africans." They wished to improve the welfare of the African people and urged the colonial powers to allow Africans greater self-government. By 1945 the leaders of the Pan-African movement were demanding full independence for Africa.

Since 1960 Pan-Africanism has been replaced by organizations composed of separate, independent African states. The Organization of African Unity (OAU), formed in 1963, is the most important of these groups. This body seeks to eliminate the remaining colonialism in Africa and develop a feeling of unity among African states. The ultimate goal of the OAU is to bring about a united Africa some day. It has helped solve border problems between Algeria and Morocco and between Kenya and Somalia. The OAU also cooperates with the United Nations to bring economic aid to African countries. However, the organization itself has at times become a battleground for rivalries among African nations. For example, in 1982 fighting between Morocco and political groups supporting an independent nation in the Western Sahara led to a boycott of OAU meetings by nations supporting Morocco.

Different routes to independence. During the colonial period the European powers had different political philosophies regarding their colonies. Britain never tried to destroy the native governments, preferring to work with them.

Leaders from many African nations gather for meetings of the Organization of African Unity (OAU). At this 1979 meeting in Monrovia, Liberia, the OAU gave official recognition to the government of Prime Minister Robert Mugabe as the only legitimate government of Zimbabwe, supplanting the all-white minority regime that had ruled for almost fifteen years.

> **Sign of the Times**
>
> *As African countries have become independent, they have also become more interested in their African cultural heritage. The following article, which appeared in* The New York Times, *February 17, 1972, is one example of the increasing emphasis on an independent Africa.*
>
> KINSHASA, Zaire, Feb. 16 (Agence France-Presse)—The people of Zaire must henceforth drop their baptismal names and adopt authentic African names, the Political Bureau of the governing Popular Revolutionary Movement has ordered.
>
> The Zaire press agency said that the bureau decided at a meeting yesterday that the changing of names was now obligatory.
>
> It added that the President, Gen. Mobutu Sese Seko, who recently changed his name from Joseph D. Mobutu, had shown the meeting a new type of identity card that would give the former baptismal name in small print and in brackets after the African name.
>
> President Mobutu has adopted a policy of changing names to African ones in Zaire, which was known as the Congo until last year.
>
> Copyright © 1972 by *The New York Times Company*. Reprinted by permission.

This is a policy of "indirect rule." The British attempted to influence local rulers to cooperate with them. They gradually permitted more self-rule until full independence was achieved. Ghana was the first of the British colonies to gain independence in 1957.

France wished to assimilate its colonies by trying to transform African into French. They considered their colonies to be a part of France, rather than future independent countries. But a bloody rebellion in Algeria convinced France to permit independence, and most of its colonies gained self-rule by 1960. The French colonies were less well prepared for sudden self-rule than the former British territories. Some, like the Ivory Coast and Senegal, have made good progress toward political stability and economic development.

Belgian policy was less constructive than the French. The people of Zaire were not given educational opportunities to prepare them for self-government. When the Belgians left suddenly in 1960, chaos and civil war followed. Separatist regimes sprang up in Kasai and Katanga provinces. Not until General Joseph Mobuto took control of the government in 1965 did efforts toward national unity begin to take hold. Tribalism continued to trouble the country into the 1970s. In May 1978, political, economic, and tribal differences caused a rebellion in the Shaba province of Zaire.

Government Since Independence

Despite a tradition of monarchy, few of the new African countries became kingdoms after independence. Only the tiny nations of Lesotho and Swaziland in southern Africa are monarchies. All of the other sub-Saharan nations are republics.

Single-party governments became typical. Most of the African republics permit only a single political party, or they have only one party that is so dominant that other parties have little influence. Major nations with one-party political systems include Guinea, Ivory Coast, Kenya, Tanzania, Zambia, and Zaire. Botswana and Gambia permit two or more parties. Nigeria and Togo are ruled by the army, and no parties are permitted. Some nations are under military control but do permit a political party to exist. Such is the case in Burundi, Central African Republic, People's Republic of Congo, Uganda, and Ghana.

Almost all of the African republics permit elections. However, since independence, elections have become less common in many African republics. Kenya has held only one election since 1963, and Chad has had only one election since 1960. In such countries as Botswana and Tanzania elections are democratic and determine the selection of government officials. In some countries elections are rigged so they become meaningless. Most of the republics have a parliament or national assembly of some kind.

Following independence, the people in the new republics generally supported the nationalist parties. To get popular support, political leaders promised many rewards for the people, especially a higher standard of living. The leaders often failed to recognize how difficult it would be to fulfill these promises. When independence did not bring expected changes, some people wanted to organize new political parties. Usually, however, their efforts were suppressed.

Role of the military. Within ten years after independence there were more than twenty military takeovers in the newly independent nations. Military rule continued to play a role in many African countries in the 1980s. Military intervention has occurred for a variety of reasons: to gain political power, to remove leaders thought bad for the nation, and to put down rival military forces created by political leaders. In other cases army officers were dissatisfied with their positions and wanted more money or more soldiers. Frustration of hopes caused many people to support seizures of power by the military. Usually after taking over the government, military leaders discovered that it was not easy to meet the demands of the people. Often the military government itself was overthrown by someone else. Such have been the experiences of nations like Uganda, Ghana, and Benin.

Ivory Coast: An African success. Ivory Coast is a West African republic about the size of New Mexico. After gaining independence from France in 1960, it was led by Felix Houphouet-Boigny, who reached 80 years of age in 1985.

Houphouet-Boigny helped transform Ivory Coast from the backward, unpromising area it was in 1960 into an African miracle. Even without the advantages of oil or mineral resources, Ivory Coast became the most prosperous and stable nation in sub-Sahara, Africa outside South Africa.

The president kept up good relations with France and benefited from French aid without selling out to the Europeans. The economy of the nation became diversified and has had remarkable growth. The gross national product – the yearly value of all goods and services produced – tripled in the twenty years to 1985.

Jomo Kenyatta, who worked hard for the independence of Kenya, was known to his early followers as "Burning Spear."

Felix Houphouet-Boigny, first president of the Ivory Coast, led his country to independence from France in 1960. On its new equal footing, the country has maintained strong ties with France.

The Ivory Coast enjoys both one of the most stable democracies and one of the healthiest economies in Africa. Farming, fishing, shipping, and lumbering play major roles in the economy. Here, boats keep control of tropical hardwood trees in the harbor of the capital city of Abidjan.

By avoiding military adventures and huge defense costs, Ivory Coast has been able to tag 20 percent of its budget for education. The nation has more than twice the literacy rate of the rest of Africa. In its first quarter century of independence Ivory Coast did not see a single political execution, nor were any political prisoners held. The capital, Abidjan, grew into the showplace of Africa with its beautiful hotels, parks, and boulevards.

Houphouet-Boigny's successors may not do as well, but the old president is certain to be remembered as one of Africa's truly great leaders. Without fanfare or personal glorification he showed what political moderation and devotion to the welfare of his people can accomplish. Ivory Coast is not without problems. There is still much poverty, especially in rural areas. But compared to the rest of Africa the nation has made remarkable progress.

People's Republic of Congo: One-party dictatorship. The People's Republic of Congo was ruled by France prior to its independence in 1958. A nation of close to two million people, Congo is divided by conflicting tribal, religious, and economic interests. The people divide into four main ethnic groups – the Kongo, Batek, Sanga, and Mboshi. These four main groups are in turn divided into 73 tribes. Political conflicts often reflect the different tribal loyalties.

Religious conflicts have also created political problems. Half of the Congolese follow tribal religions. The other half are mainly Roman Catholics, although there is a small Muslim minority. Religious conflict arose soon after independence when the Roman Catholic Church was accused of trying to start an opposition political party. Further conflict has accompanied the rapid increase in the number of wage earners in towns, especially Brazzaville. Congo has one of the most rapid rates of urbanization in Africa. The interests of the urban workers are different from those of the rural people.

The differences among the people of the Congo have contributed to the political instability of the People's Republic. Since 1963, Congo leaders have been drawn to the socialist philosophies of both the Soviet Union and China. Conflicts have broken out between pro-Soviet and pro-Chinese Congolese. In 1970 a new constitution provided for a one-party Marxist government. The name "People's Republic of Congo" was adopted.

Since independence, Congo has experienced much internal conflict. The presidents have been removed by army seizures of power which occurred in 1963 when President Fulbert Youlou was forced out and again in 1968 when Alphonse Massemba-Delbat had to resign. In 1968 the country came under military rule. In 1969 Major Marien Ngouabi, head of the pro-Soviet National Council of the Revolution, took control. He remained as head of Congo for eight years, until his assassination in 1977. Former President Delbat was accused of killing Ngouabi and executed. Another military leader took control of the government, and he in turn was replaced by Colonel Denis Sassou-Ngnessou in 1979. The country has only one political party. As yet, democratic government has not developed to any significant degree.

Challenges to African Independence

The new African nations have enjoyed independence only since the late 1950s or early 1960s. Many westerners believed that these nations would fail within the first ten years of their independence. Such gloomy predictions have not come true. However, the African nations are facing many difficulties.

Tribalism: A liability and an asset. Tribalism is a major problem in many of the nations. Centuries of distrust and hostility between tribes are not easily

The African independence movement took many forms, some peaceful, some revolutionary and violent. In 1956 British Togoland became part of Ghana through an election. Members of local political parties held meetings and rallies to discuss and promote the drive for independence.

forgotten. In Nigeria, Sudan, and Chad tribal hostilities caused internal wars, and more conflicts may occur in the future. Some of the world's most serious violations of human rights have occurred in Africa. Idi Amin slaughtered an estimated 300,000 people during his rule in Uganda, from 1971 to 1979. In 1972 in Burundi the ruling Watusi massacred 200,000 Hutus to ensure their own continued control of the government. Hatred between tribes makes such crimes possible.

On the other hand, tribal membership gives an individual security and the sense of belonging. Both remain important in a rapidly changing society. Moreover, the new governments are unable to provide the social services the tribe offers.

The nationalist leaders are seeking solutions to lessen the influence of tribalism. One suggestion is the construction of centrally located boarding schools to be attended by children from different tribes. In addition, greater urban economic opportunities should make tribal identity less strong. African governments hope to develop a sense of nationalism in all their people. This desire for national unity is reflected in the Nigerian national anthem:

Blacks and whites work together to try to change the racist apartheid policies of the South African government. This interracial protest meeting of a group known as the Union Democratic Front was probably illegal, but an overflow crowd turned out in defiance of the laws they considered unjust.

Oh God of all creation,
Grant this our one request:
Help us to build a nation
Where no man is oppressed.

Racism and apartheid. Racism is almost as great a problem in Africa as tribalism. It takes many forms and is not confined to white prejudice against Africans. The Bantus in central Africa dislike the Pygmies, calling them "monkeys." The Ethiopians consider themselves to be of a better racial stock than the Bantus. In Rwanda the seven-foot-tall Watutsi oppressed the shorter

Bantus for centuries because the Watutsi considered themselves a master race. A few years ago the Bantus rose up and massacred great numbers of the Watutsi. In East Africa, Africans are prejudiced against Asians because of their business success.

Apartheid is the most brutal form of racism, and it involves the greatest number of people. Officially the goal of apartheid (apartness) is a complete separation of the races. White leaders of South Africa have claimed that eventually each race will have its own homeland. Each group would then be able to develop its culture as it wished without outside interference. The white minority government has plans to set up ten tribal homelands. By 1983 four of these homelands – Transkei, Ciskei, Venda, and Bophuthatswana – had opened.

Few persons who are knowledgeable about South Africa believe that these goals are realistic. The nation's economy is too vast for a white population of less than 5 million to maintain without help. The labor of nonwhites is indispensable. Furthermore, the land allowed for black settlement is only 15 percent of the territory, although blacks make up about 70 percent of the population. Much of this small area is arid and nonproductive. It would be impossible for 19 million people to take their livings from it. By contrast, 85 percent of the land would go to the whites, who make up only 17 percent of the population. How the 9 percent who are racially mixed "Coloureds" and the 3 percent who are Asian would fare is not entirely clear.

Here is how an opponent of apartheid described it in 1961:

> The apartheid laws . . . mean no vote for the African, no political standing of any kind, no right to work, to travel, to change his address, no recognized right to protest against anything. They mean . . . preventing Africans being trained as artisans, . . . defining where the African may live . . . exclusion of Africans from citizens' buses, hotels, restaurants, schools, toilets, booking offices, and even roadside seats.*

The situation remains bleak. This is only a partial listing of what is denied by law to black Africans in the Republic of South Africa. The real damage caused by the system is the fear, humiliation, and lack of hope for the future. The whites are not spared the feelings of fear either. Their nightmare is that someday the blacks will rise up against them.

The apartheid system is not only cruel and unjust but impossible to carry out. Neither whites nor nonwhites could adjust to it. Thus the philosophy of apartheid seems to be an effort to provide some kind of respectability for a system that shamefully exploits the vast majority of the nation's people.

Responses to apartheid. Protests against apartheid grew in the 1980s in the United States. One of the chief forms of protest was the effort to get American firms to stop doing business in South Africa. Some college students, for example, pressured trustees to divest – to sell university-owned stock in companies that did business in South Africa. These protesters said it was immoral to support the government of South Africa by bolstering its economy. Divestiture would have an impact on the economy, they argued, and force white politicians to change their racial policies.

South African Bishop Desmond Tutu won the Nobel Peace Prize in 1984 for his firm public stand against apartheid and violence.

---

*James Cameron, *The African Revolution*. Published by Thames and Hudson Ltd. London. Used by permission of David Higham Associates Limited, London.

Other Americans argued that the United States firms doing business in South Africa were in the vanguard of the movement for social change. Fair treatment of blacks in offices and factories was setting new standards – and even forcing the government to alter apartheid rules in some instances. Many American companies had signed the Sullivan Principles. These were a set of guidelines drawn up by the Rev. Leon Sullivan, a black leader in Philadelphia and a pioneer in job training for young blacks. The Sullivan Principles set forth a number of conditions that employers agreed to follow in hiring, paying, and promoting black workers.

A similar system of white dominance prevailed in Zimbabwe until the late 1970s. In 1980 a black coalition government headed by Robert Mugabe came to power. Like so many new governments, Mugabe's government was troubled by factionalism. The two guerrilla groups that had fought for black majority rule now fought each other. This caused political instability and wasted the nation's valuable human and economic resources.

African Foreign Relations

African countries desire assistance from developed nations. The United States, the Soviet Union, Israel, Cuba, and the People's Republic of China all provided help.

Africans reject both capitalism and communism. They believe that their problems are different from those elsewhere and require African solutions. They talk a great deal about "socialism" but insist that they mean a special African variety, emphasizing freedom from foreign control and plans for economic improvement.

African socialism has been defined in various ways by different leaders. Julius Nyerere of Tanzania sees African socialism as the application of traditional communal cooperation on a large scale. To increase production on the land, all work and share equally. In Tanzania, kibbutz-like communes have been organized where all work for the common good. In a similar collective fashion needed industries will also be developed. Capitalistic enterprises are not rejected if they can be organized, but communal or socialistic methods are emphasized.

CHAPTER REVIEW

Recalling Names and Places

apartheid	Organization of African Unity	racism
Biafra	Pan-Africanism	socialism
Felix Houphouet-Boigny	primitive democracy	
negritude		

Understanding This Chapter

1. Describe African political systems prior to colonial rule.
2. How did colonial rule change African political systems and feelings of loyalty?

3. How was Pan-Africanism a reaction to colonialism? What do present-day believers in Pan-Africanism hope to achieve through the Organization of African Unity?
4. How is tribalism both a liability and an asset to national unity?
5. Compare the philosophies of the different European powers toward their colonies.
6. What factors help contribute to growing African nationalism?
7. Government-supported schools attended by young people from different tribes have been suggested as a way to reduce tribalism. Why might such a plan help? What else could be done?
8. White South Africans say that despite apartheid, black Africans are materially better off in South Africa than elsewhere in Africa. What is wrong with that argument?
9. How does racism, particularly apartheid, affect the lives of millions of Africans.
10. What is African socialism?

Chapter 15

Africa's Rich Cultural Heritage

To understand a people's culture, we study their literature, music, and their other forms of expression. These are the ways a people communicate their feelings and beliefs to other members of their culture as well as to the rest of the world.

Africans developed distinctive forms of expression, especially in music and art. Their styles have influenced artists and composers elsewhere. When Africans became slaves in the Americas, they spread their music, dance, and literature wherever they went.

A Rich Literary Heritage

Thousands of years before Africans had much contact with the outside world, African tribes had developed an extensive oral literature. Poems, folk tales, myths, and dramas were passed on by word of mouth from one generation to the next. Some of them are now in written form. New writing has been influenced by the style and subject matter of oral literature. Many modern African writers draw their subject matter from this ancient African tradition.

Philosophical content in oral tradition. Certain key ideas appear frequently in traditional stories. One is that the universe has a moral order. God expects people to obey certain rules. If they do not, they will suffer misfortune. Africans also believe they are as much a part of nature as the plants and animals. They must show respect for the laws of nature if they hope to be happy.

Moreover, one must be responsible to others. Africans are taught that people must fulfill their moral and legal responsibilities toward others, and the oral literature teaches that they must fulfill them. The oral literature teaches that those who do not will be punished.

African poems and songs often contain a moral or rule for living. A typical example is the following song from Benin that ends with a recommendation for caution and common sense:

> When I am on the river
> I whisper and say,
> 'Flow softly.'
> And for that my two feet
> Know the earth of the farther bank.
> One who is in a boat at sea
> Does not quarrel with the boatman.*

---

*Melville J. and Frances S. Herskovits, *Dahomean Narrative*, 1958, Northwestern University Press, Evanston, IL.

This Ghanaian woman, herself more than 100 years old, recounts tales told by her great-grandparents. A tape recorder preserves this oral history for future generations.

The art of storytelling. In most African societies the ability to tell stories well is much admired. Usually a storyteller has a great fund of tales, jokes, riddles, and tongue-twisters. Storytellers are not merely clever with words. They use their whole bodies as they imitate and act out the characters.

We have noted that the animal story is a favorite form of oral literature. Told to children, it usually ended with a moral. These tales became a part of American culture in the United States. The slave women, who cared for their owners' children, told their charges these ancient tales from faraway Africa. Popular children's animal stories by such American writers as Joel Chandler Harris, the author of the Uncle Remus stories, reflect this influence. Many of the tales are almost exactly like those brought from Africa.

Current literature reflects African problems and concerns. Today, literature by African authors is much concerned with problems arising from prejudice and discrimination. Some have written eloquently about the injustices the black man has had to endure in his struggle for independence.

Autobiographical writers like Albert Luthuli, author of *Let My People Go;* Jomo Kenyatta, author of *Facing Mount Kenya;* and Kenneth Kaunda (kah-*oon'* duh), who wrote *Zambia Shall Be Free,* belong to this group of protest writers.

Much of current African literature concerns problems of adjustment the individual must face in a rapidly changing world. Many authors write sadly of the loss of tribal values and customs. The South African writer Peter Abrahams describes his painful childhood in Johannesburg, South Africa, in his novel *Tell Freedom,* while the writer and critic Ezekiel Mphahlele vividly depicts life in a black ghetto in Pretoria in *Down Second Avenue.* A third South African novelist, Alex La Guma, shows what apartheid in Cape Town is like for blacks in *And A Threefold Cord.*

African Thoughts on Immortality

Most people of the world have thought a lot about life, death, and immortality. The Africans are interested in these topics. For example, they have more than 700 stories describing how messengers went to God, requesting eternal life for man. Because of some mishap, the possibility of immortality was lost. Usually the messengers were animals, as in the examples below:

THE CHAMELION AND THE LIZARD

When Death first entered the world, men sent the chameleon to find out the cause. God told the chameleon to let men know that if they threw baked porridge over a corpse, it would come back to life. But the chameleon was slow in returning and Death was rampant in their midst, and so men sent a second messenger, the lizard.

The lizard reached the abode of God soon after the chameleon. God, angered by the second message, told the lizard that men should dig a hole in the ground and bury their dead in it. On the way back, the lizard overtook the chameleon and delivered his message first, and when the chameleon arrived the dead were already buried.

Thus, owing to the impatience of man, he cannot be born again.

a Margi story (Central African Republic)

C. K. Meek, *Law and Authority in a Nigerian Tribe* (Oxford: Oxford Unitersity Press).

An especially beautiful version of these African immortality stories comes from Nigeria. It expresses the great love that Africans have for their children. Man decided to accept death in order to experience the joy of having children:

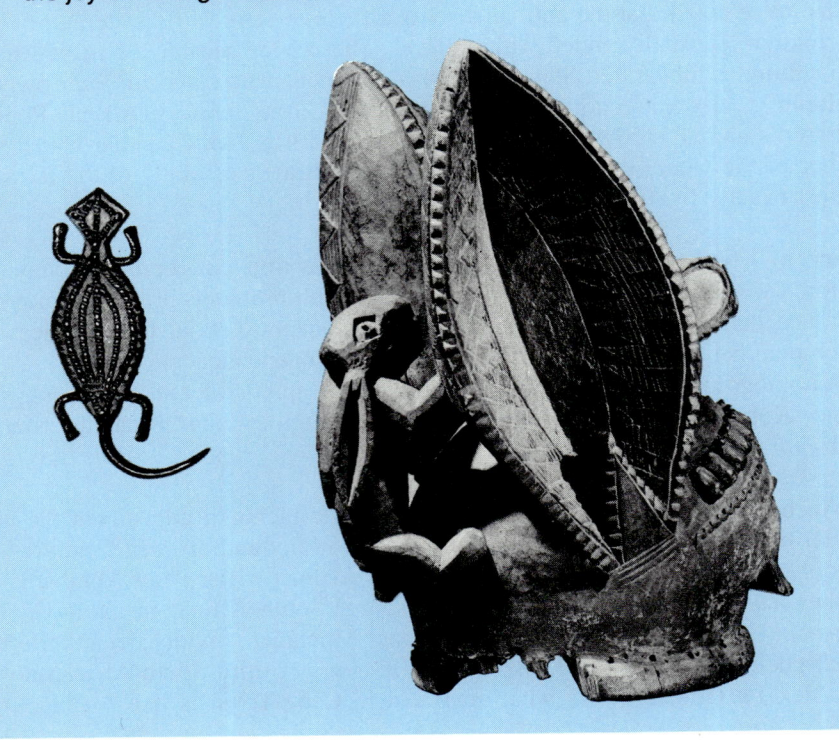

TORTOISES, MEN, AND STONES

God created the tortoise, men, and stones. Of each he created male and female. He gave life to tortoises and men, but not to the stones. None could have children, and when they became old they did not die but became young again.

The tortoise, however, wished to have children, and he went to God. But God said:

"I have given you life, but I have not given you permission to have children."

But the tortoise came to God again to make his request, and finally God said:

"You always come and ask for children. Do you realize that when the living have had several children they must die?"

But the tortoise said:

"Let me see my children and then die." Then God granted his wish.

When man saw that the tortoise had children, he too wanted children. God warned man, as he had the tortoise, that he must die. But man also said:

"Let me see my children and then die."

That is how death and children came into the world. Only the stones did not want to have children, and so they never die.

a Nupe story (Nigeria)

Ulli Beier (ed.), *The Origin of Life and Death: African Creation Myths* (London: Heinemann Educational Books, Ltd., 1966).

The negritude writers, a group of poets most of whom write in French, are represented by Leopold Sedar Senghor, David Diop, and Birago Diop, all of Senegal. A fourth negritude poet, Camara Lye, is also a novelist. His best known novel, *The Dark Child,* describes his childhood in Guinea and his later life in Paris.

The negritude writers are most expressive when writing poetry. The following poem by David Diop suggests the major themes of negritude literature.

Africa*

Africa my Africa
Africa of proud warriors in ancestral savannahs
Africa of whom my grandmother sings
On the banks of the distant river
I have never known you
But your blood flows in my veins
Your beautiful black blood that irrigates the fields
The blood of your sweat
The sweat of your work
The work of your slavery
The slavery of your children
Africa tell me Africa

Is this you this back that is bent
This back that breaks under the weight of humiliation
This back trembling with red scars
And saying yes to the whip under the midday sun
But a grave voice answers me
Impetuous son that tree young and strong
That tree there
In splendid loneliness amidst white and faded flowers
That is Africa your Africa
That grows again patiently obstinately
And its fruit gradually acquire
The bitter taste of liberty.

Nigeria has also produced several outstanding writers. Amos Tutuola's *The Palm-Wine Drinkard* is a highly imaginative tale of ancient Africa which mixes Yoruba folk tales, myth, and the supernatural. Perhaps the best known of Nigerian writers is Chinua Achebe. Both *Things Fall Apart* and *No Longer at Ease,* Achebe's first two novels, describe changing Ibo village life.

African drama. Acting ability is much admired in Africa. for centuries the most popular storytellers of a tribe acted out the characters of their tales, dancing with masks and using puppets. A favorite comedy act included an actor wearing a long-nosed European face mask who imitated European mannerisms.

Contemporary playwrights are building upon this tradition. Among the most widely respected of the African dramatists is the Nigerian Wole Soyinka. He is probably best known in the Western world for his humorous play, *The Lion and the Jewel.*

Leopold Sedar Senghor, one of the leading literary figures of modern Africa, was also the first president of the republic of Senegal. He held that office from 1960 to 1980.

---

*The poem *Afrique* ("Africa") first appeared in David Diop's *Coups de Pilon* published by *Présence Africaine,* Paris (1956). This translation by Gerald Moore and Ulli Beier appears in *Modern Poetry from Africa* published by Penguin Books, Harmondsworth (1963).

African Sculpture

African artists and artisans have been especially fond of carving wood and molding metal to make useful and religious objects. Such artisans are often highly respected members of their communities and may teach apprentices their skills that are centuries old.

Africa's finest art form is carving. The wood carvings of the Congo region are world famous. Being of wood, these carvings do not go back earlier than the nineteenth century, since termites and wood-eating white ants prevent wooden objects from lasting.

These wood carvings take many forms but frequently are of human figures. They are small statues, rarely more than twenty-four inches high. Equally famous are the carved wooden masks of this region. These are made to fit over the face, the entire head like a knight's helmet, or on top of the head. The masks are worn at religious ceremonies, representing a supernatural being or a special person. While a person wears a mask he is believed to assume the powers of the god or person the mask represents.

Carving in ivory is also a highly developed art. The source of ivory is elephant tusks. Small figures, jewelry, charms, and other objects are carved from this material. They are highly developed and sophisticated forms of expression created over many centuries.

Metal carving developed in Nigeria. Like wood carving, metal sculpture is an ancient art form in Nigeria. Ife (*ee'*fay), in southwestern Nigeria, became the center of beautiful metal work, especially in bronze, brass, and gold. The

This loom holds several designs of Kente cloth. The cloth is made of four-inch rectangular strips of woven material sewn together. The cost of the cloth may be as high as one-sixth of an African teacher's annual salary. Thus few people own more than one — if they own one at all. The weaving of Kente cloth originated in Bonwiri, Ghana, and today the industry dominates the town. There is a Kente loom on almost every front porch.

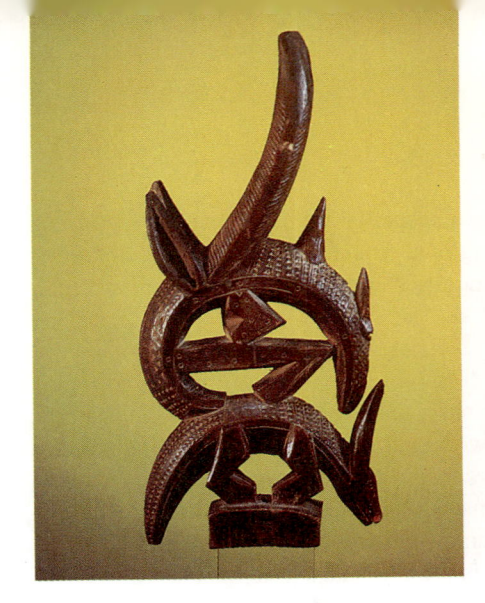

African sculpture takes a variety of strong and exciting forms: a Bambara Tji-wara wooden antelope headdress from Mali (top left); a Nigerian Yoruba "Gelede" mask (top right); a Nigerian Benin bronze head (center left); a Mbala hardwood statue of a drummer, from Congo (center right); and a horseman statuette from the Senufo people of the Ivory Coast (right).

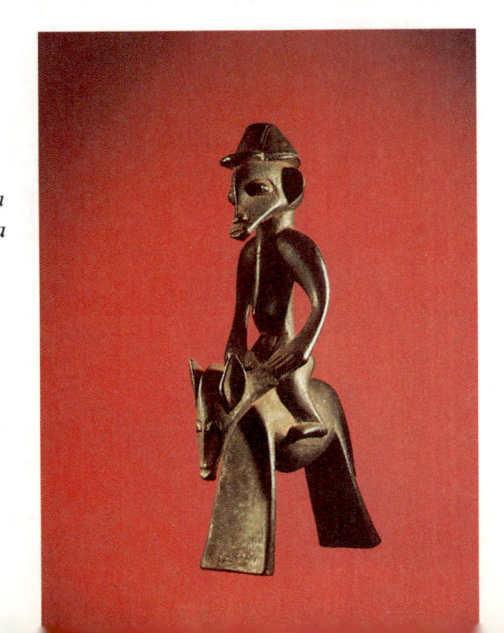

carved heads of ancient Ife kings are considered to be among the world's greatest art. When the Europeans first saw them in the nineteenth century, they refused to believe that the "primitive Africans" could have produced them. When it was learned that some of them were made in the twelfth century, it was realized that only the Africans *could* have produced them.

The art of metal sculpture spread from Ife to Benin around the thirteenth century. Benin was a kingdom in southeastern Nigeria about two or three hundred miles east of Ife. Benin produced detailed bronze carvings of kings and soldiers in very elaborate dress.

Influence of African art. In the arts Africa has had a great influence on other cultures. The great modern painter Pablo Picasso acknowledged that African art made such a deep impression on him that it changed his style. He is only the most famous of many painters and sculptors who have been affected.

African Music Is Distinctive

One of the many stereotypes people hold about Africans is that their only music is the beating of drums. Although African music shows greater diversity, drums are widely used, not only for music but also to send messages. The so-called "talking drums," which imitate human words, can be heard for many miles. However, in addition to different kinds of drums, there are many varieties of horns, flutes, stringed instruments, and xylophones. Some of these instruments look somewhat crudely made, but they usually have good tonal quality.

Different instruments are important in different regions. The xylophone, for example, is used mainly in East Africa around Mozambique. Stringed instruments are also prominent in East Africa and Nigeria. In southern Africa flutes are especially popular.

African musical instruments can highlight the distinctive rhythms of African music. In the Ivory Coast, these young men play a xylophone-like instrument called the balafon.

African rhythms are very complex. African rhythms can be enormously intricate. In Western music there is usually one rhythm at a given time, occasionally there are two, as in counterpoint when a pianist plays a different rhythm with each hand. In African music as many as five rhythms may be played at the same time. An African dancer may dance to these five rhythms simultaneously. His head may move to one rhythm, shoulders to another, hands to a third, body to a fourth, and feet to a fifth. Different instruments in the orchestra supply the different rhythms.

African music is characterized by much improvisation. The player of an instrument, the singer, or the dancer can create freely as the mood strikes him. There is, of course, an overall traditional framework within which the improvising takes place.

Music is a part of African life. Music in its various forms plays an important part in African life. When a team of men have to labor long and hard, they often sing to the rhythm of their work. It helps keep them going, lightens the burdens, and lifts their spirits. When an African woman works through the long day, she sings too. Music plays an important part in observances of births, deaths, marriages, religious ceremonies, holidays, and other special days. It contributes to the personal, individual meaning of an event.

Looking ahead. As contacts with the rest of the world increase, Africa is changing. What will the new Africa be like? A new African culture is emerging. African leaders are leading their countries towards modernization while preserving the best of the old culture. Benin bronzes and beautiful carvings are no longer produced in West Africa, except as cheap imitations for tourists. The new Africa is creating new art forms. As literacy spreads, African scholars attract the interests of the world. These men and women will be expressing the genius of a new Africa, which will have its own unique character.

CHAPTER REVIEW

Recalling Names and Places

Chinua Achebe Ife oral literature
Benin Ezekiel Mphahlele

Understanding This Chapter

1. How does the literature and the art of a people reveal their culture? Give some examples.
2. Define oral literature. Name some themes that frequently occur in it.
3. Do we have any oral traditions in America? List examples.
4. Describe the major themes in modern African literature.
5. Much modern African writing is classified as protest literature. What is the purpose of such writings?
6. Describe the types of carving African artists and woodcarvers do. How is their artwork used?
7. How is African music distinctive?

UNIT 4
Exploring
India

| 3000 | 2500 | 2000 | 1500 | 1000 | 500 B.C. | 1 A.D. | 500 | 1000 | 1500 |

- HINDUISM 1500–
- BUDDHISM 250–
- ISLAM 700–
- MUGHAL EMPIRE 1526–1857
- HARRAPAN CIVILIZATION 3000–1500
- GUPTA EMPIRE 320–535
- BRITAIN RULES 1858–1947
- ARYAN INVASIONS 1500–1200
- MAURYA EMPIRE 321–185
- EUROPEAN COLONIALISM 1498–1961
- BRITISH EAST INDIA COMPANY 1619–1858
- INDEPENDENCE 1947–

A TRAVELER TO INDIA IS BOTH SURprised and delighted by the vastness and variety of its land and people. Tropical rain forests contrast sharply with the dry plains of the northwest, the treeless mountain ranges, and the palm trees of the lowlands. The style of life ranges from that of the nomadic shepherds of Rajasthan to the wheat growers of the Punjab, wet rice farmers of Tamil Nadu, assembly line workers of Bombay, and airplane pilots of New Delhi. India's cultural variety is exemplified by its religious buildings. Hindu temples surge with life, bearing dense decorations of gods, people, plant and animal life. Unadorned Muslim mosques are still in their symmetrical balance.

For all of India's cultural differences, Hinduism provides an underlying unity. It is the religion of most of the subcontinent's inhabitants. Hinduism not only provides its followers with an answer to their quest for peace and meaning in life; it is also central to India's social structure. Yet, Hinduism is not the sole religion in India. Islam has many followers in India, while in Pakistan and Bangladesh it is the major religion.

As with many other countries of the world, India has a very marked range of wealth and poverty among its people. Because of the country's generally low level of economic development, poverty is widespread in India. Its elimination presents an awesome undertaking. India's leaders are meeting this challenge in a variety of ways.

Modern science, technology, and medicine can provide the means to improve the quality of life for the Indian people. The application of scientific farming methods to agriculture has provided a means of dramatically increasing food production. Likewise, modern industrial methods can increase factory production. However, there are many economic, social, educational, and political barriers to be overcome in India before science, technology, and medicine can fulfill their potential. In this unit we will see both tradition and change in an India that clings to its past while struggling toward a better future.

| 1500 | 1600 | 1700 | 1800 | 1900 |

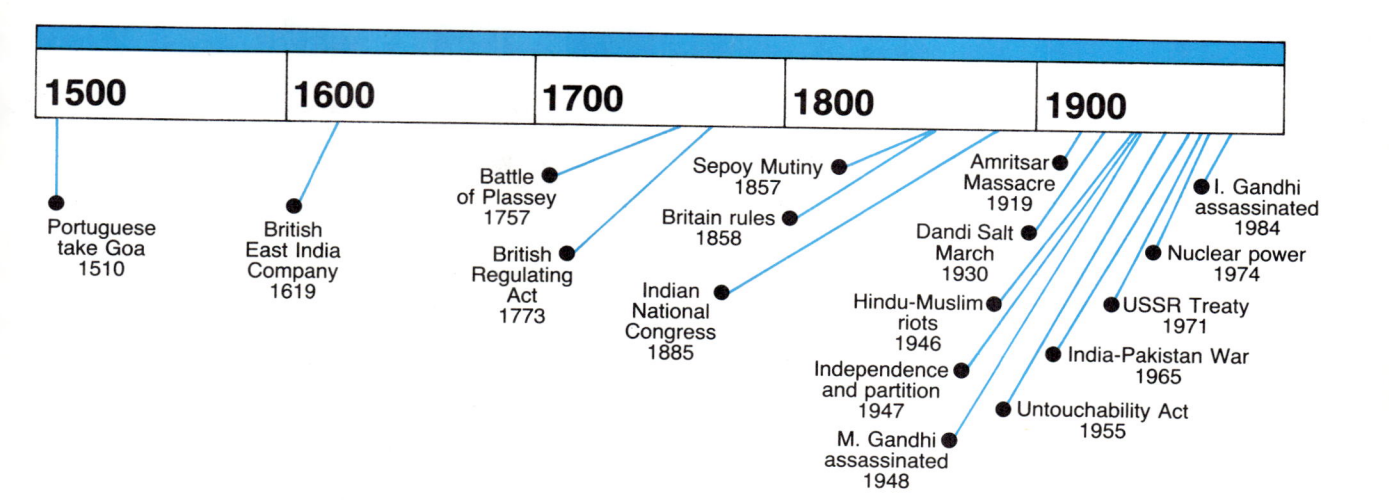

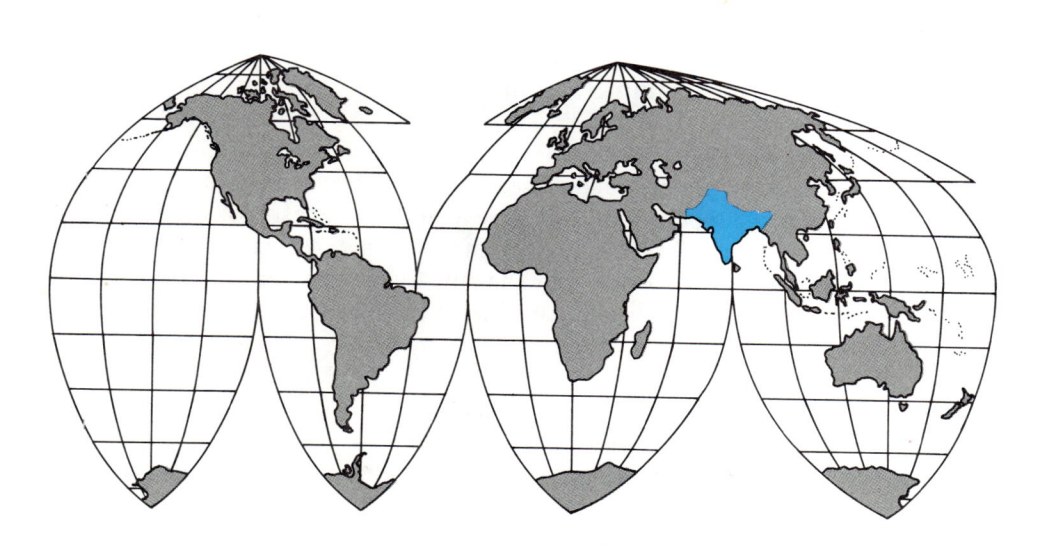

- Portuguese take Goa 1510
- British East India Company 1619
- Battle of Plassey 1757
- British Regulating Act 1773
- Sepoy Mutiny 1857
- Britain rules 1858
- Indian National Congress 1885
- Amritsar Massacre 1919
- Dandi Salt March 1930
- Hindu-Muslim riots 1946
- Independence and partition 1947
- M. Gandhi assassinated 1948
- Untouchability Act 1955
- India-Pakistan War 1965
- USSR Treaty 1971
- Nuclear power 1974
- I. Gandhi assassinated 1984

Chapter 16

India: Land and People

India, with 1,261,211 square miles, is the seventh largest nation in territory. It is second only to China in population. India belongs to a region of Asia called a subcontinent, which also includes Pakistan, Bangladesh, and several smaller nations. Geographers define a subcontinent as a large landmass, usually smaller than any of the continents but with some similarities in languages, customs, religions, and occupations of its people.

Landforms of the Indian Subcontinent

The Himalayas. The 1500 miles of the Himalayan (him-uh *lay'*-an) mountain system of northern India separates the subcontinent from the rest of Asia. This towering mountain range has several of the tallest peaks in the world. Mount Everest, rising 29,028 feet, is the most famous. As you can see from the maps on pages 189 and 241, this mountain frontier borders the countries of India, Pakistan, China, Nepal, Sikkim (*sick'*kim), and Bhutan (buh-*tahn'*).

The Himalayas have been important for many reasons. While they gave India some protection from its enemies, mountain passes in the northwest, such as the famous Khyber (*kuy'*bur) Pass, served as invasion routes throughout history. The three great northern rivers of the subcontinent have their sources in the Himalayas. This high mountain range also has religious significance for many Indians for it contains several sacred Hindu shrines.

The Indo-Gangetic Plain contains India's most fertile land. Around 40 percent of India's people live on the Indo-Gangetic Plain. Located at the foot of the Himalayas, it extends from the Indian state of Assam and the Bay of Bengal in the east to the Arabian Sea in the west. The Indus, Ganges (*gan'*jeez), and Brahmaputra (*brah'*muh-*poo'*truh) rivers flow through the plain and supply water for irrigation. In the dry northwest, farmers grow wheat. On the eastern part of the plain, rice and jute are the main crops because this region gets more rain. In the Thar Desert, along the Pakistan border, little farming is done.

The Deccan Plateau covers much of the peninsula. The southern edge of the Indo-Gangetic Plain is bordered by rugged hills which stretch east-west across the peninsula. South of these hills lies a huge plateau called the Deccan. The hills hindered but did not totally stop invasions of South India from the north. Yet they are the dividing line between North and South India and are partly responsible for the regional differences between the two areas.

Along the western edge of the Deccan, the highland wall of the Western Ghats (*gotz*) faces the Arabian Sea and helped to prevent European conquest of

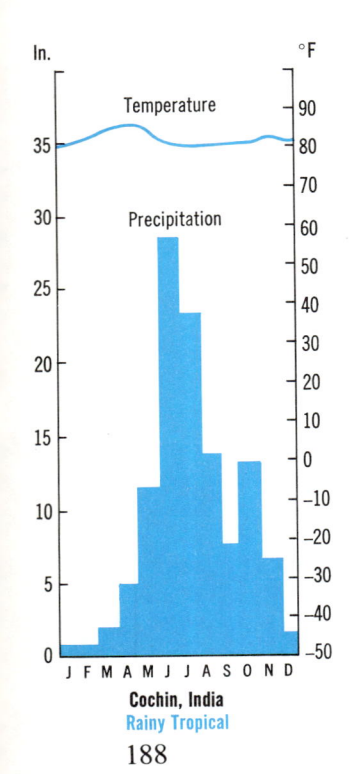

Cochin, India
Rainy Tropical

THE INDIAN SUBCONTINENT: PHYSICAL

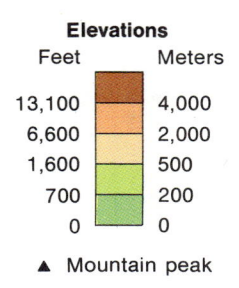

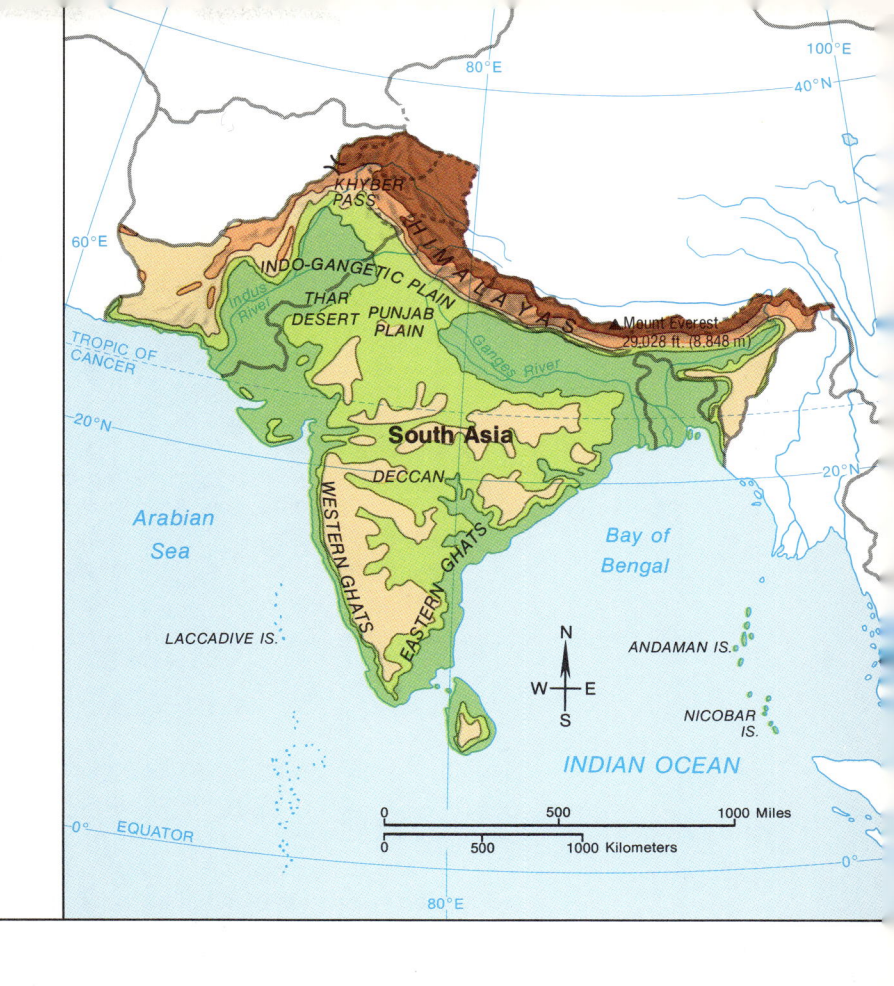

the interior. The Eastern Ghats, on the east coast, is a disconnected range of hills. Near the city of Madras, broad valleys helped to pave the way for Europeans to enter South India.

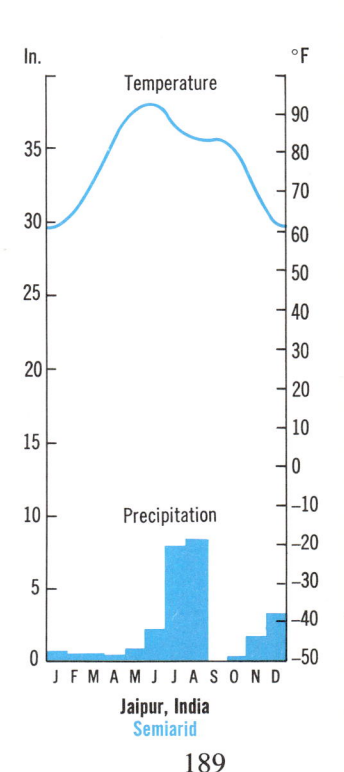

India's Climate Controlled by the Monsoons

The people of India depend heavily on the monsoons: the seasonal winds that usher in the heavy rains from June to late October and the dry season from December to March. Overnight the rains of the wet season turn dry, brown fields green with crops. An insufficient rainfall spells disaster for farmers and their families. Two seasons of drought mean severe crop failures and widespread famine.

The path of the monsoon. Eighty percent of India's rainfall comes during the five-month summer monsoon. In this season, winds flow into the subcontinent, sweeping across the Arabian Sea picking up moisture from the water below. When they hit the Western Ghats, rain is released. Winds in the east cross the Bay of Bengal and move toward the Ganges Delta and Brahmaputra Valley in northeast India. Heavy rains fall on the area before the humid air moves westward across the Ganges Valley.

The monsoon arrives in southwest India early in June and reaches Bombay a few days later. Calcutta in the east receives it in mid-June, and the monsoon moves up the Ganges Valley to the area called the Punjab by the end of the

> **The Coming of the Monsoon**
>
> *The importance of the monsoon to India can be understood by the following extract from an Indian novel:*
>
> To know India and her people, one has to know the monsoon. . . . it is not only the source of life, but also their most exciting impact with nature. . . . it is preceded by desolation . . . [for ninety days] the sky becomes flat and colorless gray without . . . a cloud. People suffer great agony . . . the thirst is unquenchable . . . then the monsoon makes its spectacular entry. Dense masses of dark clouds sweep across the heavens. . . . the deep roll of thunder . . . lightning flashes against the black sky. Then comes the rain itself . . . in fat drops; the earth rises to meet it. Then . . . in torrents . . . where there was nothing, there is everything: green grass, snakes, centipedes, worms, millions of insects. . . .
>
> Khushwant Singh, *I Shall Not Hear the Nightingale*, pp. 101–102. Copyright © 1959 by Khushwant Singh. Reprinted by permission of Grove Press, Inc.

month. It begins to retreat in mid-September and ends in Bombay by mid-October and by the end of the month in Calcutta. By early November the monsoon ends in South India.

The change between the winter and summer seasons is very abrupt. In the winter the monsoon wind directions are reversed. Rainless northwest winds travel down the Ganges Valley, turning south and southwest over the subcontinent. Lasting from October to the end of February, it produces India's dry season. Only a few inches of rain fall in northern India and the southeast near Madras.

India's searing summer winds, the loo, make water a precious commodity. Here a glass sells for about one cent.

MONSOONS OF SOUTHERN ASIA
→ Wind direction

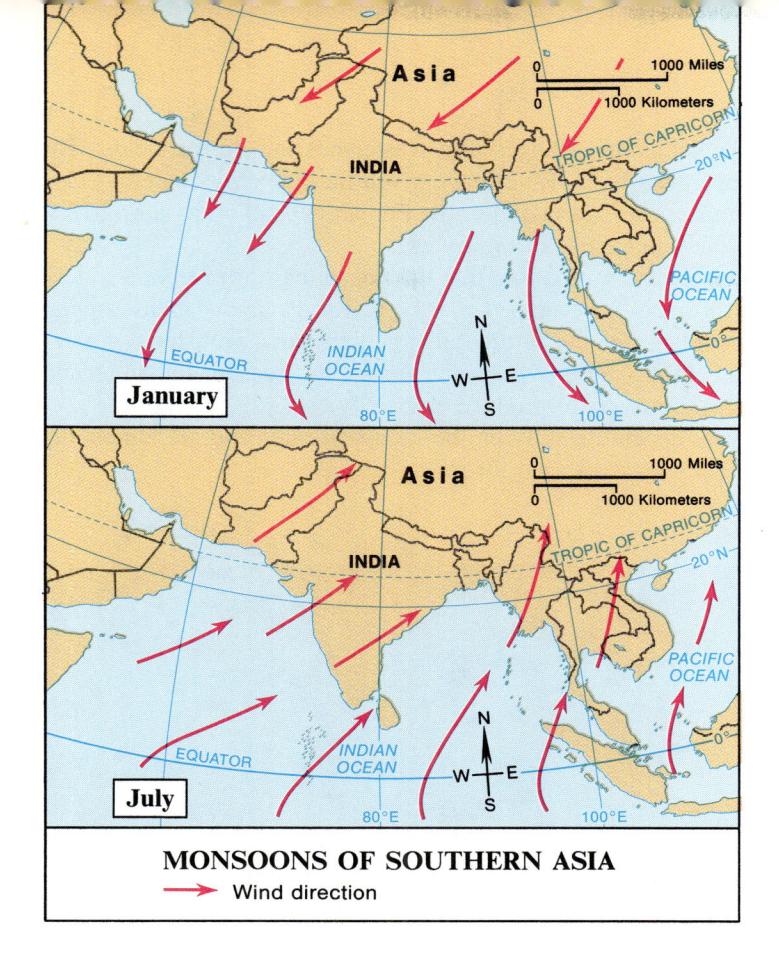

Annual rainfall varies from region to region. The slopes of the Western Ghats average 100 inches per year, while the Assam hills in the northeast have one of the world's highest annual averages, at 425 inches. The Thar Desert receives less than five inches. In the Ganges Valley, 66 inches fall on Calcutta, while New Delhi receives 28 inches annually.

Few regions of India receive a dependable quantity of rain at the right time. Forty inches is adequate for farming; with less rainfall, irrigation is required. One-quarter of the farmland is irrigated, and Indian farmers historically have depended on rivers and wells for irrigation water.

All of India does not have the four alternating seasons to which people of the United States are accustomed. From June to September the monsoon makes it hot and humid. A cool, dry season follows the end of the monsoon and extends from late November to February. The hot season begins in March and lasts into July. Under a glaring sun and in still air, a blistering heat makes activity almost impossible. Those who can, go to the hills.

Indian Rivers

The three great rivers of North India – the Indus, Ganges, and Brahmaputra – originate in the snow-covered Himalayas. Though the amount of water coming from these rivers varies through the year, they have a dependable flow.

One of the older forms of irrigation, the Persian water wheel, has earthen jugs attached to a circular belt. Camels or oxen pull the wheel, which dips into a well and then empties its water into a trough. From there it flows through shallow dikes to the fields.

The waters of the Indus and Ganges turn wastelands into fertile fields. The five large tributaries of the Indus River have given the Punjab its name – "Five Rivers." Fifty million acres of farmland in the Punjab depend on modern irrigation canals to help them make use of the rivers.

Dams raise the level of the rivers so that the canals can receive water at all seasons. Irrigation projects have helped many previously empty areas support millions of peoples. Plans for the future call for high dams with large storage reservoirs to prevent floods and provide water for the dry season. Indian technicians hope to harness the rivers to produce electricity.

South India's rivers depend heavily on the monsoon rains and are almost dry during the winter. They are also used for irrigation.

> **Along the Holy Ganges**
>
> In addition to its importance as a source of irrigation water, the Ganges is also considered a sacred river. Many holy cities that Hindu pilgrims visit are found along its banks. The city of Benares is regarded as the holiest city in India. A maze of narrow lanes, it hugs the Ganges River and contains thousands of shrines. As a part of worship a pilgrim visits the shrines and walks along a particular road outside of the city. Anyone dying in the area of Benares enclosed by this road is believed to be released from the continual cycle of rebirth and death in which Hindus believe. For this reason many old people come to pass their last days in Benares. A dead person wrapped in white cloth on a wooden litter is carried to a funeral pyre along the river. After the body is consumed by flames, the ashes and the unburned portions are cast into the river.
>
> More important than visits to the shrines of Benares are immersions in the holy Ganges River. Several dozen stone stairs are built into the river. From early morning, pilgrims descend the stairs into the muddy river, bathe, pray, and make their offerings to the Hindu gods.

Natural Resources

India has some of the important mineral deposits needed for a modern industrial economy. One-fourth of the world's total iron ore reserves are found in India. India has large deposits of manganese, which can be used to remove impurities from steel and to strengthen it. These deposits are second in size only to those of the Soviet Union. However, only limited supplies of coal needed for steel production have been found in India.

Bauxite for aluminum is mined in India, as are copper, lead, zinc, and mica. The known petroleum and gas deposits do not meet India's domestic needs. In addition, these minerals are in scattered localities, very often away from power sources and markets. Before India can develop its industries, new methods of mining and transporting its mineral resources must be found.

Transportation has always been a problem in India. The lack of good roads historically has hampered internal trade and made political unity difficult to achieve.

India's 5000 miles of coastline has few natural harbors. Until the British came, there was only limited trade across the Arabian Sea and to Southeast Asia. Even coastal shipping was little developed. Now, the cities of Cochin and Bombay are important ports on the west coast, and Madras on the east coast has a harbor that has been enlarged to aid shipping. Visakhapatnam has been dredged for a deep-water port and is to be the site of India's shipbuilding industry. Calcutta is India's busiest port.

Because river water levels vary greatly, few rivers are navigable for great lengths by motor-powered vessels. Sometimes the rivers flood, while at other times they dry up and are reduced to a trickle.

While the present rail coverage is over 38,000 miles, it is based on at least two different track systems, and connections between them are difficult to accomplish.

CHAPTER REVIEW

Recalling Names and Places

Benares	Deccan Plateau	Indus River
Bombay	Ganges River	monsoons
Brahmaputra River	Ghats	New Delhi
Calcutta	Himalayas	Punjab

Understanding This Chapter

1. What is the geographic importance of the Himalayas?
2. Why are the monsoons important to India?
3. What are the chief rivers of India? Where are they found? How are they used by Indians?
4. What natural resources are found in India?
5. Describe India's transportation network.

Chapter 17

Exploring India's Past

India's long history is filled with great human achievements and adventures. Its civilization was created by the original inhabitants of the subcontinent. Various elements of Indian culture were carried beyond its borders and had a profound influence in China, Japan, and Southeast Asia. As we shall see, India was also influenced by its foreign conquerors and rulers. The Aryan, Muslim, and Western peoples who came to India touched many aspects of Indian life and left permanent marks on its culture.

Ancient Indian Civilization

Early settlements of Indian people appeared thousands of years ago in the area which is today northwestern India and Pakistan. In time, permanent communities formed the Harappan (huh-*rahp'* un) civilization.

Harappan civilization (3000 B.C.-1500 B.C.). Along the Indus River Valley in Pakistan are ruins of an ancient civilization known as the Harappan culture. Its two chief cities were Mohenjo Daro (ma-*hen'*joe *dah'*row) and Harappa. Although 400 miles apart, these two cities were connected by a navigable river. From the discoveries of archaeologists, we know that the Harappan civilization spread over 1000 miles. Little is known about this civilization because no written records were preserved, although clay seals with undeciphered pictorial writing have been found.

In each city a fort dominated the town of brick houses. Wells, baths, and an excellent drainage system were used by inhabitants. The city streets, wide and straight, intersected at right angles. The city plan and an efficient irrigation system for farming suggest that the Harappan peoples had a strong and well-organized central government. Farming yielded wheat, barley, and cotton. Excavated bones show that farmers domesticated cattle, elephants, camels, sheep, and pigs.

The Harappans were also skilled at crafts. Earthenware pottery was made with the potter's wheel. Copper and bronze vessels, tools, and weapons were common, but no iron utensils have been found. Archaeologists have found jewelry of gold, silver, and semi-precious stones. Clay seals depicting the bull and elephant may have been used in commerce. While no temples have been found, the Harappan people appear to have worshiped a mother-goddess and a bull.

Aryan invasions destroyed the Harappan culture. The Aryans were fair-skinned nomads who lived in the steppes that stretched from Poland to Central Asia. They herded animals and also farmed. Between 1500 and 1200

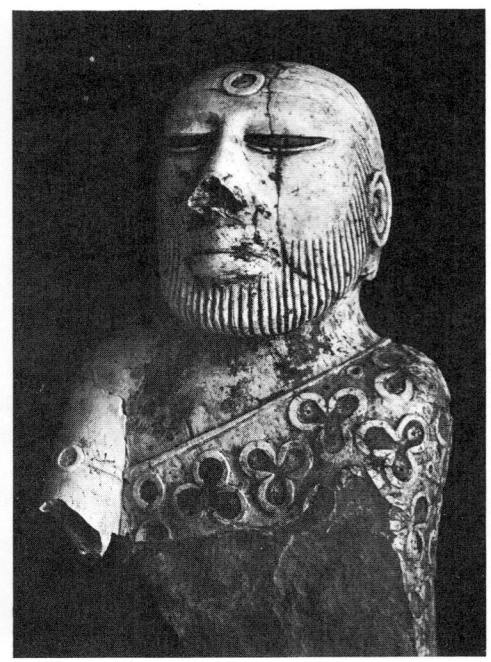

Excavations of the site of Mohenjo Daro (above) have uncovered an ancient well. In the background, a Buddhist stupa sits atop unexcavated ruins. Archaeologists think the stern looking figure (top right) may represent a priest-king. The clay ox-cart and dog (right) were probably toys for the children of the Harappan culture.

B.C., Aryan nomads made a series of invasions into India. Led by warriors fighting from horse-drawn chariots, they occupied the Indus River Valley. Next they conquered the land to the east and established themselves in the area of the Ganges River. While they destroyed the Harappan civilization, they were also influenced by it. This blending of two cultures provided the foundation for the subsequent development of Indian civilization.

Alexander the Great in India (327–325 B.C.). After the Greek ruler Alexander the Great defeated the Persian empire, he set out to conquer the rest of the world. Crossing the Indus River, his armies marched into northwestern

196

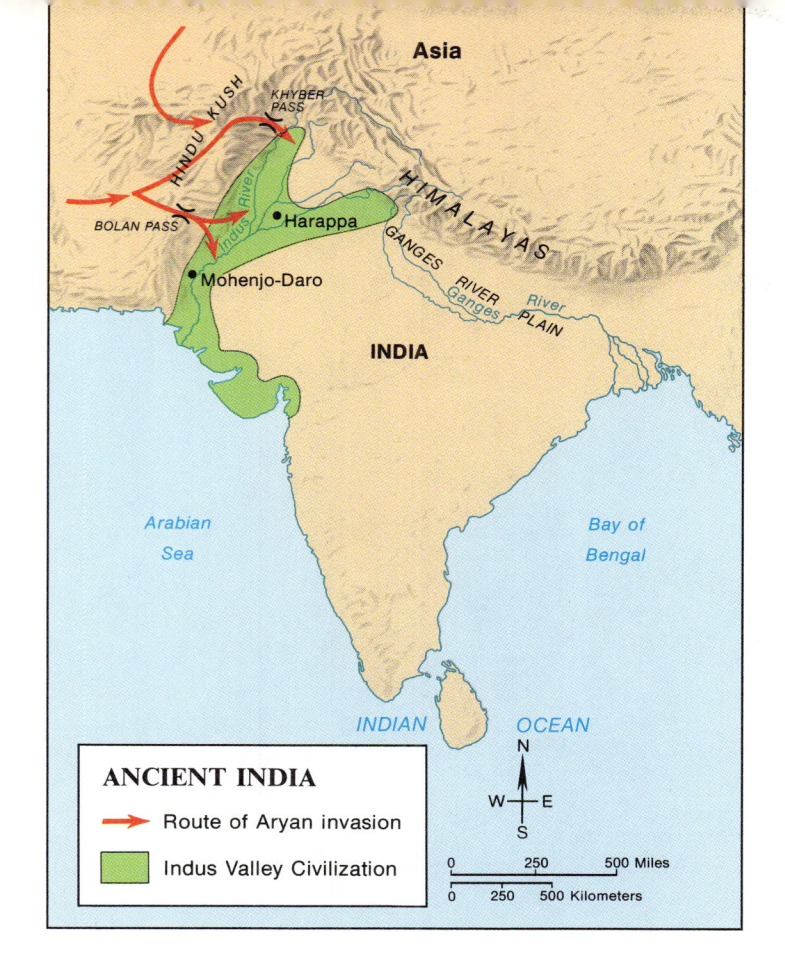

ANCIENT INDIA
- Route of Aryan invasion
- Indus Valley Civilization

India. When the Greek soldiers grew tired of fighting and refused to go deeper into India, Alexander and his army sailed down the Indus River to the Arabian Sea. Walled cities were built for Greek settlers, to be permanent colonies for Alexander's empire. However, Greek authority collapsed in India when Alexander died in 323 B.C.

The Greek conquest of India was a brief episode in Indian history. Although Greek culture had a limited effect on the subcontinent, it had a great influence on Indian art, as we shall see later.

Maurya empire (321–185 B.C.). Chandragupta Maurya (*chun'*druh *goop'*-tuh *mow'*rhea) established the first Mauryan empire, and it grew under his grandson Ashoka (uh-*show'*kuh). At its peak the Mauryan empire extended from the Bay of Bengal in the east to the Hindu Kush mountains in the west, and from the Himalayas in the north to the Deccan in the south.

From the accounts of visitors to the court of the Mauryan emperor, we know that the empire had a vast army and a centralized government under an autocratic king. Viceroys, officials of the emperor, administered the provinces for the ruler. Every person had to register and carry identification papers. Foreigners were closely watched and were required to have passports. Justice was swift and harsh, although graded according to the offender's position in society.

THE MAURYA EMPIRE

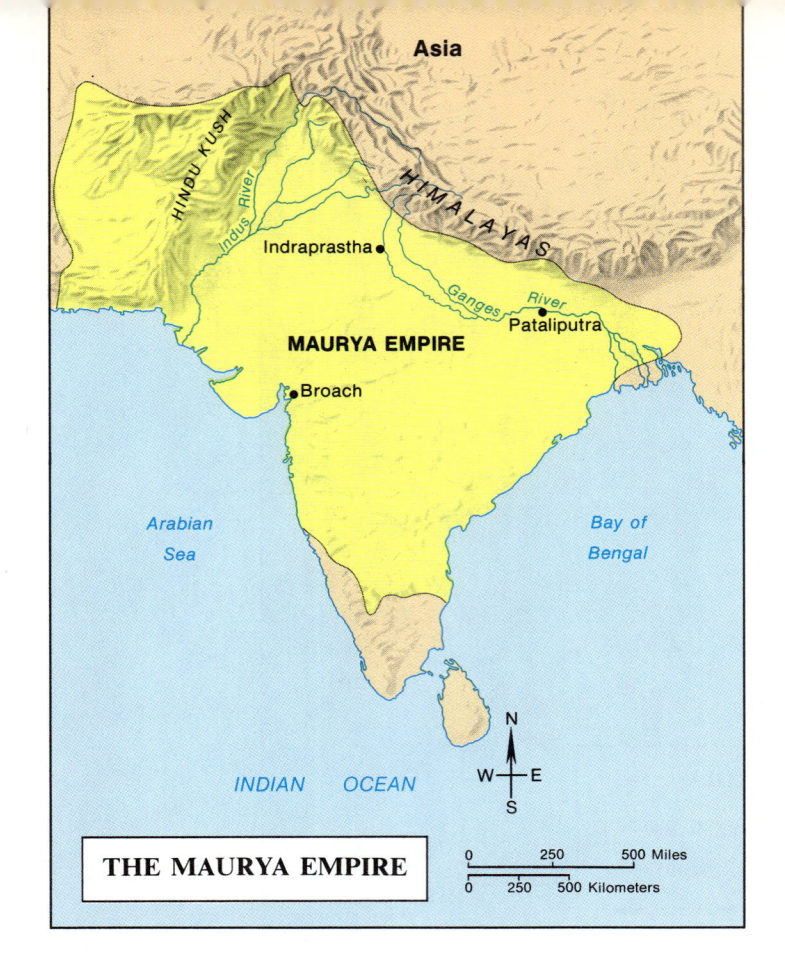

Emperor Ashoka established Buddhism in India. Chandragupta's grandson, the great Mauryan emperor Ashoka, remorseful after a savage war, resolved to lead a righteous life. He became a Buddhist and governed by Buddhist ethics. Ashoka was a great moral reformer. Opposed to injuring person or animal, he banned animal sacrifices and put regulations on the use of animals for food. He forbade the eating of meat in his palace. Pilgrimages to holy places replaced hunting, the traditional sport of kings. Although capital punishment was not abolished, a condemned prisoner had several days to prepare an appeal or to prepare for death.

Although Ashoka abandoned war-making, he continued to add land to his empire. He replaced conquest by arms with conquest by righteousness. He sought to influence neighboring countries by his example of enlightened government. Ashoka was not a complete pacifist, however, for he did not reduce his army. Today, Ashoka's "Wheel of the Law" is part of the Indian flag.

Gupta Empire (320–535 A.D.). For several centuries after the decline of the Mauryan empire, various warring rulers sought control of India. None of them, however, was ever able to unify the kingdoms of the subcontinent. In the fourth century Chandragupta I, a strong ruler, founded the Gupta empire. It stretched across northern India, but did not extend all the way into the south. Its rulers had absolute power and governed with the aid of a council. An orderly

One of the wall frescoes of the Gupta period, 100–700 A.D. These paintings on Buddhist themes decorate the walls of the Ajanta caves near Aurangabad, India.

bureaucracy administered the empire. All the Gupta emperors were Hindu rulers, and religious tolerance prevailed.

The Gupta era was the Golden Age of Hindu culture. The customs, practices, and arts firmly established during this empire became the standard for later times. Succeeding waves of Huns from Central Asia weakened the Gupta empire around the middle of the fifth century, and India was once again broken up into smaller kingdoms.

South India resists conquest. The last region of India invaded by the Aryans was the south. The region long preserved its independence from the later North Indian empires. The Pallava kingdom was the dominant power in the south from 300 to 888 A.D.

On the main sea route between Persia in the west and China in the east, the Pallava merchants engaged in the profitable commerce of the Indian Ocean. Large vessels carried hundreds of passengers and Indian goods. Hindu merchant colonies were established in Burma and along the east coast of Indochina. Hindu priests and Buddhist monks followed the merchants. In turn, pilgrims from these areas visited the holy places of India. These settlers and travelers carried Buddhism and Hindu civilization into Southeast Asia, and their influence can be seen in the religions, architecture, and script of the languages of the area to this day.

Reviewing Your Reading

1. Describe the chief creations of the Harappan civilization.
2. What effect did the Aryans have on the Harappan civilization?
3. What effect did the Greeks have on ancient India?
4. Describe the political and economic achievements of the Mauryan empire.
5. How did Ashoka promote Buddhism in India?
6. Describe the spread of Indian civilization throughout Southeast Asia.

The Muslims Come to India

Although Islam first touched India in the seventh century, not until the thirteenth century did the Muslims establish a permanent capital in Delhi. They dominated the subcontinent until the eighteenth century, when the French and British traders began to influence Indian life.

A legacy of bitterness. By 712, Muslims had laid claim to the Indian state of Sind. Like the Turkish and Afghan Muslims who followed the first Arabian raiders, these warriors saw India not only as a source of plunder, but also as a people to be converted to Islam.

In the clash between the Turkish Muslims and the Indians, religious and social differences loomed large. The Turks believed in the equality of all people before Allah, while most Indians supported the Hindu caste system, which was based on human inequality. The slaughter of Hindu priests, the killing of their sacred cattle for food, and the desecration of Hindu temples left a permanent legacy of bitterness between Muslims and Hindus. Muslim rulers further angered their Hindu subjects by levying a special poll tax on all Hindus. If they paid the tax, they were left alone. In time, an uneasy peace developed between Hindus and their Muslim conquerors. To escape the caste system, some lower-caste Indians converted to Islam.

Mughal Empire (1526–1857). The rule of the Mughals (a corruption of the word Mongol) began with the Turkish-Mongol prince Babur, who defeated the Muslim ruler of Delhi in 1526 at the Battle of Panipat. In the following year North Indian Hindu forces were defeated at the battle of Kanua. Babur died only a few years after his victories. It was left to Babur's grandson Akbar to complete the conquest of the Indian kingdoms.

Emperor Akbar enlarges the Mughal empire. Akbar (1542–1605) ascended the throne in 1556. He expanded the Mughal domain and made it larger than any previous empire.

Akbar set out to unite all his subjects into one great Indian empire. By a policy of tolerance and compromise he won the support of many Hindus. Akbar married a Hindu princess. He allowed conquered Hindu rulers to remain in authority if they submitted to him. He did not interfere in their kingdoms. Akbar abolished unfair practices against Hindus, including the poll tax and the tax on Hindu pilgrims. Hindu customs were carefully observed, and the slaughter of cattle was made a capital crime. Hindus were welcomed in his court and served in the government. Consequently, some of Akbar's strongest defenders were Hindu rulers and officials.

Persian was the language of the Mughal court. Though illiterate, Akbar had many intellectual interests and enjoyed the company of scholars and poets. His marvelous memory enabled him to remember much of what was read to him from his large library.

Downfall of the Mughal empire. None of Akbar's successors managed the government as smoothly as he did. Orthodox and intolerant Muslim rulers rein-

Emperor Aurangzeb with his third son, in a Mughal miniature painting from around the year 1658.

stated the unfair taxes and removed Hindus from all high government positions. Fights among Mughal rulers over succession to the throne sapped their resources. Officials became more cruel and oppressive.

While the Mughal rulers built many beautiful buildings, this construction was a heavy tax burden which contributed to the economic decline of the empire. Frequent famines added to the misery of the Indian peasant and worsened the economy. Hindu uprisings were not easily suppressed by the slow-moving Mughal armies. Nor were they able to prevent foreign invasions. The once great Mughal empire had fallen into political decay before the British appeared in India.

Reviewing Your Reading

1. What led to the tensions between Muslims and Hindus?
2. How did Akbar seek to promote harmony between Muslims and Hindus? Why did it not last beyond his reign?
3. Describe the decline of the Mughal empire by the eighteenth century.

European Expansion into India

In the fifteenth century, Portugal led Europe in the exploration of Asia and Africa. Sailing southward along the west African coast, Bartholomeu Dias reached the tip of South Africa in 1488. Seeking legendary Christian kingdoms and the fabled spices of the Orient, Vasco da Gama reached the spice port of Calicut on the west coast of India in 1498. The Portuguese established a series of bases in the Persian Gulf, at the port of Goa (*go'*uh) in India, the port of Malacca, and in China and Japan. They soon monopolized the very profitable spice trade between Europe and Asia. Pepper, cloves, nutmeg, and mace were not solely a luxury. Lacking refrigeration, Europeans needed spices to preserve meat through the winter and to disguise the taste of decay.

Goa was the capital of Portugal's eastern empire. While Portuguese traders did not seek to conquer India, they became involved in Indian affairs and brought Western civilization with them. Portuguese men married Indian women and settled in Goa.

Tiny Goa remained Portuguese until India annexed it in 1961. This was the first Western intrusion of India, the forerunner of further European expansion that would have far-reaching consequences in the future. Yet it was barely noticed in India.

Britain and France vie for profitable Indian trade. The British East India Company, a great commercial and empire-building corporation, was established in 1600 by a charter from Queen Elizabeth I of England. The charter gave the company a monopoly "of commerce in eastern waters," and it traded in western India in 1619. Trading centers were set up at Madras in 1640, Bombay in 1669, and Calcutta in 1690. These small villages grew as the British built forts, warehouses, residences, and offices. People from the surrounding countryside settled in them for protection and economic opportunity. In time they became the great cities of modern-day India.

The French East India Company was organized in 1664 with a monopoly to trade with Asia. French settlements were established near many of the British towns.

Both the British and French companies sought spices, cotton and silk textiles, indigo, and sugar, for which they exchanged silver, copper, zinc, and various fabrics. The British acquired opium, which they traded in China for tea. The opium trade made the British company more profitable.

Commercial rivalry leads to armed conflict. Both companies sought peaceful trade, but they became involved in the political chaos and turmoil of

India and the worldwide rivalry between Britain and France. Two men, the Frenchman Joseph Dupleix (doo-*playks*) and the Englishman Robert Clive, dominated their respective companies. Their policies led to the eventual British dominance in India.

To gain a foothold in India, Dupleix became involved in the power struggles among the Indian princes, supporting one who was friendly to the French. With Indian allies, he eliminated his European trading rivals. Dupleix organized Indian soldiers, known as *sepoys* (*sea*'poise), into a well-trained, regularly paid fighting force. The British imitated the French practice and hired sepoys to fight in their behalf.

Under Dupleix, the French were initially successful against the British; but under the direction of Robert Clive, British forces defeated the French in South India. The British triumphed because they had better leaders and greater resources, and because their control of the seas kept French reinforcements and supplies from reaching India.

Clive in Bengal. Bengal was part of the Mughal empire. It was governed by an Indian viceroy who paid an annual tribute to the Mughal rulers in Delhi. Otherwise, it was virtually independent. The British East India Company was authorized by the Mughal emperor in Delhi to carry on trade in the state of Bengal. But the Company became involved in disputes over trade with the Muslim

The Mughal emperor gives Robert Clive a proclamation making the British East India company the diwan, *or official tax collector.*

viceroy of Bengal. While Clive was fighting the French in southern India, Calcutta was captured by the Bengali viceroy's forces. British soldiers who did not escape were imprisoned. Enclosed in a small room, many of the prisoners suffocated to death overnight.

Upon his return to Bengal, Clive supported a rival candidate for viceroy. In 1757 at the Battle of Plassey, the former viceroy was defeated, leaving the British in control in Bengal. In 1765 the Mughal emperor reached an agreement with the British East India Company, making it the *diwan,* or tax collector, of Bengal and authorizing it to collect taxes in the area.

This agreement marked the beginning of the British Empire in India. With the power to collect money from the people, the East India Company was no longer a mere trading corporation. Company officials were able to extract great sums of money from the Bengal ruler, and many Britons returned home to live a high life, returning to Bengal for more plunder.

Building a base for empire. The abuses of the East India Company eventually came to the attention of the British Parliament. A series of parliamentary acts beginning with the Regulating Act of 1773 separated the Company's trading and governing roles. The Company was made answerable to the Parliament, and an efficient administrative system was created to replace the corrupt Company officials. A governor-general, assisted by a council in Calcutta, supervised all Company territory in India. Parliament abolished the private trade, which low-paid Company officials had engaged in to supplement their incomes, and raised their salaries. New Company employees were carefully recruited and trained. Britons replaced Indian workers, particularly in the higher-level administrative positions. More British officers were brought into the Company's army. While Indian religious and social customs were left alone, English became the language of government.

Reviewing Your Reading

1. Describe the expansion of Portugal into Asia.
2. How did the British establish themselves in Bengal?
3. How did the British Parliament regulate the affairs of the East India Company?

British Rule Brings Both Reform and Domination

During the nineteenth century many changes were taking place in Britain. It was a time of rapid technological change and increased production of goods and crops. Optimistic British leaders were confident that life was getting better and better through the use of reason, free enterprise, and representative government. During this period, reform, however irregular and difficult to achieve, marked British history.

This reform-mindedness was extended by many Britons to their country's role in distant India. British leaders felt that everyone would benefit by the introduction of Western practices and ideas. Christians saw India as a fertile field for missionary activity. However, there were people who objected to changing India's life. Some Britons did not want to introduce changes in India, lest its people become upset, rise up against them, and drive them out. Others urged respect for Indian religions and customs, while still others attacked these customs. Slowly, change was introduced into India.

British rule leads to many improvements. The governors-general did introduce many social reforms up to 1857. Infanticide and human sacrifice were abolished. *Sati* (suh-*tee'*), the practice whereby a widow threw herself on her husband's funeral pyre, often against her will, and *thugi,* which combined robbery with ritual murder in honor of the goddess Kali, were suppressed. Widows were permitted to remarry. Slavery was abolished. The ban on Christian missionary activity was lifted, and Western-style education was introduced. Irrigation canals were built. Communication was improved with the use of steamboats, railroads, telegraph, and the Grand Trunk Road from Calcutta to Delhi.

Changes in the tax collection system upset Indian life. As the new ruler with different cultural values, Britain introduced changes that upset some Indian practices. One good example was the change made in the collection of the land revenue.

Originally, peasant farmers who had a hereditary right to the land paid taxes to the Mughal government by way of a *zamindar* (zuh-*meen'*dahr), or tax collector. The zamindar usually lived close to the peasant and knew his ability to pay.

To provide a more dependable system of revenue for themselves, the British changed this system in 1793. Each zamindar was assigned a fixed amount of tax to give to British officials and was regarded as the landowner.

Thus a new class of zamindars, often Calcutta financiers, acquired the land. They became absentee landlords. The personal link between the zamindar and the peasants was broken. Failure to pay the tax now meant eviction for the peasants. There were few laws to protect them. The profits from the land benefited absentee zamindars who had only to pay their fixed quotas to the British government. The new zamindar class developed close links with the new government.

The British expand their holdings in India. To secure its borders and to preserve peace, the British East India Company's army fought and defeated, or made treaties with the Indian states of Mysore, Hyderabad, Maratha, Sind, and Punjab and with Burma, Afghanistan, and Nepal. Some of these territories were ruled directly by the British. Others had a British official and army to "advise" and protect the Indian ruler's kingdom. Misgovernment was also reason enough for British annexation. By this method several Indian states were added to the Company's holdings.

Sepoy Mutiny. The mere presence of the Western world with its different religion, values, and customs created tensions between the colonial rulers and the Indians. Changes in land tenure and the loss of political power angered many Indians. Both Hindus and Muslims saw Christian missionary activity and British reform efforts as a threat to their religion.

The mutiny, siege, and recapture of the town of Lucknow, 45 miles north of Delhi, were among the most destructive battles of the Sepoy rebellion.

The last straw came when Indian soldiers were issued a new rifle which required that greased cartridges, smeared with cows' and pigs' fat, be bitten before loading. Flesh for the Hindus was polluting, and the pig was unclean to the Muslims. The sepoys mutinied in May 1857, near Delhi and captured the city the following day. They proclaimed the aged Mughal who had once ruled India their emperor. Though the mutiny spread beyond Delhi, it did not become a popular uprising against the British. A number of Indian princes supported the British and supplied troops to aid them. The fighting was fierce, and atrocities were committed by both sides. In a year's time the mutiny was crushed.

The British crown replaces the Company as ruler of India. British officials were surprised by the mutiny and decided that policy changes were needed. By proclamation, Queen Victoria in 1858 promised a general amnesty to the rebellious sepoys, complete religious freedom to the people, and no further encroachment on Indian states. The governor-general was replaced by a viceroy in the service of the Queen. Most important, the British East India Company was abolished, and India officially became a possession of the British government. The Indian army was reorganized. Under the new arrangement all officers were British, and British soldiers alone controlled the artillery.

Although the Queen had announced that neither race nor religion would bar Indians from service with the British government, Muslims were blamed more than Hindus for the mutiny and were discriminated against in government employment. The gulf in understanding that had existed between the British and Indians before the rebellion widened. The British rulers were now less confident about westernizing India and more cautious with reform efforts.

Hindu forerunners of the independence movement. Seeing Hinduism in a deteriorating condition, and sensitive to Christian criticism of their religion, some Bengalis set out to reform it. A brilliant linguist and intellectual, Ram Mohun Roy (1772–1833) was the first modern Indian reformer. Though attracted to Christianity, he remained a Hindu because he wanted to restore it to its original form. He founded his own religious group, the Brahmo Samaj, in 1828. This group rejected idols and sacrifices and the use of priests. Although it was open to all castes, reform-minded Brahman Hindus were its chief members.

Many orthodox Hindus opposed Roy's activities because he favored such reforms as the abolition of sati (p. 205). Though Roy founded no political body, he called for a free Indian press and an end to racial discrimination in court. He also urged that British officers consult with educated Indians before making laws. His support for these measures marked the start of Indian involvement in British rule and the struggle for individual rights. While never a mass movement, the Brahmo Samaj was influential.

Review Your Reading

1. How did the British change the tax collecting system? How did this change affect the Indian peasant?
2. Describe the expansion of British territory in India.
3. What were the causes of the Sepoy Mutiny?
4. How did British rule change after the Mutiny?
5. What effect did British rule have in Bengal? How did Bengalis respond to this?
6. How did Ram Mohun Roy try to reform Hinduism? What other reforms did he support?

The Indian Nationalist Movement

Never in India's history had its many diverse peoples considered themselves members of a single nation. The concept of nationalism, allegiance to one country, was very foreign. Thus the task of developing a nationalist movement was exceptionally difficult. No single group led the nationalist movement. Many groups took up the cause of Indian unity, and they often argued bitterly with one another in age-old religious, racial, and regional disputes. Hindu and Muslim nationalist movements disagreed the most sharply. They worked in opposition to one another and helped to produce two nations rather than one.

Urban dwellers led the movement. A small group of Western-educated Indians from the cities provided the leadership for the nationalist movement. These leaders shared a common background – their English education. Their experiences had exposed them to Western political, social, economic, and religious ideas which helped them develop a concept of a united India. At the same time their common education and language separated them from illiterate or traditionally educated Indians who spoke various Indian languages. Because of the differences between this group and most of India's people, they were unable to create a mass national movement.

Educated Indians had many grievances against their British rulers. Recognizing the benefits of British rule, most educated Indians sought to enter the British civil service. Although many were hired for lower level positions, their ambitions were frustrated when they tried to get higher level government posts. Because of their Western education many felt cut off from Indian culture. They were neither fish nor fowl, neither Indian nor British. Britons and Indians occupied separate railroad compartments, and Indians were excluded from British social clubs. This discrimination was especially hurtful to educated Indians. They were stunned by the outcry from British subjects serving in India when it was proposed that British lawbreakers be tried before an Indian judge. The British insisted that separate courts be maintained for Britons and Indians.

Prosperous and educated Indians worked as clerks, teachers, and journalists. Without social position or property, they formed a rootless, educated middle class. Ambitious and articulate, they turned to the press, set up political movements, and used political techniques learned from the British to achieve their goals. Although they became loyal British subjects, they also developed unexpected ambitions. Educated Hindu Indians competed with the British for government jobs, criticized British imperialism and government, and called for "India for Indians."

Sensitive to British criticism of Indian civilization, educated Indians developed a nationalist movement that emphasized pride in India's cultural heritage, criticized British rule, and called for self-government. What the Indian nationalists thought about British rule and their own heritage was not always accurate. But that did not matter, for they believed their criticisms and assessments to be true and based their campaign against the British on their beliefs.

Nationalists try to instill pride in the Indian heritage. Indian nationalists looked with pride to their country's past. They felt that the ancient Hindu culture must be restored and combined with the modern knowledge and political institutions introduced by the British. They called for a return to Sanskrit, "the language of the Gods," and a reliance on Hinduism to improve the morality of the people.

The nationalists argued that ancient India was once the greatest manufacturing and commercial region in the world. Its present poverty resulted from exploitation by foreigners. Nationalists believed that the British ruled India to benefit themselves. They pointed out that cheaper, imported British manufactured goods had ruined India's handicraft markets while providing new markets for British industries in India. Indians bought inexpensive British cloth rather than handwoven goods of India. India's wealth was drained to Britain, the nationalists argued, to pay for its foreign government and army in India.

Nationalists felt that India's potential wealth must be developed for its own benefit. They asked Indians to boycott foreign goods and purchase only Indian-produced goods. They felt that Indians should help themselves by organizing savings banks, which would pool savings and make loans to Indian business owners. To get skilled technical workers, nationalists suggested that Indians follow the Japanese example – go abroad to learn skills and return to benefit India.

In 1897 members of the Indian National Congress posed for this formal portrait at their yearly meeting.

India's Muslim minority organizes. When the British took control of India, they replaced the Muslims as the country's rulers. British officials distrusted the Muslims because of their participation in the Sepoy Mutiny. Their hostility was increased by the unwillingness of the more conservative Muslims to take advantage of Western-style education. Consequently Muslims were treated less favorably than the Hindu population by the British officials.

One early Muslim leader who hoped to improve the Muslim position was Sayyid Ahmad Khan (1817–1898). He favored Western education as a means of bringing new life to the Muslim religion. He tried to show that the study of modern science was not contrary to Islamic beliefs. He founded the English language Muhammadan Anglo-Oriental College (now called Aligarh University) to produce westernized doctors, lawyers, and teachers. He hoped its graduates would provide leadership for India's Muslims. Sayyid at first favored cooperation between Hindus and Muslims, but he later opposed it because Hindus outnumbered Muslims.

As the more militant Hindu nationalist groups became increasingly anti-Muslim, Muslim leaders formed the Muslim League in 1906. The League's leaders called for separate elections in which Hindus would vote for Hindus and Muslims for Muslims with a certain number of seats reserved for each group in the national legislature. This demand was granted by the British in 1909. The British hoped this action would counterbalance the influence of the powerful Hindu nationalist group, the Indian National Congress.

Indian National Congress. The Indian National Congress was formed in 1885 under the sponsorship of a retired British official. It was composed mainly of Hindus and represented India's middle-class urban intellectuals. At first it met once a year to discuss political questions and social-reform issues. The Congress called for more opportunity for Western-educated Indians in British government offices, the use of Indians as commissioned army officers, and Indian representation on the Viceroy's Council. While the British made some concessions to the Indian Congress, they never fully met its demands.

Gandhi and the Drive for Independence

Mohandas Gandhi (1869–1948) transformed the nationalist movement from a small Western-educated middle-class movement into a mass political movement that used nonviolent action to achieve Indian independence.

Married at age 13, Gandhi left India as a young man to study law in London. Later he went to South Africa seeking a more profitable law practice. In South Africa he experienced the legalized racial discrimination that Asians and non-whites suffered under the white South African government. Taking up the cause of the Indians of South Africa, he developed nonviolent techniques to fight governmental injustice. His success was limited, and he returned to India in 1915. Loyal to the British, Gandhi supported them in World War I and urged Indians to serve in the British army.

Amritsar Massacre. Throughout World War I, Indians loyally served the British war effort. Many nationalists hoped the British would reward their efforts by giving them greater political power. However, when the war ended, the British passed the hated Rowlatt Acts.

These laws provided that a terrorist suspect could be imprisoned without trial or tried secretly without a lawyer. This violated British legal procedures and aroused intense anti-British feeling among Indian nationalists. After riots broke out, the British banned all public meetings. In the town of Amritsar (uhm-*riht'*-sur) in 1919, thousands of people ignored this order and met inside an open space surrounded by brick houses and a high wall. The enclosure had only one narrow entrance. Under a British general, fifty soldiers fired without warning on the peaceful unarmed crowd, resulting in the death of 379 people and over 1200 wounded. Though a government committee investigated the tragic event, the British general was not tried. This massacre helped to end Gandhi's loyalty to the British.

Gandhi's peaceful political method. Gandhi devised a method of nonviolent resistance which he called *satyagraha* (*sut'*ya-gruh-ha), "soul force," to help gain Indian independence. Gandhi taught that the realization of God comes from service and sacrifice toward others. Gandhi turned Hindu attitudes of personal spiritual freedom into tools for political and social change. He taught that *ahimsa* (ah-*heem'*-sah), or nonviolence, was the way to win over an opponent, by self-control, patience, sympathy, and suffering. To end the "injustices" of British rule, the nonviolent resister was prepared to be beaten, arrested, and imprisoned. He believed these unselfish actions would help to change the ruler's heart. Gandhi preached that "suffering opens the eyes of understanding."

The nationalists' goal was *swaraj*, self-rule for India. In order to accomplish this goal, Gandhi developed several resistance techniques. These techniques included civil disobedience (that is, the refusal to obey what the resister considers an evil law), fasting, and work stoppages with the time spent in prayer. Between 1920 and 1930 Gandhi led several peaceful boycotts using these methods. He urged Indians not to buy British cloth but to wear Indian homespun cloth. He asked his followers to refuse to pay taxes, to give up British honors, and to use Indian languages instead of English. He announced that Indians should refuse to cooperate with new governmental reforms instituted by the British. While Indian

Mohandas Gandhi, in simple peasant dress, leads followers on a march to protest the salt tax.

Gandhi's Influence on Martin Luther King

Gandhi's technique of nonviolent civil disobedience influenced the American civil rights leader, Martin Luther King. In Stride Toward Freedom *King wrote:*

Like most people, I had heard of Gandhi, but I had never studied him seriously. As I read I became deeply fascinated by his campaigns of nonviolent resistance. I was particularly moved by the Salt March to the Sea and his numerous fasts. The whole concept of "Satyagraha" *(Satya* is truth which equals love, and *agraha* is force; "Satyagraha," therefore, means truth-force or love force) was profoundly significant to me. As I delved deeper into the philosophy of Gandhi my skepticism concerning the power of love gradually diminished, and I came to see for the first time its potency in the area of social reform. Prior to reading Gandhi, I had about concluded that the ethics of Jesus were only effective in individual relationship. The "turn the other cheek" philosophy and the "love your enemies" philosophy were only valid, I felt, when individuals were in conflict with other individuals; when racial groups and nations were in conflict a more realistic approach seemed necessary. But after reading Gandhi, I saw how utterly mistaken I was.

Martin Luther King, Jr., *Stride Toward Freedom* (New York: Harper & Row, 1958), pp. 96–97.

nationalists did not always follow his suggestions, Gandhi's efforts caused enough unrest throughout the country to bring him to the attention of British authorities. He spent many years in prison because of his nationalist activity.

The Dandi Salt March showed widespread support for the independence movement. Gandhi's 1930 civil disobedience campaign centered on a salt tax that every Indian had to pay. Gandhi urged his followers not to pay it, and to dramatize his plea he organized a march to the sea. With seventy-eight followers, Gandhi walked for over three weeks, covering the 241 miles from Ahmedabad (*ah'*mad-ah-*bahd'*) to Dandi on the west coast. When he reached the seashore, he distilled salt from the evaporated seawater of the mudflats.

The anti–salt tax movement became nationwide. People made and sold their own salt illegally. As civil disobedience spread, tens of thousands of Indians were arrested. Hoping to stop the movement, the British arrested Gandhi and imprisoned him without trial. Jawaharlal Nehru (juh-*wah'*hur-lahl *nay'*roo, 1889–1964), President of the Congress Party, and later independent India's first prime minister, was also arrested. Although this campaign attracted worldwide attention, the salt tax remained.

Independence Follows World War II

In 1939, without consulting Indian leaders, Britain proclaimed India at war against Nazi Germany. The Indian Congress Party (formerly the Indian National Congress) denounced this action, stating that it would not support the war effort unless India became an independent nation. Congress Party leaders resigned from government posts, passed a "quit India" motion, and boycotted the war. All Congress Party leaders including Nehru were arrested and imprisoned. The Muslim League supported the British war effort on the condition that no constitutional changes be made without its approval. Nonetheless, more than two million Indians served in the Indian armed forces and fought side by side with the British in World War II.

Disagreements between Hindus and Muslims delay independence. After the war was over, Great Britain promised independence to India. Weakened by two major wars and no longer a great power, Britain could not afford to retain India. However, before giving up control, the British wanted to devise a plan to insure the peaceful transfer of power. This was not a simple task.

Hindu and Muslim leaders disagreed strongly on the best means of dividing the country. Britain's willingness to grant independence had not lessened the hostility between the Congress Party and the Muslim League. Riots between Hindus and Muslims in Calcutta in 1946 resulted in the death of 5000 people.

Working intensely to avoid a civil war and to live up to a promise to withdraw by 1948, the British in 1947 convinced Indian leaders to agree to its partition plan. The plan created an independent Muslim state of Pakistan, broken into two areas and separated by almost 2000 miles of Indian territory. A separate India was also created.

The partition plan was not carried out peacefully. It was marred by the flight of Hindus from Pakistan and Muslims from India. Many thousands were killed in these migrations, and much property was lost or destroyed. On August 15, 1947 the Indian flag replaced the Union Jack in New Delhi. India was independent, free to work out its own political destiny.

India under Prime Minister Nehru. Nehru had long been involved in the Indian nationalist movement. Although he and Gandhi disagreed on many policy matters, Nehru was attracted to him by the force of Gandhi's personality and his idealism. Gandhi chose Nehru to be his political successor. As India moved closer to independence, Gandhi's influence in the Congress Party lessened. Nehru became India's first prime minister. Six months after independence, Gandhi was killed by a Hindu extremist who objected to Gandhi's efforts to ease the hostility between the Hindus and Muslims.

Uncertain democratic rule. In 1967 Indira Gandhi became prime minister. As crises mounted, her rule became more dictatorial. Governing under emergency powers, she censored the press, imprisoned political foes, suppressed trade union rights, and moved India toward compulsory birth control. Thousands of her political foes were imprisoned. In the 1977 national election, the Janata (People's) Party, an opposition coalition, defeated her government. The new prime minister, Morarji Desai, ended emergency rule measures and the rule of law was re-established. But political infighting grew within the Janata Party. In 1980, Indira Gandhi regained the prime minister's office in a surprise landslide election victory. Since that time Gandhi's political party, the Congress-I (C-I), has succeeded in keeping control of the government. Even after Gandhi's assassination in 1984 (p. 245), her son Rajiv succeeded her as head of the party and as prime minister.

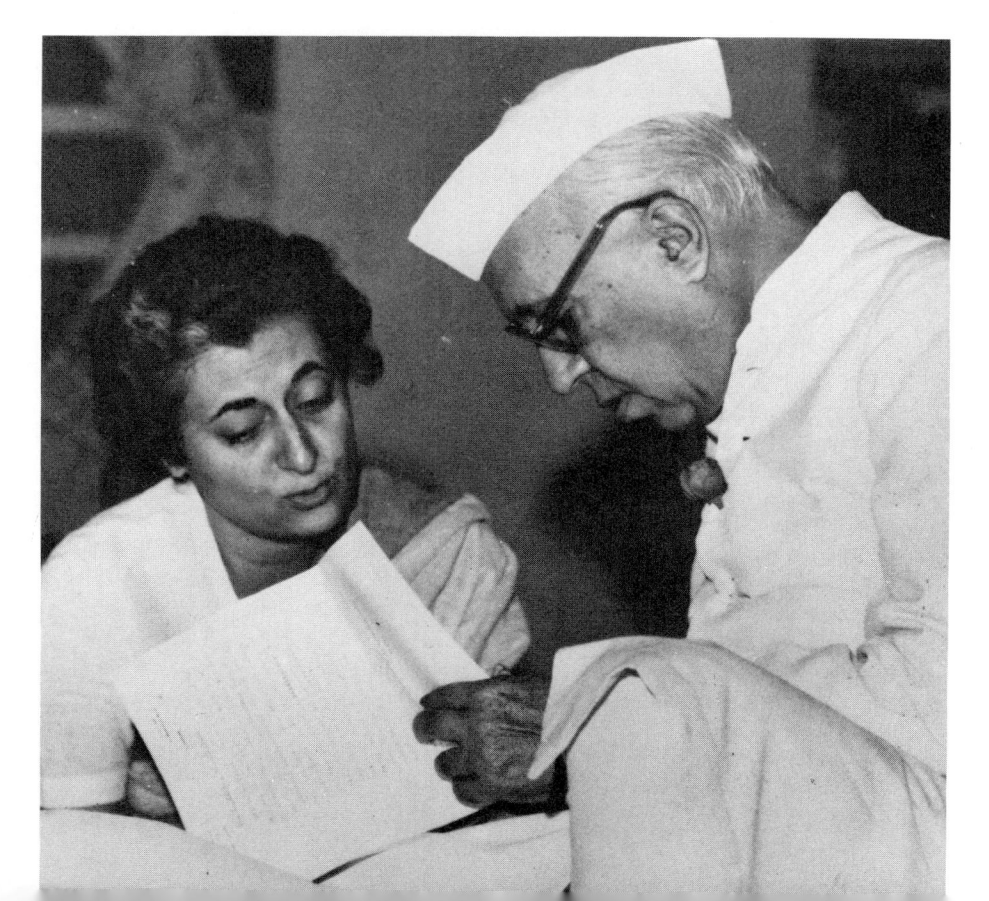

Jawaharlal Nehru served as India's first prime minister, from independence in 1947 to his death in 1964. His daughter, Indira Gandhi, eventually succeeded him in 1967, and ruled for all but three years until her death in 1984.

India becomes a nuclear power. With an underground nuclear explosion in the Rajasthan desert in 1974, India joined the world's nuclear powers. The Indian government assured the world that atomic research was to harness nuclear energy for the needs of the people. Research continues at the atomic center at Trombay as India builds several nuclear electrical generating plants.

Reviewing Your Reading

1. Describe the grievances of the Indians against the British.
2. What economic changes did nationalists propose to improve Indian life?
3. How did the English education system in India promote Indian nationalism?
4. Why was Muslim nationalism slow in developing? What part did Sayyid Ahmad Khan play in its development?
5. What were the goals of the Muslim League?
6. Why was the Indian National Congress formed? Who were its members? In what ways did members disagree on the course of action for the Congress?
7. Describe Gandhi's nonviolent campaign methods and his anti–salt tax campaign.
8. What was the Congress Party's reaction to Britain's involvement of India in World War II?
9. What led Britain to grant independence to India? Describe the terms of the division. Was it satisfactory to both Muslims and Hindus? Explain.

CHAPTER REVIEW

Recalling Names and Places

ahimsa	Dandi	Mughal
Akbar	Joseph Dupleix	Muslim League
Amritsar Massacre	Indira Gandhi	Jawaharlal Nehru
Aryans	Mohandas Gandhi	sati
Ashoka	Harappa	satyagraha
Bengal	Indian National Congress	sepoys
Robert Clive	Sayyid Ahmad Khan	thugi
Congress Party	Mohenjo Daro	zamindar

Understanding This Chapter

1. Trace the roots of conflict between Hindus and Muslims in Indian history. Why has this conflict arisen? Has it changed at all in nature over 13 centuries? Has it ever relaxed? If so, how? What might this mean for future relations between the two groups?
2. Trace the growth of British and French rivalry in India. Why did European powers want to rule India? Why did they feel they could or should? Why did the British triumph?
3. What changes did Britain make in Indian culture?
4. What prevented the development of an all-Indian outlook before the arrival of the British? How did British rule help to develop the idea of a united India? Was this experience shared in any other lands colonized by the Europeans?
5. Gandhi's ideas about nonviolent action were derived from thinkers of many cultures, and they have influenced thinkers of many other cultures. What about them seems distinctively Indian? What seems universal? How have Gandhi's ideas changed when adapted by leaders in places other than India?

Chapter 18

Changing India

The origin of the caste system is uncertain. The word "caste" originated with the Portuguese. The caste system is based on social inequality. A person's caste is determined at birth. He or she is trained in its customs and marries and dies within the caste. The caste system is not utterly rigid. While there has been some change within the system, its disappearance in India is not likely in the foreseeable future.

The Caste System Affects All Aspects of Indian Life

Under the caste system, an important part of Hindu philosophy, Indian society was organized into four main classes or *varna* – the *Brahmin, Kshatriya, Vaishya,* and *Shudra*. Each varna had specific duties. The Brahmin officiated at

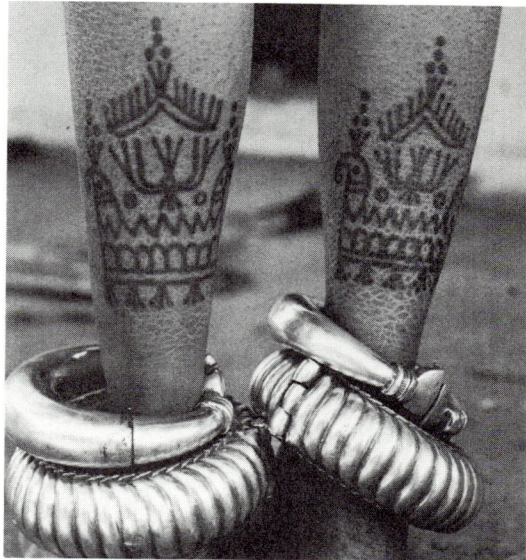

The man at left belongs to the kumbhara, *or potters' caste. According to a study of village life in Bhoringa, India, the potters' caste was ranked eighth in status — below priests, merchants, and tailors, but above shoemakers, barbers, and shepherds. Occupations with the lowest status were sweeper and folk musician, both jobs for "untouchables." The woman at right wears leg tattoos indicating the high position of her caste.*

religious ceremonies, studied, and taught the *Vedas,* Hindu religious texts. The Kshatriya (kuh-*sheh*'tree-yuh) were the rulers and warriors who protected their subjects. The Vaishya (*vash*'yah) engaged in trade, tended cattle, and tilled the soil. The Shudra (*shoe*'drah) were farm laborers. They performed services for the three higher varna. Below and outside of these four groups were the untouchables, or outcastes.

The four varna were further broken down into more than 2000 castes. Every Indian is born into a caste. Each caste lives in a separate part of the village. Yet although the individual castes are socially and culturally self-contained, they are linked with one another in economic matters. Every caste has a certain pattern of behavior, a specialized occupation, and a name such as *kayastha* (scribe) and *chamar* (leather worker).

Others included the landowning farmers, priests, carpenters, blacksmiths, potters, weavers, barbers, and latrine cleaners. Each caste has a duty (*dharma*), and according to Indian custom it is better to do one's own duty badly than to do another's well. When a person did his duty properly, society functioned smoothly.

Criteria for ranking castes. Many castes are found in a village. The castes are ranked from the highest to the lowest, theoretically, according to the number of ritually pure practices each caste observes. Ritually pure practices include vegetarianism, avoidance of alcohol, and avoidance of occupations that require the handling of the products of dead cows or human secretions and excretions, such as cutting hair or childbirth.

Another way castes are set apart is by what food its members will accept from others. Foods prepared in a certain manner are thought to retain the pollution of the cook. Consequently, food must not be accepted from people in a lower caste than oneself. Since food may always be accepted from someone who is in a higher caste than oneself, Brahmins are valued as cooks.

Other criteria in the village caste ranking are the services that a Brahmin priest performs for different castes. The more religious rites a priest performs for a caste, the higher its status is.

The panchayat settles caste disputes. To try those who fail to carry out caste practices, each caste has a *panchayat* (pahn-*chah*'yut), a council of elders. All caste members are expected to follow certain standards of ritual purity. Such an action as eating with improper company or working in an occupation beneath caste dignity is considered an offense. Although only one person might commit such an offense, it reflects badly on the entire caste. For a minor offense the panchayat might decree a fine and ritual purification. Ritual purification involves bathing in flowing water while reciting certain prayers. A major offense could lead to expulsion from the caste.

When Gandhi went to London to study law, he committed a punishable offense against his caste. Hindu scripture banned travel over oceans. Living in foreign places also led to polluting influences. Gandhi was expelled from his caste. Upon his return to India, he petitioned for readmission, went to a sacred site to purify himself, and was reinstated by his local caste.

Harijans have little chance to improve their position. Some groups are thought to have permanent pollution. Their members are called the untouchables, or *harijans* (ha-re-*johns'*), "children of God" as Gandhi called them. Pollution arises from their occupations—for example, working with leather or washing clothes. Harijans must keep their distance lest they pollute high-caste Hindus. This pollution is thought to offend the deities, so for many centuries harijans could not enter temples or receive the services of Brahmin priests. Harijans were not allowed to use public wells or attend schools used by the other castes. The harijans' position contributed to their extreme poverty, ignorance, and economic dependence on higher castes.

The government makes efforts to improve harijan conditions. The national government has legally eliminated untouchability. The Constitution abolished it. The 1955 Untouchability (Offenses) Act made it unlawful to use social and economic boycott to enforce untouchability. Yet, untouchability still exists. Many evade the law, and enforcement is weak. Harijans are still forced to use separate wells, and they still do the dirtiest jobs.

Special government programs have been established to aid the harijans and to prevent members of other castes from taking advantage of them. Government jobs, houses, and scholarships are available to talented harijans. The government pays their educational fees throughout their time in school. Seats are reserved for harijans in the legislatures, and their position in schools has improved. Despite these efforts, progress is slow. For example, from 1968 to 1978 only seven harijans were among the 1,000 candidates assuming India's most important administrative positions.

According to government plans, these special measures are only temporary, and will end when untouchability disappears. To date this has not happened. While there is now generally less discrimination against the untouchables than in the past, it continues because of weak government enforcement and deeply rooted customs.

Reviewing Your Reading

1. What are the four varna? What role did each play in ancient Indian society?
2. What criteria are used to rank castes in a village?
3. What is the caste panchayat? What role did it have within each caste?
4. What are harijans? Why were they placed outside of the four varna?
5. What does the Indian government do to try to improve the position of the harijan? How successful has this been?

Traditional Indian Family Life

The ideal Indian family is the joint family, consisting of two or more married men – father and sons or brothers – living together in one household with their wives and children. Families eat from a common kitchen and share property and money. All brothers have equal property rights and an equal social position.

A young Indian mother and her son. The woman uses kohl, a cosmetic, to darken the area under her eyes.

However, younger brothers are subordinate to the oldest, who will one day become the head of the family. Hostility can develop between brothers and between their wives. With the death of the father, brothers divide family property equally among themselves and then break up into nuclear families.

Men rule the family. As husband and father, the male is superior to his wife and children, and both defer to him. The wife serves him first at meals and eats when he finishes. If a man's wife dies, he may remarry. Although a man can have more than one wife, it is unusual to do so. If a couple has no son, one can be adopted, usually from one's own caste.

The birth of a son is more welcome than that of a daughter. Such an event is greeted with drumming, singing, and public announcement. A son means an additional laborer, someone to care for the parents in their old age and someone to carry out the father's funeral rites and the family religious observances.

Women have few chances for independence. The Indian woman has little personal independence, for she is protected by her father while unmarried, by her husband as a wife, and by her eldest son when widowed. Today, marriage in the early teens is still quite common; in the past, marriage as a small child was not unusual. Widows cannot remarry because they are considered persons who accumulated bad merit in a previous existence and had been punished for it by the loss of their husbands. Divorce is not permitted except for women in lower castes.

In the past, women had little educational opportunity. Except for such personal property as jewelry, a woman could not inherit family property. *Sati*, in which a woman burned herself on her husband's funeral pyre, was a religious ideal. *Purdah*, the seclusion and the complete covering of a woman in public, is still practiced in North India.

Marriages are arranged and considered more a family matter than one of individual choice. The wishes of the prospective couple are rarely considered. The heads of the families, with or without a go-between, conduct the marriage negotiations. Each family hopes to gain wealth and prestige and to improve the welfare of its children by the marriage. Marriage is within the caste. The amount of dowry is agreed to. Horoscope readings are taken to determine the compatibility of the couple.

If a family has no sons, a marriage can be arranged for a daughter in which the man joins her family and helps with the family work. The family property is passed on to the daughter's children. This is not a desirable marriage for a man, but a poor man will weigh the value of the family assets against the stigma of such a marriage. Once all the details are agreed to, an astrologer sets an auspicious day for the wedding.

Legal reforms give women greater equality. Several laws have been enacted since independence to improve the status of women in Hindu society. The minimum marriage age for the male is 18 and the female 15. Polygamy has been banned, and widow remarriage and divorce permitted. Women have equal inheritance rights in family property. However, since these reforms go against Hindu practice, they are not apt to affect the lives of the vast majority of the Indians who live in villages.

Despite the minimum-age requirements, many low-caste daughters marry below the age of 12. Since many families are extremely poor, an early marriage often offers the daughter a little economic security.

An Indian bride in purdah follows her husband from the wedding ceremony.

> ### Advertising for a Mate
>
> *Some urban, middle-class Indian families use the advertisement columns of newspapers to find a spouse for their children. The following were taken from an Indian newspaper:*
>
> Bridegroom required for Saiva Vellala girl, 29, vegetarian, graduate, employed as a teacher.
>
> * * *
>
> South Indian (Brahmin) youth, company executive drawing Rs. 1200, settled in Maharashtra, seeks beautiful educated bride, 24–27. Caste no bar.
>
> * * *
>
> Young man, 33, M.A. in mathematics, well placed in computer systems with . . . [an American Corporation] seeks suitable Vadama Brahmin girl for marriage. Girls should be tall, fair, pretty, college-educated, preferably in lower twenties. Fluency in English and willingness to adapt to living in America are must. This is only to locate ideal match. Well-placed parents . . . may contact mother . . . for further details. Horoscope if desired. . . .

Changes in the family system. Increased education, urbanization, and industrialization are beginning to affect the traditional Indian family system. Today a son may live and work apart from his family, earning an income on his own. He thus becomes independent of his father's authority at an earlier age than in the past. Employment may force a young villager to move to the city with his wife and children. No elder who cares deeply about traditional practice lives with the couple in their new home to make sure these traditional ways continue. Nonetheless, urban nuclear families usually have strong ties with the villages and families they left behind.

Greater educational opportunities have changed the woman's role. The idea of educated, urban, high-caste women holding paid jobs is no longer frowned upon; and some women work in shops, offices, schools, and professions, and take part in politics.

While parents continue to arrange marriages, some educated young people may be consulted, even see their prospective mate, and, very rarely, veto the choice.

The degree to which Indians change their way of life depends on their education, residence, occupation, wealth, social position, and caste. For most Indians whose world is their village, laws and modern customs do not touch them. But the direction of change is there, for those who may wish to follow it.

Reviewing Your Reading

1. Describe the ideal Indian family. What often causes the joint family to break up?
2. Describe the position of the male in Indian society.
3. In what ways was the Indian woman subordinate to the man?
4. How did legal reforms change the position of Indian women?
5. How have education and urban life affected the Indian family?

Hinduism

Hinduism, the religion of 80 percent of the Indian people, is difficult to define. It has no founder, no uniform belief system that all Hindus must accept, and no group of national religious leaders. While the religion has its sacred texts, not all Hindus regard one of them as the equivalent of the Bible or the Koran. Hinduism attracts followers of many different beliefs. One Hindu may believe in one God, another in several, while yet another may be an atheist. Such diversity is considered normal.

Hindus share certain common beliefs. Hindus consider two major religious works to be important to their religious training – the *Vedas* (*vay*'dahs), which are considered divinely revealed sacred knowledge, and the *Upanishads*

Participants in Hindu religious festivals wear colorful masks or face paint and march in dramatic processions.

221

Brahma, *the creator of the world, has four heads to show his great intelligence and to represent the four quarters of the earth.* Shiva, *the destroyer, has several personalities. He is often portrayed as Lord of the Dance. His frenzied movements destroy the world in preparation for a new creation.* Vishnu *is depicted with four arms bearing his emblems — the conch, the discus, the club, and the lotus. Vishnu works constantly for the welfare of the world. For this he changes himself into human or animal form. His two most popular forms are Rama and Krishna, heroes of the Indian epics* Ramayana *and* Mahabharata.

(up-*pan'i*-shadz), philosophical works on the nature of the universe. Hindus also consider the cow a sacred symbol of motherhood and fruitfulness. The caste system is another integral part of Hinduism. A person is not a Hindu unless he belongs to a caste.

The most important Hindu deity is Brahman. Brahman, the Absolute, is the totality of all existence – God, people, universe. He is everywhere, and all things are a part of Brahman. Every person has a portion of the Absolute, which is the human soul.

Most people cannot know Brahman, the Absolute, directly. The many Hindu dieties serve as aids in religious life and help the worshiper approach Brahman. There are three leading deities – *Brahma*, creation; *Vishnu*, preservation of life; and *Shiva*, destruction.

Hindus believe in the rebirth of the soul. Hindus believe that when a person dies his or her soul is reborn in another living creature or in a different caste group. This process continues indefinitely until the individual soul unites with the universal soul, Brahman, the Absolute. Freedom from the cycle of death and rebirth, along with spiritual union with the Absolute, is the ultimate goal of Hindu religious life.

The form of a person's next life is determined by *karma* (*car'*muh), that is, actions in the present life. The form of a person's present life – caste, for example – was determined by past karma. Good karma results in rebirth at a higher level; bad karma results in rebirth at a lower level, or even as an animal.

Karma can be earned by fulfilling one's *dharma* (*dar* muh). Each caste has a dharma, or duty – morally correct behavior that each caste member is expected to follow. The dharma of a warrior caste is to be a brave soldier. A cowardly soldier does not fulfill this dharma, and so earns bad karma.

Jagannath Car Festival

In the city of Puri on the east coast is the popular Jagannath temple, dedicated to Vishnu. Every year in June or July the temple statues are moved from their temple to their "summer house" and two weeks later back to the temple. The event is known as the Jagannath Car Festival. For the return trip the deities are placed in several wooden cars 45 feet high, supported by 16 wheels, each 7 feet in diameter. The platform above the wheels has a high wooden frame covered with bright yellow, blue, and red cloth, which houses the deity. Prancing horses are at the front of the platform.

Four thousand people take up the thick ropes and pull the massive cars along the two-mile road to the temple. The movements of the car pullers are accompanied by the rhythmic chanting, cymbal banging, and swaying of those on the platform. Periodically the cars and the chanting stop, lest an accident occur. When the cars reach the Jagannath temple, the deities are removed and placed in the shrine.

The Jagannath Car Festival in Puri, India.

Hindu worship centers around the family. Hindu worship is primarily an individual or family matter and takes place in the home rather than the temple. As prayers are recited, the image of the deity is bathed, honored with flowers and incense, and given food. According to Hindu belief the deity eats the essence, leaving the material form to be eaten by the worshiper or given to the poor. Each upper-caste family has its own household Brahmin priest who conducts the religious rites connected with birth, initiation, marriage, and death.

The Life and Teachings of the Buddha

The founder of Buddhism lived over 2500 years ago. He was born Gautama Siddhartha (*gow*'tuh-muh sid-*dahr*-tuh, 563–483 B.C.), the son of a ruler of a small kingdom near Nepal. He married, had a son, and lived a sheltered life. According to legend, one day outside the palace grounds he saw an old man, a sick person, a corpse, and a religious beggar. From this experience he learned of suffering quite suddenly. He renounced his luxurious life and quietly left the palace one night to become a wandering ascetic. When his wanderings failed to give him the peace of mind he was seeking, he resumed his normal way of life.

While meditating, Gautama Siddhartha gained insight into the meaning of life. His insights are called the Four Noble Truths: (1) life is suffering; (2) suffering is caused by desire for living and physical pleasure; (3) suffering can be stopped; and (4) living by the Noble Eightfold Path ends suffering. With this understanding Siddhartha was able to escape from the cycle of death and rebirth.

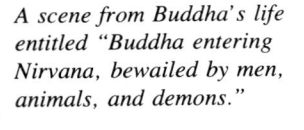

A scene from Buddha's life entitled "Buddha entering Nirvana, bewailed by men, animals, and demons."

As a result of this understanding, he was called the *Buddha* (*boo*'duh), the enlightened one. He continued his wandering life, preaching and establishing religious communities that were open to all people, regardless of caste or sex. He died around 483 B.C. at the age of eighty.

No written account was kept of the Buddha's teachings while he lived. His followers memorized his words and passed them on orally until they were finally written down in the first century B.C. The Buddha's goal was to break the circle of rebirth by ending the longing for earthly rewards and pleasures, which tie a person to rebirth and death. This was done by following the Noble Eightfold Path – right action, right speech, right livelihood, right effort, right mindfulness, right concentration, right views, and right intention.

By following the Noble Eightfold Path one could eventually achieve *nirvana* (near-*vah*'nuh). The Buddha refused to say what nirvana was. As a religious experience, words could not describe it. One who has experienced it lives a tranquil, blissful life.

Buddhism separated into two major movements. In time Buddhism was divided into two branches. One movement became known as Theravada Buddhism. Its members believe Buddha was a human teacher and not a god. They also claim that nirvana can be achieved only by a select few.

The other major branch, Mahayana Buddhism, differs in several important ways. Mahayana Buddhists believe anyone can achieve nirvana, not only monks or nuns. The Mahayana religious ideal is the *bodhisattva,* a being who out of love for humanity delays his entry into nirvana to lead everyone from the world of suffering into the blissful Western Paradise where no one is subject to rebirth. Finally, Mahayana Buddhism involves elaborate rituals with many *sutras,* or scriptures, and the worship of many gods.

Although Buddhism originated in India, it is now more significant in other areas of Asia. Theravada Buddhism is especially strong in Ceylon. Mahayana is found in China and Japan. Both appear in Southeast Asia.

Reviewing Your Reading

1. Describe the Hindu understanding of the God Brahman.
2. What is the Hindu concept of the rebirth of the soul?
3. What is karma? What is dharma? How does it lead a Hindu to accept his or her caste position?
4. What are the Four Noble Truths? What is the Noble Eightfold Path?
5. How is a Buddhist expected to achieve nirvana?
6. What are the differences between Theravada and Mahayana Buddhism?

Indian Education and the British Influence

After the Aryan conquest of India, education was available to all castes except the Shudras and the harijans. Eventually it was practically monopolized by the Brahmins. The children of the three high castes were prepared for adult life in different ways. Brahmins studied the Vedas, the Kshatriya learned warfare, and the Vaishya learned arts and crafts, farming, and trading. Most boys probably learned their skills from their fathers.

Several cities had Hindu universities. At Benares, a stronghold of Hinduism, students collected around a teacher and lived with and learned from him. There were no prescribed courses or examinations. The Buddhist University at Nalanda attracted students from China, Japan, Korea, Sumatra, and Java.

Education changes under the British. Traditionally, Indian governments had always given financial support to education. Not wishing to disturb Indian society and culture, the East India Company granted limited aid by supporting a Muslim and a Hindu college. In 1816 a group of Indians, including Ram Mohun Roy, established the Hindu College of Calcutta. Here the English language was taught.

Because they could pay Indians less, the East India Company employed them as clerks for routine work. Though Persian at first remained the official language of government, many Indians were eager to learn English to work for the new foreign rulers. Other Indians favored education in English because it would open the doors to English literature and modern knowledge. Indians crowded any facility, including Christian missionary schools, where English was taught.

What kind of education for Indians? A debate developed among the British as to which type of education the Company should support. Those who favored English education argued that there was little of value in Indian civilization, and it would be foolish to waste money supporting Indian learning. Western teaching methods and knowledge would eliminate superstition and make

---

India Through an Englishman's Eyes

When he was a young man, nineteenth-century English historian Thomas B. Macaulay was employed by the British East India Company. With little knowledge of Sanskrit or Arabic literature, Macaulay wrote in favor of English education for India:

I have never found one . . . [British Oriental scholar] who could deny that a single shelf of a good European library was worth the whole native literature of India. . . .

. . . We have to educate a people who cannot at present be educated by means of their mother-tongue. We must teach them some foreign language. . . . Whoever knows . . . [English] has ready access to all the vast intellectual wealth, which all the wisest nations of the earth have created. . . . In India, English is . . . spoken by the ruling class . . . . by the higher class of natives. . . . It is likely to become the language of commerce throughout the . . . East. . . .

. . . We must . . . form a class who may be interpreters between us and the millions whom we govern; a class of persons, Indian in blood and colour, but English in taste, in opinions, in morals, and in intellect. . . .

Macaulay Prose and Poetry selected by G. M. Young (Cambridge, Mass.: Harvard University Press, 1967), pp. 722, 723, 729.

India a better country. Missionaries also favored English education to aid them in the conversion of the Indian people to Christianity. Britons familiar with Indian literature and learning wanted both systems of education to exist side by side. The supporters of English education carried the day. English became the official language of the government. Teachers paid little attention to classical Indian languages or local dialects spoken by rural people.

Education in India Today

When India gained its independence in 1947, only 16 percent of its population could read or write. The 1981 census revealed a 36 percent national literacy rate, with many more males than females literate. Literacy rates are highest in the cities and along some coastal areas and lowest in the interior. High-caste groups, particularly Brahmins, have a higher literacy rate than low-caste groups.

A typical primary school in India. According to 1984 UNESCO data, fewer than 40 percent of the pupils who begin primary school eventually enroll in secondary school. What might be some reasons for this tendency to leave school at an early age?

This increase reflects the attention given by the Indian government to improving the educational system it inherited from the British. Its goal was to provide free compulsory education for all children up to 14 years of age and to increase opportunities for high school and college education.

Elementary education. State governments are essentially responsible for education. By the mid-1970s about 79 million students in the six-to-fourteen age group were enrolled in schools. Two decades earlier only 22 million students in this age group had attended school. The quality of education varies enormously. In the countryside the class might be taught in the open air or in a simple building. Instruction is in the local language, and the children learn reading, writing, and simple arithmetic. Some urban schools have better facilities and offer a wider variety of subjects.

Indian education officials believe that five years of primary education is sufficient to make a child literate. However, fewer than half the students who start this minimum program complete it. Children are often needed to supplement family income. Compulsory school attendance is not enforced by the states. Even some of those students who complete the five-year program slip back into illiteracy for the lack of facilities and activities to keep them interested in reading and writing.

Secondary education. Less than half of the children who start in the primary schools continue into the secondary schools. Secondary schools are geared to produce students for the universities. The curriculum includes social studies, science, mathematics, and perhaps three languages – the local one, English or Hindi, and one other Indian language.

At the completion of their studies, students take examinations set and graded by outside examiners. They spend a week writing essays on the various subjects they studied. Success in these examinations is regarded as the more important goal of schooling. This system emphasizes cramming and memorization. Doing well is crucial, for only those with the highest grades can hope to enter a university.

Today educational experts are considering establishing a more comprehensive secondary school program that will prepare students for the wider world of work.

Higher education. Today about 4 percent of the university-age groups receive higher education. Although less than one-fifth of India's college students are women, this is an impressive figure considering the traditional prejudice against female education.

Vernacular languages have slowly replaced English in the classroom, but the shift has been hampered by a scarcity of textbooks written in the languages of the people.

Many Indian graduates study in foreign universities for advanced degrees. Once they have completed their studies, many of these highly trained Indians remain abroad because they cannot find suitable employment in India. The loss of thousands of medical doctors, scientists, economists, historians, and mathematicians is a severe blow because these skills are badly needed within the country.

Reviewing Your Reading

1. How did Hindu education prepare the different caste members for their role in Hindu society?
2. Describe the current elementary and secondary schools in India. What problems keep education from reaching all Indian youngsters?
3. What were the arguments for and against the introduction of English education in India?
4. What possible loss does India face when its university students study abroad?

CHAPTER REVIEW

Recalling Names and Places

Brahma	Kshtriya	Gautama Siddhartha
Brahman	Mahayana Buddhism	Theravada Buddhism
Brahmin	Noble Eightfold Path	Upanishads
caste panchayat	sati	Vaishya
Four Noble Truths	Shiva	Vedas
harijan	Shudra	Vishnu

Understanding This Chapter

1. How did different castes fit into village life? How did caste occupations regulate village life?
2. How successful have reforms designed to change the position of Indian women been? Why is this so?
3. What makes it difficult to characterize Hinduism? What beliefs do all Hindus share?
4. What effects did the introduction of an English educational system have on India? Where these effects anticipated by those who proposed this introduction? Why or why not? Might they have been anticipated?

Chapter 19

Working toward a Modern Economy

Throughout India's history, most of its people have lived in villages. Families were interdependent, and each village was largely self-sufficient. Most villagers were farmers, and their produce was used in the villages.

The caste system provided an orderly system in the village for the exchange of goods and services. Under an associated family system, one family in a caste of carpenters did the woodwork for a particular farming family. No money was involved in this exchange. No other family in the carpenter caste served that particular farm family. If another family tried to take the place of one of the associated families, it was punished by the caste council. As one associated family died out, another family was chosen by the caste council to replace it. By this system, goods and services were exchanged for food, and a stable economic system was provided.

The Indian Economy under the British

Prior to India's contact with the Europeans, changes came about quite slowly. Contact with the British culture brought great and rapid changes in Indian life. While not all of these changes were favorable to the Indians, some were.

One of the more important achievements of the British colonial government was to reduce the ravages of famine. The British increased the amount of irrigated farmland to increase food production. The 1883 famine Code provided direct help to famine victims. Under this act able-bodied men hit by famines were paid to work on public works projects. Food was distributed to those unable to work. Tax payments were suspended during famines, and farmers could get loans to buy seed or work animals.

The British-built railroad system also provided famine relief by making it easier to move grain to an area where the crop had failed. While the British did not totally eliminate the prospect of famine, they were able to reduce the number who starved.

Other changes made by the British were less favorable to the Indian farmer. As we saw on page 000, the changes in the zamindari tax collection system were greatly resented by Indian farmers who often lost their land to absentee landlords.

The introduction of British goods upset the Indian economy. During the eighteenth century large quantities of Indian cotton cloth were exported to Europe. The Industrial Revolution and Britain's free trade policy changed that.

Workers at a cotton mill in the Damodar valley. The mill produces mainly shirts and saris.

With the factories of England producing great amounts of inexpensive cloth, British manufacturers looked the world over for new markets for their goods. British colonies became the salesrooms for their products.

The sale of British manufactured goods in India during the nineteenth century seriously undercut India's handicraft industry. Indian cotton cloth, which was made on handlooms in the home, could not be produced as quickly or as cheaply as cloth made with modern mass-production techniques. The British could ship their cotton cloth thousands of miles and still sell it for less than the cotton cloth made in India. Except for some luxury fabrics, Indian spinners and weavers produced rough cloth for the villages. Indian artisans working in iron, glass, and jute lost their jobs as British imports of these products were sold in India. They joined the displaced weavers and turned to farming.

In 1853 the British built their own modern cotton mills in India. A year later the first joint Indian-British owned textile mill appeared in Bombay. As the number of Indian owned mills grew, their cloth was sold in China and Japan in competition with British textile producers. However, after the Japanese developed their own textile industry, they soon took over the Chinese market.

British manufacturers disliked the prospect of greater competition from Indian manufacturers. They got the British government to place a tax on Indian-made textiles, which made it difficult for Indians to sell their products abroad. Indian objections to this tax were ignored until 1926, when the tax was abolished.

The introduction of modern technology brought many changes. The British revolutionized transportation in India with the introduction of steam power. Over 41,000 miles of railroad track were laid. Goods and people moved about the country cheaply and more quickly.

The growing use of kerosene reduced the demand for vegetable oils for lamps. Synthetic dyes cut the demand for Indian indigo. While the advantages gained from the new technology benefited European industrialists and various groups in India, many other Indian laborers were hurt by the loss of traditional jobs.

THE INDIAN SUBCONTINENT: LAND USE AND RESOURCES

- Manufacturing
- Farming
- Subsistence farming
- Forest
- Herding
- Fishing
- Unproductive land
- Coal
- Gold
- Iron ore
- Manganese

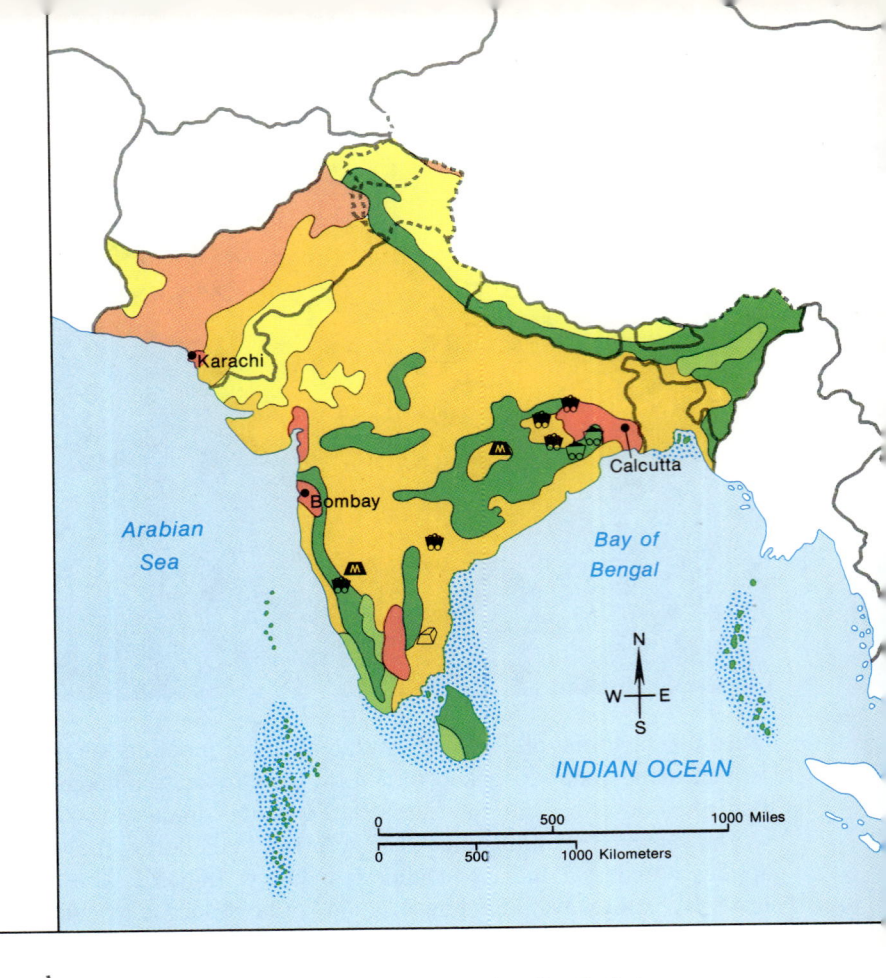

However, the new technology led to significant gains for India's economy. The cotton mills, coal mines, the iron and steel industry, and the construction of railroads and irrigation canals brought new employment opportunities. Workers were needed for British-owned tea and coffee plantations. British commercial houses and government offices hired Western-educated Indians. In addition, Indians used the technology and business methods introduced by the British to establish businesses of their own.

While the British generally ran India to the advantage of British economic interests, they did bring a modern economy to the colony. New industry required new methods of production and new types of skilled workers. A new form of business organization, the corporation, was introduced. So was a modern banking system. All these and more were left by the British when they gave up political power. The present Indian economy is based on this economic foundation.

The Indian Economy Depends Heavily on Agriculture

Almost 75 percent of India's people earn their living by farming, and 40 percent of India's national income comes from agriculture. If India's growing population is to be fed, agricultural production must increase. If its economy is to become more industrialized and provide employment and a better life for its people, part of that growth must come from funds derived from increased farm production.

Since independence, state government leaders have enacted land-reform measures. They did so with the hope that peasants might be more willing to improve their land and thus grow more crops if they owned their own farmland.

Land divided among the farmers. The zamindar's tax-collecting role was abolished, and farmers now paid their taxes directly to the state government. The zamindars were allowed to keep some land for themselves and hire farm laborers to till it. Farm tenants were to become landowners by purchasing from their landlords the land they had farmed. Under new rules the landowner was to collect no more than half of a tenant's crop as rent. Restrictions were placed on the amount of farmland a person could own. To promote more efficient production, efforts were made to combine scattered small plots of land into larger farms.

While some tenants have benefited from the legal reforms, most have not. Various ways have been found to evade the reform laws. For example, excess farmland was transferred by owners to relatives, thus keeping the land within the family. Almost half of India's farmers own less than one acre of land or no land at all. Only one percent own 50 acres of land or more. Consequently most Indian farmers have too little farmland and are too poor to improve their land and increase their farm production.

Farm cooperatives. The Indian government has encouraged the organization of cooperative farms. In a cooperative, members combine their land, tools, work animals, and labor. Each member continues to own property but shares in the benefits of large-scale farming. Large farm owners who hire workers for their land find it profitable to form such cooperatives, but some farmers have such small holdings and so few tools that even the cooperative effort is not worthwhile for them.

Government sponsors Community Development Program. To transform the economic and social life of the villages, the Indian government set up the Community Development Program. Its goal was to increase farm production with new methods of farming and to improve the villager's life by introducing better sanitation, housing, education, communication, and village industries.

This ambitious program centered on a group of 300 villages with about 200,000 people. The 300 villages were divided into three development blocks, and each block was further subdivided into groups of five villages. Village-level workers took charge of the smaller group. Their job was to help put the ideas of the villagers into action. Where there was a strong desire, much was accomplished. Villagers dug wells, organized primary schools and adult education programs, built roads, and set up health centers. In villages where there was great resistance to change and weak village-level workers, the program failed. While not entirely successful, the Community Development Program serves as a model for future farm improvement programs.

The Green Revolution. The green revolution involves the use of science and technology in agriculture to increase farm production. Farm output has soared as industrial production did when science and technology were applied to the manufacturing process. India turned to science to help solve its food problem. By

Different farmers use old and new technology to achieve the same effect. The farmer in the Punjab (left) uses cattle to pull his plow, while the group at the Nirmal Hriday Ashram secondary school in Midnapore uses a power tiller provided by CARE. The power tiller is also rented out to farmers on nearby farms, and the proceeds invested to support the school.

using hybrid wheat and rice seeds produced by the Rockefeller and Ford foundations in Mexico and the Philippine Islands and new grain seed produced by Indian research stations, some Indian farmers were able to double or triple farm output. To make these high yielding seeds work, the farmer needed a dependable water supply, high doses of chemical fertilizers and pesticides, and the proper farm machinery. If one element in this package was missing or applied at the wrong time, the high yield would not result.

Results of the pilot programs with the new seeds were fantastic. But by the mid-1970s the promise of abundant harvests looked far off. Costs of needed fertilizers soared, and India had to use limited funds to import food for hungry people today. Meanwhile India pressed its exploration for oil, a raw material for fertilizers.

Most farmers are too poor to profit from the Green Revolution. One-quarter of all farmers are tenants who till someone else's land. Tenants pay all costs of producing the crop, while the landowner gets at least half the harvest. For most Indian farmers, the high costs of new farming methods prevent the use of the new high-yielding seeds.

Many changes must be made before new farm techniques can be widely used in India. New seed farms are needed to produce the high-yield varieties of seed. Additional chemical factories are needed to supply agricultural chemicals. Factories which produce sprayers, dusters, and water pumps must be expanded. Storage facilities are needed for the enlarged food crops. Highly skilled workers are needed for continuous research.

Reviewing Your Reading

1. How were goods and services exchanged in the villages?
2. What British changes helped to lessen the dangers of famine?
3. What effect did the sale of British goods have on India?
4. Describe the land reform program after independence. How successful was it?
5. How were farm cooperatives and the Community Development Program intended to benefit the farmers? How successful was this effort? Why?
6. What is the Green Revolution? How might it affect Indian agriculture?

Central Planning in the Indian Economy

The government guides the economic development of India under five-year plans that set the production goals to be met by various industries. These plans are quite different from those in socialist countries like China and the Soviet Union in that producers are not forced to accept government production quotas. In Indian planning, private businesses have much freedom, but on occasion may be pressured to accept government goals.

In India modern large-scale industries and small farms, cottage industries, and small businesses exist side by side. To lay the foundation for a modern industrial economy, economic plans call for the establishment of so-called heavy industries – iron and steel, machine tools, electrical, mining, chemical, and cement factories. Officials hope that these industries will end India's dependence on foreign goods, promote the development of its own resources, and provide a base for more rapid economic growth.

Large-scale industries. Textiles are the oldest and best organized industry in India. Indians produce enough cotton, silk, wool, and jute to meet their needs at home and sell their products in foreign markets. The iron and steel industry can supply most of Indian needs for these metals. Located near iron ore and coal deposits, Jamshedpur (*jahm'*shed-poor) in eastern India is the chief site of the iron and steel industry. Other plants are planned or are being built with foreign financial and technical assistance.

With the exception of coal, India's minerals are inadequately developed. Most mines are worked by hand and are not very efficient. India has recently built an atomic power plant, relying for the most part on its own nuclear scientists and technologists.

Cottage industry and small-scale enterprises. India's smaller factories and cottage industries provide more jobs than its modern industries do. Individually owned factories produce such consumer goods as bicycles, electric fans, sewing machines, hardware, and hand tools. Government agencies lend support by providing loans and improved production methods.

India is noted for its handmade objects, such as brass work, carved ivory, rugs, and handloomed fabrics. These are made by individuals in their cottages.

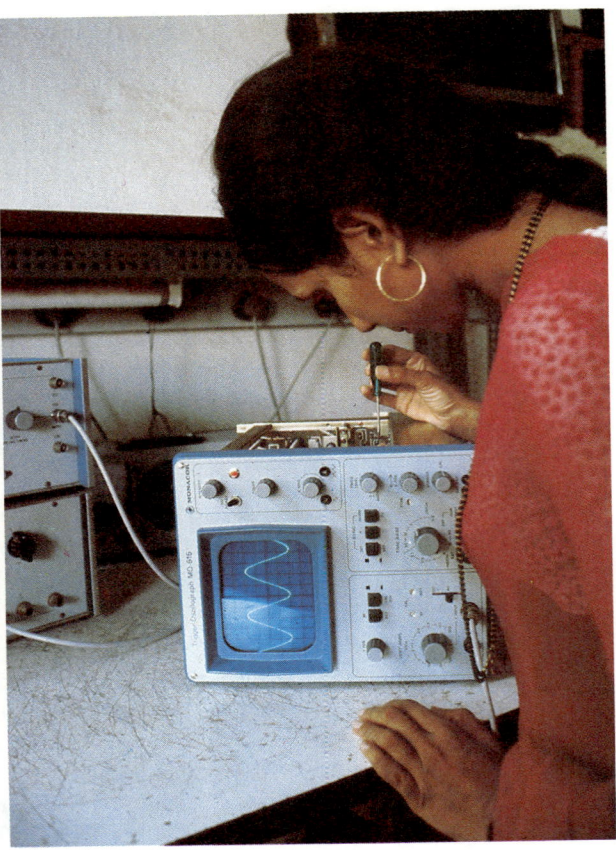

Cottage industries like this carpet weaver (left) are still quite important to India's economy, but modern technology is taking hold. The woman at the right is calibrating an oscilloscope manufactured in Bombay for export to the West.

Cottage industry provides the vegetable oil, pottery, bricks, and wood plows used in the villages.

Considering India's great size and the smallness of its modern economy, fairly steady progress has been made under the five-year plans. Although plan goals are not always achieved and much more economic development must occur before the country can provide more employment opportunities for its people, India is intent on becoming an industrial nation.

Foreign aid supports many Indian industrial programs. Many foreign governments, including the United States and the Soviet Union, give economic aid to India. Some is in the form of grants which are not repaid. The aid agreements require India to buy goods in the country giving the aid, even if such goods can be purchased more cheaply abroad.

Privately owned foreign businesses are encouraged by the Indian government to build plants in India if they fit the into government's economic plans. Such a practice gives the multinational corporation access to a foreign market. In addition, it supplements Indian investment funds, adds to India's technical knowledge, reduces its imports, and provides additional employment. Then, in time, it leads to more purchases – of raw materials, parts, tools, and basic services – from Indian businesses. The use of foreign workers is discouraged. As soon as Indian workers are trained and available to operate a facility, foreign workers must leave.

Bhopal Disaster

As Indian industrialization progresses, environmental problems like air and water pollution appear. They are seen, however, as a symptom of economic growth. Laws have been enacted to prevent and control such pollution, but they are scarcely enforced.

In December 1984, at Bhopal, toxic chemical fumes were released at a pesticide plant owned by an Indian subsidiary of the Union Carbide Corporation. Within hours, tens of thousands of people were killed or injured in the world's worst industrial accident.

Stopping industrialization is not the way to prevent such accidents. A modern economy can help provide a better life for many people. But modern plants must be properly operated. This requires trained workers, experienced technicians, and close supervision by plant managers. Plants that work with toxic or hazardous materials must have "fail-safe" equipment. Companies must see to it that local managers implement safety procedures. And government officials must enforce tough safety and antipollution laws.

The most deadly industrial accident in history occurred in Bhopal, India, in December 1984. Deadly methyl isocyanate gas escaped from a U.S.–owned pesticide plant, killing several thousand and forcing tens of thousands, like this family, to flee.

Rapid population growth handicaps economic development. Only about a dozen countries have higher gross national products than India, but in per capita income it is one of the poorest nations in the world. In 1977 per capita income was $150. India's rapid population growth has prevented it from making greater economic progress. The country has more than 730 million people, and that number increases naturally by 1.9 percent each year. Some 85 percent of the people live in villages. It is a youthful nation: 1979 estimates indicated that 43 percent of the people were under fourteen years of age and only 5 percent were over sixty.

While people can be one of the greatest resources of a nation, they also can be a serious problem for a country seeking to improve its economy. Gains in economic growth are wiped out as the population grows. No significant improvement in the living standard can occur because more people must share in any improvements.

Why has population increased so rapidly? In this century, India's population has almost tripled. Greater availability of food and improved public health have made this possible. Food production has increased as more farmland has been irrigated. Modern medicine reduced the death rate from diseases. Life expectancy in India rose in five decades from 27 years in 1931 to 56 years in 1981. At the same time, the increased rate of population growth threatens further dietary and economic improvement.

India has a high birth rate. Almost all Indians marry young and rear families. More child-bearing couples survive as the death rate declines. Cultural customs promote births, for sons are desired to help in the family work, to support aged parents, and to officiate at the father's funeral rites.

India's political leaders favor family planning. Since 1952 the Indian government has actively promoted voluntary family planning with the hope of cutting the rate of population growth. Publicity is carried on to promote the idea of a small family. People are trained to administer the program and to encourage Indians to use the available family planning assistance.

This is an extremely difficult task in a hugh, populous land with a high rate of illiteracy. Progress is slow and uncertain.

Reviewing Your Reading

1. What are five-year plans? How does the Indian version differ from the Chinese and Russian versions?
2. Describe the main features of India's economy.
3. What is the role of foreign aid in Indian economic development?
4. Account for the rapid growth of the Indian population in this century.
5. What is India doing to limit rapid population growth?

CHAPTER REVIEW

Recalling Names and Places

Community Development Program
cottage industry
Famine Code
five-year plan
Green Revolution
Jamshedpur

Understanding This Chapter

1. What changes in the Indian economy resulted from British economic innovations?
2. How has technology changed Indian agriculture in recent years? What has it left unchanged?
3. What function do five-year plans serve in a noncommunist economic system? What advantages do they offer? What are their drawbacks?
4. What might be seen as a proper role for large multinational corporations in a less developed country like India? What can the multinational corporation do to make this interaction work? What can the government of a country like India do? What can happen when foreign corporations and host governments fail to cooperate fully?
5. How can rapid population growth become a problem for an economically undeveloped country?

Chapter 20

Monarchy, Colonialism, and Independence

Monarchy was the principal form of government in ancient and medieval India. Kings took such titles as "Great King of Kings, Supreme Lord" and served the role of gods on earth. Failure to obey the king meant punishment both by the gods and the king's soldiers. The king regarded all people as his children. He was expected to keep his subjects content and render prompt justice. If he failed to protect them or if he were harsh, the king could be overthrown by an uprising.

For all the intense fighting that was carried on, no monarch was able to establish a permanent empire. The subcontinent was too large, and no king was able to organize a civil service capable of administering it.

After the Turkish Muslims conquered much of India in 1527, they established a centralized government organized along military lines under an absolute emperor. The system prevailed for centuries and influenced the British in their rule of India.

British Government in India

After the Sepoy Mutiny (p. 205) was put down, the British government assumed direct responsibility for governing the subcontinent. The Viceroy and his Council in India were responsible to the Secretary of State for India in London and, through him, to the British Cabinet and Parliament.

Most of India was divided into provinces controlled by a governor. Each province was further divided into districts presided over by the district officer, who collected taxes, maintained law and order, and dispensed justice. The British controlled the princely states by providing a resident British official as an "advisor."

The British Indian Army and a small number of powerful British officials in the Indian Civil Service governed and protected the whole of India. Key government positions were held by civil servants who were carefully recruited and trained. In general, these men were highly efficient and honest. Gradually, Indians were assigned to lower-level government positions. By 1947, when the British left India, the Indian officials outnumbered the British members of the civil service.

The development of self-government in British India. By a series of British parliamentary acts beginning in 1861, India slowly moved in the direc-

THE INDIAN SUBCONTINENT: POLITICAL

✹ National capital

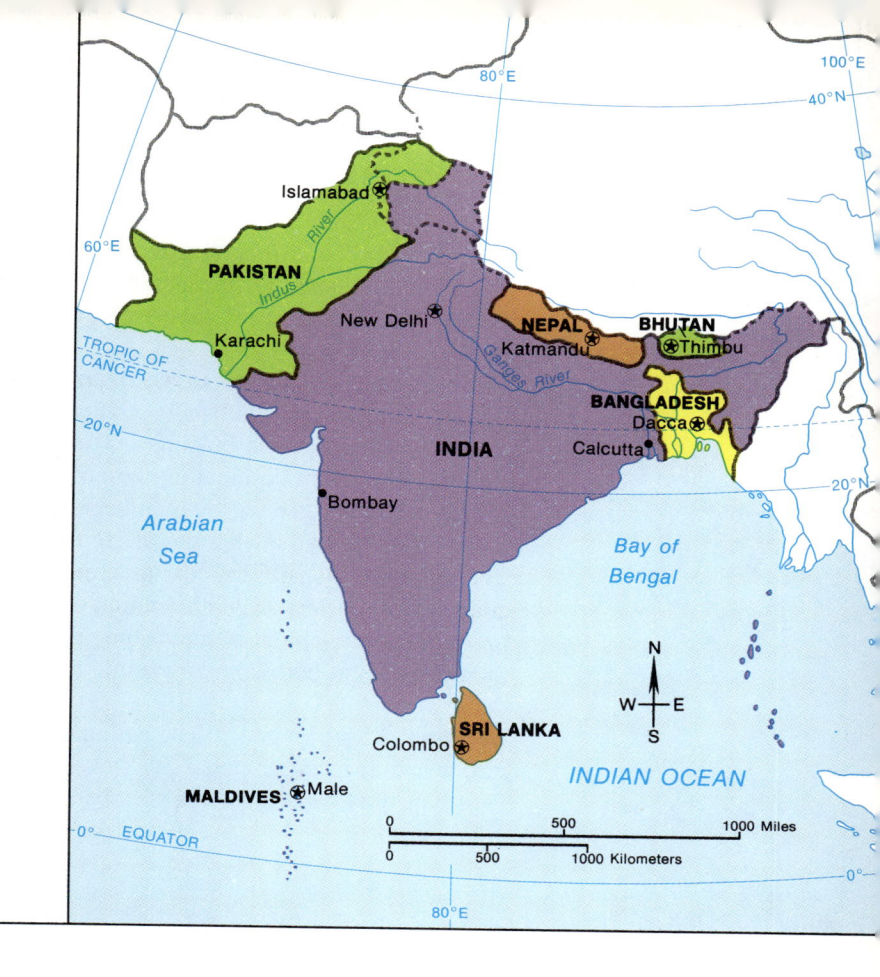

tion of self-government. These concessions were not granted solely out of kindness by the British, but in response to the demands of the Indian nationalist movement. Over the years the Council was enlarged, and the number of Indian members increased.

In the provinces, Indians gradually gained more responsibility. Until 1935 British governors ruled the provinces with legislatures composed of both British and Indian members. Then the governor and his council were made accountable to the legislature where Indians were granted greater authority. Thirty-five million voters, including 6 million women, were eligible to vote in the provincial elections at this time. Though many Indian nationalists were dissatisfied with the provincial governments, they participated in the 1937 elections. The Congress Party won control of many state governments and governed the provinces well. This experience in self-government ended after Britain involved India in World War II, when the Congress Party boycotted these governments. In the last year before Indian independence, the prewar provincial governments were again reestablished.

Hence, in less than a century after the British government assumed direct responsibility for India, Indians exercised increasing responsibility in democratic government. They have continued to operate such a form of government since independence.

Indian Government Today

India's constitution provides for a democratic republic with a parliamentary government. It is a federal government in which authority is divided between the central and state governments. The government is to be neutral in religious matters, and there are no separate legislative seats for specific religious groups.

Indian government has three branches. The 1950 constitution follows the British example by establishing a three-branch government – executive, legislative, and judicial. Each branch was to be able to check the other to prevent any single branch from dominating the government.

The president, elected by members of parliament and the state legislatures, is the head of the nation, but the office deals primarily with ceremonial functions. The actual responsibility for governing lies with the prime minister and the council of ministers, who are members of parliament. The leader of the majority party in the parliament becomes the prime minister. The prime minister appoints the council, but both are responsible to the parliament.

Bicameral legislature. The national legislature meets in New Delhi, the capital, when it is in session. The lower house, *Lok Sabha* (loke sah-*bah'*), the House of the People, has 544 members, 525 of whom are directly elected by the

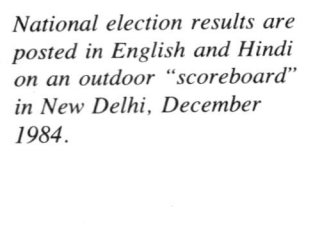

National election results are posted in English and Hindi on an outdoor "scoreboard" in New Delhi, December 1984.

voters for a five-year term. The president appoints the rest. The Lok Sabha is the more important house, for the prime minister and the council come out of it, and all money bills originate in it.

The states are represented in the upper house, the Council of States, or *Rajya Sabha (rah-*jyah sah-*bah')*. It has more than 250 members. In 1980 state legislatures elected 232 of its members while the rest, who represent "literature, science, art, and social service," were appointed by the president. This body has limited powers. The rules followed by the parliament are similar to those of the British Parliament. Debates are usually in English, though Hindi is used. A member who cannot speak either language can speak his or her own tongue.

Judicial system. There is a single judicial system for all of India. Each state has lower courts and a high court. Cases can proceed to the Supreme Court, which can pass on the constitutionality of any law.

State and local governments play an important part in national affairs. While the central government in India has great authority, it depends on the state governments to carry out all major programs. The federal government in New Delhi must work through state and local officials who have direct contact with the Indian people and are more familiar with the problems that concern them most. State political figures are less westernized, less familiar with the English language, less concerned with the world beyond their own state, more tradition-bound and influenced by caste. In addition to the usual governmental tasks, state governments have a new role – to raise the villagers' minimum standard of living by promoting economic development and social welfare.

India has seventeen states, some of which have more land and people than many European countries. Each state governor is appointed by India's President, but a Chief Minister and Cabinet responsible to the state legislature have the real governing power. Legislators are elected directly by the voters.

Indian Political Parties

India suffers from widespread illiteracy. Many villagers have little understanding of voting or experience in it. Thus elections in India are somewhat different from elections in democratic countries where the literacy rate is higher. All adults over age 21 are eligible to vote. To aid the illiterate voter, each political party has a symbol that is placed alongside its candidate's name on the paper ballot. Voters put their marks beside the symbol of their choice and cast their ballots in secret. Indelible ink is put on their hands to prevent them from voting more than once. Elections are spread over many days to enable people in remote areas to vote.

India's government is based on coalitions. The Congress Party dominated the political scene and controlled the national government in India from 1947 to 1967. In 1969 the Congress Party split into two factions supporting different candidates. In 1971 Mrs. Indira Gandhi's wing of the Party won the national elections. The general election of 1977 resulted in the first victory for a coalition party, the Janata Party, an alliance of four noncommunist parties. In 1980, however, Gandhi returned to power when the Congress-I party won a parliamentary

Congress Party

CPM

Swatantra

SSP

Jan Sangh

Many of India's voters are illiterate, so each political party identifies itself in its literature and on the ballot by a symbol.

243

Prime Minister Indira Gandhi (center), with her son Rajiv (left) and three of her grandchildren, at the funeral of her other son, Sanjay, in 1981. Indira Gandhi was grooming Sanjay to be her successor as head of the Congress-I Party and the government, but he crashed his private plane and died. Rajiv Gandhi eventually succeeded his mother, despite electoral challenges from, among others, Sanjay's widow Maneka (at extreme right in this picture).

majority in the national elections. Four years later, after Gandhi was assassinated, her son Rajiv, general secretary of the party, succeeded her. Just over a month later, in December 1984, Rajiv Gandhi and the Congress-I party won a landslide victory in new national elections

There are a number of conservative political parties as well as several socialist and communist parties. Communal political parties based on religious belief, language, or caste exist. While such parties seldom do well on the national level, some have won state and local elections.

Language and politics. With independence, the great language diversity of India had to be faced. In addition to the 14 major languages listed in the constitution, over 700 languages and dialects are spoken in India today. A common language for all India would help unify the country.

In 1950 English and Hindi were made the official languages of government. English continues to be used in the central government. However, non-Hindi-speaking people objected to the proposed exclusive use of Hindi because it would be a disadvantage in employment. Others feared it would lead to North Indian domination of the country.

Under growing pressure, India's state boundaries were redrawn starting in 1952 to conform to the language of the most people in the area. Eleven states have been reorganized along language lines. These states, with tens of millions of people each speaking the same language and sharing a common history and culture, could weaken the unity of the nation.

India's human rights concerns are deeply rooted in religious and caste friction, which frequently erupts into violence. A major conflict in 1984 involved the Sikhs, a religious minority. Hard-working and relatively prosperous, the Sikhs are prominent in the army, industry, and government. They are largely responsible for the success of the "Green Revolution" (p. 234). Despite these achievements, some Sikhs feared their absorption by the Hindu majority.

To secure their religion and language the Sikhs formed a political party, the Akali Dal. This party's efforts to wrest more political control of the Punjab region from the government of Prime Minister Indira Gandhi failed. Then Sikh extremists turned to violence. In June 1984 the Indian army attacked and defeated armed Sikhs at the Sikhs' most sacred temple, the Golden Temple, at Amritsar in the Punjab. On the last day of October of that year, Indira Gandhi was killed by two members of her bodyguard who were Sikhs. A more flexible government policy might have achieved an accommodation with the Sikhs. Nevertheless, separatist sentiment was temporarily stilled and a united India preserved.

Sikhs crowded into the Golden Temple at Amritsar to celebrate its reopening in February 1985, several months after government forces laid siege to the sacred building and routed a rebellious Sikh militia. Some members of this religious minority, which is heavily represented in the armed forces, want to make the Indian state of Punjab an independent Sikh nation.

Foreign Relations

India plays a significant role in world affairs, despite the fact it has neither the economic nor military might to be a major power. It is influential among Asian and African nations and, as a former colony, has been critical of colonialism wherever it exists.

Nonalignment has been a major feature of Indian foreign policy. It has steadfastly refused to bind itself in any alliance with either the United States or Soviet power blocs, although India has at times accepted economic and military aid from both countries.

In 1971 India and the Soviet Union signed a twenty-year friendship treaty. Each country pledged to hold "mutual consultations" and "take appropriate effective measures" if either is attacked by a third country.

Several facts have influenced India's foreign policy. India shares a 1500-mile border with China along the Himalayan frontier, and it is separated by only a few miles from the Soviet Union. Its policies are also affected by its need to develop its economy and by its years of colonial rule.

Indian relations with Pakistan. Since independence, the internal rivalry between the Muslims and Hindus on the subcontinent has been transformed into an international rivalry between India and Pakistan.

Tension ran high over the possession of the former state of Kashmir and over the use of the waters of the Indus River system. Pakistan is heavily dependent on rivers for irrigation of its farmland. Of the six rivers that flow into the Indus River, three flow through northwestern India into Pakistan. These could be diverted for Indian use rather than flowing into the irrigation canals of Pakistan. In 1960 the Indus Water Treaty settled the dispute. India now uses the waters of the three eastern rivers and Pakistan the three western rivers. At the same time, with the assistance of the World Bank, a fund of almost $1 billion was created for further expansion of the irrigation system.

Disagreement over Kashmir causes friction between the two countries. The Kashmir question still remains a sore point between the two countries. The majority of the population of the Indian state of Kashmir at the time of the partition was Muslim. The ruler was a Hindu who associated himself with India. While India promised to hold a national election to enable the inhabitants of Kashmir to vote for their political future, the election was never held. Negotiations between India and Pakistan over the status of Kashmir failed, and United Nations mediation did not succeed. A border incident between the two countries grew into a war in 1965. While India regards the Kashmir question as settled, Pakistan does not. The problem will smolder for some time to come.

East Pakistan becomes Bangladesh. When British rule ended in the subcontinent in 1947, its former colony was split into two countries, Pakistan and India. Pakistan was divided into West and East Pakistan with India between the two parts. West Pakistan was almost six times the size of East Pakistan, but the eastern portion of the country had a larger population. The Punjabi people dominated in the West, with the Bengalis dominant in East Pakistan. While both sections are heavily agricultural, the West is more economically developed.

Bangladesh, the most densely populated nation in the world, has been struck by disasters both political and geographic in the years since it gained its independence from Pakistan. Wars, famines, floods, and tidal waves have struck time and again. This mother and child fled to a refugee camp after heavy flooding drove them from their homes in 1974.

Constitutional rule in Pakistan ended shortly after independence, and Punjabi military officers ran the national government. Relations between West and East Pakistan became strained shortly after independence. East Pakistanis had little voice in the government and felt that not enough was being done to promote their economic development.

The first national election since independence was held in 1970 as the first step in the restoration of civil government. After an East Pakistan political party won the election, the president of Pakistan postponed the opening of the parliament. Demonstrations took place in East Pakistan in 1971 against this action. As the call for an independent nation, Bangladesh, grew, the Pakistan army moved to crush the movement. Thousands of East Pakistanis were killed, and millions of Bengali refugees fled into India. As India aided the Bangladesh guerrillas, clashes between Indian and Pakistani troops erupted into a full-scale war. When the Indian army entered East Pakistan, in support of the East Pakistanis, an independent Bangladesh came into existence. Indian troops left the country in 1972.

India and China. After the Communist victory in China in 1949, India established diplomatic relations with the People's Republic of China and fought for its admission to the United Nations. The friendly relations between the two Asian nations began to decline within ten years. India had a special interest in the smaller nations of Nepal, Bhutan, and Sikkim (annexed in 1974), which border China. It is responsible for their foreign relations. China's occupation of Tibet after 1950 created a major security problem for India and was seen as a threat to its northern borders.

The ruthless suppression by the Chinese of an uprising in Tibet in 1959 and the flight at that time of the Dalai Lama, the spiritual and political leader of Tibet, and thousands of his followers to India turned many Indians against China. Since then, border incidents over the Ladakh region of Kashmir and the border area between Burma and Bhutan have seriously strained relations between the two countries.

India and the Soviet Union. Some Indians are impressed with the Soviet Union's economic progress and think it is a model for them to follow. Trade agreements exist between the two countries, and Soviet economic aid has helped to build port facilities, a steel mill, and a jet-fighter factory. The USSR supported India's invasion of Portuguese Goa and its position on the Kashmir question.

India and the United States. The United States gives economic aid to India in the form of development and technical assistance grants and loans. The United States has tended to see itself as the principal defense against the threat of world Communist domination. India is less convinced of this threat and refuses to be allied with the United States. Consequently, the two countries do not always see eye to eye. In 1980, for example, the Indian government did not join the United States in strong opposition to the Soviet occupation of Afghanistan.

CHAPTER REVIEW

Recalling Names and Places

Bangladesh	Indira Gandhi	Lok Sabha
communal party	Indus Water Treaty	Rajya Sabha
Congress Party		Sikhs

Understanding This Chapter

1. Trace the growth of self-government in India under the British.
2. Describe India's executive, legislative, and judicial branches of government.
3. Describe voting procedures in India.
4. What are the various types of Indian political parties? Describe their policies.
5. Why is language such an important matter for India? What barriers are there to a common language for India?
6. What is meant by nonalignment? What importance does it have to India's foreign policy?
7. Describe India's relations with Pakistan and Bangladesh.
8. Describe India's relations with China, the Soviet Union, and the United States.

Chapter 21

Indian Culture Shaped by Religion

India's religions have had a strong influence on Indian art, architecture, and science. The temples and sculpture of India are unique. One needs a knowledge of Hinduism and Buddhism to appreciate their complexity. Indian architectural techniques and artistic expression influenced other Asian countries, as we shall see when we study China, Japan, and Southeast Asia.

Buddhist Art

Early Buddhist art used no human image of the Buddha. He was depicted in symbols: the lotus for his birth; the bodhi tree, his enlightenment; the wheel, his teaching; footprints, his renunciation. Around the first century A.D. Greek sculptors in northwestern India and Afghanistan created the first Buddha in human form. The sculptors created a youthful-faced Buddha dressed in a Roman toga with many folds. This Greek Buddha was the model for later works by Indian, Chinese, and Japanese artists.

The distinctive marks which appear on the image of the Buddha are signs of his physical perfection and supernatural powers. A lump on his head, sometimes disguised with wavy locks of hair or a top knot, represents the supreme wisdom attained in enlightenment. A large circular halo signifies divine radiance. *Mudras,* or hand gestures, are clues to understanding the Buddha statues. When the Buddha is seated in a crosslegged lotus position with his hand as shown on page 382 he is in the mudra for meditation.

Buddhist architecture. A *stupa* is a dome-shaped earthen mound covered with plastered brick containing relics of the Buddha. It is topped with an umbrella, a symbol of royalty, made of circular stone disks. The stupa at Sanchi has a stone railing with four gateways, or *torana,* one facing in each direction. Each gateway is covered with carvings depicting scenes from the life of the Buddha. These carvings of people, trees, plants, animals, and buildings show ancient Indian life.

Stupa worship was quite popular among Buddhists. It must have presented a colorful pageant as the pilgrims walked in devotion with flags, flowers, and musical instruments around the white-plastered stupa.

The earliest Buddhist sanctuaries were cave temples. Buddhists often carved temples out of the hillsides. One of the best known is the Buddhist cave temple at Karli. It has three doorways to let light into the 124-foot-long hall. At the far end of the hall is a solid stone stupa topped with a wooden umbrella. Inside the temple are massive pillars. On the tops of these pillars are carvings of riders mounted on horses and elephants. These pillars support the 46-foot-high roof.

Mudras are hand gestures used to express ideas or emotions.

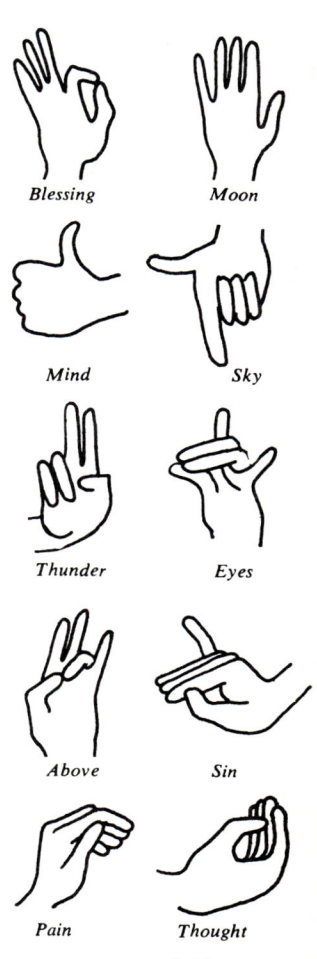

Blessing *Moon*

Mind *Sky*

Thunder *Eyes*

Above *Sin*

Pain *Thought*

249

Adjacent to the temple are the monk's cells, each with a doorway and a solid stone bed.

Another striking example of Buddhist cave temples is the Ajanta (ah-*jan*'tah) caves. The twenty-nine caves at Ajanta were carved from almost sheer cliff. Most of the cave temples have richly carved doorways, some with a horseshoe-shaped opening to admit light. Inside the caves are stupas and large Buddhas, seated or reclining in nirvana. Some cave walls are covered with lovely paintings.

Hindu Art

Although Hindu temples vary greatly in architectural style, they had to conform to strict guidelines as to their general design. A standard temple has a shrine room topped by a tower. The room contains the image of the chief deity and a hall for worshipers which is approached by a porch.

Hindu temples are free-standing. Ellora is an example of the type of structure that replaced the cave temples. This eighth-century Hindu temple was carved by masons out of the black volcanic rock of a sloping hillside. Starting at the top of the hill, workers chiseled their way down to its base to create the tem-

An Indian bodhisattva or deity shows the influence of Greek sculpture in his toga and facial features.

ple. An estimated 200,000 tons of stone were chipped away to produce an enormous pit. The solid stone temple rises 96 feet from the floor of the pit. The temple is dedicated to the god Shiva. It is flanked by two lofty stone columns.

The temples of Khajuraho, the capital of an ancient Indian kingdom, typify the North Indian style. Built on a stone platform, each temple has circular towers that narrow as they rise. Smaller towers accent the principal tower. Hundreds of figures adorn the interior and the exterior of the temple from top to bottom. The massive temples appear rooted to the earth, tying the religious shrine with the natural world.

The enormous double temple of Madurai, in South India, has high outer walls with four entrances. Most of the temple is covered by a flat roof supported by hundreds of pillars. Some are unadorned, while others are intricately carved with Hindu deities or fantastic mythological creatures. Some of the deities are stained with red powder or grimy with *ghee,* a kind of butter that Hindu worshipers use. On the temple grounds is the large Pond of the Golden Lilies where worshipers bathe.

Hindu sculpture. The sculpture of India is regarded as an instrument of worship and is often inseparable from temple architecture. Although the statues were made according to strict guidelines, individual sculptors produced widely

The Hindu temple at Ellora (on the facing page) was carved out of the solid rock of a hillside. The double temple at Madurai (this page) is an example of the extremely intricate southern Indian style of architecture.

different sculptural styles. Figures from Hindu literary epics and religious texts were favorite subjects for sculpture.

South Indian bronze figures were first designed in wax over a core and then covered with a clay coating. When heated, the wax melted leaving a mold that was filled with melted bronze. These bronzes varied in size. The base was fitted with handles for carrying in procession.

Islamic Architecture

Muslims were prominent patrons of the arts. A visitor to India remembers their red stone forts, palaces, and mosques, but their white marble tombs remain most vividly in the mind of the traveler. Such a tomb has a large dome, decorated with floral designs and an intricate network of Arabic inscriptions from the Koran delicately inscribed by Hindu artists. Inside the tomb the white marble floor may be lavishly decorated with semiprecious stones arranged in an elaborate floral pattern. Marble screens on the walls of the tomb are perforated in geometric patterns. This reduces the intensity of the sunlight in the interior and permits the breeze to pass through to ease the heat of a very hot land.

Taj Mahal. Perhaps the most beautiful Muslim tomb is the Taj Mahal. Built in twenty-two years during the seventeenth century, the Taj Mahal is a tomb for

An interior view of the Udaipur Lake Palace Hotel. Pierced marble and tinted glass are highlights of this Muslim building. Europeans were influenced by Muslim architecture in their creation of stained glass windows.

the wife of the Mughal emperor, Shah Jahan. Placed in a formal garden with fountains, the Taj Mahal rises above a white marble platform with a minaret at each corner. The tomb is 243 feet high.

There are no human figures depicted in the tomb because the Koran forbids it. The tombstones of the Shah Jahan and his wife are surrounded by a floral-patterned white marble screen.

Few examples of early Indian painting remain. Royal palaces and homes of the wealthy were adorned with murals painted by professional artists. Unfortunately, little has survived of ancient Indian painting. The walls, ceiling, and pillars of some Ajanta caves were covered with paintings. Clay mixed with straw or hair was applied to the wall and covered with white gypsum. Scenes from the life of the Buddha were painted on the wall when it dried. Cave paintings are filled with figures from everyday life and royal courts. In one, for example, a youthful bodhisattva holding a white lotus and wearing a crown is surrounded by divine figures. The skillfully drawn figure is called "Lord Who Looks Down in Compassion."

Reviewing Your Reading

1. How was the Buddha represented in early Buddhist art? What change did Greek sculptors introduce?
2. Describe the various types and features of Buddhist architecture.
3. What were the literary sources used for Hindu sculptures?
4. What architectural devices did Muslims introduce into India?

Indian Literature

India's two great ancient epics, the *Mahabharata* and the *Ramayana,* were memorized and recited orally long before they were written in Sanskrit. The *Mahabharata* is an account of a long war of succession and is filled with battle descriptions and feats of bravery by the heroes of both sides. It contains the *Bhagavad Gita* (*bug*'uh-vud *gee*'tuh), a major philosophical poem of the Hindu religion. Both the *Ramayana* and the *Mahabharata* express Hindu ideals of manhood, womanhood, and ethical behavior. These popular works were translated into many Indian languages.

Fables and plays. The *Panchatantra* (*pahn*'chah-*tan*'trah) is a collection of fables in prose and poetry in which animal characters speak and act like humans. The fables suggest ways of attaining wordly success and overcoming everyday problems. Translated into many languages, these stories provided themes for the *Fables* of La Fontaine and Hans Christian Anderson's stories.

Indian drama was performed privately for kings or wealthy persons or publicly in temples on festival days. There was no scenery and very few props. A highly developed system of body gestures helped the audience understand the characters and events. The viewers immediately recognized the heroes, heroines, villains, and other characters by their traditional costumes. The goal of

Stories from the Ramayana *have been a major source of artistic inspiration since the work's creation. This early seventeenth-century painting depicts the siege of Lanka.*

Sanskrit drama was to convey a mood. *Shakun-tala*, written by Kalidasa *(kah-lee-dah'suh)*, illustrates the mood of love and compassion. The play tells the story of the love of a hermit's daughter for a king, their separation and reunion.

Modern Indian literature. Prior to the introduction of the printing press by the British, books in India were handwritten. Only the wealthy could afford them. Much of Indian literature was in verse, though prose was sometimes used. The British encouraged the development of prose for government communications and for religious works used by missionaries. Indian writers adopted the novel form from British literature. Indian authors used the novel in the nationalist cause to glorify their country's past and to urge reforms.

Written in Hindi, *The Gift of a Cow* by Prem Chand is a vivid account of village life and a farmer's efforts to scratch a living from the soil. Raja Rao's *kanthapura*, as told by a grandmother, describes the efforts of a young man influenced by Gandhi to cut across caste barriers in a nonviolent protest.

Novels by Indian authors written in English supply much information about Indian life. The *Untouchable*, by Mulk Raj Anand, is a fast-moving account of a day in the life of a latrine cleaner and the humiliations he endures. R. K. Narayan's novel *Waiting for the Mahatma* depicts the influence of Gandhi on a young man. His *The Bachelor of Arts* deals with a recent university graduate who unsuccessfully seeks to find a job and a wife by himself. His protests at the marriage his parents have arranged disappear as he falls in love with his intended bride. Khushwant Singh's *Train to Pakistan* reveals the horrors of the India-Pakistan partition in a town where Hindus and Muslims had lived peacefully for centuries.

Indian Motion Pictures. India is the world's second largest producer of films, after Japan. A very popular type of movie is the mythological and historical film. It is based on traditional Hindu literature and features a good deal of songs and dances. The popular film is quite different from the realistic films of India's most renowned director, Satyajit Ray. *The Apu Trilogy*, directed by Ray, is a beautifully photographed story of an Indian boy's passage from childhood to manhood and fatherhood.

Ancient Indian Science, Mathematics, and Medicine

Much of Indian science, astronomy, and physics developed from religious thought. Astronomical knowledge was essential to set the date and time for religious sacrifices. Astrology was used to predict the future. Astronomers understood the causes of eclipses and could accurately forecast their occurrence. Scientific knowledge passed between Indians and Arabs and, through them, on to Europeans. Indian astronomers took the concepts of the seven-day week, the hour, and the signs of zodiac from European scholars.

Indian mathematical discoveries were impressive. Indian mathematicians used geometry to build altars and sacrificial places. They studied elementary algebra, trigonometry, and calculus. What are called Arabic numerals – nine dig-

Rabindranath Tagore (1861–1941), Bengali poet and Nobel Prize–winner, was highly respected both at home and abroad. Knighted by the British government, he gave up his title in 1919 to protest the Amritsar Massacre.

Advice to Indian Physicians

The physician was a highly respected member of Indian society. The following sermon was given at a religious ceremony to apprentices who completed their medical training.

If you want success in your practice, wealth and fame, and heaven after your death, you must pray everyday on rising and going to bed for the welfare of all beings, especially of cows and brahmans, and you must strive with all your soul for the health of the sick. You must not betray your patients, even at the cost of your own life. . . . you must not get drunk or commit evil, or have evil companions. . . . You must be pleasant of speech . . . thoughtful, always striving to improve your knowledge.

When you go to the home of a patient you should direct your words, mind, intellect and senses nowhere but to your patient and his treatment. . . . Nothing that happens in the house of the sick man must be told outside. Nor must the patient's condition be told to anyone who might do harm by that knowledge to the patient or to another.

From the book *The Wonder That Was India*, 3rd rev. ed., by Arthur L. Basham. (New York: Taplinger Publishing Co., 1968), p. 502.

Indian director Satyajit Ray is widely recognized as one of the world's great filmmakers.

its and a zero – were known by the Arabs as "Indian reckoning." This system of numbers was better for calculation than the Roman numeral system and aided further mathematical development.

Religion influenced Indian medicine. Indian medicine developed from interest in religion and yoga breathing exercises. Although scientists understood the importance of the spinal cord and knew of the existence of the nervous system, there was a religious taboo against contact with dead bodies. This discouraged dissection and the study of anatomy in India. Chemistry was devoted to developing medicines, potions for long life, poisons and their antidotes. A system of surgery with over a hundred surgical instruments existed. Indian doctors set bones, performed caesarian sections, and used plastic surgery to repair noses, ears, and lips scarred by battlefield wounds.

Reviewing Your Reading

1. What are India's two great literary epics? How were they preserved before they were written down?
2. Describe Indian drama.
3. How did the British influence the development of modern Indian literature?
4. Describe Indian scientific and mathematical achievements. What role did religion play in their development?
5. Describe Indian medical developments. How did Indian religion promote interest in medicine?

CHAPTER REVIEW

Recalling Names and Places

Ajanta	*Mahabharata*	Satyajit Ray
Bhagavad Gita	mudra	stupa
"Indian reckoning"	*Panchatantra*	Taj Mahal
Kalidasa	*Ramayana*	torana

Understanding This Chapter

1. Why didn't an Indian or other Asian artist prepare the first likeness of Buddha in human form?
2. Discuss some of the similarities of Hindu, Buddhist, and Islamic art. How is art from these groups different from art you have seen in your own culture? How is it similar?
3. Investigate the oral preservation of epic poems in cultures other than India's. Is this a common situation, or is it unique to India? What gets preserved in this way? How does this vary from culture to culture?
4. In many former colonies of European powers, writers have written important novels and other works in the language of the colonizers. How are Indian works written in English similar to, say, African works in English or French? How are they different? Why might an Indian writer choose to write in English?
5. How might a relatively poor country like India become one of the world's leading producers of a technologically complex art form like motion pictures? Why?

UNIT 5
Exploring
China

2000	1500	1000	500 B.C.	1 A.D.	500	1000	1500

- CONFUCIANISM/TAOISM c. 551
- BUDDHISM c. 1 A.D.
- MANCHU RULE QING DYNASTY 1644–1912
- HAN DYNASTY 206 B.C.–220 A.D.
- TANG DYNASTY 619–907
- EUROPEAN INFLUENCE 1514–1912
- SHANG DYNASTY c. 1750–c. 1122
- QIN DYNASTY 221–206
- REPUBLIC 1912–1949
- ZHOU DYNASTY c. 1100–c. 200
- CIVIL WAR 220–589
- COMMUNIST RULE 1949–
- DYNASTIC CHINA 1750 B.C.–1912 A.D.

MEASURING ALMOST 3000 MILES EAST to west and over 2500 miles north to south, China is the third largest nation in the world, larger than the United States. More than one billion people live in China, making it the world's most populous nation. The Chinese language is spoken by more people than any other in the world, for one out of every four people on earth is Chinese.

China has a 4000-year history. For much of that time the Chinese called their country the "Middle Kingdom" because they believed it to be the center of the world. Europeans called it China, taking the name from the Qin dynasty, which started the Chinese Empire. For more than 2000 years China dominated East Asia. Through the Chinese language, China's Confucian civilization spread beyond its borders to other Asian lands. Many aspects of Chinese civilization where borrowed by the Koreans, Japanese, and the Vietnamese.

Chinese dominance was challenged with the appearance of Westerners in Asia. For much of China's history it had little contact with the Western world. However, after the Industrial Revolution began in Europe in the eighteenth century, British, Dutch, American, and other Western traders began to travel the world over looking for new markets and new sources of raw materials. Christian missionaries wanted to preach the Scriptures to people beyond Europe. Pressures from the Western world eventually forced China into a century-long struggle that led to the collapse of its ancient Confucian way of life.

From the fall of the Middle Kingdom in 1912 until the Chinese Communists established the People's Republic of China in 1949, China suffered from both a civil war and a war against Japanese invaders. During this period China's leaders tried to modernize China and to remove all foreign presences from the land. In this effort the Nationalist leaders failed and, under Generalissimo Chiang Kai-shek, abandoned the Chinese mainland. They established themselves on the island of Taiwan, where they remain, claiming to be the rulers of all China.

Timeline

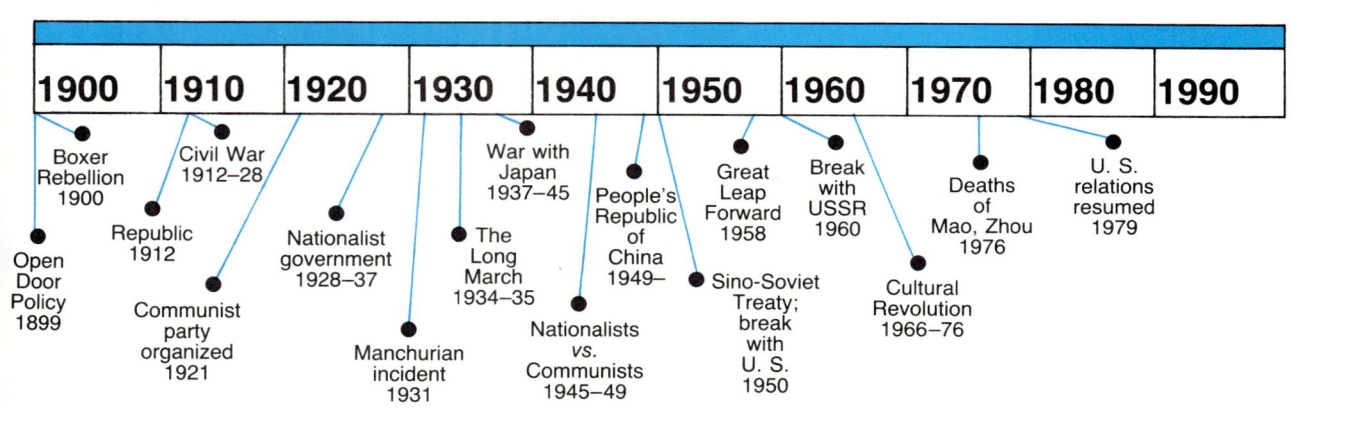

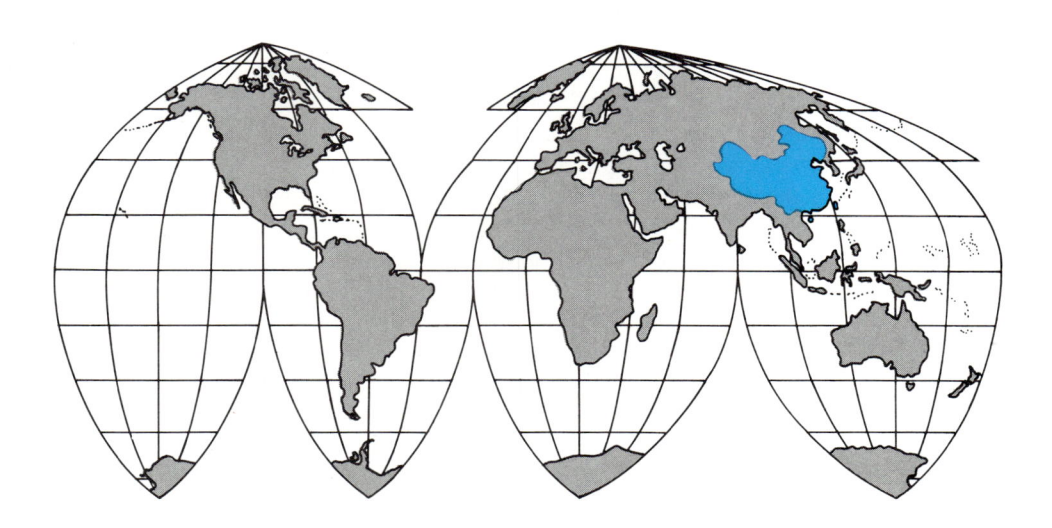

1899	Open Door Policy
1900	Boxer Rebellion
1912	Republic
1912–28	Civil War
1921	Communist party organized
1928–37	Nationalist government
1931	Manchurian incident
1934–35	The Long March
1937–45	War with Japan
1945–49	Nationalists vs. Communists
1949–	People's Republic of China
1950	Sino-Soviet Treaty; break with U.S.
1958	Great Leap Forward
1960	Break with USSR
1966–76	Cultural Revolution
1976	Deaths of Mao, Zhou
1979	U.S. relations resumed

For the last three decades, China has been under the direction of the Communists. It has embarked on an enormous experiment to transform itself into a modern industrial nation, capable of defending its land against all foreigners and improving the quality of life for the Chinese people. In this experiment many traditional Chinese values have been abondoned. The Communist ideology has provided a new value system. How successful this new way of life will be is not yet certain. The success of the Chinese Communists in transforming a land of farmers into a modern industrial nation will certainly influence people in other underdeveloped countries.

An understanding of Chinese civilization and history will enable us to appreciate China's past achievements. An understanding of the Communist effort to modernize China will give us a more realistic view of China today.

Chapter 22

China: Regions of Contrast

China, with 3,691,502 square miles, is the third largest country in the world. However, less than half of China's land can support human life. Ninety-six percent of China's billion people live in the eastern third of China, the region that contains virtually all of the cities shown on the map on page 218.

For many centuries the Pacific Ocean, deserts, rain forests, and high mountain ranges cut China off from the rest of the world. As the map on page 261 shows, the Pacific Ocean is China's eastern boundary, while the Yalu and Amur rivers are the boundaries of its northeastern territory. The Gobi (*go'bee*) Desert and the Altai Mountains border China in the north and northwest. The Tianshan and Pamir Mountains form China's western boundary. The Himalayan Mountains separate China from India in the southwest. Rugged mountains and jungles mark China's boundary with Burma, Laos, and Vietnam.

Historically the desert was the least effective of China's geographical barriers. Mongols and other invaders swept into China across the Gobi Desert. The Great Wall of China was started during the third century B.C. to protect China from the raids of the nomads of Central Asia. The wall stretches more than 1500 miles from the coast into northwestern China.

Climate and Terrain Divide China into Two Regions

The heavily populated area of eastern China is called China Proper. There are many contrasts between the landscape and climate of temperate northern China and the semitropical southeastern part of China Proper. These two areas are so distinct that geographers divide them into two regions, North and South China. The Qingling (*ching'ling'*) Mountains and the Huai (*hway*) River in central China mark the division between them. This mountain range prevents the monsoon rains which originate in the South China Sea from getting through to the northern plains. Consequently, 40 to 100 inches of rain per year fall on South China, while North China often gets less than 20 inches. The differences in rainfall between the two regions have played a large part in setting them apart. It has affected the types of crops that are grown, the houses that are built, and the clothing worn in these areas.

South China. Fertile plains are found around the rivers of this hot, humid region. The coast and the Xi (*she*) River valley have hilly land. During the monsoon season, heavy rains and water from the rivers are used to flood the rice paddies and make South China green. Rice is the main crop of the area. Because this region is warm almost year round, two or three rice crops can be grown in a single year. Corn, soybeans, and cotton are also grown in these rice provinces.

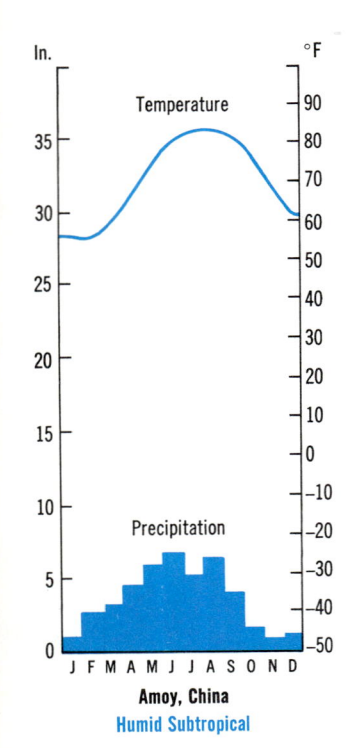

Amoy, China
Humid Subtropical

CHINA: PHYSICAL

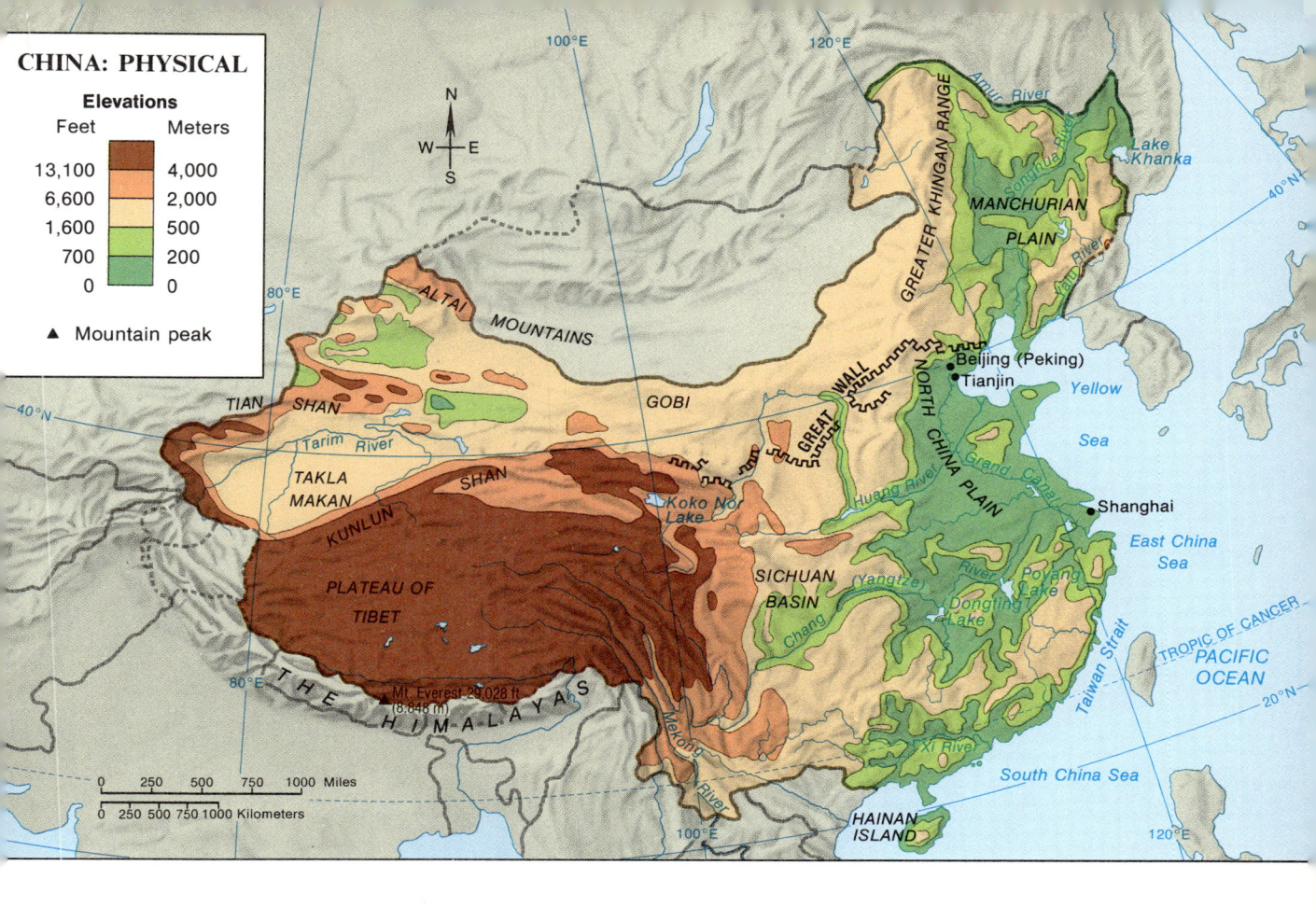

Elevations

Feet	Meters
13,100	4,000
6,600	2,000
1,600	500
700	200
0	0

▲ Mountain peak

Winter crops include wheat and barley. Tea is grown on the sides of hills. South China's farmers use the water buffalo for a work animal, and it is often seen in the streams and canals of the area.

North China. The climate of North China ranges from hot summers to very cold winters. Much of the region receives little rainfall. The rain that does reach North China comes chiefly in July and August and in irregular patterns. Eight inches of rain may fall in June one year, but less than an inch may fall during the same month the next year. This uncertainty in a crowded land is a fearsome matter. A drought one year may lead to severe famines. Sparse rainfall makes irrigation a necessity.

Wheat, which needs much less water than rice, is the main crop of the region. Such cereal grains as millet and sorghum are grown along with soybeans, sweet potatoes, corn, and cotton. Oxen, horses, and donkeys are the work animals of North China.

Outlying areas. To the north and west of the more populated regions of China are Mongolia, Xinjiang [Sinkiang] (*shin'jih-ahng'*), and Manchuria. Most sections of the area have not yet been developed, although Xinjiang is the site of China's nuclear center. Mongolia and Xinjiang are very dry lands. The Gobi Desert stretches across the southern part of Mongolia, and much of Xinjiang is also desert. With scant rainfall, little farming is possible. For the most

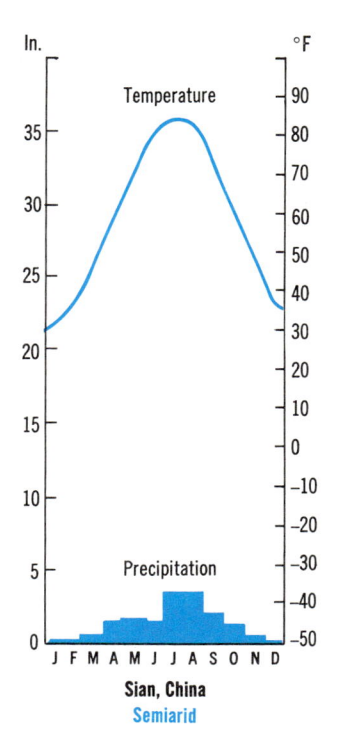

Sian, China
Semiarid

261

part the people are nomads who herd cattle, sheep, horses, and camels. Tibet is located in the mountain ranges of the Himalayas and the high barren plateau to the north. The Tibetans are herders, traders, and farmers. Manchuria to the northeast is rich in natural resources and is one of China's leading industrial centers. Many Chinese have recently migrated to this area from China Proper.

Ways of Writing Chinese Names

The Chinese language does not have an alphabet. It has thousands of written or printed characters, each one of which stands for a word (see page 329). This presents difficulties when we write about China and the Chinese in a language that uses an alphabet, such as English. Chinese words must be *transliterated* (or *romanized*) into strings of letters that reproduce something like the original's sound.

Until about 1978, most English-language works on China, including earlier editions of this book, used a method of transliteration devised by two nineteenth-century Englishmen. This *Wade-Giles* system (named after its developers) was thorough and helpful, but it had some problems. For example, the letters *k, p, t,* and the blend *ch* did not represent the sounds we normally associate with them unless they were followed by an apostrophe. Otherwise they stood for the sounds we associate with *g, b, d,* and *j.* A person who read the word *ching* would have to pronounce it "jing"; *ch'ing* would be pronounced "ching."

The Chinese government uses another method of transliteration in the English-language versions of its official publications. This system, called *pinyin,* was developed by the Chinese in the 1950s. Between 1978 and 1980 most American research libraries, universities, and journals switched from Wade-Giles to *pinyin,* at least for place names and modern historical figures.

Exploring World Cultures now generally uses the *pinyin* method of transliteration. Because this method is still unfamiliar, we often include the Wade-Giles spelling of a name or place in brackets after its first appearance. And, as in the rest of this book, we provide pronunciation guides for difficult names in parentheses. This can make for some long strings of names. When you read about "Zhou Enlai [Chou En-lai] (*joe' en-lie'*)," you are seeing the *pinyin* spelling, the Wade-Giles spelling, and the pronunciation, in that order.

Pinyin solves some of the pronunciation problems that arose in Wade-Giles, but it is not perfect. No method ever will be. Still, you are off to a good start in *pinyin* if you remember that the letter *q* is pronounced "ch" and the letter *x* is pronounced "sh". Most other letters bear some resemblance to their standard English pronunciations.

Pinyin versions are not given for the names of present or past Nationalist Chinese leaders or their organizations, because that is the strong preference of the government of the Republic of China (Taiwan). Thus Chiang Kai-shek, Sun Yat-sen, and the Kuomintang appear with only Wade-Giles versions and pronunciation guides. And some English versions whose origins are shrouded in the distant past—"Canton" for *Guangzhou,* "China" for *Zhongguo,* "Confucius" for *Kung Fuzi*—are left in their traditional forms.

A man looks down on China's Great Wall.

Many of Mongolia's herders, like the colorfully dressed group above, live in yurts — domed tents of animal skin stretched over a collapsible framework. Historically, yurts have been convenient homes for these nomadic peoples. Entire towns (right) often moved from place to place in search of good pasture land.

These areas have played an important role during some parts of China's history. The people of these areas are non-Chinese whose nomadic way of life has set them apart from Chinese civilization. While these border regions, with the exception of Manchuria, were held by China at various times, they were annexed in the last century.

China's Rivers Helped Shape Its History

The major rivers of China have been important in its development, but they have sometimes been as much a curse as a blessing. They originate in the west, flow eastward, and empty into the Pacific Ocean. Their abundant waters make irrigation possible and allow them to serve as aquatic highways. As China becomes more industrialized the usefulness of these rivers will certainly be increased. Construction of dams and reservoirs will help to control these rivers and provide places to store water for irrigation and flood prevention. The hydroelectric potential of these rivers can also be used.

The Huang River. Chinese civilization developed in the area of the Huang [Yellow] River in North China. However, few major cities have grown up along its banks because it cannot be navigated for great stretches of its 2,700 miles. The river was named for the yellow silt it carries along. The silt built up the river bed, raising the water level, and the Chinese had to build dikes to contain it. Because of this embankment, the Huang is in some places 16 to 40 feet above the level of the surrounding land.

Irrigation dikes in Zhejiang, China, enable farmers to regulate their water supply. The water is pumped into the rice paddies seen in the background.

At the Sanjiao People's Commune in Anhui province, farmers bring water to their fields from a series of criss-crossing artificial waterways.

The dikes allow North China's farmers to regulate the flow of water into the irrigation systems that cover the farmland. However, when the dikes break, large areas are flooded. Since the flood waters cannot drain into rivers, the water remains on the land until it is absorbed or evaporated. Since the flooded land cannot be farmed, famines have resulted in which millions of Chinese died. Understandably, the Huang is called "China's Sorrow." Under Communist rule the construction of large dams has brought the river under control.

The Chang River. The Chang [Yangtze] River is 3,200 miles in length and is China's most important river. Oceangoing vessels can travel to Wuhan, 630 miles up river, and smaller steamships can get 1000 miles farther up the river. Important agricultural and industrial centers have grown up along the banks of the river. Four major cities border the river – Chongqing (jong *ching'*) Wuhan, Nanjing, and Shanghai *(shang'* high), China's leading port.

Water transportation throughout central China is enhanced by a network of canals, including the famous Grand Canal. It was started 1300 years ago and eventually connected Hangzhou with Beijing to provide a waterway for travel from north to south. In imperial China it took forty days to move rice from Hangzhou to Beijing, as barges were pulled and poled by canal workers along its 1100 mile length.

The Xi River. The port of Canton is near the mouth of the Xi, or West, River in South China. Below the port is the British colony of Hong Kong, and across the bay from it is the Portuguese colony of Macao (muh-*cow'*). From these two colonies came the foreign influences that helped to shatter the ancient Chinese empire.

CHAPTER REVIEW

Recalling Names and Places

Chang River
Great Wall
Huang River
Manchuria
Middle Kingdom
Mongolia
North China
South China
Xi River
Xinjiang

Understanding This Chapter

1. Using a map supplied by your teacher, show the location of the mountains, rivers, and cities mentioned in this geography chapter. Include the Great Wall and lightly shade in the area where most Chinese live.
2. What are the features of the principal regions in China?
3. How have the major rivers affected Chinese historical development?
4. How has China's remoteness helped to shape its civilization?

Chapter 23

The Old China Gives Way to the New

Chinese history, prior to the early twentieth century, is divided into periods that coincide with the reign of dynasties. The Xia (shee-*ah'*) was the first dynasty but no archaeological remains have been found as yet.

Early Dynasties

Shang dynasty. The first historic dynasty, the Shang appeared around 1750 B.C. Nobles ruled their individual states and were united under the Shang king. He protected them, and they fought for him and gave him tribute.

Knowledge of the Shang dynasty comes from relics that Shang priests used in their religious ceremonies. The Shang rulers made sacrifices to the gods and to their ancestors. Believing in the supernatural, the rulers used the art of divination, foretelling the future, to answer important questions. Diviners wrote questions on animal bones and turtle shells. The bones were heated, and the cracks that resulted were interpreted for the king. These "oracle bones" were the earliest examples of Chinese writing. Glazed pottery and bronze vessels were made, and the wheel came into use.

China's classical age – the Zhou dynasty. Peoples from western China, the Zhou [Chou] (*joe*), conquered the Shang kingdom during the twelfth century B.C. and ruled China for nearly nine centuries.

The Zhou era was marked by feudalism under which the nobility kept the king from asserting his power over them. The economy grew with the use of iron tools, the iron-tipped plow, and irrigation. As trade expanded, new towns developed. A simple eating device, the chopstick, came into use.

The age of philosophers. Almost all of the Zhou era was marked by wars. This absence of peace and order may have prompted a search for new ethical principles. It was a period that produced many of China's most honored philosophers. Thus in later centuries it became known as the "Age of Philosophers," for thinkers sought answers to the meaning and purpose of human life and society. Some of these thinkers attracted followers and established their own schools.

Two systems of belief that began at this time, Confucianism and Taoism (*dow*'ism), played an especially important part in China's later history. Confucianism is the philosophy based on the teachings of Confucius and

ANCIENT CHINA
— Present-day boundary

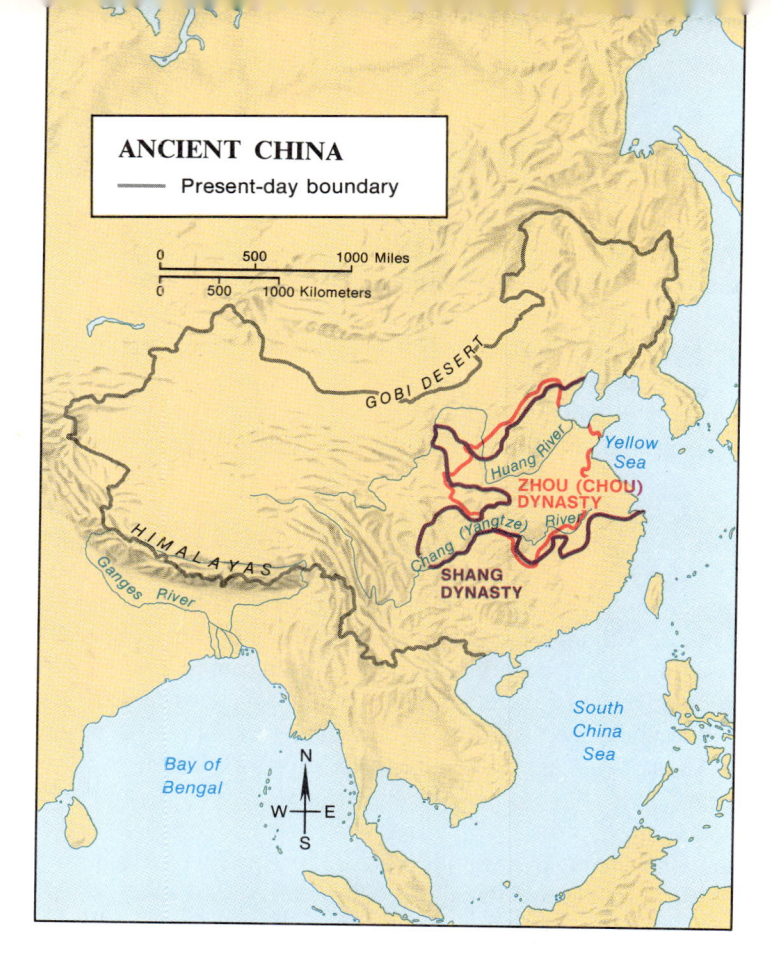

A ruler of the Zhou, whose priestly duties gave him the title "Son of Heaven." The Zhou reigned until the third century B.C., but the feudal rulers of China's many city-states held the real power.

Mencius (*men'*shih-us), his chief disciple. Taoism is based on the thought of Lao Tzu (*lah* oh dzuh). These philosophies will be described in Chapter 24.

Legalist philosophy. A philosophy called Legalism was also created at the close of the Zhou era by a group of scholars concerned about the disorder that plagued China. Under Legalism the ruler made the law and applied it equally to all people. Obeying the law was rewarded. Not obeying was punished. Minor offenses were punished severely to discourage more serious ones. The Legalists believed order would prevail when it was impossible for people to do wrong. According to the Legalists war strengthened a ruler and made his subjects strong and submissive.

China's first empire. Legalist principles helped the Qin [Ch'in] ruler unite China in 221 B.C. Under him a uniform system of writing was established, making possible contact between areas of China where dialects kept people from understanding each other. Although the Qin dynasty lasted only fifteen years, it marked a turning point in Chinese history. An empire with a central government ruled by a strong emperor replaced the independent feudal states led by Chinese kings. The Qin ruler expanded the territory of the Chinese empire and began construction of the Great Wall (p. 260). Work on this fortification was to continue for 1500 years.

Han dynasty. The Han *(hahn)* dynasty (206 B.C.–220 A.D.), which followed the Qin, reunited China and consolidated the Qin imperial system. As the economy improved, China prospered and expanded. Roads were built to accommodate the growing commerce. Chinese goods were carried on the Silk Road, which connected China with Rome and other Mediterranean countries as

---

An Ancient Book Burning

Under the Qin emperor, Legalism became the official philosophy of the land. All other philosophical works were destroyed, although one copy of each was preserved in the imperial library. Medical, agricultural, and magic books were exempt from destruction. According to an imperial decree:

. . . those who dare talk to each other about the *Book of Odes* [a collection of hymns and love poems] and the *Book of History* [historical documents of the Zhou era] should be executed and their bodies exposed in the marketplace. Anyone referring to the past to criticize the present should, together with all members of his family, be put to death. Officials who fail to report cases that come to their attention are equally guilty. After thirty days from issuing of the decree, those who have not destroyed their books are to be branded and sent to build the Great Wall. . . . People wishing to pursue learning should take the officials as their teachers. . . .

W. T. DeBary, *Sources of the Chinese Tradition*, (New York: Columbia University Press, 1960), vol. I, paperback p. 141.

This lavish burial vestment, made of more than 2,500 polished jade pieces wired together with gold, was found by archaeologists in 1968. It once held the remains of Prince Liu Sheng of the Han dynasty.

well as India and Persia. In exchange for their precious cloth, the Chinese received glass, linen, and valuable minerals. The use of such grains as wheat and barley became widespread, as did the terracing rice fields, the use of bamboo, and of water buffalo as draft animals on farmlands.

The Han rulers banned the Legalist philosophers, preferring Confucian scholars. They believed that Confucian values (p. 296) would strengthen the empire. Confucius was deified and worshiped. However, the major Legalist contribution remained the strong central government.

Members of the civil service were needed to manage the elaborate bureaucracy that tended China's vast and populous empire. Civil servants were chosen by a competitive examination system based on Confucian philosophy. The emperor used several devices to prevent officials from becoming a threat to the throne. Officials could not serve in the province of their birth, nor could they hold the same position for more than three years.

The censor was a unique Chinese creation. Searching for misgovernment and treason, he reported misconduct directly to the emperor. Censors also criticized the conduct of the emperor and his court. Such criticism often required great courage. According to a saying, "the censorate is like a sleeping tiger. Even when it does not bite, men still dread its tigerishness."

End of the Han dynasty. Under the last Han emperors, court battles for political control of the empire led to civil war. The dynasty vanished in this turmoil. Confucianism, because it was associated with the Han rulers, became unpopular. Scholars seeking a new philosophy as a replacement for Confucianism turned to Buddhism.

China was without a strong central government for four centuries. Barbarians invaded the land and gradually intermarried with the Chinese. Under the Sui *(swih')* dynasty, China was reunited in 589 A.D. The Tang [T'ang] dynasty, which followed the Sui, brought China into a period of great cultural achievements.

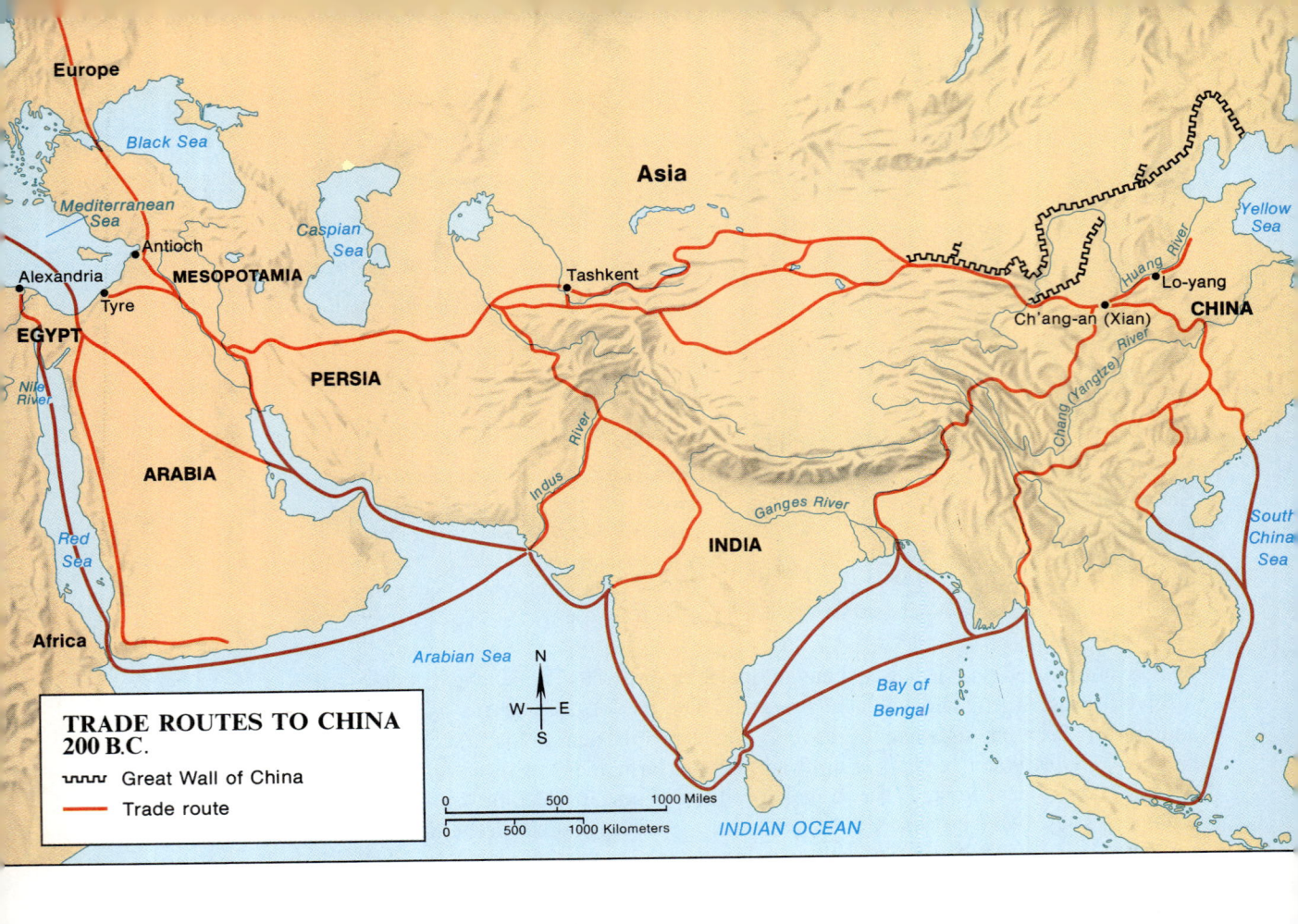

TRADE ROUTES TO CHINA 200 B.C.
- Great Wall of China
- Trade route

China's golden age. Under the Tang emperors (619–907 A.D.) Chinese civilization reached great heights. The Tang emperors firmly encouraged the establishment of state schools in the provinces. Tang armies brought parts of present-day Korea, Tibet, and Central Asia under their control. It was a most creative period for poets and artists.

Succeeding dynasties matched the political power or cultural achievements of the Tang era, but in different ways. For more than a century after the fall of the Tang dynasty, the Mongols ruled China. In 1368 the Chinese again took control of their country from their Mongol rulers.

Three centuries of Manchu rule. The Manchus, nomads from Manchuria, established the Qing [Ch'ing] dynasty in 1644. The Manchus preserved, as had previous foreign rulers, Confucian society and government. Most of the government officials were Chinese, but the Manchus controlled key government positions and the army.

Although they made up less than 2 percent of the Chinese population, the Manchus kept their identity as a distinct people. They retained their own language, clan structure, and religion. Manchus were forbidden to marry Chinese, wear Chinese apparel, or become traders or workers. Chinese men had to wear their hair in the Manchu style, a long pony tail or queue, and to shave the rest of their heads. Chinese could not settle in Manchuria.

The Qing dynasty ruled China for nearly three centuries. In addition to China and Manchuria, its large empire consisted of Mongolia, Xinjiang, and Tibet. These countries were governed under the tributary system, so called because the nations that participated paid tributes to the Qing rulers. In return for their gifts, tributary states received gifts from the Qing rulers and the promise of protection in case of outside attacks. The present-day countries of Burma, Thailand, Laos, Nepal, Vietnam, and Korea participated in this form of international diplomacy. Even Japan and several European countries that traded with China participated in the tributary system.

The Manchu rulers, while carefully keeping their own customs and practices, encouraged Chinese culture as well. They sponsored Confucian studies. Thousands of scholars were set to work producing encyclopedias, dictionaries, and other scholarly research. While assembling these works for an imperial library, a Manchu emperor also collected two thousand books that he considered anti-Manchu. Most of them were burned.

Under the greatest of the Qing emperors, Kangxi [K'ang-hsi] *(cong' she')* and Qianlong [Ch'ien-lung] (chee-*en' loong'*), China compared favorably with Europe in material wealth, resources, political organization, and cultural development. China lagged behind the West in modern technological and scientific development. The Qing emperors successfully limited Western expansion, restricting European traders to the port of Canton in South China and stopping the Russians in the north at the Amur River.

Reviewing Your Reading

1. What changes appeared in China during the Zhou dynasty?
2. Name the three belief systems that appeared at this time.
3. What were the principal features of Legalist philosophy?
4. How was the Chinese government organized?
5. Describe the tributary system.
6. How did the Manchus preserve their ethnic identity while ruling China?

European Traders and Missionaries Reach China

In 1514 the Portuguese were the first Europeans to reach China by sea. They later established the port-colony of Macao near Canton.

Jesuit missionaries followed the Portuguese traders. Believing they would win more converts if they gained the respect of Chinese scholars, the Jesuit missionaries adopted certain Chinese practices and studied Chinese learning. Matteo Ricci founded a Jesuit mission in Beijing. His pleasant manner and knowledge gained him the emperor's friendship.

The Chinese admired the Jesuit missionaries' scientific knowledge and found it useful. When a Jesuit missionary accurately predicted an eclipse, he was made chief astronomer of the imperial court. The Jesuit library included scientific, mathematical, and medical books. With the aid of Chinese scholars, these works were translated into Chinese. In this way Western scientific discoveries were introduced to East Asia. Unknowingly, the Jesuits served as the first modern technical experts in China.

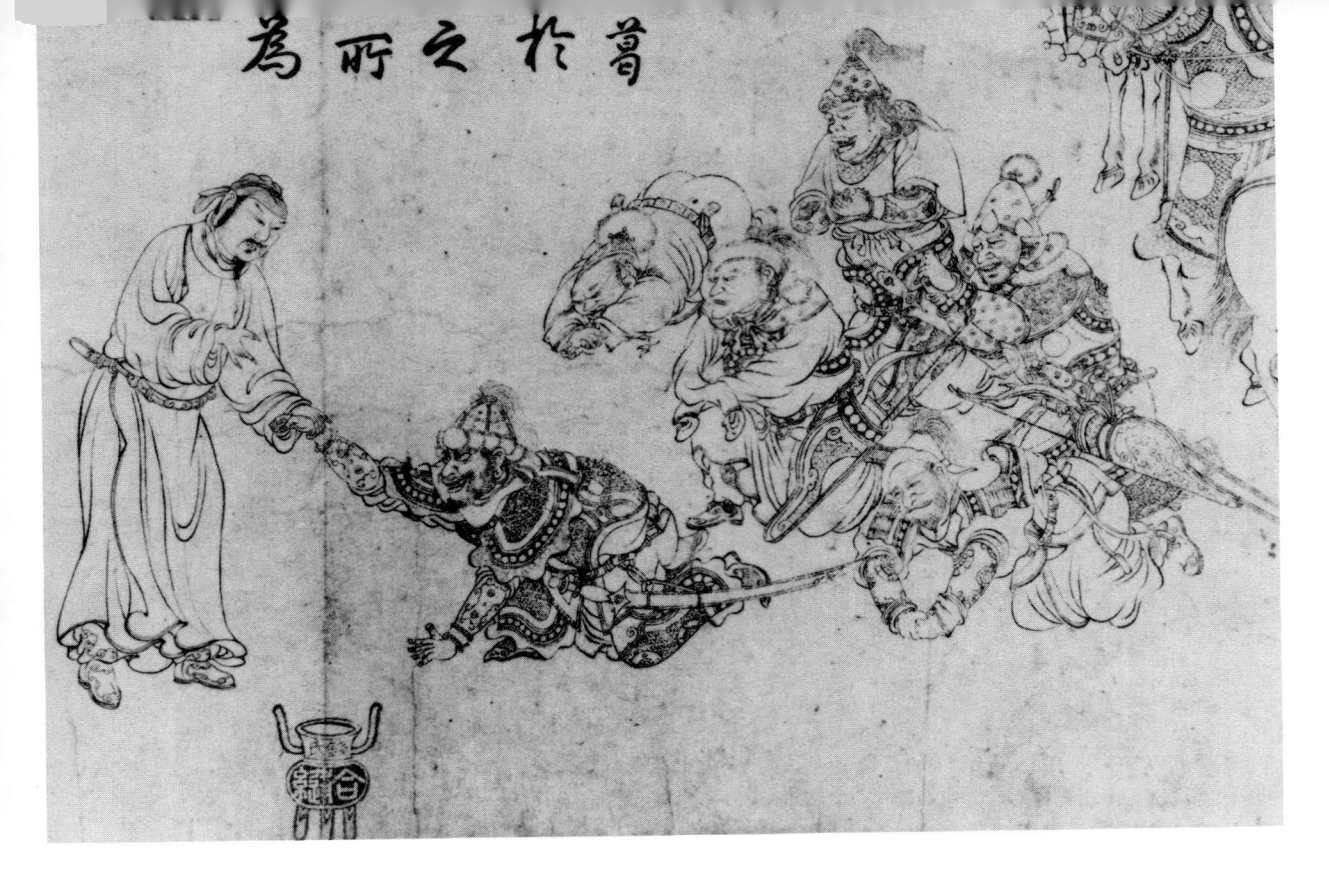

A Chinese painting entitled "The Emperor and the Barbarians" illustrates the practice of the kowtow.

Missionary activity comes to an end. The missionaries also translated Christian books into Chinese. Believing that certain Chinese beliefs could be adapted to Christianity, they used Confucian quotations to support Christian teachings. Jesuit missionary efforts were moderately successful.

Other Catholic priests appeared in China and opposed the Jesuit acceptance of Chinese customs. The Pope objected to the Jesuit adaptations of Confucianism to Christianity. A disagreement between the Chinese emperor and the Pope finally led to the departure of most of the Jesuit missionaries in the early eighteenth century.

Thus a century and a half of cultural contact ended unhappily. Western science and knowledge were more welcomed than Christianity, but neither changed Chinese thought. The Chinese people, accustomed to looking at life with a Confucian philosophy, strongly resisted Western ideas.

Uneasy relations with Europe continue. As time passed, contact with Europeans became more frequent. However, foreign relations were hampered by the Chinese belief that their civilization was superior to all others and by their lack of interest in the rest of the world. The Chinese regarded members of all other civilizations as "barbarians."

One major source of friction was the tribute system (p. 273). Under this system, non-Chinese brought gifts to Beijing and expressed their submission to the emperor. The foreign ambassador performed the *kowtow,* which involved kneeling to the emperor so that one's forehead knocked the floor. Such an act made clear who was the inferior party. After the kowtow, the emperor bestowed great

The treaty port of Canton in the early 1800s.

An Imperial Rejection

A British mission headed by Lord Macartney went to Beijing in 1793 to expand the China trade. Since he brought gifts, Macartney was regarded as a tributary envoy. He was given many presents, but increased trade was refused. The Qianlong emperor's reply to King George III below illustrates the gulf between China and the rest of the world as well as the Chinese desire to remain isolated.

You, O King, live . . . beyond many seas . . . impelled by your humble desire to partake of the benefits of our civilization, you have dispatched a mission respectfully bearing your memorial. . . . To show your devotion, you have also sent offerings of your country's produce. . . . your memorial . . . reveal [s] a respectful humility on your part. . . . Your Ambassador and his deputy have come a long way with your memorial and tribute, I have shown them high favor and have allowed them to be introduced into my presence. . . .

Our dynasty's majestic virtue has penetrated unto every country under heaven, and kings of all nations have offered their costly tribute. . . . As your Ambassador can see for himself, we possess all things. I set no value on objects strange or ingenious and have no use for your country's manufactures. . . . It behoves [sic] you, O King, to respect my sentiments and to display ever greater devotion and loyalty in the future, so that, by perpetual submission to our Throne, you may secure peace and prosperity for your country. . . .

Franz Schurmann and Orville Schell (eds.), *Imperial China* (New York: Random House, Inc., Vintage Books, 1967), pp. 105–108.

gifts on the envoys and entertained them. After 1795 the Westerners refused to take part in the tribute system. They wanted a relationship based on diplomatic equality.

Trade with Europeans was permitted only in the city of Canton, where a guild of Chinese merchants sold goods at fixed prices and rented property to foreign traders. The Europeans stayed in the city during the trading season, a period of only four months. They were forced to live in a restricted area. Forbidden to learn Chinese, the traders dealt with officials through Chinese merchants only and also had to employ Chinese clerks. In addition, they paid numerous taxes. Because their profits were great, the foreigners tolerated these restrictions but later came to resent them.

The Chinese legal system added to the friction between China and its European traders. According to Chinese law a suspect was guilty until proven innocent. A witness to a crime as well as the accused could be tortured for a confession. One official served as judge, prosecutor, investigator, and jury. Foreigners objected to this kind of treatment. They demanded extraterritoriality, whereby an accused European could be tried in China according to his own national law.

Sale of opium leads to war. The Chinese rarely used opium before the Westerners appeared. British merchants bought opium in India and sold it in China. By the early 1800s opium addiction touched all levels of society.

Traders eagerly met the increasing demand for this narcotic. As more opium was imported, more silver left China, upsetting the Chinese monetary system. Although the Qing emperors decreed the death penalty for users and smugglers, the trade continued. Some Chinese suggested that opium use be legalized instead so that it might be taxed.

Commissioner Lin Zexu [Lin Tse-hsu] arrived in the port city of Canton in 1839 and ordered the surrender of all opium. The British were forced to give up their opium supply, and it was destroyed. The British government immediately sent military troops and ships to China, and the Opium War began.

While the destruction of the narcotic was the immediate cause of the Opium War (1839–1842), there were more basic issues involved, such as Britain's refusal to accept inferior status as a tributary nation. Steam-powered British warships easily defeated the Chinese warships.

Unequal treaties weaken China. The Treaty of Nanjing (1842) ended three years of war. It was the first "unequal treaty" China accepted from other countries. It was unequal because the Chinese made more concessions than they received. China paid for the destroyed opium and gave the island port of Hong Kong to the British. Several so-called treaty ports were opened to foreign trade and residence: Canton (Guangzhou), Shanghai, Amoy (Xiamen), Foochow (Fuzhou), and Ningpo (Ningbo). Moreover, the Chinese were not allowed to set tariff rates for these ports. Similar treaties were made with France and the United States.

The Chinese tried to weaken the effects of these treaties, but the Westerners wanted them fully enforced. European merchants wanted to trade in the interior regions of the empire, and missionaries desired greater freedom to do their work.

Later treaties permitted Western diplomats to live in Beijing and gave Christian missionaries the right to travel inland, build churches, and own property. The opium trade was legalized in China and then taxed. Additional ports were opened to foreign trade.

These unequal treaties seriously reduced China's political and economic power. They also damaged the prestige of the Qing dynasty. Dissatisfaction among people led to more than a half century of peasant revolts.

The Taiping Rebellion. The Taiping *(tie'ping')* Rebellion swept across south and central China from 1850 to 1864. With 20 million people killed, it was among the most destructive and severe civil wars in history. The Taiping rebel leader, Hong Xiuchuan [Hung Hsiu-ch'uan] *(hoong' she-*oo'choo-*ahn')*, attracted a large following by founding a religious cult based on Christian missionary teachings. Hong and his followers captured Nanjing in 1853 and made it the capital of their government.

Taiping Rebellion collapses. The Taiping leaders made several mistakes that led to the failure of their revolt. Hong never received the support of the scholar class because he attacked Confucianism. Anyone who wanted to establish a new dynasty needed the support of this important class. The Taipings failed to link themselves with other peasant rebellions underway in China at this time. Foreigners also failed to support Hong because he wanted them to kowtow to him as they would to the Qing emperor.

The Manchu rulers of the Qing dynasty survived this rebellion because they had the support of the scholar class. Armies organized by Chinese bureaucrats and merchants helped the Qing dynasty regain control of the country. In 1864, when government forces captured Hong's capital at Nanjing, he committed suicide. In the same year the bloody rebellion was finally suppressed.

Reviewing Your Reading

1. How did the Jesuits conduct their missionary effort in China? Explain why their religious work was less successful than their scientific effort.
2. What does the emperor's reply to the British desire for more trade on page 275 say about China's view of other countries?
3. What restrictions did China place on European traders? Why?
4. Describe the events that led to the Opium War.
5. What made the Treaty of Nanjing an "unequal" one?
6. Describe the Taiping uprising. Account for its collapse.

Manchu Leaders Undertake Limited Reforms

The treaty settlement with the Western nations and the defeat of the Taiping rebels removed two great threats to the Qing dynasty. The Manchus restored order and strengthened their hold. However, the defeat of the Chinese by European forces convinced some officials of the Qing dynasty that changes had to be made. The tributary system was replaced by a reluctant acceptance of Western nations as diplomatic equals. A government office to deal with foreign representatives was created.

"Learn the superior techniques of the barbarians to control the barbarians." Under this slogan industrial and military modernization were promoted. China was defeated, the reformers said, because its weapons were inferior to Western arms. From 1861 to 1895, arsenals and dockyards were built to produce guns, cannon, and steamships. Railroads, telegraph lines, and modern factories were constructed. Officers were trained in new naval and military schools. Western military, scientific, and technical books were translated, while Chinese students went to Europe and the United States for training.

This effort marked the start of modern industrialization in China. New facilities in treaty ports contributed to the growth of Canton, Shanghai, Nanjing, and Tianjin. Two new social classes appeared – industrial workers and a professional class made up of engineers and business managers. Students who studied abroad became leaders in the armed forces, schools, and government.

Empress and scholars hinder reform. During the last years of the Taiping Rebellion, Cixi [Tz'u-hsi] (*tsuh' she'*), a powerful and domineering woman who had entered the emperor's harem in 1851, gained control of the Qing dynasty. She directed the government of China for thirty-seven years and became known as the Empress Dowager. The Empress Dowager was more interested in gaining power for herself than in reforms. In addition, Confucian scholars scorned Western technology, fearing their social position would be weakened. Money was scarce for starting new activities.

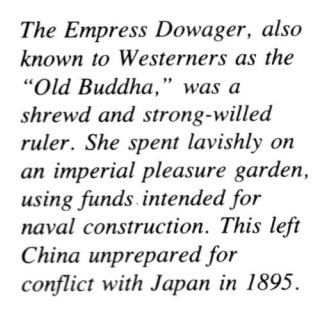

The Empress Dowager, also known to Westerners as the "Old Buddha," was a shrewd and strong-willed ruler. She spent lavishly on an imperial pleasure garden, using funds intended for naval construction. This left China unprepared for conflict with Japan in 1895.

One hundred days of reform. Not all members of the imperial court were opposed to reform. In 1898 Guangxu [Kuang Hsu] *(gwahng' shoe')*, nephew of the Empress Dowager, took control of the government from his aunt. He issued daily edicts calling for various reforms. Support for the emperor's announcement came from a Confucian scholar, Kang Yuwei. Continued foreign humiliation prompted Kang Yuwei to write *Confucius as a Reformer*. This work reinterpreted Confucianism to support changes in Chinese life. Kang favored the emperor's reform edicts, which called for modern schools to teach Western knowledge and to enable students to study abroad. He called for an end to extraterritoriality and the reform of the armed forces to help China deal more effectively with foreigners.

These changes threatened the vested interests of many people. Educational reforms upset Confucian scholars, while officials and officers opposed government and military modernization. After three months the Empress Dowager regained control of the government. She imprisoned the emperor and had other reform leaders imprisoned or executed. Kang Yuwei fled to Japan. While the One Hundred Days made some changes in the army, the 1898 effort was largely a failure.

Chinese resent missionary efforts. During the last decades of the nineteenth century, the Europeans expanded their influence in China. By 1870 hundreds of missionaries served China's half million Christians. They established orphanages, hospitals, and schools. However, missionary efforts to stop child marriages, infanticide, and foot binding angered many Chinese. Criticisms of Confucianism by missionaries also annoyed Confucian scholars, who felt criticism threatened their social position.

France supported Catholic missionary work in China. Catholic nuns in the port city of Tianjin paid fees to Chinese people for orphans left in their care. Many believed that this encouraged kidnapping. A mob attacked a church mission in Tianjin in 1870. A number of foreigners lost their lives. Chinese officials punished the attackers and thus prevented a war with France. Christian missionary activity remained unpopular with many of the peasants.

Western Nations Fight to Divide China

After 1870, Western nations sought new markets for their products and new supplies of natural resources. European countries wanted colonies to serve as military and naval bases. Other Europeans sought new sources of religious converts. Some wanted to spread Western knowledge and science to assist nonwestern peoples.

Russia begins territorial division of China. Chinese treaties with Russia in 1689 and 1727 checked the expansion of the Russian troops into China. But in 1860 a weakened China was forced to give Russia a large stretch of land between the Amur and Ussuri rivers and the Pacific Ocean. There Russia built the port of Vladivostok. France added the tributary state of Annam, which today is Vietnam, to the colony of Indochina.

In 1894 China and Japan entered the Sino-Japanese War over the control of Korea. Japan had no difficulty defeating its huge mainland rival. In the treaty ending the conflict in 1895, the Japanese acquired Taiwan. This short war demonstrated the weakness of the Qing dynasty and encouraged foreigners to seek greater economic concessions from the Chinese.

Russia built a railroad across Manchuria linking its Trans-Siberian line with Vladivostok and also occupied Port Arthur and Dalian [Dairen] on the coast of China. Germans took land on the Shandong [Shantung] peninsula. Britain leased the port of Weihaiwei in the north and added other new territories to its holdings in Hong Kong. Thus the treaty ports, in which foreigners had the right to trade and develop industries for their own profits, were increased in number from five in 1842 to nearly a hundred by 1900.

Open Door Policy. The United States did not want to be excluded from the China trade. Americans watched as other nations began to partition China into special trade areas or spheres of influence. United States officials encouraged the other powers to accept the Open Door Policy (1899) which guaranteed equal commercial opportunities for all nations and respect for China's territorial integrity.

Boxer Rebellion expresses China's anti-foreign feeling. The Chinese bitterly resented the way foreign nations were dividing up their country. One of the most strongly anti-foreign groups was a powerful secret society called "The Righteous and Harmonious Fists." They became known to the Westerners as the Boxers. Their magical practices led them to believe that foreign bullets could not kill them.

The men of the 14th US Infantry march through the Imperial Palace grounds in Beijing during the Boxer Rebellion.

The Chinese had genuine grievances. Imported foreign goods had destroyed local industries, while railroad and mining development upset their grave sites.

Chinese Christians, who claimed special privileges through the missionaries, were attacked by the Boxers. The Boxers also burned churches and destroyed railroad and telegraph lines. The Empress Dowager and her court secretly supported the Boxers, hoping the foreigners would be expelled. When the Boxers entered Beijing in 1900, they destroyed foreign property and killed Chinese Christians and members of several foreign embassies. The foreign delegations were besieged for 55 days until an international relief force rescued them. Three hundred foreigners died during the uprising, while Chinese casualties numbered 15,000.

When the Boxer Rebellion was crushed, the Chinese government was compelled to punish and execute those involved. It also had to pay large sums of money to those foreign nations whose citizens and property had been destroyed. The American share of this money was later used to finance the education of Chinese students in the United States.

Reviewing Your Reading

1. What led the Qing dynasty to attempt modernization of China? What changes did its leaders make? Why were these reforms unsuccessful?
2. What effect did the Sino-Japanese War have on China?
3. What was the Open Door Policy? Why did America press for it?
4. Who were the Boxers? What led to their rebellion?

Revolutionary Parties Begin Drive for Change in Government

Various revolutionary political parties developed after the Sino-Japanese War ended in 1895. Revolutionary newspapers and magazines appeared. The revolutionaries collected money and arms, led uprisings, and attempted assassinations. Many were arrested and executed, while others fled to Japan.

Sun Yat-sen. The most prominent revolutionary was Sun Yat-sen *(soon' yaht' sen')*. Of peasant origin, he was born in a village near Canton. Joining his brother in Hawaii, he attended a mission school and later became a Christian. He then studied medicine, but decided to spend his life as a professional revolutionary. Sun was opposed to the Manchu government. He wanted to see his country under Chinese republican rule. He organized the *Kuomintang* (*gwoh'min-dahng'*), or Nationalist Party.

When a rebel group under his leadership failed in a plan to seize Canton in 1895, Sun fled to Japan. He traveled widely, preaching his message and raising funds for his movement. While in London, he was kidnapped by Manchu agents who hoped to return him to China. However, when a British friend roused public opinion, Sun was released.

Sun's program to change Chinese government and society was stated in the book *Three Principles of the People*. The principles were nationalism, democracy, and livelihood. Nationalism meant the overthrow of the Manchu dynasty

Sun Yat-sen (1866–1925) founded the Kuomintang and called for the establishment of a democratic, nationalist government in China.

and the restoration of Chinese rule. Democracy called for a constitutional republic with equality for all and a popularly elected president and legislature. Livelihood called for equal ownership of land so that all people would have a decent level of living.

The end of imperial China. The downfall of Manchu rule started with a controversy in which Chinese officials and investors protested the government takeover of Chinese-owned railroads. The protest against the government takeover of the railroads coincided with a revolutionary plot by Sun's followers, begun in the south in 1911. The uprising spread as officials in southern and eastern China declared their independence from their former Manchu rulers.

At the time of this revolt, Sun was traveling abroad. Upon his return to China from the United States, Sun was elected temporary president. To get the support of General Yuan Shih-k'ai (you-*ahn' shir'kye'*), who controlled the Beijing army, Sun resigned as president in Yuan's favor. In February 1912, the Manchu emperor abdicated, thus ending China's two-thousand-year-old empire.

First efforts at representative government fail. China had no experience with representative government. It had always been ruled by one person. Western-style political parties, free elections, and individual rights were new concepts for the Chinese.

Initially, Sun's Nationalist Party controlled the Parliament, but General Yuan used force, bribery, and murder to silence his opponents. He dissolved the parliament, banned the Nationalist Party, and became a military dictator. Yuan's effort to make himself emperor and establish a new dynasty ended with his death in 1916.

From 1912 until 1928, China was torn by civil war. Warlords, ruled by terror, using their armies to control the people of an area, forcing them to feed and supply their troops. Local residents feared and hated these warlords because they imposed high taxes and destroyed property. Although these warlords could not build a national following, they were powerful enough to disrupt the government. Under these men, government worsened, and the Chinese people suffered.

Defeat by the Japanese increases unrest. The Japanese invasion of China in 1914 disrupted the country further. The Japanese had entered World War I on the side of the Allies and used the opportunity to seize German territory in China. The Allied nations – Great Britain, France, and later the United States – supported Japan's claims to Germany's holdings in China. When the Versailles Treaty at the end of World War I failed to return this territory to China, Chinese nationalists accused their leaders of selling out to Japan.

Criticisms of Chinese policies take many forms. On May 4, 1919, university students demonstrated against the Japanese control of Shandong. This protest became known as the May Fourth Incident. The demonstrators attacked pro-Japanese officials and burned a house. An anti-Japanese national movement, supported by the press, merchants, and workers, developed. Japanese goods were boycotted. The Chinese government resigned and refused to accept the Versailles Treaty. But Japan kept Shandong.

Around this same time a cultural movement, critical of much of Chinese life, started at Beijing University and spread across the nation. Some said China needed a national spoken language for literature as a step to unifying the country. Classical Chinese as a spoken language was as dead as Latin in the West. The use of the common language of the people was urged by many Chinese scholars, and by 1922 all school textbooks were printed in the vernacular.

Such Confucian values as filial piety, loyalty, and parental dominance were attacked. "Overthrow Confucius and Sons" became the cry. "Mr. Democracy" and "Mr. Science" were praised. Greater freedom for women was demanded, and arranged marriages were rejected.

Soviet Communist Party serves as a model for the Nationalists. The 1917 Communist Revolution in Russia showed that a well-disciplined party could seize control of Russia and organize a nation. Sun Yat-sen sought help to gain political control of China. Refused by the United States and Britain, he used the Communists to strengthen his Nationalist Party. He hoped to create a socialistic and democratic China.

Russian agents helped to reorganize the Nationalist Party. Chiang Kai-shek (jee-*ahng' kye'shek'*, 1886–1975), Sun Yat-sen's brother-in-law, trained with the Soviet Army in Russia. A military academy with Russian advisers was created. A Russian Communist taught propaganda techniques to the Chinese. The Nationalist Party copied the structure of the Russian Communist Party for their own political organization.

Chiang Kai-shek (top) on the Nationalist side and Mao Zedong (bottom) on the Communist side were the key figures in China's civil war.

Nationalists and Communists Become Bitter Foes

In 1921, nine men met in Shanghai and organized the Chinese Communist Party. The Chinese Communists worked in two directions. They worked within the Nationalist Party to gain control of it. They also formed their own organizations and began preparing to seize control of the government by force.

Following Sun Yat-sen's death in 1925, Chiang Kai-shek became the leader of the Nationalists. The next year he began a successful military campaign to defeat the warlords. While the Communists initially aided the Nationalists in this effort, rivalry between the two groups grew. Then in 1927 Chiang Kai-shek struck quickly to destroy the Communist movement. Numerous Communists were executed. Many others were put in prison.

The Long March. The surviving Communists fled to the mountains of southeast China, where they remained until 1934. Chiang launched "extermination campaigns" against them. Inadequate supplies and weapons forced the Chinese Red Army plus the wives and children of the soldiers to evacuate. Led by Mao Zedong [Mao Tse-tung] (*mah'*-oh dzuh-*dong'*, 1893–1976), they fled through enemy lines in an attempt to save their lives.

Mao Zedong's forces, 100,000 strong, retreated from their mountain base toward the northwest. This was a distance of 6000 miles, much of it through mountains, rivers, marshes, and barren stretches of land. Fewer than 20,000 survivors reached Shaanxi [Shensi] province in northwest China a year later. One of Mao's brothers and two of his children were among the casualties. Those who survived had a deeper sense of mission and commitment to the Communist

A woodcut entitled "The Chinese Red Army Passes through the Marshland" shows the struggles of the Long March through the eyes of a Chinese Communist artist.

cause. They became the core of the Communist Party. During this period of terrible struggle, Mao Zedong emerged as the leader of the Chinese Communists.

Chiang's government undertakes reforms. Under the Nationalists, Nanjing became China's capital. From 1928 to 1937, Chiang's government was plagued by political corruption, warlord revolts, battles with the Communists, and attacks by the Japanese. The Nationalist leaders attempted to follow Sun Yat-sen's plan for reforming the nation. They formed a government with executive, legislative, and judicial branches.

Few real efforts at reform were made, however. The Nationalist Party headed by Chiang Kai-shek was the only legal political party. The people did not elect national officials. Members of the legislature were appointed by the party. A small circle of Nationalist leaders controlled the party and through it the government and the army. No effective opposition parties were allowed.

Economic reforms never reached the peasants. To modernize the Chinese economy, new banks were established. Limited industrial development took place. While boats continued to be widely used, the construction of railroads and highways improved transportation. Telephone and telegraph lines were erected. Public and private education was promoted.

However, these innovations did not affect the lives of most of China's people. Land was unevenly distributed. While 80 percent of the Chinese people were farmers, 10 percent of these farmers owned more than half of the land. Peasant farmers who rented land from the wealthier landowners paid rents of up to 70 percent of the value of their crops.

The 1930 Land Law passed by the Nationalist government prevented landlords from receiving more than one-third of a farmer's crops as rent. Had this law been enforced, the Nationalists might have won the peasants' support.

Manchurian Incident. After the Sino-Japanese War, relations between the Chinese and Japanese remained unfriendly. Japanese-held territory was returned as a result of the Washington Conference in 1922. However, the Japanese were still determined to control the Asian mainland. They had already annexed Korea in 1910 and hoped to acquire Manchuria with its rich mineral and agricultural resources.

In 1931 the Japanese army captured the Manchurian capital of Mukden (Shenyang) after Japanese soldiers exploded a bomb on one of their own railroads. The soldiers used this explosion as an excuse to take control of the country. All of Manchuria was occupied by the Japanese army within five months.

At China's request the League of Nations investigated the incident and condemned Japan as an aggressor. But the League could not force the Japanese to leave Manchuria. No Western power offered to help China. The Western nations were too preoccupied with threats from Hitler and Mussolini as well as the effects of the Great Depression to come to China's aid.

Chiang forced to accept Communist cooperation. The Manchurian Incident left the Nationalists with a hard decision. On the one hand Chiang Kai-shek wanted to crush the Communists and strengthen his hold in China. On the other hand, he needed their support against the Japanese. While Chiang debated this decision, anti-Japanese demonstrations and boycotts took place throughout the country. In 1936 government troops refused to carry out the orders of their Nationalist leaders to attack the Chinese Communist forces. The soldiers protested that they wanted to fight the Japanese, not their own people. When Chiang went to the city of Xian to investigate the situation, he was "kidnapped" by his aides. He was released when he agreed to a "united front" with the Communists against the Japanese.

The Japanese launched an all-out war in 1937, occupying northern and coastal China and penetrating deep into the Huang and Chang valleys. The Japanese aggression presented the Nationalists and the Communists with an opportunity to rally the Chinese people against the enemy. Both sides, however, also used the war to strengthen their own positions. Each knew that when war with Japan ended, the power struggle for control of China would resume.

The Nationalists bore the brunt of the Japanese attack. Much of its army was destroyed. Chiang did not use all of his forces against the invaders. Many of his best troops maintained a blockade of Communist-held territory. Army morale among the Nationalist forces declined as supplies became scarce or were sold by corrupt officers and officials.

Chiang's government faces enormous economic problems. Japanese control of the ports kept China from importing war supplies. Entire factories had to be transported inland to western China, and new ones were built. But these factories lacked skilled workers and necessary raw materials. Food prices soared. Inflation worsened as more paper money was printed to meet war expenses.

While Western nations sympathized and gave moral support to China, they gave very little material aid. Soviet Russia was the major supplier to the Nationalists prior to the United States entry into World War II. The Flying Tigers, an American volunteer air force, fought for the Nationalists. Otherwise, China fought the Japanese alone until the Japanese attack on Pearl Harbor.

Communists use the war to win new members. The Communist army was poorly armed and smaller than the Nationalist forces. The Communists used guerrilla warfare and avoided large battles with the enemy. Captured Japanese weapons were used by the growing Communist units.

The Communists followed a moderate policy in the areas of China they controlled because they wanted to win support for the Communist cause. The property of absentee landlords and of those who collaborated with the Japanese was confiscated. The peasants were allowed to rent this land and give one-third of their crop to the Communists. Cooperatives, owned and managed by the people, were encouraged.

Communist Party members shared the hard life of the village peasants. They joined all local groups and used art, drama, and literature to propagandize and to strengthen party programs. Farmers were encouraged to participate in local government. By the "three-thirds system," Communist membership in all government units was limited to one-third. This enabled many non-Communists to participate in government and won the Communists more supporters. The Communists combined a patriotic war with a social revolution in the villages and won popular support in the areas they controlled.

By late 1941 numerous European nations and the United States were involved in World War II against the Axis powers – Germany, Italy, and Japan. The Chinese received limited aid from the Allies. At the Yalta Conference in 1945 the Soviets agreed to attack the Japanese army in Manchuria once the German army was defeated. By a Sino-Soviet treaty, Russia recognized the Nationalist government and was given the right to use Manchurian ports and railroads. China became a permanent member of the Security Council of the United Nations and was recognized as a leading world power.

Civil war is renewed. In August 1945, the Japanese surrendered. Both the Nationalists and the Communists rushed to control the Japanese-occupied territory. The Nationalist armies used American planes and ships to reach these areas. Thus, the United States appeared to be supporting the Nationalists. The Russians also entered China. They allowed the Communists to seize Japanese arms and to occupy Manchuria. Both sides eyed one another with suspicion, and soon the civil war began again.

Although the Nationalist troops were at first victorious, the long war with Japan had weakened their forces. The Nationalist troops began to suffer defeats. A well-organized and disciplined Chinese Red Army went from victory to victory. Beijing fell to the Communists in 1949, and before the end of the year Chiang Kai-shek's forces withdrew from the mainland and established themselves on the island of Taiwan.

Why were the Nationalists defeated? The United States did not totally support the Nationalist government. Once World War II ended, American public opinion called for a sharp reduction of its armed forces. Thus there were not many soldiers available to help the Nationalists. More military and economic aid alone could not ensure victory. Greater American help might have delayed the Nationalist collapse but could not prevent it.

The Chinese Communists received some aid from the Soviet Union. When the Chinese civil war resumed, Stalin discouraged the Communists from an all-out war with the Nationalists because he didn't think they could win. Mao ignored his advice and went on to victory.

The control of China was a matter chiefly decided by the Chinese themselves. The Nationalists failed to gain wide popular support because they did not develop a broad program of economic and social reform. Finally, people were tired of war, inflation, and corrupt government.

Communist military victories were always followed by efforts to form political organizations among the peasants of a village. The Communist success owed much to their vigorous political work and to the intense desire of the Chinese people for peace.

The People's Republic of China

Communist victory in the civil war was only the beginning of the Chinese Revolution. The Communist leaders began to direct all of China's human and material resources toward the political, economic, social, and cultural growth of the country. This was a tremendous task for the most populous and third largest country in the world. But the Chinese were determined to achieve their goals. The family system was reformed. Medical and health facilities were improved. A birth control program was begun. More schools were built. Greater educational and job opportunities were made available for people from all levels of society as long as they agreed to support official Communist policy.

In 1949, when it became evident that the Kuomintang was fleeing, the city of Nanjing was in an uproar. Mass looting occurred, much of it done by children. Famed French photographer Henri Cartier-Bresson took this and many other photos of China around the time of the Communist triumph.

Revolutionary changes in China have taken place under the firm control of the Communist Party. Party members control all sources of information and expression. In the process of changing the country, the Chinese have become one of the most regimented people in the world. The Chinese Communists seem to feel that this control is necessary if they are to provide a better life for the people and create a China strong enough to resist foreign aggressions and maintain its independence.

Reviewing Your Reading

1. Trace the collapse of the Chinese empire.
2. What problems did China face between 1912 and 1928?
3. How did World War I affect China?
4. Why did Sun Yat-sen seek Communist support for his cause?
5. Trace Chiang Kai-shek's efforts to unite China and defeat the Communists.
6. How successful were Chiang Kai-shek's efforts to strengthen China?
7. How was the Chinese "united front" formed?
8. How did the Nationalists and Communists use the war with Japan in their struggle for control of China?

CHAPTER REVIEW

Recalling Names and Places

Boxer Rebellion	Manchus	Sun Yat-sen
Chiang Kai-shek	Mao Zedong	Taiping Rebellion
Kuomintang	Qin dynasty	treaty ports
Legalists	Qing dynasty	unequal treaties
Long March	Shang dynasty	Zhou dynasty

Understanding This Chapter

1. Confucius, Mencius, Lao Tzu, and the Legalists all influenced the development of Chinese government and ways of life. Have philosophers exerted this kind of influence in any other cultures? In our own culture? Name and discuss some examples.
2. What brought Europeans to China in the sixteenth century? How did the Chinese react to them? How did the Europeans react to the Chinese? What was similar and what was different about each group's reaction to the other?
3. Research and discuss: Why *didn't* the Chinese come to the West in great numbers when European and American traders and missionaries were coming to China?
4. What was the significance of the Long March to the Communist struggle? Do any peoples or groups in other lands recall similar events and invoke them for similar reasons? Can you think of examples in our own culture? In another culture you have studied?
5. Why did the Nationalists lose the Chinese civil war?

Chapter 24

Tradition and Change

Our study of Chinese society will be divided into two parts. We shall examine the social structure, religion, and values prior to the formation of the People's Republic of China. Then we shall see how the society has changed in recent decades.

Social Structure in Traditional China

All people were not considered equal in old China. In Chinese society a person's social class depended on moral character, education, political position, and wealth. Most people belonged to one of four social groups: scholar, farmer, artisan, or merchant. These groups were based, in part, on a distinction between physical labor and mental labor. Farmers and artisans were considered physical laborers because they made goods or provided services. Mental effort was required to become a scholar. The scholar scorned physical work and expressed his contempt for it by his long fingernails.

Scholars. Membership in the scholar class was not hereditary. It was open to all men who passed the public civil service examinations (p. 294). Scholars held all the government positions. In addition, they served their community by settling conflicts between individuals, families, and villages. They established schools, led the local militia, and directed the maintenance of roads, bridges, and irrigation canals. These duties were assumed by the scholars without

---

A Place for Everyone

Social mobility, the ability to move from one class to another, was less important in Confucian thought than maintaining harmony among the classes. People were expected to carry out their particular social roles to the best of their abilities. Mencius (372–289 B.C.), an important Confucian philosopher, wrote:

There is the work of great men and there is the work of little men. . . . Some labor with their minds and some labor with their strength. Those who labor with their minds govern others; those who labor with their strength are governed by others. Those who are governed by others support them; those who govern them are supported by them. . . .

From *A Source Book in Chinese Philosophy*, translated and compiled by Wing-tsit Chan. Copyright © 1963 by Princeton University Press, Princeton Paperback, 1969, p. 69.

A rice and noodle merchant in pre-Communist China sells his wares on the street of a Yunnan village.

specific governmental orders. As members of the elite class, they were exempt from compulsory labor and were allowed to pay a fine to escape physical punishment.

Peasants. Agriculture was the mainstay of Chinese life. Farmers held the second highest position in Chinese society because they produced the grain and rice that the country depended on. They grew cotton for the cloth most people wore and the silk for finer apparel. Thus, farming was an important and honorable occupation.

Artisans. The third class in Chinese society was composed of skilled workers, or artisans, who were organized into guilds according to their craft. Each guild set the prices and the standards for the products its members made and provided welfare services for them.

Merchants. The merchant belonged to the lowest class in the social system. Wealth was not important in the Confucian system of values. While it provided comfort, it could not give one either wisdom or prestige. According to Confucian thought, merchants' profits were squeezed from their customers. The merchant was subject to legal restrictions as well as low social status. At various times merchants were not allowed to wear silk, use horses, or ride in sedan chairs.

Not all Chinese belonged to one of these four classes. Members of the nobility had their own social group. Nor were soldiers included in the formal Confucian social system, because they used force rather than persuasion to establish themselves. According to a Chinese proverb: "Good iron is not used to make a nail, nor a good man to make a soldier."

The Traditional family

Chinese society stressed family participation rather than individual activities. The ideal family included a husband and wife, the husband's parents, his unmarried children, his married sons, and their wives and children. Family members all lived in separate quarters within one house. This arrangement is called the joint family. Wealthy merchants, landlords, and scholar-officials typically had joint families. Smaller nuclear families – consisting of a man, his wife, and their unmarried children – were more common.

The family supported and trained its members and supervised their moral and political behavior. The family was held together by Confucian values, which set forth a clearly defined set of obligations between fathers and sons, husbands and wives, and younger and older brothers. Families were also drawn together by the eldest male's control of the family wealth and by his command over family members. Whether the family was nuclear or joint, there was one family budget. All property was mutually owned. Upon the death of the family head, property was equally divided among the sons. The joint family was then dissolved.

The government dealt with the head of the family rather than with its individual members. If a person committed an offense and was not caught, other family members might be punished for the crime. The individual was accountable to the family, and the family was responsible for all of its members. Confucianism stressed the belief that well-regulated families led to an orderly society. Chinese

A section of a silk scroll showing Chinese ladies preparing newly woven silk. Here the women are ironing the silk.

subjects were expected to show the same obedience to the emperor and his officials as to the family head.

Family roles of men and women were quite different. Men dominated traditional Chinese society. The father was the chief authority in the household. The relationship between father and son was expected to be harmonious, with the son submitting to the father's authority. Sons never achieved equal status with their fathers. The father supported the son and provided a wife for him.

Women were considered inferior due to their low economic value to the family and their role in ancestral lineage. Positions of ownership, wealth and status were restricted to males. Sons, not daughters, had the obligation to provide for their parents before and after death. Only male children could continue an ancestral line. During a famine, girls were the chief victims of infanticide (child-killing). Footbinding was a mark of a female's subjection. A young girl's feet were tightly wrapped to prevent their normal development. These "lily feet" kept women close to home. Almost all women were illiterate, since it was believed that "a woman well educated is apt to cause trouble." Despite this, female poets and artists existed.

Arranged marriages. Marriages were considered a family matter and were arranged. Parents rarely considered romantic love important. A son and daughter-in-law were expected to help the parents in their work, to satisfy their desire for grandchildren while they lived, and to honor them after their death.

The bride left her home and joined that of her husband. She was subject to her mother-in-law, who trained her in the practices of her new home. The birth of a son made her position in the family more secure, for it ensured the continuation of the family line. Children were considered a form of social security, as this saying illustrates: "Grain is stored against famine; sons are brought up against old age."

Filial piety was the keystone of family life. Respect and obedience to family was a highly prized virtue. Children were expected to revere and obey their parents throughout their lives. Their love and devotion was to be absolute and unconditional. This reverence, love, and devotion to family, called filial piety, was reflected in Chinese law. For example, if a condemned prisoner had old or ill parents, he might be excused from punishment so that he could look after them.

The *Twenty-four Paragons of Filial Piety* were stories of exaggerated concern for parents. They were used to train children. One story was of a son who sold himself as a servant to pay for his father's funeral expenses. Another permitted himself to be bitten by mosquitoes to spare his parents. One son laid on the ice of a frozen lake so that the heat of his body would melt it to get fish for his stepmother.

A male child in an educated family read the *Twenty-four Paragons*. While girls and children of illiterate families did not read the book, they were likely to be familiar with sayings that stressed filial piety. People with a reputation for filial piety were cited as examples to be imitated, and memorial arches were often built in their honor.

These Taiwanese stamps depict examples of filial piety: Tsai Hsun was picking mulberries when he was captured by bandits. He told the bandits the ripe berries were for his mother and the unripe ones for himself. Impressed, they freed him.

Tseng Sun was away from home collecting firewood. His mother became concerned about him, and she bit through her fingers as a message. He appeared at once, having felt a pain in his heart.

The Mutual Loyalty of Father and Son

According to Confucius, the father and son were not to report each other to authorities for an illegal act. Under Chinese law, children who testified against their parents were punished for an offense against filial piety.

The Duke of She told Confucius: "In my country there is an upright man called Kung. When his father stole a sheep, he bore witness against him." Confucius said, "The upright men in my community are different from this. The father conceals the misconduct of the son and the son conceals the misconduct of the father. Uprightness is found in this."

From *A Source Book in Chinese Philosoph*, translated and compiled by Wing-tsit Chan. Copyright © 1963 by Princeton University Press, Princeton Paperback, 1969, p. 41.

Filial Piety

Children were expected to look after their parents' needs and heed their wishes, as this segment from the Book of Rites *illustrates:*

[Sons and sons' wives] should go to their parents and parents-in-law [on the first crowing of the cock]. On getting [there] . . . they should ask if [the parents'] clothes are [too] warm or [too] cold, whether they are ill or pained, ... They should . . . help and support their parents in quitting or entering [the apartment]. In bringing in the basin for them to wash, the younger will carry the stand and the elder the water; they will beg to be allowed to pour out the water, and when the washing is concluded, they will hand the towel. They will ask whether [the parents] want anything, and then respectfully bring it. All this they will do with an appearance of pleasure to make their parents feel at ease. . . .

While the parents are both alive, at their regular meals, morning and evening, the [oldest] son and his wife will encourage them to eat everything, and what is left after all, they will themselves eat. . . .

No daughter-in-law, without being told to go to her own apartment, should venture to withdraw from that [of her parents-in-law]. Whatever she is about to do, she should ask leave from them. A son and his wife should have no private goods, nor animals, nor vessels; they should not presume to borrow from, or give anything to, another person. If any one give the wife an article of food or a dress . . . she should . . . offer it to her parents-in-law. If they accept it, she will be glad. . . . If they return it to her, she should decline it, and if they do not allow her to do so, she will take it as if it were a second gift, and lay it by to wait till they may want it. . . .

From *Chinese Religion: An Introduction* by Laurence G. Thompson (Belmont, Calif.: Dickenson Publishing Co., Inc., 1969), pp. 40–41. From Li Ki (Chi) translated by James Legge Book Ten, pp. 450f, 453, and 458 (Clarendon Press, Oxford, 1885).

Kiang Kei carried his widowed mother on his back to escape danger. He was captured by bandits, but they freed him when they learned of his care for his mother.

On a cold winter day, Meng Chung's ailing mother wanted bamboo shoots for soup. There were none at the market, so Meng Chung searched the bamboo groves until he found some. He made soup, and his mother recovered.

Families also belong to clans. Clans were groups of families that traced their ancestry back to a common male ancestor who had settled in an area. Families within the clan had a common name, although not all people with the same name belonged to the same clan. Only patrilineal descendants – that is, members of the father's family line – belonged to the clan. A daughter married outside her clan, and her children became members of her husband's clan.

The clan was an important source of financial help. Wealthy clan members cared for orphans and penniless elderly members. A clan's temple recorded the accomplishments of its ancestors. These records served as an example to its living members.

Education in Traditional China

The Chinese educational system was designed to produce officials for the government. At the completion of his education a student would take a competitive civil service examination based on the Confucian classics. It was believed that the study of Confucian teachings developed the scholar's moral virtues and enabled him to set a good example for the rest of the local community.

Private tutors were employed by the family, clan, or village to teach the classics to male students. The books were first memorized by reciting them aloud. The curriculum did not include scientific or technical training.

The examination system selected the country's civil servants. The examination system was theoretically open to all, providing a channel for improving one's position in society. There were three parts to the examination. Success at the first level led to the "bachelor's" degree. The recipient became a scholar-commoner, legally and socially a member of the leading class. He wore distinctive clothing and enjoyed certain privileges. However, this degree did not lead to government employment. If the scholar-commoner had no independent income, he often worked as a private teacher.

If a scholar passed the second level, he earned a "master's" degree and became eligible for government service. The final hurdle led to the "doctor's" degree, which automatically placed the holder in the middle level of the civil service. So prestigious was the scholar status and a government appointment that unsuccessful candidates in their forties and fifties repeatedly took the test to earn the degree.

Shortcomings of the system. While Confucian teachings taught that "in education there are no class distinctions," in reality education or the lack of it created real social differences. Only members of wealthy families had the leisure for lengthy schooling. However, a clan might sponsor the education of a promising student. The possession of a degree was not simply a personal achievement. It also brought honor to a scholar's family and clan.

Sometimes a degree could be purchased. At other times the government set quotas for the number from each province to become government officials. Their papers were marked separately.

As long as China was isolated from the rest of the world, the examination system served its people well. However, when Western powers intruded into the Chinese world, many of the officials selected by this system were too inflexible to deal wisely with new problems.

Reviewing Your Reading

1. Name the four social classes and describe the role each played in society.
2. What groups were not part of the four classes? Why?
3. What was a clan? What was its role?
4. Describe the joint family and the nuclear family.
5. What were the roles and duties of males and females in the family?
6. What is filial piety? How was this value taught?
7. What functions did education have in China? Describe the learning process.
8. What was the examination system? What were its weaknesses?

Chinese Religion and Philosophy

The great philosophies of China are Confucianism, Taoism, and Legalism. Although these three systems of belief and worship existed separately and independently of each other, they influenced one another. An individual might adhere to all three.

Confucianism. Confucius (551–479 B.C.) was a member of the lower aristocracy who held minor political posts until he established a private school in which he taught his philosophical views. He hoped his students would become political advisers to rulers, applying his ideas and bringing peace, order, and prosperity to the land.

Confucianism is not a religion. The *Analects,* which contain the collected thoughts of Confucius, is not a holy book. Confucianism is a system of ethics, a guide to right behavior. Confucius sought to create a "gentleman" of good character.

Confucius delivers a lesson on moderation. Too much water in the bucket causes the loss of all. The moral: Nothing in excess.

Confucian virtues. Righteousness, loyalty, reciprocity, and above all, humanity were qualities that made a Confucian gentleman. To be righteous meant doing what ought to be done because it was the right thing to do. Confucius taught a golden rule: "Do not do to others what you do not want them to do to you."

Humanity, meaning goodness or love, was an important Confucian virtue. It included courtesy, trustworthiness, hard work, generosity, and kindness. The man who possessed humanity was a loyal subject to his ruler, a devoted son to his parents, and a faithful friend.

Another Confucian virtue was proper conduct or decorum. Decorum meant doing what was appropriate in every situation. This virtue helped a ruler to govern. Confucius believed, "If a ruler can administer his state with decorum and courtesy, then what difficulty will he have?" His subjects would follow his good example. Confucius described the influence of gentlemen on lesser people in this manner: "The essence of a gentleman is that of the wind, the essence of small people is that of grass. And when the wind passes over the grass, it cannot choose but bend."

Confucius believed that society would be orderly if people everywhere performed the duties of their particular positions in society. This concept is explained in the sentence, "Let the ruler *be* a ruler, the minister *be* a minister, the father *be* a father, and the son *be* a son." When all people fulfilled their duties and responsibilities, society would be harmonious.

Taoism. Although it is uncertain whether the philosopher Lao Tzu (*lah'*-oh *dzuh*) lived, the book *Tao Te Ching, The Way and Its Power* (dow'duh *jing'*) is attributed to him. It is a central book of the Taoist philosophy.

The Taoist ideal was simplicity. The art of living meant doing what was natural and instinctive, not interfering with nature and not living by the social and governmental rules of a highly organized Confucian society. By an intuitive, emotional method Taoists learned of and merged their spirits with the Tao, the source of life, and lived their earthly lives in union with it. Worldly position, power, honor, and material wealth were unimportant. Self-knowledge and contentment were Taoist goals.

Non-action is a key Taoist concept. The Taoist believed that while Heaven and Earth did nothing and left all living things free to develop spontaneously, everything prospered and grew. Only when the natural order was upset by people did trouble arise. Thus the Taoist believed that the best government places the fewest controls on people, allowing them to live in harmony with the natural world.

Taoism and Confucianism. It was not possible to organize a society and govern a nation by Taoist principles. Thus, a man might practice Confucian teachings in his work as an official and as the head of a family, but turn to Taoism in his private life. Confucianism stressed social conformity and placed limits on an individual's freedom. In Taoism, the individual's mind was free to contemplate nature and try to understand the mysteries of life.

Buddhism in China. By the first century A.D., Mahayana Buddhism passed by way of northwestern India through central Asia into China. In a divided and weakened China, scholars sought a new way of looking at the world. Many found it in Buddhism. This foreign religion helped unite China in 589 A.D. and remained important through the ninth century. Buddhist monasteries became centers of learning and culture. Chinese pilgrims made perilous journeys to India to copy Buddhist scriptures.

Buddhism adapted to the Chinese way of life. Buddhism became important in the social and economic life of the countryside. Buddhist monks encouraged such charitable activities as the creation of hospitals. Some monasteries had water mills and oil presses for use by the peasants. Other monasteries owned much land, which provided the income to support their members. The practice of celibacy, which forbade a monk to marry, seemed unusual to the Chinese. Nor did monks pay taxes or perform any compulsory labor. Public resentment grew when some Buddhist communities became religiously lax. This resentment aided the Confucian and Taoist opponents of Buddhism. During the ninth century anti-Buddhist persecutions reached their peak, and thousands of temples were destroyed. Monks and nuns were forced to leave their monasteries. Buddhism recovered from this attack, but it never regained its place in Chinese life.

Buddhism never became the dominant religion in China. It did not provide the Chinese with a philosophical tradition comparable to Christianity in the West or Islam in the Middle East. However, it did have an effect on Chinese life. The

A worshiper at a Buddhist shrine in pre-Communist China. Buddhism came to China from India before the first century A.D. It never became the dominant religion of China, but it had a great influence on Chinese life.

practice of doing charitable works comes from Buddhist teachings. The Buddhist belief in compassion and respect for life convinced Chinese officials to modify the cruel punishments called for by the Chinese penal codes.

Ancestor veneration. The essential Chinese religion was ancestor veneration. It was a family religion, not a public or personal one. The ancestral altar in the home had wooden spirit tablets, each inscribed with the name of a deceased ancestor. The father led the worship ceremonies.

Performance of these rituals showed love and remembrance by the living for their ancestors. The ancestors in turn were thought to respond by giving health, sons, and long life to the family. The ancestors also protected the family from calamities.

The oldest male performed the ceremony and thus enhanced his authority. A loyal son not only looked after his parents while they lived, but also served them after their death. Ancestors with no descendants or those who were not remembered were thought to wander through the world as ghosts.

Reviewing Your Reading

1. Describe the qualities of a Confucian gentleman.
2. What were the chief elements in the Taoist philosophy?
3. How did Confucianism and Taoism complement each other?
4. How did Buddhism affect the economic life of China? Which Buddhist practices and privileges led to the persecution of Buddhists?
5. Describe ancestor veneration. How does it reflect Confucian values?

Chinese Family Life Today

The 1931 Civil Code passed by the Nationalist government made many reforms in the Confucian family system. Men and women were granted greater legal equality in matters of marriage, divorce, inheritance, and property ownership. But the new law was not vigorously enforced. The reforms had their strongest impact on educated city dwellers. The majority of the Chinese people, living in rural areas, were not touched by them.

Communists abolish the traditional family system. The new Communist government made sweeping changes in family life. Under the 1950 Marriage Law, marriage became a free contract between individuals. It could be ended in divorce by either husband or wife. Parents and children became responsible for each other's support. Husband and wife were given equal rights in property ownership, inheritance, and the control of their children. Both were free to choose their own occupations.

The 1950 Marriage Law and the abolition of private property put an end to the joint family. Under the Communist system there is very little private property. Thus the head of the family has no property to pass on to his children, and his authority is severely weakened.

> **The Government Comes First**
>
> *Under the Communists, public confessions of loyalty to the government were common. These confessions were considered lessons on good behavior and were used by the Communists to encourage others to reform their ways. A statement by a college student which appeared in a newspaper in 1951 shows how loyalty to the family was replaced by loyalty to the new China. The student's father has been accused of disloyalty to the government. The student discusses his changing reactions to his father's predicament.*
>
> My father . . . participated in a rebellion and fled from home. . . . I blamed the government for . . . [not] understanding: my father had been forced into action by bandits, and the government was unjustly accusing him. . . . After repeated "study" [indoctrination] I . . . [saw] many things wrong with my father. . . .
>
> . . . he . . . embezzled . . . government rice. . . . his rebellion . . . was [a] premeditated action against the revolution and against the people.
>
> . . . my attitude towards my father . . . change[d] from sympathy to hatred. . . . [I located my father; we talked and he said], "When you get home be sure to bring me some money."
>
> . . . I . . . could not sleep. New and old thoughts were struggling within me. . . . How could I have taken him back to be shot. . . . [But] without repentance he continued to be an enemy of the people. . . .
>
> Though he was hateable, he was my own father. . . . Wouldn't it be all right if I went home and told people that I . . . failed to find my father?
>
> That would not do. I would save my father . . . but . . . I would become a counterrevolutionist. . . . I was forgetting that I was a youth of a new China. . . .
>
> . . . I . . . shattered my incorrect thoughts . . . on the principle of "no compromise in revolution, and no sentimentalism in struggle." . . .
>
> I went to the police . . . [and] to my father . . . [demanding] . . . he recant his past and reform. He said, "How could you do this to me?" and tried to escape. . . .
>
> . . . I waited until he wrote out his . . . confession before [returning home]. . . . My duty was at last done. I felt lighthearted; I was happy, for I rid the people of a dangerous character."
>
> C. K. Yang, *Chinese Communist Society: The Family and the Village* (Cambridge, Mass.: The MIT Press, 1965), pp. 176–178.

Several other changes made by the Communists also weakened the father's authority. Ancestor veneration was forbidden. This ended the father's traditional role as the leader of family rituals. The father's position declined because his wife could divorce him. The individual's ties with his family were further weakened through involvement in Communist political organizations. Children were encouraged to report parental disloyalty to the new China. Women and youth gained the most from these changes.

While the joint family is dead, the nuclear family survives. The Communists stress a harmonious relationship between husband and wife, the need for respectful children, and the family's responsibility to care for the aged. However, since Communist farm communes and factories also help to care for the elderly, old people rely less on their children for support. Parents are encouraged to have only one child. Families with more children face economic penalties and social disapproval.

Women under communism. Since 1950 women have enjoyed political, legal, social, and economic equality with men. They have played an active role in changing society. Because the Communist Party encourages them to participate in political life, women serve as party leaders and hold high-level government jobs. Greater educational and economic opportunities for women have increased the number of women in the labor force. Child care centers, which free women from household duties, have made them more active. The newspapers praised "labor heroines" and urged women to respect industrial jobs. The Chinese Communists have won many supporters among the women of China because of the benefits and opportunities provided for them.

Since 1950 women have had virtual job equality in China. These two women are welders at the Hubei Chemical Fertilizer Plant.

Communists Build a New Society

Communist Party members are the new elite. Communist Party leaders hold the most important and responsible positions in the country. Communist leaders recruit peasants and factory workers into the party, and they move up through the ranks of the party to become important party leaders.

The life of a Communist Party member is not easy. Members are expected to carry out party decisions regardless of hardships or personal sacrifices. They are expected to be an example to the people by promoting hard work and thrift. Yet no shortage of candidates for party membership exists. Some join to help modernize China, hoping to restore it to its former position of power among the nations of the world. Others belong because the party gives purpose to their lives and provides the highest status in the country. Power and prestige attract others. Membership is not required for the better positions in government and economic enterprises, but preference is given to those who belong.

Education under the Communists

Educating vast numbers of illiterate Chinese has been a great challenge. In addition to teaching reading, the Communists tried to replace all Confucian ideas with the thought of Mao. Since Mao's death, Mao's thought is being replaced by the philosophy of Marx and Lenin.

Educational opportunities for the poor increase. Mass education opened the schools to the children of farm and factory workers. Today, students with needed skills and a commitment to the Communist Party can rise in Chinese society. Approximately 93 percent of school-age children attend some type of school. Full-time workers attend "spare-time" schools attached to communes and factories. Both young and old workers are taught reading and new skills at these schools. Education of workers is encouraged because people who cannot read instructions are of limited use in modern industries. In half-work and half-study schools, education and production receive equal attention. People work half a day, or week, or month, and attend school the rest of the time. Such schools serve many students and make good use of China's small supply of trained teachers.

The backbone of the Chinese educational system is the full-time school. These schools range from kindergartens to universities. In addition to political indoctrination, students can attend courses in all academic subjects, vocational training, or agricultural training.

Between 1966 and 1976 China underwent a period of social upheaval during which radicals controlled the Communist Party. During this period, high school and college students and professors were sent to work on farms or in factories. Millions of city teenagers were forced to move to rural areas. This experience was meant to contribute to the econmomic development of the countryside, and also to teach the young people the dignity and honor of physical work. Great emphasis was also put on teaching the revolutionary ideals and philosophy of Chairman Mao. Since Mao's death, Chinese education has returned to an emphasis on high academic standards.

The Communists have thoroughly reorganized the Chinese educational system, but their work is not finished. Books, desks, and other educational materials are in short supply, and there are not enough classrooms. The shortage of trained teachers hampers the improvement of educational standards. However, China's leaders realize that education is indispensable in their nation's march into the modern world.

A New Philosophy for China

Communists have called religion the "opium" of the people. They oppose all forms of religious activity. Confucian and Taoist philosophies have been replaced by the philosophy of Marx and Lenin. Ancestor veneration has been attacked, and ancestral graves have been cleared to make more land available for farming.

While Buddhism has not been openly persecuted, the government supervises Buddhist leaders and services. The Communists have revised many Buddhist teachings to fit the party line. Because Christianity was a "foreign import," it

---

An English Lesson

Education seeks to impart knowledge and to instill the values of a society. Confucianism stressed the moral improvement of human nature, teaching loyalty to family, father, and emperor. Maoism seeks to instill loyalty to the people, the Communist Party, and party leaders.

The exercises in a 1983 Chinese textbook, A Practical Guide to English Grammar, *include sentences that illustrate Maoist political values and emphasize the importance of the technological and scientific education fostered by the Four Modernizations campaign.*

Children need many things, but above all they need love.

Through my childhood I hungered for education.

Our main task is to develop the student's ability to carry on independent work.

The Party's educational policy has always been that education shall serve working class politics and should be combined with productive labor.

Socialism will surely triumph over capitalism.

I am ready to do whatever the Party wants me to.

The Chinese people are not to be bullied.

In this respect, the Soviet Union is the more deadly of the superpowers.

Free of these household chores, the women can concentrate their energy on production.

These electronic computers were made in Shanghai.

Expectant mothers may not work with radioactive isotopes.

was cast off. Chinese Christians have been cut off from Christians in other countries, and foreign missionaries have either been deported or imprisoned.

Marxism has replaced Confucianism as a guideline for living. To remake the nation, the Communists are changing Chinese thinking and behavior. They claim that the old way of life taught people to be selfish and think only in terms of their own happiness. In the schools, children learn that the modern Chinese must be hard-working, modest, plain-living, honest, and serve the people of China. The goals of the Communist Party come before personal goals, and people are expected to work for the party rather than seek gains or comforts for themselves or their families.

Mao Zedong is called the "liberator" of his people. As chairman of the Communist Party, prior to his death in 1976, he was known as Chairman Mao. His writings are contained in a small red book called the *Quotations of Chairman Mao*. The "red book" became required reading. Today's schools put less stres on the political thought of Mao and pay more attention to such subjects as math and science. Mao is still honored, however, for founding the communist state.

Workers at Shanghai State No. 17 Cotton Mill study an article written by Chairman Mao Zedong, whose portrait looks out over them.

303

> **Applying Mao's Ideas**
>
> *The aim of Chinese Communism during the Cultural Revolution was to transform Chinese society by applying the ideas of Mao Zedong. His thought blends the ideas of Marx, Lenin, and Stalin with his own experiences in the Chinese revolution. Mao's ideas held the Communist Party together and tied it to the rest of the Communist world. The Communists claimed that the mastery and application of the red book,* Quotations of Chairman Mao, *made possible the production of more crops and more coal, and even enabled a person to win ping-pong games.*
>
> *The possession of "the ever victorious and all conquering thought of Mao Zedong" reportedly made possible certain technical developments.*
>
> Formerly we consulted Chairman Mao's work only when we encountered ideological problems. We referred exclusively to foreign books when we met technical problems. . . . After repeated failure . . . in . . . practical scientific research, we finally realized that the thought of Mao Zedong was not only the best weapon for transforming society and man's thinking, but also the best guide to disclose the secrets of science and technology. We succeeded quickly in making important achievements . . . because were were enlightened and guided by . . . [the] works by Chairman Mao.
>
> Some people may be curious as to how the thought of Mao Zedong can solve technical problems. It is true that the thought of Mao Zedong cannot solve concrete technical problems. However, by revolutionizing the people's thinking, it first gives them courage and awakens their intelligence, leads them to change their attitude toward technical innovations, and encourages them to carry out technical innovations for the sake of the people and the revolution. . . . The thought of Mao Zedong is thus able to solve the problem of the direction for technical development.
>
> *Bulletin of the Atomic Scientists.* February 1969. Vol XXV, No. 2, p. 82. By permission of Random House, Inc.

Thought reform. Thought reform was a technique used by the Communists to change thought and behavior through a psychological process of coercion. A person was remolded into a useful citizen. The Communists also used thought reform to get captives to confess.

The prison where a person underwent thought reform was a controlled environment. Every aspect of the prisoner's life was regulated by the captors. New prisoners were placed with selected inmates who were "advanced" in their own "reform." Daily activity in the cell focused on the new arrivals. Encircled by fellow inmates, new prisoners were denounced. Cell mates demanded that they recognize their "crimes" and "confess." This "struggle session" usually lasted all day. At night, handcuffed and chained at the ankles, the prisoners were questioned by the jailers. The prisoners' diets were poor but adequate.

Physically and emotionally weary, prisoners became confused and forgot who and what they were. Feeling that there was no help or release from prison, they would stop resisting the pressure of their captors in order to live.

Re-education. With a group, the prisoners would then study Communist doctrine, applying it to all aspects of their life. Under the control of their jailers, they would accept and confess to all the charges they were accused of. Self-confessed prisoners might then finish their sentences or be released. A foreigner might be expelled from China.

Thought reform was also used to indoctrinate party members and others and to change the thinking of Chinese officials so that they would work for the party. In "re-education" camps, heavy physical work replaced handcuffs and chains, but the "struggle sessions" and intense study of Maoist thought were still practiced.

Looking ahead. Most Chinese are enthusiastic about their country's recent achievements. They support the new China. However, old attitudes and habits persist among many people. Four decades is too brief a time to measure the Communist success in China. The Communist Party has a long journey ahead before its new society is finished.

Reviewing Your Reading

1. Why were Nationalist family reforms ineffective?
2. What is the most important social group in China today?
3. Why do people want to join the Chinese Communist Party?
4. How was the Chinese family life changed by the 1950 Marriage Law? What other factors also changed the family role?
5. How has the position of women changed?
6. How have the Communists changed religious and philosophical beliefs?

CHAPTER REVIEW

Recalling Names and Places

Analects	Confucianism	joint family
ancestor veneration	Confucius	Lao Tzu
Buddhism	examination system	*The Way and Its Power*
clan	filial piety	thought reform

Understanding This Chapter

1. Who was Confucius? Is Confucianism a religion? Explain.
2. What problems do the Communists face in transforming education in China?
3. What features of Chinese society under the Communists are significant departures from traditional Chinese ways of life? What features are in keeping with traditional ways? List your answers in two columns. Which column is longer?
4. Which reforms introduced by the Communists would have been most difficult for traditional Chinese to accept?

Chapter 25

The Chinese Economy

Agriculture dominates the Chinese economy today just as it did before the Communists came to power. Farming employs approximately 80 percent of the work force, although the government is trying to mechanize various farm tasks to release workers for the newly created industries. Planners must face such problems as a lack of knowledge of modern technology and machinery as well as an inadequate transportation system. Moreover, the average peasant, who is often poorly educated and conservative, is reluctant to try new methods of farming.

Chinese Agriculture

Although agriculture is China's main source of income, only 11 percent of the land can be tilled. Thus the Chinese farmer must use every acre of land profitably. Wide use of irrigation and terraces carved from hillsides has increased land use somewhat from former times. Animal and human manures are still used to fertilize the soil, but the production and use of chemical fertilizers is growing.

Lacking machines and using simple technical aids, traditional agriculture relies chiefly on human labor. It is known as intensive agriculture. Foot treadles and water buckets provide the water for irrigation. Terraces, carved from the hills by hand, require constant attention.

South China's farmers practice wet-rice cultivation. Warm climate, abundant rainfall, and a long growing season make the southeastern part of China the most productive. Because rice is a very nourishing cereal with a short growing season, it is South China's most important agricultural product. The rice crop requires intensive human labor and great care. Hillsides must be terraced. The paddies, small level fields, have to be bordered with dikes. Seeds are first planted in nursery beds. Weeks later farmers, often knee deep in soft mud, transplant these seedlings one by one by hand in water-filled rice fields. The ripened rice is then harvested.

North China's farmers grow wheat. In northern China the green fields of the south are replaced by brown grain fields. During the four to six month growing season, wheat is raised along with millet, sorghum, sweet potatoes, and cotton. Soybeans, an important source of protein, are grown in Manchuria as well. Although some pigs and chickens are raised, meat is a scarce item in the diet of the average person.

Terraced fields (top) check soil erosion and provide flat land for farming in hilly areas. Enormous amounts of human labor are needed to plant, harvest, and irrigate the steep slopes and to keep the terraces in good condition. The flooded rice paddies in the Xi River delta region of southeast China (bottom) also require intensive human labor. In addition, rice farming depends on land that is relatively flat, warm, and extremely wet.

Communist Farm Policy since 1949

China's growing population requires an ever-increasing food supply. Moreover, if the Communists are to achieve their goal of industrialization, China has to produce enough food to sell some of its crops abroad to obtain foreign currency. This money can then be spent to buy needed foreign industrial equipment and to develop natural resources. Hoping to achieve greater production, the Communists abolished privately-owned farms and combined them into collective farms where newer farming methods could be used to increase farm output. This was done in three stages.

Land is redistributed. First, all land, work animals, and farm tools were taken from the large landowners and redistributed to the landless peasants. Under Communist leadership public trials were held at which the landless peasants charged the wealthy landowners with various offenses. Such crimes as charging excessive interest on loans and overworking their laborers were recalled. If the landlords "confessed" their wrongdoing and were "re-educated," they lived and were allowed to work with the other farmers. However, many landlords resisted and were put to death. Having gained land of their own, the peasants supported the new government.

Cooperative farms were established a few years later. While on cooperative farms land remained privately owned, the farmers of a cooperative worked the land together. In addition to the cooperative's land, the farmers had small private plots near their own homes. The farmer tended this land and sold its produce privately. While farm output increased, the government's share was not enough to feed the growing urban population.

Communes – the final stage in the government's program. In 1958 cooperative farms were merged into communes of at least 20,000 people. The commune became the basic economic and political unit. In addition to farming, the communes engaged in industry, trade, and public works projects. The communes took care of their members' health and educational needs. They also provided social welfare services and cultural activities.

All private property was turned over to the commune. Dormitories, dining halls, and kitchens replaced private houses. Family members no longer lived together but with others belonging to the same commune. Each person was paid a wage. In addition, the commune provided food, clothing, and housing. In return, the commune member was expected to do the work assigned by the commune leaders.

The commune program was a failure. Too much was attempted without sufficient planning. Production goals were set by Communist policymakers, many of whom had little or no experience in farm management. The peasants disliked group living, the loss of their private plots, and their often unbearable workloads. Sabotage and passive resistance spread. Farm animals were killed, and grain was hidden instead of being sold to government agencies. Work slowdowns took place.

From 1959 to 1961, peasant opposition coincided with bad weather conditions. China suffered three disastrous crop failures. The government was forced

Workers at the Hongshan Commune gather the tea crop.

to ration food, control prices, and purchase foreign grain to keep people from starving. Since the government wanted to be economically self-sufficient, its leaders decided the commune system needed changes.

The communes are made smaller and more manageable. Each commune was divided into production teams of about forty households. These households were responsible for farming a specific portion of the land. Private plots were again given to the farmers. Communal living ended. Each person was guaranteed twelve hours a day for personal activities – eating, sleeping, and recreation. In addition, since 1979 farmers have been allowed to sell the fruits and vegetables they grow on their private plots.

China's 1982 constitution changed the communes yet again. They would no longer be the basic political unit of the community. Responsibility for local government was returned to town officials elected by the voter. Still, the commune remained the most important economic entity in rural areas.

The China-Korea Friendship Commune near Beijing is a model commune often shown to foreign visitors. It consists of 240,000 acres with 75,000 people.

309

CHINA: LAND USE

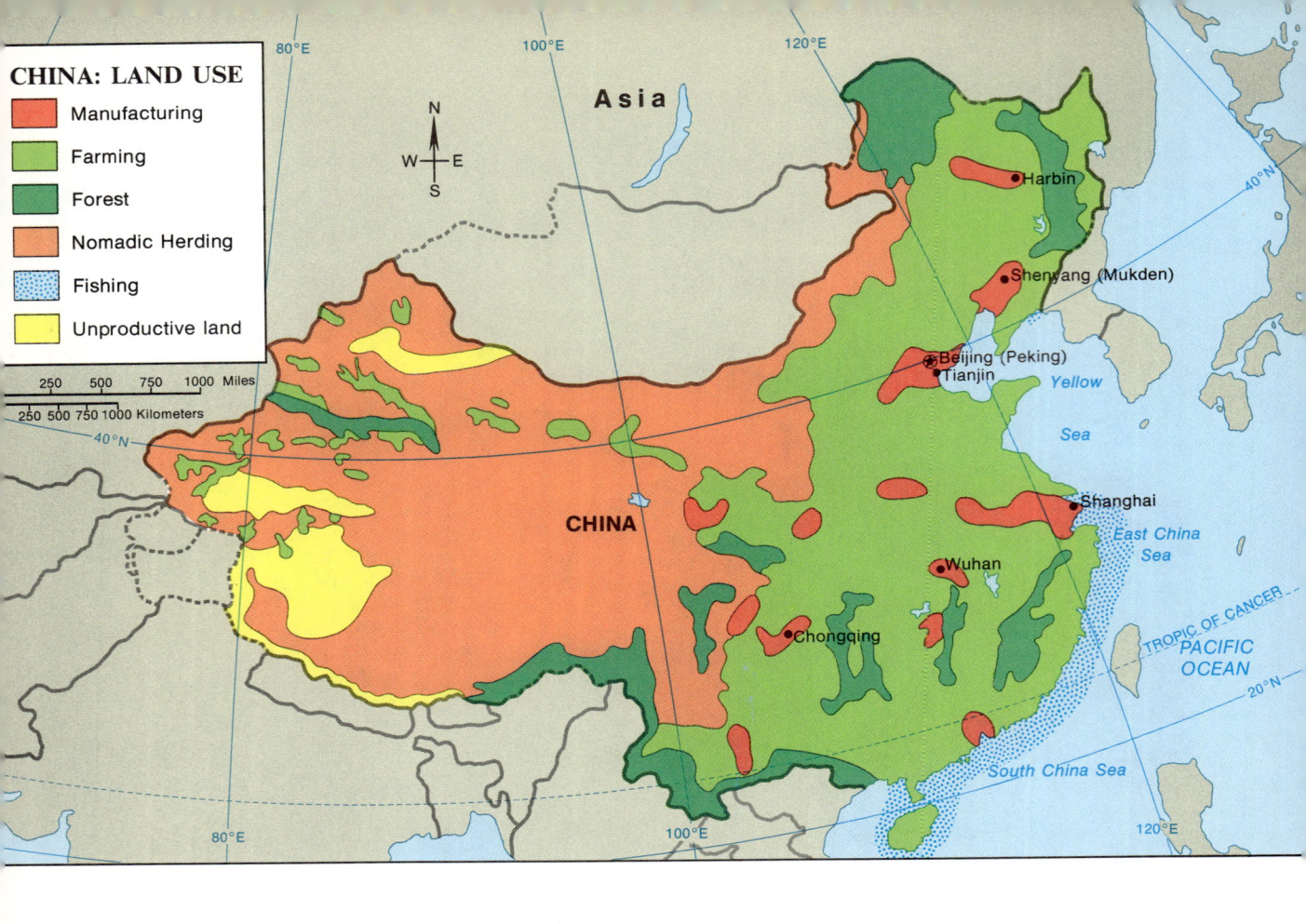

- Manufacturing
- Farming
- Forest
- Nomadic Herding
- Fishing
- Unproductive land

Using an extensive irrigation system, the farmers grow rice, wheat, sorghum, vegetables, and cotton and raise thousands of hogs and cattle. A power plant supplies the commune's electrical needs. Factories on the commune produce farm equipment and bricks. Such farm-factory communes are intended to make the various regions of China more self-sufficient.

By 1985, however, communes in many places were being dismantled. Land was still owned collectively, but rural production brigades began adopting what was known as the "responsibility system." Under this program, the use of a plot of farmland was allocated to an individual or a household for up to thirty years. Such farmers were allowed to make their own production decisions once they met their state quotas. In addition, by this time 15 percent of Chinese farmland was held in private plots. Markets where farmers sold their own produce directly to buyers were becoming common.

Chinese Industry

For most of its history, China's local handicraft industries supplied farm tools and household utensils. Imperial China's larger factories produced silk, paper, iron, and salt, which were used locally or traded in other provinces. Except for some luxury goods, the Chinese were self-sufficient.

China's trade with the West, and especially with the United States, has increased enormously since the death of Mao and the U.S. recognition of the Communist government. At Shenyang No. 1 Machine Tool Works, this power lathe is being prepared for export to the United States.

Foreigners first bring modern industries to China. Modern industries came to China with the Westerners, who built cotton and flour mills in the treaty ports, and with the Japanese, who created an iron and steel industry in Manchuria. Foreigners also built railroads and dockyards.

The unequal treaties (p. 276) prevented the Chinese from using a protective tariff against foreign goods to stimulate development of Chinese industries. Thus many foreign companies dominated China's industries. While China's natural resources such as its petroleum deposits remained undeveloped, Western oil companies supplied most of the kerosene for lamps and oil for China's industries.

Foreign conflict and civil war during the 1930s and 1940s made a shambles of the Chinese economy. Agricultural and industrial production lagged. The transportation system was shattered. Russia stripped the machinery from the Japanese factories in Manchuria after World War II.

Communists assume control of China's economy. When the Communists took over in 1949, inflation was widespread. However, by 1952 inflation had been checked, and industrial production had risen to its prewar levels. The following year the government began its most serious efforts to industrialize China. Officials outlined a series of five-year plans that set goals for each of China's major industries.

The First Five-Year Plan concentrated on the iron, steel, coal, oil, construction, and machinery industries. China's leaders hoped that such industries would produce materials needed for further economic growth. Loans, equipment, and technical experts from the Soviet Union helped the Chinese reach their first goals. As China's economy became more stable, these loans were repaid.

Heartened by this success, the Chinese continued to stress heavy industry in their 1958 Second Five-Year Plan. Government leaders in Beijing announced that China would surpass Britain as an industrial power in fifteen years. Under the slogan the "Great Leap Forward," a massive propaganda program was undertaken to encourage workers to support the Second Five-Year Plan. All the country's resources were directed toward greater industrialization. Communist leaders announced that China would walk on two legs – developing their industries by modern methods, while continuing to use traditional techniques. Communist planners believed that modern steel plants and small, backyard steel furnaces could both be used to increase production.

The Chinese worked with great enthusiasm to make the Great Leap a success. Production rose quickly. Most of the goods, however, were of poor quality. Pig iron produced in the backyard furnaces was useless. Raw materials and products that might have helped the Communists achieve their goals sometimes went unused because of poor transportation. The withdrawal of Soviet aid in 1960 (p. 319) was another severe blow to Communist planning. By the end of 1960 the Great Leap Forward had collapsed, and the nation suffered a severe economic recession.

The failure of the Great Leap set China's economic development back by several years. The 1966 Third Five-Year Plan emphasized agricultural production as the best means of promoting industrialization. Chinese leaders decided to improve the technical and farming skills of their people and purchase industrial equipment from Western Europe and Japan when necessary. Communist leaders decided against asking the Soviet Union for any further assistance.

In 1978 China embarked on a Four Modernizations campaign to improve its agriculture, industry, science and technology, and national defense. The five-year plan drawn up at that time called for less emphasis on "heavy industry," such as the production of iron, steel, and machinery. The central government also experimented with giving more control of factories and communes to local managers.

In the five-year plan for 1983–1987, China's leaders called for efforts to raise the standard of living of the Chinese people. To do this they would produce more consumer goods, use loans from foreign countries to finance modernizations, and raise the prices farm communes received for their produce without raising food prices for city workers. By 1985 they had begun to relax state control over much of the industrial and scientific sector, while retaining a core of centrally planned economic activity. A new policy called for looser planning, rationalized prices and wages, and decentralized management in an attempt to promote greater freedom for market forces and individual initiative.

A better life under the Communists. Although the standard of living of the well-to-do peasant of pre-Communist times has declined, life for most Chinese has improved since 1949. China has not had a famine since the Communists came to power. While peasants' standards of living vary in different parts of the country, all are assured a minimum living standard. Although the average farmer's cash income may seem low by United States standards, it represents money remaining after all food, housing, medical, and educational needs are met.

Factory workers are assigned jobs and paid according to skill, length of service, and "total contribution to the country." Men and women receive equal pay. If a worker's pay cannot meet his or her family expenses, the factory must pay additional money to meet the minimum living standard. Factories provide free nurseries for working mothers. Women retire at age 50, men at 60. Both receive 70 percent of their regular salary after retirement. Though most parents prefer to live with one of their grown married children, the factory will provide an apartment in its housing units for them if they wish.

Consumer goods are still in short supply. Cotton cloth used for clothing is rationed, but more expensive wool, silk, and synthetic fabrics are not. Such consumer items as bicycles and transistor radios are available. Although the prices of these items are the same throughout the country, they remain too high for some to afford.

Prospects for future industrial growth. Compared to its production levels before World War II, China has an impressive record of economic growth. While it had previously imported many industrial items, Chinese factories today produce machinery, trucks, locomotives, and electronic equipment. Its engineers design bridges and factories. China was the first agricultural nation to become a nuclear power.

Nonetheless, China remains an agricultural country. China has the mineral resources — especially coal, iron, oil, and uranium — to build a modern industrial economy. It has the human resources and organization, and a more balanced economy than in the past. Unless wars or internal conflicts intervene, China may one day be a major industrial power.

CHAPTER REVIEW

Recalling Names and Places

commune
cooperative
First Five-Year Plan
Four Modernizations
Great Leap Forward
Second Five-Year Plan
Third Five-Year Plan

Understanding This Chapter

1. What is China's main source of income?
2. Describe the two agricultural areas of China today.
3. Describe the stages by which the Communists changed farming from an individual to a cooperative activity.
4. What changes did the Communists introduce to make commune farming more productive? Why did it fail?
5. What modern industries were introduced by foreigners? What prevented China from developing its own industries to compete with the foreigners?
6. What was the Great Leap Forward? Why was it unsuccessful?
7. What are the strengths and weaknesses of China's economy today?

Chapter 26

China's National Policies and International Relations

In many ways modern China, in its official ideology, its political framework, and its strong central government, resembles the former empire. While the imperial government was founded on Confucian principles, the present leaders rely on Communist philosophy. However, new dimensions have been added. The Communist government reaches the most remote villages and seeks to involve the Chinese people directly in the life of the nation.

The Cultural Revolution

Although Communist leaders have been able to agree on the long-range goal of building a new China, they have not always agreed on the most effective methods of doing so. Mistakes have been made in the process of remaking Chinese society as seen in the failure of the Great Leap forward and the communes. No doubt other mistakes will be made. But the task of remaking China goes on.

Opposition to Mao's programs. In the 1950s some Communist leaders were displeased with Mao Zedong's program of rapid collectivization of farms into cooperatives and communes. They disliked his plans for industrial growth, the constant mass political rallies and propaganda campaigns he demanded, and his insistence on giving the acquisition of Communist beliefs greater weight than learning the technical skills. Some leaders also resented the loss of Soviet economic and military aid. Led by the President of the People's Republic, Liu Shaoqi (*lyoo' shah-oh-chee'*), Mao's opponents favored cooperation with the Soviet Union and a slower pace of economic development.

For his part, Chairman Mao feared that Communist Party members would become a new privileged group and lose contact with the common people. Mao also feared that lack of revolutionary experience among young people, by then half of the Chinese population, and the desire for a better life might cause people to be less willing to make sacrifices to create a new China. The aging Mao also wanted to be certain that there would be a peaceful and orderly succession in leadership on his death. Though Liu Shaoqi was his apparent successor, Mao feared that Liu might make compromises to remedy China's urgent economic and foreign problems. Mao felt that changes might undercut the revolutionary program he had worked to build.

The disagreement over party policy became a political struggle for power in 1965. On one side was Chairman Mao Zedong with army support, and on the other President Liu Shaoqi, who had the support of party leaders.

In 1966, student members of the Red Guard formed propaganda teams and toured factories, villages, and schools to publicize the thought of Chairman Mao. The Cultural Revolution disrupted Chinese life for almost ten years, closing down schools, turning family members against one another, and resulting in the death, persecution, or imprisonment of thousands upon thousands of Chinese.

Disagreement in many areas. The battle for control between Mao and his opponents took place in educational, governmental, economic, scientific, and cultural fields. Because it affected all aspects of Chinese life, it became known as the Cultural Revolution. In 1966, the Maoist Red Guards, consisting of high school and college students, appeared. With the little red book of Mao's quotations as their guide, they upheld their leader's thought and strongly criticized his opponents. They ransacked private property and harassed foreign diplomats. They wrote large wall posters, that attacked Mao's foes as "anti-party, anti-socialist monsters" who were "taking the capitalist road." Liu was stripped of all party and government positions.

The army emerged from this struggle with a decisive voice in Chinese politics. Its role was expanded as soldiers were placed in important party and governmental posts. The Minister of Defense, Lin Biao (*lynn' byow'*), became Mao's new right-hand man. He was in this position until 1971, when he died under mysterious circumstances. Some Western observers of China believe he may have been involved in a failed attempt to overthrow or assassinate Mao.

The Cultural Revolution was more than a struggle for power. Those who won were to decide the direction China would take in its future development. The ideals of the Communist revolution were reaffirmed, and any leader who hesitated to support the revolution was removed from power. Since Mao's death in 1976, the Cultural Revolution has been declared a serious mistake. The new leaders believe that education, science, and technological development were hurt by the Red Guards and their supporters.

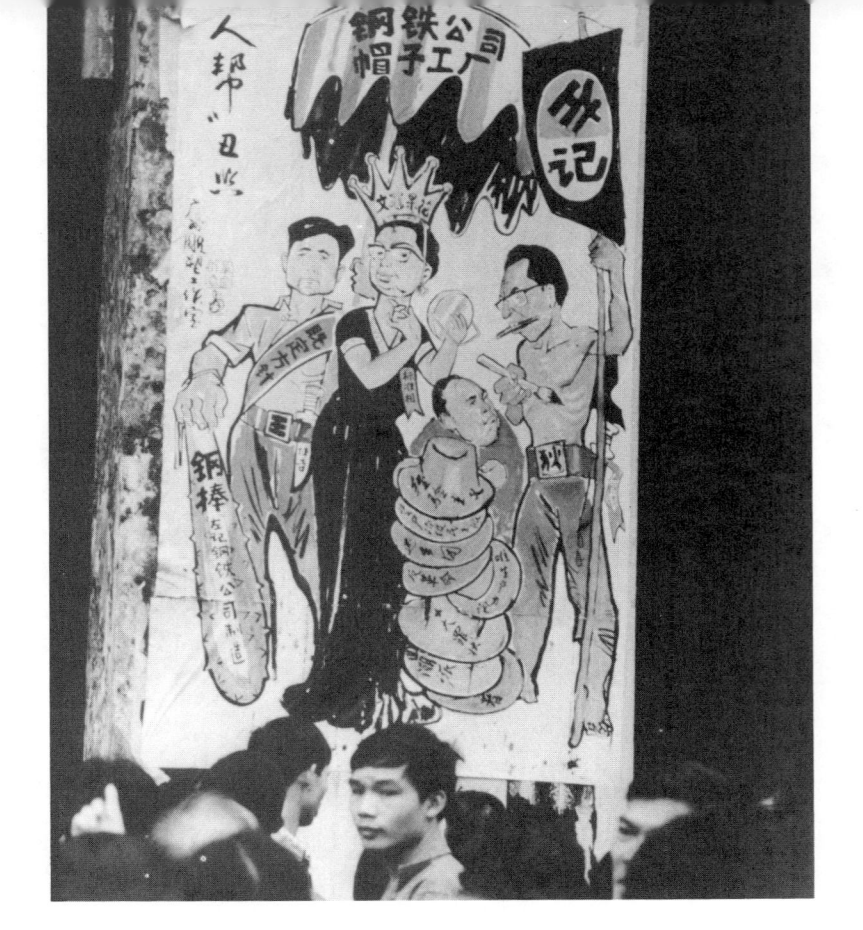

A poster denounces the "Gang of Four" as brutal and power-hungry. Jiang Qing, widow of Mao Zedong, wears a crown and studies her image in a mirror. In this way the artist reminds the viewer of Jiang's prerevolutionary career as an actress as well as of her alleged desire to be treated like royalty.

In 1980 four leaders who had supported the Cultural Revolution, among them Mao's widow Jiang Qing [Chiang Ch'ing] (jee-*ahng' ching'*), were accused of trying to overthrow the government after Mao's death. The members of this so-called "Gang of Four" were tried by a special court. In 1982 they received sentences of life in prison. The trials of these former radicals seemed to show that China's new leaders wanted to take a more moderate direction.

Political Organization

The control of China requires three legs – the Communist Party, the government, and the army.

Communist Party. The Communist Party is a pyramidal organization made up of less than 3 percent of the Chinese population. The base consists of a million branches in factories, mines, farms, schools, offices, the army, and other units of society. City, county, provincial, and regional party congresses make up the succeeding levels. These lower units elect the National Party Congress. Its power is delegated to a Central Committee of 200 party leaders.

The top governing body is the *Politburo* (Political Bureau). The all-powerful Politburo has nineteen members and sets all national policy. A seven-member Standing Committee is the inner circle of the Politburo. The first Chairman of the Standing Committee of the Politburo and the Central Committee of the National Party Congress was Mao Zedong. He served from 1935 until his death in

1976. From 1976 to 1981, Mao's hand-picked successor Hua Guofeng held this post. He was succeeded in 1981 by Hu Yaobang.

Policy is discussed within the party, and a small group makes the final decisions on establishing party policy. Once set, policy is strictly obeyed.

The *cadres,* groups of party workers, are the backbone of the party. They organize and direct the people at all levels of Chinese society to carry out party policy. The majority of the population belongs to branches of such national organizations as the All-China Federation of Trade Unions and the All-China Federation of Literary and Art Workers. Local party leaders direct each group, and its members become involved in party tasks.

The Young Pioneers and the Young Communist League enroll young people for party training. School children between nine and fifteen join the Young Pioneers. Those between fifteen and twenty-five join the Young Communist League, which serves as a stepping-stone to party membership.

Chinese government. The government issues and enforces the policy established by the Communist Party. The National People's Congress meets annually. Other than electing the Chairman of the Republic, it has no real political power. Its Standing Committee functions when the Congress is not in session. The highest government authority is the cabinet-like State Council, headed by a premier. The State Council supervises all government agencies. Zhou Enlai [Chou En-lai] (*joe' en-lie'*), a founder of the Chinese Communist party and a veteran with Mao of the Long March and the civil war, was the first to serve as premier. Zhao Ziyang assumed this position in 1980. But the real leader of China in the years after the deaths of Mao and Zhou was Deng Xiaoping [Teng Hsiao-p'ing] (*dung' she-ow-ping'*), a vice premier and chief of staff of the army.

The judiciary consists of the Supreme People's Court, provincial, and county people's courts. However, trials can be held in open meetings outside of the courts where an accused person faces mass denunciations.

The 1954 Constitution, which organized the present government, did not mention the Communist party. But every level of government had party members from a parallel unit. For example, State Council members belonged to the Central Committee of the party.

A new constitution in 1982 restored the post of president. This position had been abolished by Mao in 1968, after his dispute with Liu Shaoqi. The 1982 constitution also limited top officials to two consecutive five-year terms in office. Before this, officials had held their jobs for life.

The army. We have already seen that military forces played a key role in the success of the Chinese Communists. Mao rejected the idea of a professional army separate from civil society. Under Defense Minister Lin Biao, a party and army figure, political control was established over the People's Liberation Army. Soldiers studied political as well as military affairs. They kept close contact with the people by their work with farmers and workers. The army became the showcase for correct Communist behavior and set the pace for the study and implementation of the thought of Mao Zedong. Under the 1982 constitution, leadership of the armed forces shifted to a Central Military Council. The leader of this council was to be elected by the National People's Congress.

Vice-Premier Deng Xiaoping wielded great power in China after the deaths of Mao and Zhou. One of his first great triumphs was to win diplomatic recognition for Communist China from the United States.

China's Foreign Relations

Once in power, the Communists removed all signs of foreign domination in the country. Western businesses, government buildings, publications, and Christian missionary facilities were closed. In this way government leaders asserted that China was its own master within its borders. But China was not totally isolated and continued trade and diplomatic relations with many nations.

China and the United States. After its consular buildings were seized in 1950, the United States broke diplomatic relations with China. However, irregular diplomatic meetings between the countries occurred in Poland for many years. In 1970 the United States government once again permitted Americans to visit and have limited trade with China. Beijing allowed American journalists and scholars to visit. President Richard Nixon visited Beijing in February 1972, ending two decades of no official diplomatic contact.

After the Indochina War, relations worsened between China and Vietnam. A 1978 treaty between Vietnam and the USSR increased China's fears of "encirclement" by its two former Communist allies. The United States wanted improved relations with China to limit Soviet influence in Asia and to improve trade. The Chinese wanted American technological aid for its modernization program. In 1979 full diplomatic relations were established between China and the United States. The American embassy in Taiwan was replaced by an

Premier Zhou Enlai and U.S. President Richard Nixon tour a garden in Hangzhou during Nixon's 1972 visit to China. Zhou, a veteran of the Long March, held considerable power in China's government from 1949 until his death in 1976. In his last years he made many more of the daily decisions of government than the aging Mao.

"institute." American military aid to Taiwan ended, except for the sale of "defensive arms." Beijing speaks of peaceful unification of Taiwan with the rest of China.

China and the Soviet Union. China's ties with the Soviet Union during the first decade of its existence were a great help to it. By the terms of the 1950 Sino-Soviet Treaty, The Soviets promised to protect China from attack by Japan or any of its allies, meaning the United States. They gave economic and military assistance to modernize China's economy and armed forces, and promised to help China develop nuclear weapons. Furthermore, they withdrew from Manchuria.

This cooperation collapsed in 1960 when the Soviet Union cut off its assistance. The split between China and the Soviets was based on differences in philosophy. The Soviet leader Nikita Khrushchev's (Kroos-*choff*) attacks on the former Russian leader Joseph Stalin upset Mao, who admired Stalin Khrushchev did not believe that war between the capitalist Western world and the Communist countries was inevitable. He felt that Communism could triumph peacefully because it would provide a better life for people than capitalism. Mao, on the other hand, believed that war between the Communist and non-Communist worlds was unavoidable. This conflict of ideas was reflected in a competition between China and Russia for leadership in the Communist world.

Relations worsened as the USSR signed a nuclear test ban treaty with the major Western powers and supported India in 1962 in its clash with China. In 1969 a border dispute between China and the Soviet Union led to fighting on the Manchurian frontier between the two nations. Although tensions mounted, a major war was averted. However, both nations kept large military forces along their common border. In the early 1980s the Soviet Union tried to ease tensions between the two Communist giants by offering to negotiate these long-standing border disputes. China was slow to respond, insisting that the Soviets first reduce their military forces along the border.

319

China and the Afro-Asian world. Today the People's Republic of China sees itself as the revolutionary example for "colonial" countries, that is, countries once dominated by foreign rulers. China has attempted to win friends among the newly independent African and Asian countries. The Chinese government tried to promote itself as a leader of the developing Third World nations, better able to understand their problems than the more industrialized powers would be. So far results are mixed. An Indonesian government sympathetic to the Chinese was replaced by an anti-Communist government in 1965, and diplomatic relations between the two countries were severed in 1967. While relations were cut off between China and several African nations, China helped Tanzania build a 1000-mile railroad that opened in 1975.

In 1984 China and Great Britain agreed that they would reunite Hong Kong with China as a "special administrative district" in 1997. Hong Kong will retain its capitalist way of life until 2047. In all areas except defense and foreign relations it will govern itself, but under the watchful eyes of Beijing. Hong King's importance in international trade will aid China's modernization drive.

Looking ahead. Twenty-eight years after the Chinese Communist Party was founded, it controlled one of the oldest nations in the world. Since 1949 peace and order have been established in China, and the country has been politically united under a strong central government. Its leaders are committed to restoring China to its former position of power in East Asia and to being involved in any international question which touches this region.

CHAPTER REVIEW

Recalling Names and Places

cadre
Central Committee
Deng Xiaoping
Jiang Qing
Lin Biao
Lin Shaoqi
National People's Congress
Politburo
Red Guard
Sino-Soviet Treaty
Standing Committee
State Council
Young Communist League
Young Pioneers
Zhou Enlai

Understanding This Chapter

1. What were the major differences between the policies favored by Mao Zedong and Liu Shaoqi?
2. What part did the Red Guards play in the Cultural Revolution?
3. Describe the structure of the Chinese Communist Party. How does each level function?
4. How is the government organized? How is it coordinated with the Communist party?
5. What part does the People's Liberation Army play in China?
6. What issues have caused conflict between China and the United States?
7. Describe the changing relations between China and the Soviet Union.
8. What has been China's goal in its relations with the Afro-Asian world? How successful has it been?

Chapter 27

China's Contributions to Civilization

China's almost 4,000-year history is rich in human achievements. From the Shang, Zhou, Han, Tang, Sung, and Ming dynasties have come discoveries and creations that have added greatly to an understanding and appreciation of our world and to everyday convenience. The world's debt to Chinese culture is great. The modern world may be enriched by the new China as well.

Chinese as Early Scientists

The Chinese made many contributions to technological and scientific knowledge. Early in China's history, scholars were encouraged by the government to undertake scientific work. The government favored the growth of applied science. It supported work on projects that had a useful, practical application.

Astronomers organized the calendar, which was used to set planting and harvesting times. The acceptance of the Chinese calendar by its neighboring countries was a sign of their tributary relationship to China.

Major technological contributions. The Chinese developed many inventions that have made work more efficient and life easier. Perhaps their four greatest discoveries were printing, paper, gunpowder, and magnetism.

Printing developed from the use of official and religious seals made of wood or metal. Carved in relief and backwards, their ink impression appeared right way round on a white background. The *Diamond Sutra,* a Buddhist text of 868 A.D., is the oldest printed book in the world. Movable type was devised by the Chinese in the eleventh century, almost 400 years before Gutenberg developed the printing press in Europe. However, because of the large number of characters in their language, the Chinese tended to use block printing rather than movable type.

Paper appeared in 105 A.D. It was made from tree bark, hemp, rags, and fish nets. Later bamboo became the most popular material for making paper.

Gunpowder was developed by Taoists interested in alchemy, an early form of science that sought the secret of long life. In their search for a substance to prolong life, the Taoists examined the chemical properties of many substances. The first explosive mixture, consisting of charcoal, saltpeter (potassium nitrate), and sulphur, came from such activity. It was initially used in making fireworks, but by 1000 A.D. gunpowder was used in simple bombs.

The Chinese also did the earliest work on magnetism. The discovery of magnetism grew from the Chinese system of geomancy. Geomancy involved the selection of sites for buildings and tombs. A good site meant honor and wealth for

321

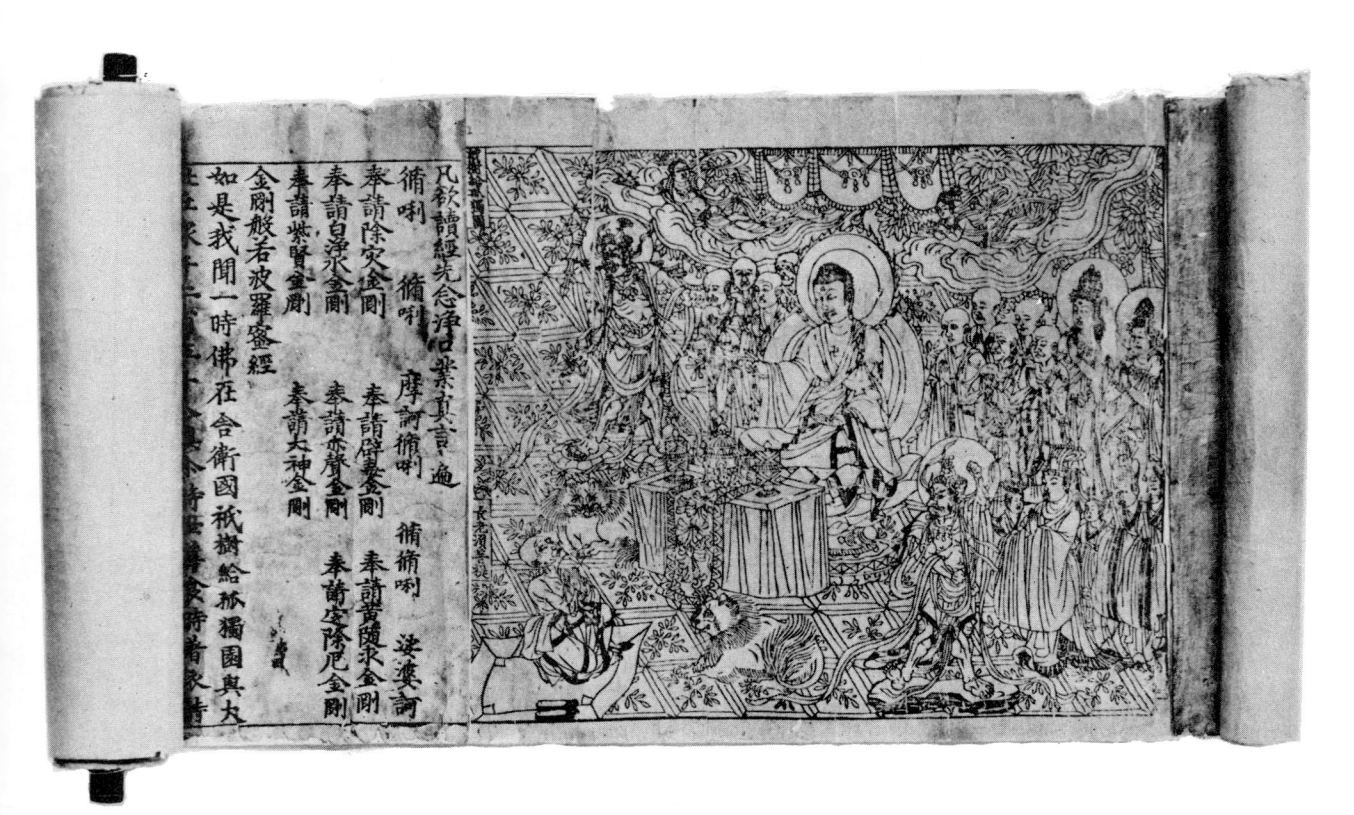

The diamond sutra, the oldest printed book in the world.

the family. The geomancer, a sort of fortune-teller, was employed to determine if a site was lucky or unlucky. He rubbed a lodestone against a steel needle, which was then floated in water or suspended from a thread.

Using their understanding of magnetism, the Chinese invented the compass. By the twelfth century, the compass was used for navigation. From the Chinese, Arab traders learned to sail by compass. They introduced the instrument to the Europeans.

Other important contributions. The Chinese developed numerous tools and techniques centuries before they appeared in Europe. Many tools were devised to make work easier, including the breaststrap harness and the collar harness for horses. Before the invention of the harness, animal power was less useful than human power to drag a plow or pull a cart. The Chinese also found that pushing an object is easier than pulling one, and they developed the wheelbarrow. The Chinese developed iron casting during the sixth century B.C. In addition to its use in tools, iron was used to protect warships and as chains on suspension bridges.

All these inventions were seen in China many centuries before they appeared in the Western world. Chinese developments made their way to Europe in clusters. Around the twelfth century, paper making, the sternpost rudder, and the idea of the windmill were transmitted to Europe. Arabic traders, Tatar slaves, European travelers, and later Jesuit missionaries carried this information westward. Possibly Europeans invented these items independently of their Chinese counterparts. For example, a seismograph used in second century A.D. China was not known by the European scientists who developed one themselves 1400 years later.

Limitations of Chinese mathematics. Chinese accomplishments in mathematics seem few in comparison to their contributions in applied science and technology. Chinese scholars studied algebra but not geometry. They never developed a widely used system of mathematical logic. Prior to the arrival of the Jesuit missionaries in the seventeenth century, the Chinese had no symbolic way of writing algebraic equations. They used Chinese characters instead. In contrast, modern European mathematics during this same period was systematic and abstract. Calculus, logarithms, analytical geometry, and the slide rule were invented in seventeenth-century Europe.

Chinese unable to develop modern science. Confucian scholars were more concerned about solving problems of human relations than about abstract, scientific problems. The Confucians sought to show people how to live together harmoniously. The Taoists were curious about the natural world. Unlike the Western philosophers of the seventeenth century who were busily working toward a modern scientific method of studying the world, the Chinese kept their mystical, religious feeling toward the universe.

For Chinese scholars, true happiness was found in self-knowledge and in a life lived in harmony with nature. While scholars wanted to enjoy a comfortable life, more goods were not essential for true happiness. The Chinese did not want what modern science offered – greater technology, power over the natural world, and an improved standard of living. Unlike westerners, the Chinese felt no need to develop modern science to conquer the natural world.

A doctor at Beijing's Children's Hospital gives an acupuncture treatment. This ancient Chinese practice involves inserting needles of various sizes into specific spots on the body. It is used in treating such ailments as arthritis and headaches.

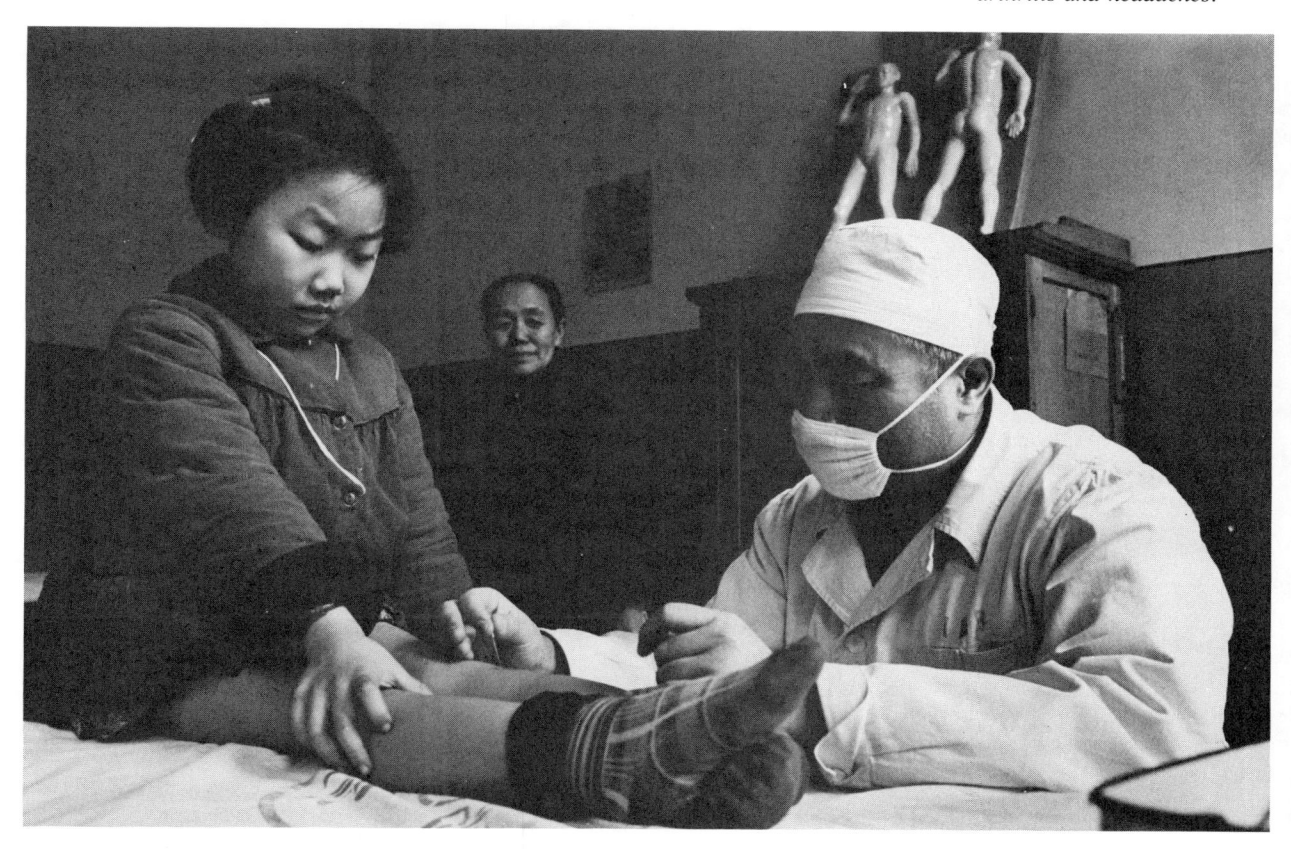

> **The Civil Service: A Chinese Invention**
>
> Until the nineteenth century the Western world had no system comparable to the Chinese method of choosing government officials by merit. Birth or political appointment was the usual channel to a government position. Admiring the Chinese examination system, some Britons called for the adoption of a similar method. In 1855 the British civil service, based on competitive tests open to all classes, was created. The United States adopted the system in 1883.

Furthermore, because of the social gulf between classes, the knowledge of the scholar and the skills of the artisan could not be combined to produce a new form of learning. Finally, Chinese scholars did not break with the teachings of Confucianism.

Modern science in China today. Unlike the scholars of the past, modern China is committed to a "march on science." Scientists today are working to supply the immediate needs of the nation. Scientists have devised an inexpensive method of producing nitrogen fertilizer and a hormone to stimulate plant growth. Discoveries like these can be used on the communes.

Chinese scientists are also working on new weapons for China's defense. Chinese scientists and engineers have successfully tested nuclear bombs and missiles and launched a satellite. Without a doubt, the Chinese are rapidly adapting modern science to meet their needs.

Chinese Art

Our knowledge of early Chinese art has come from the excavations of archaeologists in the tombs of ancient Chinese civilization. The Chinese custom of surrounding the dead with objects that might be needed in the afterlife made possible the preservation of numerous art treasures.

Bronzes and ceramics. Thousands of bronze vessels were excavated from tombs of the Shang and Zhou dynasties. These vessels were used in sacrificial offerings to Heaven, Earth, and ancestors. The beauty of these food containers, caldrons, wine vessels, and goblets is in their shape and decoration. Some are cast in the form of birds and elephants. Others are decorated with dragons, reptiles, and mythical beasts, which were probably religious symbols of some kind.

When archaeologists opened the tombs of the Tang dynasty, they uncovered amazing collections of ceramic articles. Realistic ceramic servants, musicians, bodyguards, and dancing girls were found along with lively horses and camels. Glazes of yellow, green, and blue set these figures apart from the ceramics of other dynasties.

Porcelain was the highest form of Tang ceramic work. To make porcelain, a person mixed kaolin, a chemical compound, with white clay and baked the mixture in a very hot oven. Porcelain plates and bowls were very serviceable, for they were hard, smooth, and nonporous. Over many centuries, Chinese porcelain has had wide appeal and influence around the world.

Compare this Chinese Buddhist statue with the Indian figures shown in Unit Three. How is it similar? How is it different? What has changed as a result of the processs of cultural exchange?

The Lung-men Buddha in central China, fifty feet high, was carved in the seventh century.

Ceramics of a single color – creamy white or iridescent blue – were often preferred during the Sung dynasty. Lavender bowls with splashes of purple were also popular. A tenth-century imperial order required some wares to be "blue as the sky, clear as a mirror, thin as paper, and resonant as a musical stone of jade." If the artisan controlled the firing, a crackled glaze like a spider web was produced. Blue-white ceramics made during the Ming period were crowded with people, flowers, and twisting dragons. All Chinese ceramics proved very popular in Europe when traders introduced them. Special ceramic objects were later made for purchase by Europeans.

Lacquerware. Lacquer, a resinous varnish, is tapped from trees. Channels are cut into the tree, and the oozing sap is collected and removed by a scraper. Lacquer can be finely polished and serves as a good insulator. Cups and bowls with a lacquer surface keep liquids hot.

To make lacquerware, the craftsman applies coat after coat of lacquer to wood until it is thick enough to carve. Boxes, trays, utensils, and furniture are often covered with red or black lacquer. They are decorated with landscapes, human figures, or animal life. Sometimes designs were carved through layers of lacquer of contrasting colors.

Chinese Painting

Most Chinese paintings were done on hand scrolls. The scroll was rolled up when not on display and placed in a wooden box for storage. In this way people

This sixteenth-century ceramic jar (left) is a fine example of the porcelain of the Ming dynasty. The red lacquer plate (right) is from the Yuan dynasty, late thirteenth or early fourteenth century.

could vary the exhibition of the scrolls in their collections. Scrolls were often stamped with red seals, bearing the names of the artist or of previous owners.

Landscape painting was the supreme form of Chinese painting. While color was sometimes used, most landscapes were in black ink with bold brush strokes. A landscape might place tiny human figures, buildings, or boats against a vast background of craggy mountains with twisted pine trees, valleys, and a lake or river. Another artist might select a single detail of nature such as a lotus, a spray of bamboo, or a bird perched on a branch of a blossoming fruit tree.

Landscape painting was closely connected to Chinese religion and philosophy. Taoist influences appeared in nature scenes in which tiny human figures are a small part of the larger natural world. These paintings expressed the feeling that people should live in harmony with nature.

Although the landscape painter copied the colors and forms of natural objects, landscape paintings were largely suggestive, often with areas left unpainted. A too accurate conformity to nature was avoided. Painters thought this robbed a picture of its beauty. Artists also felt that their work was better if it reflected the style of a great artist from the past. Sometimes an artist would copy a poem relating to the scene on the scroll.

Contemporary art. There are many styles of modern art in China today. Woodcuts depict industrial scenes, cooperative farm life, dam construction, and political meetings. Under the Communists, artists have been encouraged to continue using such traditional Chinese art forms as landscape painting but to paint "correct" modern subjects. For example, one "correct" modern subject is Chinese soldiers crossing a suspension bridge over a river gorge. Today art is very much in the service of the Communist Party. It is used for propaganda purposes and to build loyalty to the new China.

Chinese Literature

Confucianism has strongly influenced Chinese literature. It has affected both the works of the writers who followed the traditions of the past and of those who did not. Because of the Confucian influence, moral lessons were an integral part of literature. The Confucian writer used the written word to teach people to be good. In traditional stories virtue is rewarded and vice is punished.

Chinese poetry. Of all of China's literary forms, poetry has had the greatest worldwide appeal. The writing of poetry was an everyday activity for the scholar, who had many occasions to write poems. The most common form of verse was a compact four- or eight-line poem, each line of five or seven words. Frequent themes were friendship and family love, nature, and a nostalgic longing for home.

The Tang dynasty was an era of brilliant poetic creation. Emperors, officials, generals, Taoist hermits, and Buddhist monks tried their hand at poetry. Poets were honored and patronized. The poems of Tu Fu *(doo' foo')* represent some of the best of Chinese poetry.

Tu Fu (712–780) came from a poor, scholar family. Although he failed the examinations, he held minor posts and served briefly as a censor. Selections from his poems reflect such Confucian values as his deep love for his family and concern over the decline of Chinese society.

"Spring Plowing," a fifteenth-century landscape painting, contains a poem inscribed in fine calligraphy. Poems frequently appear in Chinese scroll paintings.

> My old wife stays in a strange land,
> Our ten mouths separated by wind and snow.
> Who would have left them long uncared for?
> So I went home to share their hunger and thirst.
> Entering the door, I heard a loud wail;
> Our youngest boy had died of starvation.
> How could I forbear from sharing this great sorrow?
> Our neighbors too sobbed and sighed.
> Ashamed am I to be a father
> That the lack of food should have caused his death.
>
> * * *
>
> The silk that was bestowed at the vermilion court
> Came originally from some poor shivering women;
> Their husbands were whipped and flogged
> So that it could be levied as a tribute to the
>   imperial city
>
> * * *
>
> Inside the vermilion gate wine and meat are stinking
> On the roadside lie the bones of people frozen to death
>
> * * *
>
> All my life I have been exempt from taxes,
> My name has not been listed in the muster roll.
> If I should feel bitter and grieved at past
>   experiences
> The commoners indeed have more reason to be angry.
> Silently I think of those who were unemployed
> And of soldiers summoned to guard the frontier.*

* From *An Introduction to Chinese Literature* by Liu Wu-chi. Copyright © 1966 by Liu Wu-chi. Reprinted by permission of Indiana University Press. (pp. 80, 82)

The ancient art of Chinese calligraphy is still practiced today.

Traditional fiction. While poetry was written in classical Chinese, fiction was written in the language of the common people. Folktales, historical events, and Buddhist stories about the supernatural originally told by entertainers were turned into novels by scholars writing under assumed names. For example, a Buddhist monk's journey to India was the basis for Wu Ch'eng-en's supernatural novel of the mid-1500s, *Monkey*. The all-powerful Monkey escorted the monk and overcame superhuman obstacles to help him reach his destination. Told with much humor, it is an allegory of a pilgrim's progress to Buddhist salvation. Ts'ao Chan's *The Dream of the Red Chamber* traced the decline of an upper-class Chinese family in the eighteenth century. *The Scholar* is a satirical novel that contrasts sham scholars with honest ones. It also criticizes officials and the examination system. Together these novels present an interesting picture of imperial Chinese society.

Twentieth-century fiction. During the late 1800s, Western writings were translated and avidly read by many Chinese. Modern writers abandoned the traditional forms of fiction writing to adopt Western literary models. Fiction became realistic, a form of protest against social injustice, and an instrument of social reform. Lu Xun [Lu Hsun] (1881–1936) wrote satirical short stories and critical essays, including "The Diary of a Madman" in which he attacked Confucian society. Pa Chin (1904-   ) wrote a sentimental autobiographical novel, *Family,* in which he described clashes in the Gao family between the desires of the young and parental authority, which resulted in tragedies of forced marriages and frustrated true love. In *Rickshaw Boy,* Lao She (1899–1966) portrayed the

Sun	Moon	High	Elephant

Chinese characters developed from simple picture images, or ideographs, somewhat like Egyptian hieroglyphics. The four columns show how the symbols for sun, moon, high, and elephant evolved from the fourteenth century B.C. to modern times.

futile effort of a rickshaw puller to improve his life. Lao She ends his novel with the conclusion that a collective effort is needed to replace a sick society.

Literature under the Communists. Literature, according to the Communists, must be used to free the people from oppression and to serve them. To the Communists this means teaching people to accept Communist doctrine and the Communist way of life. In *Dragon Beard Ditch*, a melodramatic play by Lao She, a foul-smelling, treacherous ditch is repaired under party direction by a cooperative effort. After the work is done, everyone is converted to Communism. The play's message is expressed in such lines as: "The government cares for us; we must care for them." "The Communist Party really gets things done!"

Other art forms. The Beijing Opera is a blend of drama and music. It is performed with little scenery and few stage properties. The actors wear elaborate costumes and color their faces to indicate their character. A performance may consist of scenes from several plays. The opera combines music, singing, acting, dancing, and acrobatics. The gestures of the actors are set. There is little freedom for the actors to develop their roles. The opera is judged less for its literary merits and more for the skill of the actors.

As with other art forms, motion pictures in China serve the party as weapons of propaganda and education. Often the artistic qualities of the motion picture have been sacrificed in the interests of teaching party policy. The movie *Five Golden Flowers* is a love story with a political theme. The characters have such names as Iron-Smelter Golden Flower and Tractor-Driver Golden Flower. *The East Is Red* describes the Chinese revolution under Mao Zedong.

Current Chinese artistic and literary works with their heavy emphasis on propaganda disappoint viewers or readers who are familiar with past Chinese cul-

Dancers perform a scene from The Red Detachment of Women, *a popular revolutionary ballet about the women of the Chinese Red Army.*

tural creations. A totalitarian government that demands that its artists follow the party line makes the appearance of genuinely creative artists and writers difficult, but not impossible. As great cultural works have been produced in other restrictive societies, no doubt Chinese artists will once again produce works which will attract worldwide admiration.

CHAPTER REVIEW

Recalling Names and Places

Diamond Sutra	Lao She	scroll
geomancy	Lu Xun	Tu Fu
landscape painting	Pa Chin	

Understanding This Chapter

1. How did the early Chinese rulers encourage scientific and technological study?
2. Describe Chinese work in printing, paper making, gunpowder, and magnetism. Why are these inventions considered especially important?
3. How can China's inability to develop modern science be explained?
4. What is the attitude of the Chinese today regarding modern science?
5. How did the examination system influence Western civilization?
6. Where has much of our information about early Chinese art come from? Describe the art objects from this source.
7. Describe Chinese work in ceramics and painting.
8. Contrast traditional Chinese fiction with twentieth-century fiction.
9. What use do the Communists make of literature, art, theatre, and cinema?

UNIT 6
Exploring
Japan

Timeline

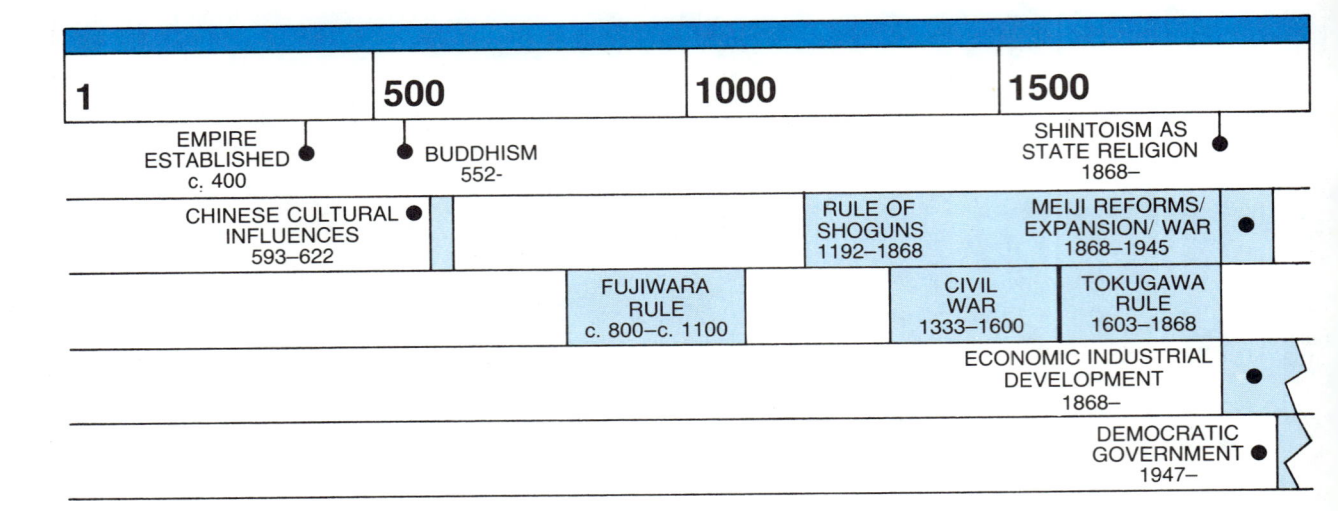

c. 400	EMPIRE ESTABLISHED
552–	BUDDHISM
593–622	CHINESE CULTURAL INFLUENCES
c. 800–c. 1100	FUJIWARA RULE
1192–1868	RULE OF SHOGUNS
1333–1600	CIVIL WAR
1603–1868	TOKUGAWA RULE
1868–	SHINTOISM AS STATE RELIGION
1868–1945	MEIJI REFORMS/ EXPANSION/ WAR
1868–	ECONOMIC INDUSTRIAL DEVELOPMENT
1947–	DEMOCRATIC GOVERNMENT

JAPAN WAS ONE OF THE FEW ASIAN NATIONS that successfully maintained its independence during the nineteenth century, when Western imperialist nations expanded or created Asian colonial empires. It was also the first Asian nation to modernize itself, defeat a Western nation, and challenge the Western powers for dominance in the western Pacific.

Although Japan failed to become a powerful nation by war, since 1945 it has done so by peaceful means. Japan today is the third largest industrial nation in the world, surpassed only by the United States and the Soviet Union. Japanese products are often eagerly purchased by other industrial nations. The Japanese have a higher standard of living and literacy rate than all other Asian people and compare favorably with many Western nations.

By looking at Japan's history and civilization we can discover how the Japanese have accomplished these feats. When confronted with the more highly developed civilizations of China and, later, the Western world, the Japanese responded by borrowing from those cultures. Cultural borrowing, adaptation, and assimilation are carried on by all people. It would be a mistake to think of the Japanese solely as imitators. As we shall see, the Japanese did not simply bring foreign elements into their own culture. Often they also changed them, improving them and thus giving them a distinctly Japanese character.

| 1900 | 1910 | 1920 | 1930 | 1940 | 1950 | 1960 | 1970 | 1980 |

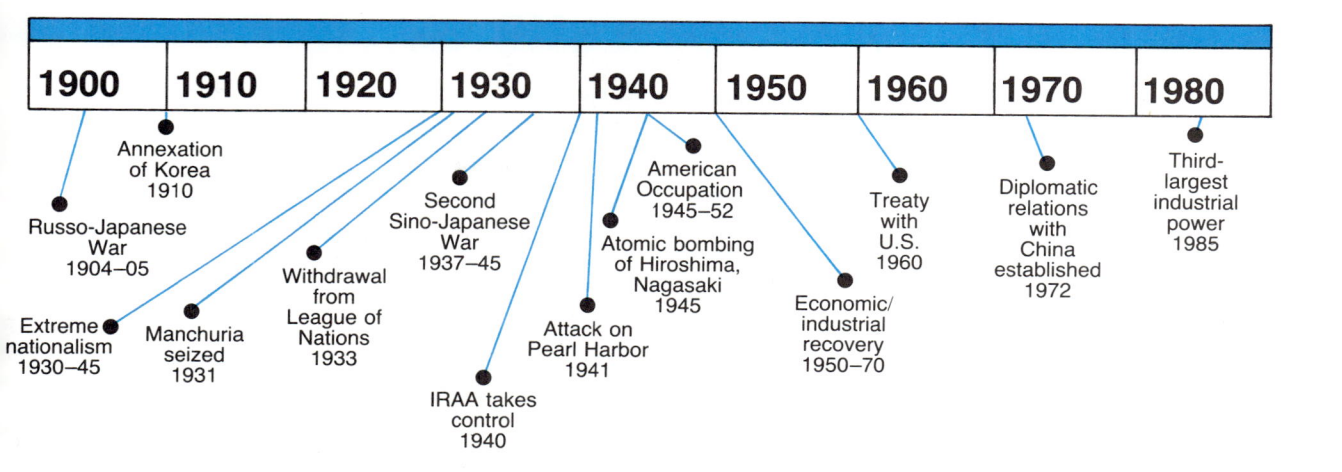

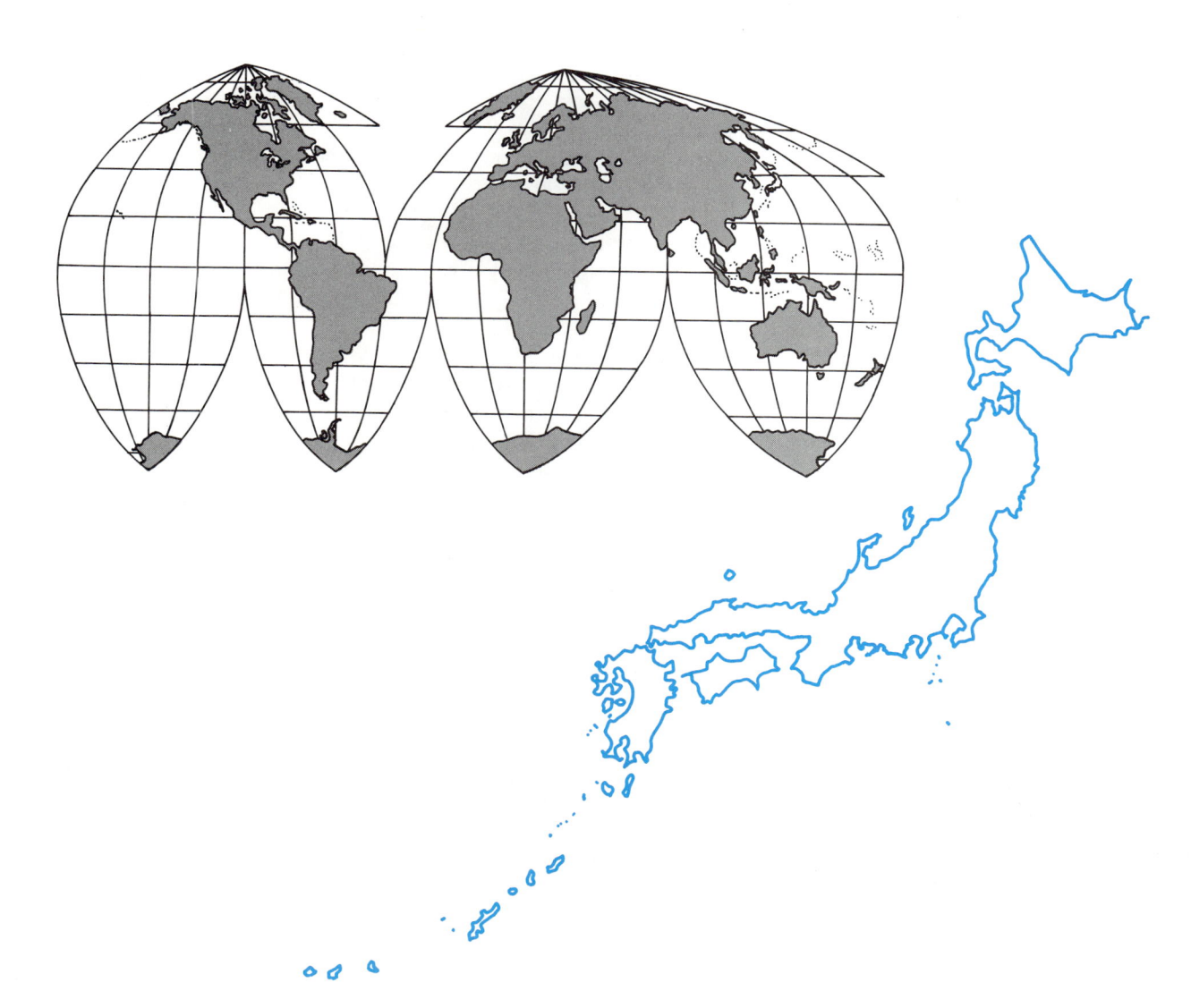

- Annexation of Korea 1910
- Russo-Japanese War 1904–05
- Extreme nationalism 1930–45
- Manchuria seized 1931
- Withdrawal from League of Nations 1933
- Second Sino-Japanese War 1937–45
- IRAA takes control 1940
- Attack on Pearl Harbor 1941
- American Occupation 1945–52
- Atomic bombing of Hiroshima, Nagasaki 1945
- Economic/industrial recovery 1950–70
- Treaty with U.S. 1960
- Diplomatic relations with China established 1972
- Third-largest industrial power 1985

333

Chapter 28

Japan: The Island Empire

Japan is an arc of islands on the eastern edge of Asia. If it were placed along the eastern coast of the United States, Japan would stretch from Maine to Georgia. Extending 1500 miles, Japan covers 142,727 square miles; thus, it is a bit smaller than the state of California. Whereas over 25 million people reside in California, more than 119 million live in Japan.

Influence of Land and Climate on Japan

As in other culture regions, climate and landforms have affected Japan's development. That it is an island country located off the Asian continent has been an especially important factor in its history.

Climate. Lying in the temperate zone, most of Japan has four seasons. Hot, humid summers prevail throughout the nation, while the winters are cold in the north and mild in the south. Spring and autumn are the most pleasant times of the year.

Japanese weather is influenced by both the Asian continent and the Pacific Ocean. Cold Siberian winds absorb moisture from the Sea of Japan and deposit heavy snow on the northern portion of Honshu* and Hokkaido islands. Kyushu and Shikoku in the south get heavy rains during the summer. The "Plum rain," important for rice cultivation, appears in June and July at the time the plum trees blossom. Typhoons from the southern Pacific arrive in late summer. Their strong winds and heavy rains endanger human lives and destroy farm crops and dwellings. No part of Japan has less than 40 inches of rain each year, and some areas have more than 100 inches.

Island nation. Of the hundreds of Japanese islands the four main islands are Honshu, Kyushu, Shikoku, and Hokkaido. Honshu is the largest and has 75 percent of the population. Hokkaido is the least economically developed and is sparsely settled. In 1984 a 54-kilometer (33.5-mile) tunnel was completed, connecting Honshu and Hokkaido, as part of the national railway system.

Japan's geographic isolation as an island nation kept it safe from outside pressures for much of its history. For example, an unsuccessful Mongol invasion attempt in the thirteenth century was the only foreign military threat Japan faced

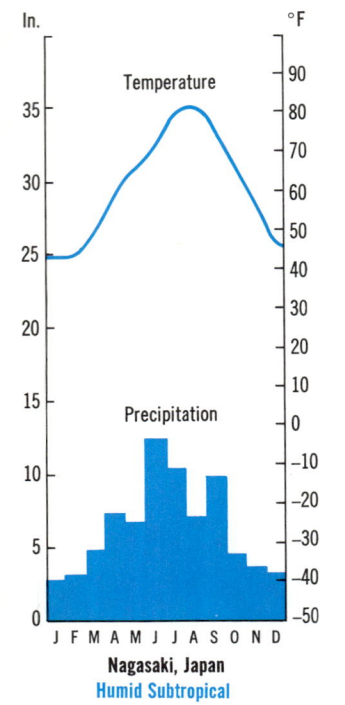

Nagasaki, Japan
Humid Subtropical

---
* Japanese is easy to pronounce because most words sound like they are spelled. Japanese consonants are usually pronounced as in English. Vowels generally have one sound only – **a** as in **father**; **e** as in **sent**; **i** as in **machine**; **o** as in **host**; **u** as in **food**. The letters **ai** are pronounced ī as in **samurai**. The letters **ei** are pronounced ā as in **geisha**.

334

JAPAN: POLITICAL AND PHYSICAL

Elevations

Feet	Meters
6,600	2,000
1,600	500
700	200
0	0

✪ National capital
▲ Mountain peak

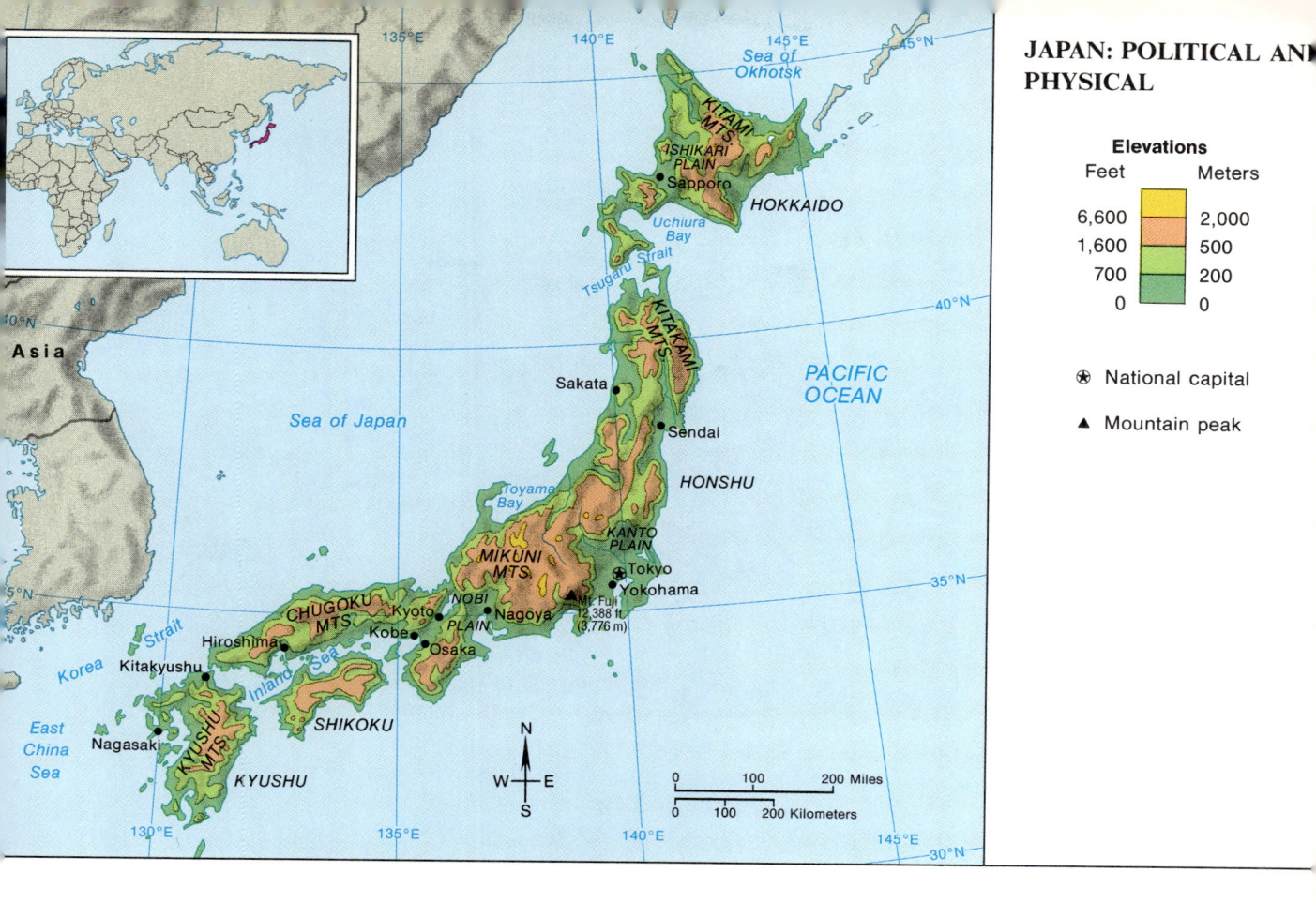

until it was defeated and occupied in 1945. Change in Japan before the last century took place slowly, more from internal than external pressure.

While the sea has limited Japan's living area, it has played an important role in its development. Japan developed its sea trade to obtain resources for its industrial needs and to transport its exports the world over. It has also taken advantage of the fact that the waters around the islands are one of the world's richest fishing grounds.

Rivers and mountains. The rivers of Japan are seldom used for travel, since they are short and fast flowing. They do, however, supply water for irrigation. Japan, more than any other Asian country, has harnessed its rivers to create hydroelectric power.

About 85 percent of Japan is mountainous, and half of the country is covered with forest. Further, almost 200 volcanoes are found in the island chain, and there are more than 1500 earth tremors each year. Mt. Fuji, Japan's most famous volcano, has been inactive since 1707. When the Tokyo-Yokohama area was devastated by an earthquake in 1923, some 143,000 people died.

While the tree-covered mountains and deep valleys make Japan a beautiful country and inspire poets and painters, the rugged land severely restricts the living area. Hence, most of Japan's population, industry, and agriculture are concentrated on a few plains and basins where every bit of available land is cultivated, no matter how small it is. Kanto is the fertile, densely populated

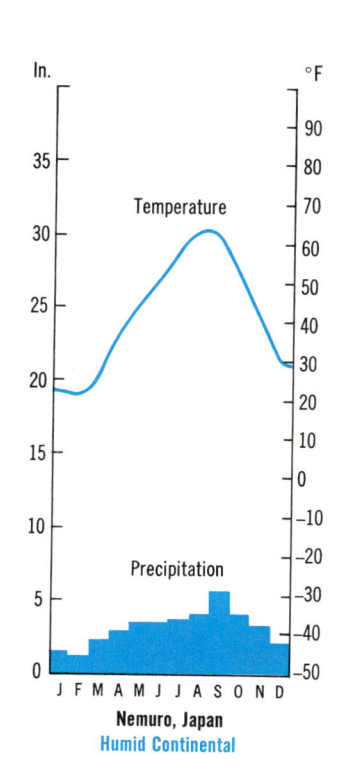

Nemuro, Japan
Humid Continental

An early morning view of the Tokyo fish market.

> **Fish in the Japanese Diet**
>
> That fish is an important food item for the Japanese can be seen by a visit to the Tokyo Fish Market. The aisles are crowded with stalls displaying sardines, cod, salmon, mackerel, crab, squid, octopus, seaweed, and various dried fish products. Large tuna labeled with numbers lie on the dock to be auctioned off.
>
> Raw fish is a unique Japanese delicacy. Sliced filets of raw fish (*Sashimi*) are dipped in soy sauce and eaten with horseradish. Tuna, abalone, sea urchin, eel, octopus, and shrimp are a delight to eat. One might finish a seafood snack with a bit of cucumber and rice wrapped in seaweed.

plain around Tokyo. Kinki includes Japan's two ancient capitals, Nara and Kyoto. Japan's principal cities – Tokyo, Yokohama, Nagoya, Osaka, and Kobe – are found in these two regions.

Japan's industries extend along an almost 700-mile corridor from Tokyo to Kita-Kyushu in northwestern Kyushu. The cities and industries developed here because the deep-water ports gave traders access to the overseas trade routes. Part of this urban industrial belt runs along the Inland Sea and also includes major agricultural areas. The Inland Sea, between the islands of Honshu, Kyushu, and Shikoku, is Japan's "Main Street," for it is crowded with vessels of all types and sizes from all over the world.

Within this 700-mile belt lies the 320-mile corridor from Tokyo-Yokohama to Osaka-Kobe. Although this belt contains about half the Japanese population, they live on less than 1 percent of the total land area of the country. Seventy percent of the industry is located there. This highly urbanized corridor is called a megalopolis, a multi-centered cluster of cities. The world's second-largest city, Tokyo, has over 10 million inhabitants, whereas rural Hokkaido, one-third the size of the main island of Honshu, has 5 million people.

Limited resources. Japan's mineral resources are very limited. Its copper mines supply two-thirds of its needs. Though Japan has abundant coal deposits, their poor quality forces Japan to import coking coal for steel production. There are small iron, sulphur, and zinc deposits on the islands. Petroleum is Japan's largest import item, with 90 percent coming from the Middle East.

CHAPTER REVIEW

Recalling Names and Places

Hokkaido	Kinki	Mt. Fuji
Honshu	Kitakyushu	Nagoya
Inland Sea	Kobe	Osaka
Kanto	Kyushu	Shikoku

Understanding This Chapter

1. How has Japan's geographic position affected its climate?
2. What is the importance of the sea to Japan? Of rivers?
3. How have the mountains affected Japanese economic and urban patterns?
4. How has Japan overcome its shortage of mineral resources?
5. How has Japan achieved prosperity with so few resources?

Chapter 29

The Making of Modern Japan

Although Japan was not a major world power for much of its history, it became one in the twentieth century. It grew from a tribal society to an aristocratic government and then into a feudal society. Finally in this century it emerged as a modern nation-state. In the following pages we will see how Japan achieved this change.

Early Japanese Society

Japanese society before the fifth century A.D. consisted of clans whose members claimed a common ancestor and worshiped the same deity. The Yamato was the principal clan, exercising power from Kanto Plain to South Korea. Its authority was based on conquest and the claim that the Sun Goddess, an important figure in Japanese legend, was its original ancestor. According to Japanese mythology she gave the Yamato clan the jewel, mirror, and sword that are still the symbols of imperial authority in Japan today. The leader of the Yamato clan established the form of government that was to continue for many centuries. From the Yamato clan came the emperor, who also served as high priest, a role the present emperor retains. An entire system of ranks and titles was worked out. Guilds of priests, weavers, and rice growers were associated with the clans.

Chinese influence in Japan. Japan's continual contacts with Korea and China resulted in much cultural borrowing by the island people. In the seventh century the great cultural developments of Tang China passed to Japan, where they found a fertile soil in which to blossom. Buddhism was one of the principal cultural carriers, for it enriched Japanese life with Chinese-style temples, pagodas, sculpture, and painting.

Ambassadors went to China and, on their return, introduced Chinese cultural and technological advances. Chinese written word symbols, or characters, were adopted, thus providing the Japanese for the first time with a written language. The Chinese calendar was adopted along with the Chinese system of government.

The Japanese learned new skills from Korean and Chinese artisans. Foreign commerce increased as trade missions went to China and Korea. Markets appeared around temples, and some even grew into towns. Prior to the period of Chinese influence, Japan had no permanent cities. Nara, the first permanent capital, was modeled after the Chinese capital of Ch'ang-an.

Modification of Chinese influences. Though certain Chinese notions changed Japanese life, the Japanese borrowed selectively. For example, Shinto, a form of nature worship, remained the religion of the Japanese. The Chinese examination system for selecting officials by merit was not adopted because family, not talent, was the key to a government service position in Japan.

Decline of centralized government. The Fujiwara family dominated the imperial court from the ninth to the twelfth century. The luxurious court life with its moon viewing and poetry contests was quite different from the lives of the rest of society. It became an economic burden on the Japanese people. Political dissenters were banished to remote areas where they built up their own groups of supporters. Ultimately the dissenters developed into a military class. Later, as we shall see, this military class broke the political power of the court and paved the way for the establishment of feudalism in Japan.

Feudalism and Early Contacts with Europe

Feudalism is a form of military government in which the ruling class is composed of a small group of landowners, who are the superior lords, and their subordinate vassals, who share the political power. Membership in the ruling group is hereditary, passing usually from the father to his eldest son. The lord protects his vassals and provides for their livelihood. In return, the vassal is expected to be loyal to his lord, defending him or his property whenever necessary and providing other services.

Japanese feudalism. As various factions in the imperial court quarreled among themselves for power, they lost effective control of the government. Other families asserted their authority in the countryside and in the court. In the struggle for control among rival court families Minamoto Yoritomo was the victor. In 1192 he forced the emperor to name him the *shogun,* the military ruler of Japan. While Kyoto remained the residence of the emperor, the shogun made Kamakura in eastern Japan his capital. There Yoritomo established a military government. Under Yoritomo the feudal system was extended throughout the land.

In time Japan was ruled by the shogun with the assistance of a group of powerful lords, the *daimyo* ("great names"), who were loyal to him. The daimyo's income came from estates worked by peasants. The daimyo's warriors, the *samurai,* were given an annual specified quantity of rice in return for providing protection for the shogun and the daimyo. The daimyo's personal officials were the *jito* and the *shugo.* The jito collected taxes, supervised roads, arrested criminals, and judged cases. The shugo were the military commanders who maintained peace and order and organized the local samurai in time of war. In this manner an orderly political system was established.

Civil war and unification. Succeeding shoguns were not as effective rulers as Yoritomo. Unsuccessful Mongol invasions of Japan in 1274 and in 1281 further weakened the shogun's authority. Many ambitious rivals appeared. From 1333 to 1600 Japan suffered from civil war. The rivals competed for political supremacy. However, in the late sixteenth century unity was finally established by three major military leaders, Nobunaga, Hideyoshi, and Ieyasu. These leaders defeated the weaker daimyo or gained their loyalty and support by granting

This painted screen from the sixteenth century is called "Views of Southern Barbarians." It shows a Japanese view of foreigners arriving in a harbor by ship.

them land. The military power of Buddhist monasteries was broken. In 1603 Tokugawa Ieyasu (1542–1616), the third of these great leaders, was made shogun of a united Japan.

Japan's first contact with Europeans. The Portuguese landed on Kyushu in 1543 and were followed by other European traders. Because the daimyo were disunited and fighting among themselves, the Europeans found it easy to enter Japan. In addition, both the Westerners and the daimyo were eager for the profits of trade. Nagasaki became the chief trading center. The Portuguese sold firearms, fabrics, and glassware; they purchased silk, ceramics, and silver.

Among many other things, the Europeans introduced tobacco and the potato from the Americas as well as European battle techniques. Japanese artisans learned to make Western-style weapons. These new weapons were adopted by some of the daimyo who were involved in the civil war. In a short time some of the contenders were using several thousand muskets in battle against rivals.

Rivalry among Portuguese and Spanish priests led the shogun to fear that Japan might be conquered and transformed into a colony. Fearing that the daimyo might organize converts to the Christian religion against him, the shogun forbade his followers to become Christians. A peasant uprising in 1637, in a Christian area of Kyushu, moved the shogun to action. With the support of Dutch vessels, which bombarded the rebel castle, the shogun savagely put down the peasant rebellion. Many Japanese were required to walk on plaques with the picture of Jesus Christ. Those who refused to do so were identified as Christians and tortured or executed. In short, while the Japanese were willing to adopt European arms and technology, they did not accept Western ideas as they had those of the Chinese in the seventh century.

The "Great Peace" of Tokugawa. The fishing village of Edo, modern-day Tokyo, became Tokugawa Ieyasu's capital in 1606. He ruled Japan with the aid of the daimyo. First Ieyasu divided them into two groups: those who were loyal to him before he united Japan, and those loyal afterward. The first group were given estates in remote areas, and the second were placed nearby so he could watch them.

Ieyasu devised an elaborate system of checks to keep the daimyo from threatening his rule. Under the *sankin-kotai system,* each daimyo lived part of the year in Edo under the shogun's eye and the rest of the year on his own estate. Whenever a daimyo returned to his estate, his family was expected to remain in Edo as hostages to insure the daimyo's good behavior. Roads and bridges leading from one estate to another were checked by the shogun's agents. Castle building was regulated by the Tokugawa shogun. Daimyo marriages were also carefully watched by the shogun to prevent the formation of an alliance that might threaten his power. An elaborate system of spies was used to watch daimyo activities.

Tokugawa seclusion policy. To secure their political authority and to preserve peace, the Tokugawa shoguns isolated Japan from the rest of the world in 1639. Christianity was banned. Except for some Chinese and a small Dutch contingent, who lived closely supervised lives in Nagasaki harbor, all foreigners were expelled from Japan. Not only were Christian books barred but so was any book, even a Chinese translation, dealing with any Western subject. Japanese were forbidden on pain of death to leave their homeland. Vessels were restricted in size so they could be used only in coastal trade and not in overseas commerce.

Such practices gave Japan about 250 years of peace. Thus, the era of Tokugawa rule is often referred to by historians as the "Great Peace." Japanese government became more stable, and cultural life flourished. Although Japanese society became more settled, economic growth was limited by the absence of foreign trade. Isolated Japan did not keep pace with Western economic and scientific development. Consequently, when Japan once again had contact with the rest of the world in the nineteenth century, it had to work especially hard to catch up with the Western world.

Reviewing Your Reading

1. Describe early Japanese society.
2. How did Chinese civilization affect Japanese life?
3. Trace the rise of the military class.
4. Describe Japanese feudalism.
5. How was Japan united under Tokugawa Ieyasu?
6. How did the Japanese respond to the European presence?
7. How did the shogun keep the daimyo from challenging his authority?
8. What was Tokugawa's seclusion policy? What was its long-range effect?

The "Opening" of Japan

Where the British and the Russians failed, the United States succeeded in "opening" Japan in 1854 to the world community. Under Commodore Matthew Perry a fleet of United States warships entered Tokyo Bay. The presence of foreign warships increased Japan's severe internal economic and political problems. Japanese leaders remembered China's recent defeat by the British during the Opium War. Fearing that their country would suffer a similar fate, the

Portraits of Commodore Matthew Perry by a Japanese artist and an American. Do the pictures reflect any differences in Japanese and American attitudes toward Perry?

Japanese granted certain rights to the United States: trade, protection of shipwrecked sailors, and access to fresh supplies. In addition, foreigners could live in Japan under extraterritorial protection. That is, foreigners in Japan who broke Japanese laws could not be tried under the Japanese legal system but were tried in courts administered by their own compatriots. Other Western nations received similar concessions. Thus after two and a half centuries Japanese seclusion ended.

Samurai oust the Tokugawa government. Japan was a country in motion. The shogun lost the confidence of many Japanese when he granted trading rights to Westerners. Seeing an opportunity to gain greater power, many samurai entered the political arena to defend Japan and to reform it. Under the slogan "expel the barbarian and revere the emperor," some samurai sought to continue the seclusion policy, but Japan was too weak militarily to expel the Westerners.

Several daimyo, through earlier contact with foreigners, purchased modern arms and strengthened their military units. With the shogun's power ebbing, they supported restoration of imperial rule to modernize their nation and safeguard it against foreigners. The shogun's effort to strengthen his forces came too late. He was defeated in a brief civil war. The Tokugawa shogunate was abolished in 1868.

Meiji Restoration. With the restoration of the emperor, Japan set out to modernize itself. The new government promised to abandon the "evil customs of the past" and seek knowledge the world over. Within the next two decades Japan underwent massive changes that affected every aspect of its life. These will be examined in succeeding chapters. Under the Meiji emperor Japan kept its independence, rid itself of unequal treaties, and began to modernize itself.

Japanese expansionism. While making improvements at home, the Japanese were also busy pursuing new efforts to expand their holdings abroad. By acquiring islands to the south and north, Japan began its expansionist policy during the 1870s. Using its naval power Japan "opened" Korea to the world and became a rival with China and Russia to dominate the peninsular nation. Long a tributary nation to China, Korea had the misfortune to be a defenseless nation in a period when more powerful nations were seeking new sources of wealth and new markets.

The first Sino-Japanese War, 1894–1895, resulted from the rivalry of China and Japan for control of Korea. The Japanese easily defeated China, proving that Japan's efforts at modernization were more successful than those of its larger neighbor. China turned over Formosa (Taiwan) to Japan and gave up all claims to Korea. Russian, German, and French intervention forced Japan to return some Manchurian territory to China, however.

Russo-Japanese War, 1904 – 1905. Japanese leaders feared that they could not protect their interests in Korea against Russia, whose Trans-Siberian Railway signaled a greater Russian role in northeast Asia. Japan was interested in the economic development of Korea. The Japanese also sought economic opportunities in Manchuria, an area the Russians wished to control. The Japanese resented Russia for keeping them out of Manchuria, an area rich in mineral resources.

In 1894 Japan went to war with China over territorial rights in Korea. As this Japanese painting from the time shows, the Chinese with their traditional weapons and equipment were no match for the modern army of Japan.

Western countries also feared Russian expansion. Britain desired an alliance with Japan to check Russian advances into East Asia, while the Japanese wanted allies to help isolate Russia. The 1902 Anglo-Japanese Alliance, the first between a Western and Asian nation as diplomatic equals, bound each to aid the other if attacked by more than one nation.

When Russia refused the Japanese proposal for Russian control of Manchuria in return for Japanese supremacy in Korea, Japan attacked the Russian fleet stationed at Port Arthur without warning. With Russian forces scattered over their own vast territory, the Japanese easily defeated them. However, with their resources strained to the limit, the Japanese called on President Theodore Roosevelt to promote a settlement. Russia gave up the southern half of Sakhalin Island and recognized Japan's dominance in Korea. In 1910 Korea was annexed by Japan, which ruled it until 1945. The defeat of a Western power by an Asian nation cheered many colonial people in Asia.

Japan and China. When the Japanese entered World War I in 1914, Japanese leaders said that they had entered the war to fulfill treaty commitments with Britain. However, they used the war to gain greater power for themselves in China by seizing German concessions in China. Japan pressed "Twenty-one Demands" on China that would have given Japan control of the Chinese police and arsenals, and indirectly of the Chinese government. The Allies secretly agreed to support Japanese claims to Germany's former Chinese holdings. In return, Japan was to get China to enter the war on the Allied side. Japanese leaders failed to do so because of intense anti-Japanese feeling among the Chinese. However, China later entered the war in hopes of strengthening its bargaining position with the Allies and Japan. At the Versailles Conference at the end of World War I, Japan received the German holdings in China.

Western concern with Japan as a Pacific rival led to the Washington Conference in 1922. At this meeting the treaty powers agreed to respect China's independence and territory. Japan returned its former German holdings to China.

The Rise of Extreme Nationalism in Japan

In the 1930s nationalistic groups appeared who declared themselves guardians of Japan's "unique" heritage – its divine origin, its divine emperor, and its destiny to rule others. These extreme nationalists resented the Western influences in their country and scorned parliamentary politics. They favored direct political action against the emperor's "enemies."

Economic depression increases nationalism. Like other nations, Japan suffered from the worldwide depression that started in 1929. Many ambitious and inadequately educated junior officers, from families who suffered from the depression and who were fearful of communism, were attracted to the idea of war. They hoped that by making war on other nations Japan could acquire colonies and solve some of its economic problems. Secret patriotic societies grew up throughout Japan. These societies preached a program of extreme patriotism and called for war. Young officers who belonged to these groups used violence to further their cause.

Schoolboys with dummy guns participate in a patriotic parade. This photo, taken in 1905, foreshadows the extreme militarism of Japan in the 1930s.

Manchurian incident. Radical officers in the Manchurian army blew up part of a Japanese-controlled railway in Manchuria. Acting on its own, the Japanese army used this as an excuse to seize all of Manchuria in 1931. Tokyo government officials, afraid to anger the military, accepted this deed. A puppet state created in Manchuria was turned into an industrial base and self-sufficient economic unit to support the Japanese army in China. In 1933 when a League of Nations commission condemned the Japanese aggression in Manchuria, Japan withdrew from the League.

Extremist officers pressed their attacks on the political leaders, and a number of government officials were assassinated. However, the military's role in government continued as strong as ever.

Second Sino-Japanese War, 1937–1945. Pressure mounted in Japan for a war against China. Some desired to control China for its mineral resources and as a market for Japanese goods. Others were fearful of the Russian Communist "menace" in East Asia. An incident at the Marco Polo Bridge near Beijing grew into a general war. By 1938 the Japanese controlled the coastal areas, the major cities, and the railroad lines, but they were harassed by Chinese guerrillas and bogged down in an unwinnable war.

Every aspect of Japanese life was affected. Factories began producing war materials at top speed. All military forces were put into action once the war began. Political parties were abolished in 1940 and replaced by the Imperial Rule Assistance Association. Under the IRAA, schools, universities, press, and radio – all social and cultural agencies – were organized to unite behind the government and to support its "imperial objectives."

The road to the Pacific war. While Britain, France, and the Netherlands were deeply involved in a war against Nazi Germany, Japan signed a pact with Germany and Italy that gave it a free hand in East and Southeast Asia. The Japanese wanted the rubber, oil, tin, bauxite, and other resources in this area. In 1941 Japan seized French Indochina.

The United States viewed this Japanese activity in the western Pacific as a threat to its security. The United States strengthened its position in the Philippine Islands and gave aid to China. American leaders wanted Japan to leave China and Southeast Asia, but Japan refused. It wanted the United States to stop its aid to China and recognize Japanese supremacy in East Asia. In the summer of 1941 the Americans, the British, and the Dutch stopped all trade with Japan, denying it vital oil supplies.

Some Japanese leaders preferred war with the United States to a withdrawal from China and a possible civil war at home. While Japanese diplomats were negotiating with the Americans, Japanese leaders were making plans for a war with the United States if there was no settlement on oil shipments by October 1941.

The Pacific war. A surprise attack by the Japanese on Pearl Harbor on December 7, 1941, destroyed most of the American Pacific fleet. The Japanese had no plans to invade Hawaii or the United States. They expected the United States to give up the fight and negotiate a settlement that would leave Japan in control of East and Southeast Asia. The Japanese miscalculated, for after the attack on Pearl Harbor the United States was determined to crush them.

By May 1942, Japan had conquered Hong Kong, Malaysia, Thailand, Burma, Indonesia, the Philippine Islands, and part of New Guinea. In June, when they lost four aircraft carriers at the Battle of Midway, the Japanese advance was stopped. In August the United States began its island campaign with the invasion of Guadalcanal. On Tarawa, Kwajalein, Saipan, Guam, Iwo Jima, and Okinawa the Japanese fought furiously, but were defeated. These island battles brought American airpower close to Japan, and its cities were devastated. Meanwhile, American submarines destroyed Japanese shipping. With its overseas supplies cut off, the Japanese economy was breaking down. In August 1945, atomic bombs were dropped on Hiroshima and Nagasaki, and Russia invaded Manchuria. On August 15, the emperor announced "the unendurable must be endured" and ended the war.

American Occupation followed. The Japanese empire was reduced to the four main islands. Japan was stripped of its armed forces. War trials were held for those accused of plotting wars and crimes against humanity. Of the twenty-five found guilty, seven were executed.

The worst fears the Japanese had about the American occupiers did not come to pass. The United States army did not punish the Japanese people, but rather

The remains of Hiroshima after the atom bomb was dropped, August 1945.

helped to improve the country. Americans initiated many reforms that some Japanese had long desired. While many of the changes might not have occurred without the American Occupation, they succeeded only because they were built on the efforts made by the Japanese in previous decades.

Reviewing Your Reading

1. Trace Japanese overseas expansion up to 1910.
2. Describe Japan's relations with China from 1914 to 1922.
3. What were the beliefs of the extreme nationalists?
4. How did these nationalists involve Japan in Manchuria? How did they threaten the Japanese government?
5. Why did the Japanese invade China? How did this war affect life in Japan?
6. Trace the events that led to the Pacific War.
7. Describe the Pacific War.

CHAPTER REVIEW

Recalling Names and Places

Anglo-Japanese Alliance
daimyo
Tokugawa Ieyasu
Kamakura
Korea
Marco Polo Bridge
Meiji Restoration
Sakhalin Island
samurai
sankin-kotai system
shogun
Minamoto Yoritomo

Understanding This Chapter

1. In the early history of Japan most of the cultural diffusion was from China to Japan. Why? Do you think that is still true?
2. What advantages does a strong central government have for a people? How is it an improvement over a feudal system? What advantages does a feudal system have?
3. Japan's first contact with Europeans was disruptive for Japan. How?
4. What long-term benefits did the "Great Peace" of Tokugawa provide for Japan?
5. List and discuss some of the causes of Japanese expansionism after the Meiji Restoration.

Chapter 30

Japan Adapts to a Changing World

A social system of four classes evolved from Japan's cultural contact with China. The separation of society into classes was supported by Confucianism. Each class had a defined code of behavior, which the individual member was expected to fulfill for the proper functioning of Japanese society.

Traditional Social Structure

Unlike the Chinese, the Japanese considered military spirit an essential quality of the gentleman. This, along with a long tradition of a hereditary aristocracy of warriors, placed the samurai at the top of the social pyramid. Farmers, artisans, and merchants made up the other classes.

Samurai. All warriors were samurai. The most powerful samurai was the *shogun*, the military ruler of Japan. He appointed the *daimyo*, governors of the provinces, who were supported by lower-ranking samurai.

The relationship between the daimyo and his warriors was a personal one based on loyalty. Fidelity, courage, self-discipline, frugality, and self-sacrifice were also highly esteemed samurai qualities. Death was preferable to disgrace or surrender. Ritual suicide, *seppuku*, was the means to atone for an offense to pre-

A law court of the Tokugawa period. Penalties were determined by the social class of the offender. The poor received the most severe sentences.

> **A Harsh Decree**
>
> A 1649 ordinance stated, "Peasants are people without sense or forethought. Therefore, they must not give rice to their wives and children at harvest time, but must save food for the future. They should eat millet, vegetables, and other coarse food instead of rice. . . . During planting and harvesting . . . when the labor is arduous, the food taken may be a little better than usual. . . .
>
> Peasants must wear only cotton or hemp—no silk. They may not smoke tobacco. It is harmful to health, it takes up time, and costs money. It also creates a risk of fire."
>
> From *A History of Japan, 1615–1867* by George Sansom (Stanford: Stanford University Press, 1963, and London: Cresset Press, 1964) p. 99.

serve family honor. The samurai alone was privileged to have a surname and to carry two swords, a long and short one.

The samurai were the leaders of Japanese society. Their military role declined during the Great Peace of the Tokugawa era, and their style of life and thought changed. Their training consisted not only of military arts but also of book learning. They governed their daimyo's estates and were expected to set a good example for other people. Other samurai became noted scholars and teachers. Those who did not assume these new roles fell on hard times.

Farmers. The farmers produced the crops that supported samurai society. Farmers led a life of endless toil. They made barely enough to live on and paid heavy taxes. A few were prosperous and educated, and enjoyed the cultural life of the towns. However, wealthy peasants who enjoyed city life were looked down on by the samurai. Their way of living was considered to have a harmful effect on their characters, because peasants who lived such a life exceeded the limits placed on their class.

Artisans. The artisans were the skilled workers—sword-makers, carpenters, sake brewers, and mat-makers. Each occupation belonged traditionally to certain families, and the sons learned the skill from their fathers. Craft associations set standards of production and made work rules.

Merchants. The lowest of the four classes was the merchant class. As a mover of goods the merchant was considered unproductive. Merchants were organized into guilds, which set prices and assured a sufficient supply of goods. In return for an annual license fee, a guild received official permission to operate and protection from samurai. While the merchants accepted their role as servants in the samurai world, they were their own masters in the world of commerce.

Traditional Household

The household was the basic social unit in Japan. Prior to 1947 the Japanese household was defined by law. All living members of a family were listed on the page devoted to each household in the legal register, the *koseki*, which was kept at the local government office. All family births, marriages, and deaths were recorded in the koseki. An adopted child's name was added, whereas the name of a daughter, on marriage, was removed and added to the record of her husband's family. There were no equals in the family. Males were superior to females, elder to younger, those born within the household to those born outside of it.

Men in Japanese society. The eldest male was the head of the house. He directed the family work, supervised the family property and officiated at ancestor veneration. The final word on marriage and employment of family members was his. But his authority was balanced by his duty to care for those under him. A widowed sister, for example, turned to him in time of need. Since the family was considered more important than an individual family member, individual desires took second place to family interests. The father, as head of the household, sought to promote the family good, so family members accepted his decisions. If a person's actions threatened the family's good name, he was expelled from it and his name removed from the koseki.

Women held an inferior position. Confucianism described the relationship of women to men by the "three bonds" – daughter to father, wife to husband, widow to eldest son. Greater emphasis was placed on the parent-child relationship than on the husband-wife relationship. A man, for example, mourned a longer period of time for his parents than for his wife. The notion that a man should love his wife offended the Japanese sense of masculine superiority. It was considered shameful for a husband and wife to walk together in the street.

The Well-Bred Wife

The Greater Learning for Women *(1672) was the classic statement of the correct behavior of a well-bred samurai wife and reflected what was expected of all Japanese women.*

More precious in a woman is a virtuous heart than a face of beauty. . . . The only qualities that befit a woman are gentle obedience, chastity, mercy and quietness. . . . [She must practice filial piety]. She must look to her husband as her lord, and must serve him with all worship and reverence, not despising or thinking lightly of him. . . . A woman must . . . keep a strict watch over her own conduct. . . . [Attend to] the duties of her household. . . . [She should not] enter into correspondence with a young man. . . .

The five worst maladies that afflict the female mind are: indocility, discontent, slander, jealousy, and silliness. . . . these maladies infest seven or eight out of every ten women, and it is from these that arise the inferiority of women to men. A woman should cure them. . . . The worst of them all, and the parent of the other four, is silliness. . . . Such is the stupidity of her character that it is incumbent on her, in every particular, to distrust herself and to obey her husband.

From Herbert Passin, *Society and Education in Japan.* (New York: Teachers College Press, 1965; copyright 1965 by Teachers College, Columbia University) pp. 174–176.

The creation of a kimono, a traditional robe worn by Japanese men and women, requires careful, skillful work. First the design is drawn on silk by the artist. Then another artist (bottom left) paints the colors. When the panels have been completed (top) they are sewn together. When a fine kimono is to be cleaned, it is unsewn and each piece is laundered separately. At bottom right, a teacher instructs a class in the proper way to wear a kimono — loosely wrapped and tied with a sash.

However, while in public the wife was obedient and respectful to her husband and not apt to openly disagree with him, she often had great influence on her husband in private.

There was a sharp division between the man's world and the woman's world. Each lived separate social lives. The woman's world was the household, for she managed it, took care of the family, and trained the daughter-in-law in the ways of the family. Relations between the daughter-in-law and the mother-in-law were often strained. In any dispute involving the daughter-in-law, her husband was expected to side with his family.

Marriages were arranged. A seventeenth-century Japanese text stated, "The fundamental reason for a man to take a wife is that she may serve his parents and bear heirs to continue the succession." Since marriages were arranged, there was little room for personal preference. It was a family matter made by the heads of the families involved. A *miai*, a contrived meeting, was arranged by the go-between so that the parents and the prospective partners could see one another. If they were not satisfied, negotiations stopped without either side being offended. If all were pleased, the go-between handled such arrangements as the amount of the groom's family's gift to the bride, the amount of the return gift, and the bride's trousseau.

Divorce was possible for all classes, but it was more frequent among peasants. Because family interests were considered more important than individual desires, divorce was uncommon among the samurai. A family's honor would be marred if the bride were sent back to her family.

The eldest son occupied a high position in the family. There was a marked difference between the eldest son and his brothers and sisters. As heir apparent, he would one day become the head of the house, and they would be dependent on him. Daughters and younger sons were considered temporary members of the family. At her marriage, the daughter left the household. The younger son might be adopted by another family or be set up in a branch house.

When a couple had no son, they adopted one to marry their daughter. A childless couple first adopted a girl and trained her in the ways of the family, then adopted a son to be her husband. The adopted son broke all ties with his natural family, assumed his new family name, honored its ancestors, and managed the family property as if he were the natural son.

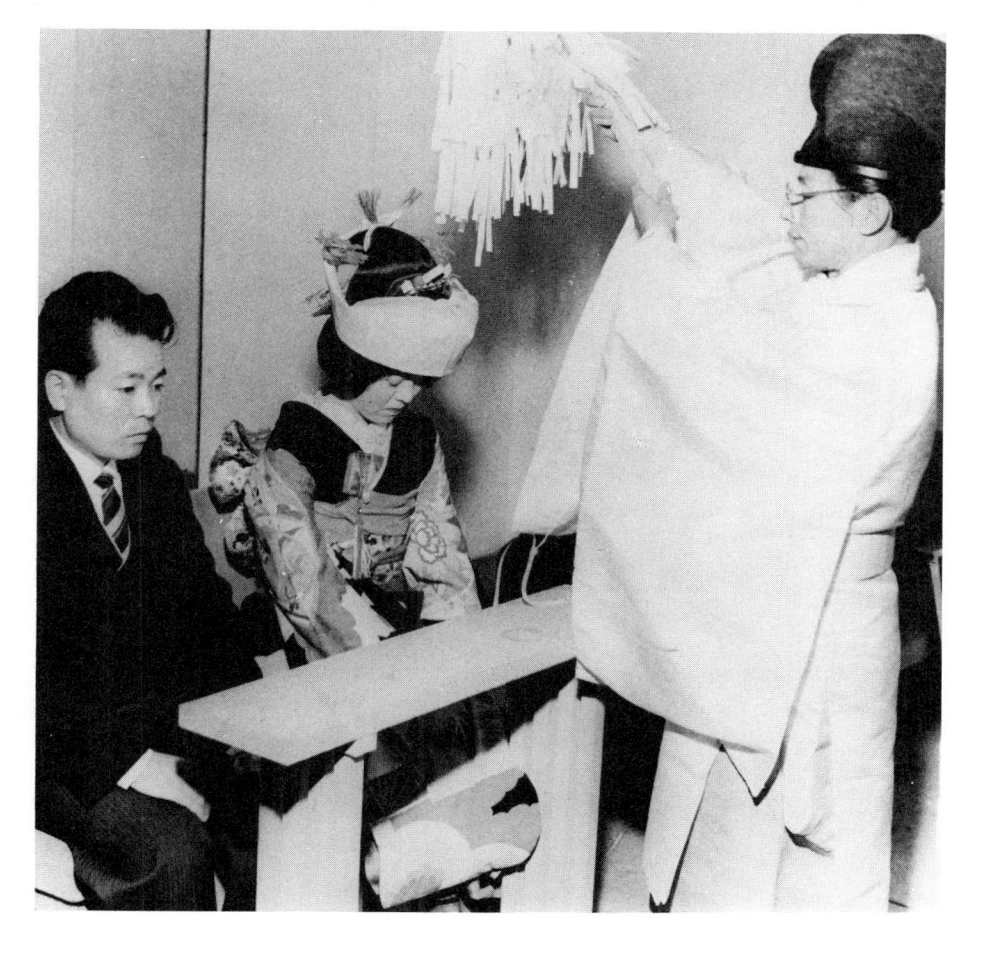

At a traditional wedding ceremony a Shinto priest drives out evil spirits with a wave of his paper streamer wand. According to custom, the bride wears a hat to cover her "horns of jealousy."

353

Reviewing Your Reading

1. Into what groups was Japanese society divided? Describe the role and values of each group.
2. Describe the relationships between family members in the traditional family.
3. What was the man's position in Japanese society? the woman's position?
4. How were marriages arranged?

Social Structure Changes

When Japan began to modernize during the Meiji era, the economic, social, and political supports of the Japanese family system were considerably weakened. Several factors contributed to the weakening of the family system: (1) the abolition of the four-class system, (2) the development of modern industry, (3) the rapid growth of cities, (4) compulsory universal education, and (5) the influence of Western ideas. Household unity declined, and a more open society emerged. Education, wealth, and political influence replaced family ties as the new measures of prestige.

The Meiji Restoration makes new laws for the family. During the last years of the Tokugawa era, economic and political pressures began to blur class lines. The roles of the farmer, artisan, and merchant intermingled. Samurai with little money engaged in work previously rejected by them.

The leaders of the Meiji Restoration were young, vigorous members of the lower samurai ranks who hoped to improve their own positions by restoring imperial rule. They were politically experienced, well educated, and well trained. Many had contacts with the Western world.

Japan established legal social equality. A conscription army was created, drawing its soldiers from the ranks of the peasants. This, in addition to the abolition of the four-class system, destroyed the last privileges of the samurai class. A new nobility was created consisting of former samurai, court nobles, and wealthy merchants. All other people were commoners, free to choose their own occupation. Some former samurai aided by the government went into business or industry. Many entered government service, becoming military officers, police officers, or teachers. However, for most samurai the changes meant a decline in their social position.

Legal factors in social change. Beginning in 1945 when the American army occupied Japan, the Americans made many changes in customary practices. The household lost its legal status, and the legal authority of the head of the house over the family members was eliminated. Today, registration in the koseki is by nuclear family, and marriage results in a new nuclear family with its own page in the koseki.

While it is still possible for the eldest son to inherit the family farm or business, the other children are legally entitled to take a share of the family property in the form of a dowry or money for an education or a business.

A young worker welds transistors to a radio at the Matsushita Electric Company in Kyoto.

Economic factors also caused changes. Modern industrial production methods, new technology, modern banks, new-style schools, and science research centers provided employment opportunities other than the craft work traditionally done in the home. Some of these new occupations were more prestigious and better paying than some old-style occupations. Skills acquired in the family were often useless in factories and offices. Educational and technical skills acquired outside the family were needed for the new jobs. Sons had different, often better, occupations than their fathers. Consequently, the son's economic security no longer depended on following the occupation of the main house.

New families were established by younger sons in the cities. While economically independent of the main house, at first the younger sons remained linked to it by kinship and ritual. However, these ties weakened and became less important in succeeding generations.

Industrialization offered new positions for women. Education and industrialization helped to change the woman's position in Japanese society. A woman's intellectual and vocational development were encouraged as higher educational opportunities opened up for her. Now she could engage in professional employment – teaching, engineering and medicine.

It became acceptable for middle-class girls to work at office jobs that required higher educational standards. Peasant girls often worked in factories and lived in company housing rather than marrying early. These developments gave women independent incomes and helped to make women more confident in their ability to make decisions for themselves.

Schools, female voting, new property inheritance laws, and protection by labor laws also helped to change women's position. Women now hold high civil service positions and sit in the Diet (parliament). Despite legal equality and the changes noted, it is still more difficult for a woman to acquire a skill and obtain a high-paying job than it is for a man.

Contemporary marriage. As the Japanese became sensitive to foreign criticism of Japanese social customs, they made other social changes. Concubinage ended, and monogamy became the ideal marriage form. Today more Japanese marry without a go-between or customary formalities than in the general past. However, arranged marriages continue to be a common practice.

The social position of each family and its connections are considered in arranging a marriage. The prospective bride is expected to preserve the prospective groom's family tradition, be a good house manager, and be able to bear children. Proficiency in flower arranging and the tea ceremony are favorable factors. The man's earning ability is an important item, for a seventeenth-century saying that marriage is a "commercial transaction that only comes once in a lifetime" remains a powerful consideration. The looks, intelligence, and temperament of the prospective couple are also weighed.

The miai (page 352) is still held. While dating is still not the accepted pattern of courtship, a couple may date for a time after the miai before a final decision is made. Not to marry after a miai is very embarrassing.

Changes in Family Relationships

The greatest single change in Japanese family life is the increased emphasis given to the husband-wife relationship at the expense of that between the parents and the children. This resulted, in part, from the influence of the Western notion of romantic love in which a couple marries to fulfill their own emotional needs. Love is no longer considered a sign of masculine weakness.

A love marriage, however, does not necessarily result in much sharing of interests and responsibilities. The man's world and the woman's world remain separate, though wives now play a greater role in family decisionmaking. In a nuclear family there is no mother-in-law to dominate the bride. Where a woman's mother-in-law lives in her son's house, the better educated and more knowledgeable daughter-in-law is less likely to follow her mother-in-law's ways. In fact, white-collar husbands, among young couples, tend to help with the housework. Although they tend to have separate recreational activities, the notion of companionship between husband and wife is gaining acceptance.

Care for retired parents. In the past, retired parents were cared for by the eldest son, who inherited all the family property. However, the abolition of this practice has weakened family ties. In addition, today crowded and often inadequate urban housing makes it difficult for retired parents to live with their children. They now look to all their children for support.

In summary, a modern economy, education, foreign influences, and legal changes contributed to altering the traditional Japanese family. The changes are more common in the cities than in the countryside. As Japan becomes increasingly industrialized and urbanized, as the number of rural residents declines, as mass communication helps spread new ideas and practices, the new patterns of family organization are likely to become more common.

Reviewing Your Reading

1. What changes were made in the social structure during the Meiji period? How did they affect the samurai?
2. How did economic changes alter the family system?
3. Describe changes in the woman's position in Japanese society.
4. How does contemporary marriage differ from traditional marriage practices?
5. How has Western influence affected family relationships?
6. Describe changes in the position of the aged in modern Japanese society.

Education in Japan

Today Japan has one of the most fully developed educational systems in the world, and its people have a 98 percent literacy rate. To have accomplished this in a century is remarkable. Several factors account for this.

In the Tokugawa period. Formal education was well established in Japan even before the country was "opened" to the world in the nineteenth century. The great emphasis Confucianism placed on learning was strongly responsible for it. However during the Great Peace of the Tokugawa era, an enormous expansion of education took place among all classes of people. Tokugawa Japan had a 40 percent male literacy rate. Former samurai who had become civil administrators, merchants, artisans, village headmen, all needed education.

Ideal Conduct for Students

Most schools had guidelines for students. The following is an extract from a common school's set of precepts.

To be born human and not to be able to write is to be less than human. Illiteracy is a form of blindness. It brings shame on your teacher . . . on your parents, and . . . yourself. The heart of a child of three stays with him till he is one hundred. . . . Determine to succeed, study with all your might, never forgetting the shame of failure. . . .

At your desks let there be no . . . idle talk . . . yawning . . . stretching . . . dozing . . . chewing paper or biting the end of your brush. To imitate the idle is the road to evil habits. . . . Just concentrate wholeheartedly on your writing, giving each character the care it deserves. . . .

You will never write a good hand unless you . . . practice . . . even when you are cold and hungry. . . .

He who is born a man but lacks . . . filial piety is no more than a beast. . . . He who thinks these precepts foolish and fails to obey them shall bring shame on himself, lose his good name, and soon live to repent his ruination. . . .

R. P. Dore, *Education in Tokugawa Japan,* University of California Press, pub. 1965, pp. 323–326.

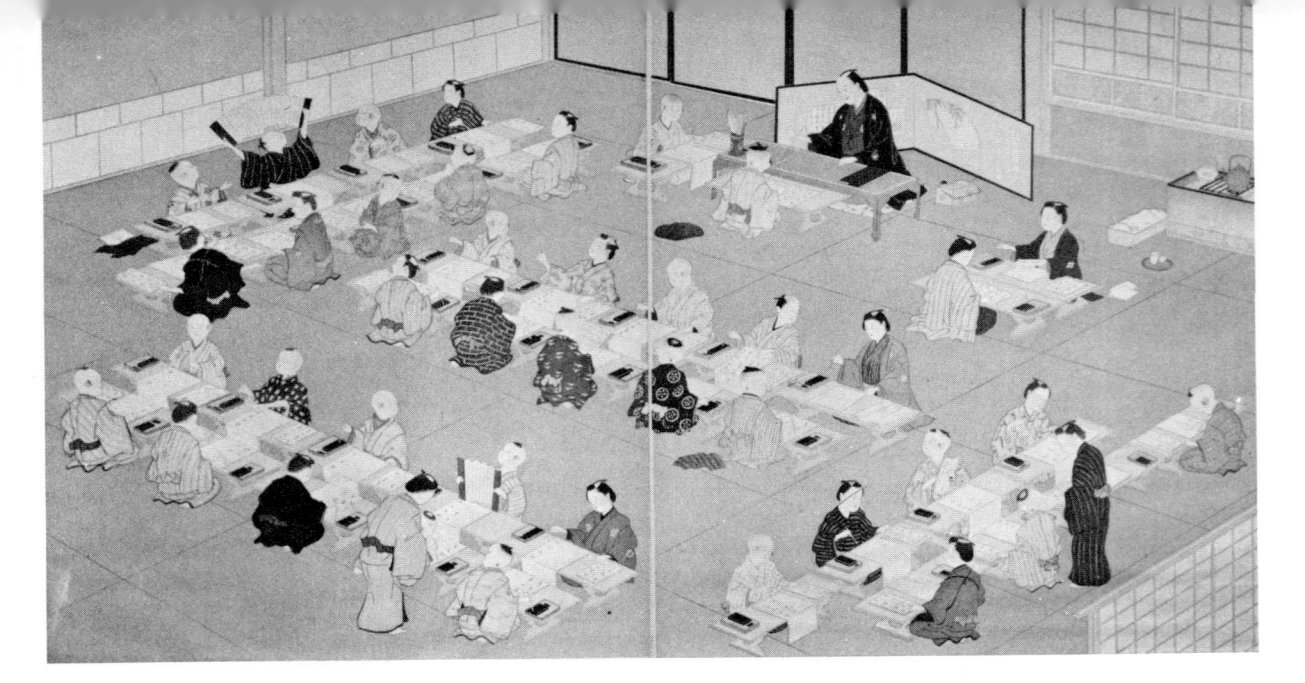

During the Tokuguawa period, Buddhist priests ran terakoya schools, where the children of commoners studied reading, writing, and arithmetic. By the end of that time such schools could be found in almost every Japanese town and village.

Samurai education. As members of the ruling class, the samurai received a distinctive education that emphasized character development rather than specialized training. Students learned Confucian virtues for future use in social relations and in government work. This ethical training helped to transform the samurai from rough, often illiterate, warriors into gentlemen. The samurai also continued to be trained in military matters. Teaching stressed acquiring the qualities of leadership and decisiveness. In addition to military duties, swordsmanship and archery were also taught to deepen the concentration of the mind. The samurai code became a guide for civil administrators as well as army officers.

Education for commoners. Common schools, often attached to Buddhist temples, provided elementary schooling for the children of farmers, artisans, and merchants. Along with Confucianism, practical subjects such as arithmetic on an abacus were taught.

Education for women. Female education was neglected or limited to subjects that enhanced a woman's marriageability. Samurai women were taught at home. They received moral training and learned to manage a household. Merchants were apt to send their daughters to school because a literate wife was needed to take orders in the shop.

Teachers in Tokugawa Japan. Teachers were deeply respected and had great authority. They were expected to be models of virtue, honored as much for their character as for their learning. One Japanese book cautioned the student to "keep seven feet behind your teacher and never tread on his shadow. . . . Every letter you know you owe to him. Never answer back to your parents or your teacher, observe carefully their admonitions, and seek their instruction that you may walk evermore firmly in the Way of Man."*

---

*R. P. Dore, *Education in Tokugawa Japan,* University of California Press, published 1965, p. 326.

Most teachers were volunteers who were supported by a wealthy patron or received "donations" – fish, rice, cloth. The teacher's authority over the students' minds and bodies was complete. The pupils memorized the knowledge their teacher passed on to them.

Dutch studies. After the closing of Japan, Western learning entered the country through the small Dutch settlement in Nagasaki harbor. In 1720 the ban on Western texts was lifted, and Western books were translated. The private study of the Dutch language was encouraged to acquire modern knowledge and military techniques. While the number of Japanese students of Dutch studies was small, the superiority of Western learning was sometimes demonstrated. Note an instance of this in the anatomy lesson below.

As the Western world forced its attention on Japan, some samurai favored using the sword to drive the foreigners away. Those who mastered Dutch studies knew the strength of the foreigners and realized such action was folly. A few samurai visited Western nations and were very impressed by their wealth and power. When they returned, they called for the adoption of modern knowledge, weapons, and industry to protect Japan.

Meiji education. The Meiji leaders realized that an educated people was necessary to unify the nation around the emperor and to acquire new knowledge and techniques with which to make Japan a world power. As one leader put it, "In the administration of all schools, it must be kept in mind, what is to be done is not for the sake of the pupils but for the sake of the country."

Asia's first public schools were in Japan. In 1886 Japan created the first modern public school system in Asia. This national school system came only fifteen years after Britain established its own elementary public school system. By the first decade of the twentieth century, the Japanese literacy rate was comparable to that of Western countries.

An Anatomy Lesson

Sugita Gempaku (1733–1817), a student of Dutch learning, used a cadaver to compare a Western anatomy text with a similar Chinese book.

"When . . . I compared what . . . [I] saw [in the dissected cadaver] with the illustrations in the Dutch book, . . . everything was exactly as depicted. The six lobes and the two ears of the lungs, and the . . . lobes . . . of the kidneys, such as were always described in the old Chinese books of medicine were not so found. The position and shape of the intestines and stomach were also quite unlike the old descriptions."

Convinced of the superiority of the Dutch anatomical texts, Sugita and a companion translated it, and modern medicine was introduced to Japan.

Donald Keene, *The Japanese Discovery of Europe, 1720–1830*, Rev. Ed. (Stanford, Calif.: Stanford University Press, 1969), p. 22.

Indoctrination in the schools. The subjects studied in Japanese schools were similar to those in Western schools except for a special "morals" course. Japanese students underwent intensive political indoctrination in the schools. The center of the curriculum was the "morals" course, which taught reverence to the emperor and patriotism.

The portrait of the emperor and the Imperial Rescript, which defined the duties of the Japanese subject, were in every school. The Rescript was read in ceremonial assemblies, and pupils had to participate in Shinto rituals in order to strengthen their loyalty and devotion to the nation. An official "morals" textbook taught a unique view of Japanese history. According to this textbook, under a divine emperor, the racially and culturally superior Japanese people had a mission — to spread their influence throughout the world.

Occupation reforms of education. After Japan's defeat in World War II, the school system linked with Shinto lost the confidence of the people. The Japanese were ready for a change and embraced the Occupation-sponsored reforms. The Occupation ended indoctrination in the schools. Teachers were investigated, screened, and certified, and those not linked with Japanese militarist-nationalism were permitted to teach. The entire school system was reformed in structure and curriculum. The schools were to promote democratic concepts.

At a modern Japanese junior high school, a teacher makes a point to his attentive students. Required subjects for these students include Japanese, social studies, math, science, music, and fine arts.

Equal educational opportunity. Nine years of compulsory schooling is now required of all children. Thereafter, one can work and attend a part-time upper secondary school or technical school, or a full-time three-year upper secondary school that will lead to a junior college or a university. The schools are coeducational, with the same curriculum for boys and girls. Women have the same educational opportunity as men do and attend the same universities.

Because a degree from a good university is the means to a better job, education is one of the most competitive areas in Japanese life. Top job positions in Japanese society are usually held by graduates of the best universities. A degree from a top university is necessary to obtain the higher positions in government, the business world, and political life. A university degree gives the holder a lifetime identification with a clique. These close informal groups can sponsor or help a graduate. Once a university clique is established in an enterprise, it tends to continue, drawing new workers from the same university.

Tokyo, with one-third of the universities and one-half of the nation's students, is the goal of the most ambitious students, and Tokyo University is Japan's most prestigious school. Entrance into the universities is difficult, for there are many more applicants than places. Admission is determined by a stiff competitive examination. Unsuccessful candidates attend special cram schools and are privately tutored for several years. Entrance examinations are often repeated several times.

Japanese education is fiercely competitive in the early stages, but the pressure eases off after admission to a university. Once a university accepts a student, he is practically guaranteed a diploma, the all-important passport to the top positions in Japanese society.

Reviewing Your Reading

1. What earlier trends in Japanese education have led to Japan's high educational level today?
2. Describe the education of the samurai, commoners, and women.
3. What was expected of Japanese students under the Tokugawa education system?
4. How did Western learning enter Japan? What role did it play in "opening" Japan to the world? How did various samurai respond to it?
5. Why was the Meiji government eager to accept Western learning? Describe the school system it established.
6. How has Japanese education changed since 1945?

Japanese Religion

Religion has always played an important part in Japanese life. Religion is woven into everyday life. At regular stages throughout life a person is taken or goes to a shrine or temple. He or she may be married in a Shinto ceremony and be buried in a Buddhist service.

Unlike Judaism and Christianity, which insist that their members belong to only one religion at a time, the Japanese religions permit simultaneous involvement in several religious traditions. According to Japanese thought, a person

Every Shinto temple is approached through a simple gateway, or torii. This torii guards the entrance to one of Japan's most sacred shrines, Itsukushima, in Hiroshima bay.

could believe in or participate in several religions and philosophies – Shinto, Buddhism, and Confucianism. A Japanese seeking religious fulfillment finds it in a blend of all the traditions.

Shinto is the native religion of Japan. Shinto does not have a founder, sacred scriptures, or organized doctrine. It combines animism, the notion that objects possess a living spirit, and nature worship.

Shinto means the way of the *kami,* or the gods. Japanese believe that a kami, a spirit, is contained in all living and non-living objects – animals, plants, rocks, storms, winds, mountains. The peak of Mt. Fuji is an example of a kami that guards the land. All things that invoke awe, are mysterious and incomprehensible, or have extraordinary powers are thought to possess a kami.

According to Japanese mythology, Isanagi (male kami) and Izanami (female kami) were married. From heaven they thrust a jeweled spear into the water and created the islands of Japan. After their descent to earth they created the rest of the universe. By this account the Japanese imperial family is descended from the Sun-Goddess, who was the offspring of Izanagi and Izanami. This legend of the divine origin of the imperial family was widely accepted. It helped to give the imperial family a position of great esteem in the eyes of the Japanese people.

Japanese Buddhism. In 552 A.D., Mahayana Buddhism reached Japan from Korea. The Buddhism that was practiced in Nara used the Chinese language, rites, costumes, and architecture.

Nara Buddhism, as it was called, introduced the Indian Buddhist philosophy in Chinese dress to the Japanese upper classes. Nara Buddhism had no real influence among the common people. However, later Japanese adaptations of Nara Buddhism spread the religion throughout the land.

Buddhism was popularized by linking Shinto deities with Buddhist divinities. Japanese Buddhism added ceremonies of purification and other rituals familiar to the Japanese people.

A Japanese adaptation: Tendai. Tendai is a Buddhist sect that combines the message of the Buddha into a single set of teachings. The *Lotus Sutra* is the major work of the Tendai sect. It is considered the greatest of the sutras, or books containing the teachings of Buddha. The Tendai teachings contain the seeds of two of Japanese Buddhism's most popular sects – Jodo and Zen.

Jodo. The Jodo, or Pure Land Sect, was popularized by Honen (1133–1212), a wandering preacher. Jodo offers enlightenment to the worshiper through faith and the intervention of a bodhisattva known as *Amida,* the deity of Infinite Light. According to Jodo teachings, the Amida Buddha vowed that he would only accept enlightenment after he shares his karma with those who call on him and brings them to the Western Paradise or the Pure Land.

Racism in Japan

In Japan minority groups are called races even when they are physically and culturally indistinguishable from the dominant population. Such is the case of the Burakumin, who are also called "Eta," the Japanese word for outcasts.

The Burakumin are the largest minority in Japan, numbering about 2 million persons. Because most Japanese associate this group with certain occupations such as butchering and tanning, they are regarded with disgust and even fear. They are seen as morally deficient and are denied opportunities in education, employment, and housing.

The second largest minority, numbering about 675,000, are the people of Korean background. Although some Korean families have lived in Japan since the sixteenth century, they are treated as resident aliens, regarded as inferior, and denied equality of opportunity.

A third minority group, numbering only about 16,000 persons, are the Ainu. They live mainly in a small area of Hokkaido and are the descendants of an indigenous population that was gradually pushed to the northernmost island. They are a Caucasoid type of people with their own distinctive culture and language.

Organizations have emerged seeking greater equality for these minorities, such as the Burakumin Liberation League. The government made some concessions in the late 1960s and 1970s, but social discrimination is difficult to combat. Rejection of persons defined as outsiders is deeply rooted in Japanese culture.

At right, a Zen Buddhist monk tends a gravel garden, notable for its stark simplicity. Below, a Zen ceremony in Kyoto.

According to Jodo, through a practice that involves the frequent repetition of Amida's name, *namu Amida butsu,* or "Hail Amida Buddha," all people could be saved. If this is repeated with genuine and heartfelt devotion and supported by an individual's moral behavior in preceding lives, the merciful Amida will bring the faithful to the Pure Land.

Zen. Zen calls for self-reliance. *Satori* – the Japanese term for nirvana (enlightenment or becoming a Buddha) – is achieved by one's own effort. The method is meditation. The truly enlightened are few in number because it is a difficult process.

Zen training is quite strict. For the novice, a young man training to become a Buddhist monk, the day starts before dawn and ends after sunset. As the Buddha renounced physical possessions, so does the novice. To learn humility, the novice takes his bowl and begs for food in the streets. All phases of daily life, even eating and washing, are part of Zen discipline. Manual labor on the temple grounds is combined with spiritual training. Temple community life involves Buddhist rituals, listening to lectures on the sutras, and joint chanting of sutras.

Buddhism in this century. There have been few notable developments in Buddhism in the past century. While many Japanese profess to be Buddhist, many seem indifferent to their faith. Some feel that Buddhism is not adequately dealing with the issues that modern man faces. Buddhist sects lost most of their income when the 1945 land reforms deprived them of their land holdings. Today many temples are in need of repairs. Today many sects operate kindergartens and perform other public services.

Zen Enlightment

Life in the temple is based on meditation. In the meditation hall the novice sits with crossed legs on a cushion on a raised wooden platform. This position encourages the proper spiritual attitude. In deep concentration the novice empties his mind of all thought. During these sessions a monk walks around the hall and strikes any novice who lapses in the meditation across the shoulders with a staff. These blows are intended as acts of kindness to aid in meditation.

Zen cannot be learned from texts. It is transmitted from a master to a pupil, who is given themes to meditate upon. The theme may be in the form of a *koan,* a paradoxical problem that cannot be logically solved. Two examples of the koan are: "What was your basic nature before your parents made you?" "What is the sound of one hand clapping?" The disciple who advances in spiritual development is given more difficult koans on which to meditate.

A long period of meditation precedes enlightenment. As the Zen disciple continuously searches for a solution to the koan, tension mounts and persists. Only a mind that is relaxed, free from all ordinary concerns and totally involved in the task, can open of itself. In this tense state, sometimes a slap or a shout will lead the disciple to a sudden flash of understanding that shows the path to satori.

New religions. Since the end of the war in 1945 almost 200 new religions have appeared in the face of the decline in interest in Shinto and Buddhism. These new religions have borrowed much from the principal religions. Buddhist influences are especially strong. Many of them claim to have begun as a revelation from a Buddhist divinity, who ordered the founder to organize a religious movement.

One of the most powerful and largest of the new religions is the *Soka Gakkai*. It teaches unquestioning faith in the *Lotus Sutra*. Soka Gakkai promises its worshipers a life filled with beauty, goodness, and such material benefits as good health and success in business. Buddhahood in this life is held out to its members. Its members are not allowed to participate in other Buddhist sects.

Shinto, 1868 to 1945. Before the Meiji era Shinto shrines and Buddhist temples were built side by side, and the priests of both religions often served in each other's worship services. When imperial rule was restored in 1868, Shinto became the most important religion in the country. It was made the sole religion of the government.

In order to stop objections from people who were forced to attend Shinto ceremonies, the government ruled that it was not a religion. The Shinto ceremonies, designed to arouse patriotic fervor, were compulsory. Shinto also received economic support from the government. Shinto priests were government officials.

Until 1945 Shinto dominated all religions in spite of the government's statement that it was not a religion. State Shinto was used to promote nationalism and militarism among the Japanese people. It was used in the schools to foster reverence for the emperor and loyalty to the nation. During this intensive nationalistic period Buddhists and Christians also supported the government's program. However, no rival religious teaching, either Buddhist or Christian, was permitted in the public schools.

Shinto in postwar Japan. In 1945 the Occupation ended the tie between the Japanese government and Shinto. The emperor announced he was not a god, but only a human being. Today, government funds no longer support shrines, and Shinto priests have ceased being government officials.

In the postwar years many people lost sympathy with Shinto because it had been closely linked to the war machine. Shinto was further weakened when the Japanese people were guaranteed complete religious freedom, for the first time in their history, by the 1947 constitution. The constitution also guaranteed that no special privileges could be extended by the government to any religion. The shrines are now supported entirely by private contributions.

Looking ahead. Though modern Japan is quite different in many ways from Japan of the past, many of its traditions remain. Many thoughtful Japanese are still trying to decide how traditional Japanese values can be blended in the new, highly technological society they are creating. In the past Japanese society created a new synthesis when it was challenged by a world of new cultural values. Possibly the same thing can occur again.

Reviewing Your Reading

1. What elements are common to all Japanese religions?
2. What are the chief features of the Shinto religion?
3. Why is Nara Buddhism called a Chinese transplant?
4. Describe the Tendai sect.
5. Describe the Jodo sect. Why did it develop a wide following?
6. Describe the training of a Zen Buddhist monk.
7. Which is the most prominent of the new religions? What are its features?
8. Describe Shinto from the Meiji Restoration to Japan's defeat in 1945.
9. What is Shinto's position in present-day Japan?

CHAPTER REVIEW

Recalling Names and Places

Imperial Rescript	koseki	Soka Gakkai
Jodo	satori	Sun-Goddess
kami	Shinto	Tendai
koan		Zen

Understanding This Chapter

1. The Japanese accorded the samurai or warrior class the highest status. In China at the same time warriors were at the bottom of the class structure. Can you think of any explanations for this difference?
2. Why did the Meiji Restoration cause a decline in the social position of most samurai?
3. Social and economic changes have brought greater freedom and opportunity for women in Japan. Have these changes had any negative consequences for women as well? If so, what?
4. Was a traditional Japanese education too hard on students? What are the advantages and disadvantages of such rigorous schooling?
5. Education is respected and valued more in Japan than in the United States. Can you name any reasons why this is so?

Chapter 31

The Economic Modernization of Japan

Under the Tokugawa shoguns, Japan's economy grew steadily. Two and a half centuries of peace in Tokugawa Japan permitted increased agricultural and industrial production. Trade within the country flourished. Farming changed from growing crops for family needs to the cultivation of crops for sale.

This steady economic growth, especially in agriculture, enabled Japan to become more prosperous than any other Asian nation by the nineteenth century. When the Meiji government replaced the Tokugawa shoguns, it undertook major economic changes. However, these changes were built on the foundation laid by the Tokugawa rulers.

Meiji Modernization Took Many Directions

Commercial treaties with Western nations during the nineteenth century led to greater foreign trade for Japan. Meiji leaders feared that their Western trading partners would take advantage of Japan and that Japan needed a more favorable trading position. Thus Japanese leaders undertook major economic changes.

The Meiji government built model factories and purchased foreign machinery for them. Foreign experts were hired to teach the Japanese how to run these factories. As soon as the Japanese workers mastered the skills taught by foreign experts, the foreigners were released. Japanese leaders also traveled abroad to learn techniques of modern factory organization and finance.

As Japanese agricultural production increased, raw silk, rice, tea, copper, and textiles were sold abroad. The income from these sales helped to pay for needed imports. Japan did not, however, encourage foreign investments. Any business started by a foreigner in Japan had to have Japanese partners. In this way, Japan avoided foreign control of its economy.

The rise of the zaibatsu. As merchants became more prosperous, enormous, family-owned business organizations appeared. These private corporations became known as the zaibatsu. The Mitsui, Mitsubishi, and Sumitomo zaibatsu had many firms engaged in banking, insurance, commerce, manufacturing, and mining. The zaibatsu amassed great wealth and political power. The families that controlled the zaibatsu were to occupy powerful leadership positions in Japan's economic and political affairs for many decades.

Popular support for economic change. The massive modernization of Japan's economy in the period before World War II was made possible by a

The Ginza district, Tokyo's main shopping area, glows brightly and bustles with activity at night.

great national effort on the part of the Japanese people. Although the living standard of the ordinary Japanese worker did not improve as the economy grew, the Japanese enthusiastically supported the modernization.

Rebuilding After the War

Japan emerged from World War II as one of the most devastated nations in the world. More than 3 million people had died. The major cities were battered by the bombing. Much of the urban population had fled to the countryside to escape the air raids. One-fourth of Japanese industry was destroyed. The railroad network was disrupted. Almost all of the maritime fleet was sunk by submarines, aircraft, or mines. The Japanese empire was reduced to the four principal islands of Honshu, Hokkaido, Shikoku, and Kyushu. Many of the advances of the Meiji period were wiped out.

Since 1959 Japan has been the world's leading shipbuilding nation. Here workers repair a hull at a Tokyo shipyard.

Today, however, Japan is the third largest industrial power in the world, exceeded only by the United States and the Soviet Union. Certain worldwide industries are dominated by the Japanese. As the principal shipbuilder, Japan produces oil supertankers that are too large to pass through the Suez and Panama canals. Some of the most modern steel, chemical, oil refining and industrial machine plants in the world are found in Japan. It is a leading producer of such sophisticated items as cameras, binoculars, and electron microscopes, and of such electronic equipment as color television, radios, and stereo equipment.

By the 1980s, with a total production of more than 11 million units, Japan had become the largest producer of automobiles in the world, as well as the largest exporter of cars and trucks. More than half of its automotive production is shipped overseas. The United States is Japan's largest customer.

The manufacture of computers is a recent development in Japan. IBM Japan, a subsidiary of the American company, dominated the Japanese market until about 1980. Since then Japanese companies have taken the lead in the domestic market, and exports of computers are rising rapidly. Japan is second only to the United States in the manufacutre of computers.

Since 1945 Japan has rebuilt its economy and gone on to accomplish an impressive list of achievements. The leaders of the American Occupation of Japan provided supervision, aid, and support for many of these accomplishments, particularly in the early postwar years. However, the Japanese people provided the energy, resources, and skills that made them possible.

Land divided among the farmers. The leaders of the American Occupation realized that major economic reforms would be necessary if the Occupation's efforts to make Japan democratic were to succeed. Land reform was one of the most successful Occupation undertakings. The Japanese government purchased land from large landowners and sold it to the tenant farmers. Japanese farmers worked harder under this new system. Any improvements farmers made now were for their own benefit.

Today, Japanese farms are more like gardens, for they average two and a half acres each. Farming is changing as Japanese eating habits change. More vegetables, fruits, dairy products, and livestock are grown than in the past. Rice is still the single most important crop.

Japan still follows the Asian pattern of intensive farming, which requires enormous amounts of time, energy, and care. It has also added modern machines. Mechanization and scientific farming methods have produced an agricultural revolution. Hand tractors, rototillers, fertilizer spreaders, power hullers, polishers, and mechanical water lifts are used. To protect the farmer, the Japanese government purchases the entire rice crop each year. The rice is then resold to consumers.

Big business loses some of its power. To make businesses more competitive, the Occupation broke up the large businesses. The big zaibatsu financial organizations were divided into separate independent firms. However, further antimonopoly reform was stopped when the Occupation feared it would hamper economic recovery by depriving the nation of the resources of the former zaibatsu owners.

Factors Contributing to Economic Recovery

Many factors led to Japan's emergence as a great industrial power:

Technological innovation. The war destroyed many of the old industries. New factories with new and more efficient machines were purchased to help Japan rebuild its economy. The Japanese applied more modern methods of production in their new factories, techniques that enabled them to produce more goods more rapidly.

Skilled labor supply. Much of Japan's economic success can be attributed to its human resources – its people. Postwar Japan has a hardworking, highly motivated, and well-educated labor force. Japanese workers have the skills needed for economic growth and are receptive to training on the job.

United States helps Japan complete its economic recovery. The victory of the Communists in China and the outbreak of the Korean War in 1950 convinced the United States that it needed a new ally in Asia. With the help of American aid and purchases, Japan's economy improved rapidly, making it a leader among industrialized countries by the 1970s.

The strength of the Japanese economy has allowed investment in other countries. Some Japanese automobiles, for example, are assembled in Britain, Australia, and the United States, and Japanese investors own other property in the United States.

Japan's Economy Today

Today government and business continue to be linked to each other. While not controlling the economy, the government does play an active part. The government has given high priority to stimulating economic growth at home. High tariffs protect Japanese industries from foreign competition. Japanese businesses are aided by special tax breaks, loans, and advice. It is very difficult for a foreign firm to engage in business in Japan.

Reappearance of the zaibatsu. In the last ten years there has been a trend toward increasing concentration of business in a few large firms. Corporations with familiar names – Mitsui, Mitsubishi, Sumitomo, and Fuji – have reappeared. Firms in the zaibatsu buy, sell, and finance one another.

The new-style zaibatsu differs from the earlier form in that it is not controlled by a single family. Nor is there a central company or a single authority for decision-making. However, the heads of firms meet regularly to deal with problems of mutual interest.

Japanese employment practices. Employment in a Japanese enterprise is compared to membership in an industrial family. Large firms offer their workers the security of lifetime employment – from the completion of school until retirement, usually at age 55. It is unusual for a worker to shift from one firm to another to attain a higher position. Employees have a strong identity with their employer. In return for lifetime employment workers develop strong loyalty to their company. Japanese employees assume that they will be taken care of. Short of bankruptcy, a place will be found for the worker in the firm.

In addition to a regular salary, employees receive two bonuses, one at the middle and the other at the end of the year. These can equal two to eight times a worker's monthly salary, depending on company profits. Since most firms do

---

All For the Company

Japanese employees, as workers and managers, share a strong sense of purpose in the well-being of their company. They feel that its success makes their nation successful, which in turn means success for themselves. The high morale of Japanese workers is reinforced every morning in a ten-minute warm-up before the start of work, during which they sing company songs, such as the following of the Matsushita Industrial Electric Company:

For the building of a new Japan,
Let's put our strength and mind together,
Doing our best to promote production,
Sending our goods to the people of the world,
Endlessly and continuously,
Like water gushing from a fountain.
Grow, industry, grow, grow, grow!
Harmony and sincerity!
Matsushita Electric.

JAPAN: LAND USE AND PRODUCTS

Land Use
- Manufacturing
- Farming
- Forest
- Fishing

Products
- Cars
- Electronic equipment (cameras, computers, radios and television se[ts])
- Rice
- Tea

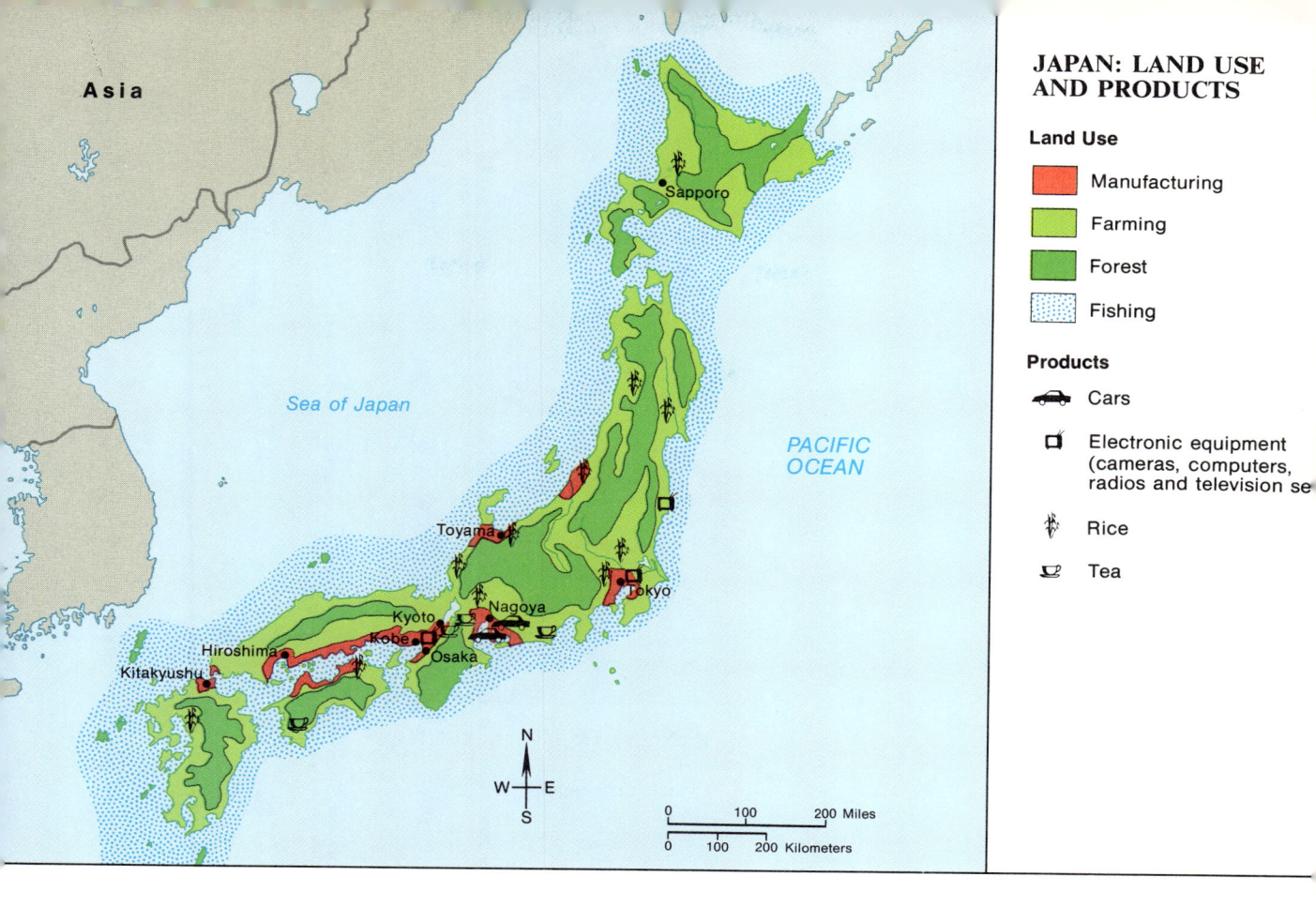

not offer pension plans, the employee at retirement receives a lump-sum payment, which may equal several years' pay. Since retired workers cannot live on this for the rest of their lives, many take jobs in smaller businesses.

Many firms also offer non-cash benefits. Company dormitories, dining rooms, recreational facilities, and medical care are offered at reasonable rates. Marriage arrangements, family planning clinics, and funeral arrangements are often offered. Sometimes workers also receive a transportation allowance. They also receive job training or retraining if they are shifted from one job to another.

Not all Japanese workers enjoy lifetime employment. Women are not thought to be hired for life in most companies. They are expected to leave their jobs at marriage or when the first child is born. Employees in Japan's many smaller firms are not assured of lifetime employment.

Living standard. With the exception of the aged and the unskilled worker, almost all levels of Japanese society have gained from Japan's economic growth through higher wages and better work opportunities. As Japanese citizens have made more money, they have become bigger consumers. A small percentage of the average worker's income is spent on food and clothing. More is spent on recreation. Almost all Japanese homes have televisions. More than half of the households have electric rice cookers, sewing machines, washing machines, and refrigerators. About 60 percent of the people own cars, and the number is growing, as is the market for air-conditioners. Japan has become a consumer-oriented country.

373

JAPAN: INDUSTRIAL REGIONS

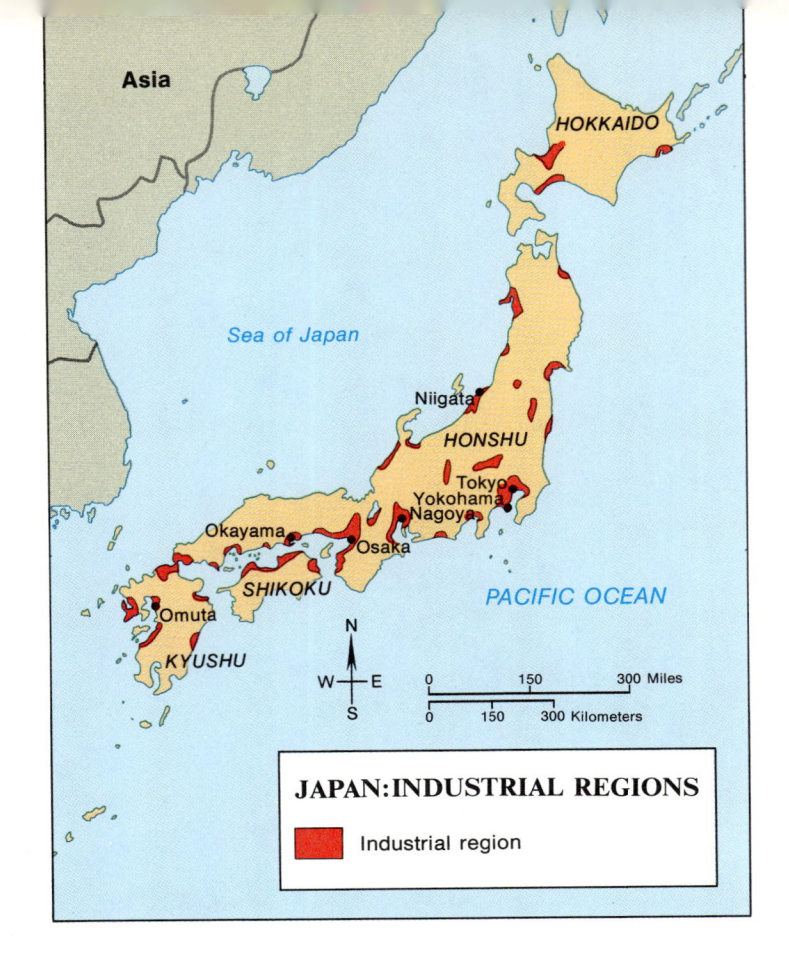

An Environmental Success Story

Japan's economic recovery following the devastation of World War II was a remarkable achievement. Only a highly skilled and motivated people could have accomplished what they did. However, all this was achieved at a heavy cost in pollution of air, land and water. This in turn had serious health consequences.

Public awareness of the pollution threat was sharpened when many residents of a town on Minamata Bay were found to be suffering from a disease of the central nervous system. They had eaten seafood from local waters that had been poisoned by mercury discharged into the bay from a nearby factory.

Pollution from automobiles and industries became so bad that much of the natural beauty from which Japan is famous was being destroyed. The beautiful view of Mount Fuji was obscured by smog.

An organized effort to control pollution was launched. The courts accepted the view that industries were responsible for the pollution they created and must deal with it. Though control is costly, industrial pollutants are now limited, automobile emission standards have been established, and once again the beautiful snow-capped peak of Mount Fuji can be seen by the citizens of Tokyo.

Challenges for the future. Although Japan's economy grew rapidly in the 1950s and 1960s, it experienced some decline in growth rate in the 1970s as higher prices for oil made manufacturing costs soar. Another factor in the decrease in Japan's rapid economic growth has been increased competition overseas from developing countries where labor costs are lower. Nonetheless, Japan is certain to remain a leader of the industrial world. In 1981 it had the highest growth rate among the major industrialized nations.

In many areas of public welfare, problems still exist. Urban water supplies and sewage need improvement. A better system of roads is needed. The traffic problems of the cities require urgent attention. The Japanese have already started making an effort to control the air and water pollution that results from industrialization. Finally, better housing is one of Japan's most urgent needs. Now that Japan has a vigorous economy, more attention is being focused on social needs.

CHAPTER REVIEW

Recalling Names and Places

land reform   lifetime employment   zaibatsu

Understanding This Chapter

1. How did the Meiji government modernize the Japanese economy?
2. What were the zaibatsu? Why were they important?
3. What economic reforms were promoted by the American Occupation authorities? How successful were they?
4. What factors contributed to Japan's economic recovery since 1945?
5. How does the Japanese government aid its business community?
6. How are the postwar zaibatsu different from the earlier forms?
7. Japan sells much more to the rest of the world than it buys. What are the immediate consequences of this favorable balance of trade? What might the long-term consequences be? What actions, if any, should Japan take on this matter?

Chapter 32

From Monarchy to Parliamentary Government

From the restoration of the Meiji emperor in 1867 until 1918, the Japanese government was ruled by the former samurai who had helped end Tokugawa rule. It was government by oligarchy – that is, a government in which a few men exercised great political power.

The Meiji Government

Although some former samurai leaders expressed dissatisfaction with the way the oligarchy ran the country, rebellions against the Meiji government were successfully put down by the imperial forces. However, in the early 1880s opposition to the Meiji government shifted from military actions to organized political party activity. The pressure put on the Meiji government by these parties as well as the desire to end unequal foreign treaties (p. 343) led to the first modern Japanese constitution in 1889.

The Constitution of 1889. One of the oligarchs, Ito Hirobumi, was given the responsibility of writing the new constitution. After a world tour to study foreign constitutions, Hirobumi produced a constitution that combined Japanese and Western political ideas. The constitution was presented to the public as a "gift" of the emperor to his subjects. The constitution proclaimed the emperor the absolute ruler of the nation.

Cabinet members and military leaders overshadow the emperor. Actually the emperor was ruler in name only. He appointed the prime minister and all cabinet ministers. These men as his close advisers held the real power in the government. The cabinet was responsible to the emperor and not to the Diet, the legislative body. Ministers held their posts as long as they held the confidence of the emperor. The army and navy also held an important check on the government. Only active generals and admirals could head the army and navy ministries. If the high command did not approve of cabinet members, it forbade military officers to head the military ministries. Thus the military had a virtual veto on the government.

Diet. The Diet, elected in 1890, is the oldest modern parliament in Asia. It provided limited popular participation in the government. The Diet consisted of an upper House of Peers and a lower House of Representatives. The new nobility – former samurai, nobles, and wealthy merchants – elected representatives from their ranks to sit in the upper house. The members of the lower house were elected by men over the age of twenty-five who met the tax qualification. There were about 450,000 voters.

The powers of the Diet were severely limited. It debated government measures and served as a forum for public opinion. It could defeat a government bill, but it could not introduce legislation of its own.

Political leaders resist political reform. Very little progress toward political democracy took place in the years before World War II. One exception was a broader suffrage law passed in 1925. All men over twenty-five were given the right to vote, thus creating almost 14 million new voters. At the same time, however, the Peace Preservation Law was passed. This law sentenced to prison anyone convicted of wanting to change the constitution or the government or abolish private property. This law was used to suppress the labor movement and the socialist parties.

Few other efforts at reform were made in the next six years. By 1931 the extreme nationalists, supported by the military, wanted to remove "corrupt" politicians and to restore direct rule by the emperor. Equally important, they wanted to see Japan take on a more aggressive foreign policy. They assassinated two moderate prime ministers and committed other terrorist acts. By the following year they had successfully intimidated the more moderate Japanese leaders. In 1932 a new cabinet was formed headed by an admiral. Until 1945 succeeding governments were dominated by the military and the bureaucracy.

American Occupation Reforms

A peaceful political revolution accompanied the American Occupation of Japan after World War II. A new constitution, written and imposed by the Americans, was accepted and put into operation in 1947. This document established a cabinet system with separate branches of government. The new constitution also provided a system of checks and balances to prevent any single branch of government from dominating the others.

Emperor retains his ceremonial position. While the emperor is no longer considered divine, the emperor system remains today. The constitution describes the emperor as the "symbol of the state and of the unity of the people. . . ." He performs such duties as convening the Diet and receiving foreign ambassadors.

The prime minister is the chief executive. The political party that has a majority of the seats in the Diet elects its leader prime minister. The prime minister is responsible to the Diet and to the party. Under the leadership of the prime minister, the cabinet does the work of the executive branch of government. The prime minister appoints and dismisses cabinet ministers. The cabinet controls and supervises the government, handles foreign relations, prepares the budget, and introduces almost all the bills enacted into law by the Diet. The cabinet is responsible to the Diet and must resign when the House of Representatives gives it a vote of "no confidence." When this happens, the House is dissolved, and all of its members are up for election.

Emperor Hirohito formally opens a new session of the Japanese parliament, called the Diet.

Diet reorganized. The Diet consists of an upper House of Councillors, which replaced the House of Peers and the abolished nobility, and a lower House of Representatives. Members of the upper house have a six-year term. Those in the lower house usually have a four-year term. Universal suffrage for those over twenty years of age has been the rule since the American Occupation decreed it. Women first voted in 1946.

The majority party in the Diet and cabinet governs Japan. It proposes legislation, submits a budget, and is responsible for foreign relations. However, its decisions are always carefully reviewed by factions within its own party, by the opposition parties, and by the public. Japan is not a one-party government. The voters can always turn out the majority party and elect another party to form a new government.

Political parties. Since 1955 Japan has had largely a two-party political system. In that year several parties united to form both the Liberal Democratic Party and the Japan Socialist Party. The Liberal Democratic Party has close business ties and is supported by many rural residents. The Japan Socialist Party gets most of its support from labor unions. The third largest party is the Komeito, which grew out of the Buddhist Soka Gakkai sect (p. 366). The Communist Party has a small representation in the Diet. There are also a few extreme nationalist political groups. Some extremists commit terrorist acts, the most spectacular of which was the murder of a socialist leader during a live television broadcast in 1960.

More popular participation needed. Political parties serve as a link between the voters and the government. They offer different policies, sponsor candidates for office, and campaign for them. Japanese political parties seem to be organizations of politicians rather than organizations of citizens. They are not grass-roots parties. Many Japanese are not yet convinced that political parties can be an effective way to express the desires of the people. Until political parties have the support of the majority of the people, democratic government cannot be considered to be firmly established in Japan.

Postwar Japan revises its defense policies. Japan's defeat in World War II was the first time in its history that it was defeated and not permitted to have armed forces. After the Korean War began in 1950, the United States pressed Japan to build, under civilian control, its armed forces.

While Japan maintains a mutual security treaty with the United States, it is now increasing its armed forces. The Japanese Self-Defense Agency has taken a leading role in calling for an expanded military to counter a growing Russian navy in the Pacific and to ensure the free movement of imported oil, a critical source of energy in Japan. The United States continues to operate its own military bases in Japan.

Good Foreign Relations Essential to Economic Growth

Although the Japanese economy depends heavily on foreign trade, 15 percent of its goods are sold abroad. Japan is a processing nation, which means that its factories transform imported raw materials into goods that can be used at home and sold abroad. Japanese businesses must export their products to earn dollars or other foreign currencies to pay for Japan's imports.

Virtually all the materials Japan imports are necessities. Almost all of its oil, iron ore, bauxite, coal, cotton, hides, and chemicals come from overseas. So do much of its foodstuffs and machinery. Japan wants good relations with its trading partners because it needs resources to keep its economy growing.

Japan and the United States. As long as the United States occupied Japan, the island country had little diplomatic contact with the rest of the world. In 1951, at the San francisco Peace Conference, forty-eight allied nations, not including Russia and China, signed a treaty with Japan ending the war. Japan's government was then free to govern itself and to enter into collective security treaties.

The only security treaty signed by Japan was with the United States. In return for a promise to defend Japan, the United States received permission to maintain military bases in Japan, but no nuclear weapons. When the Mutual Security Pact was renewed in 1960, demonstrations by neutralists, socialists, and radical students were so intense that President Dwight Eisenhower had to cancel a scheduled visit to Japan. The treaty remains in effect. When it was renewed in 1970, the United States agreed to return the island of Okinawa to Japan in 1972. Since the early 1980s the United States has put increased pressure on Japan to expand its defense budget. Many Japanese are opposed to such defense spending. The Japanese government has put more money into defense, but not as much as the Americans had hoped. This issue has caused tensions between the United States and Japan to grow.

Nakasone Yasuhiro became leader of the Liberal Democratic Party and prime minister of Japan in 1982.

Commercial trade between Japan and the United States is one of the most delicate and complex issues in Japanese-American foreign relations. After Canada, Japan is the United States' leading trading partner. About 24 percent of Japan's exports go to the United States, and 17 percent of its imports are from the United States. The United States is Japan's biggest supplier of foodstuffs, accounting for 35 percent of Japan's total food imports. It is also Japan's largest supplier of raw materials.

Since the 1970s the balance of trade between the United States and Japan has run heavily in favor of Japan. Japan's exports to the United States are significantly greater than its imports from the United States. The gap shows no signs of diminishing. It is a large portion of the overall United States trade deficit. This deficit, along with the strong Japanese presence in certain American markets, has caused some loss of good will toward Japan in the United States. Japanese barriers to American exports have added to the resentment of Japanese trade policies. Both sides are trying to reduce the imbalance. Efforts have included quotas on Japanese goods and Japanese pledges to open their markets more.

Japan and China. Japan's prewar trade pattern in Asia is gone. China, Korea, and Taiwan are no longer as important to Japan's economy as they once were. Japan has traded with both the Chinese Communist and Chinese Nationalist governments, although until 1972 the Japanese government maintained formal diplomatic relations with only the Nationalist Chinese.

In 1972, Prime Minister Tanaka Kakuei made a trip to the People's Republic of China. The agreement between Japan and China that resulted from this visit ended the thirty-five-year state of war between the two countries. It also acknowledged Taiwan as a part of China and established diplomatic relations between Tokyo and Beijing. At the same time Japan cut its diplomatic ties with the Nationalist government on Taiwan, though it continues its economic ties with Taiwan. Thus Japan opened a new era in foreign relations in Asia.

Japan and the Soviet Union. At the end of World War II the Soviet Union regained the Kuril Islands and the southern half of Sakhalin Island. While the Russians refused to sign a peace treaty with Japan after the war, Moscow and Tokyo established diplomatic relations in 1956. Relations between these countries have at times been strained by the presence of American military bases in Japan and Japan's close alliance with the United States. In 1982, however, the two countries announced that they would begin talks on improving relations. One issue that has kept them apart is Japan's demand that the Soviet Union return the four southernmost Kuril Islands. Increased trade between the two countries is a real possibility. Japan needs the raw materials of Siberia, and the Russians need capital to develop Siberia.

Japan and Southeast Asia. An anti-Japanese feeling persists in those parts of Asia that were overrun by the Japanese during World War II. Since the war Japan has paid more than a billion dollars in reparations for war damages to Southeast Asian countries. In addition Japan gives substantial economic aid to these nations, both long-term loans and outright grants. Japanese business leaders have been active in the economic development of Southeast Asia, opening up Japanese-owned industries in many parts of the area. Some of the smaller nations of Southeast Asia fear that Japan will dominate the region economically.

As Japan regains its self-confidence and as the United States reduces its willingness to be involved in Asian conflicts, Japan faces the prospect of assuming greater responsibility for the security of the Asian world. As it does so, new and different diplomatic and economic ties will begin to form in the Asian world.

Chinese Premier Zhou Enlai shakes hands with Japanese Prime Minister Tanaka Kakuei on Tanaka's arrival at the Beijing airport in 1972.

CHAPTER REVIEW

Recalling Names and Places

| Article 9 | Ito Hirobumi | oligarchy |
| Diet | Mutual Security Pact | Peace Preservation Law |

Understanding This Chapter

1. What pressures led to the writing of the 1889 constitution?
2. Who were the actual rulers of Japan under its first modern constitution?
3. What was the Diet? How powerful was it?
4. Describe the political situation in Japan between 1918 and 1945.
5. What are the positions of the emperor, the cabinet, and the Diet under the 1947 constitution? Why is the position of emperor retained?
6. What has been the position of the military in Japanese political life since 1945?
7. Should Japan have a role in the defense of the Western Pacific? What difficulties might this create?
8. What role does foreign trade play in Japan's relations with the United States? the Soviet Union? China? Southeast Asia?

Chapter 33

Japanese Cultural Contributions

The world has been enriched by the cultural creations of the Japanese. Their native talent was evident before it was influenced by the highly developed Chinese culture. As in so many other areas, the Japanese capacity to create a distinctive Japanese style is evident in the arts.

Diversity of Japanese Art

Like artists the world over, the Japanese worked in many media and used various techniques to express their values in their art. They also developed art forms that were uniquely Japanese.

The Great Buddha at Kamakura, made of gold and copper, weighs 124 tons.

Buddhist influence on sculpture.   Buddhism, like Christianity in the Western world, was a great patron of the arts. Temples housed figures of the Buddha and bodhisattvas. Incense burners, bells, candle holders, and gongs were used by the Buddhists in their worship.

Bronze was often used, whether the image was several inches in size or towered over the worshiper. The two largest bronze figures in the world are found in Japan. All that remains of the original Great Buddha at Nara are a few petals of the lotus flower base. The rest of the 53-foot-high figure is newer than its eighth-century bronze base. The Great Amida Buddha at Kamakura is smaller, but a more imposing and serene image.

Wood was the material that best suited the talented Japanese carvers. Wood was carved in its natural state and then polished, or it was painted with lacquer and then covered with gold leaf. A skilled wood carver could make a delicate human figure emerge from a bulky tree trunk. By the flow of the drapery, the bend of the arm, and the placement of the fingers on the smiling face, the artist could create a figure that radiated much calm.

The Japanese were also fine sculptors of lacquerware. Cloth was draped and folded over a hollow wooden frame and then covered with the sap of a lacquer tree. As the lacquer dried, the cloth stiffened into a rigid light shell. The hands, feet, and head were made separately and then stitched to the body. Layers of lacquered cloth covered the seams. The figure was then painted.

Zen influenced all the arts.   Zen monasteries were centers of learning and the arts. Books, paintings, ceramics, and even skilled artisans were brought from China by the monks. The monks helped set styles of art that continue to influence the Japanese sense of beauty today.

Zen stresses close ties with nature. Zen also teaches that awareness of nature is tinged with sadness, since it makes people realize their own insignificance. Zen teachings rely on intuitive thinking and indirect statement. They support the tendency of Japanese artists toward illusion and suggestion in the arts. Zen also stresses that poverty and detachment from worldly values – wealth, power, and reputation – are essential. Zen monks believe that one should be satisfied with a modest hut and a bowl of vegetables.

In line with Zen philosophy is the belief that beauty is found in ordinary objects, ones that are imperfect, old, plain, natural, small, and simple. Zen art is often of subdued colors and varied textures.

Scroll painting.   Chinese landscapes and portrait painting supplied the model for the Japanese Zen painter. Artists seldom painted from life. They spent years painting such conventional subjects as bamboo or rocks. With careful use of the brush for ink drawings the disciplined artist could complete a drawing with only a few brush strokes. Much of the painting was left blank, leaving the viewer to complete the scene. A small fishing boat on a lake might make one think of the boundless sea and at the same time convey peacefulness, contentment, and the Zen sense of aloneness.

Another variety of scroll painting was the long horizontal scroll. It was not meant to be hung, but unrolled horizontally on a mat. Artists painted stories and

"Pea Fowl and Flowers," by Massuyama Sessai (1755–1820), is a fine example of scroll painting.

historical events. *The Tale of the Genji* depicted beautifully attired members of the imperial court. Other scrolls described battle scenes full of action with galloping horses, tense archers, flying arrows, and raging fires. Buddhist scrolls showed the horrors of hell, where murderers and thieves burned in a river of fire.

> **The Japanese Tea Ceremony**
>
> The path to the teahouse is curved to conceal the entrance until the last moment. The teahouse has varied textures — natural wood, mud straw walls, thatch roof, and straw-matted floors. Guests and the teamaster sit on the floor of the small square room. In an alcove is a hanging scroll and below it a flower arrangement. The tea utensils — bowl, caddy, bamboo whisk, and spoon — are usually valuable art objects with a rich historical association. Several teaspoons of powdered green tea are put in an irregularly shaped tea bowl. Next hot water from an iron kettle is poured into the bowl and beaten into a froth with the bamboo whisk. The bowl is placed before the honored guest who, after bowing to his fellow guests, picks it up and takes a sip. He compliments the host on the excellence of the tea, takes a few more sips, and carefully wipes the edge of the bowl before passing it on to the next guest. This is repeated until all have tasted the tea. The three-hour ceremony passes quickly as the guests speak on the beauty of the scroll, flower arrangement, and tea utensils.

Signs of the old and the new can be seen in this tea ceremony at the Sokenin Temple.

Landscape gardening. A talented landscape artist can create a scenic composition with rocks, trees, and water. These elements are carefully placed to make even a small garden give the impression of a vast landscape. The landscape artist tries to make certain that a garden's arrangements do not seem artificial.

At the famous rock garden in the Ryoanji Temple in Kyoto fifteen stones are placed in carefully raked white sand. Oiled mud walls enclose three sides of the small rectangular garden. The abstract design of stones and sand might represent islands in the sea or mountains piercing a layer of clouds. The trees outside of the wall complete the composition.

Tea ceremony. The Zen notion of beauty can also be found in the tea ceremony. This takes place in a teahouse in a separate part of the garden to suggest solitude and detachment from the world. When a monk first introduced tea into Japan from China, it was used as a medicine or to prevent drowsiness during meditation. Zen monks made tea drinking into a ritual used in the attainment of enlightenment and mental calmness.

While only Zen monks and samurai enjoyed the discipline and the tranquility of the tea ceremony in the past, today it is a necessary element in the finishing touches of a young lady's social training. Cultured men practice it as well and often serve as teamasters.

Influence of Tokugawa urban culture. Life in the cities of seventeenth-century Tokugawa Japan, with its flamboyance and frivolity, contrasted sharply with Zen artistic standards. Osaka, Kyoto, and Edo offered social freedom for the merchants who had the money to purchase luxuries in the amusement centers. In the bath houses, restaurants, and theaters, relief was found from the restrictions of Tokugawa society. Those who could afford it enjoyed the polite company of the geisha, the professional women entertainers. The way in which Tokugawa artists described the "floating world," as Japanese called the gay city life, expressed the Buddhist notion that the pleasures of this life are only temporary and soon come to an end.

Wood blocks. Artists were attracted by the "floating world." They loved to capture it in many types of art work. While at one time their work was considered vulgar, wood-block artists are highly regarded today. The vivid colors and the striking designs of the kimonos were captured in the woodblock prints that flourished during this time. Scenes of home and city life, famous actors and actresses, nature scenes, and historical places were depicted by the artists. These prints, with their brilliant colors and shading, required great skill and attention. Many different wood blocks were made for each color in a print. These were printed one over the other for the finished work.

Among the most famous of these artists were Utamaro, Hokusai, and Hiroshige. Utamaro (1753–1806) revealed the beauty of Japanese women. The "Thirty-six Views of Mount Fuji" by Hokusai (1760–1849) depicted the Japanese landscape in color, with the famous mountain in each scene.

One of the prints in the series 53 Stages of the Tōkaidō *by the well-known woodblock artist Andō Hiroshige (1797–1858). The Tōkaidō highway connects Tokyo with Japan.*

Japanese Literature

Japanese literary works first appeared with the adoption of Chinese writing. Novels, short stories, plays, and poems were written in both the Chinese and Japanese languages.

Japanese poetry. Japan's greatest poet, Matsuo Basho (1644–1694), was a samurai who gave up his privileges to live as a commoner, teaching poetry to people from all classes. He is the master of the *haiku,* in which he dealt with such natural objects as the crow on the branch and a monkey shivering in the rain. In his poems he created pictures of a small bit of the world to suggest the entire world, or to suggest a universal truth.

The *haiku,* a brief poem of 17 syllables in three lines of 5, 7, and 5 syllables, is the verse form of the finest Japanese poetry. Although quite short, it is always in two parts divided by a break. The first sets the general scene, and the second gives the poem its larger meaning. Following is an example taken from *Japanese Literature,* translated by Donald Keene.

The sea darkens,	The ancient pond
The cries of the seagulls	A frog leaps in
Are faintly white.	The sound of water.*

*From *Japanese Literature* by Donald Keene, pp. 39–40. Copyright © 1955 by Donald Keene. Reprinted by permission of Grove Press, Inc.

"A Snowy Night at Kambara," also by Hiroshige.

The first part of the poem sets the scene. A mood of serenity is created. In the second part the splash of the frog disturbs the stillness of the pond. The sudden movement of the frog and the sound it creates startles the observer into looking at the scene and the world differently. The poem suggests that any sudden awareness might lead to *satori,* the Zen state of greater understanding.

The novel has a long history in Japan. *The Tale of the Genji* by Murasaki Shikibu is the world's first novel and one of its greatest. Written about 1000 A.D., it depicts the loves of the ideal courtier, Prince Genji, and the splendor and decline of an aristocratic society. A melancholy tone reflects the awareness that all things, including youth and beauty, pass. Sei Shonagon wrote the *Pillow Book* during the same period. Both books were written by women who lived at the imperial court and so present much information about court life. These novels show the large amount of freedom court ladies enjoyed.

Modern Japanese novels often blend Western style and writing techniques with traditional Japanese subjects. The works of Tanizaki Junichiro (1886–1965) and Kawabata Yasunari (1889–1972) give the reader a vivid picture of Japanese life and a feel for the beauty of the country. *The Makioka Sisters* by Tanizaki is a detailed account of the lives of a merchant family from the city of Osaka that has seen better days. The difficulties in arranging a marriage for one of the sisters is contrasted with the success of an assertive Western woman who finds her own husband. Kawabata won the 1968 Nobel Prize for literature for such novels as *Snow Country* and *A Thousand Cranes*. Mishima Yukio's (1925–1970) *The Temple of the Golden Pavilion* concerns the burning of one of Japan's most cherished Buddhist temples by a mad monk who dreamed of perishing with the building he adored. It gives a vivid feeling of life in a Zen temple.

Japanese Theater

Plays originated from symbolic dances performed at the imperial court and pantomimes by commoners. While they may move too slowly for Westerners, Japanese plays provide many insights into the Japanese character and values.

Nō drama. The oldest Japanese drama form is the *nō* play, which includes songs and dances. The plays are performed by actors whose roles have been handed down from generation to generation. The play has from one to five characters and a chorus that chants some of the lines. The actors' movements are restrained and stylized. Emotions are suggested by movements and gestures. Drums and flute provide the music. The small, highly polished wooden stage has little scenery. A stage may have only one stylized pine tree, which stands in sharp contrast to the beautiful brocaded costumes and the wooden masks worn by some of the actors.

Drums beat the rhythm to an actors graceful dance as he performs a nō play

A program will include five one-hour plays, which deal with gods, warriors, women, madmen, and devils. The tragic plots are based on history and legend. Comic relief is introduced between the plays by actors wearing masks who often make fun of the plays. While originally of secular origin, the nō plays reflect a Buddhist view of life. Zen influence may be seen in the sparseness of the lines, the simplicity of the stage sets, and in the discipline of the actors.

Kabuki theater. Unlike the aristocratic nō plays, the *kabuki* is the popular drama. All the roles are played by male actors. A chorus chants the narrative portions to the musical accompaniment of the three-stringed *samisen*. Against a background of realistic scenery, actors deliver elaborate speeches in a measured artificial voice. Great acrobatic skill is demonstrated by an actor portraying an animal, as he leaps about the stage and pops in and out of hidden doors. The makeup and the costumes are flamboyant, and an actor will wear an elaborate animal wig.

Japan's most noted playwright and the founder of its modern theater was the samurai Chikamatsu Monzaemon (1653–1725). Although he wrote many plays for the puppet theater, many of his works are performed by the kabuki. History was the source of some of Chikamatsu's plays. *The Battles of Coxinga* deals with a famous pirate who fights a tiger in a fantastic dance. *The Treasury of Loyal Retainers* depicts 47 ronin, masterless samurai, who avenge their master's death and then commit hara-kiri.

Japanese motion pictures. A few years after the first foreign film appeared in Japan in 1894, the Japanese produced their own motion pictures. The plots and settings are as varied as the films of any country. Some recount incidents in Japanese history. A prominent theme is the pain of having to adjust to new mores and valuesd in a changing society. One of Japan's best-known modern directors is Kurosawa Akira. His movie, *The Seven Samurai,* is the story of warriors who defend a village against bandits. It is considered one of the cinema's great battle epics. *Rashomon* is Kurosawa's psychological study of several people who tell their versions of a double crime.

Summing up. Many modern Japanese writers began their literary careers with a fondness for Western literature and civilization. After some years these artists often shifted from modernism to an appreciation of their own history and culture. Japanese writers have skillfully blended the old and the new in their imaginative writings.

CHAPTER REVIEW

Recalling Names and Places

Basho	Hokusai	nō plays
Chikamatsu Monzaemon	kabuki	Ryoanji Temple
haiku	Kawabata Yasunari	*The Tale of the Genji*
Hiroshige	Kurosawa Akira	Utamaro

Understanding This Chapter

1. How did Buddhism influence Japanese art?
2. What materials were most often used in sculpture? Describe each form and give examples.
3. Describe the Zen elements in the various art and literary forms.
4. What elements characterized the art and the literature of the "floating world?" Describe each form and give examples.
5. How does traditional Japanese theater differ from the modern western theater?
6. The American influence on Japan since World War II is obvious. List some examples of the less obvious Japanese influence on American ways of life.

UNIT 7
Exploring
Southeast Asia

| 900 | 1000 | 1100 | 1200 | 1300 | 1400 | 1500 | 1600 | 1700 | 1800 | 1900 |

- RISE OF ISLAM c. 900
- CHINA RULES VIETNAM 11 B.C.–938 A.D.
- VIETNAM KINGDOM OF CHAMPA 192–1471
- SRIVIJAYA DYNASTY 800–1200
- CATHOLIC MISSIONARIES 1500–c. 1650
- DUTCH EAST INDIA COMPANY 1602–1800
- FRANCE CONTROLS INDOCHINA 1884–1954
- INDOCHINA WAR 1946–1954
- U. S. INVOLVEMENT IN VIETNAM 1956–1973
- INDEPENDENCE FOR CAMBODIA, PHILIPPINES, BURMA, INDONESIA, MALAYA 1946–1957

SINCE THE END OF WORLD WAR II, SOUTHeast Asia has attracted a good deal of the world's attention. Vietnam, Laos, and Cambodia have been a bloody battleground long torn by war. The horror and destruction of war will not soon be forgotten by the peoples of these nations.

In other parts of Southeast Asia long wars of independence or peaceful negotiations have given Southeast Asian colonies political freedom. However, self-government has not resulted automatically in a more peaceful life for Southeast Asians. Rather, most countries of the region have been plagued by political instability. By studying this region, we can see more clearly the complexity of government and the challenges of independence.

Unlike such countries as Japan or China, most nations of Southeast Asia do not share a common history or culture. In languages, customs, religions, and practices, there are many differences. Ten independent nations are found in the region today. In most of these countries there are many distinct groups of people with their own culture. All together they make up the ethnic mosaic of Southeast Asia. Their similarities and differences and their political and artistic achievements make Southeast Asia an interesting region to study.

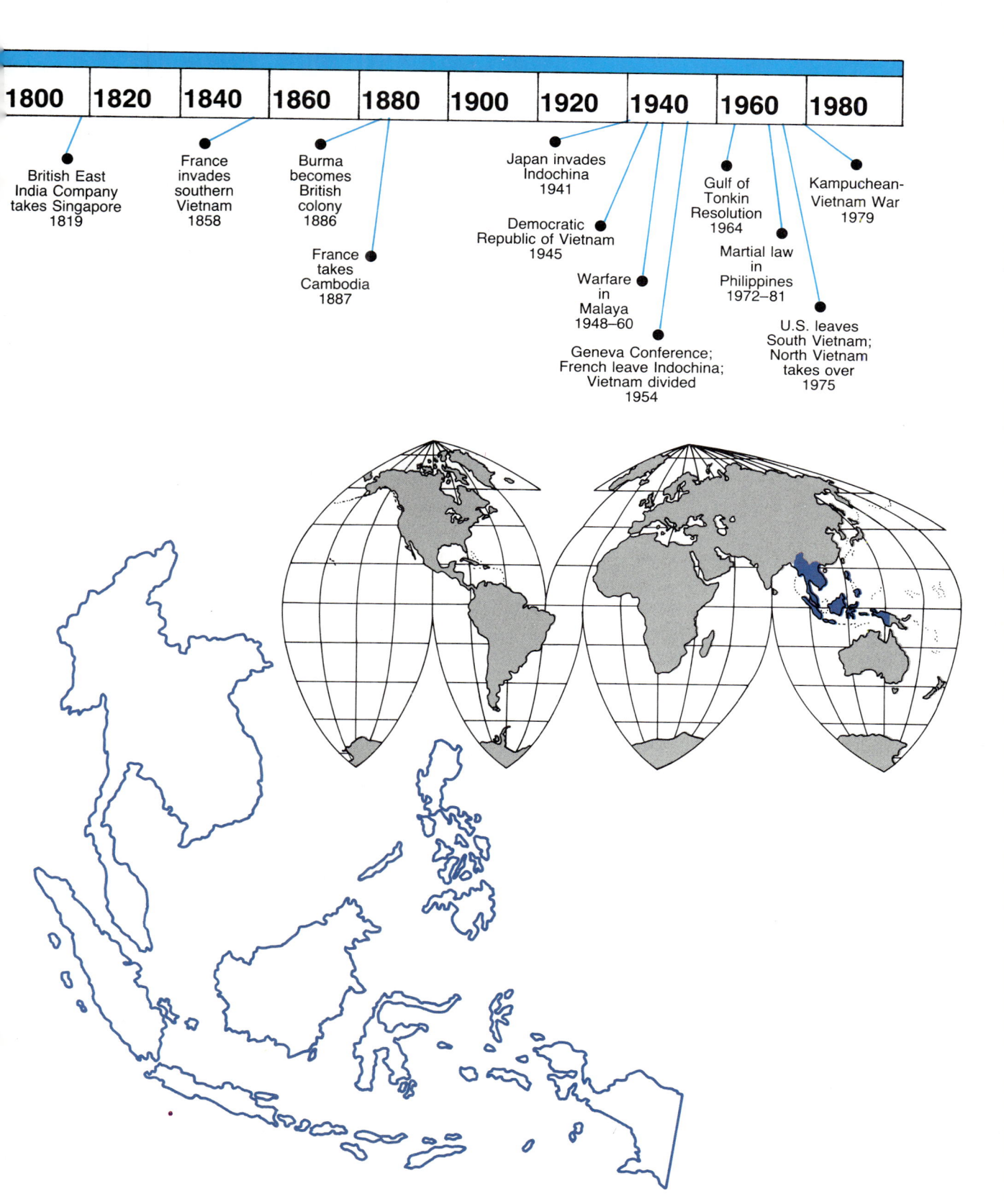

| 1800 | 1820 | 1840 | 1860 | 1880 | 1900 | 1920 | 1940 | 1960 | 1980 |

- British East India Company takes Singapore 1819
- France invades southern Vietnam 1858
- Burma becomes British colony 1886
- France takes Cambodia 1887
- Japan invades Indochina 1941
- Democratic Republic of Vietnam 1945
- Warfare in Malaya 1948–60
- Geneva Conference; French leave Indochina; Vietnam divided 1954
- Gulf of Tonkin Resolution 1964
- Martial law in Philippines 1972–81
- U.S. leaves South Vietnam; North Vietnam takes over 1975
- Kampuchean-Vietnam War 1979

393

Chapter 34

The Variety of Southeast Asia

Lying between the two large nations of India and China, Southeast Asia covers an enormous area. As you can see from the map on page 436, it stretches approximately 4000 miles from Burma on the Bay of Bengal to the eastern border of Indonesia's West Irian on the large island of New Guinea. From north to south almost 3000 miles separate the northern portion of Burma from the southern coast of Java. Half of the Southeast Asian area consists of seas. Ten nations are found in this region – Singapore, Burma, Thailand (*tie*'land), Malaysia, Cambodia, Laos (*lah*'ohs), Vietnam, Indonesia, Brunei (brew-*nie*'), and the Philippines.

Southeast Asia has no single cultural or political center. The closest thing to an economic and transportation center is the port of Singapore and the nearby Strait of Malacca. At Singapore, travel from the Indian and Pacific oceans converges. Bangkok has recently become important, for it is a key point in airline travel between Calcutta and Hong Kong.

Southeast Asia Can Be Divided into Two Sections

Geographers usually divide Southeast Asia into two regions: the peninsula or continental realms and the island realms. The peninsula is characterized by a series of river valley societies. The islands, on the other hand, are much more varied in their cultures.

Peninsular or continental Southeast Asia. Peninsular Southeast Asia is separated from the rest of the Asian continent by a rugged plateau and mountain system that begins in Tibet and stretches through the province of Yunnan in China. Mountain ridges extend southward from this area into the peninsula and divide it into distinct valleys. One ridge separates Burma from India, while another forms the mountainous border between Burma and Thailand and extends into the Malayan peninsula. Another ridge extends into east-central Thailand. The easternmost range straddles the border between Laos and Vietnam.

In the valleys between these mountain ranges flow the great rivers of the area. Originating in Tibet, the Irrawaddy and Salween rivers, each over 1000 miles long, flow through Burma and empty into the Gulf of Martaban. Over 2800 miles long, the Mekong River flows through China and separates Laos from Thailand. It continues through Cambodia, enters Vietnam and flows through the delta area into the South China Sea. The Red River is more than 700 miles in length. It makes its way through southern China into northern Vietnam until it empties into the Gulf of Tonkin. Thailand's principal river is the Chao Phraya (*chah'oh prah'yah*). Less than 300 miles long, it empties into the Gulf of Thailand.

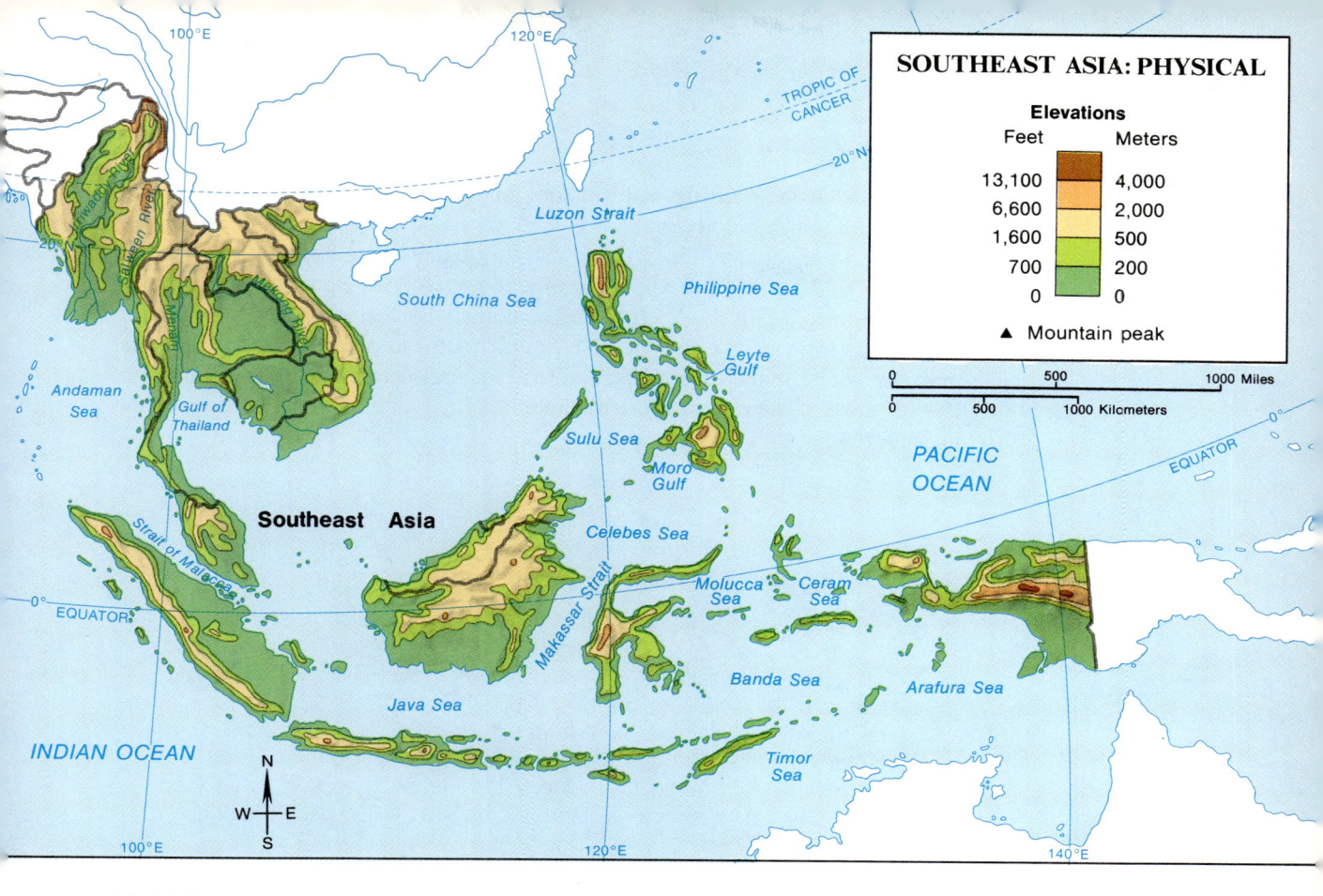

The capitals of Burma, Thailand, Laos, Vietnam, and Cambodia are located along the rivers. Some capitals such as Rangoon and Bangkok are also the chief ports of their countries.

The islands of Southeast Asia. Both Indonesia and the Philippines are archipelagoes. Geographers define an archipelago as a group of islands extending over large areas of water. Each nation consists of thousands of islands.

More than 13,000 islands make up the Republic of Indonesia. Most of the land area, however, consists of the islands of Java, Sumatra, Kilimantan [Borneo], Sulawes: [Celebes], and West Irian. Of these, the principal island is Java. Two-thirds of Indonesia's more than 166 million people live on Java. The other Indonesian islands have 90 percent of the land area and one-third of the population. To promote the economic development of these areas and to ease the population pressure on Java, the Indonesian government encourages immigration from Java to the outer islands.

More than 7000 islands make up the Philippine archipelago. Ninety-four percent of the almost 54 million Filipinos live on eleven islands. Most of the other islands are uninhabited.

Luzon is the largest and most populous island. The chief farming area lies between the mountains to the north and to the west. Manila Bay, one of the finest natural harbors in the world, is the site of the port-capital of Manila.

Climate, Resources, and People

Southeast Asia lies in the tropical zone, mostly north of the equator. The high temperature and humidity make this area very hot and muggy. As one moves away from the equator, the average monthly temperature range increases. It is only 78°F to 81°F near the equator at Singapore, while at Bangkok farther north, it is 78°F to 87°F. In the Vietnamese mountains bordering China, the temperature ranges from winter days of 40°F to maximums in April at 107°F. Temperatures are cooler in the mountains, and frost appears occasionally in the far north. But for most of the region, the temperature is high with only an infrequent cooling breeze.

The Greatest Volcanic Explosion Ever Recorded

Indonesia has several hundred volcanoes, most of which have been inactive for centuries. The greatest volcanic eruption ever recorded took place on Krakatoa, an island in the strait between Java and Sumatra. Two-thirds of the island disappeared in 1883. The sound was heard in Singapore, more than 500 miles away, and in even more distant Australia. The fine ash was blown miles into the sky and carried completely around the world. A 100-foot-high ocean wave was created by the volcanic explosion. It drowned 36,000 people on an island six miles away.

The erupting volcano of Krakatoa in the Sunda strait.

Southeast Asia is one of the wettest regions on earth. Much of Southeast Asia receives 80 inches or more of rain annually. The highest recorded 24-hour rainfall – 46 inches – fell at Baguio, Luzon, in July 1911. From June to September rainfall is very heavy as humid monsoon winds from the seas to the south move northward and are forced to rise over the mountains. With the exception of a few places on the northern coasts, winter is generally dry as winds flow from the Asian continent to the sea. Among the islands near the equator, the extreme wet and dry seasons caused by the monsoons are less pronounced. This is because tropical showers provide rain throughout the year.

From April to December the Southeast Asian area is hit by typhoons, the "hurricanes" of the eastern hemisphere. Typhoons often start just north of the equator in the Pacific Ocean. Moving west and then north they cause great property damage and sometimes loss of life.

Rain forests hold abundant natural resources. Where the annual rainfall exceeds 80 inches, and temperatures are constantly over 65°, tropical rain forests develop. Ferns, shrubs, and bamboo grow close to the ground. A second layer of plants consists of trees. Forming a canopy above these layers are trees that flourish in the sun and grow to several hundred feet in height. Woody vines grow from tree to tree, and orchids thrive in tree branches.

Although important mineral resources are found in Southeast Asia, only a few specific types are mined to any extent. The full mineral wealth of the region is not yet known, for the dense tropical forest has made geological exploration difficult. One-third of the world's tin supply comes from Malaysia, which also has the bauxite from which aluminum is made. Northern Vietnam has the only good coal deposits in the area. Oil is found in Burma and Indonesia.

Southeast Asia's population is mostly rural. Over 400 million people live in Southeast Asia. Most of these people live in the plains along the major rivers and along the coasts. Since the region is almost entirely agricultural, more than 90 percent of the people live in the countryside.

Every country has one major city, usually the capital, with a population of over one million. Some include Rangoon, Burma; Jakarta, Indonesia; Bangkok, Thailand; Manila, Philippines; and Ho Chi Minh City, Vietnam. (Ho Chi Minh City is not the capital, but as Saigon it was the capital of South Vietnam before Vietnam was reunited in 1975.) Cambodia's capital Phnom Penh, with a prewar population of 600,000, has steadily lost population in the 1970s and 1980s as a result of years of war and political unrest.

These cities are pockets of modernity in the midst of traditional, more slowly changing village life. They have newer sections with modern office buildings and industries. Leading international corporations have branch offices in these cities. At the wharves of the port-capitals are vessels from many nations unloading manufactured goods and picking up the rubber, oil, timber, and minerals needed by the industries of the world.

Centuries of migration have resulted in an urban population that reflects many languages and cultures. Chinese, Indians, Europeans, and to a lesser extent Japanese and Americans form important minority groups. In Singapore, Chinese actually make up 77 percent of the total population and outnumber all culture groups, including the Malays.

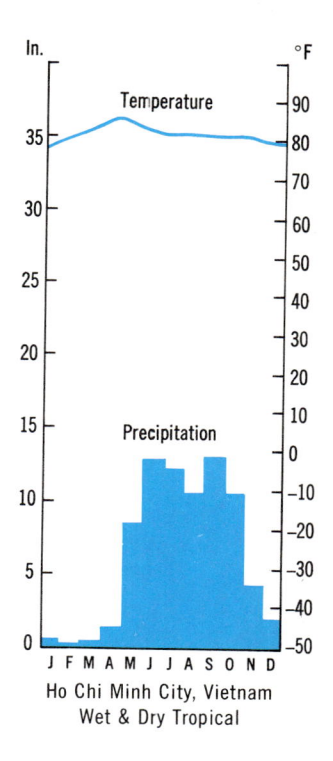

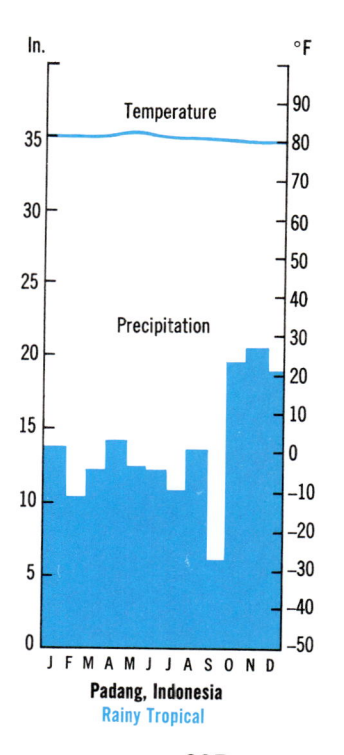

Ho Chi Minh City, Vietnam
Wet & Dry Tropical

Padang, Indonesia
Rainy Tropical

Bamboo: Useful and Beautiful

Bamboo is a common plant over much of Asia. It is the fastest growing plant in the world. It completes its growth in about two months and remains the same size as long as it lives. It flowers once every hundred years and then dies.

Although bamboo is tough and strong, it is also flexible and light. A skilled workman finds the material easy to work with. It splits easily and can be bent into a new shape when heated.

Bamboo is one of the most useful plants known. Half of the world uses it in daily life. Its importance to the people of Southeast Asia can be seen in a Vietnamese proverb: "The bamboo is my brother." Houses and fences are built of bamboo. Chopsticks and water ladles are made of bamboo. Fruits and vegetables are carried in a bamboo basket. Fish are caught in bamboo nets or traps. Farm fields are irrigated with bamboo pipes. To produce salt the Chinese placed bamboo pipes several thousand feet into the earth to draw out the salt water. Young bamboo shoots are fried crisp and eaten.

Bamboo also has refined uses. Chinese used strips of bamboo linked with silk as books. A bamboo stem is part of a writing brush. Paper was made from bamboo, as were flutes and the utensils used in the Japanese tea ceremony. Gardens are decorated with it.

Bangkok's many miles of klongs, or canals, are major transportation routes for the city's inhabitants. Rice and lumber from the farms and mills farther inland come into the city through the canals.

Automobiles, trucks, buses, trolley cars, and motor scooters vie with bicycles, rickshaws, ox carts, and pedestrians along the crowded streets. Western clothing contrasts with colorful Asian dress. The residential sections of these cities, with their local markets, are a vivid contrast to the modern sections.

Most people travel on foot or in carts. Dense forests and mountains have always limited the movement of goods and people in Southeast Asia. People use pack animals, bullock carts, and carrying poles to transport goods over the area's dirt roads. These roads are muddy during the wet monsoon and dusty during the dry season. While improved highways and railroads are found throughout the area, they do not reach all villages.

The entire area has over 130,000 miles of roads that can be used by trucks and buses. With the exception of Laos, every nation has a railroad network. They range in mileage from a little over 400 in Cambodia to over 4,264 in Indonesia. With such limited modern facilities, the people of Southeast Asia still rely mainly on traditional means of transportation.

Since half the area of Southeast Asia consists of water, boats have always been a most important means of transportation. Sampans and motor boats carry people and goods along the rivers and canals of Southeast Asia. Modern boats go back and forth between the many islands of Indonesia and the Philippines.

CHAPTER REVIEW

Recalling Names and Places

archipelago   Krakatoa   Singapore
Irrawaddy River   Mekong   typhoon

Understanding This Chapter

1. Describe the land formations and rivers of peninsular Southeast Asia.
2. What makes the Philippines and Indonesia archipelagoes?
3. Describe the climate of Southeast Asia. How does it make tropical rain forests possible?
4. What are Southeast Asia's natural resources?
5. Describe the different methods of transportation found in Southeast Asia.
6. Has the geography of Southeast Asia contributed to the large amount of conflict in the region? If so, how?

Chapter 35

The Road to Nationhood

The modern nations of peninsular or continental Southeast Asia are based on cultures that developed in the major river valleys. While each valley civilization has its distinguishing traits, they also reflect the historical influences of the Chinese, Indian, and later, European cultures.

Before the fifth century A.D. Indian cultural influences reached Burma, for example, by way of traders and migrants. Indian languages brought literacy to much of Southeast Asia, and political, religious, artistic, and scientific ideas spread throughout the area as the educated read Indian literature.

Ancient River Valley Kingdoms of the Peninsula

Many of the early kingdoms of the peninsula area represent close connections with China. These kingdoms were often created by people migrating from China.

The rulers of Pagan left their mark on Burma. Early settlers in most of the great river valleys in Southeast Asia migrated from the north and were of Mongolian descent. These included the people who established the Mon and Pagan (pah-*gahn'*) empires. They grew rice and were skilled artisans, shipbuilders, sailors, and traders. By the mid-thirteenth century, the Pagan

This wood carving is found on a book cabinet made in Ayutthaya, the capital of Thai kingdom from the late fourteenth century until the Burmese overran it in 1767. It is now a part of the collection of the National Museum in Bangkok.

government had lost its power. In 1271 Mongol armies from China invaded Burma, and it became a tributary nation to China.

After that, various dynasties ruled Burma for almost four centuries, during which the country was torn by civil war and battles with Thailand, Laos, and China. Not until the eighteenth century did Burma reassert its power, driving off foreign invaders.

The Khmer organize the ancient Cambodian state. Little is known of early Cambodian history. Scholars think that during the first century A.D., such tribes as the Funanese, the Khmer (*kmehr*), and the Cham fought for the fertile land along the Mekong River. Eventually the Khmer became most powerful. Jayarvarman II organized the Khmer kingdom around 800 A.D. This empire formed the foundation for the modern country of Cambodia. At its peak, it extended from the mouth of the Mekong River to the Gulf of Siam. Angkor, the capital, housed some of the most beautiful art treasures in the world.

Thailand, to the west, repeatedly attacked Cambodia during the thirteenth and fourteenth centuries, and in 1432 the Thais captured Angkor. They looted the capital and carried thousands of artists and scholars into slavery. Angkor's elaborate waterworks fell into decay, the temples were neglected, and the tropical rain forest embraced the buildings, almost totally hiding them from view. For the next four centuries Cambodia was a vassal state under its Thai or Vietnamese neighbors.

Nan Chao, ancient home of the Thai. The ancient home of the Thai people was Nan Chao on the border of China. The influence of Chinese culture was reflected in the language and culture of Nan Chao. Thai rulers married the daughters of prominent Chinese families and sent their sons to China for an education.

A Boastful Thai King

The following quote is from a fourteenth-century inscription. In it, a Thai king boasted of the manner in which he ruled his kingdom by Buddhist values:

This king rules by observing the ten kingly precepts. He has pity on all his subjects. If he sees rice belonging to others, he does not covet it, and if he sees the wealth of others, he does not become indignant. . . . When a father dies, he lets the children have his possessions; when an elder brother dies, he lets the younger brother have them. He has never once beaten to death someone who has done wrong. . . . Whenever he captured warriors . . . he has neither killed them nor had them beaten, but has kept them and fed them so as to preserve them from ruin and destruction. If he catches people who are guilty of deceit and insolence . . . he never kills them nor beats them, but is merciful to all who display evil intentions toward him. The reason why he represses his feelings and curbs his thoughts and refrains from anger when anger is called for, is that he desires to become a Buddha and to lead all creatures beyond the sea of suffering of transmigration.

G. Coedés, *The Making of Southeast Asia* (Berkeley: University of California Press, 1966), p. 145.

Nan Chao successfully resisted Chinese efforts to conquer it until 1253 when the Mongols finally gained control. A migration began before the Mongols took Nan Chao and ended in the fifteenth century when the Thais formed a new kingdom to the south.

During the next several centuries, Thailand was plagued by civil war and clashes with its neighbors. Cambodia regained its independence, and Burma destroyed the Thai capital in 1767. The present royal family, the Chakri dynasty, was established in 1702 with the city of Bangkok as the new capital.

River valley kingdoms of Vietnam. The Red River delta was the ancient center of the Vietnam kingdom. In 11 B.C., China conquered the Red River area and ruled Vietnam for the next 1000 years.

The Chinese influence resulted in many improvements in the Vietnamese economy. They introduced the water buffalo and the iron plow. The Vietnamese also adopted the Chinese written language of characters, their military and governmental organizations, and many social customs and clothing styles.

In 938 A.D. the Chinese were finally driven out of Vietnam, and a tributary relationship was maintained. Vietnam remained independent until the nineteenth century, when it became a French colony.

South of the Red River valley the kingdom of Champa (192–1471) occupied the Mekong Delta. Champa and Vietnam fought for supremacy along the east coast of Indochina. In 1471 Champa was finally conquered by its northern rival. The Vietnamese cleared the land and turned it into rice fields, which supported newly established villages. Schools and settlers followed. The Champa culture soon disappeared.

Reviewing Your Reading

1. What were the major river valley kingdoms of the continent?
2. Which peninsular peoples were hostile to one another?

Early History of Island Civilizations

Unlike the continental regions of Southeast Asia, the islands did not allow for the development of great river valley civilizations. Rather, a number of smaller kingdoms developed. They were exposed to a variety of cultural influences, such as Islam, from merchants and travelers who crossed the seas. This area also came under the influence of Western colonizers much earlier than its neighbors to the north.

Malaya, crossroads of Southeast Asia. Malaya's importance in Southeast Asia rests on its key position at the oceanic crossroads of the area. Control of the Malacca Strait meant the power to tax vessels using the ocean passageway between the Malayan peninsula and the island of Sumatra. Because of this strategic position, Malaya's first rulers, the Srivijaya, became the wealthiest and most powerful monarchs in the area. They controlled the Malayan peninsula until the thirteenth century.

Early in the fifteenth century, with the development of the port of Malacca, new influences began to affect the Malayan peninsula. The Malaccan ruler became a Muslim and encouraged the spread of Islam among the islands. Even today, Islam remains a strong cultural force in the island area.

Indonesian dynasties. Between the ninth and the thirteenth centuries, the Srivijaya (*shree'* vah-ji-yah) dynasty on the island of Sumatra dominated the islands of Southeast Asia. Controlling the Malaccan Strait, it became a wealthy, commercial kingdom, taxing vessels that passed through the strait from as far away as China and Arabia. (The Arab traders brought eastern spices and luxury goods into Europe.) As an important Buddhist center, the Srivijaya kingdom also attracted scholars and pilgrims from the entire region.

The Srivijaya dynasty began to decline in the eleventh century. By the time Europeans appeared in the area during the sixteenth century, Indonesia consisted of many small rival Muslim kingdoms with little power beyond their own borders. This situation helped to make creation of Western colonies an easy process.

The Europeans Arrive

Portuguese traders were the first Europeans to arrive in Southeast Asia. In 1511 they captured the port of Malacca and built a fort there. The Portuguese grew wealthy in the profitable spice trade, and for over a century they resisted repeated attacks intended to oust them from the islands.

At the beginning of the seventeenth century, the Dutch began to challenge the Portuguese for commercial control of the islands. In 1602, Dutch traders formed the Dutch East India Company. The Company was authorized to make treaties and to defend and govern the lands where it traded. Fearing Portuguese control

The islands of present-day Indonesia were once known as the Spice Islands. At port towns like Bantam in Java, Dutch and English mercants traded Javanese pepper for Chinese silk.

of Malacca, the Dutch allied themselves with a Malayan ruler to capture Malacca. In a series of seventeenth-century wars the Dutch eliminated their Portuguese rivals from the area, except for part of the island of Timor, which the Portuguese continued to hold until 1975.

Dutch rule in Southeast Asia. The fortified port of Batavia (modern Jakarta), founded in 1619, was the center of Dutch activity in Southeast Asia. The Dutch were primarily interested in the valuable spice trade – mace, nutmeg, clove, and pepper. They earned handsome dividends for the stockholders of the Dutch East India Company.

During the eighteenth century, the Dutch started a plantation system of farming. Sugar, coffee, tea, cotton, indigo, and pepper were grown. Local rulers had to supply a fixed quantity of each crop and sell it at fixed prices to the Dutch. The Dutch limited the spice supply by destroying the surpluses to keep prices high in Europe. Farmers bore a heavy burden. To meet Dutch demands, they were forced to grow less rice, their essential food.

Because of poor management and political problems in Europe, the Dutch East India Company was dissolved in 1800. The Dutch government assumed responsibility for the islands. Later the Dutch extended their control from Java to Sumatra, Borneo, and the western half of New Guinea.

The culture system. Commercial farming was placed under government control. Java became an enormous government plantation. The Dutch rulers received 20 percent of the crop or two months of labor from each farmer. Forced labor built and maintained roads and irrigation systems.

When the poor Javanese living conditions became known in the Netherlands, humanitarian interest in the Javanese farmer grew. Under humanitarian prodding, reforms were made. Slavery was abolished, forced labor was regulated, and laws were enacted to protect local Javanese industries. But these measures were not effective, for they were not fully enforced.

In 1870 the government monopoly of agriculture ended. Private economic development of Sumatra and other islands took place. Tin was mined, oil was pumped out of the earth, and rubber plantations were started.

Early Philippine life under the Spanish. At the time the Spaniards landed on the Philippine Islands in the sixteenth century, the Filipinos lived in scattered communities with very little contact between them. Each community was led by a local chief. Since the self-sufficient economy produced no significant crop surplus, there was very little trade.

Ferdinand Magellan came on the Philippine Islands in 1521. After Magellan was killed in a battle, the surviving Spanish sailors left the islands. Succeeding Spanish explorers established Spain's authority in the port of Manila on the main island of Luzon. The area was governed by a Spanish governor-general and officials, while Filipinos, guided by Spanish priests, looked after the villages.

The land was divided into large estates called *encomiendas* (en-koh-myen'dahs) and assigned to individuals or church groups. Taxes were collected, sometimes in the form of labor services. The landlord was to protect the residents and teach them the Catholic religion. The encomiendas eventually became the basis for large plantations. Life for the Filipino on these estates was often quite harsh.

The Catholic Church played a major role in the Philippine Islands. Spanish missionaries lived and worked among the Filipinos. They established schools and were active in social and economic programs. Except for the Muslims in the south, almost all Filipinos became Roman Catholics.

Britain dominates Malaya. In 1819 the British East India Company acquired the island of Singapore at the southern tip of the Malayan peninsula. With its good deep-water port, it became a shipping lane to India and Africa.

Malaya's economic development grew under the British. Singapore became the leading port in Southeast Asia. Modern transportation and communication facilities were introduced. The British brought in seedlings from Brazilian rubber trees, and plantations expanded to meet the growing world demand for rubber. Indian workers were imported to work on the plantations. Because sufficient local labor was unavailable, Chinese were also brought in to work the tin mines.

At first the British had no intention of expanding their land holdings in the peninsula. When battles broke out in the tin-mining areas, the Chinese, who were British subjects, called for protection. Britain moved in to "rescue" the Malayan states before they fell into "ruin."

Modern Singapore came into being in 1819 when Sir Stamford Raffles made a treaty with the sultan of Singapore allowing the British East India Company to establish a trading post at the mouth of the Singapore River. Today it is a modern port, a shipping and shipbuilding center, and the fourth-largest city in Southeast Asia.

Reviewing Your Reading

1. What areas did the Srivijaya rulers control? How did their geographic position contribute to their wealth and power?
2. Describe Dutch rule in Indonesia, Spanish rule in the Philippines, and British rule in Malaya.

European Influence in Continental Southeast Asia

Europeans became interested in the continental kingdoms of Burma, Thailand, Cambodia, and Vietnam over two hundred years after their colonization of the island area. The northern river valley states were far from the heavily traveled routes around Southeast Asia's islands.

British rule in Burma. In the eighteenth century, British and French traders appeared in Burma. However, there was little prospect for profitable trade with Burma at this time. The British East India Company had established control of India, and Burmese rebels were using Indian territory as a base from which to attack Burma. Eager to expand into India and stamp out the rebels, the Burmese troops invaded India in 1824. But the Burmese had underestimated British power in India and were forced to surrender in 1826. A second war in 1852 resulted in the loss of Lower Burma to the British. Burmese kings tried to modernize the country to strengthen it against foreign invasion but reform efforts were largely unsuccessful. After a third war with Britain in 1886, all of Burma became a British colony.

Britain ruled Burma as a part of India, restoring peace and order to the country. The British reorganized the Burmese government and abolished slavery. Burma became a leading exporter of rice, much of which was sold to India. Indian workers helped to build railroads, canals, roads, docks, and factories. Rubber plantations were laid out.

While the Burmese economy grew, most of its people did not share in its prosperity. Their situation was often worsened. The Burmese competed with Chinese and Indian managers, laborers, and professionals for jobs. The British did little to help or to protect the Burmese.

This lithograph of a European's "country house" in the island city of Batavia was made in 1883. Batavia was the center of Dutch colonial power in the islands of Southeast Asia. The Dutch built the city in 1618 on the site of the town of Jacatra, which they had burned to the ground. Today the Indonesian capital of Jakarta stands on the same spot.

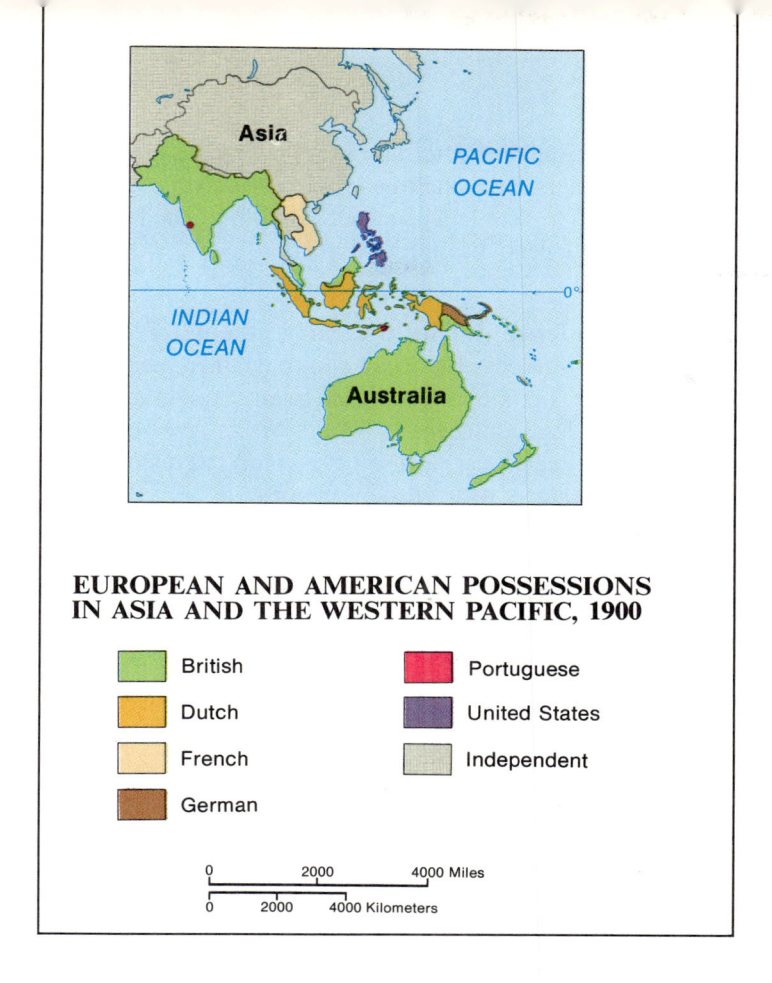

EUROPEAN AND AMERICAN POSSESSIONS IN ASIA AND THE WESTERN PACIFIC, 1900

- British
- Dutch
- French
- German
- Portuguese
- United States
- Independent

Burmese nationalism begins under the British. As in their other colonies, the British established modern English language schools in Burma. A small number of well-to-do city families sent their sons to these schools, and Western-educated Burmese replaced the traditional Burmese elite. They became lawyers or teachers in the modern schools or competed for the few low-level positions in the civil service. Yet many did not find positions equal to their training and ambitions.

The Buddhist religion helped to hold Burmese society together; the religion became a rallying point for Burmese nationalists. Buddhist associations assumed a wide political role. Politically minded monks led hunger strikes and rebellions and went to prison. Political parties were formed. They pressed for more self-government and successfully boycotted elections to get a greater Burmese role in government. The nationalists called for more Burmese in the civil service, free elementary schools, a Buddhist university, and the abolition of English as the teaching language in the University of Rangoon. On the eve of World War II, the nationalists demanded the promise of independence in exchange for Burmese support of the British war effort. The British refused to meet this demand.

Burma in World War II. During World War II, the Japanese army occupied Burma. The Japanese freed the nationalist prisoners and established a puppet government with the assistance of some nationalist leaders. Yet in general, the Japanese treated the Burmese poorly.

When the British returned to Rangoon after the war, prewar conditions were restored. But the nationalist leaders, with their newly experienced political role and sense of power, called for complete independence. Britain granted Burma a new constitution in 1947 and independence the next year.

Thailand retains its independence during the early colonial era. Thai rulers encouraged foreign trade with both European and Asian merchants. While foreigners were welcomed, the Thai king played each against the other to prevent one foreign country from dominating his kingdom. When foreign intrigue grew, the king expelled all foreigners, fearing Thailand would fall under foreign control. Later rulers renewed contacts with Western nations.

Beginning in 1851 Thailand was led by two strong rulers who set out to modernize Thailand, develop its economic resources, preserve its independence, and limit foreign influences. Under King Mongkut (*mong*'guht) and his son Chulalongkorn (choo-lah-*long*'corn), Thailand gradually modernized itself.

Thailand's two very able rulers were also sharp political figures. They balanced British and French influence against each other. Chulalongkorn yielded territory to both nations yet avoided a direct conflict with either.

Britian and France favored an independent Thailand. The British controlled Burma to the west, and the French controlled Laos, Cambodia, and Vietnam to the east. Both wanted a neutral Thailand to serve as a buffer between their colonies. While this arrangement was made without consulting Thailand, it meant its continued independence.

Many changes took place in Thailand during the first decades of the twentieth century. It freed itself from unequal treaties with foreign nations and abolished the extraterritorial rights of outside countries. In 1932 an uprising occurred which changed Thailand into a constitutional monarchy. Limits were placed on the political power of the king. Six years later conservative army officers seized control of the government and established a military dictatorship. While the king has remained, he has no political power. Military leaders have, to the present day, been the actual rulers.

Vietnam becomes part of French Indochina. French Jesuits entered Vietnam in 1615. As men of learning and science, the Jesuits were welcomed at the court, and missionary activity led to many conversions. In 1802 the Nguyen dynasty was established with the help of a French bishop. Grateful for French assistance, the emperor allowed French missionary activity to increase. However, the new values of Christianity were seen as a threat to traditional Confucian values, and French missionaries were persecuted.

French Catholic organizations called on their government for protection. French business interests and expansionists who wanted French colonies called for intervention by the French government. Using the murder of a French priest as an excuse, the French invaded southern Vietnam in 1858. Within 26 years they occupied all of Vietnam.

Under French policies, the Vietnamese were to become French in language, customs, and citizenship in order to participate in the operation of the colony. However, the Vietnamese were given lower level civil service positions, with the French in all the important posts. Since government jobs required a French education, educated Vietnamese turned to the modern French schools. When educated Vietnamese could not obtain employment equal to their talents and ambitions, their resentment of foreign rule increased.

The Cambodians also fell under the domination of the French. As Europeans expanded into Southeast Asia during the nineteenth century, the Cambodians became alarmed. Fearful of the British, who were occupying Burma and Malaya, Cambodia turned to the French for assistance. The French at this time were fighting Cambodia's traditional enemy, the Vietnamese. When Cambodia lost more territory to Thailand in 1864, it accepted French protection. In 1887 Cambodia became a part of the French colony of Indochina along with Vietnam and Laos.

The French made few changes in Cambodia. Slavery was largely abolished. Rubber plantations worked chiefly by Vietnamese were organized by the French. Modern French language schools were established in Cambodia as in Vietnam. French archaeologists studied and restored the ancient monuments of Khmer greatness at Angkor. But these changes hardly affected the life of most rural Cambodians.

Japanese occupation of Indochina. By 1941 the Japanese army moved into french Indochina and occupied it. In 1945 Japanese leaders declared Vietnam, Cambodia, and Laos independent as a part of their wartime empire. After the surrender of the Japanese, however, Indochina again became a French colony.

The Indochina War

French education had unexpected results in Vietnam. Vietnamese learned about European nationalism and such Western political ideas as liberty, parliament, political parties, and elections. Such political ideas added fuel to the already strong anticolonial feeling in the country. A small group of Western-educated Vietnamese intellectuals began to form. This group wanted independence and concluded that revolution was necessary.

Ho Chi Minh leads the independence movement. Under Ho Chi Minh (*hoe' chee min'*, 1890–1969), a nationalist and Communist who was trained in the Soviet Union, the Indochinese Communist Party was formed in 1930 in Hong Kong. Although the French attempted to suppress the party, the Communists built a following among the Vietnamese people.

Ho Chi Minh's Communist organization joined with non-Communist nationalists to form the Vietnam Independence League, the *Viet Minh*. Viet Minh guerrilla bands attacked French and Japanese soldiers during World War II. Since the Viet Minh fought the Japanese, Nationalist China and the United States gave them limited military assistance.

After the defeat of the Japanese army in 1945, Ho Chi Minh proclaimed a Democratic Republic of Vietnam. However, French troops returned to Vietnam, for the French government had no intention of losing its Southeast Asian colony.

In 1946 the French government recognized the Democratic Republic of Vietnam as a "free state" within French Indochina, but it soon became clear that the

Ho Chi Minh (1890–1969) founded the Vietnamese Communist party, wrote his country's declaration of independence, and led North Vietnam in its wars against South Vietnam and several foreign powers, including the United States.

The Vietnamese people saw their country turned into a battleground for nearly half a century. Troops and arms became part of the backdrop od everyday life. In this 1954 scene near Thai Binh, a farmer plows his rice paddy without even stopping to watch the French task force stopping on the road nearby to avoid a confrontation with snipers ahead. Robert Capa, the acclaimed war photographer who took the picture, was killed when he stepped on a land mine a few months later.

French did not intend to give the nation full self-government. After fruitless negotiations, war broke out between the French and the Viet Minh.

The Indochina war lasted eight years. It became a part of the international cold war between the Western powers and the Communist world. The Chinese and Russian Communists recognized the Democratic Republic of Vietnam and extended military and economic assistance to it. Great Britain and the United States recognized the French-supported nation of Vietnam. The French received American military and economic assistance.

Negotiations at the Geneva Conference end the war. With a frustrating war that the French could not win, pressure grew within France for withdrawal. At the Geneva Conference in 1954 the French and all Indochinese representatives met with Britain, Russia, and China, with the United States as an observer.

The Geneva settlement ended French rule in Indochina. Vietnam was divided at the seventeenth parallel into North Vietnam and South Vietnam. Provision was made for Vietnamese people to move freely from one state to the other. The French would leave North Vietnam, and the Viet Minh were to leave South Vietnam. A general election was to be held in 1956 to determine the future status of the divided nation. An International Control Commission would supervise the implementation of this agreement. Thus, less than a century of French colonial rule ended in Indochina. Cambodia, Laos, and a divided Vietnam regained their independence.

Reviewing Your Reading

1. What changes did the British introduce in Burma?
2. How did the Japanese help to end Western colonial rule?
3. How did France acquire Indochina?
4. How did the changes the French introduced help Vietnamese nationalism grow?
5. Trace the Vietnamese war for independence from 1941 to 1954.

Peninsular Southeast Asia since World War II

Since World War II Burma and Thailand have continued to maintain fairly stable, autocratic governments. Cambodia has suffered greater political instability. King Norodom Sihanouk (*see*'ah-nook) led the Cambodian drive for independence from French rule. In 1953 Sihanouk went into exile in Thailand, saying he would not return until the French granted independence to Cambodia. With its hands full fighting the Vietnamese war for independence, the French granted independence to Cambodia in 1953. Sihanouk returned to his capital, a hero to his subjects.

A divided Vietnam suffered the greatest problems in the postwar period. South Vietnam emerged from the war against the French with a devastated land and many problems. In 1955 Ngo Dinh Diem (ngaw din dzi-*em'*), a Catholic, gained control of the government. He and his brothers jealously guarded their power. They were suspicious of all organizations they did not control. Many Buddhist officials were replaced by Catholics. As the government came under increasing control of the Diem family, much of its early popularity was lost. However, Diem's divided opponents were not able to defeat him.

According to the Geneva accords, Vietnam was to have free elections to decide its political future. However, the Diem government claimed that there could be no free election in North Vietnam and maintained that the South did not have a fair chance to determine the future of a united Vietnam. Thus, with the consent of the United States, no elections were held as required by the Geneva agreement.

Despite the Geneva agreement, North Vietnam kept an underground network in South Vietnam, which became the National front for the Liberation of South Vietnam, known as the *Viet Cong*. The Viet Cong terrorized the countryside and attempted to defeat the Diem government.

Fall of the Diem government. In his effort to crush the Viet Cong, Diem neglected to carry out social and economic reforms that might have won him the support of the South Vietnamese peasants. In addition, there was much friction between Diem and other political leaders of the country. Buddhists resented the rule of the Catholic minority in the government. To protest anti-Buddhist actions

South Vietnamese troops pass through the village of Chieu Hoi in 1963. The village, whose name means "open arms," was established as a re-education center for former members of the Viet Cong.

by the Diem government, several Buddhist monks set themselves on fire. Buddhists demanded freedom of worship and equality with Catholics. Anti-government demonstrations increased, and in 1963 a group of army generals overthrew the Diem government. Diem and his brother were killed, and military leaders took power.

The United States and the Vietnamese war. When the French left Indochina, the United States became a firm supporter of South Vietnam. The United States government gave economic and military assistance to the country, and American military advisers helped to train its army and develop strategy to fight the Viet Cong. After North Vietnamese gunboats were reported to have attacked an American naval vessel in the Gulf of Tonkin in 1964, President Lyndon Johnson, supported by a congressional resolution, stated a United States policy of assisting its South Vietnamese ally by all necessary means. After that resolution the United States widened its role in the war. American soldiers were sent in to fight. The United States, as France before it, was frustrated by guerrilla warfare.

As war casualties rose, pressure grew in the United States to end the war. Negotiations among warring nations began in Paris in 1968. An agreement to end the war and restore peace in Vietnam was signed in 1973. A neutral four-nation team supervised the cease-fire, the withdrawal of United States troops, and the release of American prisoners. Elections were to be held. Early in 1975, however, the Viet Cong and North Vietnamese troops launched heavy attacks against remaining government outposts in the Central Highlands. Retreats of the South Vietnam troops turned into a rout, and the government in Saigon surrendered in April 1975. A provisional Communist government took control.

Independence for the Islands of Southeast Asia

The desire for independence spread among the island colonies of Southeast Asia. While strong nationalistic feeling did not appear at the same time in all of the colonies, it often followed a similar pattern. As the desire for political freedom grew, the peoples of this area developed an intense interest in their cultural heritage and their history. Pride in their past added fuel to their drive for independence.

Malayan nationalism. Nationalism developed later in Malaya than in other European colonies in Southeast Asia. Its varied population of Malays, Chinese, and Indians may have contributed to this delay. The prosperity of the country and the certainty that the British would protect Malayan interests were other probable factors. While a few small reform and anticolonial organizations were formed, most Malays were not attracted and remained loyal to their sultans and the conservative Muslim leaders.

Road to independence. During World War II, Malays fought a guerrilla war against the Japanese army. After the war the British returned to Malaya and prepared to grant independence to the colony. In 1948, while negotiations were going on, the Malayan Communist Party, consisting mainly of Chinese, started a revolution. Fighting a guerrilla war in the jungles, they resorted to terrorist activity, killing British and Chinese residents. British and Malayan troops fought the Communist guerrillas for twelve years before finally suppressing them in 1960.

With many Chinese and Indians in the population, Malays had to be reassured they would not be politically dominated by them. Malayan political life was organized into separate Chinese, Indian, and Malayan groups within the country's major political organization, the Alliance Party. A constitution that satisfied all racial groups was produced in 1957. Malays were given special privileges in government employment, education, and business. Some land was reserved for their exclusive use. Non-Malays were assured that they would be given fair treatment. With the acceptance of this constitution Malaya became an independent nation in 1957.

Singapore temporarily joins Malaya to become Malaysia. Singapore, with its 80 percent Chinese population, was not part of Malaya. If its Chinese population were added to the Chinese living in Malaya, it would outnumber the 3 million Malays. After accepting certain political restrictions, Singapore, along with the British colonies of Sarawak and Sabah on the island of Borneo, joined with Malaya to form Malaysia.

Achmed Sukarno (1901–1970), first president of Indonesia.

This union did not work smoothly. Two years later Singapore broke its ties with Malaysia and became a separate, self-governing nation. Malaysia retained its name.

Sukarno leads Indonesian nationalist movement. In 1927 the Indonesian Nationalist Party was established. One of its members was Achmed Sukarno (1901–1970), who later became Indonesia's first president. Many of its members had been educated in Western countries. The Nationalist Party called for a program of non-cooperation with the Dutch. The colonial rulers became alarmed at the success of this program and suppressed all nationalist groups. Leaders were arrested and sent into exile on islands far from Java.

During World War II Indonesia was occupied by the Japanese. When the Japanese surrendered in 1945, Sukarno declared Indonesia independent and established a government. The return of the Dutch, who sought to restore colonial rule, led to a colonial war in 1946. After a cease-fire and a brief period of joint rule with the Dutch, Indonesia became completely self-governing in 1954.

Growth of Filipino nationalism. As a small, educated elite group of Filipinos grew, young men went to study in Madrid, Hong Kong and Tokyo. In Europe they learned liberal political ideas. Students in Japan admired the Japanese ability to modernize while remaining independent. Through their letters, pamphlets, and books, a "Propaganda Movement" developed. It called for free speech, racial equality, and a greater Filipino role in governmental and church affairs.

United States acquires the Philippine Islands. With the outbreak of the Spanish-American War in Cuba in 1898, the United States entered the Philippines and replaced Spain as the colonial power for the next half century. Under Commodore George Dewey, United States warships destroyed the Spanish fleet in Manila Bay. The 1898 Treaty of Paris gave the Philippine Islands to the United States for $20 million.

Emilio Aguinaldo's revolutionary troops joined the fighting against Spain. A Filipino government was organized with Aguinaldo as president. But the United States did not recognize this revolutionary government, and war broke out between the American army and the Filipino rebels. More than 100,000 American soldiers fought for three years before suppressing the guerrillas in 1901.

Jose Rizal

Jose Rizal (1861–1896) was the leading figure in the "Propaganda Movement." Educated in Manila, the brilliant Rizal studied medicine and philosophy in Spain. He mastered a number of European languages and traveled widely in Europe where, in 1887, he published his first political novel, *Noli Me Tangere (Touch Me Not)*. The abuses of Spanish colonial rule were depicted, and the novel's characters called for reform. Upon his return to the Philippines, Rizal organized a reform group. After a revolution broke out in which he was not involved, Rizal was arrested, tried for treason, and shot in 1896.

A civil government based on that of the United States was established with William Howard Taft as the first governor. Political parties were permitted, and Filipinos were elected to various government offices. The Filipino demand for independence continued, and in 1934 the United States promised independence in ten years.

The Japanese invasion of the Philippines in 1941, and the subsequent occupation, delayed the grant of independence. Although some Filipinos cooperated with the Japanese occupiers, many others organized resistance groups and fought the Japanese.

From 1899 to 1901, American troops fought in the Philippines to suppress the government of Emilio Aguinaldo and retain possession of the islands.

Philippine independence achieved. Despite the devastated condition of the islands, the United States granted the Philippines independence on July 4, 1946. The government of the United States provided financial aid for the enormous task of rebuilding the country's economy after World War II. Today, the United States has military bases in the country and helps train and equip the Philippine armed forces.

Elections were held in 1946 for the new government, and Manuel Roxas was elected president of the Republic of the Philippines. Filipino Communists, known as the Huks (*hooks*), won six seats in the legislature but were kept out of the body because they were charged with using terror and fraud. Denied access to political life, the Huks led a rebellion in the forests of central Luzon.

Under President Ramon Magsaysay, peasant grievances were heard and reforms were made. Rural centers were built, wells dug, medical care provided, and corruption removed from government. Huk rebels who surrendered were resettled on the island of Mindanao. After ten years of guerrilla fighting, the Huk rebellion was suppressed.

After Ramon Magsaysay's election as president of the Philippines in 1954, he led the nation's army in suppressing the Huks and brought order to the country.

Reviewing Your Reading

1. Trace the Vietnam War from 1954 to 1975.
2. What were the terms of the 1973 agreement that ended American involvement in the Vietnam war?
3. What groups had to be satisfied before Malaysian independence? Why?
4. Trace the Indonesian path to independence from 1927.
5. Describe the role of Filipino nationalists in the drive for Philippine independence. What part has the United States played in its history?

CHAPTER REVIEW

Recalling Names and Places

Emilio Aguinaldo	Khmer	Jose Rizal
Chulalongkorn	Ferdinand Magellan	Norodom Sihanouk
Ngo Dinh Diem	Ramon Magsaysay	Srivijaya
Dutch East India Company	Mon	Achmed Sukarno
Gulf of Tonkin	Nan Chao	Viet Cong
Ho Chi Minh	Pagan	Viet Minh

Understanding This Chapter

1. Describe the growth of nationalism in Burma.
2. How did Thailand preserve its independence during the colonial period.
3. Vietnam is a poor nation, but neither the French nor the Americans could defeat Vietnam militarily. Why was this so?
4. Why was Malaysian nationalism slow in developing?
5. Compare the Filipino transition from colony to independent country with that of other Southeast Asian countries. How was it different? Has that difference had any long-term significance?

Chapter 36

Southeast Asia's Ethnic Diversity

As there is variety in the land of Southeast Asia, so is there diversity among its people, not only between countries but also within countries. Burma, for example, has many ethnic groups – Burman, Karen, Shan, Chin, Kachin, Mon, and Arakanese, among others. Other Southeast Asian countries can match Burma's ethnic mosaic. However, each country tends to have one dominant group – the Burman, Thai, Vietnamese, Khmer – who live in the lowlands and control the government.

While these ethnic groups may have some similar customs, their differences have kept them apart. Many have their own language or political and economic organization. Some hill people have no political system beyond the village level. Many lowland dwellers grow rice in paddy fields and sell it for cash, while many highland people move from place to place farming, hunting, and fishing to keep alive.

Relations among the various ethnic groups have not always been peaceful. Many of these groups resist efforts of a central government to incorporate them into national life. They are reluctant to give up their traditional ways of life.

Chinese and Indians in Southeast Asia

For centuries Indians and Chinese have migrated to Southeast Asia and added to the variety of cultural patterns. Indians first came as traders and carriers of Hinduism and Buddhism. Later, they followed the British flag to the market-places of Burma and the rubber plantations of Malaya. The Chinese began businesses in many Southeast Asian cities and worked in the tin mines of Malaya. Because of their strong attachment for their traditional customs and their closely knit families, many separate Chinese and Indian communities were established. Often they attracted resentment from the native population because they were different and fairly successful economically.

The Traditional Family

Most Southeast Asians live in villages and work as farmers. Family organization reflects the agricultural way of life. The family is not simply a social group; it is also an economic and a religious group. Family members live together, work together, and take their pleasure together.

The joint family, with three generations in a household, is the ideal. It consists of the senior couple, a married son, his wife and children, and his unmarried brothers and sisters. The eldest son usually remains in the parental home. However, in a few areas it is the youngest son who cares for his aging parents.

Houses in Sumbawa, Indonesia, are built on stilts with trap-doors that can be closed at night. The roof of such a house slopes down to the floor.

Only the well-to-do can maintain the joint family ideal. For most Vietnamese, the nuclear family, with the husband, his wife and children, is the most common form of family.

Unlike other traditional Asian cultures, women in Southeast Asia have a significant decision-making role in society. Although a woman is expected to be dutiful and respectful to her husband, her role as housewife and mother gives her great importance in the family. She manages the family finances and works with her husband in the fields. Many women are merchants.

Communists in Vietnam have influenced social customs there. In Vietnam the Communists have attacked the traditional family system and made laws that they hope will change many former customs. A marriage and family law abolished polygamy and arranged marriages. Youthful marriages are discouraged, as are large dowries and elaborate weddings. Parental consent is not required for those over seventeen. Communist Party members must inform their superiors before they marry; high officials must obtain the Party's approval.

The Batak, a mountain people of Sumatra, Indonesia, are noted for their beautiful homes. This Batak roof is inlaid with wood, ivory, and copper.

The rights of women and children are championed by the Party. Women were made equal with men, and many hold prominent political positions. Family planning is promoted. A small family will not only decrease pressure on the economy but also enable the parents to free themselves for further work and political study. Despite these attempts at change, traditional patterns and values still persist in some areas.

Reviewing Your Reading

1. What is meant by Southeast Asia's "ethnic mosaic?"
2. How does a Southeast Asian woman's role differ from that of a woman in other traditional Asian family systems?

Southeast Asian Education

Various forms of education existed in Southeast Asia before the Europeans appeared. Practical skills such as farming, carpentry, and metal work were learned by children from their fathers or other skilled people. Buddhist and Islamic religious schools taught reading and writing. Vietnamese schools concentrated on the teaching of Confucianism.

Traditional village education in Thailand. Most villagers are illiterate. However, men training to become Buddhist monks have to learn to read to study religious texts, and singers of folk opera have to memorize written songs. Such people attend Buddhist temple schools.

The monks teach basic reading, writing, and arithmetic in a two-year program. Boys who are to become monks have further educational training. Much of their time is spent memorizing religious chants.

Most men remain monks until their early twenties, when they marry. A promising monk may be sent to a district and provincial monastic center for further education. Those who spend their lives as monks become detached from the world, intent on achieving nirvana.

Traditional Vietnamese education. Vietnamese education followed the Chinese model. Confucianism, taught in the Chinese language, stressed the cultivation of moral character. Scholars taught students in their homes or in Buddhist pagodas. While education was open to all boys, only well-to-do boys had the leisure for such an opportunity. Such training prepared students for the competitive examinations that led to degrees and positions in the governmental civil service.

European rulers introduce modern education. At first the European rulers depended on their own people to do the variety of work colonial government required. Later they organized Western-style schools to train local workers for lower level government jobs and business positions. Europeans also built universities. The University of Santo Tomas was founded in Manila by the Spanish in 1611, twenty-five years before Harvard University was organized in the British colony of Massachusetts. These European schools provided educational opportunity for only a small portion of the region's families.

Education in Present-day Southeast Asia

The political leaders of Southeast Asia, building on the educational system left by their former colonial rulers, are committed to promoting wider educational opportunity for their people. In Vietnam, for example, officials have started a crash program to end illiteracy. Officials say that ten weeks are re-

Bangkok is the center of Thailand's higher education system. Chulalongklorn University (in photo) provides an education in the liberal arts. Law students attend Thammasat University. Agriculture and forestry are taught at Bangkok's Kasetsart University.

quired for a Vietnamese to learn to read and write. However, this literacy can easily be lost if it is not continuously used.

In general, more people are attending schools in Southeast Asia since independence. Literacy rates have risen throughout the region. They range today from 41 percent in Laos to almost 94 percent in Vietnam. All countries have both elementary and secondary schools. All except Laos have universities.

A Student's Ambition

Many educated young people from Southeast Asia have come to the United States to continue their education or to seek opportunities in their professions. Still more seek to come. Arranging such a move is difficult, and students will eagerly explore every possible way of making it possible. One American traveler in Thailand told of this encounter:

While walking away from the Reclining Buddha, I was approached by a young Thai named Somdat. He said he was studying English, and offered to show me aound the ruins for practice. I suspected a tour guide in disguise but agreed.

Somdat led me to a clearing and I found myself in something called the elephant *kraal*. The *kraal* is an enclosure of teakwood fence walls where wild elephants were captured and tamed for work and warfare. The wood still looked strong enough to withstand an elephant charge or two.

After visiting a monastery and several other *wats*, I thanked Somdat and offered him payment.

"No," he said, "Just your address, please."

"My home address?"

"Yes, I need a sponsor to go to school in America."

"But I hardly know you."

"So come with me for a meal at my family's house."

My curiosity about Thai home life overcame any hesitation, and I accepted. I was led to a wooden house on stilts by the bank of the river, and, after removing my shoes, entered to a warm welcome by Somdat's parents.

They accepted my arrival as if it were preordained and quickly set a table in front of me. Was this the way all strangers were welcomed in Thailand or was Somdat in the habit of inviting potential sponsors to his home? I never found out.

Somdat's mother introduced me to two of the seasonings popular throughout Thailand, *nam plaa* and *prik*. The former, a fermented fish sauce, seems saltier than soy sauce but is rich in vitamins and quite tasty. *Prik* are hot chile peppers that take some getting used to. They adorned the quick-fried cabbage I was served, along with several small whole fish. The rice acted as a coolant after the chilies; it was all delicious. I left after thanking them and promising to keep up a correspondence with Somdat.

Peter Aiken, "Into the Heart of Thailand," *Travel/Holiday*, November 1980, pp. 45–46. Reprinted by permission.

Obstacles to educational progress. Compulsory education, from three to six years, is the rule in all Southeast Asian countries. While a large percentage of six- and seven-year-old children start school, there is a high dropout rate. Poverty, poor health, and the distance from schools keep many from finishing. Failure of parents to appreciate the value of education and of government to enforce compulsory attendance are other factors.

A great need exists in all Southeast Asian countries for technical, vocational, and modern farming skills. Governments plan their educational programs to teach people these skills. However, many Southeast Asians prefer to train for a civil service post, medicine, or the law, because these jobs are considered more prestigious than engineering, forestry, and veterinary studies. Consequently, there are often more people trained for such work than there are jobs available.

Another problem faced by these countries is the reluctance of students attending urban schools to return home to apply their training. Many find city life more attractive than the harsher life in their villages. Bright young college students are also reluctant to return to their countries after being educated at foreign universities.

Religion in Southeast Asia

Southeast Asia was influenced by religious and philosophical ideas from many countries. Confucianism and Taoism came into Vietnam from China. Buddhism came from both China and India. India also was the source of Islam. The Europeans brought Christianity to Southeast Asia.

> **Nat Worship**
>
> Buddhism is not concerned with the crises of everyday life. A Burmese Buddhist does not appeal to the Buddha for assistance in worldly matters. He turns to various **nats,** spirits of trees, rain, or natural objects. Nat worship is a form of animism. Rituals are performed in front of box-shaped shrines with an image of the nat. Food or a flower offering is placed in front of it, for example, to help guard the house.

Burmese Buddhism. Theravada Buddhism is the religion of most people in Burma and much of Southeast Asia. Most Burmese men spend part of their lives as monks. A man may enter the monastery and leave it when he wants, and he may do so more than once.

A boy's first initiation into monastic life comes at age twelve or younger. It is an important event in his life. The boy is dressed in brightly colored silk robes and jewelry and paraded around the village. There is much music, dancing, and feasting. Afterwards his head is shaved, he is given a new name, and he wears a simple yellow robe. His initiation symbolizes the Buddha's renunciation of worldly riches and his becoming a religious beggar.

A Buddhist monk is not a priest. He is not an intermediary between an individual Buddhist and his progress toward nirvana. Like everyone else in Buddhist society, he is involved in working out his own nirvana. A monk is specially honored because he is closer to the life of the Buddha than a lay person. His life helps others to understand the Buddha's teachings better.

Each Burmese village has a monastery, and the villagers invite monks to live there. By having a monastery in the village, the villagers may be able to earn good merit, *karma*. Feeding, digging a well, or building a pagoda for a monk earns good merit for a person. In his relationship to the people, a monk has two important roles: to teach in the monastic school and to attend Buddhist rituals when invited.

Islam. The religion founded by Muhammad in seventh-century Arabia reached Southeast Asia in the tenth century. Not until Indian Muslim traders appeared on the scene four centuries later did Islam develop a wide following in Indonesia. Islam spread over the region and reached Malaysia and the Philippines during the fourteenth century. Today, Islam is the religion of 90 percent of the Indonesians and almost half of the Malaysians. There are sizeable numbers of Muslims on the island of Mindanao in the Philippines, with smaller numbers in other Southeast Asian countries.

Christianity in Southeast Asia. In the sixteenth century, Catholic missionaries followed Portuguese and Spanish traders into Southeast Asia. When European interest in the area faded during the seventeenth century, Christian

Imposing golden statues guard the doors to a Buddhist wat in Bangkok. Wats are temple and monastery complexes. They often form the center of community social life in Thai villages.

Muslim merchants from India introduced Islam to Southeast Asia in the fourteenth and fifteenth centuries. Today more than 160 million Southeast Asian Muslims worship at mosques like this one in Kuala Lumpur, Malaysia.

missionary activity declined, except in the Philippine Islands. During the nineteenth century, interest in Southeast Asia revived, and various Christian churches sent many missionaries into the region.

In the Philippine Islands 92 percent of the people are Christians. Elsewhere in the region, fewer than 5 percent of the people have become Christians. Christian missionaries continue to operate schools and hospitals throughout the region.

Reviewing Your Reading

1. Describe traditional education in Thailand and Vietnam.
2. How do Southeast Asian governments promote education? What problems do they face?
3. What is the role of a monk in Burmese Buddhism?
4. What other religions are found in Southeast Asia?

CHAPTER REVIEW

Recalling Names and Places

Buddhist initiation   nat worship   temple school

Understanding This Chapter

1. Compare the assimilation of Indian and Chinese immigrants in Southeast Asia with their assimilation in the United States. Are there any great similarities? Differences?
2. Most people in Southeast Asia are rural. Is education any more important for them now than it was in the past? If so, why?
3. Not long ago the entire graduating class of a Thai medical school moved to the United States to practice medicine. What causes this kind of "brain drain" in Southeast Asian nations? What can be done to reverse it?

Chapter 37

The Economy of Southeast Asia

The farmers of Bali, Indonesia, have organized cooperative water control boards to manage the irrigation system that floods their rice paddies. Rice is the major crop on the terraced fields of this hilly island, but farmers also grow yams, sweet potatoes, cassava, corn, coconuts, and date palms.

Like much of the tropical world, Southeast Asia is economically underdeveloped. The annual revenue of the two largest corporations in the United States exceeds Southeast Asia's combined gross national product (the money value of all goods and services produced in the region). Agriculture is the chief source of employment and wealth for more than 80 percent of the area's work force.

Agriculture in Southeast Asia

Before Europeans appeared in Southeast Asia, the land in most countries belonged to the ruler, and was assigned by him to a village and its inhabitants. Villagers worked the land without owning it as long as they paid the taxes. The idea of legally enforced private ownership and the right of inheritance came with the European influence.

SOUTHEAST ASIA: LAND USE AND RESOURCES

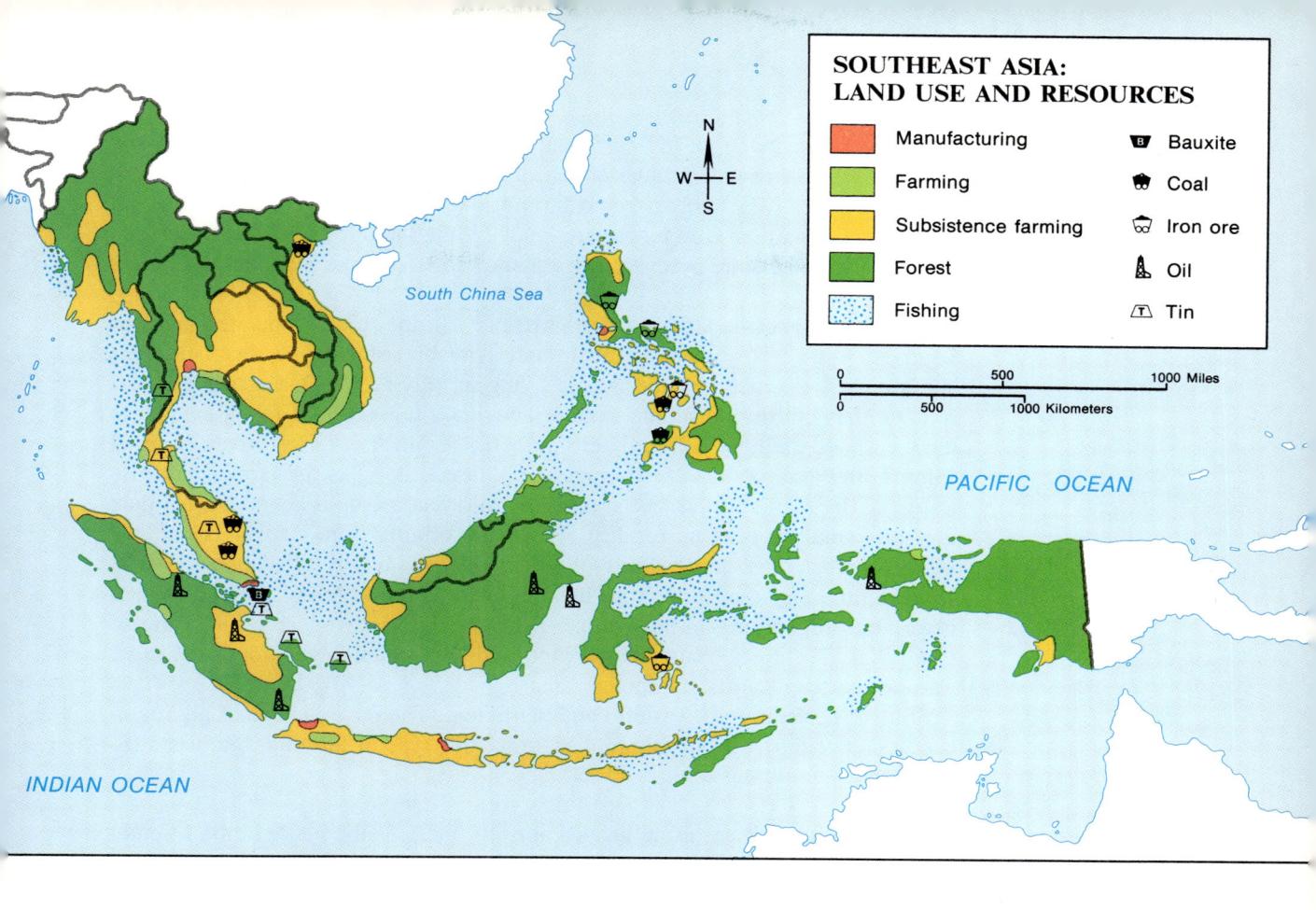

- Manufacturing
- Farming
- Subsistence farming
- Forest
- Fishing
- Bauxite
- Coal
- Iron ore
- Oil
- Tin

Today the pattern of land ownership varies throughout the nations of the region. Some countries permit foreigners to own land, while others do not. Vietnam has farm communes, and members are paid according to the amount of work they do. Each family also has a small private plot to grow crops for its own use or sale. In 1984, three-quarters of the land in southern Vietnam was still privately owned. The Vietnamese government was urging the collectivization of this land. Private land ownership is the rule in most other countries. Legal limits have been placed on the size of a farm a family can own. Laws have been enacted to enable farm tenants to own the land they work. But these reform programs are not always enforced. Consequently, many farmers in the area are still hired laborers or tenants who must share the crop with the wealthy landowner.

Subsistence farming is typical. Most Southeast Asian farmers engage in subsistence farming, which produces only enough food to keep their families alive. The average farmer lives in a village of a few hundred families. Farmers rarely travel and are apt to spend their entire lives no more than a few miles from the village center. Houses are made of matted reed, coconut leaves, and bamboo. They have dirt floors. Some are built on stilts to keep the inhabitants dry during the floods caused by monsoon rains.

A wealthier farmer with more land might live in a more comfortable wood or masonry-tile house. He might even own a motorbike and a transistor radio. If he has enough money to hire laborers, his sons will have the time to attend school.

The farmer tends to be self-sufficient. Subsistence farmers live a life that has changed little in centuries. Just about all of a family's needs are provided by their own labor. The tools used in farming, such as a broad hoe, sickle, and wooden plow with an iron blade, are made by the farmer or the village carpenter. The metal parts are purchased in a market town or from a traveling peddler.

Hill people practice shifting agriculture. In the thinly populated areas of Southeast Asia where there is much land available, shifting or slash-and-burn agriculture is practiced by the people living in hilly areas. During the dry season, farmers cut the brush and smaller trees on a few acres of forest land. It is then burned, and the ash provides mineral fertilizers. Larger trees, burned stumps, and tree roots make it impossible to use a plow, so the farmer must use a stick to dig a hole for his rice seeds. The first year's crop is abundant, but then the soil rapidly looses its fertility. When the original forest cover is cut, the heavy tropical rains can easily erode or carry soils down hillsides along with valuable nutrients that food crops need in order to grow. Many years must pass before the soil can regain its fertility. After the third harvest, crop yields are so small that the farmer abandons the plot, and the natural vegetation takes over. The farmer then "shifts" to another area.

Shifting agriculture is wasteful and inefficient. The governments of all Southeast Asian countries are trying to discourage this type of farming, but it is difficult to change old customs.

A typical diet. Rice, usually eaten at every meal, is the major crop of Southeast Asia. Its importance is seen in a Cambodian proverb, "To destroy growing rice is as serious as to insult one's mother and father." Vegetable gardens with peas, beans, squash, and onions add some variety to the diet. Fresh, dried, or pickled fish are the chief sources of protein. Bananas, pineapples, and mangoes are commonly eaten fruits.

Cooking oil is pressed from peanuts or sesame seeds, and the leftovers are used as cattle food or fertilizer. The juice of a coconut is drunk fresh, and shredded coconut is used in many food dishes. Copra, dried coconut meat, is sold, and its oils are used in making margarine or soap. The sweet potato and the cassava are poor people's staple food.

Animals of the village might include chickens, ducks, and pigs. The eggs and meat from these animals are sometimes sold for cash. Water buffalo and oxen are the main work animals.

Commercial farming grew as a result of European plantations. In contrast to small-scale subsistence agriculture, Europeans organized the plantation farming system to produce crops sold on the world market. These farms required large sums of money to establish and years of work before they were profitable. Using plentiful and inexpensive local labor, the plantations grew tea, jute, hemp, cocoa, and pepper. The Spanish introduced South American tobacco, and the British brought rubber trees from Brazil.

Today most of the world's natural rubber comes from the countries of Southeast Asia. Malaysia is the principal supplier. Colonial plantation crops still contribute much to the economy of the area. But many of these products are no

An aerial view of fields of rice paddies in the Mekong delta, one of the world's greatest rice-growing areas.

> **Rubber-Making in Southeast Asia**
>
> A warm, moist climate with an annual rainfall of more than 80 inches is an ideal environment for the rubber tree. Rubber plantations average less than 50 acres in size, with trees widely set apart in regular rows. Seeds are started in a nursery, and seedlings are then transplanted to the fields. The tree must be at least five years old before it can be tapped. Then it will yield latex for up to forty years, although it is most productive in the ten years after the first tap. Once the yield declines, the tree is cut down, and another seedling is planted in its place.
>
> Latex is collected in cups that are placed at the end of diagonal cuts or slashes made through the bark of the tree. A tapper or collector can handle several hundred trees daily. The latex is strained to remove the dirt and then placed in a tank and treated with acid. Otherwise it will decompose. The acid also makes the rubber float to the top in a soft doughy slab. The slab is then passed through metal rollers and emerges as sheets. To preserve the rubber, the sheets are placed in a smokehouse. Treated latex is sent abroad in liquid form in tanker vessels.

longer used as much as they once were. They are also subject to frequent, unfavorable price fluctuations in world markets. As a result, most nations are trying to find more profitable crops for export.

How has the Green Revolution affected Southeast Asia? In 1962 the Ford and Rockefeller foundations, in cooperation with the Philippine government, established the International Rice Research Institute, south of Manila. An international staff of scientists crossbred a rice plant from Taiwan with another from Indonesia to create a new, high-yielding rice known as IR-8. This new rice along with a new wheat variety started the Green Revolution. When properly cared for with a regulated water supply, artificial fertilizers, insecticides, and pesticides, the new rice plant could at least double the rice output. The shorter growth cycle made it possible to grow three crops a year, thus diminishing the prospects of hunger and diseases from malnutrition.

In the 1960s the Green Revolution seemed to be a giant step toward the elimination of hunger in many parts of the world. Since then this optimism has been tempered. The new crop varieties demand close attention. They are highly vulnerable to diseases, and their fertilizing and irrigation must be closely timed. Rising costs of fertilizer have been another limitation in the Philippines and other Southeast Asian countries. As a result, increases in yield have been smaller than anticipated. Since the mid-1970s, the annual increase in rice production in Indonesia has been only 1 percent — far less than the annual increase in population. Southeast Asia is not likely to achieve self-sufficiency in grain production in the near future.

Forest products are sources of potential income. Much of the land of Southeast Asia is covered with forest. While forests cannot be fully developed until more access roads are built, the forest has always provided many valuable

Latex from rubber trees is strained, then placed in vats and treated with acid (above) until it forms a soft slab. The slab is then cleaned in a washing trough (left) and fed through rollers to form sheets of rubber.

431

products. Rattan, the tough and flexible stem of the palm tree, is used for baskets, rope, tables, and chairs. Teak from peninsular Southeast Asia is a durable wood used in shipbuilding, fine furniture, and flooring. Mahogany from the Philippines is also used for furniture and wall paneling. Other useful products include pulpwood, plywood, and timber for heavy construction.

Indonesia has the most substantial forest resources in the region, with more than 300 million acres of tropical hardwoods. Many of these hardwoods are in great demand in world trade, and at the current logging rate Indonesia's forests could be depleted in twenty to thirty years. Poor logging methods often destroy more trees than are harvested. Forests are also depleted when population growth brings settlers into forest areas, increasing both harvesting and the danger of fire. A vast fire burned for three months in Indonesian Kalimantan in 1983, destroying more than 8.6 million acres of forest – an area as large as Taiwan.

When hillside forest cover is removed, flooding can become a problem. Reforestation of steep slopes in the Philippines has been speeded up to reduce this danger. Forests are a valuable resource in Southeast Asia, and the need for better forest management is being recognized.

Industry in Southeast Asia

As in the past, most of the manufactured items used by Southeast Asians are made by hand. Pottery, woven cloth, and bricks are produced by village workers in cottage industries.

A Bangkok silversmith hammers a design onto a plate.

Modern industry came with Europeans, who developed the region's natural resources for their own benefit. The Europeans built agricultural processing plants for their plantation crops but kept the skilled, higher paying jobs in the economy for themselves. Consequently, when independence came, few Southeast Asians had the technical or managerial skills needed to operate modern factories.

Independent nations seek ways to economic improvement. All Southeast Asian governments are trying to promote industrialization. Industrialization will permit better use of the region's natural resources, provide additional opportunities for skilled employment, and improve the living standards of the people. All governments are constructing modern communication, transportation, electric power, education, and water facilities to help their economic development. Tax benefits and protective tariffs have been used to encourage businesses to build new factories. Singapore, for example, hopes that low taxes on foreign industrial investments will put some of its large unemployed population to work.

Much of the present industry is based on processing various agricultural products. Mills grind corn or sugar and convert unhusked rice into polished rice. Vegetable oil is produced from copra, peanuts, and sesame and cotton seeds. Canning factories process fruits, vegetables, meat, and fish. Cotton, jute, and hemp are processed into fiber and cloth. Tea, coffee, and carbonated beverage plants operate throughout the region.

Vietnam and Burma have small steel complexes using local supplies of iron and coal. All Southeast Asian nations hope to have their own industries to supply fertilizers and cement for the construction of buildings, dams, and roads.

In terms of power sources, only Burma, Malaysia, and Indonesia have enough petroleum for their own needs. Recent offshore discoveries have led many Southeast Asian nations to explore for oil under the seas.

Setbacks to economic growth. Decades of war in Indochina have put a severe strain on the economies of Vietnam, Laos, and Cambodia. Wartime disruptions during the 1950s, 1960s, and 1970s and then fighting between Vietnam and Cambodia destroyed roads, railroads, and irrigation systems. Regular cycles of planting and harvesting were also disrupted.

The economic growth of these countries has also been upset by the loss of skilled workers. In 1979 thousands of Chinese living in Vietnam fled, claiming economic and political discrimination. Many of these refugees escaped by sea to such countries as Thailand, Malaysia, Indonesia, and Hong Kong. For this reason they became known as "boat people." Their flight greatly affected Vietnam's economic development. Farmers have fled Cambodia and Laos because of economic hardship or disagreement with the policies of their Communist rulers. The presence of these refugees has meant new economic problems for other Southeast Asian nations.

Looking ahead. Despite the problem of repairing war-torn economies, modern industry plays a minor but growing part in the economic life of Southeast Asia. Industrial workers make up less than 10 percent of the work force, and they are not yet a major factor in the regional economy. Before modern industries can play a greater role, the area's natural resources must be explored further, and transportation improved. More skilled workers and plant managers are needed. Low income and a shortage of capital are additional hurdles to be overcome before Southeast Asia can be industrialized.

CHAPTER REVIEW

Recalling Names and Places

Green Revolution   Mekong valley scheme   shifting agriculture

Understanding This Chapter

1. What is the pattern of land ownership in Southeast Asia today?
2. How do the farming methods of lowland and hill people differ?
3. How does commercial farming differ from subsistence farming?
4. What benefits has the Green Revolution brought Southeast Asia? What problems? What possible solutions are there to these problems?
5. What useful products do the forests of Southeast Asia provide?
6. How have governments promoted industry in Southeast Asia?

Chapter 38

Political Uncertainty in Southeast Asia

Since independence the nations of Southeast Asia have followed several paths to government organization and political stability. Some nations have been dominated by military regimes. In other countries where the military has been influential, a constitutional framework for government also exists. Vietnam has taken the Communist road to political organization. The nations of Malaysia and the Philippines have made somewhat successful attempts at Western-style democracy, although martial law has been imposed frequently in the Philippines since 1972.

Political Instability in Continental Southeast Asia

Almost all the Southeast Asian countries have a long history of strong, one-man rule. Since independence, this absence of democratic experience has contributed to political unrest in their brief experiments with representative government.

Burma under military rule. Burma was a deeply troubled land for more than a decade after independence. Civil war threatened to break up the country. Various ethnic and Communist groups carried on guerrilla warfare. In addition, the Burmese had little experience with a political party system, which made the operation of democratic government difficult.

In 1963 the army under General Ne Win (neh win) seized control of the government. He formed the Revolutionary Council that has ruled the country ever since. The Council suspended the constitution, outlawed opposition political parties, and retired or arrested political leaders.

The government-sponsored Burmese Socialist Program Party encourages the people to participate in politics under General Ne Win's direction. Those who reject the Party must either remain quiet or join a guerrilla group. It is not likely that Burma's military dictatorship will permit the country to return to democracy in the near future.

Cambodia struggles to achieve stability in a war-torn land. In 1955 Norodom Sihanouk abdicated as king of Cambodia, formed his own political party, and became chief executive. Under Sihanouk the nation had a policy of neutrality in the cold war between the Communist and Western nations.

During the Vietnam War Sihanouk allowed Communist troops to buy rice and move supplies through Cambodia to South Vietnam. In 1971 General Lon Nol overthrew the Sihanouk government, abolished the monarchy, and created the Khmer Republic. Lon Nol called on the United States and South Vietnam to assist him in driving the Communist troops out of Cambodia. Both United States and South Vietnamese troops entered Cambodia in pursuit of Communist soldiers. The American troops withdrew after two months but continued military and economic aid.

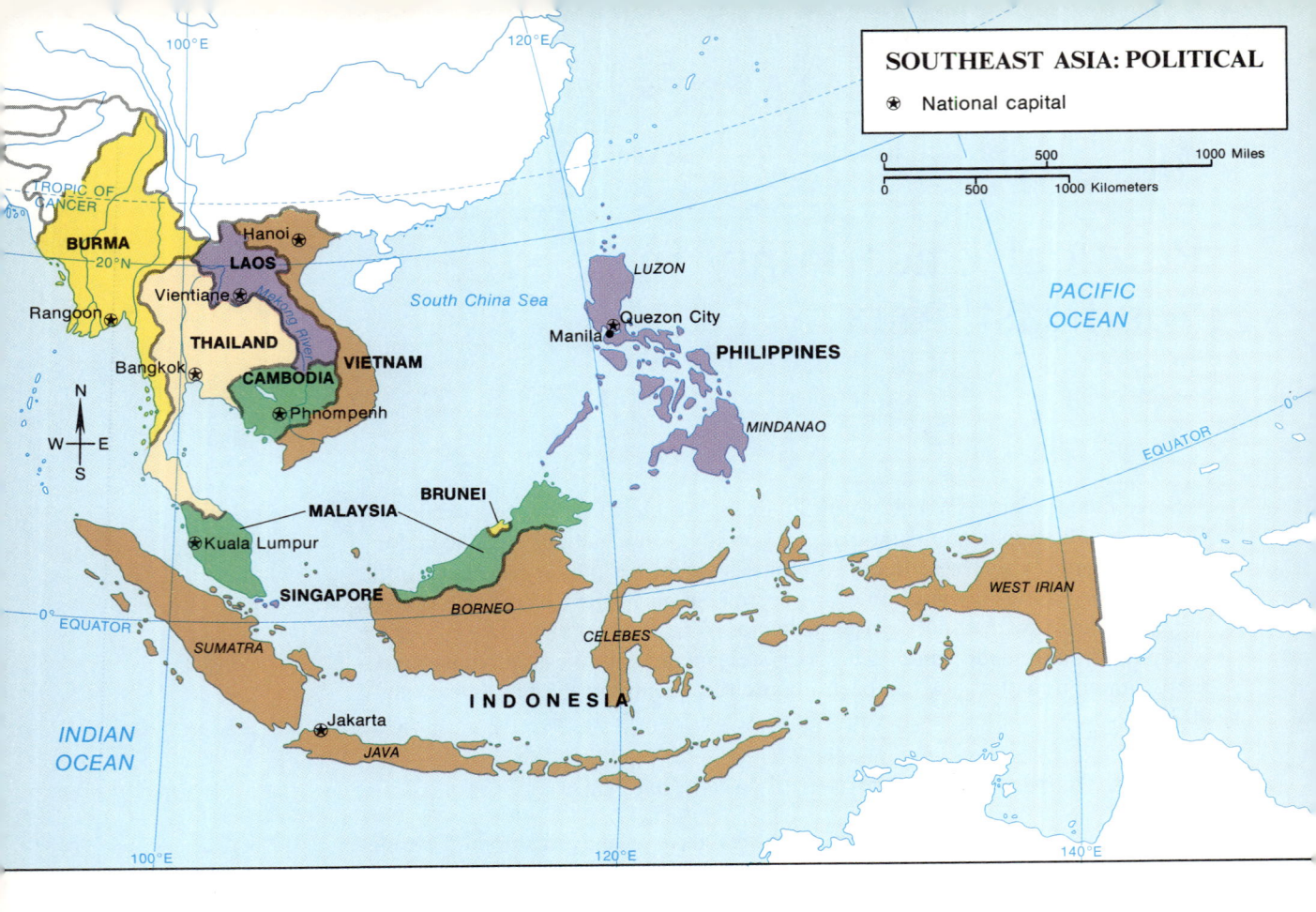

The 1973 agreement that ended the Vietnam War was followed by another agreement to end the fighting in Cambodia. However, just as in Vietnam, the Communists completed their takeover in April 1975. Early in 1976, the Communist Khmer Rouge declared Cambodia "Democratic Kampuchea."

Cambodia as Kampuchea. Under Communist Prime Minister Pol Pot, Kampuchea was reorganized. The elite of the previous society was eliminated. Former government officials and military officers of the Khmer Republic were executed along with wealthy landowners, business leaders, and educated Cambodians. By this harsh stroke, almost all of the skilled people needed to operate a modern society were eliminated.

Phnom Penh became a deserted city as its inhabitants were forced to move to the countryside to live and work on agriculture cooperatives. Millions of Cambodian deaths were reported by refugees able to escape to Thailand. Pol Pot planned to improve agriculture and to develop industry by following the principles of "independence, sovereignty, and self-reliance."

War with Vietnam. Kampuchea and Vietnam have a long history of rivalry in Southeast Asia. As an extreme nationalist and radical, Pol Pot sought to rid Kampuchea of all foreign influence and to insure full and complete authority within Kampuchea. Pol Pot did not want Kampuchea to be subordinate to Vietnam, as had happened to Laos. Border clashes between Kampuchea and Vietnam grew into a war in 1979. With aid from its Soviet ally, Vietnam defeated Kampuchea and installed a new government under Heng Samrin. China assisted Kampuchea during the war and continued after the war to aid Pol Pot in guerrilla warfare against the new Vietnamese-supported government.

Communists control Laos. The former kingdom of Laos came under the complete control of Communist forces closely associated with Vietnam. Laos is an isolated and undeveloped country. Since the end of the Vietnam War, this bankrupt nation has tried to cope with great odds. Many of its people had fled to Thailand because of food shortages.

Communists dominated North Vietnam's government. The 1960 North Vietnamese constitution established a "People's democratic state." The most important government organization was the National Assembly. Its 453 members included delegates from South Vietnam. When the National Assembly was not in session, the Standing Committee elected by the Assembly exercised its powers. The president and vice-president of North Vietnam were also elected by the National Assembly.

All key government positions were held by the top leaders of the Workers Party, the official Communist party. The Workers Party was the only political party permitted in North Vietnam. Whenever there were three or more Party members – in factories, government offices, schools, armed forces, government cooperatives – a Party branch was formed.

War complicated South Vietnam's efforts at democratic government. South Vietnam had several constitutions after independence. The one in 1967 divided government power among executive, legislative, and judicial branches. The president appointed the nation's prime minister. The National Assembly, a bicameral legislature, was elected by popular vote. The judiciary was headed by a Supreme Court.

South Vietnam had several legal political parties. Although the Communist Party was outlawed, it was important in the politics of the country. After 1963, when a group of generals overthrew the civilian government, the military was dominant in South Vietnam. The end of the war in Vietnam gave North Vietnam control of the government.

Reunited Vietnam. After two decades of division, North Vietnam and South Vietnam were reunited into the Socialist Republic of Vietnam. Privately owned businesses were replaced by state enterprises and mutual aid farm teams. Tens of thousands of former South Vietnamese government officials and workers, soldiers, teachers, and religious leaders were sent to "re-education" camps. To ease urban unemployment and shortages, many urban dwellers were relocated to new economic zones in unsettled and remote areas. Vietnam's economic

Families of Cambodian refugees wait patiently in a camp in Thailand.

Vietnam invaded Cambodia in 1979 and set up a new government there to replace the Khmer Rouge reign of terror. The occupation continued into the 1980s. Armed Vietnamese troops became a common sight around Phnom Penh and in the countryside.

reconstruction was limited by wars with Kampuchea and China and the flight of thousands of skilled refugees.

Vietnam's war with China. Historic tensions between Vietnam and China were intensified by the clash of mutual interests after 1975. China wanted small, weak neighbors on its southern borders, while Vietnam sought a dominant role in the region. The Chinese were upset when Vietnam signed a treaty in 1978 with the Soviet Union, an opponent of China.

In 1979 Vietnamese forces invaded China's ally, Kampuchea. This attack, as well as other tensions between Vietnam and China, led to heavy fighting between the two countries in several Vietnamese border provinces in 1979. The results were inconclusive militarily but led to tragic consequences for tens of thousands of ethnic Chinese living in Vietnam. Increasing Vietnamese hostility and the abolition of private businesses forced many to flee in boats. Many of these "boat people" drowned in ships unfit for the sea.

War refugees. The wars of the 1970s in Southeast Asia resulted in other refugees. Fearful of cruel punishment, some Vietnamese fled their country. Others left Vietnam because they did not want to live in a socialist society. Many Laotians fled their country when the Pathet Lao, Communists under Vietnamese control, ruled Laos. The Kampuchea–Vietnam War of 1979 added additional refugees to those who earlier fled the savage rule of Pol Pot. Many refugees suffered, and thousands died. A number settled in China and Hong Kong. More lived in squalid camps, waiting to migrate to other countries.

Military control in Thailand. Since 1938 army officers have controlled the government of Thailand, and the military has played a major role in Thai politics. In l968 Thailand experimented with democratic government, issuing a new constitution and holding elections for the national legislature for the first time in ten years. The legislature showed its independence by refusing to give automatic consent to all government-proposed laws. Its members wanted to make the parliament more powerful by weakening the authority of the prime minister and the military.

In November 1971, Premier Thatnom Kittikachorn (*that'* nom kit-ti-*kah'*-chorn) and leaders of the army seized political power. They abolished the constitution, dissolved the parliament, and established martial law. This political upheaval was barely noticed by the nation's rural residents.

Several times in the 1970s and early 1980s power passed back and forth between constitutional governments, democratically elected, and military governments who seized power. After a student uprising ended the Kittikachorn government, a new constitution brought a new elected government to power in 1973. Internal violence erupted three years later, and by 1977 a military government under Kriangsak Chamanand was in power. A 1979 constitution led to the formation of a new elected government, which lost support and was replaced in 1980. Another constitution was adopted in 1983. In that year, responding to significant popular pressure, the National Assembly fought off an attempt by the military to limit the political freedoms guaranteed in the new constitution. The elected government was returned to power in a vote of record numbers.

Reviewing Your Reading

1. What led to the establishment of military rule in Burma and Cambodia?
2. Contrast political life in North and South Vietnam before reunification.
3. Trace the course of Thailand's experiments with a democratic form of government.

Some Island Governments Make Progress toward Democracy

Countries in the island area are also having problems with national unity, for the spread of distant islands makes political stability difficult. However, the countries of Malaysia and the Philippines have made a start.

Malaysia strives for national unity. Malaysia's 1957 constitution created a federal system based on parliamentary democracy with a king who has no real political power. The Alliance Party controlled the government and relied on cooperation between the Malay, Chinese, and Indian groups within the organization. Each of these groups elected its own political representatives who were Alliance Party members. After independence, cooperation among these groups began to decline.

Race, language, and religion are the three issues that threatened to break up the Alliance Party and possibly Malaysian unity. With independence, the Malay language became the official language of the country. Chinese and Indian

The assassination of Philippine opposition leader Benigno Aquino in August 1983 gave rise to a wave of demonstrations against the regime of President Ferdinand Marcos. In 1984 an official panel of inquiry reported that high-ranking military officers had been involved in planning and carrying out the Aquino assassination.

Malaysians are not pleased with this. Islam is Malaysia's official religion. Muslim extremists would like to see the religion receive stronger support from the government, while the Chinese and Indian groups who economically dominate the country resent its special position. Extremists on all sides have used these explosive issues to their advantage. Riots broke out between Malays and Chinese in 1969.

While the Alliance Party kept control of the government, its appeal to the voters was slipping. Other political parties, based more on ethnic and religious interests, increased their voter strength. Conflict among Malaysia's three major culture groups clouds Malaysia's future.

Uncertain democracy in the Philippines. The Republic of the Philippines was the first Southeast Asian nation to become independent after World War II. The constitution, written in 1935 when the country was still a territory of the United States, provides for separation of governmental power among executive, judicial, and legislative branches. It calls for a strong president with an appointed cabinet, a bicameral legislature, an independent judiciary, and civilian control of the military.

The Philippines have two major political parties, the Nationalist and Liberal. Other parties exist, but the Communist Party is outlawed. Before independence, only upper-class Filipinos voted. In 1953, village farmers and urban workers received the vote.

In 1972, President Ferdinand Marcos declared martial law in the Philippines, shutting down newspapers and television stations and jailing his political opponents. Marcos began imposing economic reforms, including a major land reform program. He forced the legislature to accept constitutional changes giving him greater power. Marcos claimed his strong-man rule was necessary for the success of the reform efforts.

After more than eight years, martial law ended in 1981. Marcos freed many political prisoners but otherwise kept tight control of the country. A major political crisis was created b the murder of opposition leader Benigno Aquino at the Manila airport on August 21, 1983. Aquino had spent most of the martial law years under arrest at Marcos's order. He was returning from self-imposed exile in the United States to lead his party's election campaign. A commission appointed by President Marcos to investigate the murder concluded that the highest military officials were responsible for the crime. Many Filipinos held Marcos personally responsible and expressed their sentiments in massive demonstrations against the president. Elections in May 1984 kept Marcos's party in power, but the opposition made great gains in urban areas. Marcos seemed likely to face renewed opposition and increasing discontent as long as he remained in power.

Indonesia starts out with "Guided Democracy." With independence, Indonesian leaders sought to create a democratic government. But many political parties formed around ethnic and religious interests. No single party was able to form a government, and coalition governments were unsuccessful. Dissatisfied with this confusing political scene, Achmed Sukarno, one of the few national leaders, abandoned plans for parliamentary democracy. Sukarno instituted a form of government known as "Guided Democracy." Under this arrangement a National Council was formed to represent all major groups in the country. These groups were to discuss national problems until a consensus was achieved. A large share of the power was kept by Sukarno as president, but he relied on support from the army and the Communists to keep him in power.

Sukarno ruled until 1965. The nation had many problems. The economy worsened, inflation grew, and Indonesia threatened to go to war with Malaysia over disputed territory. The Communists launched a coup in 1965, which the army rapidly crushed.

In 1967 General Suharto, who had led the drive against the Communists, became president. Civilian experts worked with the military to solve the nation's economic problems. With an improved economy and greater political stability, the government held an election in 1971. Nine political parties offered candidates who were screened by Suharto's government. The Communists were not included. The army-sponsored Golkar Party easily won control of the national legislature, and retained that control in elections in 1977 and 1982. Indonesia's political stability depends on its continued economic growth.

Oppression of minorities.   Sukarno and Suharto both made it their policy to annex territories they considered strategically important, regardless of the opposition of the inhabitants. In 1963 Indonesia took control of West Irian (now Irian Jaya), the western half of New Guinea. "Indonesianization" has been forced on the racially and culturally distinct people of West Irian. This policy and the exploitation of West Irian resources have aroused their hostility. An even more brutal action was Indonesia's takeover of East Timor, a former Portuguese colony, in 1975. More than 10 percent of the people of East Timor were killed, large numbers were tortured, and many more were starved by the deliberate destruction of crops. The West has largely ignored this vast human tragedy.

Looking ahead.   Southeast Asia has a history of rivalry among the different countries of the region and among its many different groups of people. This historic hostility threatens to plague the area with political instability. The area is also involved in worldwide rivalry between Communist and non-Communist nations and will probably remain an area with a short fuse.

Reviewing Your Reading

1. How does Malaysia's varied population challenge its democratic government?
2. What factors make it difficult to establish democratic government in Southeast Asia?
3. Trace the rise of Suharto to power in Indonesia.

CHAPTER REVIEW

Recalling Names and Places

Alliance Party	General Ne Win	Suharto
Golkar Party	Pathet Lao	General Nguyen Van Thieu
General Lon Nol		

Understanding This Chapter

1. Pol Pot and the Khmer Rouge murdered more than 1 million of their own people when they ruled Cambodia (Kampuchea) from 1975 to 1979. What was their purpose for such destruction? How did their Southeast Asian neighbors respond to these events? How did the United States and other western powers respond?
2. The United States went to war in Vietnam to prevent a Communist takeover of South Vietnam. Did we succeed? Why or why not? What have been the consequences for Vietnam? For the rest of Southeast Asia? For the United States?
3. What has caused unrest in the Philippines in the 1980s? What has the United States done in response to these conditions in its longtime ally? How might it have responded?

Chapter 39

Cultural Contributions of Southeast Asia

Southeast Asia's cultural indebtedness to India and China is evident in the region's various art forms. Both Hindu and Buddhist influences can be seen in architecture and literature. Chinese influence is strongest in Vietnam.

Buddhist Architecture in Southeast Asia

On the parched plain of Pagan, along the Irrawaddy River, between Rangoon and Mandalay, are the ruins of thousands of Buddhist temples and stupa-like structures that were erected between the eleventh and the thirteenth centuries. A few have been restored to their former glory.

The Ananda temple. The largest and most impressive of the Pagan monuments is the Ananda temple, built in 1105. It is almost 180 feet high and almost 300 feet long. In the center of the temple, on each of the four sides of a square column, is a 31-foot tall gilded Buddha standing in light that passes through a lofty window.

A more recent creation is the Shwe Dagon *(shway' dah'gan)* temple in Rangoon, built to entomb eight hairs of the Buddha. Elaborately carved woodwork, showing animal and human figures, decorates various buildings in the shrine. The main stupa of Rangoon attracts the viewer. Rising over 300 feet above its platform, its spire is covered by layers of gold leaf placed there by worshipers.

Beautiful remains of the Khmer empire. Angkor served as the capital of the Khmer empire for several centuries. During the twelfth and thirteenth centuries temple-mausoleums were built by kings. These works surpassed the architectural creations of Khmer's neighboring countries. An army of workers was needed to cut, transport, place, and shape the stone according to an elaborate design. Many skilled sculptors decorated the walls with figures.

The temple of Angkor Wat is dedicated to the Hindu god Vishnu. The temple design, with its moat, walls, and towers, reflects the Indian idea of the World Mountain, the center of the world and the kingdom. The temple is approached from the west over the moat, which has a long stone crossing with a serpent handrail.

Angkor Wat consists of three levels, with a tower at each corner of the wall. The central tower rises more than 200 feet above the roadway. It is connected by galleries to eight smaller towers, all of which were originally covered with gold leaf.

One of the gateways to Angkor Thom is formed by statues representing giant devils. Note the unique expression on each face. Angkor (the word means capital or city) Thom and Angkor Wat are located in central Cambodia near Tonle Sap. Angkor Thom was built by the Khmer ruler Jayavarman VII as his capital. In its center stand the remains of the Bayon temple, which housed a statue of the Buddha and was crowned by 541 towers.

Angkor Thom was built later than Angkor Wat. By the time of its construction Hinduism had lost its following among the Khmer, and Theravada Buddhism was the faith of the country. The temple of Angkor Thom was dedicated to the Buddha. For protection, the city was surrounded by a stone wall with a gate in each direction. The gates were topped by towers that were shaped into massive heads, each of which represented a bodhisattva.

The architectural design is not the only glory of Angkor Wat and Angkor Thom. The walls are covered with an incredible variety of sculpture. One scene shows the judgement of the dead before Yama, the Hindu god of the underworld. The Indian epics the *Mahabharata* and the *Ramayana* are the sources for the vigorous battle scenes, which include chariots and war elephants. Beautiful, graceful, heavenly dancers with elaborate headdresses are carved in stone. Vines and flowers flow from the mouths of mythological creatures, while people, gods, and animals inhabit a dense tropical forest of stone.

The Borobudur monument of Java. One of the greatest Buddhist monuments is found at Borobudur on a plain in central Java. It has four stories, each of which is smaller than the one below. On the top story are 72 perforated bell-shaped stupas, each of which contains an image of a seated Buddha. At the center of these smaller stupas is a large closed stupa, which may have contained a statue of the Buddha.

Each of the four stories has an enclosed gallery lavishly decorated with sculpture. These sculptures show scenes from daily life. Other sculpture depicts the previous lives of the Buddha – his life as Gautama Siddhartha, the growth of his spiritual life, his attainment of enlightenment, and the delivery of his first sermon. As Buddhist pilgrims make their way through these galleries to the top of the monument, they symbolically pass through the various stages to Buddhist enlightenment.

While the Borobudur monument shows its Indian origins, the skill of the Javanese artists in adapting the style to their culture is evident. The settings and the dress of the men and women in stone tell us much about the life of the eighth-century Javanese people.

Literature and Dance

In addition to architecture, the literature and the dances of Southeast Asia reflect Indian and Chinese influences. The Indian epics, the *Ramayana* and the *Mahabharata,* were translated into various Southeast Asian languages and adapted to the theatre. But there is much original Southeast Asian art as well.

Vietnamese culture is strong in literature. The importance of the Confucian scholar and a high regard for the written word are ingrained in the Viet-

Indonesian puppets in a wayand kulit, *or shadow play. The puppets are moved between a lamp and screen while the puppet master tells a story, usually an episode from the* Ramayana *or* Mahabhrata. *An orchestra of four xylophones accompanies the telling of the story.*

namese. Even illiterate people are familiar with the literature. It was memorized and passed from person to person by oral recitation, a practice that continues today.

Written in the eighteenth century, *Kim Van Kieu* is Vietnam's most famous poem. It relates the story of a beautiful woman who gives up the man she loves to save her family's honor. After many years of adventures and sufferings, she meets her first love in a Buddhist temple. Both realize that they can never marry. The hardship she endured was to cleanse her from the bad karma she earned in a previous life.

Cambodian classical dance. Dancing as an art form in Southeast Asia ranges from the village folk dances to the formal classical dances. In the past, many of the rulers of the region patronized royal dance groups.

One such group was the Classical Khmer Dancers of Cambodia. Most of the dancers were women who begin their difficult training at an early age. They spent years learning the various hand gestures and body positions that help to tell the story they performed. Stretching the thumb and the index finger forward while curling the other three fingers back showed picking flowers. Rubbing the palms of the hands together in a circular motion indicated greed.

The Cambodian dancers were beautifully dressed in velvet, silk, and cloth of gold. They wore jewelry of gold and precious stones and gold leaf tiaras. Musicians played bamboo flutes, xylophones, stringed instruments, and drums as the barefoot dancers performed.

CHAPTER REVIEW

Recalling Names and Places

Ananda temple	Angkor Wat	*Kim Van Kieu*
Angkor Thom	Borobudur	Shwe Dagon

Understanding This Chapter

1. Give examples of Indian and Chinese influences in Southeast Asian art.
2. Should other lands and peoples help preserve the art treasures of Southeast Asia, as has been done in Egypt? Why or why not?
3. What Buddhist ideas are found in the Vietnamese poem *Kim Van Kieu?*
4. Describe the body gestures used by Cambodian classical dancers to tell a story.

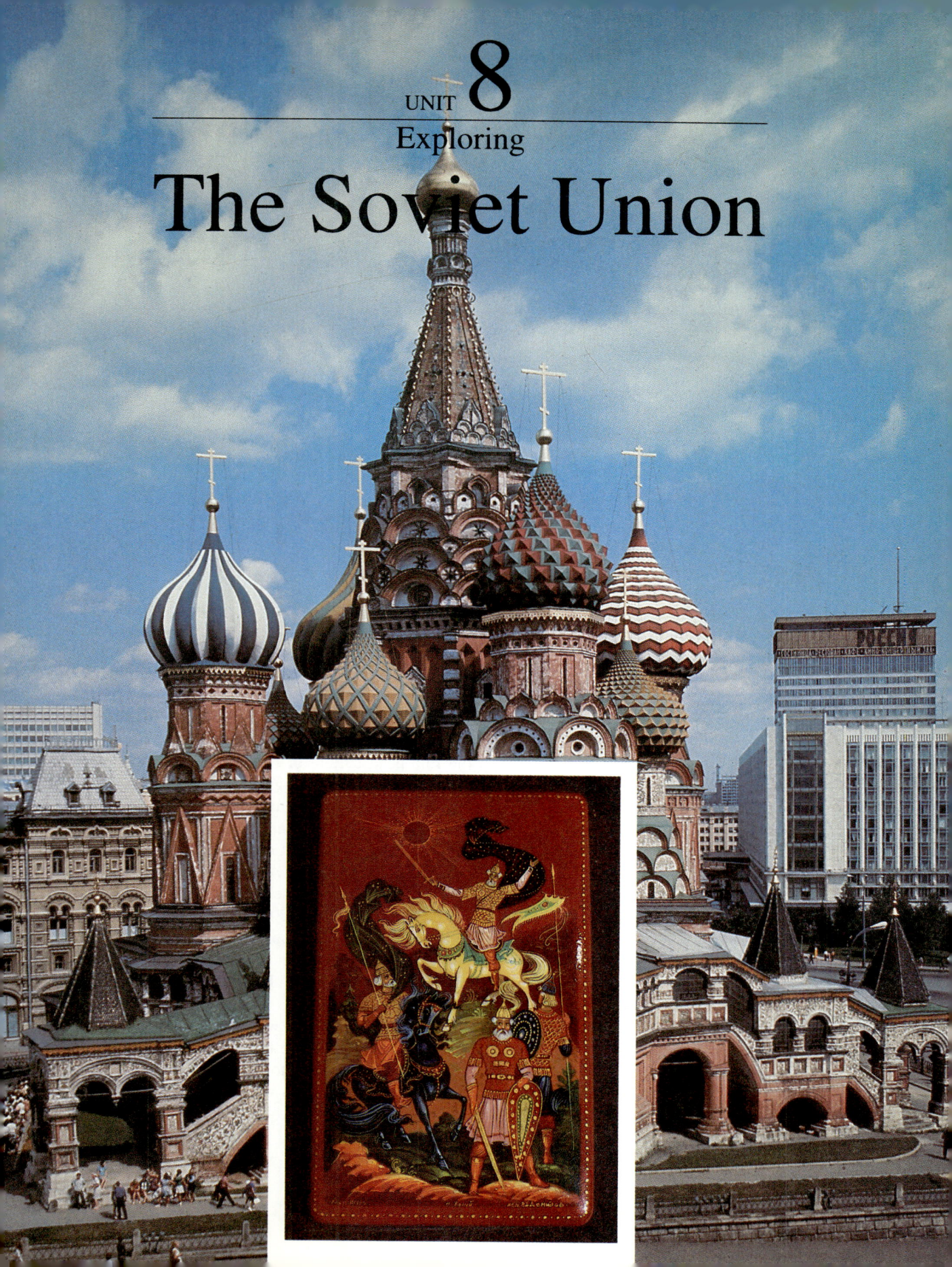

UNIT 8
Exploring
The Soviet Union

| 800 | 900 | 1000 | 1100 | 1200 | 1300 | 1400 | 1500 | 1600 | 1700 | 1800 | 1900 |

RISE OF TSARIST RUSSIA (NOVGOROD, KIEV, MOSCOVY)
c. 862–1584

ROMANOV DYNASTY
1613–1917

● RISE OF CHRISTIANITY
c. 850

TATAR DOMINATION
1223–1480

PETER THE GREAT
1682–1725

GOLDEN AGE OF NOBILITY
1725–1796

TIME OF TROUBLES
1519–1613

COMMUNIST RULE
1917–

THE UNION OF SOVIET SOCIALIST REPUBlics is the official name of the Soviet Union. Although some refer to the nation as Russia, this is not quite accurate. Only a portion of the land is Russia, and only half of the total population is Russian.

Over 100 different nationalities and cultural groups live within the Soviet Union. Numbering over 280 million people, the nation has the world's third largest population. Both Europeans and a variety of Asian peoples make up the population, many speaking their own languages and preserving their traditional cultures.

The Soviet Union is a vast cultural bridge between Europe and Asia. Long contact with other Asian countries and centuries of rule by Mongol conquerors brought Asian influences to the European culture of the Soviet Union. On the other hand, European people, customs, and technology have also diffused into Soviet Asia. The end result has been an exciting mixture of many cultures.

The European portion of the Soviet Union occupies about one-fourth of the country's total area, although it has nearly 70 percent of the population. Three-fourths of the Soviet Union, the area of Siberia, is in Asia. Despite some settlement of this area by Europeans, Siberia remains sparsely populated. Many of its peoples are nomads who live as herders, hunters, and food gatherers.

The Soviet Union is so large and plays such an important part in world affairs that it is often called a superpower. It is by far the most influential of the non-Western nations. Few international problems can be solved without the cooperation of the Soviet Union.

The Soviet Union is a complex of cultures about which most people in the United States know too little. It is important that we have some knowledge of this huge country, its culture, and its contributions to the world. Without this understanding agreements between our two countries will be difficult to reach.

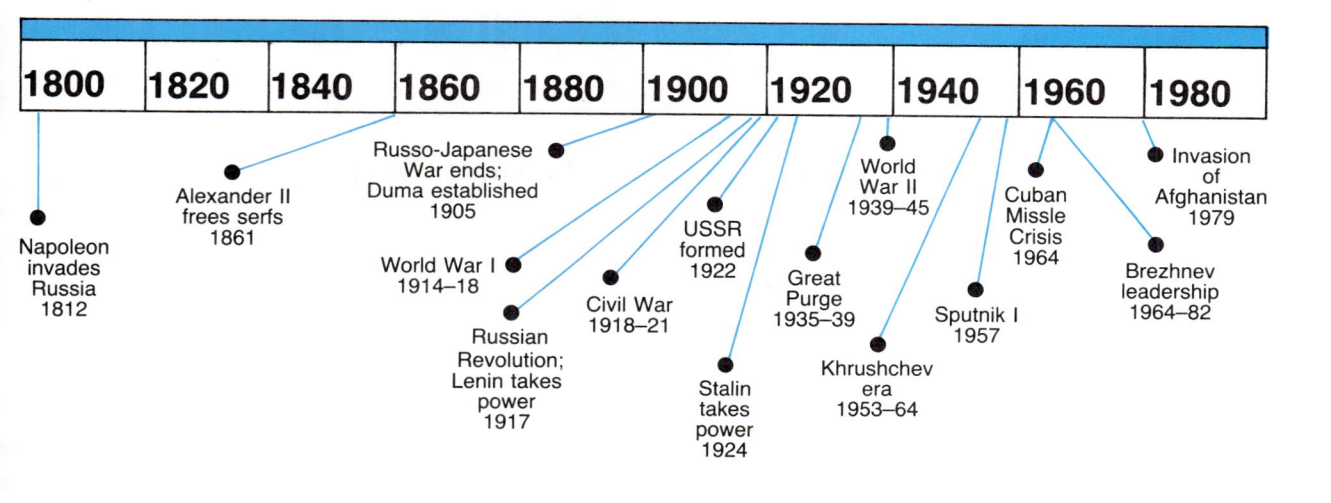

| 1800 | 1820 | 1840 | 1860 | 1880 | 1900 | 1920 | 1940 | 1960 | 1980 |

- Napoleon invades Russia 1812
- Alexander II frees serfs 1861
- Russo-Japanese War ends; Duma established 1905
- World War I 1914–18
- Russian Revolution; Lenin takes power 1917
- Civil War 1918–21
- USSR formed 1922
- Stalin takes power 1924
- Great Purge 1935–39
- World War II 1939–45
- Khrushchev era 1953–64
- Sputnik I 1957
- Cuban Missile Crisis 1964
- Brezhnev leadership 1964–82
- Invasion of Afghanistan 1979

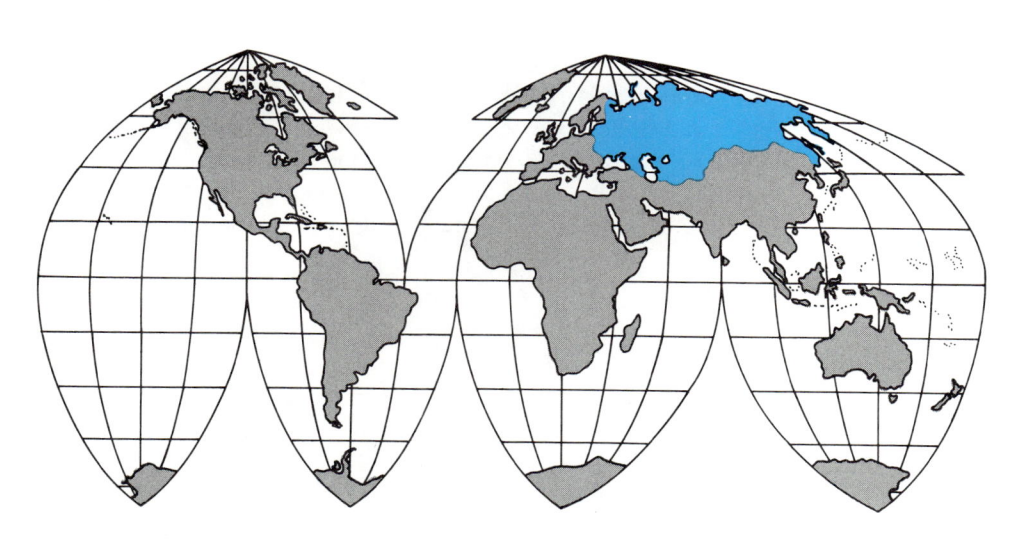

449

Chapter 40

Land, Climate, and People of the Soviet Union

The Soviet Union is the largest country in the world. With an area of 8,649,500 square miles, it is more than twice as large as the United States. From its most western boundary on the Baltic Sea to its most eastern point on the Pacific coast, the Soviet Union covers about 6000 miles. West to east the Soviet Union extends almost halfway around the world. This huge nation covers about one-sixth of the earth's surface.

Look at the map on page 451. If we compare the latitude of the Soviet Union with that of the United States, we see that the Soviet Union is farther north. Leningrad and the southern tip of Greenland are at the same latitude. Moscow is as far north as southern Alaska. Only the desert region east of the Caspian Sea and the Caucasus region extend more southward than the northern border of New York State.

A Cold Country

Because of its northerly location much of the Soviet Union experiences long, cold winters. Perhaps the lowest temperature ever recorded in any community in the northern hemisphere was −96° at Oymyakon (*oi' me yah' cone*), a town in eastern Siberia.

The Soviet Union is also cold because of its land formations and the location of its water bodies. In many regions oceans help to make the climate along their shores milder. They do so because air temperatures change more slowly above water than over land. Thus coastal areas are usually cooler in the summers and warmer in the winters than inland areas. However, most of the Soviet Union is located far from the oceans. Moreover, its longest shoreline is on the Arctic Ocean.

The extreme cold in much of Siberia is also due to the land formations. Except for some lowlands in the west, most of Siberia is a vast plateau ringed by mountains. The mountains block off what warming winds might come from the Pacific Ocean and from the south. The city of Oymyakon is the "Pole of Cold" in the Siberian plateau because it is surrounded by mountains, keeping out winds that might scatter the bitter cold air surrounding this community. Oymyakon illustrates on a small scale what is true in so much of Siberia.

One could draw three straight lines on a map of the Soviet Union to form a triangle. The first one connects Leningrad on the Gulf of Finland and Odessa on the Black Sea. The second line connects Leningrad with the southern end of Lake Baykal in south central Siberia. The third line joins Odessa with Lake Baykal. Within this triangle lives much of the population. Most farming also

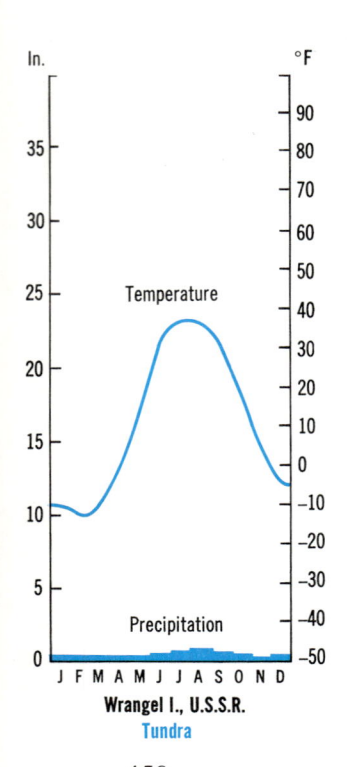

Wrangel I., U.S.S.R.
Tundra

takes place within this area. North of this triangle the climate in most areas is too cold, while to the south it is too dry.

Rainfall is light. Most of the Soviet Union has only light precipitation because of its distance from the ocean. Winds that have gathered moisture over the ocean have already lost it by the time they move farther inland. The southern and eastern mountain ranges prevent moisture from being carried to Siberia from the south and east. Fortunately, the cool weather in most of the country slows the rate of evaporation and prevents the land from rapidly losing the little moisture it has accumulated.

Four Major Vegetation Belts

The land of the Soviet Union can be divided into four zones set apart by differences in vegetation and in the quality of the soil. Along the Arctic shore is the *tundra*, a region where the climate is cold for most of the year. Little vegetation exists except for mosses and lichens. About a tenth of the Soviet Union is tundra, a vast, treeless plain, largely permanently frozen.

The permanently frozen ground is called *permafrost*. Its depth varies from one location to another, extending hundreds of feet into the earth in some places. Most of the land north and east of the Leningrad-Baykal line has permafrost, especially in Siberia.

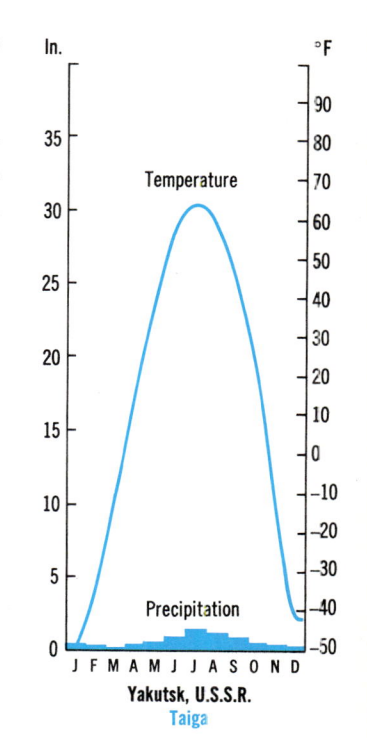

451

Anthropologists remove a mammoth bone from an excavation on the Berzovka River. Several carcasses of the now extinct woolly northern mammoth have been kept in good condition by the Siberian permafrost. The mammoths, members of the elephant subfamily, grew to be almost ten feet high. Fossil ivory from mammoth tusks is sold for industrial uses.

Permafrost Problems

Building a house on the permafrost calls for special techniques. If it is built on the ground in the usual fashion, heat from the house thaws the ground, and it will begin to sink into the mud. The house must be built on posts driven into the earth. By forcing hot steam into the ground, it will soften enough to push in the posts. The ground quickly freezes again, holding the posts securely. The house is then built on a platform above the surface. Open space under the house keeps the earth frozen.

Although the summers are short in the permafrost region, the days can be warm. In Oymyakon, for example, temperatures may rise to 100°. A few inches of the top layers of soil will thaw out. However, the frozen ground below prevents the water from draining, and the land becomes muddy and swampy.

The tundra is a vast wilderness of untapped wealth. Such minerals as coal, oil, and diamonds exist beneath its surface, but thus far no one has discovered a practical means of removing them from the frozen earth.

The Soviet Union contains one-fifth of the world's forests. South of the tundra is a vast forest belt extending across the Soviet Union and covering about half of the country's land surface. The northern portion of this forest region consists of such evergreen trees as pine and spruce. It is called *taiga*. The southern portion of this forest belt has evergreen trees mixed with such broad leaf trees as maple, birch, and elm. The soil of the taiga is poor because much of it is also permafrost. Even where there is no permafrost, the cold slows the decay of vegetation which produces the humus, decomposed plant and animal matter, needed to make rich soil. The southerly forest region has more humus and better quality soil.

The steppes have the richest soil. South of the forest region, extending from the Ukraine to Kazakhstan in central Asia, is a prairie country called the *steppe*. This grassland region has the richest soil of the Soviet Union, called *chernozem*. It is a black soil containing much humus. Most of farming takes place within this area. Wheat, rye, barley, sugar beets, and potatoes are among the major crops raised in this region.

In the Caspian and Aral Sea region, covering parts of Central and South Asia, is an arid or semi-arid region which geographers describe as the desert belt. Some of the soil in this region would be productive if water were found for irrigation. Large areas south of the Aral Sea are sandy or have too much salt in the ground to be useful to farmers.

Land elevations vary. Although much of the Soviet Union is not flat, the populated part of the country is. Except for the low-lying Ural Mountains, which divide Europe from Asia, and the high Caucasus Mountains near the border of Turkey and Iran, the European part of the nation is mostly level. This is sometimes called the "Great Russian Lowland." The northern half is covered with forest. The southern part is grasslands, the "bread basket" region of the country where the grain grows.

East of the Ural Mountains, the lowlands continue. A vast and mostly level terrain extends eastward as far as the Yenisei (*yeh'nuh-say'ih*) River. A huge area is forest and marshland, except in Kazakhstan where desert conditions exist. Long rivers like the Ob (*ahp'yih*) cross the western Siberian lowlands as they flow northward to the Arctic Ocean. Mountains help form the southern frontiers bordering Iran, Afghanistan, and China.

East of the Yenisei River is eastern Siberia, which covers nearly one-third of the nation's area but has only 5 percent of the population. This is almost entirely permafrost country.

As one travels east of the Yenisei River, the land elevation rises and forms a plateau. Some regions are quite mountainous, especially east of Lake Baykal and of the Lena (*lyeh'nah*) River. This land experiences long and bitterly cold winters.

Warm weather by the sea. Although the major waterways in the Soviet Union are its rivers, some bodies of water are quite large, among them the Caspian Sea and the Aral Sea. The Black and Caspian seas are in the southwestern region of the Soviet Union.

From the southeastern shore of the Crimean peninsula to the town of Poti in the Georgian Soviet Socialist Republic is a major recreational area. It is sometimes called the "Russian Riviera" because the area has the type of vegetation and climate found along the Mediterranean coast of France. Since the rule of the tsars, there have been many beautiful homes, hotels, and recreational facilities along the coast.

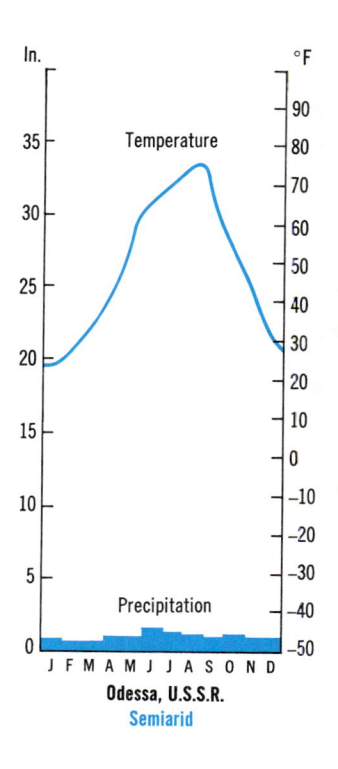

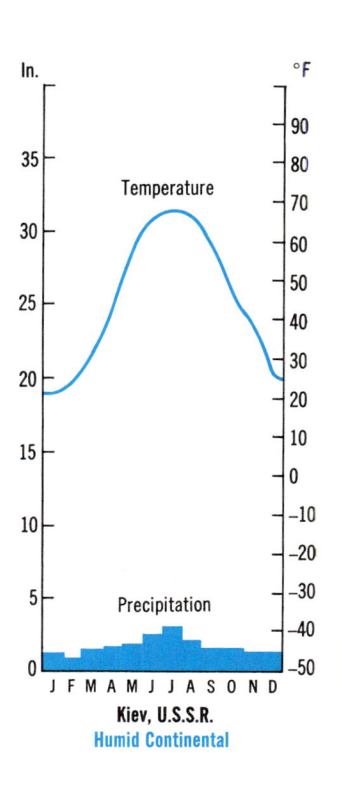

Odessa, U.S.S.R.
Semiarid

Kiev, U.S.S.R.
Humid Continental

453

Warm weather and a coastline on the Black Sea make Yalta (above) a favorite resort city for Russian vacationers. Even on the tundra (right), the changing seasons bring changing colors to vegetation. Here autumn colors are evident in Chukotka, near the Arctic Circle.

Much of the Caspian shore is very dry and for the most part is not as attractive to vacationers as the Black Sea area. However, the west shore near the town of Baku is a major source of oil. Where water is available for irrigation, the warm climate makes such semi-tropical crops as citrus fruits possible. About half of Russia's cotton is grown east of the Caspian Sea. This sea is also the source of Russia's famous caviar.

Except in Karelia on the border of Finland, the Soviet Union has few lakes. One of its well-known lakes is Lake Baykal. This fresh water lake is the deepest in the world.

Rivers are the Soviet Union's most important inland waterways. The Soviet Union's rivers are among the longest in the world. Siberia has three mighty rivers, each over two thousand miles long. They are the Ob-Irtysh system, the Yenisei, and the Lena. Despite their great length, their value for transportation is limited, because long cold winters keep them frozen for several months a year. The Volga River is by far the most important river. It is a main transportation route whose usefulness has been increased by the building of canals. The Volga River system now connects the Baltic and White seas with the Black Sea.

Other major rivers are the Don and the Dnieper (*dnyeh'purr*), which are in the European portion of the country. Both rivers flow through the fertile region of the Ukraine and are used to transport grain, coal, and other important products of the area.

Land of Ethnic Diversity

Today the Soviet Union is divided into fifteen union republics or Soviet Socialist Republics (SSR's). Within the SSR's there are 109 different ethnic or nationality groups. Most of these groups have maintained the customs, dress, childrearing practices, and languages that have given them their cultural identity. Although only nineteen of these groups have over a million members, each SSR has one nationality group which predominates.

The Great Russians are the largest nationality group. The largest republic in the Soviet Union is the Russian Soviet Federated Socialist Republic (RSFSR). The capital of this republic is Moscow. About 80 percent of the people in this republic are Russians, or Great Russians. Along with the Byelorussians (White Russians) and the Ukrainians, these three Slavic peoples make up nearly three-fourths of the population of the Soviet Union. Members of these groups speak Slavic languages, a branch of the Indo-European language family, and earlier generations of Russians were members of the Russian Orthodox Church. Byelorussians compose 81 percent of the Byelorussian SSR, and Ukrainians make up 77 percent of the Ukrainian republic.

Another five republics are grouped together by their geographic location and the language and religion of their populations. The Kazakh, Uzbek, Kirghiz, Tadzhik, and Turkmen SSR's are located in Central Asia. The peoples of these republics speak languages of the Turkic language group, and the influence of the traditional culture of the Turks can be seen in their music, art, dress, and folklore. Many Uzbeks, Tadzhiks, Kazakhs, Kirghizians, and Turkmens continue to follow the Islamic faith despite efforts of Soviet authorities to rid them of their customary practices.

The republics of the Caucasus. Three SSR's are located in the Caucasus region of the Soviet Union: the Georgian, Armenian, and Azerbaijan SSR's. This area is located within the Caucasus Mountains and between the Black and Caspian seas. Around 65 percent of the Georgian SSR is composed of Georgians, a nationality group descended from Christian converts who speak a language unique to the area. In the Azerbaijan SSR the people speak a Turkic language and follow Islam. The Armenians are Christian and speak Armenian, an Indo-European language.

Along the banks of the Dnieper stand Russia's oldest towns. Kiev, the first capital, grew up there, serving as a trade route to Byzantium and the Baltic. The 900-year-old Pechora monastery, now an architectural preserve, looks across the river to the high-rise buildings of the modern city.

The peoples of the Estonian, Latvian, and Lithuanian SSR's have had many rulers in their history. After the Russian Revolution of 1917 they became the independent countries of Estonia, Latvia, and Lithuania. They remained independent until 1940, when they again came under Soviet domination. Together these SSR's are known as the Baltic republics because of their position along the southern coast of the Baltic Sea. Both Latvians and Lithuanians speak languages of the same language family, while the Estonians speak a language similar to Finnish.

The Moldavian SSR is in the southwest corner of the Soviet Union next to Romania. Prior to 1940 parts of this republic belonged to Romania. Other parts came from the Ukrainian SSR. The Moldavians make up 65 percent of the population and speak a language akin to Romanian.

Many other nationality groups in the country's subdivisions. In addition to the fifteen SSR's, the country is also divided into several other administrative units known as autonomous republics, autonomous regions, territories, and national areas. Many other nationality groups live within these divisions. Such groups as the Yakuts, Karelians, and Abkhasians continue to maintain their separate identity. The Jews also represent a significant minority. On pages 505–510, we will look at the status of some of these groups in the Soviet Union in greater detail.

CHAPTER REVIEW

Recalling Names and Places

Aral Sea	Lake Baykal	taiga
Byelorussians	Lena River	tundra
Caspian Sea	Ob-Irtysh River system	Ural Mountains
Dnieper River	permafrost	Volga River
Don River	steppe	Yenisei River
Great Russians		

Understanding This Chapter

1. How have land formations and the location of oceans affected the climate in the Soviet Union?
2. Where do most of the Soviet people live?
3. What is permafrost? How does it affect living conditions?
4. Describe the "Great Russian Lowland."
5. Name the major rivers in the Soviet Union. Which are most frequently used as transportation routes?
6. Identify the Soviet Union's four major vegetation zones. How do they differ from one another?
7. With more than twice the area of the United States, the Soviet Union still has a smaller agricultural production. How does geography help explain this difference?
8. What are the largest nationality groups in the Soviet Union?

Chapter 41

The Path to the Russian Revolution

Since the early Stone Age, people have lived in the Soviet Union, but an organized state probably did not exist in Russia before the ninth century A.D. Until that time many different peoples moved back and forth across the vast Russian plains. The Scythians, Alans, Finns, Magyars, Turks, and others migrated into this area. Finally, Slavic tribes moved in and eventually controlled the region. These people were farmers, raising crops of barley, rye, and wheat. They also traded in forest products, like timber and furs, and in fish. The word *Russian* comes from *Rus,* a term applied to these Slavic tribes who finally became dominant in this part of Europe. The origin of the word is unknown.

The Early Russian State

The beginnings of the Russian state in the ninth century are rather hazy, since records of this period are poor and mixed with legend. Vikings came eastward, probably by crossing the Gulf of Finland and Lake Ladoga *(lahd' uh-guh)* in the middle of that century. They were looking for trading opportunities and followed the many rivers of this region.

Most Slavic people lived in settlements and were peaceable. But they were often attacked by hostile tribes, and they had no unified defense system. Thus the Vikings, probably hired first as paid warriors to protect the Slavs, were able to gain political control. According to legend, the first Viking ruler was Rurik. Rurik's successor, Oleg, captured the town of Kiev and made it his capital. Novgorod (*noff'* guh-rut), Pskov, and other communities also came under control of the Vikings who soon adopted Slavic ways and were absorbed into the local population.

Kiev becomes prosperous. In the ninth century, wilderness surrounded Novgorod. Kiev (key-*ef'*) was better located for trade. Situated on the Dnieper River, which flows into the Black Sea, ships from Kiev could easily sail to Constantinople. Refer to the map on pages 6–7. Recall that Constantinople was the wealthiest city of the Mediterranean world at this time. Kiev could trade timber, furs, and fish for the manufactured goods of the Byzantine empire. This trade became so profitable that Kiev was soon the most prosperous town in Russia.

Cyril and Methodius. With the growth of the Byzantine trade came new ideas. Perhaps the two most important ones were a system of writing and the Christian religion. Around 850 A.D. two missionaries named Cyril and Methodius left Constantinople and journeyed north to spread the Christian faith. To help convert the Slavs, they taught them an alphabet of Greek letters and others they had created to fit Slavic sounds. This alphabet, called Cyrillic, is still used in the Soviet Union, Bulgaria, and some parts of Yugoslavia.

Since there was no important rival religion in Russia, Christianity was readily accepted. The efforts of Cyril, Methodius, and later missionaries were finally rewarded when Vladimir I, the ruler of Kiev, officially accepted Christianity in 988. Eleven years later inhabitants there were ordered baptized.

Christianity splits in 1054. When the citizens of Kiev were converted, eastern and western Christians were united by one faith. This unity ended in 1054 when the Bishop of Constantinople, called the Patriarch, refused to accept the supremacy of the Pope in Rome. This east-west division in Christianity continues today.

Eastern Christianity became known as the Eastern Orthodox, or Greek Orthodox, Church. Until the middle of the fifteenth century, the center of the eastern Church was within the Byzantine empire with its capital at Constantinople. When, in 1453, Constantinople fell to the Turks, the power of the Patriarch was reduced. As the Byzantine empire began to decline, Russian Church leaders assumed greater control of the Russian Church.

In the sixteenth century the Church in Russia became independent of the Greek Orthodox Church. The Russian Church rejected the control of the Patriarch of Constantinople, and Moscow became the center of the Russian Orthodox Church. The Patriarch of Moscow was strongly influenced by the tsars, and supported their efforts to maintain strong controls over the peasants of Russia.

With the separation from the Church in Rome, the Russians were also cut off from Western ideas. The state controlled the Church. Moreover, use of the native Russian language rather than Latin, an international language, isolated Russian scholars from the intellectual ferment taking place in western Europe. The liberal ideas of the eighteenth century, which stressed greater control on the power of royalty, had little influence on Russian thinking. The Russian tsars escaped the challenges to their authority which were confronting the kings of

The medieval city of Voin in Kiev served as a center for river ships going to Byzantium. Founded by the Grand Duke of Kiev in the tenth century, it was destroyed by foreign invaders in 1240.

France, Italy, and other western European countries. However, while new ideas and the technology of western Europe hardly touched Russia, Byzantine art and culture had a lasting effect on Russian life. The influence of Byzantine culture is especially evident in Russian religious art and music.

Decline of the Kievan state. Kiev seemed well situated to become rich and powerful. On a large river flowing to the Black Sea, it could trade with the outside world. Its farmers tilled the richest farmlands in all of Russia. They paid tribute to the grand duke of Kiev who kept the loose federation together. Despite these advantages, problems arose which were destined to plague Russian society in later centuries.

Major difficulties in Kiev were the succession of rulers, threats from external nomads, and the eventual loss of trade. The law for choosing new rulers moved dukes through a series of territorial seats before attaining the Kiev position. The law was changed in 1097 to allow dukes to retain their seats as family dukedoms. The appearance of dangerous nomads in the south created unsafe conditions for living and trade, pushing the center of trade north. With loss of its central role both in government and trade, Kiev declined.

The Golden Horde invades. Mongols from Central Asia, called Tatars by the Russians, threatened the nation for many years. The Tatars were also called the "Golden Horde" because their leader, Batu Khan, used a gold-colored tent for shelter. These warriors on horseback roared out of the vast Siberian steppes many times to attack their terrified neighbors – the Chinese, Indians, Persians, and Arabs. Surrounding their enemy quickly, the Tatars cut them down. For a long time they seemed invincible.

Around 1223, the Tatars entered Russia. Seventeen years later they took Kiev. They advanced westward as far as Poland and Germany. Novgorod was the only important center not taken, but it was forced to recognize Tatar rule. The Asian tribesmen controlled Russia for over 200 years.

Tatar rule. The Tatars established a rather loose control over the territories they conquered. As long as the Russians continued to pay heavy taxes to the Tatar Khan, they were allowed to manage their own affairs. Novgorod and Pskov continued their trade with western Europe, but other cities suffered setbacks to their development. Under Tatar rule Russian states were sometimes asked to provide soldiers for the Tatar army.

Russian princes planned to drive out the Tatars as soon as they showed signs of weakness. The people hated the Tatar conquerors for the acts of cruelty they committed to remind the Russians of their power.

When the Tatars first attacked, the Russian princes pleaded with the western Europeans to come to their aid. No help came because Swedes, Germans, and Poles were anxious to expand their territories at Russia's expense. Shut off from western Europe for a long time, the Russians were at the mercy of the Tatars.

During this period many Asian customs and standards became part of Russian life. The status of women declined, and they were treated as inferiors. Slaves and other people of lower status enjoyed fewer rights. Tatar words crept into the Russian language; clothing styles became more Oriental; and autocratic government became firmly established.

A Russian icon of the sixteenth century, entitled "Madonna and Child." Among medieval Russia's greatest art forms was iconography, the creation of religious pictures on portable panels. Such pictures are called icons, *from a Greek word meaning "image" or "reflection."*

In the sixteenth century Saint Basil's in Moscow became the center of the Russian Orthodox Church. Built by Ivan the Terrible from 1554 to 1560, it has nine chapels capped by colorful domes and spires. According to legend, Ivan had its architects blinded on completion of their work so they would never again build anything so beautiful.

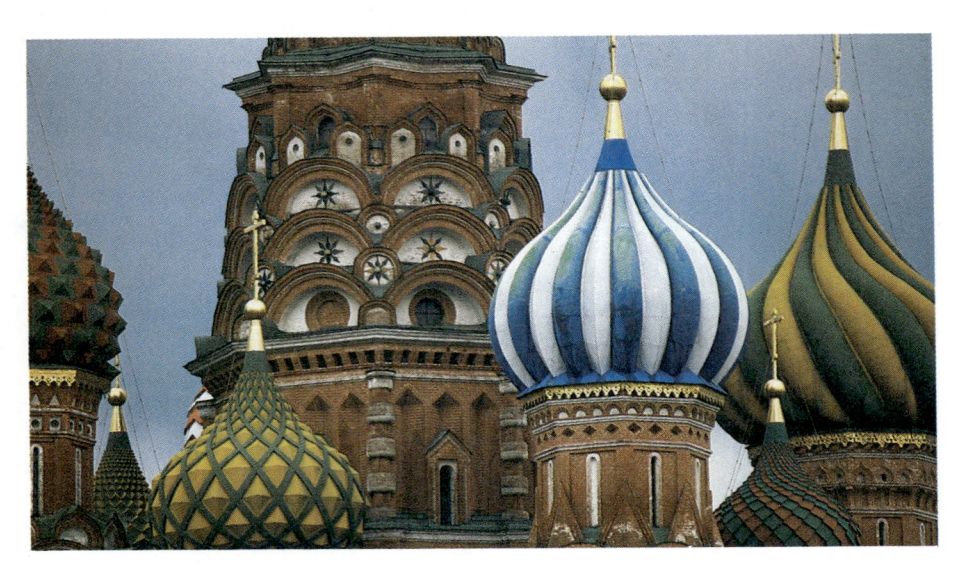

Moscow gains in importance. Under Tatar rule Kiev declined, and Moscow gained greater importance. During the Tatar period Moscow had several able princes who ruled for long periods of time. These princes secured many favors from the Tatars. For example, they received the right to collect the taxes the Tatars demanded for tribute, thus reducing Tatar interference in Russian affairs.

Moscow's geographical location aided its rise to power. The city is located on the Moscow River, one of the tributaries of the great Volga River system. As the Russians traded with the Tatars, the Volga River replaced the Dnieper as the main trade route.

Growth was further stimulated by the transfer of the head of the Russian Orthodox Church from Kiev to Moscow in 1299. The Church gained in importance under Tatar rule. Although they were not Christians, the conquerors were very tolerant of the Russian Church, granting it freedom from taxation. The Church became a unifying force for the Russian people during the period of Tatar rule.

Because of its religious and commercial importance Moscow grew from a town into the most important Russian state. Moscovy, as it was called, gradually added surrounding territory to its control. From these small beginnings a vast Russian empire began its development.

Reviewing Your Reading

1. Name some of the peoples who migrated into present-day Russia. How did they make a living?
2. How did Cyril and Methodius contribute to Russian culture?
3. Account for the growth of Kiev. Why did it lose importance later?
4. Who were the Tatars? How did their rule change Russian culture?
5. Why did Moscovy become the most important Russian state?

A Russian State Develops

In the period of Tatar control Moscovy became the strongest and largest of the many small Russian states. The larger Moscovy grew, the more powerful the princes of Moscow became, and the more easily they could bring the lesser princes under their control. In this fashion a Russian national state gradually evolved.

From the beginning the Russian rulers were autocrats. Autocracy is a system of government in which there is no recognized limit to the powers of the ruler. Autocrats may do whatever they want to do or are able to do.

Tatar rule had been absolutely autocratic. The khans not only owned all the lands of the empire, but also all the people. They could do anything they pleased. As was noted earlier, Tatar ideas of government were adopted by the Russian princes. Russian autocracy was further strengthened by the Orthodox Church, which maintained that the ruler of a state performed the will of God and could do no wrong.

Ivan the Great, founder of modern Russia. A prince of Moscow, Ivan III (1462–1505), is remembered in Russia as Ivan the Great. The founder of the Russian nation used the title *tsar,* which is the Russian word for "caesar" or "emperor." (Ivan IV formally took the title in 1547.) Ivan III refused to pay any more tribute to the Tatars. Disunity among Tatar leaders prevented them from challenging Ivan's refusal. As a result, the Mongol invaders gradually lost power. Ivan then added Tatar lands to Moscovy.

461

Ivan married Sophia, the niece of the last Byzantine emperor, in 1472. The Byzantine Empire had already ended when the Turks conquered Constantinople in 1453. Now that Constantinople, the Second Rome, had fallen to the Turks, Moscow was the new holy city.

The spread of serfdom. Although the record is not entirely clear, it seems that peasants were quite free to move about the country before the Tatars came. The Mongols' invasion destroyed fields, animals, and numerous buildings. To start over again, many peasants sold their labor or promised part of their crops to get loans. The poorest people were frequently unable to get out of debt and became serfs. Under debt serfdom one cannot leave the land as long as he owes an unpaid debt to the landowner.

During and after the reign of Ivan the Great, life became increasingly difficult for the poor. Debt serfdom was replaced by legal serfdom. People who became serfs for debts could still hope to be free after they repaid their debts. Legal serfdom meant that the peasant family was permanently tied to the land by law and was not free to move.

The growth of serfdom seems to be related to growth of the nobility as Muscovy expanded in size. To keep the nobles contented and to reward them for services in war, the tsar allowed former ruling princes to become nobles holding large estates. These estates needed farm labor. Laws were passed requiring the peasants to stay on the land and work for the landowner. Peasants were not allowed to leave without permission of the noble.

The tsars needed the nobles' support, especially that of the more powerful, land-owning nobles, or *boyars*. The government passed laws that helped the landowners keep the peasants under control. By the time the tsars became strong enough to force obedience from the boyars without granting them special favors, serfdom was firmly established in Russia.

Serfdom had a deadening effect on the Russian economy. The system was inefficient. Working only for others, serfs were seldom motivated to do their best. They did only what they had to do. The serfs also remained poor. When a large portion of the population is kept in poverty, the whole nation is affected. New business and industries do not develop because no market for new goods exists. Few people are rich enough to purchase anything but the barest necessities.

The serfs used primitive farming methods. Most Russian land has always been poor, and when it was seldom fertilized and improperly farmed, crop yields were very small. To make matters worse for the peasants, the nobles kept demanding more of their labor and crops as time went on. Conditions became so miserable that peasants either ran away or revolted. Before serfdom was abolished, hundreds of such rebellions were brutally crushed. The nobles looked on the serfs as property. When serfs ran away, they were hunted like animals. Before their emancipation in 1861 nearly half of the Russians were serfs.

Ivan the Terrible. Ivan IV (1533–1584), usually referred to as "Ivan the Terrible," was a grandson of Ivan the Great. Orphaned at the age of three, he spent an unhappy childhood. After becoming tsar at age seventeen, he extended Russian boundaries and began the first drive into Siberia. Ivan strengthened his position by challenging and finally destroying the power of the boyars. Although some plotted against him, he was insanely suspicious of all those around him. He slaughtered tens of thousands of people suspected of disloyalty by the end of his reign. However, he expanded Russia's boundaries and strengthened the central government. When he died in 1584, he left the Russian state much stronger.

The years following Ivan's reign are remembered in Russian history as the "Time of Troubles." His incompetent son Fyodor ruled for fourteen years. Then for fifteen years, around 1598 to 1613, a period of anarchy and suffering prevailed. Many men sought the crown and murdered each other trying to get it. Russia's enemies invaded, and for a short time Polish troops occupied Moscow. Meanwhile crops failed, and people starved. This period finally ended when a National Assembly elected a new tsar in 1613. From about fifty towns came delegates representing the free classes. This group elected Mikhail Romanov (1613–1645) the first tsar of the last Russian dynasty, which ruled until the Revolution of 1917.

From an unimpressive wooden fortress on the Moskva River, the Kremlin grew to become the center of Moscovy. Within the Kremlin's stone walls stood the palaces of grand dukes and boyars, monasteries, and other administrative buildings of the state.

Reviewing Your Reading

1. Define autocratic rule. In what ways was Russia an autocratic state under the tsars?
2. Why is Ivan III regarded as the founder of the Russian nation?
3. Describe the difference between debt serfdom and legal serfdom.
4. How did Ivan IV's leadership change Russia?
5. What was the purpose of the National Assembly meeting in 1613?

Peter the Great

Russia Becomes a Major Power

In the eighteenth and nineteenth centuries Russia expanded its territory. Much of this land was gained during the reigns of Peter the Great and Catherine the Great.

Peter turns Russia towards the West. Mikhail Romanov's grandson Peter became one of Russia's most important tsars (1682–1725). A huge man, over six feet eight inches tall, he possessed a violent temper. As a boy he had some contacts with Western merchants in Moscow and learned some mathematics and engineering from them. Peter also developed a great interest in military matters and shipbuilding. He visited the Netherlands and England to learn more about ship construction.

Peter's enthusiasm for ships arose from his interest in making Russia a naval power capable of extending the Russian empire to the Black Sea to fight the Turks. However, the Russian navy's longest battle was waged with Sweden. Between 1700 and 1721, in a conflict known as the Great Northern War, victorious Russia took lands along the Baltic Sea. Here Peter built a new capital at the eastern shore of the Gulf of Finland. This new city became St. Petersburg, which today is called Leningrad.

After winning in the Great Northern War, the tsar was called Peter the Great. He now had a "window to the West," with control of a large stretch of Baltic coast. Although Peter forced certain Western ways on the Russian people, such as shaving of beards and wearing Western-style clothes, there was little deeper

---

Etiquette for Young People

Peter the Great was determined to transform Russia from a barbaric and isolated nation into a Western power. During his reign a collection of rules for proper behavior was published. It was intended to help transform uncouth young people into cultured young men and women. Among these rules, first published in 1717, are the following:

When you are at table with other persons, behave according to these rules: First, trim your nails, wash your hands and take your seat in a mannerly way; sit straight, and don't grab first at the dish; don't gorge like a pig; don't blow into the soup to make it splash in all directions; don't snort while eating.... Don't leave your hands in your plate too long; don't swing your legs; when preparing to drink, don't wipe your lips with your hand, but use a napkin; don't drink until you have swallowed the food in your mouth. Don't lick your fingers, and don't gnaw at bones, but use a knife.... Don't hold bread to your chest while cutting it. Eat what is in front of you and don't grab elsewhere .... Don't champ on your food like a pig; don't scratch your head; don't talk with your mouth full—those are all peasant manners.... When you eat an egg, cut a piece of bread first, and be careful not to let the egg dribble.... Don't build a barrier of bones, crusts, and other things beside your plate. When you have finished eating, give thanks to God, wash your hands and face, and rinse your mouth.

westernizing of Russia. Peter made the authority of the tsar even more complete by bringing the Church under closer control of the state. War and territorial expansion continued as in the past.

The "Golden Age of Nobility." Peter died in 1725. For the next seventy-five years, Russia was ruled by women: Catherine I (1725–1727), Anna (1730–1740), Elizabeth (1741–1762), and Catherine II (1762–1796). Strong willed, they depended heavily on the support of the Guards, an elite military unit composed largely of nobles. With their assistance, Catherine II had her husband Tsar Peter III murdered so she could rule in his place. She was neither a Romanov nor a Russian, but a German princess before her marriage to Peter III.

Exercising great influence, the Guards persuaded the empress to pass many laws to help the nobles. Peter the Great had insisted that everyone must give service to the state. Catherine passed a series of laws that permitted only hereditary nobles to own serfs and relieved them of any obligation to the state. These nobles could not be punished for any wrongdoing. They had complete ownership of their estates and did not have to pay any taxes. In other words, they exercised great power and influence without assuming any responsibility. The "golden age" of the nobles had come. But the gains of the nobles were losses for the peasants who had to accept even greater financial burdens.

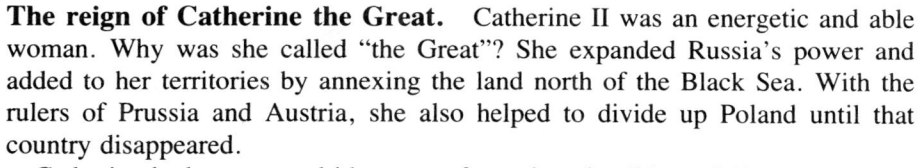

Catherine the Great

The reign of Catherine the Great. Catherine II was an energetic and able woman. Why was she called "the Great"? She expanded Russia's power and added to her territories by annexing the land north of the Black Sea. With the rulers of Prussia and Austria, she also helped to divide up Poland until that country disappeared.

Catherine had some good ideas on reform, but she did not follow through on them. She had intellectual interests and corresponded with famous European philosophers and writers. This period of the eighteenth century was called the Age of Reason in western Europe. At this time well-educated people believed that they could solve problems through reason and intelligence. While Catherine knew the writings of such French thinkers as Rousseau and Voltaire, she felt that their views on human rights could not be applied to the Russian social system. The French Revolution, which overthrew the monarchy of France in 1789 so upset Catherine that she cast away her liberal beliefs. Fearing that greater freedom might lead to an uprising among her own subjects, she ruled as an autocrat until her death in 1796.

Western influences strong among nobility. As we have noted, many cultural exchanges are likely to occur when people of different ways of life come in contact. During the eighteenth century, western European influences, especially French, affected the Russian nobility. The French language became the language of "cultured people." Only peasants spoke Russian. The nobility dressed in the French fashion. The men wore knee breeches and powdered wigs, and the women dressed in silk and satin gowns and had elaborate hair styles. They also pursued the same leisuretime interests as the French.

The division between the nobility and most of the Russian people, who had been reduced to serfdom, was already deep enough. Now, increasingly, they could not speak the same language. The peasants continued in their ancient ways with little change, except that each year it seemed to get more difficult to stay alive.

Alexander I, a tsar of contradictions. Catherine the Great was not fond of her son Paul and preferred that her grandson Alexander follow her to the throne. Paul I (1796–1801) became tsar when Catherine died in 1796, but he ruled for only five years. With Alexander's knowledge, Paul was strangled by some military officers in 1801.

Alexander I (1801–1825) became tsar as Catherine had wished. He was a handsome and intelligent man who had received a liberal education. Later, Alexander surrounded himself with friends who held democratic views. Yet his record of liberalism is not impressive.

Perhaps Alexander's most democratic acts were his granting of constitutions to Finland and Poland. Of the two, the constitution for Finland was most noteworthy. When Finland was annexed by Russia in 1809 after a war with Sweden, the tsar guaranteed that Finland could have self-rule under a constitution. For the most part this freedom was respected until 1917, when Finland became an independent republic. Unfortunately for Poland, its constitution was not honored long.

Perhaps Alexander would have been more liberal had it not been for Napoleon Bonaparte. In the early nineteenth century this Corsican colonel, who made himself emperor of France, kept Europe in turmoil.

Napoleon invades Russia. Napoleon was determined to make himself master of all Europe. To achieve this goal, he had to defeat Russia. By 1812 Napoleon controlled most of western Europe. With an army of about 600,000 men he invaded Russia. As Napoleon's armies approached Moscow, the Russians burned all shelters and retreated far inland. When the French army reached Moscow, they found the city burning and abandoned. Napoleon awaited word of a settlement from the tsar, but Alexander refused to negotiate. With the coming of winter the French army had to withdraw from Russia. Thousands froze to death while the Russian forces sniped at the living. Of the 600,000 men who started out so proudly, less than 100,000 survivors ever saw their homes again. Although Napoleon made several major efforts to regain control of Europe after his Russian disaster, he never fully recovered from this setback. He was finally defeated in 1815.

First Signs of the Coming Revolution

Alexander I died suddenly in 1825. This event prompted a small group of young officers to make a public demonstration on December 26, 1825; hence they were called *Decembrists*. The Decembrists had been officers stationed in Paris following Napoleon's defeat. There they had been exposed to new ideals, such as constitutional government and freedom of the individual. They wanted these rights for Russians too.

The Decembrists eagerly awaited the succession of Constantine, Alexander's brother, to the throne. Believing that he would be less conservative than his brother, they demanded "Constantine and Constitution," reflecting their belief that Constantine would be willing to rule under a constitution. However, unknown to the people, Constantine had already refused the throne, and Alexander had named his brother Nicholas to succeed him. The Decembrists were all arrested by the new tsar Nicholas I (1825–1855), but their revolt was only the first in a long series.

Criticism of tsarism spreads. In the following decades more people joined a variety of organizations opposed to the autocratic rule of the tsars. They were not only enlightened nobles, but also common people.

Various groups held different views on what type of government they desired. Some organizations wanted to keep the monarchy but place it under a constitution. Some wanted Russia to become a democratic republic. The Nihilists wanted no government at all. The first organization holding the beliefs of Karl Marx, a German philosopher of the nineteenth century who favored socialism, appeared in 1883.

Autocracy changes little in the nineteenth century. If the tsars had possessed greater foresight and the courage to act decisively, Russia might have evolved differently. Unhappily, few of the Romanovs were good leaders, and most lacked proper concern for their nation's future.

Nicholas I realized that reforms were needed. He knew that serfdom had to be abolished, but he was afraid to act. He was too fearful of the conflict and confusion that might follow when more than twenty million serfs were suddenly freed. Nicholas became known as the "Iron Tsar" because he struck down any rebellion.

The Hermitage in Leningrad was built between 1754 and 1762 as a winter palace for the tsars. Later three annexes were added to house the royal art collections. In 1852 Nicholas I opened the Hermitage to the public, and today it is one of the world's finest art museums.

A terrorist bomb kills Alexander II. This reform-minded tsar introduced unprecedented liberties to the Russian people. In the 36 years after Alexander's death, his son and grandson returned to the repressive ways of earlier tsars, leading ultimately to a revolution.

When Nicholas died in 1855, his son Alexander II (1855–1881) came to the throne. Alexander had the courage to do what his father dared not try. In 1861 he gave the serfs their freedom and thereby earned the title of "Tsar Liberator." This was two years before Abraham Lincoln issued the Emancipation Proclamation in the United States.

The abolition of serfdom created some problems. For example, land had to be provided for the freed peasants. Nevertheless, the changeover went quite well. Alexander II was assassinated by a revolutionary in 1881. During his reign he had been busy with reforms. On the day he was killed, he was planning to sign a new law introducing representative government for the Russian people.

Alexander's son was Alexander III (1881–1894). Rejecting his father's reforms, he returned to autocratic ways. He was determined to crush all liberal and protest movements, but he did not restore serfdom. At the same time factories and railroads were being built, providing jobs for many of the former serfs. An educated class to whom ideas of freedom and equality might appeal continued to grow. It was clear that an explosive situation was developing.

Tsardom comes to an end. When Alexander died in 1894, his son was crowned the new ruler. Nicholas II (1894–1917) was destined to be Russia's last tsar. He was a man of weak character who lacked an understanding of events around him. He was determined to be an old-fashioned autocratic tsar. His strong-willed wife, Tsarina Alexandra, reinforced his determination with the aid of Rasputin, an unscrupulous and power-hungry monk.

In 1905 Russia suffered a humiliating defeat in the Russo-Japanese War (p. 000). Under pressure Nicholas made a few concessions, such as the creation of a parliament called the *Duma*. But he also tried to preserve much of the old autocratic system.

Reviewing Your Reading

1. How did Peter the Great westernize Russia and expand its territory?
2. Describe Catherine the Great's accomplishments.
3. How did the Russian nobility live during the eighteenth century?
4. Who were the Decembrists?
5. Why was Alexander II called the Tsar Liberator?
6. What were social conditions in Russia like when Nicholas II came to power?

Russia in the Twentieth Century: A Vast Empire

In the early twentieth century, Russia was a vast empire larger than the Soviet Union is today. From a small state around Moscow the nation had grown into an empire extending from the Baltic Sea to the Pacific Ocean. How had this happened?

The Russians began to move into Siberia in the sixteenth century when the *Cossacks,* poor peasants and pioneers, followed their leader, Yermak, to Siberia on an expedition of conquest in 1581. By 1644 the Russians had explored the Amur (ah-*moor'*) River, bordering Manchuria, a Chinese province. At this time China was a prosperous and mighty empire. Russia and China established diplomatic and trade relations through the Treaty of Nerchinsk in 1689. It provided that China would control both sides of the Amur River as well as Mongolia. Both sides were satisfied with the treaty at the time.

During the mid-nineteenth century, China was a far weaker nation than it had been 200 years earlier. European nations scrambled to take advantage of its weakness, demanding territorial concessions of all kinds. Ignoring the Treaty of Nerchinsk, the Russians moved into Chinese territory. In 1858 the Chinese were forced to sign the Treaty of Peking, which allowed the Russians to annex the Amur River region. Two years later China had to give up more territory, accepting the Ussuri River as the new boundary. The Russians built the city of Vladivostok on land that had always been Chinese territory.

Russians take the Caucasus region. In contrast to the ease with which the Russians occupied Siberia, the southern regions around the Black and Caspian seas were much harder to conquer. These territories were held by Turkey and Persia. The inhabitants were mainly Georgians and Armenians. The Russians found them to be tough fighters, and only after a long struggle was this area conquered. Russian control was recognized by the Treaty of Adrianople in 1829.

The greatest engineering feat of tsarist Russia was the building of the Trans-Siberian Railroad across the entire length of Russia and Siberia. It aided in the development of Siberia and helped unify the nation. Construction began in 1891 and was completed to Vladivostok and Port Arthur by 1903.

Annexation of central Asia. From Peter the Great's time, Russians were interested in central Asia. On a modern map of the Soviet Union, this area lies east of the Caspian Sea and extends to the Chinese border. Encountering bitter resistance at times, the Russians gained control of central Asia between 1865 and 1885. The British finally halted the Russian advance. Worried about the safety of India, Britain first gained control of Afghanistan. Britain informed the Russians that it would defend the northern border of that country. Russian expansion southward came to an end.

The sale of Alaska. After the Russians had colonized Siberia, their ships reached Alaska in 1741. Soon afterward, the Russians moved southward along the Pacific coast until they reached California. British and, later, American protests finally persuaded them to withdraw to the north. In Alaska the Russians established settlements and developed a fur trade.

In 1869 the Russian government sold Alaska to the United States for $7,200,000. Russia was having troubles in Europe and needed money badly. Moreover, fur trading in Alaska had become less profitable. Although President Andrew Johnson was much criticized for buying a vast area of "snowdrifts and icebergs," it was the greatest bargain for the United States since the Louisiana Purchase.

Reviewing Your Reading

1. Trace relations between China and Russia over the last 400 years.
2. Why did the Russians wish to gain control of the Caucasus region?
3. Why did Russian expansion southward stop?
4. Why did the Russian government sell Alaska?

World War I and the Revolution

By 1914 when World War I began, the Russian army had already fought in one major conflict, the Russo-Japanese War (1904–1905), and had helped restore order after the Revolution of 1905. The further suffering experienced during World War I increased dissatisfaction in the army; as a result, many soldiers became revolutionaries in 1917.

War comes to Russia in 1914. Before the outbreak of World War I the major European nations were divided into two alliance systems. Britain, France, Russia, and Serbia were on one side and Germany, Austria-Hungary, and Italy on the other. Serbia was a small state which later became part of Yugoslavia. When a Serbian nationalist murdered Archduke Francis Ferdinand of Austria in June 1914, the Austrians moved to punish Serbia, and war began.

The Russian armies achieved some success against Austria-Hungary, but when Germany turned its troops against the Russians, the armies of the tsar suffered one disaster after another. Russian soldiers fought bravely; however, they were so poorly supplied that by 1917 about 30 percent of them had no rifles. Russia's transportation system was inadequate to supply its armies. Disaster at the front and poor management in the government badly damaged the prestige of the tsar.

The Revolution begins. By early 1917 food supplies were running low. When people began rioting for food in March, troops sent to control the mobs joined the rioters. The rioters caused the government to collapse, and Nicholas II gave up his throne. The Duma attempted to carry on by establishing a Provisional Government. This group also began to lay plans for some kind of democratic government while continuing to fight the war.

The common people, however, were fed up with the war. Many soldiers deserted the army and returned home. The Bolsheviks, who were the radical wing of the Social Democratic Party, seized this opportunity to lead the crowds. They adopted the slogan of "Peace, Land, and Bread."

Lenin takes over. In April the leader of the Bolsheviks, Vladimir Ulyanov (1870–1924), returned to Russia from exile in Switzerland. He had earlier adopted the name "Lenin" to conceal his identity from the tsarist police. He called for immediate peace with Germany and land for the peasants.

In the following months the Provisional Government tried to carry on the war against Germany, but conditions at the front deteriorated. Moreover, peasants seized land, and workers took over factories. By October Lenin was convinced that the Bolsheviks could seize power. They organized the workers and the soldiers in the chief cities, attacked the Provisional Government, and took over in early November 1917. Lenin took power in the name of the *Soviets* – councils representing the workers, soldiers, and peasants. The Soviets had first been formed in the Revolution of 1905 and were re-established in 1917 after the fall of the tsar. Lenin declared that peace would be arranged immediately and the new government would begin to carry out a socialist revolution. Lenin headed the new government. He won the support of the peasants by telling them they could keep the land they had recently seized.

Lenin addresses a crowd in Moscow's Red Square.

A harsh peace with Germany. The Communist party, as the Bolsheviks now began to call themselves, controlled the Soviet government and most of the country. It secured peace with Germany in March 1918, when it signed the Treaty of Brest-Litovsk.

The terms were harsh, and the Russians were asked to give up much territory. The Soviet leaders accepted the treaty because they wanted to retain power in Russia and to avoid German occupation of all of western Russia. Lenin believed that Europe would soon be swept by communist revolutions, so the treaty really would not matter for long. Actually the terms of the treaty lasted only a few months because Germany was defeated in 1918 by the Western Allies.

Little force was necessary to overthrow the tsarist government. The old system practically collapsed from lack of support and the burden of the war. But a major conflict began in the summer of 1918 between the supporters of the Soviet government, the "Reds," and those who opposed the Communists, the "Whites." This civil war lasted until 1921. Before it was over millions were killed or suffered great hardships. The White forces included supporters of the old system – nobles, intellectuals, former landowners, and many officers of the tsarist army. At times both Reds and Whites had to struggle with such non-Russian nationality groups as the Latvians, Ukrainians, Georgians, and Uzbeks, who were fighting to establish greater freedom or, in some cases, full political independence for themselves. The Western Allies supported the Whites out of fear that if the Reds won, communism might spread to the rest of Europe.

The White Army was widely scattered and lacked plans for the future of the nation. By contrast, Lenin offered an economic and political program to the nation, while his associate, Leon Trotsky, built up a strong Red Army. This combination finally won the struggle.

In July 1918, Nicholas II, Alexandra, and their five children were taken to Ekaterinburg (now called Sverdlovsk). When the civil war began, the Reds feared that the royal family might be rescued. To prevent that from happening, they were executed.

The Red Army is victorious. By 1921 civil war in Russia was over. The Reds had won, but the nation was severely damaged by the conflict. The people were hungry and weary of war, but Lenin and the Communist party were in firm control.

The government's immediate task was to deal with famine and the threat of anarchy. Long-range programs of communism had to be postponed until the immediate problems of survival were solved. Between 1914 and 1921 twenty million people lost their lives as a result of the fighting, executions, famine, and epidemics. The condition of the nation required Lenin's full attention.

One of the new government's first tasks was reorganizing the state structure and establishing relations with the non-Russian peoples who had not succeeded in becoming independent. Only the Finns, Estonians, Latvians, Lithuanians, and Poles were able to set up separate states.

The government's approach to this task was to divide the country into a union of republics which were, in theory, independent of one another. The first of these republics was the Russian Soviet Federated Socialist Republic (RSFSR). To this were added three other states under the control of the Communist Party – the Ukrainian Soviet Socialist Republic, the Byelorussian SSR, and a Caucasian SSR, which was later subdivided into Georgian, Armenian, and Azerbaijan SSR's. All were declared a part of the Union of Soviet Socialist Republics (USSR). As we saw in Chapter 40, the number of Soviet Socialist Republics has grown to fifteen.

Stalin succeeds Lenin as dictator. In January 1924, Lenin died from a stroke. Two men competed for his position. One was Leon Trotsky, creator of the Red Army. Joseph Dzhugashvili (1879–1953), better known as Joseph Stalin, was his rival. Stalin, whose name meant "steel," was a revolutionary imprisoned many times for his anti-government activities. Lenin did not like Stalin very much and felt that he was not the man to lead the country.

Stalin won the struggle for leadership, forcing Trotsky to go into exile. Trotsky was hounded for years by Stalin's agents and finally assassinated in Mexico City in 1940. The two men disagreed because of their political beliefs. Trotsky felt the Soviet Union should encourage worldwide revolutions immediately. Stalin maintained that the revolution first must be completely successful in Russia before it could be spread elsewhere.

In 1934 Sergei Kirov, the Leningrad party secretary, was assassinated. He was an important government official, considered by many as Stalin's second-in-command. Many believed Stalin ordered the assassination because he feared Kirov's influence. The death of Kirov set in motion a reign of terror called the "Great Purge," which began in 1935 and lasted four years. Thousands were executed or imprisoned, charged with treason and plotting to overthrow the government to restore capitalism. How much truth there was to these charges no one knows. Somehow those accused were persuaded to confess to the charges.

> **Marxist-Leninist Philosophy**
>
> Lenin's dream was to bring about a communist world revolution. Taking the philosophy of the German philosophers Karl Marx and Friedrich Engels, he revised it to make it applicable to conditions in Russia in the twentieth century. The blend that resulted is described as Marxist-Leninism.
>
> Marx thought that revolution would come only when most of a nation's people were proletarians, laborers of the lowest class. The workers could then seize power and establish a "dictatorship of the proletariat." Unlike Marx, Lenin believed that revolution could be carried out by a small group of dedicated revolutionaries, thoroughly disciplined and loyal to the cause. Revolutionary leaders need not wait for a country to become industrialized. In his writings Marx never stressed the importance of peasants in a revolution. In applying Marxist theory to his own country, Lenin saw that the support of the peasants was quite necessary to the success of the revolution.
>
> Unlike Marx, Lenin believed that revolution should be a worldwide effort. He was convinced that the struggle between communism and capitalism would be fought throughout the world. His theory was that capitalism, the private ownership of the means of production, naturally leads to imperialism, the control by one country over other, less-powerful countries. He felt that the dominated countries and colonies would be most likely to respond to the call for world revolution.

Joseph Stalin

By the time the Great Purge ended in 1939, most of the important officials in the government and the armed forces were eliminated. In the end even those whom Stalin ordered to carry out the purges were executed, notably Nicholas Yezhov, head of the secret police. Some believe that the purges ended in 1939 because the nation was greatly weakened by the fear that gripped the country and the loss of efficiency in the economy.

Although the reasons for the purge are not fully understood, many believe that Stalin feared a conspiracy against him. There were important people who did not agree with his policies. The mass execution of high officials removed most of the people likely to challenge him.

World War II and the Postwar Period

In Germany in 1933 the National Socialist Workers' Party, called the Nazi Party, became powerful under the leadership of Adolph Hitler. The Nazis were determined to gain control of Europe. The Soviet leaders feared that their homeland might be invaded. They increased their production of military supplies to be prepared.

As the threat of war increased, Stalin and Hitler made an agreement in August, 1939. They pledged they would not go to war against each other, and they divided Poland between them. Although the rest of the world was shocked by this agreement, both the Soviet and the Nazi leaders felt they gained by this understanding. Hitler did not have to worry about an attack from the east, and Stalin gained territory westward toward Europe and time to improve his defenses.

World War II breaks out. Hitler began the war by attacking Poland on September 1, 1939, while Stalin's forces invaded Poland from the east. The Soviet Union then demanded and got military bases in the three small Baltic countries of Estonia, Latvia, and Lithuania. However, when Stalin made similar demands on Finland, the Finns refused. They were willing to grant some requests but not all of them. Early in December 1939 the Soviet Union attacked Finland by land and air. To the world's amazement the Finns stopped the invasion for three months. Finally, exhausted by the endless Soviet attacks, the Finns were forced to surrender. They had to give some of their territory to the Soviet Union, but they preserved their independence. Such was not the case with the Baltic states. In 1940 the Soviet Union annexed Estonia, Latvia, and Lithuania.

Hitler invades the Soviet Union. The German army invaded in June 1941. In a few weeks the Germans drove deep into Russia, and in November they were within forty miles of Moscow. They also reached the outskirts of Leningrad and occupied most of the Ukraine.

Just as in Napoleon's invasion, the Soviet army slowly retreated, trading space for time. As in 1812 the Russians followed a "scorched earth" policy, destroying anything that would be useful to the enemy. When the terrible Russian winter began in November, the Germans, like the French earlier, were slowed down. Then the Russians counter-attacked, aided by guerrilla bands in the rear of the German lines.

In 1942 the German armies continued their advances, however, until they reached Stalingrad on the Volga River. A tremendous struggle took place which completely destroyed the city. But the Russians surrounded a German army there and stopped the German offensive.

The German army's failure to take Moscow and Stalingrad marked the turning point of the German invasion. Soviet counter-attacks became more and more effective, and the Germans began a long retreat. In June 1944 the Western Allies invaded France, which had fallen to the Nazis in 1940, and began a steady advance eastward. The Russians drove the Germans out of the Soviet Union and advanced on Berlin. The Germans surrendered in May 1945. The war in Europe came to an end, but at a tremendous cost.

The Soviet Union suffered enormous losses. More than 20 million people lost their lives. Close to 2000 cities and towns and over 70,000 villages were destroyed along with bridges, dams, mines, and factories. In spite of these losses the Soviet Union emerged as a major world power. It began setting up Communist-controlled governments in the countries of Eastern Europe. With Germany defeated and other nations weakened by war, the Soviet Union assumed a powerful position in world affairs.

Soviet leadership in the postwar years. After the war Stalin continued his dictatorial rule. Upon his death in 1953 a struggle for power developed among the top leaders. Georgi Malenkov (mah-lyen-*kawv'*) exercised leadership briefly. He was soon replaced by Nikita Khrushchev and Nikolai Bulganin (bool-*gah*'neen), who shared power for a short while. Gradually Khrushchev took control and assumed top leadership until he was ousted in October 1964.

Khrushchev was a colorful personality. After many years of rule by Stalin, who seemed sinister and withdrawn, many found the sociable and talkative Khrushchev a welcome change. More important, he denounced the cruelty and terror of Stalin's rule. The Soviet people could live their lives with less fear.

While in office Khrushchev was quoted as saying that if a nuclear war broke out it would be so terrible that the "living would envy the dead." Because such a war would be a disaster for the entire world, Khrushchev advocated a policy of "peaceful coexistence." While the final goal of Soviet foreign policy remained the eventual victory of communism over capitalism, the Soviet leader wanted this to be achieved without the risk of nuclear war. Any means short of war — economic competition, propaganda, and shrewd diplomacy — would be used to bring about a Communist victory.

With less fear of the government the people began to demand a higher standard of living. After long years of sacrifice they felt they deserved a better life. Under Khrushchev the Soviet Union continued to invest heavily in armaments, space technology, and heavy industry. Nevertheless, the demand for consumer goods could not be entirely ignored. More and better clothing, appliances, and housing were produced.

Khrushchev was removed from office by other top Communist leaders because some of his programs failed. His most serious failure was in agriculture. He could not fulfill his promise to raise enough food to catch up with the United States. In 1962 he tried to install missiles in Cuba and had to back down when the United States threatened to take strong action. Accused of "hare-brained schemes," he was dismissed and allowed to retire to his country home where he remained until his death in 1971.

The Brezhnev years. After Khruschev's removal, a period of collective leadership followed. Leonid Brezhnev became first secretary of the Communist party. Aleksei Kosygin (koh-*see*'ghin) became premier. Both men were described as "colorless technocrats." They came up through the party ranks in the years after the Revolution. Working quietly and more closely with the Soviet bureaucracy, they provided less of the dynamic and even flamboyant leadership associated with Khrushchev and Stalin.

In 1977 Brezhnev was elected chairman of the Presidium of the Supreme Soviet and emerged as the nation's central leader. He continued Khrushchev's policy of improving the Soviet standard of living. Relaxation of some economic controls in the areas of consumer products and farm ownership has not been accompanied by greater freedoms for the arts, the news media, or the intellectuals. The generation that has grown up since World War II has demanded greater freedom of expression, the right to travel abroad, and other rights enjoyed in the West. Communist leaders have not responded to these demands from citizens.

During the Brezhnev era the Soviet leaders showed more interest in foreign affairs and overseas trade. Under Stalin's leadership the Soviet Union had been more isolated from the rest of the world. At the time of his death in November 1982, Brezhnev had been head of the Soviet Union for eighteen years. Only Stalin had led the country for a longer period of time. Under Brezhnev's leader-

Leonid Brezhnev

ship the standard of living improved for most Soviet workers. But there was a slowdown in the overall growth of the nation's economy.

The next two Soviet leaders were old – and ailing – men who together served hardly more than two years. Yuri Andropov died fifteen months after taking over from Brezhnev. Then Konstantin Chernenko won the top post, but he died a year later in March 1985.

This time the Politburo saw its youngest member become head of the party and the government. Mikhail Gorbachev (*gor'ba choff*) at age 54 was the youngest top Soviet leader in fifty years. Experts saw the personable Gorbachev as a symbol of change from the Old Guard who had served the nation so long.

Mikhail Gorbachev

Reviewing Your Reading

1. Trace the events leading to Lenin's takeover of the government.
2. Why did the Soviet government sign the Treaty of Brest-Litovsk?
3. Why were the Reds victorious in the civil war?
4. How did Stalin's and Trotsky's political views differ?
5. Why did Stalin and Hitler sign a treaty in 1939?
6. Describe the German invasion of the Soviet Union.
7. How did Khrushchev's leadership differ from Stalin's?
8. Name the four top Soviet leaders who followed Khrushchev.

CHAPTER REVIEW

Recalling Names and Places

Amur River	Mikhail Gorbachev	Reds and Whites
autocracy	Nikita Khrushchev	Mikhail Romanov
Bolsheviks	legal serfdom	Joseph Stalin
boyars	Lenin	Tatars
Leonid Brezhnev	Mongols	Trans-Siberian Railroad
Catherine the Great	Nicholas II	Treaty of Brest-Litovsk
debt serfdom	Nihilists	Leon Trotsky
Decembrists		

Understanding This Chapter

1. How did religion affect the early political development of Russia? Did it have lasting effects?
2. Russians are often called *xenophobic* (suspicious of foreigners). How might the experience of Tatar rule and the "Time of Troubles" have developed this trait?
3. Does Catherine II deserve to be called "the Great"?
4. Can you see a link between repeated invasions of Russia, like those of Napoleon and Hitler, and modern Russian expansionism? Why or why not?
5. Tsarist Russia could not prevent the diffusion of outside ideas. What nineteenth-century ideals began to undermine the old way of life?
6. Distinguish between the Russian Revolution and the civil war that followed. Why was the civil war a much harder struggle?
7. Since nuclear war would be a disaster for everyone, Khruschev said world communism would be achieved by peaceful means. How did he plan to do this?

CHAPTER 42

Social Life in a Soviet Society

More than a hundred nationalities live within the Soviet Union. The customs of these groups vary greatly. However, since Russians and Ukrainians with very similar customs comprise more than two-thirds of the population, this chapter concentrates on the social customs, religious practices, and social organization of these groups.

Russians are by far the largest nationality group and have the most power. Although local languages are tolerated, the Russian language is taught in all schools and is the official language. Many non-Russian regions have been heavily colonized by Russians. As a result, many things throughout the Soviet Union are done in the Russian way.

Tsarist Society Had Rigid Social Divisions

We usually think of India when we think of a caste system. In such a society people must remain members of the caste into which they were born. On the other hand, in an open-class society like the United States, people may be able to move up to a higher class if they have ability and determination and are given enough opportunities to improve their life situation.

Tsarist Russia fell between these two degrees of social stratification. Its social system allowed very few opportunities for people to improve their social position, particularly during the period when serfdom was legal. Peasants could escape from the lower class but such cases were rare.

Peasants held the lowest position in society. As we noted earlier, the vast majority of the people were peasants in the nineteenth century, and before 1861 most were serfs. Serfs belonged to the estate on which they worked. If the estate was sold, they went with the property as did the cattle, pigs, and tools. Generation after generation of children followed in their parents' footsteps.

The nobility and the small group of wealthy manufacturers and merchants belonged to the upper class. In many ways they lived in a different world from that of the peasants. Life was comfortable, and servants attended to every need. But just as the peasants' life was predictable so was that of the nobles. They, too, would follow in their parents' footsteps.

The priesthood was another division in tsarist Russia. Two groups of priests existed. The black priests were the higher clergy who did not marry. The majority were the white priests. They did the regular parish work, married, and usually had large families. These priests could only marry daughters of priests. The eldest son of a priest was expected to become a priest. In that way the class continued.

Although life for the nobility seemed unchanging, by 1850 social changes were beginning to set the stage for the Revolution of 1917. The development of industry did not at first seem to endanger the old social system. Many of the industrial workers were serfs rented out to factory owners. However, other workers were free and lived in the cities. Although they were usually as poor as the serfs, the workers were later to join with the growing professional class in the cities to overthrow the tsar.

Few Russians liked the bureaucracy. Many Russian writers of the nineteenth century, notably Gogol, described the government bureaucracy of the tsars as a vast, inefficient organization with little interest in serving the people. Similar charges frequently appear in the newspapers of the Soviet Union today.

Peter the Great, more than anyone else, helped to found the Russian bureaucracy. He hoped to provide opportunities for citizens in government service.

The Russian nobility of the nineteenth century lived in a different world from that of the peasants — a world full of waiting servants, huge estates, and lavish entertainments.

Therefore, in 1722 he established what was called a "Table of Ranks," which consisted of fourteen classifications of positions in both civil and military services.

Admission to these various levels of government service gave a person prestige and power. Often the honor made these officeholders arrogant toward common people. Hence they were often hated and feared. They were attacked by writers in books and sometimes attacked physically by the common people.

The intelligentsia "rock the boat." The real threat to the system came in the last half of the nineteenth century from a group known as the *intelligentsia*. These people were intellectuals critical of Russian society. They opposed the authoritarian rule of the tsars and resented the oppression of the Russian peasant by the Russian nobility. Many intellectuals were the children of nobles or priests. They had traveled widely, becoming familiar with the outside world. The intelligentsia called for social changes, including the abolition of the monarchy.

Most people paid no attention to the intelligentsia, because few could read or understand what they were talking about. The tsar's secret police, however, understood only too well. Whenever possible, they seized these agitators, executing some and sending others to Siberia. Nevertheless, the writings of this small group started a reform movement that was eventually to transform Russian life completely.

The Traditional Russian Family

The Revolution brought many changes in the family. Equality between husbands and wives is emphasized today, although some earlier customs are still preserved in rural areas. In the past families were usually large. They were extended families, consisting of husband, wife, and their unmarried children, plus married sons and their wives and children.

The traditional Russian family was strongly patriarchal. Guides such as the *Domostroy* (p. 481) instructed men to be stern fathers and husbands.

Fear and respect toward the father and obedience from the wife and children were all important. Fathers were counseled not to be too strict but to use a whip on disobedient wives and children.

In the last half of the nineteenth century a poor peasant often left his family in the village and got a job in a factory to earn enough money to pay his taxes. In these situations the mother usually took the role of head of the family.

Fathers arranged marriages. Before the Revolution, fathers arranged marriages. A father with a son of marriageable age would reach an agreement with a father of an eligible daughter. Often the young people had nothing to say about the arrangement.

Among the nobility, merchant class, and the more prosperous peasants, property was important in marriages. The size of a girl's dowry and possible land to be gained through marriage were discussed at great length before agreement was reached. Among the poor peasants property was not important in arranging marriages because most peasants had none.

The intelligentsia attacked the emphasis on property in marriages and the authority of the father in the family. They argued that young people should have the right to decide their own marriage partners and that divorce ought to be permitted. The Revolution's leaders were familiar with the ideas of the intelligentsia and enacted many of their suggestions when they came to power.

Cramped quarters. The nobility lived in palaces, sometimes having hundreds of rooms. Today many of these buildings are art museums, and the visitor is dazzled by their elaborate interiors. Gilded designs and paintings decorate the ceilings, and magnificent marble staircases are reminders of the luxurious life the nobility had in tsarist times.

Peasant families were large, and three generations often lived under one roof – the peasant couple, their unmarried children, and their married sons with their families.

The majority of the people crowded into humble houses. Each peasant home had one large room where everyone lived. In one corner was an enormous stone or brick stove which took up about a third of the space. This heated the building

---

A Family Code

In the sixteenth century a guide to family living called the Domostroy *was compiled. The name means "Household Book" or "Household Code." Among other things it advised husbands and fathers on the supervision of their families. As the following excerpts reveal, the father expected respect and obedience from members of the family:*

How to instruct children and save them by fear: In his early years and he will comfort you in your old age. Do not spare your child any beating, for the stick will not kill him but do him good. When you strike the body, you save the soul from death. . . . If you love your son, punish him often so that he may later gladden your spirit. . . . Raise your child in fear and you will find peace and blessing in him.

How to keep your house clean and well ordered: In a good family, where the wife is careful, the house is always clean and well-arranged. . . . All this is the wife's job; she must instruct the servants and children in a friendly manner or in harsh: If words don't help, let blows do the job. . . . If she completes and does everything as it should be done, she deserves love and favor; but if she fails . . . let her husband discipline her and scare her in private. . . . But if wife, son, or daughter pay no heed to word or instruction, if they will not listen, obey, and fear, if they refuse to do what they are told by father or mother, they should be whipped according to their offense. . . .

In no circumstance should you beat on the ear or face or in the midriff with your fist or foot, nor strike with a stick or any wooden or metal instrument. Such blows struck in anger or rage may cause great harm: blindness, deafness, dislocation of arm or leg or finger, injury to head or teeth. The whip should be used wisely, in a painful, frightening, and profitable manner. . . .

Marthe Blinoff, *Life and Thought in Old Russia* (University Park: The Pennsylvania State University Press, 1961), pp. 35–36.

Life for the peasant in pre-revolutionary Russia was physically exhausting. The peasant's earnings were eaten away by heavy taxes for the tsar. Here a peasant woman carries water from a well.

and cooked the food. During the bitter cold winters the family slept as close to the stove as possible. Shelves below the ceiling and a wooden platform hung by ropes provided warm places to sleep, especially for the children. Curtains hung as room dividers provided a little privacy.

The typical peasant home had little furniture. Usually benches lined the walls. A table was in one corner. A spinning wheel and perhaps a loom made up the rest of the furniture. An image of a saint with a lamp burning under it was a common feature. Windows were few and small to keep out the cold.

In the winter, animals were brought indoors to prevent them from freezing to death. Smaller animals like chickens and pigs stayed with the peasants in their houses. More prosperous peasants had a lower level to the house where these animals and perhaps a cow were kept.

Scattered individual farms like those found in the United States were not customary in Russia. Families usually lived close to their neighbors in small villages. The heads of all the families in a village formed an organization called the village commune, or *mir* (meer), which regulated village life. The tsarist government levied taxes on the village, and the mir distributed the taxes among the families of the village. The mir also divided any available land among the villagers.

> **Survival in a Cold Climate**
>
> *Winters are long in the Soviet Union. Wright Miller, who knows the Soviet Union well, has described the Russian winter:*
>
> In the worst weather it is so cold that it seems to burn. You launch yourself out of double doors into the street and you gasp. You narrow your shrinking nostrils to give your lungs a chance to get acclimatized, but you gasp again and go on gasping. Ears are well covered against frostbite, but eyebrows and moustache grow icicles in bunches. . . . Another moment, surely, and the whole nostril will freeze over; in a panic you warm your nose with your glove, but the nostrils do not freeze, and you go on warming your nose and stinging cheeks with your glove, and you go on gasping. Half an hour's walk gives you the exercise of an ordinary afternoon.
>
> How does one protect himself in such a climate? Considerations of fashion and style are no longer important . . . nothing will keep frostbite from your toes except the clumsy felt boots called *valenki*. These are simply right-angled tubes of felt closed at one end, and you must wear them several sizes too big, after you have first wrapped your feet and legs in strips of cloth. . . . For short journeys goloshes pulled over shoes will do, and some people stretch outsize goloshes over the feet of their *valenki,* not to keep out the wet, except for a short period in spring and autumn, but to keep out the cold. . . . The only effective alternative to *valenki* are the soft skin boots worn with the fur inside – a Siberian invention called *oonty*.
>
> *The gray and dreary days of winter finally give way to the bright promise of spring. After the long cold months, this is a joyous time. Now it is possible to give some thought to fashion.*
>
> From the book *Russians as People* by Wright Miller. Copyright, ©, 1960 by Wright Miller. Published by E. P. Dutton & Co., Inc.

Religion in Tsarist Russia

After Constantinople fell in 1453, the tsars gained greater control over the Russian Orthodox Church. By the time of Peter the Great the Church had become a servant of the tsar. The government appointed important church officials and gave them financial support.

Church officials were expected to support the government. Priests reported to the police anyone suspected of disloyalty. Members of the secret police sometimes dressed as priests and heard confession. In this way the Church aided the government's ability to watch and arrest anyone considered dangerous to those in power. Moreover, the Church did not criticize Russian society nor discuss serious social problems.

Many members of the intelligentsia left the Church because they disapproved of the priests' loyalty to the tsar. Leo Tolstoy, the great nineteenth-century writer, was a very devout Christian. He helped numerous poor peasants, but finally left the Church. Others strongly criticized organized religion, contributing to the Communists' later hostility toward it.

For the common people, however, the Church was a tremendous comfort. They could not read and knew little about the Scriptures. The *icons,* (paintings of religious scenes on small wooden panels), rituals, and music made them feel close to God. Life frequently contained so much hardship and suffering that the Church offered great comfort to the average peasant.

Reviewing Your Reading

1. Describe the class system in tsarist society.
2. Who were the intelligentsia?
3. Who arranged marriages?
4. Describe the mir and the living conditions of the peasants.
5. What role did the Russian Orthodox Church play in government and in the lives of the peasants?

Life in the Soviet Union

When the Communists came to power, they wanted to create a "classless society." They tried to make all citizens equal to one another. All titles and class distinctions were abolished. People called each other "comrade," and women were to have full and equal rights. Efforts were also made to reduce discipline in the schools and factories. But it was soon realized that some discipline and different rates of pay for different levels of work were necessary if people were to be encouraged to do their best.

In tsarist times little mobility of any kind existed. Classes were clearly defined and few people had new job or educational opportunities. Although the opportunities of the Soviet people are greater today, traces of the old social system remain.

Soviet education. Perhaps the greatest Soviet achievement has been the almost total elimination of illiteracy in less than fifty years with a basic education of ten years available to all. In the fifth grade, students begin an intensive study of a foreign language, most often English, which they continue for at least six years. In the university they learn other languages. Russian young people show remarkable command of at least one foreign language. In 60 percent of the schools, instruction is in Russian. The rest use local languages but Russian is a compulsory subject.

The other areas of great strength in Soviet education are the sciences and mathematics. By the time students complete seventh grade, they have had algebra and geometry as well as biology, chemistry, and physics. By the time they are eighth graders, they know more science and mathematics than most American high school graduates.

Perhaps the greatest weakness of Soviet education is in the social sciences. History, economics, political science, and sociology are taught in accord with

A doctor teaches a class of physicians. In 1972, 60 percent of the Soviet Union's physicians were women. This compared with 10 percent in the United States.

the writings of Marx and Lenin. Propaganda against the "evils" of the capitalist world distorts the teaching of all the social studies. Truly open and free study in this field is impossible in the Soviet Union at the present time.

To qualify for the highest positions, one must have a university degree. Because far more students seek university entrance than can be admitted, competition is very intense. In a recent year, for example, university openings existed for only one-fifth of the applicants.

Efforts are made to encourage applications from children of workers and peasants, but inevitably those whose fathers are professionals, government workers, or members of the Communist party have an advantage. Young people from small towns or rural areas have difficulty getting a place. Limitations on the educational opportunities open to peasants have created new social distinctions.

The Revolution changed family life. Following the Revolution the Communist leaders believed that most people would be more loyal to their families than to the government. They wanted to weaken the family as much as possible.

Marriage and divorce laws were simplified. Except for regulations on minimum age and restrictions against marriage between close relatives, marriage was permissible. Originally men had to be eighteen and women sixteen to wed. Later both had to be eighteen. The government opposed church weddings, and government offices became the site for marriage ceremonies. Obtaining a divorce became simpler. If either the husband or wife wanted a divorce, it could

485

be granted for any reason or no reason at all. A man did not even have to notify his wife directly, or a woman her husband. A postcard mailed to the proper office was enough. Few restrictions existed; the partner earning the higher income paid alimony for child support. The divorce rate spiraled, and in some cities more divorces took place than marriages. Lax marriage and divorce laws continued until 1935. Since then stricter regulations have been in effect, and the family has been emphasized as an important social unit, even in a communist society. New laws passed in 1935 ended easy divorces. One could still get a divorce, but the procedure became more difficult and expensive. Before a divorce was granted, social workers first offered marriage counseling to help the husband and wife reconcile their differences.

In the early years of revolutionary fervor, the Soviet government planned to have all children cared for in government nurseries and schools, while the men and women worked on the farms and in the factories. Morever, separate kitchens were to be eliminated, and all the people on a collective farm or factory would eat at one big dining hall. They would use a common kitchen. Instead of separate family units, a large number of families would live together on what was called a *commune*. However, the communal system was never fully realized because the government was unable to provide enough kitchens, laundries, nurseries, and other facilities to make it possible. In 1933 the idea was finally rejected as unworkable. The Chinese Communists tried to institute a similar system in China in the 1950s (page 308) with limited success.

Men and women declared equal. Following the earlier thinking of the intelligentsia, a strong emphasis was placed on insuring equality between men and women: All the rules discriminating against women were swept away. Women were no longer barred from any occupation, and soon they were driving tractors, handling steam shovels, and laying bricks. Women doing these jobs are a common sight in Moscow, Leningrad, and other cities today. Women also became highly skilled professionals. About 70 percent of Soviet doctors are women as are a large percentage of the lawyers.

Equality of men and women became more necessary after World War II, when the Soviet Union found itself with far more women than men. Because of the Revolution, civil war, and other disasters in the 1920s and 1930s there were already fewer men than women when the Soviet Union entered World War II in 1941. Since many more men than women were killed in the war, the Soviet Union had the greatest surplus of females of any nation in the world when the war ended in 1945. To rebuild and repair the damage caused by World War II, the women had to do much of the job.

Decline of the extended family. Although extended families still exist among Russians and the other nationality groups, their number has declined. Reasons for this change are numerous.

During the 1920s and 1930s Stalin ordered rural inhabitants to join collective farms, and many people were forced out of their villages. Consequently families were broken up. Because the prosperous peasants, called *kulaks,* were especially opposed to losing their lands, they were dealt with brutally. At least a million kulak families became scattered throughout the Soviet Union; many of them were sent to labor camps. Family members were often permanently separated.

Newlyweds in Moscow traditionally travel to Red Square to have their picture taken next to Lenin's tomb.

    The Nazis occupied huge areas of the western Soviet Union during World War II. Millions of people fled before their advance and resettled elsewhere. After the war other resettlements took place. These population movements broke up numerous families.

    Since World War II many people have moved from rural areas to cities. Moreover, the creation of many new cities during the past few decades has required the movement of thousands of people to these new centers. Because city apartments are very small – usually only two rooms – families larger than the husband, wife, and children cannot be provided for. Consequently the small nuclear family is becoming typical.

> ### "What's in a Name?"
>
> It is customary for Russians to address a person by his first name and a possessive form of his father's first name. Last names are used for formal purposes, but not among friends. Boris Ivanovich Surikov is not addressed as "Comrade Surikov" except in a formal situation. As soon as two people became acquainted, they exchange first names and their father's first names. When Surikov informs his acquaintance that his name is Boris and his father's name is Ivan, he is promptly addressed as "Boris Ivanovich" (Ivan's son Boris). Boris' sister might be addressed as "Tanya Ivanovna." Even government officials may be addressed in this fashion. Thus, Leonid Brezhnev was called "Leonid Ilyich," and Aleksei Kosygin was called "Aleksei Nikolaevich." The Russians like to use the first name and the *patronymic*, the form for indicating the father's name. The custom implies a warmth and acceptance of a fellow human being into one's circle. Even foreigners are quickly included in this fashion.

Limited housing has had another important effect. The birth rate is steadily dropping, and some Soviet officials are becoming alarmed. Because Russian birth rates are dropping faster than those of other nationalities, the Russians may soon make up less than half of the Soviet Union's population.

Communists Are Hostile to Religion

Karl Marx, the founder of communism, attacked religion in his writings, calling it the "opiate of the people." An opiate is a drug that puts one to sleep or gives one a feeling of well-being. Marx felt that religion was used to lull people into accepting social injustice rather than struggling against it.

The influence of Marx and the intelligentsia, as well as the record of the Russian Orthodox Church in cooperating with the oppressive tsars, made the Communist attack on religion more acceptable to the people. As soon as the Revolution was successful, the vast lands of the church were seized, and most of the beautiful cathedrals became museums or were put to other uses.

All religions affected. The drive against religion was directed not only against the Orthodox Church but also against other religions in the Soviet Union. Such groups as the Jews, Baptists, Jehovah's Witnesses, Buddhists, and Muslims were persecuted. Mosques and synagogues were closed in all parts of the country.

When these open attacks on religion first began, religious people clung harder to their faith. By the 1930s the campaign against religion no longer took the form of outright persecution. Ridicule of religion and those who are religious took the place of direct attack. Although older people were rarely affected by this ridicule, younger people were often persuaded to discard their religious beliefs. As a result those who attend the few churches still open today are mostly older women. The future of religion in the Soviet Union is uncertain. The old *babushkas*, or grandmothers, who frequently care for Soviet children while their parents work, may teach the children something about religion. However, it is difficult to counteract the constant propaganda waged against religious observance.

Communism is the new faith. Some people feel that the Soviets have tried to make communism into a religion, with Lenin as the major deity. One can see many similarities between religious instruction and the way communism is taught. Portraits of Marx and Lenin, like those of saints in tsarist times, are displayed everywhere. Parades honoring Communist heroes are like religious processions.

The individual serves the state. Communism teaches that the individual owes service to the state. The needs of society as a whole, as determined by the Communist party, must overrule personal needs. The party and the government demand the labor and complete loyalty of each citizen.

This philosophy was not entirely forced on the people by communism, however. A strong feeling of loyalty and devotion to the larger Russian community has always been characteristic of Russians. The peasant always cooperated with the mir, or village community. The Communists simply built on this traditional value to obtain the social discipline and control they needed to rule unchallenged and to begin the task of industrialization.

Long lines wait patiently to visit Lenin's tomb in Red Square. Inside the body of Lenin lies preserved, with a light shining on his face. Every day of the year, in rain, heat, or cold, the long lines can be seen outside the main shrine of the Soviet Union.

Since the Revolution the government often publicly honors individual high achievers as models for others. In 1925 a miner named Alexei Stakhanov (stah-khah'-nawv) broke records in production. Since then, extremely industrious production workers have been called "Stakhanovites." They have been rewarded with honors and special bonuses. Conversely, "shirkers" are shamed publicly, urged to confess their shortcomings, and made to promise to do better.

Looking ahead. Soviet society has changed enormously since the Revolution. Although the Communist party tries to control these changes, the direction of change is sometimes unpredictable. Education makes people curious about the whole world. The more freedom people have, the more they want. Increased cultural and economic exchange between the U.S.S.R. the countries of the Western world, greater affluence at home, and changes in economic policy may eventually bring many changes both to the lives of the average citizen and to the Soviet Union's relations with the rest of the world.

Andrei Sakharov won the Nobel Peace Prize in 1975 for his work in monitoring and protesting human rights violations of the Soviet government. In the 1980s he and his wife Yelena Bonner have been banished to the city of Gorky, 250 miles east of Moscow; kept away from foreign reporters; and frequently placed under house arrest.

Reviewing Your Reading

1. How is the class structure of the Soviet Union different from that of tsarist Russia?
2. What are some strengths and weaknesses in Soviet education?
3. List some of the changes in family life since the Revolution.
4. How have women's roles changed since the Revolution?
5. Cite some reasons for the decline of the extended family.
6. Why are the Communists hostile toward religion?

CHAPTER REVIEW

Recalling Names and Places

black priests	intelligentsia	patronymic
commune	mir	white priests

Understanding This Chapter

1. A rigid class structure in a society can sometimes lead to stability and sometimes to instability. The class structure in tsarist Russia had both effects. Give examples, and explain why this happened.
2. Why are the "intelligentsia" often seen as a threat by governments? Are they as powerful as some governments fear? Why or why not?
3. Describe four basic changes in Russian family life that have taken place since the Revolution of 1917.
4. Does the Soviet educational system create social class differences? If so, how? Is this true of education in other countries as well?

Chapter 43

A Planned Economy

For centuries Russia was a land of farmers, herders, and hunters. Farming was most successful in the region of present-day Ukraine. From early times the farmers of this region traded their products for the timber and furs of the forest region. Trade developed between the north and the south because each region needed the products of the other.

Tools were simple and usually made of wood. Farmers raised rye, wheat, oats, and barley. Flax was grown for clothing in some areas. Primitive farming methods and poor weather led to low crop yields and frequent famines. Moreover, the growth of serfdom did little to improve agriculture, since serfs often lacked the incentive to work hard. Even after their emancipation in 1861, the peasants did little to change agricultural techniques.

Industrialization Begins with Peter the Great

Little industrialization occurred before Peter the Great's reign. He encouraged the development of an iron industry to meet his war needs, obtaining iron from the Urals. To get industrial workers, Peter allowed manufacturers to buy entire villages of peasants to work as factory serfs.

Russian industries did not grow as rapidly as those in western Europe and the United States. Until the late nineteenth century most Russian manufacturing was in the form of cottage industries. Under this system a family made a product at home. Textiles were woven in this way.

Following the emancipation of the serfs, large-scale industry developed rapidly. Between 1890 and 1900 total industrial production doubled, while textiles, coal, and iron production tripled. Large factories began to replace cottage industries. Between 1900 and the outbreak of the Revolution, Russian industry expanded more slowly because of the losses suffered during the Russo-Japanese War in 1905 and World War I. Despite the growth of industry Russia remained primarily an agricultural nation.

Internal conflicts damage the Russian economy. Although the Revolution was largely bloodless, the civil war which followed took a heavy toll both in human lives and in property damage. By 1921 the economy of the nation was a shambles. Industrial production had declined to about one-sixth of what it was in 1913. Millions of people were starving.

Money became worthless through inflation. The government tried to arrange the barter of manufactured goods for food from the countryside. However, not enough goods were manufactured to pay for the needed food. When the government tried to seize food supplies, the peasants hid or destroyed them. Droughts in 1920 and 1921 worsened conditions.

Lenin tried to reorganize the economy along Communist lines as soon as he came to power. However, conditions had become so bad that his efforts did not succeed. Violent riots, especially among the peasants, forced a change of tactics. To help speed up recovery, Lenin announced what he called a New Economic Policy (NEP). Under this program some private businesses were allowed to operate even though the government controlled land and heavy industry. According to Lenin's strategy, after the economy recovered Communist planning would be enforced. Such planning would include setting production goals for agriculture and industry and allocating the country's resources.

By 1928 the country was on the road to recovery from World War I. The production levels for some goods had returned to their 1913 levels. Although agriculture had not quite reached its 1913 levels, the New Economic Policy had been successful. Now the time had come to make the nation into an industrial leader.

Soviet Agriculture Is Collectivized

The First Five-Year Plan was launched in 1928. It was aimed at the development of the iron and steel industry and at the complete reorganization of agriculture. Major iron and steel mills were built, especially in the Ural Mountains region. An even more dramatic reorganization of agriculture took place. By persuasion if possible and by force when necessary, small peasant farms were combined into fewer large farms called collectives. As many as 300 peasant families worked together on one large collective.

By the time World War II began in 1939, Soviet industrial output had risen to four times its 1914 levels. Agricultural production had not increased as rapidly. The peasants never fully accepted the system. Furthermore, much of the capital which might have aided agricultural development was channeled into industry instead. Industrial development has always been the main concern of Soviet planners.

Bitter opposition to collectivization. One goal of the First Five-Year Plan was the creation of collective farms, or collectivization. Stalin hoped to combine 25 million small, private farms into a much smaller number of larger, cooperative ones. Most peasants bitterly opposed loss of their private holdings. Stalin went ruthlessly ahead, and those who resisted were either killed or sent to labor camps in Siberia. Rather than submit, many peasants burned their fields and slaughtered their cattle. Countless people starved to death. Livestock deaths were so great that even today there is a shortage of cattle in the Soviet Union.

To the Communist planners, combining small farms into larger units seemed to make sense. Fewer farm machines could do the job, and the latest scientific methods could be employed more easily. If industrialization was to succeed, the rural population would have to supply the produce to help industry grow and to feed the factory workers and miners.

Because of the intense resistance to collectivization and the damage to farmlands and livestock which followed, the First Five-Year Plan completely failed

Much of the Soviet Union's richest farmland is in the Ukraine. On this farm, Ukrainian workers gather potatoes.

to meet its goals in agriculture. Serious food shortages occurred in the cities, and famines threatened some rural areas. Stalin relaxed some of the demands on the peasants, and eventually the new system of agriculture began to show more promising results.

Farm production today. Farms are divided into two categories, collective farms and state farms. Around 27,000 collective farms, called *kolkhozi*, provide about 40 percent of Soviet farm produce. Workers are paid according to how well they work and what they do. A productive worker on one of the best collective farms earns about $200 a month, which is good pay in the Soviet Union. As a bonus he or she may receive some cheese, vegetables, and grain. On poorer farms, conditions are not this good.

The peasants' desire for some land of their own was so strong that Stalin made a small compromise. Each family on the collective farm may have a private plot of land not more than two and a half acres in size. Farmers can grow vegetables or fruit, perhaps raise some chickens, and have a cow. They may also sell this produce for their own profit in special open markets. Frequently peasants seem to work much harder on their own private plots than on the collective farm. The rather low yield of Soviet agriculture is due partly to the lack of peasant enthusiasm. Less than 2 percent of all farmland is in private plots, but these lands account for about a quarter of all farm output.

The second type of farm in the Soviet Union is a state farm, called a *sovkhoz*. These are like factories in the fields. A worker is hired for regular wages as in a factory. There are about 20,000 state farms, and they are generally larger in size than the collective farms. By the mid-1970s about two-thirds of the Soviet Union's farmland was devoted to state farms. One purpose of the state farm is to carry on experiments in breeding livestock and developing better strains of grain and other food plants. A worker on a state farm is not permitted to have a private plot of land as on the collective farm. The output goes entirely to the state.

Many agricultural problems remain. Although about 25 percent of Soviet workers are on farms as compared to less than 5 percent of American workers, Soviet leaders constantly worry about harvests. The major problems of soil and climate remain. In tsarist times 7 percent of the land was cultivated, while today about 10 percent of the total area is under cultivation. About half of this farmland is in the so-called "dry areas" such as Kazakhstan where rain is unreliable. In some years there is enough rain, but often there is too little. Poor soil management has also led to loss of topsoil. Soviet experts have reported that "two-thirds of the plowed land in the Soviet Union has been subjected to the influence of various forms of erosion."

There are about two acres of farmland per person in the Soviet Union. In the United States there are four acres per person, and these acres are far more productive. The Soviet people cultivate every bit of land they can. Much land in the United States that is not cultivated would be considered choice farmland in the Soviet Union. United States agricultural experts estimate that Soviet cornfields yield less than half the amount of corn per acre that American fields produce. The same is also true for other staple crops.

In addition to increasing the number of acres under cultivation, Soviet farm specialists are working to improve the yield per acre. This has been difficult because fertilizer and machinery are often in short supply. Since industry gets more capital investment than agriculture, the means to produce and distribute chemical fertilizer and equipment are frequently unavailable. Spare parts to repair machinery may not exist.

Although progress has been made, agriculture remains a backward area in the Soviet economy. In the early 1980s, the government even allowed state farms and collective farms to make purchases from farmer's private plots to meet production quotas. This was especially common in the area of animal production. As the Soviet standard of living has risen, the demand for beef and pork in the Soviet diet has grown. Soviet planners are attempting to find other ways to increase production while retaining control of the collective and state farms.

Reviewing Your Reading

1. How did most Russians earn a living before the Revolution?
2. What was the goal of the New Economic Policy?
3. How did the First Five-Year Plan change agricultural methods?
4. How is a *kolkhoz* different from a *sovkhoz*?
5. How has agriculture changed since the Revolution?

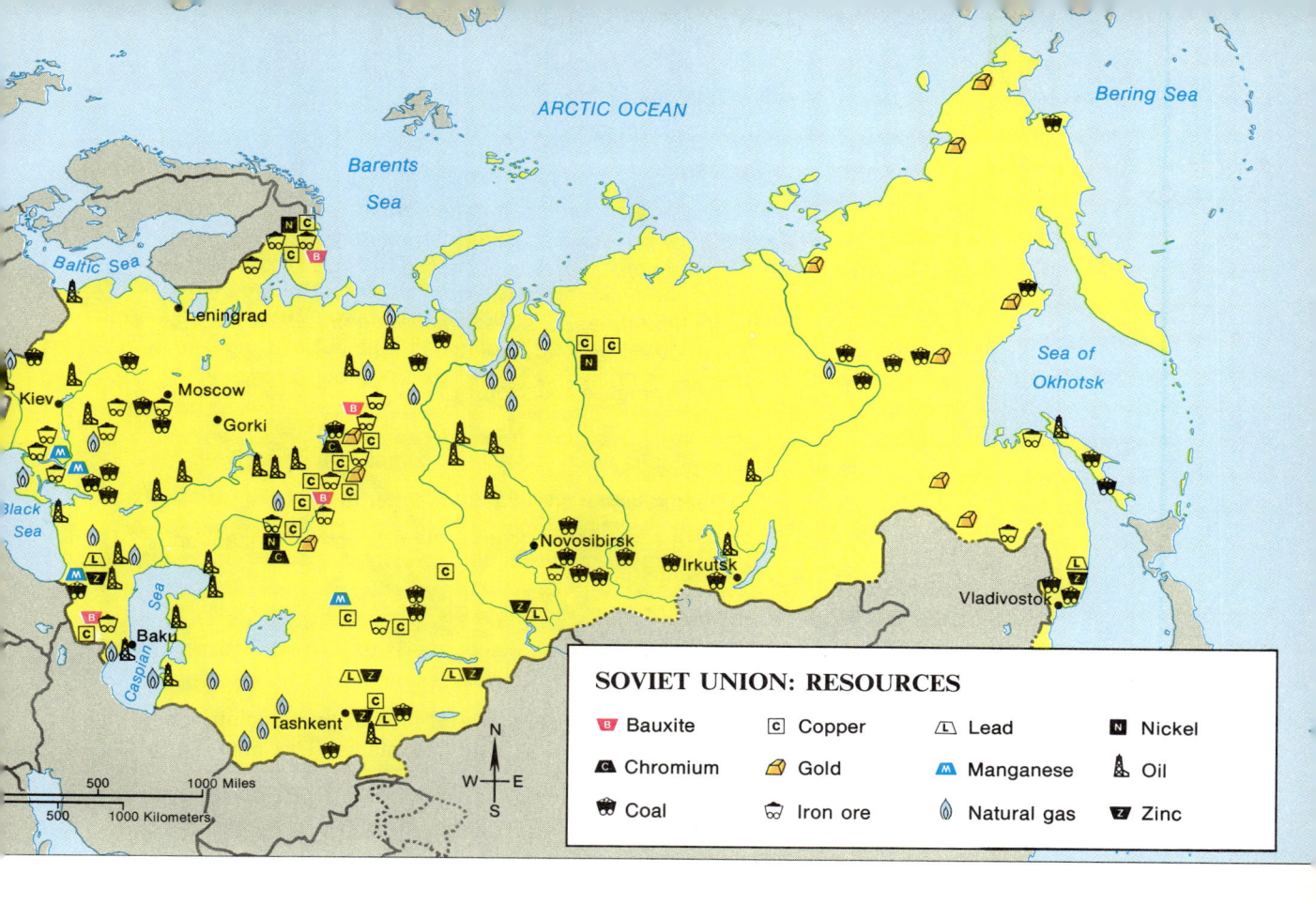

Soviet Industry Expands

The First Five-Year Plan in 1928 was designed to transform the Soviet Union from an agricultural to an industrial nation. More than an economic plan, it was intended to change people's entire way of life. Production goals for a five-year period were set for numerous items, including coal, iron, steel, oil, and machinery. Goals were also set for the number of schools, homes, and roads to be built.

By 1932 the Soviets had exceeded their goals in machine making and oil production. They failed to meet their quotas in railroad construction. They were also unable to produce enough consumer goods. The leaders justified the hardships as a small price to pay for the glorious future which lay ahead.

When the First Five-Year Plan ended in 1932, another began with new goals. The emphasis continued to be on heavy industry, such as steel and mining. Light industries that produced consumer goods did not get much attention, thus the level of living remained low. However, by the time that the German army invaded Russia in June 1941, the Soviet Union had been transformed into a major industrial power.

The Germans did enormous damage during the Second World War. The Ukraine, a main center of industry and agriculture, was the chief area of fighting. At one point in the war, the Nazi army occupied most of the Ukraine.

> **Labor and Proverbs**
>
> *The Soviet People are famous for their many proverbs. When Khrushchev was premier, he was noted for inserting salty, peasant sayings into his speeches. Since work takes a large part of one's waking hours, many proverbs deal with this aspect of life. Of the following sayings, the first three urge responsibility and hard work. The last comments on Soviet efficiency.*
>
> The crop doesn't come so much from heavenly dew as from the sweating you do.
>
> He who discipline does not shirk, always comes in time for work.
>
> A slacker in a factory is the same as a deserter at the front.
>
> Situation normal: the sleigh is in Kazan, the harness in Ryazan, and the driver in Astrakhan.
>
> Bernard G. Guerney (ed.) *An Anthology of Russian Literature in the Soviet Period from Gorki to Pasternak* (New York: Vintage Books-Random House, Inc., 1960), pp. 438–451.

About a third of Soviet industry was destroyed. Much of the remaining industry was moved to safer positions east of the Ural Mountains. This move served to open up Siberia and led to its industrialization.

Postwar industrial growth. After World War II Stalin struggled to rebuild the Soviet economy. He took what machinery and materials he could from the defeated nations, especially Germany. By 1953 the level of industrial production exceeded the prewar level, but the people remained poor.

Following Stalin's death in 1953, the government continued its emphasis on heavy industry. However, the production of more and better consumer goods began. The Soviet people are demanding more of the items available to Western shoppers. As the country has become more prosperous, it is likely that even more consumer goods will become available.

The Eighth Five-Year Plan, 1966–1970, set high goals for heavy industry just as in the past. However, a 43 to 46 percent increase in the production of consumer goods was also recommended. With the assistance of foreign companies, especially French and Italian, in developing a Soviet automobile industry, the plan was successful and the standard of living did improve for the average citizen. The 1971–1975 Plan was successful in many areas, but was notably off target in agriculture and consumer goods.

The Tenth Five-Year Plan (1976–1980) was more modest and realistic in its objectives than the previous Plan. Its most significant feature was the increase in resources to agriculture which received more than one-quarter of investments during the period. The plan called for a moderate increase in consumer goods.

In the Eleventh Five-Year Plan (1981–1985) Soviet planners continued to set only modest goals for economic growth. The labor force was growing much more slowly, and it was costing more to mine coal, drill for oil, and obtain other raw materials. The plan called for an increase in consumer goods and a lower rise in the output of heavy industry. Past failures in the farm sector led the planners to set lower growth targets in agriculture. But they did plan for a big rise in grain production. An important goal throughout the 1980s would be boosts in the output of oil and natural gas in Siberia. Even though the plan's targets were modest, it was clear early on that most of the goals could not be met.

Soviet industry is highly centralized. Since the Communists came to power, centralization has been characteristic of the Soviet economic system. The government in Moscow has tried to direct and control the economic activity of the entire nation. In theory, major decisions reached by planners in Moscow are to be put into effect quickly. Factories receive orders which are expected to be followed immediately. According to Communist theory, an economic system organized in this manner finds it easier to put plans into operation.

Although a centralized government is able to act quickly, Soviet leaders have found that serious weaknesses exist in such a system. A wrong decision may be made in Moscow, the capital, because the planners do not know enough about local conditions in distant parts of the country. Perhaps the raw materials cannot be found locally, or the necessary transportation is not available.

A major weakness of the system has been the tremendous pressure put on the local factories to fulfill orders set by Soviet leaders. For example, if a factory is ordered to produce 10,000 electric generators in a given period, the manager must produce them or lose his job, or maybe go to jail. The order has to be filled even if it means falsifying records or producing low-quality products.

In the 1960s government leaders realized that the Soviet economy would become more efficient if officials in Moscow permitted local factory managers to

The thoughts of this Soviet worker seem to be far from her job in this chocolate factory.

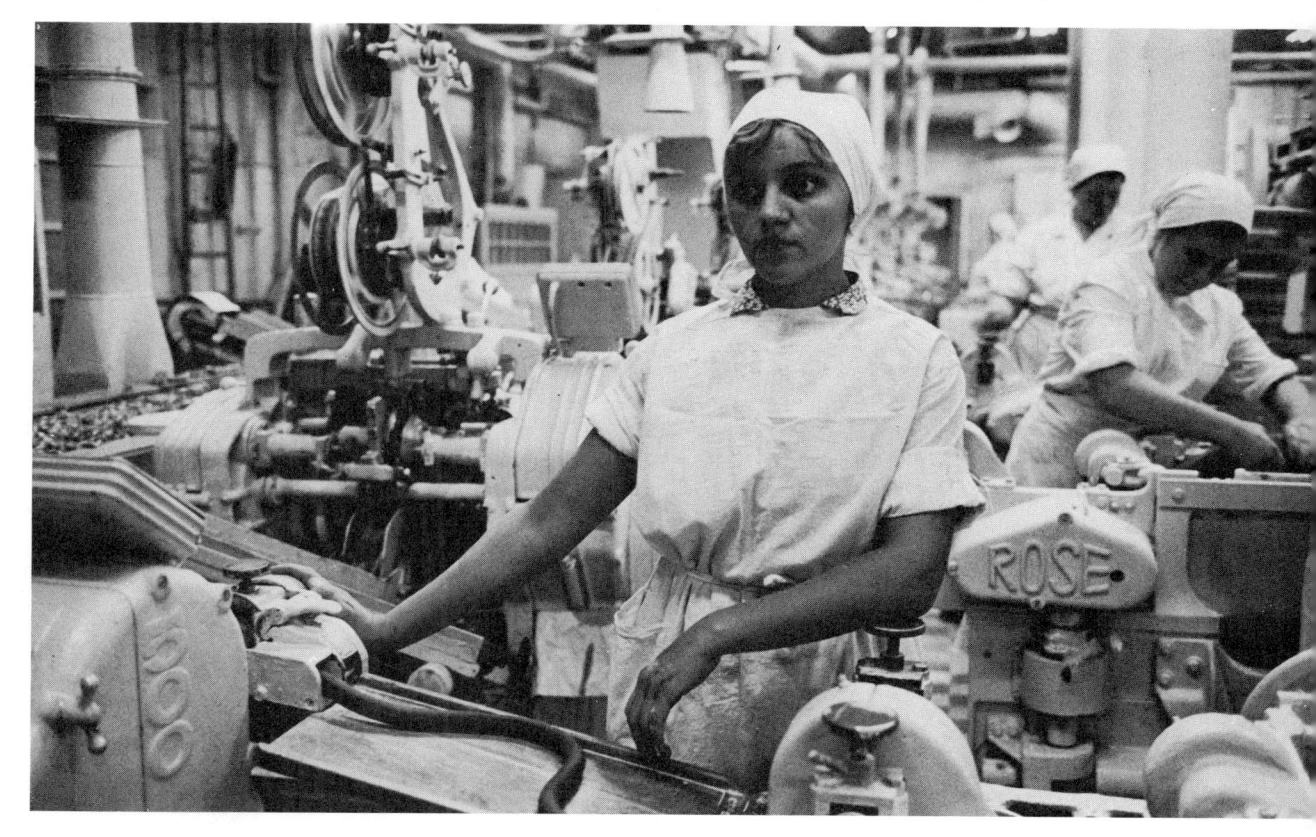

make some of the planning decisions. Soviet economist Yevsei Liberman proposed that government planners decide *what* to produce and let the directors of an industry decide *how* to produce it. He also suggested that an industry's efficiency be judged by its profits.

To some Soviet leaders Liberman's suggestions sounded too much like capitalism. However, since 1965 there has been a trend away from complete centralization of the Soviet economy.

The problem of quality continues. Achievements in space exploration and development of long-range missiles show that the Soviet economy can produce high-quality goods if the need is important enough. It is in consumer goods that quality of goods seems to be poorer.

An average industrial worker earns about $240 a month. However, it costs $100 or more to buy a suit. The cost of clothing is a heavy drain on the budget of the average family.

Electrical appliances are expensive and often faulty. Small television sets cost around $250 in Moscow. They do not always work well. In the production of military supplies and space equipment, the government insists on high quality and gets it. The low quality of Soviet consumer goods is partly due to an economic system in which industrial and government needs are given higher priority than the wishes of the consumer.

Great contrasts in the Soviet system. A visitor in the Soviet Union sees great contrasts of efficiency and inefficiency and of cultural advance and cultural lag in the economy. The Moscow subway system is an example of excellent engineering and construction. The stations are beautifully designed and

Life in a Soviet Factory

Hedrick Smith in his book *The Russians* tells how a typical Soviet factory operates. Russian workers told him that a working month divides in three ten-day periods.

The first period is one of low output for three main reasons: Workers are worn out from the rush to complete last month's quota; they suffer the aftereffects of the heavy drinking they did to relieve the stress of overwork; and deliveries of raw materials for the new month are rarely on time.

In the second ten-day period, factory production starts to move more normally. But essential materials and parts may still be coming in late.

The last ten days tend to be a frenzy, which Russian workers call "storming." The quota must be fulfilled one way or another. Workers put in long hours, including weekends, and end up utterly exhausted. The quality of the product gives way to meeting the quota.

It is custom that Soviet products have the date of productions stamped on them. Consumers try to avoid buying items that were made after the twentieth of the month. They know what happens to the quality of the product when meeting a quota becomes all-important.

> **High-Status Jobs in the USSR**
>
> In a questionnaire distributed by Soviet sociologists, Russians were asked to list in order of importance the occupations which they considered most prestigious. The results of this survey are shown below. Of the top 74 occupations, 24 are shown here. As you read through the list try to decide how a ranking drawn up by Americans would compare with this one.
>
> 1. Physicists
> 2. Pilots
> 3. Radio mechanics
> 5. Mathematicians
> 7. Geologists
> 8. Doctors
> 9. Writers and artists
> 12. University instructors
> 13. Civil engineers
> 18. High school teachers
> 25. Miners
> 28. Steelworkers
> 30. Automobile drivers
> 36. Nurses, doctor's assistants, midwives
> 39. Lathe operators
> 40. Electricians
> 41. Postal workers, mailmen, telephone and telegraph operators
> 50. Tailors, dressmakers
> 51. Tractor and combine harvester operators
> 68. Carpenters
> 70. Salespeople
> 72. Accountants
> 73. Public Service Workers
> 74. Clerks
>
> Vladimir Shubkin, "The Occupational Pyramid," *Soviet Life,* September, 1971, p. 21.

clean. The trains are fast, comfortable, and seemingly spotless. A ride on one costs five cents. At the same time public housing is so poorly done that buildings begin to crumble almost as soon as they are completed.

Most products are supplied by the state. State-owned industries provide most products and services for the Soviet people. Transportation, housing, machinery, and appliances are provided by organizations owned by the state. The government takes all profits and losses. Managers and supervisors are hired by the government to operate these businesses. These managers are given quotas to meet. If they do better than what is required, they receive rewards such as bonus payments, vacations, or better housing.

A small part of Soviet economic production is carried out by cooperative enterprises. The government provides the money to operate these cooperatives, and profits are heavily taxed. Any profit over 15 percent of the cost of production is taxed 90 percent. Such products as furniture, clothing, and musical instruments are produced by cooperatives.

Private enterprise is not entirely missing in the Soviet economy, but it is a very small part of the total. People are allowed to make such goods as hats or shoes and sell them. Many farmers sell fruit and vegetables grown on a private plot of land. However, they cannot hire anyone to work for them, nor can a person buy merchandise from a private seller in order to resell it for profit.

The underground system. One not surprising result of the government's efforts to control the economy – and the lives of people in general – is that a vast "underground" system has developed. On the surface, nearly everyone seems to

Shopping Russian Style

The foreign visitor who would like to shop in the Soviet Union must go forth with limitless patience. A quick shopping trip, in the Western style, is hardly possible. Near the Moscow Centralnaya Hotel on Gorki Street is a large, old-fashioned bakery. In order to sample foreign breads, the author visited the shop, fragrant with freshly made bread and cakes. He soon learned how shopping is done in the Soviet Union.

In front of every counter was a line of people waiting to make a selection. At the counter selling sweet rolls the author joined the line. Finally he reached the counter and told the clerk what he wanted. She made out a bill and set the rolls aside. He then joined another line leading to the cashier. Finally he was able to pay the money and was given a receipt. With the receipt he returned to the original counter and waited in line again. The "paid" receipt was handed to the clerk who had first waited on him. It then took her a few minutes to locate the rolls. By this time he was not really sure whether he wanted the rolls any more.

In the Soviet Union one lines up for almost everything. The people seem endowed with unlimited patience. Five or six cashiers at the bakery shop, instead of one, would have speeded up the process enormously. However, in Russian eyes such an investment in expensive cash registers would be wasteful extravagance.

A cashier in a Moscow restaurant uses an abacus to add up the bill.

submit to the official rules. But most of the people, experts say, engage in activities to beat the system one way or another. In this hidden world, theft of goods from the state – for example, by walking off with tools or goods from the work place – is widespread. So is selling one's services on the side – from doing repair work, perhaps with stolen supplies, to lecturing in apartment "classrooms" on subjects not offered in the official curriculum of the schools and colleges. Managers as well as workers take part in this game. They go outside the official channels to obtain resources to meet the goals set by the planners in Moscow.

Time after time the Soviet leaders have tried to crack down on the underground system. Yet the system seems to grow rather than diminish. In some cases, not only in the Soviet Union but in the other eastern European countries where the underground also flourishes, the Communist leaders have decided to cash in on individual and group efforts to beat the system. Allowing managers more freedom in running their state enterprises and encouraging sales from private farm plots are examples.

Employment rules have eased. Under Stalin, workers had very little freedom to improve their situation by changing jobs. They could not move until they were transferred by higher officials. Today jobs are changed more easily. Most people are free to quit a job if they wish and get another that suits them better. They are given a month to find other work. This greater freedom has helped push up wages and improve working conditions. If the conditions in a certain place are too harsh, people can now refuse to work there.

All employees are required to belong to the appropriate trade union, and one percent of their pay check is deducted for dues. Unlike American unions, Soviet trade unions are not allowed to call a strike, picket, or slow down production to force demands on a factory. Unions can do little about wages; however, they can sometimes negotiate changes in work rules and working conditions.

Looking ahead. The Soviets have achieved great success economically. Record production has been attained by industry. Although there are problems, agriculture has been successful enough so that no one goes hungry. However, many Soviet people are unhappy with the economic conditions in their country. Soviet citizens want more of such consumer goods as televisions, shoes, and furniture than the economic system is willing to provide. Needs of heavy industry, the military, and space technology get top priority.

Reviewing Your Reading

1. How did the early five-year plans change industry?
2. How is Soviet industry organized?
3. Why is the quality of manufactured goods a problem?
4. How are products supplied?
5. How are Soviet labor unions different from those in the United States?

CHAPTER REVIEW

Recalling Names and Places

cottage industry *kolkhoz* *sovkhoz*
five-year plans New Economic Policy underground system

Understanding This Chapter

1. Industrialization began a hundred years later in Russia than in Western Europe. What delayed it in Russia?
2. Small family farms are being replaced in the United States by large commercial farms like in the Soviet Union. Are there similar reasons for this trend? How is the trend in the United States different?
3. Why are Soviet farm workers able to produce more per acre on their private plots than on the collective farms? What problems might this entail for the Soviet economic system?
4. When all the important decisions on industrial production are made in Moscow, what problems arise? Would benefits come from decentralization? If so, is such decentralization likely? Why or why not?

Chapter 44

Soviet Government at Home and Abroad

When the Communists came to power, they radically reorganized the government, removing the autocratic tsar and the nobles. However, a new kind of autocracy emerged in Russia. The Communist party and the state continued to exert strong controls on the people.

The New Government Is Organized

Following the teachings of Karl Marx, Lenin believed that the government should go through two stages of development toward communism. During the first stage the nation should move from *capitalism,* a system in which goods are produced by private enterprise, to *socialism,* a system in which the state owns factories, railroads, and other business enterprises. During this first period the government would be directed by the leaders of the Communist party. The second stage would come when the nation had become strong, production was at a high level, and the people were educated in the ways of communism. In the second stage a government would no longer be necessary, and everything would belong to all the people. True communism would have arrived.

Soviet leaders now claim that they are moving toward the second stage of communism – a higher standard of living and the withering away of government. Although there have been some improvements for the average citizen, the government still controls every aspect of life.

The Communist party makes the decisions. The Soviet Union is run by a fairly small number of Communist party leaders. Even though it is the only political party allowed, membership is limited. Less than 10 percent of the people belong to the party. A person must get the recommendation of several party members and submit to a thorough investigation for loyalty and enthusiasm before being allowed to join. Lenin believed that the party should be made up of a small number of loyal, devoted members.

More than 40,000 local party units organized in factories, schools, farms, the military services, and elsewhere meet regularly and report to the district committee above them. Above the district or city committee is a regional organization. At the very top of the party organization is the national Central Committee which elects a small executive body called the *Politburo,* or Political Bureau. Its leader is the General Secretary of the Communist Party. He is the most important person among the party leaders. The Politburo members make all the important decisions.

THE COMMUNIST PARTY AND THE SOVIET GOVERNMENT

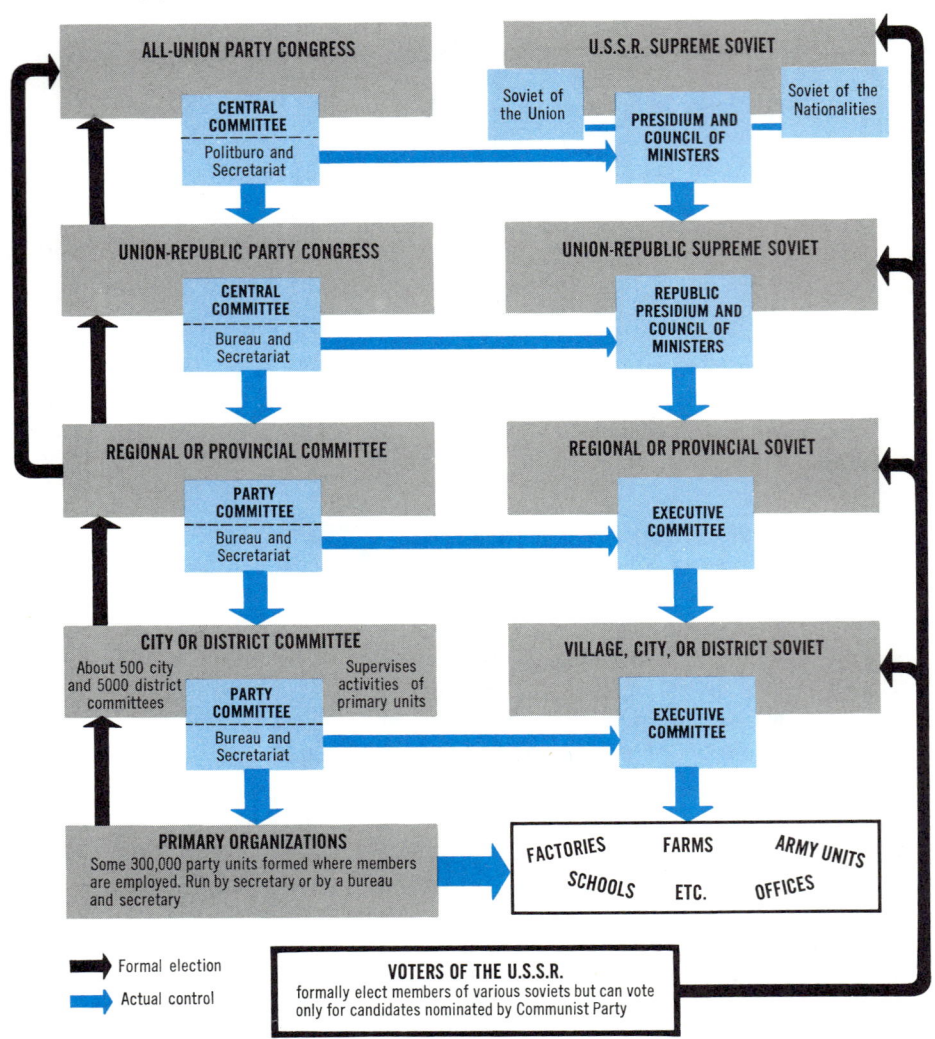

[Chart showing the hierarchical structure of the Communist Party (left column) and the Soviet Government (right column):

Party side (left):
- ALL-UNION PARTY CONGRESS — Central Committee, Politburo and Secretariat
- UNION-REPUBLIC PARTY CONGRESS — Central Committee, Bureau and Secretariat
- REGIONAL OR PROVINCIAL COMMITTEE — Party Committee, Bureau and Secretariat
- CITY OR DISTRICT COMMITTEE (About 500 city and 5000 district committees; Supervises activities of primary units) — Party Committee, Bureau and Secretariat
- PRIMARY ORGANIZATIONS (Some 300,000 party units formed where members are employed. Run by secretary or by a bureau and secretary)

Government side (right):
- U.S.S.R. SUPREME SOVIET — Soviet of the Union, Soviet of the Nationalities, Presidium and Council of Ministers
- UNION-REPUBLIC SUPREME SOVIET — Republic Presidium and Council of Ministers
- REGIONAL OR PROVINCIAL SOVIET — Executive Committee
- VILLAGE, CITY, OR DISTRICT SOVIET — Executive Committee
- FACTORIES, FARMS, ARMY UNITS, SCHOOLS, ETC., OFFICES

Legend: Black arrows = Formal election; Blue arrows = Actual control

VOTERS OF THE U.S.S.R. formally elect members of various soviets but can vote only for candidates nominated by Communist Party]

The Supreme Soviet is the legislature. The constitution of 1936 provides for a legislature called the *Supreme Soviet,* meaning "supreme council." This legislature consists of two houses, the *Soviet of the Union,* which has one member for approximately every 300,000 people, and the *Soviet of the Nationalities,* with members from each of the republics and different nationality areas. Both houses have 750 members.

The Supreme Soviet does not really engage in lawmaking. It simply meets once or twice a year for one week or less to give approval to policy decisions made by the top party leaders. It also formally elects members of two governing groups — the Soviet *Presidium* and the *Council of Ministers.*

The Soviet Presidium is an executive committee of the Supreme Soviet. It calls meetings of the Supreme Soviet, presents legislation to that body for approval, appoints certain officials, and carries out other business of the Supreme Soviet when that body is not in session. Its members are leaders of the Communist party. The chairman of the Soviet Presidium serves as president of the Soviet Union. The office is more honorary than one of real power.

The Council of Ministers, whose chairman is the premier, is made up of fifty or more members chosen for their managerial skills and their leadership rank in the party. The Council directs the day-to-day work of running the government and the economic system. The chairman is usually the General Secretary of the Communist party. Thus Gorbachev and his predecessors were all heads of the party as well as of the government.

Popular participation expected. All citizens are pressured to vote in elections, and in important elections 99 percent of the eligible voters go to the polls. But the voters have no real power. There is only one political party, and its leaders select the one candidate who may run for office. The voter's only choice is to vote for the name on the ballot or cross it off. There is no opportunity to write in another name. At election time a great effort is made to encourage support of the government and to make people feel that the government and party are acting in the best interest of all the people.

People are urged to join countless organizations and listen to endless speeches. There is no end to the petitions they are urged to sign and meetings they must attend. Political posters and slogans are everywhere.

Nationality Groups Struggle to Maintain Their Identity

The Soviet Union has a complicated system of federal government. The central government is in Moscow, and local governments exist in the union republics, the autonomous soviet socialist republics, the autonomous regions, and the national territories. These are designed to encourage self-rule in areas where different nationalities and ethnic groups live. However, political independence is not permitted. The Communist party exercises centralized political control over the whole Soviet Union. But the union and autonomous republics, autonomous regions, and national territories are not simply political and cultural divisions, having different languages, customs, and traditions. The people in these regions have considerable freedom to follow the practices of their nationality group.

Real power in Russian hands. For the most part each nationality has about its proper proportion of representatives in the Supreme Soviet. But there is serious discrimination against Jews, who are listed as one of the nationalities. Although officially there are more than 2 million Jews in the Soviet Union, they have only five representatives. By comparison, 65,000 Abkhazians in the Caucasus region are allowed seven representatives. Actually, less than half of the representatives in the Supreme Soviet are Russians.

But even within the non-Russian republics, Russians – and occasionally Ukrainians – hold the higher positions. The most powerful office in the government of each republic is the Secretary of the Communist Party. In almost every case this key position is held by a Russian. Since this is the most powerful office, Russians are assured of control.

The 1936 constitution, still in use, gives the separate republics the right to secede from the Union if they wish to do so. However, Soviet authorities have admitted that actually the possibility of secession is highly unlikely. When Nikita

Khrushchev headed the government, he made it clear that even the slightest evidence of separate nationalist feeling in the republics would not be tolerated. The present leadership has continued to reject any efforts at greater independence from nationalist groups.

Non-Russian nationalism. Currently, Russian historians are under orders to rewrite the historical relationship between the Russians and the other nationalities in the Soviet Union. They must show that from earliest times a great friendship between Russians and the non-Russian ethnic groups existed. This has been a difficult task. Earlier Soviet historians admitted that many of the nationalities bitterly resisted domination by the Russians.

Even under Soviet rule many national groups have resisted Russian planning and control. In the 1930s the Communist party tried to force Kazakhs, among

The Soviet Union's many ethnic groups give a colorful variety to the faces and dress of its peoples (clockwise from left): a Mongol boy and man from Central Asian republics; a girl with typical Slavic features; and a Caucasian in Cossack dress.

others, to settle on collective farms. Hundreds of thousands of Kazakhs died in the struggle, and great numbers of their animals were slaughtered. Stalin finally had to compromise by allowing some Kazakhs to continue their nomadic way of life. These people are likely to remain a distinct group for a long time, even though today the majority of the people in the Kazakh Republic are Russian.

Nationalism among the Baltic peoples. People living in the Baltic republics of Estonia, Latvia, and Lithuania probably have the strongest nationalistic feelings. The three small republics were originally annexed by tsarist Russia in the eighteenth century, but gained their independence after the Revolution of 1917. This independence ended when the Soviet Army invaded these countries in 1940 and annexed them.

Although the Baltic republics have no hope of gaining independence from the Soviet Union, they do not wish to be dominated by Russians living in their region. They have tried to develop a kind of national communism as free from Moscow's control as possible. This effort to maintain their national identity has caused Moscow to remove some of their leaders from office, but the feeling of separateness continues.

Nationalism in the Ukraine. The Ukraine is the largest non-Russian republic in the Soviet Union. Although they share a long common history, a common religion, and a similar language, many Ukrainians have yearned to be independent from the Russians for a long time. During the Revolution there was a brief period when independence seemed a possibility. However, the richest farmlands of the Soviet Union and great mineral resources are located in the Ukraine. The Russians could not afford to lose this valuable territory.

Many Russians have moved into the Ukraine; nevertheless, differences between the two peoples remain. Russians settle mainly in the cities, whereas the Ukrainians usually stay in rural areas. Added to the cultural differences between the two peoples is the age-old suspicion of the country man for the city slicker and the city man's contempt for the country yokel.

Stalin tried to Russify the Ukrainians. However, since his death the situation has changed. Although the Ukrainians have little chance of winning their independence, the Russians now recognize them as their chief partners in the building of the Soviet state. Some friction remains, but relations between Russians and Ukrainians seem somewhat better.

The Muslims remain culturally separate. There are more than 40 million people of the Islamic faith living in the Soviet Union. About 55 per cent of them live in the Kazakh and central Asian republics, 20 percent in the Volga and Ural Mountains area, and about 25 percent in the Caucasus region. Although they have been split into many separate republics, around 85 percent of the Soviet Muslims are of Turkish ancestry and speak related native languages.

Since the time of the tsars, there has been an effort to Russify the Muslims. Although campaigns against polygamy and child marriage have been quite successful, the Muslims seem determined to maintain a separate identity. Economically their standard of living has been raised under Soviet rule, but they have limited political independence. Nine-tenths of their mosques have been closed, and contacts with Muslims elsewhere are very limited. Still the faith persists, and many old traditions are continued.

An embroidery worker in Bukhara, in the Uzbek SSR, adds tiny, delicate stitches to her design.

People of the Soviet Far East. The vast territory north and east of Lake Baykal is the highland region of Siberia. Its sparse population is due to the harshness of the climate. Although the Soviet government urges people to move there, it is still an empty land.

The original peoples of the Soviet Far East are members of numerous nationalities. Thinly scattered over the territory, most are of Mongolian racial stock. When the Russians came into this region during the seventeenth century, these tribes lived by hunting and food gathering.

The coming of the Russians resulted in a two-way cultural diffusion between the Europeans and the Asians. The natives taught the Russians much about how to live successfully in the severe climate. The Russians in turn brought the natives better tools and taught them how to raise such crops as the potato to increase the food supply. The standard of living in these areas has improved.

An important group in this part of Siberia are the Yakuts. They are people of Turkish descent who migrated into this cold country between the tenth and thirteenth centuries.

The development of the Yakut Autonomous Soviet Socialist Republic (YASSR) has continued under Soviet rule. Soviet interest in the YASSR is strong because of the valuable mineral resources of this area. Gold exists in several places, and in the 1950's diamond deposits, considered among the richest in the world, were discovered.

The difficult position of Jews. The Jews are one of the larger minority groups in the Soviet Union. Few if any important government positions are filled by Jews, even though they probably have a larger proportion of well-educated people than any other group.

The Soviet hostility toward the Jews comes from several sources. First is the long tradition of anti-Semitism in the Soviet Union, especially among Russians and Ukrainians. If the government does not suppress it, discrimination against Jews arises very easily. Second, the Soviet government believes that many Jews have strong emotional ties with both the United States and Israel, two countries considered unfriendly to the Soviet Union. Therefore, many Soviet leaders feel

At a synagogue in Riga, capital of the Latvian SSR, men gather for a daily worship service. The practice of religion is officially discouraged in the Soviet Union, but many Jews, Christians, and Muslims manage to find ways to practice their faith.

Religious Groups in the Soviet Union

The plight of Jews in the Soviet Union has been widely publicized. They have many sympathizers in the western world, especially in Israel and the United States. Less known is the treatment other religious groups have received.

From the time of the Revolution the Soviets have expressed hostility toward religion, and it continues with varying intensity. When Khrushchev was in power he learned that there was an increase in church weddings and baptisms among the people. He began a new effort to eliminate religious groups and practices. After his ouster pressure on religious groups eased somewhat.

The intensity of the government's hostility varies depending on the religious group. Although under stress, the Russian Orthodox Church perhaps suffers less pressure than some others. The Roman Catholic Church, centered mainly in Latvia and Lithuania, has suffered more. Its clergy looks to a supreme leadership outside the Soviet Union, and this puts it under suspicion.

Discriminatory measures taken against religious groups have included the outlawing of whole denominations, the closing of places of worship, the restriction of religious activities, and discrimination in employment, housing, and public life. Although many of these actions are prohibited by the Soviet Constitution, they are carried out nevertheless.

Why does the Soviet government continue to pursue a hostile policy toward religions when it has not been successful in its goal? Even some Soviet officials have admitted that such measures have been counterproductive. It may be that the government sees religion as an ideology that competes with communism for the people's loyalty, and finds this hard to tolerate.

Based on Michael Bourdeaux, *Religious Minorities in the Soviet Union,* (London: Minority Rights Group, 1977).

that they cannot be sure of Jewish loyalty. Some are convinced that if such institutions as Hebrew schools and synagogues are eliminated, the Jews will be forced to assimilate. Paradoxically, discrimination and the listing of "Jew" on the internal passports that all citizens must have do not permit the Jews to forget their faith.

Only a very few elderly rabbis are left, and no more can be trained because the proper schools have been closed. No courses on Jewish culture, liturgy, or history are taught in either Yiddish or Hebrew. Nonetheless, despite government efforts to discourage religious practices, many young Jews are interested in their heritage. They crowd the few remaining synagogues on Jewish holidays and secretly study Hebrew even though most of them have had no religious instruction.

Immediately after World War II there were more career opportunities for Jews in the Soviet Union than there are today. Now there are no Jews in high positions in either the government or the army. It is also more difficult for Jewish students to get into universities. Without higher education the most rewarding professions are closed to an applicant.

Many Jews want to leave the Soviet Union. When a person applies for permission to leave, he is often regarded as a traitor and sometimes imprisoned. Nevertheless, some Jews are allowed to leave, and recently the number increased dramatically. In 1970 only about 1000 were able to go to Israel. By 1979 the number increased to 51,000. The increase in exit visas for Jews came about partly because of pressure by the United States, which made this policy a condition for a trade agreement with the Soviet Union. So an average of 4,200 Jews per month left Russia for Israel or other western countries. By the early 1980s, however, the number of Jews allowed to emigrate had dropped sharply again. In all of 1981 only 9,000 were permitted to settle in other countries.

Reviewing Your Reading

1. Describe Karl Marx's theory on the evolution of a Communist government. How did Marx and Lenin differ in their ideas on revolution?
2. What is the role of the Politburo in Soviet government?
3. What are the functions of the Supreme Soviet?
4. Summarize the relations between the Russian and non-Russian groups in the Soviet Union.

Soviet Union and the Western World

When World War II ended in 1945, two great powers existed – the United States and the Soviet Union. The wartime friendship between them quickly cooled after 1945, when a Cold War, political and economic rather than military, began.

To help Europe recover from World War II the United States launched an aid program called the Marshall Plan. It provided food and building materials to the war-torn nations of Europe. Countries in Western Europe accepted this aid, but those in the eastern section did not. The Eastern European countries came under the firm control of the Soviet Union and are often referred to as the "Communist

A young private leads members of the Oldest Soviet Rifle Regiment in a tactical drill.

satellite states." Yugoslavia, however, is an exception. It broke with the Soviet Union in 1948. Although it has a Communist government, it has been able consistently to pursue a course independent of Soviet influence and control.

In general when popular uprisings demanding more freedom have occurred, as in East Germany in 1953 and Hungary in 1956, Soviet military power has been used to suppress such protests. In the summer of 1968 the Soviet Union sent troops into Czechoslovakia to force reorganization of the Communist government of that country. The Czech government had become increasingly liberal, allowing greater freedom of the press and other personal freedoms to its citizens. The Soviet leaders feared that greater freedom for the Czechs would lead to similar demands within the Soviet Union and from other satellite nations. Liberal Czech leaders were forced to resign and were replaced by party leaders who followed Soviet policy more closely.

Peace is precariously maintained. Tensions between the Soviet Union and the United States grew after the 1979 Soviet invasion and partial takeover of Afghanistan. In protest of this invasion the United States decided to boycott the 1980 Olympic Games held in Moscow and to restrict grain sales to the Soviet Union. The suppression of Poland's labor union *Solidarity* by the Soviet-backed Polish government in 1981 also helped to worsen relations between the Soviet

Union and the West. The death of long-time Soviet leader Leonid Brezhnev and the eventual succession of Mikhail Gorbachev may signal the start of a new era in United States–Soviet relations. Both the United States and the Soviet Union fear the possibility of nuclear war. Such a war would devastate both countries, no matter who started it. Negotiations to slow down the buildup of military weapons may lead to more peaceful conditions in the future.

With the reelection of Ronald Reagan in 1984 a new interest in reaching agreement on arms limitations appeared on both sides. Meetings began in Geneva in March 1985 with the expectation of prolonged negotiations. Mutual fear of a nuclear holocaust compels both sides to seek an agreement to control the arms race.

Communist giants disagree. On October 1, 1949, the People's Republic of China was established in Peking, the capital. The new rulers of China were promptly recognized by the Soviet Union and other Communist nations. The following year, Chinese and Soviet leaders signed a thirty-year treaty of friendship and alliance. This was probably the high point of the Sino-Soviet friendship. Although trade relations between the countries were never broken in the next twenty years, a steady worsening of relations took place.

Mao Zedong, the leader of the government of the People's Republic, considered himself more faithful to the teachings of Marx and Lenin than were the Soviet leaders in Moscow. Each government has attacked the other over the issue of Communist doctrine. Until about 1955 the Soviet Union sent some supplies and technicians to China to help develop industry there. As the friendship between the two countries cooled, this assistance came to an end.

In 1960 Chinese leaders warned the Soviet Union against friendship with the United States, declaring that war against the Western "imperialists" was inevitable. Soviet officials argued that war could be avoided. Throughout the 1960s Chinese leaders continued to accuse the Soviet Union of drifting away from true Marxist-Leninist thought, while Soviet leaders said that the Chinese were guilty of advocating nuclear war.

Border disputes and disagreements over territorial claims have further damaged relations between the two countries. Chinese leaders in 1964 accused the Soviets of starting border incidents in the area of Sinkiang. In 1969 fighting broke out along the Ussuri River, which separates the Soviet Union from northeastern China. Each side accused the other of provoking the attack. Soviet and Chinese forces also clashed on the frontier between Soviet Kazakhstan and Sinkiang and along the Amur River. These border disputes continued into the 1970s with each side accusing the other of increasing military preparation for an attack.

The early 1980s saw some easing of tensions, but serious problems remain. From time to time the Soviet leaders have called for better relations with China, and denied that they are a military threat. The Chinese have responded slowly. They want the return of their territories taken by the tsars through unequal treaties (page 279). So far, the Soviet Union shows no willingness to return any of these Chinese territories.

The Soviet Union and the Asian subcontinent. The Soviet Union has maintained good relations with India, the largest nation on the subcontinent. In

Half of the foreign students studying in the Soviet Union come from Asia, Africa, and Latin America. These African students are working in a laboratory at Moscow Friendship University, which was founded to train students from developing nations.

1962 ranking Soviet officials openly criticized China for aggression against India. The Soviet Union has given military and economic aid to India. On occasion Soviet leaders have eased strained relations between India and Pakistan. In 1971 the Soviet Union sided with India in its support of Bangladesh's struggle for independence. Since December 1979, when the Russians invaded Afghanistan and put a Soviet-backed government into power there, relations with Pakistan have been strained.

Latin American relations. Although Communist parties were established in many Latin American countries soon after the Russian Revolution, Stalin was not strongly interested in Latin American affairs. However, with the overthrow of the dictator Fulgencio Batista in Cuba in 1959, Fidel Castro came to power. Soon Castro declared himself a Communist, and Latin America gained new importance for the Soviet Union. The election of Salvador Allende as the first Marxist president in Chile increased Soviet interest in South America, even though Allende was ousted by the military three years later in 1973. In the 1980s the Soviet Union continued to give strong support to Cuba and tried to increase trade and cultural relations with Latin America. The Soviets were eager to support any important trend toward communism.

Relations with the Middle East. Ever since the creation of the state of Israel in 1948, the Middle East has been an area of conflict. Although the Soviet Union cooperated in sponsoring the new state of Israel, it later became a champion of Arab hostility toward Israel. As a result, Soviet prestige and influence have greatly risen in the Arab world.

Relations between the Soviet Union and the Arab nations have not been entirely harmonious, however. The Arabs have resented Soviet efforts to reorganize their economic and military affairs. In particular, relations between Egypt and the Soviet Union have continued to worsen since the 1970s. The Soviet leaders have resented Arab suppression of local Communist parties. Culturally there are many differences between the two peoples. Nonetheless, the Soviet leaders have considered it politically advantageous to support the Arabs. It greatly increases their influence in the Mediterranean region. Although they have supported the Arabs against the Israelis, they have opposed a widespread Middle East war.

Relations with sub-Saharan Africa. Until the African states won their independence, the Soviet Union had very little contact with that part of the world. The Russians never had colonies in Africa. However, after many of the African nations gained their independence, the Soviet leaders became more interested in the region.

Some countries, like Tanzania, have been led by people who seemed to share many ideas with the Soviet Communist leaders, but they have not entirely accepted the Communist system. While many African nations have been happy to get economic assistance to develop their countries, they have resisted domination by outsiders, either from the West or from the Communist world. In such countries as Angola and Ethiopia the Soviet Union gave strong support to pro-Communist rebels seeking to gain control of the government. Throughout the developing world the Soviet Union has supported groups that seek to install Soviet-style Communist governments in their countries.

The Soviet Union is changing. The harshest features of the Communist system have been softened in recent years. Tight controls still exist, but there are fewer arbitrary and illegal actions taken against citizens. Soviet citizens know they are not likely to be arrested if they obey the Soviet laws and support the policies of the Communist party. The Soviet Union has worldwide interests. Growing contacts with the rest of the world may affect the Soviet Union profoundly.

Reviewing Your Reading

1. What do the Communists regard the final goal of communism to be?
2. Trace the changes in Soviet relations with the West.
3. What does the term "Communist satellite states" mean?
4. How have political philosophies of Soviet and Chinese leaders differed?
5. What role has the Soviet Union played in the Middle East?
6. How have Soviet relations with Africa changed?

CHAPTER REVIEW

Recalling Names and Places

autonomous regions	Marshall Plan	Presidium
autonomous republics	national territories	socialism
Council of Ministers	Politburo	union republics

Understanding This Chapter

1. Is the final stage of communism that the Soviets claim will come about, with no government and shared ownership of everything, possible? Why or why not?
2. The Politiburo makes all the important political and governmental decisions. Why does the Soviet Union continue to have a legislature?
3. Why does the Soviet Union see more freedom in its eastern European satellite countries as a threat?
4. Discuss and evaluate the different ways the Soviet Union tries to influence governments of Third-World countries in Latin America, the Middle East, and Africa. Are some ways more successful than others? Why?

Chapter 45

Russian Contributions to the Arts and Sciences

The Soviet Union has a rich intellectual heritage. The nineteenth century was a remarkable literary and musical period. The twentieth century has been most notable for advances in science.

Earlier developments made later major contributions in the arts and sciences possible. During Peter the Great's reign the Academy of Sciences was established (1725). In the years that followed, the Academy encouraged a high level of scholarship. A scientific tradition was established which has been generously supported by the Soviet government.

The great achievements in literature and music, especially in the nineteenth century, were often an outgrowth of folk culture. Traditional songs and dances, folktales, and epics inspired musicians and writers. Russia's growing problems also encouraged many writers to express themselves. While careful not to criticize the tsarist government directly, writers portrayed the aspirations and problems of their fellow countrymen. Modern Soviet writers also draw on the life and problems of today for their creative works.

Science and Mathematics Receive Government Attention

Mikhail Vasilievich Lomonosov was born on the bleak shores of the Arctic Ocean in 1711. A fisherman's son, he was a poet, historian, and a chief founder of modern chemistry. Lomonosov was one of the first Russian scientists to gain international recognition. The official name of Moscow University is Lomonosov University in his honor.

American students who study chemistry have heard of the Russian scientist Dmitri Mendeleev (1834–1907). He was the chemist who first devised the periodic table of elements, the most basic reference used by chemists.

Mathematics also became a major interest of the Russians. Many outstanding mathematicians lived during the nineteenth century, including Nikolai Ivanovich Lobachevski. He gained an international reputation as the inventor of non-Euclidean geometry.

The study of earth science has also been important. Russian scientists have particularly concentrated on the examination of bedrock and soils in hopes of finding more mineral resources and increasing crop acreage. The founder of modern Russian earth science was Vasily Dokuchayev (1846–1903). He constructed the first adequate soil map of European Russia and the Caucasus region. One of his students, Konstantin Glinka (1867–1927), mapped the soil zones of Siberia and central Asia.

Visitors examine an aerospace display at a Moscow exhibition hall.

Soviet science is strongly supported. The nineteenth-century scientists laid the groundwork for scientific advancement after the Revolution. Today science enjoys a very high status in the Soviet Union. Since Marxism teaches that material progress depends in part on the human ability to control nature, scientific studies are encouraged.

Scientists are much honored in the Soviet Union. They receive some of the highest salaries in the nation, paid vacations at luxury resorts, and other special privileges. Although scientists have suffered from censorship, restrictions have been less severe than on other intellectuals.

One example of official encouragement of scientific inquiry is the establishment of a community called Akademgorodok (Science Town) in western Siberia. Scientists and their families are provided with attractive homes in woodland surroundings. There are about twenty research centers where people look for ways to use natural resources more fully.

Outstanding achievements in space technology. The space age began in 1957 when the Soviet Union orbited the world's first earth-launched satellite. They called the 157-pound satellite a *sputnik*, meaning "fellow traveler of earth." In 1961 Russian astronauts Yuri Gagarin and Gherman Titov were the first men to orbit the earth and return safely. Nine years later an eightwheeled driverless car was delivered to the moon by an unmanned space vehicle to explore the lunar surface.

These impressive space achievements by the Soviet Union stirred the United States into action with a space program. Both cooperation and competition between the two countries in space exploration continue today.

Reviewing Your Reading

1. Name some well-known Russian scientists and mathematicians and describe their achievements.
2. How has the Soviet government encouraged scientific research?
3. Describe some of the Soviet space achievements.

Development of Literature

Until the eighteenth century the Russian Orthodox Church was the source of most written literature. These writings were on religious subjects and had a limited audience. Ordinary people knew the oral literature which consisted of heroic poems, epics, and folk tales. There is a vast collection of these stories, many of which were eventually written down. Some of these tales, like the epic of Prince Igor, the story of Sadko the Minstrel, and the folk tale of the firebird, inspired Russian composers to write music based on their plots.

The great period of literature. The greatest writers of Russia appeared in the nineteenth century. The most loved of them all was Aleksandr Pushkin (1799–1837), an outstanding poet. Young people in the Soviet Union today say that Pushkin is still their favorite writer. Two of his works, *Eugene Onegin* and *Boris Godunov,* are well known as operas.

The first great genius of prose was Nikolai Gogol (1809–1852), best known for his play *The Inspector General* and his novel *Dead Souls.* Both deal with corruption among government officials.

The nineteenth century produced an impressive number of great writers. Among them were Ivan Turgenev (1818–1883), writer of *Fathers and Sons;* Fëdor Dostoevski (daw-stau-*yehv*'ski) (1821–1881), author of *Crime and Punishment* and *The Brothers Karamazov;* and, perhaps the greatest of all, Leo Tolstoy, author of such books as *Anna Karenina* and *War and Peace.* While these Russian writers expressed a deep love for their country, they also effectively portrayed human suffering. Without openly criticizing their society, they inspired their readers to work for change.

Special mention should be made of Tolstoy's long novel *War and Peace,* which many have considered one of the greatest novels of all times. The story, written between 1865 and 1869, deals with events during the time of Napoleon. The author blends scenes of life among aristocratic families with accounts of battles waged between the Russians and the invading French armies in 1812. Tolstoy described the lives of the chief characters with great realism and sympathy. His portraits of men in battle are among the greatest ever written.

Aleksandr Pushkin (above) is considered the greatest Russian poet. Leo Tolstoy (below) gave world literature two of its greatest masterpieces, War and Peace *and* Anna Karenina.

In his comic yet moving plays, Anton Chekhov dramatized the changes that were taking place in Russia at the turn of the century and the inability of many Russians to deal with them.

> **A Russian Folk Tale**
>
> *Russians are fond of ghost stories and tales of the supernatural. Among the peasants, pagan superstitions linger and are blended into their folk tales. The following story reveals an ancient belief that the dead may mingle among the living. The tale suggests, however, that these walking dead are no longer entirely trustworthy.*
>
> A TALE OF THE DEAD
>
> Once a carpenter was going home late at night from a strange village: he had been at a jolly feast at a friend's house. As he came back an old friend met him who had died some ten years before.
>
> "How do you do?"
>
> "How do you do?" said the walker, and he forgot that his friend had long ago taken the long road.
>
> "Come along with me: let us have a cup together once more."
>
> "Let us go."
>
> "I am so glad to have met you again, let us toast the occasion."
>
> So they went into [a hut], and they had a drink and a talk. "Well, good-bye; time I went home!"
>
> "Stay, where are you going? Come and stay the night with me."
>
> "No, brother, do not ask me: it is no good. I have business at home to-morrow and must be there early."
>
> "Well, good-bye."
>
> "But why should you go on foot? Better come on my horse, and he will gallop along gaily."
>
> "Thank you very much."
>
> So he sat on the horse, and the horse galloped away like a whirlwind.
>
> Suddenly the cock crowed: it was a very terrible sight! Graves all around, and under the wayfarer a gravestone!
>
> Aleksandr N. Afanasev, *Russian Folk Tales* (ed. Leonard A. Magnus) (London: Routledge & Kegan Paul Ltd., 1915), p. 8.

One of Russia's greatest playwrights was Anton Chekhov (1860–1904). Such plays as *The Seagull* and *The Cherry Orchard* are still performed frequently all over the world. Like the novelists, Chekhov in his plays gives us a picture of nineteenth-century life in Russia. He portrayed the lives of the well-to-do as empty and dreary.

Increase in "protest literature." As the nineteenth century drew to a close, the amount of underground writing grew. Newspapers, pamphlets, and newsletters attacked the government and the social system.

Any criticism of the tsar or the government was considered a serious crime by government officials. The tsar's secret police arrested people who wrote or spoke out against the system. Such offenders could be punished without a trial. One form of punishment was exile to Siberia. Dostoevski was sent there because of his political activity.

Censorship is an old problem. Censorship existed during tsarist times, and it continues today. During tsarist times a writer would be told what was not allowed. If the subject was not forbidden, he could usually write about it freely. Soviet censorship is of two kinds. Not only are some subjects forbidden, but writers are also told what they should write about. Similar pressures are put on artists and musicians. Soviet censorship leaves creative people with much less freedom than existed before the Revolution.

During the 1920s many writers experimented with various forms of expression. This was the time of the New Economic Policy when freedom in economic life was matched by a fair amount of freedom for writers and artists. Authors were able to write on many subjects.

Conditions changed greatly after 1928, however. Stalin launched his First Five-Year Plan, and the period of relative freedom came to an end. Everybody was ordered to join together to build a communist society. This meant that writers had to produce work which would inspire people to labor harder for communism. Writings were expected to be simple so all could understand them. They had to be optimistic in spirit and express loyalty to Soviet leaders, especially Stalin. Writers produced stories about such subjects as collective farms, electric power plants, and steel mills.

Good literature cannot often be produced by order of politicians, and few books of value were written. In spite of the lack of freedom, Mikhail Sholokov (1905–1984) wrote *And Quiet Flows the Don,* which received the Nobel Prize for literature. Works of such high quality were few, however.

In the 1930s Stalin became increasingly fearful that enemies were plotting against him. Many people were put in prison or executed in what were called "purges" to clean out "traitors." Among the victims were many writers who had aroused Stalin's suspicions. This was a period of great terror for the Soviet people. Fear of arrest destroyed the writer's creativity. They had to grind out the kind of propaganda and literature that Stalin would accept.

The post-Stalin period is uncertain. When Stalin died in 1953, people seemed to become less fearful. With the promise of greater freedom, writers dared to produce articles and books revealing some of the weaknesses of the system. These works are not critical of Communist theories, but rather of their application by administrators. For example, in *One Day in the Life of Ivan*

The Worship of Stalin

By the 1930s Stalin's power was so complete that he was hailed like a god. Newspapers, magazines, and children's textbooks were filled with praises of Stalin. Below is a brief excerpt.

Who broke the chains that bound our feet, now dancing,
Who opened lips that sing a joyous song,
Who made the mourners change their tears for laughter,
Brought back the dead to life's rejoicing throng,
Most loving, true and wise of Lenin's sons —
Such is the great Stalin.

Warren B. Walsh (ed.), *Readings in Russian History,* 4th edition, p. 761. Copyright © 1963 by Syracuse University Press. Reprinted by permission of the publisher.

Denisovich, Aleksandr Solzhenitsyn (*sole'shen-nit' sin*) describes the terrible conditions in a concentration camp during the Stalinist era.

However, in some ways the situation was easier under Stalin, since the writers knew where they stood. Either they wrote the way Stalin wanted, or they kept quiet and did not write at all. Today, although writers have a bit more freedom, they can never be sure how the government will react to their work. When Boris Pasternak (1890–1960) wrote *Doctor Zhivago* he was denounced by Soviet authorities. In many ways *One Day in the Life of Ivan Denisovich* is much more critical of the Soviet Union than *Doctor Zhivago,* yet it was published. Pasternak's book was published outside of the Soviet Union. He was offered the Nobel Prize, but the government would not let him accept it.

Solzhenitsyn's novels, including *Cancer Ward* and *The First Circle,* have been published in the West and received much praise. Many regard him as the greatest Russian writer of his time. Nevertheless, he was expelled from the Soviet Writer's Union in 1969 and was unable to leave Russia to accept his Nobel Prize in Stockholm the following year. His "crime" was criticizing Soviet conditions. In 1974 Solzhenitsyn authorized the foreign publication of *The Gulag Archipelago*, which describes in detail the oppression of the Soviet system and the author's own experience in Stalin's prison camps. He was charged with trea-

Aleksandr Solzhenitsyn produced a brilliant, enormous record of the atrocities of Stalin's regime in The Gulag Archipelago.

A Romance with the Russian Land

Love of country has long been a traditional theme of the Russian writers and poets. This deep feeling for the Russian countryside has remained characteristic of the Russian people despite changing times and changing political systems. Such modern writers as Boris Pasternak and Alexander Solzhenitsyn expressed their reluctance to leave the land of their birth despite repeated attempts by the government to stifle their creativity. This feeling for "Mother Russia" is also common among ordinary people.

Michael Lermontov (1814–1841), a nineteenth century romantic writer, describes the way many Russians feel about their land in the passage below. Although Lermontov is describing tsarist Russia, the emotion he is describing would be no less true today.

I love my native land . . . the cold silence of her steppes, the waving of her boundless forests, the oceanlike expanse of her flooded rivers. . . . I love to speed in a *telega* (wagon) along the country road, when, as I sigh for the night's lodging, my slow gaze pierces the shadows of the night and glimpses the trembling lights of melancholy villages.

I love the smoke of the burnt stubble, the wagons bivouaking at night in the steppe; and on the hill, among the yellow fields, a couple of white-glimmering birches. With a gladness unfamiliar to many, I see the heaped threshing floor, the thatch-roofed *izba* [peasant hut] with its carved shutters; and on a holiday, in the dewy evening, I am ready to spend half the night looking at the dancers as they whistle and stamp, and listening to the tipsy peasants' talk.

Marthe Blinoff, *Life and Thought in Old Russia* (University Park: the Pennsylvania State University Press, 1961), p. 5.

son and deported from the Soviet Union. Shortly thereafter, he came to live in the United States.

Why can some writers be critical while others cannot? There is some evidence that a struggle has been going on in the Kremlin between liberals, who favor more freedom of expression, and conservatives, who favor strong censorship. There is no doubt that Soviet leaders worry about what might happen if intellectual freedom were greater.

Eisenstein: Master of Epic films

Sergei M. Eisenstein (1898–1948) is remembered as a genius in the art of motion picture making. Trained as an architect and engineer, he became a director of plays at an early age. From his theater work he became interested in films and produced his first movie *Strike* in 1924.

Fame came to Eisenstein with the film *Potemkin* (1925), which portrays key events in the nationwide uprising against the tsarist government in 1905. The climax of the film is an exciting portrayal of an uprising by sailors aboard the battleship *Potemkin* in the port of Odessa. This film is known worldwide to film buffs for Eisenstein's development of a film technique known as montage.

In two of his other famous films – *Ten Days that Shook the World* (1928), which portrayed the events leading to the seizure of power by the Bolsheviks in 1917, and *Ivan the Terrible* (1944) – Eisenstein introduced other new techniques which added to the dramatic impact of his films. Because of the difficulties of government censorship, Eisenstein did not make many films. However, those he did make are epic portrayals remembered by lovers of cinema everywhere.

The most famous scene from Sergei Eisenstein's film Potemkin *shows soldiers firing on the people of Odessa as they flee down a long stairway in terror.*

The cultural underground. We have seen that people under Communist regimes find ways to get ahead by taking part in an underground economy (p. 499). The same is no less true in religion, the arts, and popular culture. Small groups gather in homes for worship. Artists paint for their friends. Writers send manuscripts to other countries for publication. Actors save their best performances for living-room theater. Some young people imitate Western fashion out in the open and go to secret cabarets and rock-music concerts. In recent years the government has compromised by allowing some rock combos to perform openly. A shadow school system operates to teach forbidden topics and banned courses with the use of self-published texts called *samizdats* and lectures on casette tapes.

Some of the dissenters openly defy the government – and take their punishment. But far more dissent permeates the society through the underground. Political dissent is supressed most vigoursly and punished more severely than other forms of nonconformity.

Development of Fine Arts

Because the Soviet Union includes hundreds of ethnic and racial groups, the forms of expression in the fine arts are enormously varied. This is especially true of the folk arts, since each culture group developed its own modes of expression in costume, painting, carving, music, and dance.

Art and architecture. Architecture was the earliest major art form to develop, and the churches received the best talent available. Since the Russian Orthodox faith came from Constantinople, the Byzantine style was imitated. To this style were added some native Russian elements. Most striking is the onion-shaped dome which is characteristic of Russian churches. Even today the visitor to the Soviet Union is impressed by the many churches and cathedrals of rich design and color with their brilliant golden domes.

Beginning in the eighteenth century Western architectural styles became more prominent. When Peter the Great designed Petrograd (now Leningrad), he invited Western architects to participate in the construction. Leningrad is considered by many the most beautiful Soviet city.

Socialist realism in art. Stalin discouraged creativity in art as well as literature. Paintings had to reflect what was called "socialist realism." Artists were expected by the government to create works which were politically inspiring. Stalin did not like abstract or impressionistic art. Outstanding artists who refused to be limited by the government simply left the country. Those who decided to stay painted or carved sculpture approved by the Communist Party. Oftentimes the results were lifeless and dull. Painting became like billboard art or photographs. A visitor to the Soviet Union still sees art of this kind everywhere.

Stalin liked buildings that were elaborately designed, overdecorated, and not very functional. He had a number of buildings constructed in a style often referred to by foreigners as "wedding cake" because of the ornate tiers on the buildings. Today the Stalinist style of architecture has been dropped, and more functional designs have taken its place. Current construction in the Soviet Union resembles Western-style buildings.

Russian music is recent. Except for folk and church music, Russian music developed largely in the nineteenth century. Mikhail Glinka (1803–1857) is often called the "father" of Russian music because he wove popular Russian tunes into his works and wrote operas about the Russian people. Several musicians followed in the tradition of Glinka, creating a national, or distinctly Russian school of music. Pyotr Tchaikovsky (1840–1893), Modest Mussorgsky (1835–1881), Cesar Cui (1835–1918), Aleksandr Borodin (1834–1887), and Nicolay Rimsky-Korsakov (1844–1908) have been called the "Mighty Five." Their music was influenced by Russian history, folklore, and their own love of country. Tchaikovsky is also well known to audiences as the creator of the ballet music to *Sleeping Beauty, Swan Lake,* and the *Nutcracker Suite.* The opera *Boris Godunov* by Mussorgsky is considered by many as Russia's finest opera. The second half of the nineteenth century was a period of remarkable musical achievement.

The Soviet Union has produced a number of outstanding performers such as the world-famous cellist Mstislav Rostropovich, pianists Sviatoslav Richter and Emil Gilels, and violinists David Oistrakh and Leonid Kogan.

Dance takes many forms A Soviet dance group that has enjoyed great popularity in the United States is the Moiseyev folk Dance Company. Organized in 1937 by a ballet master, Igor Moiseyev, it has grown over the years into a company of 110 dancers. Its repertoire has more than 300 dances. Many consider this group the finest of its kind in the world.

Being a nation of hundreds of different cultures, the Soviet Union has an enormous wealth of folk dances. The "Polyanka," a Russian quadrille, the Moldavian "Zhok," and Kurd dances are especially popular. Most Soviet nationalities have their traditional dances. Some are sedate, and others are very lively. Dancing on toes and spectacular leaps by men characterize the dances of Georgia in the Caucasus. The Ukrainian "hopak" also features high leaps into the air.

The Yunost (Youth) Ensemble from Lvov in the Ukrainian SSR performs the hopak, *with colorfully dressed dancers leaping high in the air.*

An elaborate stage set of St. Basil's highlights a scene from Mussorgsky's opera Boris Godunov *at the Bolshoi Theatre in Moscow.*

Classical ballet is especially popular. An outstanding dance art form in the Soviet Union is ballet. Young people get as excited about ballet as Americans do about football. Ballets with Communist themes have been produced and performed, but beautiful classical ballets like *Swan Lake* are enormously popular. Ballet came to Russia from Italy during the first half of the eighteenth century. The Russians adopted it and have made it a great art. Their largest company, the Bolshoi Ballet, is one of the world's finest dance troupes.

An All-Tatar Musical Evening

In addition to outstanding classical music and ballet, Russian audiences are treated to a wide variety of entertainment from the many ethnic groups within the country. The center of Russian cultural life is Moscow. Performers come from all over the Union to entertain Moscow's citizens with the unique songs and dances of their homeland. The following article from The New York Times *suggests that even sophisticated city dwellers cling to the culture of their birthplace.*

Moscow has been playing host to a song-and-dance ensemble from the Soviet Union's Tatar Republic. . . .

The emcee, Nadir Satdinov, a dark-haired man with fashionably long sideburns, dressed in a striking embroidered green velvet jacket, used scarcely a word of Russian through the entire evening, from opening introduction to the final encores, and, judging from laughter and applause, the audience liked it that way. . . .

Moscow often plays host to stage shows from the various ethnic republics of the Soviet Union, but those performances are usually designed to show off the local talent to Russian audiences in the Soviet capital. But the Tatar troupe had evidently come to entertain some of the 109,000 Tatars living in Moscow. . . .

The Tatars, who are related to the Turks and typically are of strong, broad-shouldered build with black eyes and [prominent] cheek bones have resisted cultural assimilation despite their widespread settlement among ethnic Russians.

[The variety show at the Railroad Workers' Club consisted of a] . . . musical program, accompanied by a four-piece band of piano, drums and two electric guitars, combined folk songs with modern tunes written by Tatar composers. There were no Russian or Western numbers.

Nail Khabidullin sang fast-paced modern songs and lilting traditional tunes written in the five-tone scale that gave the Tatar melodies some of the singsong quality associated with Chinese music. . . .

The featured dancer, Raisya Sharafi, wore a . . . long white chiffon dress over black tights . . . [and, while she danced, tapped] out the rhythm on two porcelain saucers in her hands.

About the only Russian word uttered by Mr. Satdinov, the emcee, was "zanaves" ("curtain") as he instructed the stage crew to open or close the fringed, gold-colored curtain between acts.

Theodore Shabad, *The New York Times,* January 23, 1972, p. 3. Copyright © 1972 by The New York Times Company. Reprinted by permission.

Summing up. The vast Soviet nation has had a major cultural impact on the rest of the world. As a cultural bridge between Europe and Asia, the Soviet peoples have helped to introduce modern technology to Asian nations. One of the most enduring contributions of this culture area is in the realm of literature, theater, and music. Soviet science is also impressive in its achievements.

Reviewing Your Reading

1. Why is the nineteenth century considered to be a great era of Russian literature?
2. How has censorship affected Soviet writers?
3. Trace the development of architecture and art.
4. Name some outstanding Russian composers.

CHAPTER REVIEW

Recalling Names and Places

Anton Chekhov
Fëdor Dostoevski
Mikhail Glinka
Nikolai Gogol
Dmitri Mendeleev
Aleksandr Pushkin
Aleksandr Solzhenitsyn
Pyotr Tchaikovsky
Leo Tolstoy

Understanding This Chapter

1. The Soviet Union has a strong science tradition because the government has always supported and rewarded scientists. Should we do more than we do in this area? How?
2. Why is good literature, art, and music difficult to create under government control? What does censorship do to the writer and artist?
3. Russian music for the concert hall largely emerged in the nineteenth century. What is there about Russian culture that gives richness and variety to the music?

UNIT 9
Exploring
Latin America

| 10,000 B.C. | 900 A.D. | 1000 | 1100 | 1200 | 1300 | 1400 | 1500 | 1600 | 1700 | 1800 | 1900 |

- MIGRATION FROM ASIA 50,000–10,000
- AZTEC EMPIRE 1400–1520
- MAYAN CIVILIZATION c. 1500 B.C.–1200 A.D.
- SPANISH COLONIAL EMPIRE 1520–1808
- MAYAN GOLDEN AGE 250–900
- INDEPENDENCE MOVEMENT 1808–1825
- INCAN EMPIRE 1000–1530
- CAUDILLO RULE 1825–1910

UNLIKE THE OTHER REGIONS DESCRIBED in this text, Latin America is in the Western Hemisphere. Its culture was greatly influenced by people from the Iberian peninsula, the people of Portugal and Spain. Spanish and Portuguese explorers were the earliest European settlers of this part of America, establishing large colonial empires. Today Spanish is the official language of most of Latin America, although in Brazil the official language is Portuguese. In a few Caribbean countries, French, English, and Dutch are spoken. Because the region was explored and colonized by people who spoke Latin languages – Spanish, Portuguese, and French – it is called Latin America.

Latin America is an exciting blend, both culturally and racially, of many different cultures and peoples. The great Indian civilizations of the Incas, Aztecs, and Mayas made the earliest contributions to the region's cultural patterns. Today millions of Indians speak their own languages and follow a life-style similar to that of their ancestors. Many of them live in the nations of the Andean mountains, such as Peru, Ecuador, and Bolivia, as well as in Guatemala.

The arrival of the Spanish and other European explorers added new elements to the population. Often these men married Indian women. Their children, of mixed white and Indian ancestry, are called *mestizos*. Such Latin American nations as Mexico, Venezuela, and Colombia have large mestizo populations.

Some of the African blacks originally came to Latin America as slaves to work on the Caribbean sugar plantations. Now they form a majority group in Haiti and most other islands and have intermarried with other racial groups on the mainland. The contributions of these African settlers can be seen in many aspects of Latin American culture, especially the arts.

For many years twenty-one countries made up the Latin American region: Argentia, Bolivia, Brazil, Chile, Colombia, Costa Rica, Cuba, Dominican Republic, Ecuador, Guatemala, Haiti, Honduras, Mexico, Nicaragua, Panama, Paraguay, Peru, Puerto Rico, El Salvador, Uruguay, and Venezuela. Since 1960

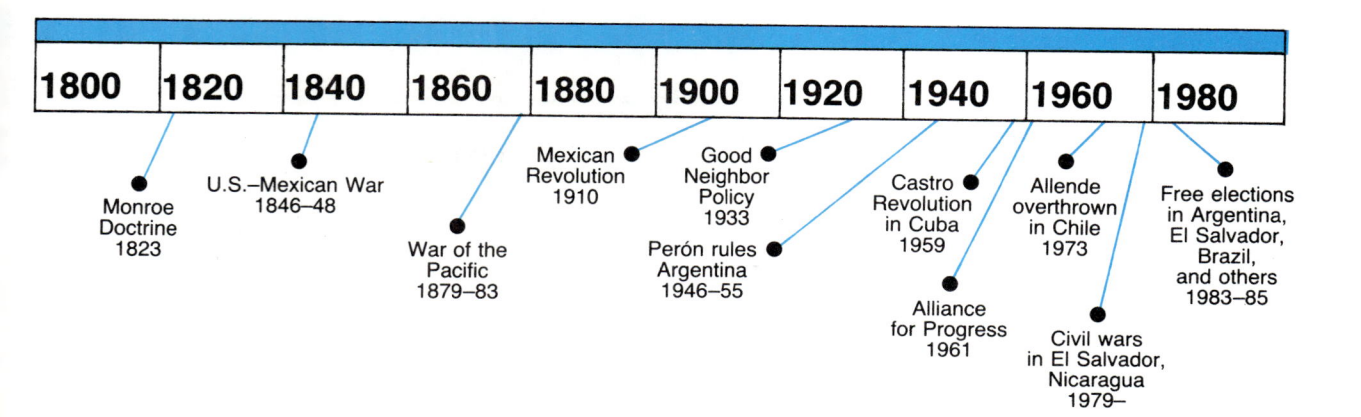

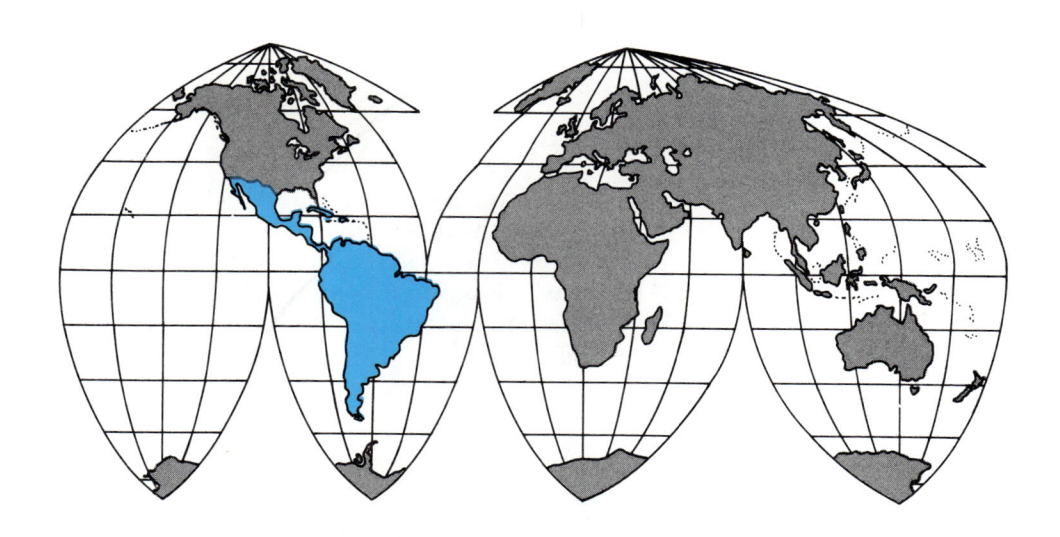

| 1800 | 1820 | 1840 | 1860 | 1880 | 1900 | 1920 | 1940 | 1960 | 1980 |

- Monroe Doctrine 1823
- U.S.–Mexican War 1846–48
- War of the Pacific 1879–83
- Mexican Revolution 1910
- Good Neighbor Policy 1933
- Perón rules Argentina 1946–55
- Castro Revolution in Cuba 1959
- Alliance for Progress 1961
- Allende overthrown in Chile 1973
- Civil wars in El Salvador, Nicaragua 1979–
- Free elections in Argentina, El Salvador, Brazil, and others 1983–85

other new nations have been created – Jamaica, Barbados, Trinidad and Tobago, Guyana, and Belize, all within the British Commonwealth of Nations. Puerto Rico is a self-governing commonwealth of the United States. Suriname became independent, but Curaçao, Aruba, and several smaller islands remained Dutch territories. French Guiana and the islands of Martinique and Guadeloupe are overseas departments of France. Despite the challenges of poverty, illiteracy, and rapid population growth, Latin America is not stagnant. Major changes are taking place. It is an area of great potential development with bright prospects for the future.

Chapter 46

Challenges of a Varied Landscape

Latin America includes South America, Central America, and numerous islands in the Caribbean. The region extends 7000 miles from the northern Mexican border to Chile. The distances between the Atlantic and Pacific oceans vary: in Panama the land bridge is only about 32 miles, while the greatest width through Brazil and Peru is over 3000 miles. Notice how close this continent is to Africa – only about 1800 miles at the nearest point. Some scientists believe that South America and Africa were once connected and over a long period of time gradually drifted apart.

Physical Features Vary Greatly

Like Africa, Latin America has plains, mountains, and upland regions. But while Africa is mainly a plateau, Latin America is more mountainous.

The mountains of the Americas. Probably the most striking geographic feature of Latin America is the series of mountain ranges and highlands that occupy much of Central America and western South America. Population clusters are separated from one another by these natural barriers, isolating people, limiting the spread of ideas, and creating local differences.

The Andes tower over western South America.

LATIN AMERICA: PHYSICAL
Elevations
Feet
Meters
13,100
4,000
6,600
2,000
1,600
500
700
200
0
0
Below sea level
Below sea level
Mountain peak
0 250 500 750 1000 Miles
0 250 500 750 1000 Kilometers
UNITED STATES
Gulf of Mexico
ATLANTIC OCEAN
TROPIC OF CANCER
Gulf of California
SIERRA MADRE OCCIDENTAL
MEXICAN PLATEAU
SIERRA MADRE ORIENTAL
Rio Grande
WEST INDIES
Yucatán Peninsula
MEXICO
Citlaltepetl 18,855 ft. (5,747 m)
Gulf of Honduras
Caribbean Sea
Central America
Panama Canal
VENEZUELA
Lake Maracaibo
Orinoco River
LLANOS
GUYANA
FRENCH GUIANA
SURINAM
GUIANA HIGHLANDS
COLOMBIA
Magdalena River
EQUATOR
GALAPAGOS ISLANDS
ECUADOR
Mt. Chimborazo 20,561 ft. (6,267 m)
Rio Negro
Amazon River
AMAZON LOWLANDS
PERU
PACIFIC OCEAN
Mt. Huascaran 22,205 ft. (6,768 m)
Madeira River
Xingu River
Tocantins River
BRAZIL
ANDES MOUNTAINS
Nevado Ancohuma 21,489 ft. (6,550 m)
Mamoré River
Guaporé River
Lake Titicaca
BOLIVIA
BRAZILIAN HIGHLANDS
São Francisco River
TROPIC OF CAPRICORN
ATACAMA DESERT
CHACO
Paraguay River
PARAGUAY
Ojos del Salado 22,572 ft. (6,880 m)
Salado del Norte River
Paraná River
Uruguay River
PAMPAS
Mt. Aconcagua 22,834 ft. (6,959 m)
URUGUAY
CHILE
ARGENTINA
Río de la Plata
SALINA GRANDE -131 ft. (-40 m)
CHONOS ARCHIPELAGO
PATAGONIA
Strait of Magellan
FALKLAND ISLANDS
Cape Horn
110°W
100°W
90°W
80°W
70°W
60°W
50°W
40°W
120°W
30°W
30°N
20°N
10°N
0°
10°S
20°S
30°S
40°S
50°S

The Andes form a long western ridge in South America just as the Rockies do in North America. However, they are higher and steeper than the Rocky Mountains. Transportation through them is more difficult since most passes are at altitudes of 12,000 feet or more. As in North America there are lower mountainous areas in the eastern part of the continent. These are the Guiana Highlands and the Brazilian Highlands.

In Central America mountains and highlands cover most of the area. Although these mountains are not as high as the Andes to the south, they sometimes inhibit trade and communication. In certain nations more people live in the central mountainous regions than on the coastal plains.

Most of the Caribbean islands are quite rugged, too. Hispaniola, divided into the nations of Haiti and the Dominican Republic, is very mountainous. Jamaica and Cuba also have small mountain ranges. Puerto Rico, the Virgin Islands, and a string of small islands extending southward, the Lesser Antilles, are actually mountain tops rising above the sea. However, a group of small islands to the northeast of Cuba, the Bahamas, are low-lying coral isles.

Few lowland areas. Unlike North America, lowland areas in Latin America occupy a small percentage of the land surface. Except for tropical rain forest areas, the major concentrations of population, agriculture, and commerce are found in the lowland regions. However, on the west coast near the equator, population concentrations are found in the cooler highlands. Quito (*key*'toe), Ecuador, and Bogotá, Colombia, are cities at very high altitudes.

Coastal plains are also less extensive than in North America. They are almost nonexistent on the Pacific coast, but they are more common on the east coast. The narrowness of the lowland plains area stems from the fact that mountainous and highland regions are often situated near the coast. By examining the map on page 531, one can see that substantial portions of the region lack natural harbors since there are few indentations in the coastline.

One of the largest plains regions is located in Uruguay and Argentina. This grassland area, called the *pampas,* is the most productive agricultural region of Latin America. There farmers grow large crops of wheat, and cattle and sheep are grazed. Two major cities, Buenos Aires (*bway*'nohs *eye*'rehs), Argentina, and Montevideo, Uruguay, developed as trading and manufacturing centers for this productive region.

Other lowland areas in South America are the river basins. The largest of these are the Amazon, Orinoco, and the Rio de la Plata.

The great rivers in South America. The exploration and settlement of North America was greatly aided by the geography of the region. Inland mountains and coastal plains in the east created rivers that flow to the sea. Rivers like the Mississippi, the Hudson, and the Saint Lawrence were like highways into the interior of the continent. After settlement began, these rivers as well as the Great Lakes continued to be the major means of transportation from one part of the continent to another. In South America the deepest penetration by waterway from the sea is along the Amazon. An oceangoing cargo ship can reach Iquitos (e-*key*'tohss), Peru – about 2300 miles from the river's mouth.

A much smaller river than the Amazon is the Orinoco. It rises near the Venezuelan-Brazilian border and flows in a broad arc through Venezuela before emptying into the Atlantic Ocean. This river is about 1500 miles long. It has

The Amazon and its tributaries serve as the main highways to the interior of northern Brazil. The Jari River rises in the Guiana Highlands near the Suriname border and flows into the Amazon near the town of Boca do Jari, site of this wood pulp plant.

gained economic importance since World War II because of extensive irrigation projects and the construction of a shipping route for high grade iron mined south of the river.

The Rio de la Plata, an estuary, is the third largest river system in South America. Flowing between Argentina and Uruguay, it is about 225 miles long and formed by the joining of the Parana and Uruguay rivers. Other rivers, such as the Paraguay and the Salado, also join this river farther upstream. Despite the size of this river system, it is not very reliable for navigation. The Paraguay frequently shifts channels, and sand bars tend to form, hindering shipping. This is serious for the landlocked nations of Paraguay and Bolivia because the river is their only access to the Atlantic Ocean. Even the broad Rio de la Plata is a problem for navigators. Mud banks form continually in the estuary. Dredges work constantly to keep shipping channels open to Buenos Aires.

The Río Magdalena in Colombia is another important river. For centuries it was the only way into the interior of Colombia and to its major city, Bogotá.

Lakes are not numerous. Although rivers are numerous, few lakes exist in South America. The largest, Lake Maracaibo (mah-rah-*ky*'bow), is part of the Gulf of Venezuela. It is an unusual lake in that the southern portion contains fresh water while the northern part is brackish. The bottom of this shallow lake and the surrounding shores are important sources of oil. Lake Titicaca, the second largest lake in the region, is at an elevation of 12,000 feet. No other lake at such a high altitude is navigable. Other lakes near Valdivia (vahl-*dee*'vyah), Chile, are small, but scenically so beautiful that they have become tourist attractions.

A Variety of Climate and Vegetation Zones

Like Africa, Latin America sits on both sides of the equator. In fact, most of Latin America extends farther south of the equator than Africa. As a result there are several climatic vegetation zones. The most extensive are the tropical zones which cover three-fourths of South America. The many mountain ranges of this

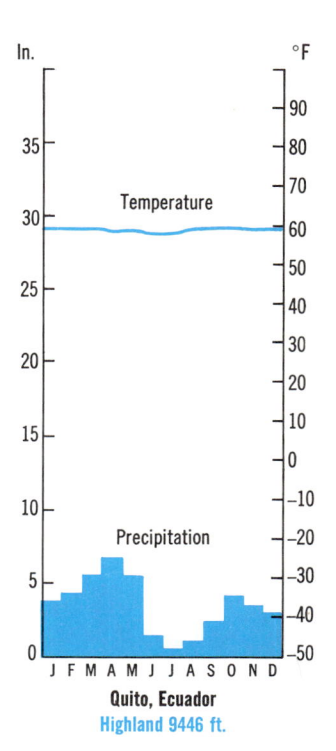

Quito, Ecuador
Highland 9446 ft.

LATIN AMERICA: CLIMATE REGIONS

- Tropical wet
- Tropical wet and dry
- Semiarid
- Desert (arid)
- Mediterranean
- Humid subtropical
- Marine
- Highlands
- Tundra

Buenos Aires, Argentina
Humid Subtropical

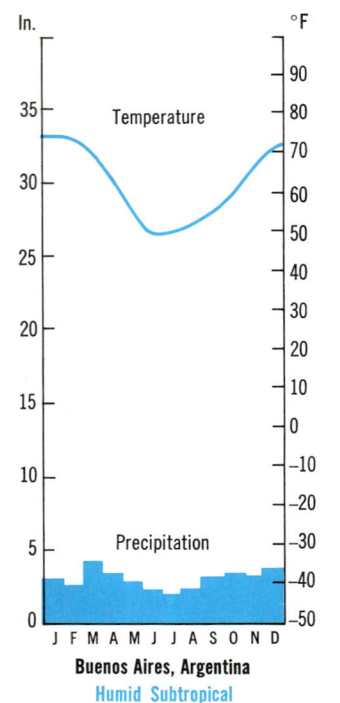

region also affect the climate. In the higher altitudes the weather is considerably cooler than in the lowland areas.

Tropical rain forest. This climate can be found in some Caribbean islands as well as along the eastern coast of Central America. In South America it extends along the northeastern coast and the lowlands of the northwestern coast. It is also found in western Brazil.

These regions are warm and moist all year long. Much of the land in these areas has not been developed because of the humidity, insects, and thick vegetation. In some places, however, plantation crops are grown.

In the mid-1980s the Brazilian government embarked on an extensive program to exploit the resources of the vast Amazon forest region. Logging, the introduction of cattle ranching, and the expansion of farming have resulted in rapid destruction of forest lands.

Loss of these forests may have serious consequences for the entire world. Plant life may be lost that could have important medicinal value. Very few of the plants have been studied and classified. Many scientists also fear that serious climatic consequences for the whole world would follow the destruction of the tropical rain forests.

Tropical savanna. In South America this climate covers the northern as well as the central portions of the continent. It is also found in western Central America and several Caribbean islands.

LATIN AMERICA: VEGETATION

- 🟩 Tropical rain forest
- 🟫 Tropical and subtropical forest and scrub
- 🟢 Mid-latitude forest
- 🟨 Grassland
- ⬜ Savanna
- 🟡 Desert shrubs and plants
- 🟧 Little or no vegetation

This warm climate has two seasons – one dry and the other wet. The length of each season depends on location. In the dry savanna regions grasses are usually the natural vegetation, while trees grow in those areas receiving more rainfall. In parts of this climatic zone plantation crops are grown and cattle raised.

Humid subtropical. In tropical zones the climate is consistently warm almost year round. There is little seasonal change. However, humid subtropical zones have a warm and a cool season. This zone is more densely populated. In both of the tropical zones, the average population density per square mile is rarely greater than 25 people. In this zone it is much higher, rising to over 250 people around the Río de la Plata estuary. This zone is mostly found in southeastern Brazil, Uruguay, and Argentina. Plentiful rainfall plus rich soil make this area the most prosperous. On the fertile pampas farmers raise beef cattle and wheat.

Dry lands. Like Africa, Latin America has arid areas. However, these do not occupy as high a percentage of the region's land surface as they do in Africa. Dry areas include parts of the Andes Mountains, the southern part of Argentina, called Patagonia, northern Mexico, and a desert area along the Pacific coast from southern Ecuador through Peru to central Chile.

Both location and altitude affect the climate of the Andes. As the elevation rises, temperatures fall. For example, Quito, Ecuador, at an elevation over 9000 feet, has temperatures in the fifties throughout the year, even though it is near

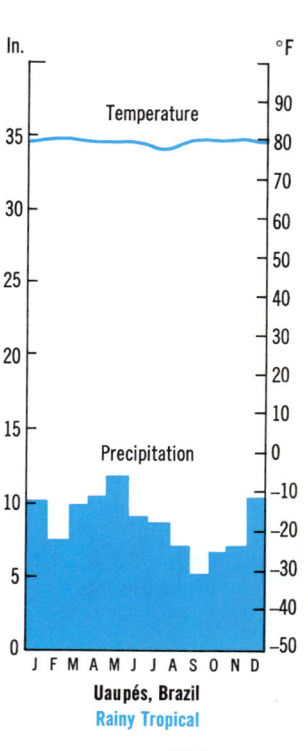

Uaupés, Brazil
Rainy Tropical

535

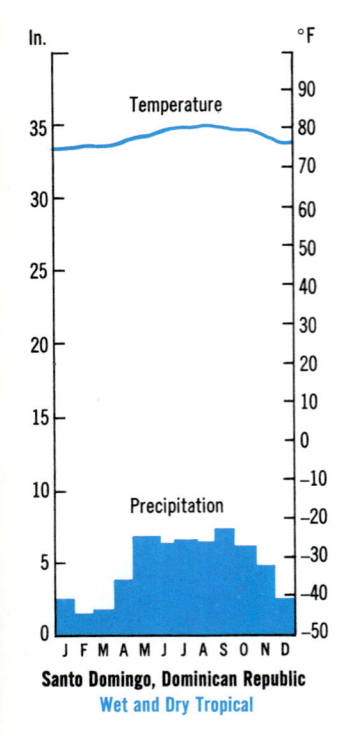

the equator. Another dry region is Patagonia in southern Argentina. This area receives less than 10 inches of rainfall per year.

Parts of northern Mexico also have a dry climate. The area is sparsely settled except for those places where irrigation projects exist. In such locations the soil becomes highly productive.

Much of the land is unproductive. Much land in Latin America is unproductive because it lacks fertility, is too mountainous, or is inaccessible. Vast areas have fewer than two or three persons per square mile because the land could not support more. Such large, nearly empty areas are found especially in the interior regions of South America and northern Mexico. Brazilian engineers have begun vast roadbuilding projects to link the Amazon region with the outside world. In Central America and Peru similar efforts are now being made on a smaller scale.

Looking ahead. Although 400 years have passed since European settlement of Latin America began, the full potential of the region has not been realized. Modern technology is helping to overcome some of the earlier obstacles to development of Latin America's resources. This part of the world is experiencing tremendous changes in all areas of life. We shall explore some of these trends in the chapters that follow.

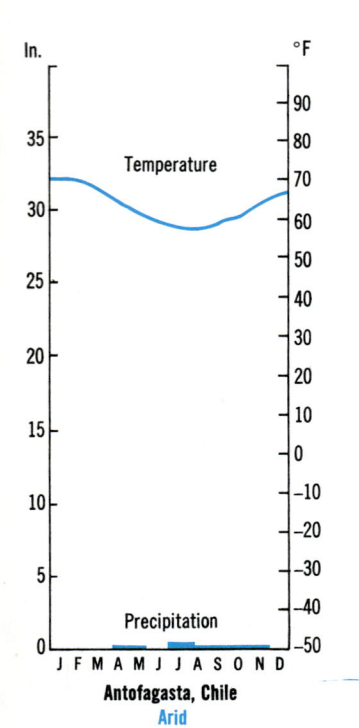

CHAPTER REVIEW

Recalling Names and Places

Amazon River	Lake Maracaibo	pampas
Andes	Lake Titicaca	Patagonia
Brazilian Highlands	Orinoco River	Río de la Plata
Guiana Highlands		

Understanding This Chapter

1. Where are the mountainous regions located? Compare them with the mountainous regions of North America.
2. Why are there few lowlands areas?
3. Name some of the large rivers of South America. Why have they often lacked economic importance?
4. In volume of water, the Amazon is the mightiest river in the world. What role has it played in the development of South America?
5. Describe each of the major climatic zones of Latin America and tell where they are located.
6. Explain why much of Latin America's land is unproductive.
7. There are 19 independent nations in mainland Central and South America. In the rest of the mainland North America – a slightly larger land mass – there are three nations. Can you think of any geographic reasons for this difference? Any cultural reasons?

Santo Domingo, Dominican Republic
Wet and Dry Tropical

Antofagasta, Chile
Arid

536

Chapter 47

The Building of Latin America

Humans lived in the Eastern Hemisphere for perhaps 3 million years before migrations to the Americas began. Some scientists believe that these migrations began between 50,000 and 100,000 years ago. Abundant evidence – tools and other aritfacts – shows that small groups of hunting and gathering peoples entered America from Siberia across the narrow Bering Straits. These migrations continued for thousands of years.

Early Inhabitants of the Americas

At the time of early migrations, great glaciers, as much as two miles thick, covered most of Canada and the northern United States. Not all the land was ice-covered, however. People could travel on land to get from the Arctic region to the south.

So much water became ice that the level of oceans may have dropped 200 or 300 feet at the peak of the Ice Age. The dry ocean bed created a land bridge between Siberia and Alaska, making migration to America easy. After the ice retreated, around 10,000 years ago, water separated the continents again. For people with boats the narrow crossing was no great problem. Migrations continued long after water again separated Siberia from Alaska.

The search for food leads to the Americas. Eventually some of these migrants and their descendants wandered 10,000 miles from the Bering Straits to Cape Horn. The routes of these early migrants were determined by the animals they hunted. Where the animals wandered, people followed. Although they ate roots and berries, the meat supply was very important. In the search for food humans populated the Western Hemisphere. When areas gained more population than the food supply could support, people were forced to move on.

Alternate theories. Other theories of the origins of American Indians have been offered at various times. Because the Mayans and Egyptians both built pyramids, some have suggested a link between these two peoples. Thor Heyerdahl, a Norwegian explorer, demonstrated in 1947 that winds and ocean currents could carry a raft from Polynesia to South America. Going from Africa to the West Indies in 1970, he sailed a papyrus boat of ancient Egyptian design to prove that it could be done. However, scholars have not found enough evidence to accept these theories.

PRE-COLUMBIAN CIVILIZATIONS

- Aztec Empire
- Inca Empire
- Mayan Civilization
- Present-day national boundary

The First Americans

Asian migrants settled the Western Hemisphere at least 30,000 years before the arrival of Christopher Columbus in 1492. Because Columbus thought he had reached southern Asia, he called the people he found Indians. Although later explorers realized his mistake, the name has remained. The migrants eventually settled in various locations and developed agriculture to provide a constant food supply. Corn became a major crop and, along with others, created an abundance of food to support a large population. The necessary conditions for the development of a civilized life had been met.

More than a thousand years before the arrival of Columbus, complex civilizations emerged. Because 1492 marks the beginning of Spanish exploration and conquest in this area, historians often divide the history of Latin America at this date. The earlier period is often called pre-Columbian history. Among the most highly developed Indian civilizations of pre-Columbian history were the Mayas (*mah*'yuhs), the Aztecs, and the Incas. Their cultures have influenced all aspects of Latin American social and cultural life.

Mayan culture was once the most advanced in the Western Hemisphere. Mayan civilization was originally centered in what is today southern Mexico, Guatemala, Belize, and Honduras. For about a thousand years Mayan culture

Maize

Most peoples of the world have tales that explain how the world began and human life was created. Human beings wonder about such things and usually evolve an account of creation.

The Mayas were a very hospitable people. A stranger was warmly welcomed and fed generously to the limits of the family's food supply. Storytelling was a favorite form of entertainment, and tales of the gods and how life began were especially popular. The Mayas believed that people were created to serve a special purpose.

The gods, according to this legend, were not satisfied with an earth which did not have creatures who could praise and worship them. So they decided to make man. They tried three times before they got what they wanted. First they made men of mud, but they were too soft and melted away. Then they carved creatures out of wood. But they did not suit either. The animals and the tools rose up in rebellion against these wooden men. The dogs said, "You beat us with sticks and order us about; why should we not kill you?" The stones used in grinding corn said, "In your service we are worn away; day after day you are always rubbing us together, making us go holi, holi, huki, huki; now we will try our strength against you." In the end, the gods sent a great flood, wiping out these unsatisfactory creatures, and finally fashioned four new men out of corn meal with corn cobs for arms and legs. "These men were our forefathers," the saga says, "four in number were the men created from maize, and afterward four women were made for these men." Then at last the sun rose, for up to that time the world had been in darkness. And the morning and the evening were the first day, and man, ruling the earth and praising the gods, was started on his way.

Corn was the staff of life for the Mayas, and it is significant that in this creation account human beings were made from corn. Note also the reference to a great flood. The biblical account of Noah is duplicated in the traditions of many peoples of the world.

Edwin R. Embree, *Indians of the Americas*. Copyright 1939, © renewed 1967 by Kate C. Embree. Published by Houghton Mifflin Company. pp. 44–45.

About 700 A.D., Mayans painted this colorful fresco and many others at Bonampok, a religious center in what is now Chiapas, Mexico.

developed, reaching its Golden Age early in the fourth century A.D. This civilization lasted for about 600 years. The land of the Mayas was rich in the resources needed to build a great civilization. Since they had large supplies of food, the Mayas had sufficient leisure to develop science, mathematics, architecture, and fine arts.

The Mayas were the only Indians to develop a complex system of writing. Their ideographs expressed ideas by means of symbols. Mayan astronomy was so advanced that they could compute the movements of planets. The Mayas developed a calendar more accurate than that of the Europeans. The Mayas were among the world's greatest mathematicians. Only Mayan and Hindu mathematicians discovered the concept of zero.

In architecture, sculpture, and painting, the Mayas were equally brilliant. Excellent limestone quarries produced a stone that could be easily cut but hardened when exposed to air. If burned, it turned into lime which was mixed with gravel to make cement. Their architecture and sculpture compare with the best works of the ancient Egyptians.

This civilization declined in the tenth century, for a variety of reasons. Some experts think the soil lost its fertility or that severe droughts, invasions, or widespread epidemics may have been the cause. The great cities of Tikal, Copan, and Palenque (pah-*lain*'kay) were abandoned, and finally the forests hid them from view. The Mayas migrated north to Yucatan (you-kah-*tahn'*), a large peninsula in southeastern Mexico. From the eleventh century until shortly before the Spaniards came, a new civilization flourished. The cities of Chichen Itza (chih-*chain'* ett-*sah'*) and Uxmal became great cultural centers at this time. Civil wars between the cities brought the decline of the Mayas.

This Aztec calendar stone was discovered by workers in Mexico City in 1790. In the center is the face of the sun god. The stone, which measures 13 feet across, today stands at the entrance to Mexico City's Museo Nacional de Antropolgía.

Aztecs control central Mexico. During the first 1000 years of the Christian era various people settled in central Mexico. By 1000 A.D. the Toltecs had created a great empire with a magnificent capital called Tula. However, early in the twelfth century the city was attacked and destroyed. Less civilized peoples, called by the name *Chichimecs* (sons of the dog), moved into the area. Learning from the Toltecs, they blended into the culture of the region.

The origin of the Aztecs is not clear. They may have been a small tribe living on the frontier of the Toltec empire and serving as mercenaries for other Indian groups. They also had legends about a distant origin. Taking advantage of local tribal conflicts after the fall of Tula, they gradually rose to a position of dominance in central Mexico. Within a century the Aztecs advanced from a small

---

A Bloody Religion and a Love of Beauty

The chief god of the Aztecs was Huitzilopochtli, a young warrior who was identified with the sun. Each sunset was his death but he was born again at sunrise to fight the darkness away and scatter the moon and stars.

In order to be reborn each day, Huitzilopochtli required the nourishment that only human blood could provide. Therefore, the Aztecs believed that regular human sacrifices were needed to assure the preservation of the sun.

Although human sacrifice to gods was a practice of some other tribes, none emphasized it so strongly as the Aztecs. Special occasions might involve the sacrifice of many people. It is reported that the Temple of Tenochtitlan was dedicated with the sacrifice of 20,000 prisoners of war. The need for a continual supply of sacrifices made the Aztecs warlike and alarmed other peoples. Captured enemies were sacrificed by priests who cut open their chests and tore out their hearts.

The Aztecs believed that if they served Huitzilopochtli faithfully the god would help them conquer the world. The Aztec king was called *Cemanáhuac tlatoani,* meaning "Ruler of the World."

Warfare and human sacrifices were not the only concerns of the Aztecs. Like people everywhere they were chiefly concerned with home, family, and other daily matters. That they had a love for beauty is revealed by some of their literature, such as the poem below:

My heart wishes with longing for flowers,
  I suffer with the song, and only rehearse songs on earth,
  I, Cuacuauhtzin:
  I want flowers that will endure in my hands . . . !
  Where shall I gather beautiful flowers, beautiful songs?
  Never does spring produce them here:
  I alone, torment my self, I, Cuacuauhtzin.
  Can you rejoice perchance, may our friends have pleasure?
  Where shall I gather beautiful flowers, beautiful songs?

*From *The Aztec: Man and Tribe* by Victor Von Hagen. Copyright © 1958 by Victor W. Von Hagen. Reprinted by arrangement with The New American Library, Inc., New York, New York.

tribe to become masters of a great empire, successors to the Toltecs. They built their capital city, Tenochtitlan (tay-nohch-tee-*tlan'*), on islands in Lake Texcoco. This lake has since been largely drained, and the site is now the location of Mexico City.

The Aztecs were a warlike people, and those they conquered had to pay tribute. When the Spaniards arrived in 1519, Aztec domination of central Mexico was only about a century old and the empire was not fully established. However, Aztec society was well-administered. Laws were effective, and antisocial behavior was rare. No one went hungry. Although people became slaves for debt or wrongdoing, they were seldom very harshly treated.

Although the Spanish forces, led by Hernán Cortés, numbered only 600 men, they had guns and horses, which gave them strong advantages. Even though the Aztecs had at least 20,000 soldiers, they were unable to stop the invaders. The conquered tribes helped the Spaniards fight their rulers. The Aztecs were also handicapped by a legend. They believed that Quetzalcoatl (kate-sahl-*koh*'atl), a deified Toltec king, would return to them from across the sea. They thought this god-king would look like a bearded white man. Thus the Aztecs hesitated long enough to permit Cortés to enter Tenochtitlan. In two years he was master of Mexico.

The Incan empire. In the Andes a series of advanced cultures existed before the Christian era. The Incan empire was the last and greatest of several such po-

This 100-foot-high pyramid temple, dedicated to a Toltec war god, stands in the ruins of Chichén Itzá in the Yucatan peninsula.

litical systems. The Incas were an elite ruling caste who were descended from a tribe living in the vicinity of Cuzco (*koos'*koh) around 1000 A.D. They extended their control over other peoples in all directions until they ruled a vast empire. It extended from southern Colombia to northern Chile and Argentina, a distance of almost 3000 miles. Quechua (*kay'*chew-ah) was the language everyone used, and it is still spoken by millions living in this region today.

The Incan empire may have been the most thoroughly organized welfare state in the world. The needs of every individual were met from birth until death. Each person served the state and was told what to do. At the age of sixteen a person was expected to work full time. At age fifty a person was permitted to do lighter work. After sixty no work was expected. In theory all land belonged to the *Inca*, the emperor, and he distributed it and indicated how it should be used.

The Incas did not have as much advanced knowledge and technology as the Mayas. Although they never developed a system of writing, they sent communications by tying knotted cords or *quipu* together. Messages were sent by runners on roads built from one end of the empire to the other. The Incan road system was one of the most impressive achievements of their civilization. Since they had no wheeled vehicles, the Incas constructed their roads for foot travel. Two parallel roads were built north to south. One followed the shore from northern Peru to Chile and the other the highlands from northern Ecuador to Chile. East-west roads connected them.

They skillfully constructed stone buildings and forts. After cutting huge blocks of stone, some weighing many tons, the Incas erected structures high in the Andes. They used no mortar, yet the stones fitted perfectly and in irregular shapes to prevent collapse during the earthquakes that are common in this part of the world. In addition to their achievements in architecture, the Incas also produced metal-work, pottery, and textiles.

The Spanish did not conquer the Incas' mountain city of Machu Picchu. They did not even know of the existence of this fortress city high in the Andes, more than 19,000 feet above sea level. An explorer from the United States discovered the ruins of Machu Picchu in 1911.

543

Incan Textiles

Some of the most beautiful textiles made in pre-Columbian America were those produced by the Incas. The Incas tended large herds of domesticated llamas, wool-bearing animals related to the camel. They were the only Indians who had wool fiber. They also grew cotton. The women spun the wool or cotton and dyed them beautiful colors. As the following passage shows, making textiles was a major activity of Incan women.

Since spinning was all done by hand, a great deal of women's time had to be devoted to this task to furnish the thread and yarn used in the great textile industry of the Empire. Women carried cotton or wool with them wherever they went. Even as they walked along the city streets or country roads or visited their neighbors, their fingers were busy making strands and winding them on spindles. When a woman went to call on a person of higher rank, she left her own work at home and immediately on arriving said humbly that she had not come to call but to see if she could help in some household task. A gracious hostess replied that she would not think of letting the guest do servant's work but that she would be glad to get some of the spinning or embroidery on which her daughters had been working. This was a compliment since it admitted the guest to the work and therefore to the social sphere of the high-born lady of the house.

Edwin R. Embree, *Indians of the Americas*. Copyright 1939, © renewed 1967 by Kate C. Embree. Published by Houghton Mifflin Company. p. 97.

The Spaniards take control of the Incan empire. As with their conquest of Mexico, the Spaniards had extraordinary luck on their side. When Francisco Pizarro arrived in Peru in 1530 with 180 men, they found a divided Incan empire.

At his deathbed Huayna, the last Inca, ordered that the empire be divided between two of his sons. This was contrary to Incan law, and civil war broke out between the followers of Atahualpa (ah-tah-*wahl'* pah), a son of a secondary wife, and the legal heir to the throne.

Pizarro first seized Atahualpa and then imprisoned and murdered the true Inca. Later Atahualpa was strangled and the empire was without a ruler. The Incan empire was paralyzed to act without orders from an Inca, and the Spaniards were able to take control.

Shortly before his death in 1541, Pizarro founded the city of Lima in Peru. It became the chief administrative center of Spanish government in South America. Incan administration was permanently ended, and Spanish governors proceeded to organize the newly conquered territories. Although missionary work among the Indians had some success, the basic way of life of the people changed little. The territories of the old Incan empire still remain largely Indian four hundred years after the Spanish conquest.

The eastern half of South America, which was to become Brazil, underwent a vastly different experience. Sparsely populated by culturally more primitive people than the Incas, Brazil was settled and developed by the Portuguese at a much slower pace than that of Spanish colonies.

Reviewing Your Reading

1. Describe early migration to the Americas.
2. Why is the Mayan civilization considered to be the most advanced Indian culture to develop in this region?
3. How did the Mayan civilization differ from that of the Aztecs?
4. How did the Incas control their vast empire?

Spain Creates and Loses Its Colonies

The Spaniards concentrated their explorations and settlements on the Caribbean islands of Hispaniola, Cuba, Jamaica, and Puerto Rico for several decades. Then they expanded their interests to Mexico and Peru. They considered three other areas less important: the Spanish Main (Colombia and Venezuela), Chile, and the Río de la Plata region. These areas did not promise quick mineral wealth. In southern South America hostile Indians prevented permanent settlement of this area until 1580. This date marked the end of the spectacular era of Spanish conquest.

How Spain controlled its empire. The colonial period in Latin America began when the age of absolutism was in full sway in Europe. Monarchs were supreme rulers with few recognized controls over their power. Nowhere was this more true than in Spain. In theory the colonial holdings belonged to the king or queen, who decided how the lands would be administered. An endless stream of rules and regulations came from Spain to the administrators whom the monarch appointed. Local government did not exist.

The Spaniards were much concerned about the administration of the territory they invaded. They immediately established a city, often before the fighting ended. When Hernán Cortés landed on the shores of Mexico, he founded Veracruz (True Cross). After the Aztec capital of Tenochtitlan fell, it became Mexico City, the capital of New Spain as the Spaniards called Mexico. In Peru, Francisco Pizarro founded Lima as the capital. Cities were the administrative centers for the surrounding countryside, and their founding was the necessary first step in governing the territory.

By the time the major conquests ended, Spanish America was divided into administrative territories called viceroyalties. The major ones were New Spain, with Mexico City as the capital, and Peru, administered from Lima. Each viceroyalty had a viceroy as its chief administrator. This title, meaning vice-king, showed he had permission to speak for the crown. He received instructions from the monarch, and although he had little authority independent of the crown, he had great power over the people he governed. Although the viceroy was the most important colonial official, he had little control over other administrators of lower rank. They also received their orders directly from the king.

Economic development: Gold and land. The discovery of gold and silver speeded the Spanish development of Latin America. Although most regions did not yield treasures in minerals, some miners uncovered fabulous riches. It is be-

The Indians of Mexico sent this letter to the king of Spain to protest the injustices they were suffering under the encomienda *system.*

lieved that in 1800, three centuries after their founding, the Spanish colonies were producing 90 percent of the world's supply of gold and silver.

Agriculture became far more important than precious metals, however. The Spaniards brought with them numerous foods that could grow in various parts of Latin America. They introduced grains and fruits, as well as sugar and coffee, which soon became major crops. They also brought goats, pigs, chickens, cattle, and sheep. Moreover, they introduced beasts of burden and the wheel, speeding transportation and making agriculture easier. They also learned to use many food-producing and medicinal plants found in the region and cultivated by the Indians.

In the early 1500s the Spanish introduced the encomienda system. *Encomienda* is a Spanish word which means "commendation" and referred originally to the arrangement between Spanish social classes in which lesser nobles, small landholders, and freemen provided services for more powerful nobles in return for protection. In Latin America the encomienda system enabled Spanish landholders to use the Indian workers in certain villages near their estates as laborers. In return, the Indians were supposed to be paid for their work, receive humane treatment, and be taught the Christian religion. This arrangement was sometimes abused by Spanish landowners who overworked the Indians.

The Church tried to protect the Indians. Spanish exploitation of the Indians might have been greater if it had not been for the Church. Not only did priests seek to convert the Indians, but they also labored hard to protect them.

The enslavement of Indians by the Spanish conquerors was often so cruel that many natives died. Several priests protested the treatment and aided the victims.

Some religious orders, for example Jesuits and Franciscans, established mission villages in which Indians could live. The priests taught the Indians agricultural skills and protected them from slave-raiding colonists. The largest center of such mission villages was in the Río de La Plata region of Paraguay and northern Argentina. They lasted until 1767 when the Jesuits were forced to leave the Spanish territories.

Toward the end of the colonial period the Church itself became a major landholder. Large and beautiful cathedrals were built in many cities as the institution became increasingly wealthy. The priestly class, which had once been concerned with the Indians' welfare, became less interested.

Portuguese settlement in America. Portuguese America was called Brazil. During voyages there in the early 1500s, some red wood, called "brazil," was found. It became a source of red dye. Although this wood became the colony's first commercial product, few people settled there.

The Portuguese were primarily interested in increasing their trade with India, other parts of Asia, and the East Indies. Lack of wealth and a shortage of workers resulted in a much slower development of Brazil than of Spanish America. The Indian population was more sparse than in Peru and Mexico. Expeditions sent into the interior did not bring back any precious metals.

In the 1530s the Dutch, Spanish, English, and French began showing an interest in Brazil and hoped to claim the territory for themselves. At that time, the Portuguese established communities on or near the Atlantic coast.

As in Spanish America, commercial farming was the major part of the economy. Commercial farming was done on estates where slaves provided the labor. A variety of crops, including tobacco and cotton were grown. However, the most profitable crop during the colonial period was sugar. On the plantation, called a *fazenda,* the owner was lord and master. Unlike pre-Civil War slave owners in the United States, however, the Brazilians were more tolerant. Racist feelings were less strong. Slaves could buy their freedom and non-whites could rise to positions of importance in Brazilian society.

Bartolomé de Las Casas, the first Roman Catholic priest ordained in the New World, documented the oppression of the Latin American Indians by his fellow Spanish settlers and struggled to put an end to it.

Learning from the Indians

A few of the more common foods and drugs developed by the Indians which were unknown in Europe include:

avocados	pineapples
beans (lima, kidney, and others)	pumpkins
cacao (source of chocolate)	squash
cashew nuts	sweet potatoes
chili peppers	tapioca (from manioc)
cinchona (source of quinine)	tobacco
coca (source of cocaine)	tomatoes
corn (maize)	vanilla
muskmelons	white potatoes
peanuts	

Fighters for independence in South America: (top to bottom) Simón Bolívar, Jose de San Martín, and Bernardo O'Higgins.

Cities were not important in Brazil as they were in Spanish America. Instead of becoming cultural and administrative centers, they served chiefly as outlets for the products from the plantations.

Independence Movements Begin in 1808

Napoleon Bonaparte's invasion of Spain in 1808 ignited the spark that started the independence movement. Napoleon imprisoned the king, Ferdinand VII, and put his own brother, Joseph Bonaparte, on the throne. His action led to the formation of Latin American councils, called *juntas,* to defend the colonies against the French. However, this temporary self-rule soon became an independence movement that spread throughout the region. The leaders were inspired by the recent revolution in North America. The writings of Thomas Jefferson, Benjamin Franklin, and Thomas Paine were read eagerly. By 1825 the Spanish forces were defeated.

Fighters for independence. Among the revolutionary war heroes were Simón Bolívar (bow-*lee*'vahr, 1783–1830) and José de San Martín (1778–1850). Bolívar, a Venezuelan, led his forces to liberate the present-day countries of Venezuela, Colombia, Ecuador, Peru, and Bolivia. San Martín freed his homeland, Argentina, and along with Bernardo O'Higgins (1778–1842) liberated Chile. He also helped free Peru – the last Spanish stronghold in South America.

While South American capitals were the centers of independence movements, the revolution in New Spain began in a Mexican village. Led by a priest, father Miguel Hidalgo y Costilla, his "people's army" first tried to overthrow Spanish rule in 1810. Although Father Hidalgo's (ee-*dahl*'goh) army failed, another led by Agustín de Iturbide (ee-tour-*bee*'day) achieved Mexican independence in 1821.

Pedro I proclaims Brazil's independence. Brazil, unlike other Latin American countries, gained its independence peacefully. Shortly before Napoleon invaded Portugal in 1807, the Portuguese royal family fled to Brazil.

The Cry of Dolores

The small village of Dolores, 100 miles northwest of Mexico City, is the birthplace of Mexican independence. In 1810 Miguel Hidalgo y Costilla, a poor parish priest, rang the bells of his little church in a call for freedom.

Father Hidalgo was a scholarly man who had read of the French Revolution and believed the time for Mexican independence had arrived. He saw the poverty of his people and wanted a better life for them.

"Long live Our Lady of Guadelupe! Down with bad government! Death to the Spaniards!" This became the slogan of revolution – the "Cry of Dolores." Father Hidalgo was captured and shot by the Spaniards, but the demand for freedom did not die. He became a hero of the people, and the struggle went on until independence was won in 1821.

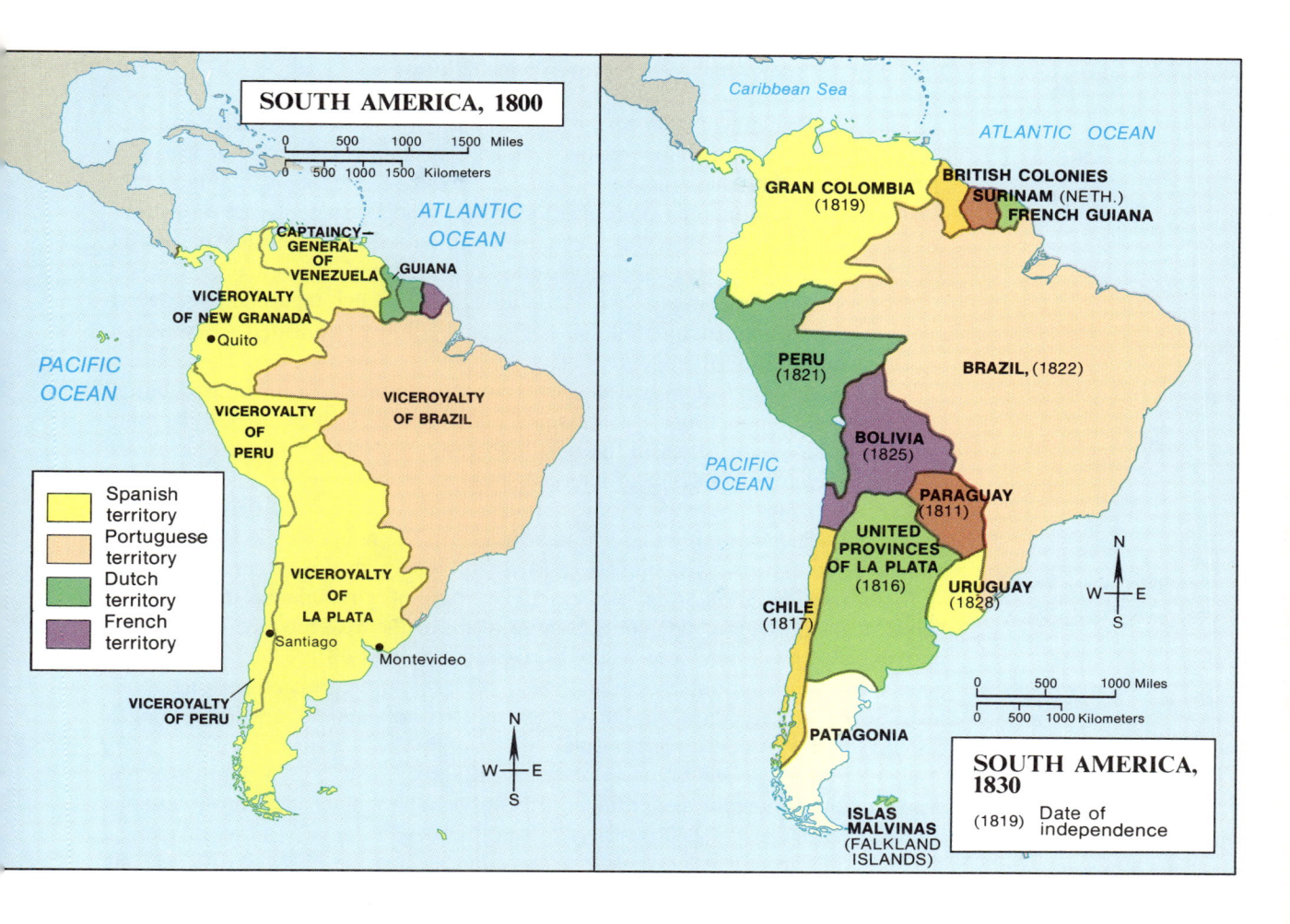

Eight years later, Brazil achieved equal status with Portugal, and the king became the ruler of both countries.

In 1821 the king, Joao VI (zhoh-*ow'*), returned to Portugal and left his son, Pedro I, in charge. Suspecting that Brazil would once more be reduced to a colony, Pedro declared the country's independence in 1822 and became emperor. Pedro I and then his son, Pedro II, reigned until 1889, when Brazil became a republic.

Reviewing Your Reading

1. Describe methods the Spaniards used to control their empire.
2. Why did agriculture become more important to the Spaniards than precious metals? What means did they use to make farming more productive?
3. How did the Church try to protect the Indians?
4. Compare the Portuguese settlement and development of Brazil with the Spanish settlement and development of their territories in the Americas.
5. Trace the events leading to independence for the Spanish colonies and Brazil. Who were some of the revolutionary heroes?

The New Republics Are Beset by Problems

Simón Bolívar dreamt that Spanish Americans would form a federation, perhaps a union such as the United States. In spite of his great prestige and leadership experience, he was unable to make his dream become a reality. Gran Colombia, a federation of Colombia, Venezuela, and Ecuador, lasted only eight years. A short time before his death Bolívar wrote in despair: "America is ungovernable. Those who have served the revolution have ploughed the sea."

Bolívar and other leaders of the new nations realized that their countries faced many hurdles before they could achieve stability. Let us consider a few of the problems confronting the new republics:

1. Geographical isolation: Lack of easy transportation between population centers created distinct local customs and loyalties. Few routes crossed the continent until air travel began in the twentieth century. National leaders have had difficulty developing a sense of nationalism in their followers.

2. Poverty and illiteracy: Some scholars think that over 90 percent of the Latin Americans were illiterate and poor in 1825. The new national leaders were unrealistic to expect such people to participate widely in government.

3. Inexperienced political leaders: The reins of government fell into the hands of inexperienced people. Although many of them were sincere and well-intentioned, they did not know how to compromise their differences. Two issues became critical: (1) Should new nations provide for some decision-making at the local level or should power be centralized in the national government? (2) Should liberals or conservatives rule?

4. Oligarchies come to power: Poverty, illiteracy, and lack of political experience made democratic government impossible. The nineteenth century became known as the Age of the Oligarchy, "government by the few." In Latin America the oligarchs usually represented wealthy landowners or military officers and were generally conservative, opposing changes that threatened their positions of wealth and power. The influence of oligarchies has often prevented social improvements in Latin America.

Caudillo rule in Mexico and Central America. The caudillo (cow-*dee'*-yoh), or political "boss," has been a familiar figure in Latin American history. He presented himself as a man who loved his people and wanted to improve their lives. He tried to cultivate *personalismo* among his followers, requiring complete loyalty to himself as the leader without concern for law or government. The caudillo often supported the interests of the oligarchy, even as he pretended to help the common people. The army, which he controlled, also served the elite.

Caudillos achieved power and leadership in a variety of ways. Frequently they won an election by promising to bring about reforms. When conflicts over powers of the Church arose, caudillos sometimes opposed Church domination as in Mexico and sometimes supported Church power as in Colombia, always to gain power for themselves.

Mexico had one of the more turbulent histories of caudillo rule in the nineteenth century. Most of the period from independence until 1855 was dominated by Antonio López de Santa Anna. A man of little real talent, though impressive appearance, he did little to help his country. Under his leadership half of Mexico

The storming of Chapultepec, a 200-foot-high fortress outside Mexico City, was the last major battle of the Mexican War. At the time Chapultepec was the site of the Mexican national military academy.

was lost to the United States as the result of a revolution in Texas in 1836 and the Mexican War in 1848.

A man much revered by Mexicans was a full-blooded Indian named Benito Juárez (*hwah'rayss*). Between 1855 and 1872 he served his country in various offices and as president. Juárez was not a military leader but a man trained in law. He tried to serve his country unselfishly. After his death Mexico was so torn by strife that only another caudillo could bring about order. In 1876 Porfirio Díaz took control and held it until 1911.

Díaz was tough and efficient. His police force eliminated bandits, political opponents, critics, and other troublemakers. Law and order were established throughout Mexico to the relief of wealthy landowners and foreign investors. The new security brought a flood of entrepreneurs from the United States and Europe to invest in various businesses in Mexico. Foreign investors, Mexico's wealthy class, and Díaz and his supporters profited from the increased economic activity. By the end of his regime it is estimated that only 5 percent of the people owned any land at all. The life of the masses remained miserable. Resentments such as these helped to fuel the Mexican Revolution of 1910, the first real social revolution in Latin America.

South of Mexico an early union of the small Central American countries failed, and most of them came under the rule of caudillos. Since that time caudillo rule has characterized their history. Costa Rica is the exception. It has been ruled democratically with only brief periods of dictatorship.

Benito Juárez served as president of Mexico from 1861 to 1865 and again from 1867 until his death in 1872.

Argentina and Chile achieve stability. While some Latin American countries suffered from political instability, Argentina and Chile achieved a high degree of stability around 1850. Two factors that contributed to this condition were their strong economies and trade markets. In neither nation was there the poverty and hunger experienced in Mexico and in the Andean region.

Following independence a major political struggle developed in Argentina between the urban population of Buenos Aires and the *gauchos,* or cowboys, of the pampas. It was a conflict between rural federalists and urban centralists. The federalists wanted greater local control while the city dwellers wanted to see a strong central government. Finally, in 1829 a caudillo named Manuel Rosas (*row'*sahss) came to power. As a rural ranch owner who had become a centralist, he understood both sides. He established a harsh dictatorship, suppressing freedom of speech and creating a secret police to eliminate all opposition. Although he was criticized for his methods of governing, his defenders say he saved Argentina from anarchy. He was finally ousted from power by another harsh leader in 1852.

Domingo Sarmiento became his nation's leader sixteen years later. He worked hard to give Argentina a government by law rather than by military force. He was an intellectual who believed strongly in advancing education and pushing other reforms.

Chile was plagued by fewer internal conflicts than Argentina. From the beginning of its independence wealthy landowners controlled politics. The constitution had such high property qualifications for voting and holding office that only members of the landed aristocracy could get into office. A powerful elite, or oligarchy, ruled the country. This group exercised such strong political control that the nation did not fall into the anarchy that plagued so many other countries. The electoral system provided by the constitution also prevented harsh strongman rule.

Brazil becomes a republic. The second emperor of Brazil, Pedro II, ruled Brazil for 42 years before he was invited to leave. He provided the country with good government and encouraged economic development. As his final constructive act he approved a bill abolishing slavery in 1888.

As in Chile, the republic came under the control of the wealthy landholders. The presidents served the interests of the upper class. The needs of the nation were not overlooked, however. Contributing to the development of Brazil was a great increase in immigration from Europe. Most immigrants came from Portugal and Italy. A large number of settlers also came from Germany.

Venezuela has a century of authoritarian rule. The years after independence were as chaotic in Venezuela as in Mexico. So much fighting was done by Venezuelans during the wars for independence that the nation was in ruins. Caudillos, often of the most brutal type, ruled the country for more than a century.

In 1908 a dictator named Juan Vicente Gómez (*go'*mace) took control. He adopted a policy very similar to that of Díaz in Mexico. He imposed order with the gun and invited foreign investors to exploit Venezuela's natural resources, especially oil. As in Mexico, the plight of the poor people remained unchanged because the oil revenues were not used to raise their standard of living. It should be noted, however, that Gómez did not give away as much to foreign investors as Díaz.

Gómez died in 1935, and the government leaders who followed tried to bring reform with little success. In the 1950s Marcos Pérez Jiménez (*he'*mennayss), a dictator with ideas similar to those of Gómez, ruled for eight years. After his ouster, a strong effort at social reform was attempted.

Reviewing Your Reading

1. Describe the problems facing the newly independent nations.
2. Why were oligarchies able to gain control of Latin American governments?
3. How did caudillos achieve political leadership?
4. Trace caudillo rule in Mexico from 1823 to 1911.
5. How did Manuel Rosas and Domingo Sarmiento try to unite their people?
6. Why was Chile able to avoid internal conflicts?
7. How did caudillo rule affect Venezuela?

Revolutionary Movements and Change

After independence, reformers demanded a better life for everyone, not just for the aristocracy. They desired universal education, the right of all citizens to elect government leaders, honest elections, and the opportunity to earn a decent living. Some believed that once independence was won these rights would be secured. They were not. Independence brought little improvement for the common people. Wealthy landowners who wanted to retain their special powers and privileges were generally successful during the nineteenth century.

Toward the end of the century pressures for change began to build. The reformers' desires had not changed, but they had often become anti-foreign. United States and other outside investors were exploiting the resources of the region and giving strong support to the dictators. This money gave the dictators the power to suppress changes and reforms. The reformers denounced these transactions as "Yankee imperialism."

By the twentieth century demands for reforms were strong throughout Latin America. In a few countries, leaders recognized that the time for change had arrived, and some improvements were allowed. The first major revolution to break out was in Mexico in 1910.

The Mexican Revolution brings changes. Porfirio Díaz succeeded in bringing order, economic prosperity to industry and commerce, and international respect for Mexico. But the poor Indians and mestizos had no share in this prosperity, and they were the majority of the population.

Criticism and discontent increased over the years. When Díaz, aged 80, announced that he would run again for president in 1910, a storm of protest broke out. By May 1911, angry mobs crowded Mexico City. Díaz resigned and left the country.

Orderly government broke down, and a murderous civil war raged. Cities and villages were destroyed, while close to a million people were killed as various

Pancho Villa (1878–1923) gallops alongside a column of his rebels. Villa was, successively, a cattle rustler, a bandit, and a revolutionary general. He joined the revolution against longtime president Porfirio Díaz in 1910 and helped bring about Díaz's resignation. After ten years of civil war, he made peace with the new government in 1920.

groups fought each other. During a lull in the fighting a constitution was drawn up. This constitution of 1917 provided for nationalization of the land, government ownership of mineral resources, and controls over the Church.

At first the various men who gained control of the government did not pay any attention to these provisions of the constitution, but they were not forgotten. Gradually in the 1920s and 1930s action was taken in all major areas referred to in the constitution. A genuine revolution took place. Land was more evenly distributed, foreign control of oil fields was ended, and Church powers were drastically reduced. A continuing program of reform has been adopted, and the way of life of the people has improved.

Not all Latin American nations have solved their political problems. As in the nineteenth century, many countries continue to resort to rule by force, although there are some differences today. In the nineteenth century many political leaders were ignorant, brutal military men who served the interests of the wealthy landowning oligarchies. Today they are likely to seek support from city workers, miners, and union members. They appeal to feelings of nationalism and popular resentments including the need for land reform or full employment. However, like the earlier caudillos, they often depend on the military.

Argentina is a good example of a country which has long lived under authoritarian leaders. Numerous problems during the past fifty years have brought a series of strong-man presidents, usually installed by the military. The best known was Juan Domingo Perón (pay-*rohn'*, 1895–1974), who held power in 1946–1955 and 1973–1974. His support came from the trade unionists and urban workers whom he rewarded by favorable labor laws. Other military rulers followed Perón until 1983. After a humiliating defeat by Britain in a war over control of the Falkland Islands (Islas Malvinas), military rulers allowed a civilian government to take control.

Since 1930 Brazil frequently has been ruled by army-supported caudillos. Like Argentina, the country has serious economic problems. Economic growth has not kept up with population increase. Inflation has been a major problem, with prices rising 100 percent in one year (1981). Still, economic growth goes on. Brazil continues to have the largest economy in Latin America. And in 1985 Brazil saw the end of more than 20 years of military rule, as a democratically elected government took office.

In 1970–1973 Chile had a freely elected Marxist president, Salvador Allende Gossens (ahl-*yen*'day), a member of Chile's Socialist Party. He was called a Marxist because he reflected many of the ideas of Karl Marx in his economic planning, especially in the need for government control or ownership of major industries. In 1973 a military coup overthrew the Allende government. Since then Chile has been ruled by military leaders who have strongly resisted opposition to their policies.

Salvador Allende, a Socialist, was the last democratically elected president of Chile. In 1973 a military junta killed him and seized power from his government.

Uruguay: Once a firm democracy. The unity of Uruguay is largely the work of one remarkable man, José Batlle y Ordóñez (1856–1929). A newspaper publisher, he was twice president of Uruguay, 1903–1907 and 1911–1915. Inspired by the example of Switzerland, Batlle (bah'yay) wanted to make his nation a genuine democracy. Fearful that a strong president might become a dictator, he successfully substituted a council for the presidency. From 1951 until 1966, a democracy without a presidency flourished in Uruguay.

Severe inflation, a decline in the demand for wool, Uruguay's chief export, and inability to effect necessary reforms caused instability in Uruguay in the early 1970s. A guerrilla movement arose but was defeated by the military. In 1973 the military disbanded congress and outlawed political parties. The leaders agreed to permit general elections in 1984, and a civilian government took over in March 1985.

Postwar revolutions of Cuba and Bolivia. Not since the Mexican Revolution had there been a genuine revolution in Latin America until Fidel Castro came to power in Cuba in 1959. Castro was determined to help the common people and reorganize the economy. Much of the Cuban industry was owned and controlled by businesses in the United States. The Cuban government took control of these holdings, and within a year the two nations opposed each other and trade between them dwindled. Castro turned to the Soviet Union for economic aid. His government embraced socialism and became the first Marxist nation in the Western Hemisphere.

During the years of Castroism, Cuba has had a close relationship with the Soviet Union. Without Soviet aid the troubled Cuban economy would have collapsed. The total embargo on trade by the United States and other hemispheric nations created many shortages. The privileged class of bureaucrats was able to obtain better food, services, housing, and goods than the masses. Still, in the early 1980s the Cuban economy was thriving. Enough food was available, and the people had many health and educational benefits.

The 1976 Cuban constitution guarantees the civil liberties of speech, press, and religion. The liberties, however, may not conflict with the aims of the communist state. The state's powers are vast: it can strip of all rights individuals accused of political crimes, reduce procedural obstacles in the courts, and control labor unions.

In cooperation with the Soviet Union, Cuba is pursuing an aggressive foreign policy that aids and abets Marxists in various African nations. In 1979 Cuban

A revolutionary force calling itself the Sandinistas overthrew the right-wing government of Anastasio Somoza and took control of Nicaragua in 1979.

troops were in Ethiopia and Angola, assisting the Communist governments in controlling border incursions, secessionist groups, and local guerrillas. Cuba's role in Africa was a major barrier to better trade and diplomatic relations with the United States.

Recent conflict in Central America has led to some Cuban involvement there. The Sandinista rulers in Nicaragua have recieved aid from Cuba in the form of military advisers and educational and medical teams. Cuba has also shipped military supplies, some of which may have been transferred to left-wing guerrillas fighting government forces in El Salvador.

Bolivia is the poorest nation in the Americas, but it is rich in some mineral resources. Its chief resource has been tin, but at times world prices have been so low that profits from the mining have been small. In 1952 working conditions in the mines were so bad that workers overthrew the government. One of the leaders of the coup, a sincere, reform-minded man, Victor Paz Estenssoro, became president. He nationalized the tin mines and attempted other reforms, but Bolivia's problems remained severe. Today Bolivia is the second-largest producer of tin, but in the early 1980s world tin prices dripped sharply and the country faced a severe economic crisis. Many believe that there are other possibilities for economic development, but the nation has neither the money nor people to do the job.

Political instability, poverty, and illiteracy remain Bolivia's chief problems. Throughout the 1970s and early 1980s Bolivia has largely been ruled by the military. From 1978 to 1982, Bolivia had nine changes of government. Bolivia lacks trained people to develop the nation's resources. It has been said that Bolivia is "a beggar sitting on a pile of gold." What is needed is a program that will use the gold to benefit the people.

Looking ahead. Latin America is a complex region of cultural lags and cultural achievements. In the 1970s and early 1980s political violence and instability greatly reduced the effectiveness of a number of goverments. Economic and political problems were worsened by a worldwide recession in the early 1980s. Still, in many parts of Latin America democratic values were taking hold and military dictatorships were giving way to freely elected governments. And despite problems of poverty, illiteracy, and overpopulation, there are great resources that remain untapped. The major problems are solvable, and there is a growing recognition throughout Latin America that economic cooperation may lead to the solution.

Reviewing Your Reading

1. What types of changes did reformers seek?
2. Describe the events leading to the Mexican Revolution. How did the constitution of 1917 help change Mexicans' lives?
3. Compare the caudillo of the twentieth century with the caudillo of the nineteenth century.
4. How were the outcomes of revolutions in Cuba and Bolivia different?

CHAPTER REVIEW

Recalling Names and Places

Aztec	Juan Vicente Gómez	Pedro II
Simón Bolívar	Inca	Juan Domingo Perón
Fidel Castro	Marcos Pérez Jiménez	Manuel Rosas
caudillo	Benito Juárez	Antonio López de Santa Anna
Porfirio Díaz	Maya	José de San Martín
encomienda	Pedro I	viceroyalty

Understanding This Chapter

1. Of the three great early civilizations of the Americas – Aztecs, Mayas, and Incas – which achieved the most advanced level? Why do you think so?
2. What benefits did the coming of the Spanish bring to the native peoples of the Americas? What losses?
3. It is said that the food products of the Americas proved to be more valuable than all the gold and silver. Why?
4. Caudillo rule has been more common than democracy in Latin American history. What reasons can you give for this? Is this changing at all? How?
5. Why were revolutions sometimes the only way that real reforms could be made in Latin America?

Chapter 48

A Region Strong in Traditions

Great distances, and natural barriers such as mountains and tropical rain forests, have preserved a diversity of life styles in Latin America. Despite efforts of leaders like Simón Bolívar to create political federations, Latin America broke up into many separate nations. These political boundaries further contributed to social and cultural diversity.

Racial and cultural patterns also contributed to social differences. Millions of Indians preserve their distinctive ways of life. There is little reason to believe that they will soon abandon their ancient ways. Considerable isolation from the rest of the world as well as the conservatism of religious and political institutions limit influences from the rest of the world. Traditions of the past have a strong hold in Latin America.

Social Stratification: Historical Roots

At the time of the Conquest, Spain and Portugal were medieval societies divided into two classes. One was the aristocracy, which included the royal family, nobles, and high church officials. The other was the lower class whose members were peasants, merchants, and a few professional people. Upward mobility rarely occurred.

When the conquistadors came to the Americas, they created a class system similar to the one they had known at home. However, the colonial social structure was more complex because race as well as wealth and family status played a part in determining a person's rank. In some parts of the Americas a new social system was easily established. In Peru and Mexico, for example, the conquerors replaced the ruling Incan and Aztec aristocracy.

Spanish-born people occupy highest social positions. Most members of the colonial upper class were *peninsulares,* or people who were born in Spain. They were influential in colonial life, since they held most of the important governmental and church positions. Moreover, many were prosperous merchants, high army officers, and university officials. All but four of the 170 viceroys named to head the colonial governments were peninsulares.

Not all members of the colonial aristocracy were members of upper-class Spanish families. Some of the conquistadors were able to establish themselves in high positions. Among them was Gonzalo Pizarro, a former swineherd. Wealthy or not, they considered themselves too important to engage in physical labor.

LATIN AMERICA: POPULATION
People per square mile
People per square kilometer
Over 125
60
25
2
0
Over 50
25
10
1
0
City with over 2 million people
City with over 1 million people
Gulf of Mexico
ATLANTIC OCEAN
Caribbean Sea
PACIFIC OCEAN
Monterrey
Guadalajara
Mexico City
Havana
Santo Domingo
San Juan
Guatemala
Barranquilla
Caracas
Medellín
Bogotá
Cali
Guayaquil
Fortaleza
Recife
Lima
Salvador
Brasília
Belo Horizonte
São Paulo
Rio de Janeiro
Curitiba
Porto Alegre
Córdoba
Rosario
Santiago
Buenos Aires
Montevideo
N
W
E
S
0 250 500 750 1000 Miles
0 250 500 750 1000 Kilometers

Closely associated with the peninsulares were the *criollos,* or Spaniards born in the Americas. Their "pure white" ancestry guaranteed them the next best position in society. They held minor church and governmental positions and became lawyers, doctors, and judges. They frequently controlled town governments and often had large estates and mines.

Mestizos rank below criollos in the social system. The *mestizos,* having a white and Indian heritage, were beneath the criollos. They were rejected by both races, and were, in effect, marginal. Not allowed to own land, they became parish and mission priests, nuns, and small shopkeepers. Others were overseers in the mines and on the huge estates. The second largest racial group, they formed the majority of the population in the towns.

Indians formed the largest social class. Indians were exploited by the classes above them. They were laborers and artisans who worked hard for little or no pay. Others became personal servants. Many Indians lived outside Spanish-American society, remaining in rural, mountain areas.

Blacks rank with Indians in the social system. The upper classes in the Caribbean countries imported black slaves when Indians proved unsatisfactory workers in the fields and mines. The blacks, unlike the Indians, had limited legal rights. They could work to purchase their freedom and were allowed to marry whom they chose.

Colonial society was not completely rigid. Criollos and peninsulares intermarried. So did some whites and blacks, whose children were called *mulattos.* Talented mestizos sometimes moved to higher positions in the social system and

Many Peruvian Indians, direct descendants of the Incas, still practice the ancient arts of metalware, pottery, and the weaving of colorful homespun cloth.

Pedestrians in downtown Sao Paolo, Brazil, show the great variety of Brazil's population.

were treated as equals by the Spaniards. Toward the end of colonial rule classes were based more on wealth than on race or birth. Many criollos gained much greater prestige in their communities than did the peninsulares.

The class system today. Wealth and family lineage remain an important basis for social stratification. For the most part members of the upper class form a tightly knit group, unlikely to accept others no matter how talented, intelligent, or wealthy they may be. This group retains much power and most of the land, and is the best educated. Industrialization is a major threat to this group's power.

The middle class, practically nonexistent in colonial times, is growing as nations become more industrialized. Members of this group, often mestizos, are slowly gaining control of the government from the aristocracy. Nevertheless, many members of this growing class continue to identify with the one above it. Like the upper class, working with one's hands is not considered honorable.

Upward mobility is difficult to achieve. It is not easy to escape the social class into which one is born and achieve a higher status. In Peru, for example, class lines are almost caste divisions. It is difficult to penetrate the barrier between the upper class and the middle class, the *cholo,* which is largely mestizo. The cholos include shopkeepers, small landowners, lesser professional people, and others of moderate achievements.

Below the cholos are the Indians. In the towns they hold only the lowest paid jobs. The majority, however, live in their own villages where they belong to a separate society with its own rules and class system.

On the other hand one can achieve upward mobility in Mexico. As a result of changes brought by its revolution, opportunities have become much greater. The old aristocracy seems to be disappearing so that the upper class consists of

The marketplace is an important center for buying, selling, and socializing with friends.

wealthy industrialists, professionals, government officials, and a few large landowners. Mexico, a largely mestizo country, has made a sincere effort in this century to improve living conditions and increase opportunities for Indians.

Reviewing Your Reading

1. How did Spanish and Portuguese customs affect the development of social classes in Latin America?
2. Name the social classes which existed during the colonial period. How did class membership determine the type of occupation one had?
3. Compare the class system during the colonial era with today.

Family Life Is Closed and Reserved

The word *familism* describes home life in Latin America well. Latin Americans are more family-centered than are North Americans. Welfare services and institutions are in their infancy in most areas. The family provides protection and security for the individual, taking care of its sick and elderly members. The absence of other agencies for the care of old people is one incentive for a couple to have many children.

Usually family life is very private. At one time Latin Americans rarely invited friends and acquaintances to meet their families or participate in family activities. This custom has been relaxed somewhat in recent years. Still, visitors tend to get very formal treatment. Moreover, the traditional style of housing emphasizes this way of life. Unlike North American homes, which open toward the street, the Latin American home usually does not. Windows are often covered with decorative grills for greater privacy.

Marriage selection is controlled by tradition. The majority of Latin Americans today follow the traditional Roman Catholic rules of marriage. Most parents strongly disapprove of marriages between two people from different classes because they are sensitive to the social acceptance of a prospective son or daughter-in-law. Although young people have a greater say in the choice of a marriage partner than in the past, parents still play an important role.

Some Latin Americans use both of the parents' surnames as their last name. The reason for this practice is to reveal the distinguished names on both sides of one's family. Thus a man may have the name Juan Gómez Martínez. Gómez is the father's surname, and Martínez is the mother's maiden name. A woman uses her maiden name as well as her husband's name.

Interracial marriages are more common in Latin America than they are in the United States. The large number of mestizos is evidence of the frequency of such marriages. While racism is not absent, it is much milder than in the United States. Marriages between whites and blacks are restricted more by social class than by race. Since blacks and mulattos tend to be concentrated in the lower classes, they rarely intermarry with the white elite.

There are many kinds of marriages. Two types of marriages are legal, one of which may be performed by a civil servant, similar to a justice of the peace, and the other by church officials. Attitudes toward the two kinds of marriages differ widely. For example, Mexicans hardly consider a civil marriage a real one and think church marriages have higher prestige. Civil marriages are increasing, however, because they are less expensive. Since church marriages continue to be popular, many people have both ceremonies. In Brazil, on the other hand, the government recognizes only civil marriages.

Many people are too poor or too isolated to have either type of marriage and establish a family without a formal ceremony. Often called "consensual unions," they are similar to common-law marriages in the United States. The stability of such marriages varies widely. Most national governments are trying to get such couples to make their marriages official.

The commercial wedding is a unique arrangement. Since most Latin Americans are Roman Catholics, divorce is not a solution to an unsuccessful marriage in most countries although a separation is possible. Some years ago the Brazilians created a new arrangement called a commercial wedding.

The commercial wedding is one in which two persons who are legally separated, or one separated and the other unmarried, sign a legal contract. They agree to support each other financially, or the man agrees to provide support for the woman. Then the couple usually gets divorces from former partners in Mexico or Uruguay, where divorce is permitted. Although the Brazilian government does not recognize divorce, such divorces seem to give the commercial marriages greater legality. Because the cost is high, few can afford them, however.

The nuclear family is predominant. Most Latin Americans are part of nuclear families, usually living separately from their relatives. Often the nuclear family is the logical unit of labor in rural areas, although relatives may work with each other from time to time. Since World War II the number of nuclear families has grown as people migrate to expanding industrial and urban centers.

In general, families in South America are strict, nuclear, and patriarchal. Some differences can be seen, however, even within those limits. At right, a Venezuelan boy with his father; below, a young couple with their child in the mountains of Peru; and below right, a boy strolling city streets with his grandmother in Peru.

The number of extended families, usually found among the upper classes, is declining. Today this style of family life occurs most frequently in Brazil. From the *fazendas,* or large estates, the patriarch directs his family from the *Casa Grande,* the "Big House." In the cities such families may occupy an entire apartment building.

Families are patriarchal. Despite the effects of increasing urbanization and industrialization on life, family patterns remain strongly rooted in their European origins, especially those of Spain and Portugal. In Brazil, Uruguay, and Argentina, with their sizable populations of Italian and German origin, other family customs are followed as well.

Most Latin American men have strong feelings about their role as husbands and fathers. They want to be *muy hombre,* that is, "very much a man." Being the dominant family member, they want their wives and children to hold them in awe and treat them with great respect. At one time the typical man would have found it unthinkable to help his wife with household chores, child care, or grocery shopping. However, this position is changing, particularly in such countries as Mexico and Argentina where the younger, sophisticated, and educated couples believe in more equalitarian ways.

A wife's role is submissive. A wife is expected to obey her husband, who sets the rules and makes all the important decisions. Traditionally a woman has been considered her husband's property. He can choose her friends. Despite her low status a wife may wield a good deal of influence within the family. It is not unusual for the husband to turn over all his earnings to his wife for her to manage. He insists, however, that she must give him money whenever he asks for it.

Female emancipation has affected only a small group of educated middle-class women who have entered careers. In rural areas and among those of little education, traditional attitudes are still strong.

Parent-child relationships are formal and strict. Generally children are submissive and obedient, regardless of their age, as long as they are living in their parents' home. A son may be an adult, but as long as he is in his father's house, he must be obedient.

Parents are concerned about their children's behavior. They do not want them to misbehave and disgrace their family within the community. They believe in physical punishment for their children when necessary because they feel that strictly disciplined children will become hard working adults. They also allow their sons more freedom of activity than their daughters.

Children's relationships with each parent are different. Since the mother cares for them daily, her children usually feel closer to her. The father tends to play a smaller role in their upbringing when they are young.

When sons are old enough to work, the father's role becomes more important, especially in rural areas. Then the father and son work together while the son learns his father's occupation. Because schooling is limited for the average Latin American child, this is often the most important and meaningful education a boy receives.

Compadres supplement kin. Kinship ties are supplemented by the *compadre* (literally co-father) who is a godparent to a child or all the children of a family. For special occasions, such as baptisms, confirmations, and marriages, godparents are chosen. Godparents may be selected from close friends of the family, employers, or people of wealth in the community.

Godparents act as additional parents for children. They provide security for a child who is orphaned or otherwise in need. If godparents have sufficient wealth they may pay the cost of baptism or other ceremonies for which they are chosen. A child may have different sets of godparents for different special occasions. If a godfather is married, his wife usually functions as godmother with him. A couple may be godparents for all the children of a family, or each child may have different godparents.

Relations between compadres and parents are very respectful, for the relationship is highly valued. They often exchange favors and aid each other in time of need. Children are very courteous toward godparents. In the past it was the custom for a child to kiss the godparent's hand at each meeting. Godparents in turn would give children a little money or some other gift when they met.

Formal Education Is Limited

Many Latin American children receive very little formal schooling. It is estimated that almost 40 percent of all Latin Americans cannot read or write. Many listed as literate have very poor command of these skills. Extension and improvement of the schools are major needs in Latin America today. Unless they are achieved progress against poverty will be difficult.

Education for the elite. Since colonial times formal education has been mainly a privilege of the upper classes. To a still considerable extent the educational system is organized to train children of well-to-do families for traditional professions. The best schools are found in the cities, and most students are from upper or middle-class homes, but this is changing.

Latin America has some very fine universities. The ones in Mexico City and Lima (*lee*'ma) were founded a century earlier than Harvard, the oldest university in the United States. These schools, modeled after European universities, provided classical curricula in law, medicine, and theology. They were not intended as schools for the common people.

In the nineteenth century, control of most education was transferred from the Church to government. During the last fifty years schools have been made more democratic and the range of studies broadened. Universities are now training scientists, engineers, and other specialists who are badly needed. However, the greatest need is for basic education in the public schools.

Difficulties in providing education. The task of eliminating illiteracy is a difficult one. The growth of population is so rapid that there is not enough money to provide the schools and teachers needed. Until this growth rate declines, large numbers of children may not receive any formal education.

The struggle against illiteracy is also handicapped by the variety of languages in some countries. In Bolivia, Peru, Ecuador, and Guatemala many of the people do not understand Spanish. In some countries like Mexico, more than a dozen different Indian languages are spoken. It is often difficult to find enough teachers who can instruct in a language the children understand. Nations like Argentina and Uruguay have few Indians, and all instruction can be in Spanish. They also have the highest literacy rates in Latin America.

Students at this school in Bogotá, Colombia, learn most subjects by rote memorization and other traditional methods of study.

Reviewing Your Reading

1. What is familism? Why is it descriptive of the typical Latin American family?
2. Describe the roles of the father and mother. How do these roles affect parents' relationships with their children?
3. Describe the role of the compadre in family life.
4. What have been the traditional patterns of education? Why is literacy so hard to achieve?

Religion in Latin America

Although wealth was the chief goal of the conquerors, many came for less selfish reasons. Devout servants of the Church suffered many hardships to spread their faith among the Indians. As a result of their work, the Roman Catholic Church became an important part of Latin American society and culture.

Indian religions. Religion played a very important part in Indian culture. The Indians often worshiped many spirits and a Supreme Being. In the ancient civilizations of Mexico and Peru the priests played an important role in the community. Great temples were built as centers for worship and rituals. All aspects of life and natural events – rains, earthquakes, and the seasons – had religious meaning. Religion gave the Indians an understanding of the universe.

Many similarities between Indian religious beliefs and Christianity existed. Thus the Catholic priests found it easy to convert the Indians. One reason was

> **Incan Monotheism**
>
> Conversion of the Incas to Christianity was not difficult for the Spanish priests. The idea of one God already existed in Peru. Although sun worship was officially prescribed by the Incan government, the aristocracy also worshiped a Supreme Being called Viracocha the Creator. Note that the image of God revealed in this hymn is quite similar to the one held by Jews, Christians, and Muslims.
>
> Oh Viracocha! Root of all being,
> God ever near,
> Lord of shining apparel,
> God who dost rule and preserve. . . .
>
> Stephen Clissold, *Latin America: A Cultural Outline* [New York: Colophon Books (Harper & Row), 1965], p 29.

that the priests often allowed Indian customs to remain. Earlier religious shrines were easily converted into Christian holy places. In Aztec times the goddess Tonantzín (Our Mother) was worshiped at a shrine near Mexico City. Today it is the Shrine of Our Lady of Guadelupe, the most important holy place in Mexico.

A noted authority on Latin America, Frank Tannenbaum, pointed out that the greatest shock the Conquest produced for the Indians was to their religion. The Spaniards were contemptuous of the Indians' faith and the things they held sacred. The temples were desecrated and holy objects made from gold and silver were broken and melted down. Because the Indians were deeply religious, the destruction of religious objects sometimes led to their demoralization.

The Indian religions still survive in remote areas of Mexico, the Andean regions, and Brazil, where Indian populations are the largest. Prayers are still made to the various gods of nature, and pagan priests conduct rituals. In the Amazon region where some tribes do not see outsiders, animism, or a belief that all objects have spirits, is practiced.

African religious influence. In Brazil and in the Caribbean regions are many descendants of the African slaves who were transported to the Americas during the colonial period. Most of them converted to Christianity, but some kept a few elements of African cults. Dances, animal sacrifices, and rituals have also been preserved. In Haiti, a cult called "voodoo" is practiced. It involves a belief in sorcery and fetishes of various kinds. People in a trance believe that they can communicate with the spirits of the dead. Very elaborate rituals have developed around these beliefs. In Haiti voodoo rituals are officially accepted. In other countries followers of such cults have been persecuted from time to time. Governments have been more tolerant in recent years.

The role of the Catholic Church in the colonial era. During the 300 years of colonial rule, the Catholic Church became well established. It has been said that the Church ruled and the state governed. The presence of the Church was everywhere. In the cities often the most impressive buildings were the churches, shrines, and monasteries. The calendar was filled with saints' days, and every town and organized group had its patron saint. On special occasions, such as the period before Lent, people participated in elaborate fiestas.

The Church affected the lives of people in many ways. It was involved in the important events of life from birth until death. Generous donations and vast land holdings made the Church enormously wealthy and powerful. The priesthood was much respected, and a family was proud to have a son become a priest or a daughter a nun.

Political and social role of the Church. The Church was involved in numerous nonreligious activities. High Church officials were appointed by the king and were given a great deal of power. The Pope and his advisers had practically no control over appointments of high Church officials to the colonies. For centuries Spain had been the most devoted defender of the faith and in return insisted on this freedom.

The Church kept records of vital statistics (births, deaths, and marriages) and established and operated schools and universities. The colonial schools and universities were intended mostly for the upper class. They prepared men for traditional professions. The earliest hospitals and welfare services were provided by the Church. They were not sufficient to meet the needs of the people, but only the Church was concerned with relief of sickness and suffering at that time. Often the Church was the only refuge for abandoned children and neglected old people.

The economic role of the Church. The years following the Conquest were a period of strenuous missionary work. The colonial Church was not wealthy, and the priests often endured hardships for the faith. They built simple open chapels for celebrating mass to congregations out of doors.

By 1600 the Church was amassing property, and a century later was the chief landholder. By the end of the colonial period at least half of all lands was held by the Church. Ownership of ranches, cattle, buildings, mills, and numerous enterprises brought a steady flow of wealth. Indians were sometimes forced to labor on these lands as hard as on the encomiendas.

As a result of its enormous wealth the Church was able to build many elaborate cathedrals. Despite the poverty of the common people, some members of the clergy lived in great luxury. Gold, silver, and precious stones decorated the altars and tapestries of the great cathedrals. The spirit of reform of the earlier churchmen was forgotten by many.

Independence produced a religious crisis. The struggle for independence created two major crises in the Church. The first was whether to support the independence movements or not. This created a split within the Church hierarchy. The top officials were peninsulares appointed by the king. They felt loyal to the Crown and opposed colonial independence. The lesser clergy, especially local priests, tended to favor independence. They were native-born and sometimes Indian or black. Their sympathies were with the common people.

As soon as independence was declared, the Church's powers in the new republics were questioned. The Church wanted to continue to enjoy all of its former powers and privileges. The problem still exists in some countries. Four issues often debated are the disposal of Church property, authority over marriage, control of education, and the right of non-Catholics to enter the country.

A colorful Christmas procession reenacting the nativity scene.

569

Roman Catholic church workers have been active among the poor and forgotten in Latin America. This French sister has lived and worked for almost thirty years among the Indians of the Tapirape River valley of central Brazil.

Relationship between the Church and governments. The Church lost many of its struggles with national governments. The degree of bitterness in these conflicts varies widely from one country to the next. Everywhere the Church lost much property, especially in Mexico following the 1910 Revolution. Although most Latin American nations still do not allow divorce, the power of the Church over marriage has weakened considerably. In many countries a civil ceremony is necessary to make a marriage legal.

All Latin American governments now keep records of vital statistics. They control their educational systems, although parochial schools are usually permitted. Most of the universities are run by the government rather than by the Church. Freedom of religion is guaranteed in all of the constitutions, and some Protestant groups have been active in missionary work. Some European immigrants in Brazil, Argentina, and Chile are Protestant, and the Lutheran Church has one of the largest Protestant memberships in Latin America.

Some Muslim and Jewish communities exist in various parts of the continent. In Guyana (guy-*ah*-nah') about 10 percent of the population is Muslim. Some Muslims also live in Trinidad and Suriname. Jews usually live in large urban areas, including Buenos Aires. Some are Sephardic Jews who came from Spain. The majority, however, migrated from Europe during the last century.

The Church and changing times. Since the 1940s the Church has become more concerned with the welfare of the urban poor and labor groups. Some priests and Catholic lay people have become active in helping to organize and strengthen labor unions. This effort to help urban workers has developed a new feeling among laboring people that the Church has a genuine interest in their welfare.

Senior officials in the Church still tend to support governments in power, but there are exceptions. The archbishop of El Salvador, Oscar Romero, condemned the violence that both government and guerrilla armies inflicted on civilians. He was a champion of the poor and a strong supporter of human rights. After repeated attempts against his life, he was murdered in March 1980 while saying Mass at the cathedral in San Salvador.

The term *liberation theology* has been applied to the beliefs of clergy who see their mission as one of actively helping the poor and oppressed to gain social and political liberation. This sometimes involves supporting movements against oppressive governments. In his visits to Latin America and at tother times, Pope John Paul II has called on governments to promote social justice and human rights. But he has opposed political activism by priests and condemned liberation theology. The Church, he believes, should take a strong moral stance for justice. But members of the Catholic clergy must not be active political leaders. He ordered three priests who were members of the Nicaraguan Sandinista government to resign.

Looking ahead. Traditional patterns of living persist in Latin America, especially in rural areas and among the Indians. The Church is, for the most part, a conservative force in Latin American life. Nevertheless, pressures for change are building. The rapid growth of population is making land reforms more urgent each year. New ideas about family living and the status of women are spreading. Despite resistance, Latin American life is changing.

Reviewing Your Reading

1. What role did Indian religions play in the lives of their followers? How were their beliefs and practices similar to those of the Europeans?
2. How have African religions affected religious beliefs in Latin America?
3. Describe the role played by the Church during the colonial period. How has its role changed since independence?

CHAPTER REVIEW

Recalling Names and Places

animism   compadre   mulatto
cholo   familism   peninsulares
criollo   mestizo

Understanding This Chapter

1. A complex stratification system emerged during the colonial period in Latin America. What importance did class position have for a man? for a woman?
2. What changes would be necessary if Latin American societies were to provide greater equality for women?
3. Why are godparents important in Latin American society?
4. Why is basic education a more important need in Latin America than universities?
5. There is a major debate in Latin America over whether the Catholic Church should confine itself to strictly religious matters or seek to improve people's material welfare. What is the case for each side?

Chapter 49

The Economic Life of Latin America

The Latin American economy is built primarily around agriculture. Millions of poor rural people, sometimes called *campesinos,* live on small plots of land, tilling the soil with primitive tools. Many peasants are peons on large estates. In debt to landlords, they are tied to the land like slaves. Others work on large plantations where cash crops such as coffee and bananas are often grown for export.

Today industry is playing an increasingly important role. Once copper, nitrates, and tin were the chief exports. Now other natural resources are being tapped. For example, oil drilled in Venezuela may be refined there. Iron ore mined in one region of Brazil is made into steel in another.

The economy of most Latin American nations is capitalistic. Many industries and large farms are privately owned. Individuals decide how to invest their money and set prices. They determine what to produce and how to distribute the things they make. Other economic systems, particularly socialism, are favored by a growing portion of the population. In such an economic system, a government often owns and runs factories, transportation systems, and other businesses. It also decides how products, land, and supplies will be distributed among the citizens. Along with Cuba, Chile has been one of the most socialistic nations in Latin America. In the early 1970s the government of Salvador Allende moved the country toward greater socialism. The military regime that ousted Allende in 1973 pledged to return the economy to privat enterprise. Still, some major industries continue to be run by the government.

Let us examine the traditional economy of the region, beginning with the original settlers, the Indians. Then we shall consider the ways in which Latin Americans have been making a living in more recent times.

Traditional Agriculture

The Indians developed a great variety of food plants that contributed to their successful economies. The Mayas, Aztecs, and Incas never invented the plow. Since much of the land they tilled was mountainous, the hoe was more practical. Where arable land was scarce, as in the Andes, using a hoe to dig the soil produced more food per acre than plow agriculture could.

The Indians of Central and South America did not have draft animals, either. They used only the llama to carry burdens in the Andes. Llamas and alpacas were bred and herded for both their meat and wool. This wool was much prized, for the weather in the mountains is often chilly. Cotton, grown from Mexico to Peru, was also used for clothing.

Llamas are raised for their meat and their wool. They also serve well as beasts of burden in the rugged terrain of the Andes, where transportation is difficult.

Land was communally owned. In many Indian cultures land was communally owned and cultivated. In a few cases the nobility owned land that was tilled by slaves. Because the territory was so rugged, the Incas of the Andes had to make every inch of land as productive as possible. Therefore, they developed scientific agriculture to a remarkable degree. They terraced the mountainsides, irrigated the soil, and grew those crops that would flourish best in each area. Families were organized into economic groupings called *ayllus*. Each ayllu had land allotted to it by the ruling Inca, and part of the land was cultivated for him as well as for the priesthood.

At the time of the Spanish Conquest, Indian agriculture was concentrated in the fertile valleys and in the carefully irrigated terraces of Peru. The Spaniards were interested in raising livestock rather than crops. When they conquered the Indians, they seized the choice lands and converted them into pastures for animals. The Indians were forced into the hills to cultivate less fertile areas. In Peru the Incan lands were overrun by livestock, and the terraced fields were ruined.

The best lands eventually became part of the large Spanish estates, while the majority of people had to cultivate lands largely unfit for agriculture. This agricultural tragedy contributed much to Latin America's poverty.

A Variety of Agricultural Systems in Latin America Today

A large portion of the rural population live by subsistence agriculture. The families are self-sufficient, producing most of their needs. Things they cannot produce they usually do without. Trade is not important in this way of life. What little trade takes place is by barter.

Communal ownership is still common. In such countries as Mexico, Ecuador, and Peru, the agricultural village is common. In these countries the Indian populations are large, and the traditional Indian custom of village land ownership persists. Agricultural villages also serve as settlements for workers on large plantations in many parts of Latin America.

Isolated subsistence farms are also typical. A family may live in a one-room thatched house in the center of a fenced-in half acre of land. They may cultivate a patch of corn, beans, and squash, and a hedge plant to provide fiber for clothing. Often the family does not have title to the land, but the soil may be so poor that no one else wants to own it.

The hacienda system of land ownership. Large estates, or *haciendas* (called *latifundios* in Peru and *fazendas* in Brazil) originated during the Spanish colonial period. Officers and members of the victorious armies were granted large pieces of land, along with the Indians living on these lands, as their reward for services to the Crown. During the colonial period, this system of land holding spread, as the sons of the *hacendados,* or hacienda owners, wanted their own lands. In a few generations most of the productive areas were taken.

Today work on the estate is done by peasant families. The hacendado gives each family a little land for growing its own food. In return the family cultivates the landlord's fields and works as servants in the house. The hacendado may even lend some workers to a neighboring landowner. This system resembles the manorial system of medieval Europe. The workers receive no pay and often are permanently in debt to the owner.

The agricultural methods used on the estates are inefficient. Since labor is abundant and cheap, the owner has no incentive to modernize. The land often is poorly managed and sometimes loses its fertility. Nevertheless, the hacendado lives a comfortable life, counting on the estate to meet practically all of the family's needs.

Plantation agriculture is the major form of commercial farming. In sharp contrast to subsistence farming is plantation or commercial agriculture. Usually a single crop is grown on a large, privately owned estate, and sold on the world markets. The plantation may employ large numbers of workers who live in a nearby village or in housing provided by the plantation owner.

More than half of the world's coffee and bananas, and almost one third of all cocoa and sugar are grown on Latin American plantations. Cattle are also an important export, especially from Argentina and Uruguay.

Banana plantations, concentrated in Central America, Colombia, and Ecuador, were first established by North Americans in Costa Rica in 1878. Although subject to diseases, the banana is a major product for international trade. One species of banana, the plantain, is an important local food. It is not sweet when raw like the commercial banana and must be cooked to be edible.

Coffee and cacao are major plantation crops. Brazil is the major producer of coffee, but it is also grown in many other Latin American countries. Many think

Young coffee plants are placed in greenhouses and tended carefully until they are ready to be transplanted to open fields. The mature plants first produce fragrant blossoms and then the ripe berries whose seeds will become coffee beans. After the beans are picked they are left to dry in the sun. Then they will be sorted and shipped to market.

575

the highland coffee grown in Colombia and Central America superior to the Brazilian variety due to better soil and climate conditions.

Plant disease and increased African production have reduced the importance of cacao as a Latin American export. Several nations grow cacao (from which cocoa is made), but Brazil and Ecuador are among the major producers. Only Ghana and Nigeria grow more cacao than Brazil.

The rise of sugar plantations encouraged the slave trade. Of all plantation crops, sugar has had the greatest importance in Latin American history. The first great sugar plantations were developed in Brazil by the Portuguese in the sixteenth century. Slaves from Africa supplied the labor. Large profits encouraged plantations elsewhere, and sugar production spread, especially to the Caribbean region. Because of ideal climate and soil conditions, the islands of Hispaniola (Haiti and Dominican Republic), Cuba, and Puerto Rico became major producers. Today, Cuba is the world's largest producer of sugar.

Management of plantation agriculture today is, to a large extent, in Latin American hands. When there is foreign control, it is often resented. In the past, foreign plantation owners, like the United Fruit Company, were accused of trying to influence local politics. When a Marxist, Jacobo Arbenz Guzmán (goose-*mahn'*), was elected president in Guatemala in 1950, he expropriated some United Fruit Company lands as part of an agrarian reform program. In 1954 a successful uprising against Arbenz broke out, led by Carlos Castillo Armas (are-*mahss'*). Whether it was true or not, it was widely believed by Guatemalans that the United Fruit Company gave support to the ouster of Arbenz. Today the company has a more favorable reputation in Guatemala, but incidents such as this have led to resistance among Latin Americans to foreign land ownership.

Many nations become one-product producers. Many Latin American countries are producers of one or two main products. People have learned there, as they have in other regions, that too heavy reliance on the sales of one product can be very risky. As long as the demand for a product is strong and the prices are steady, the producing nation may enjoy prosperity. However, if production becomes greater than demand, prices will fall, leaving the country in financial difficulty.

Excess production may come about in several ways. It may be that the producers in a country increase output. Expansion of Brazilian coffee plantations sometimes has led to overproduction. Other nations may begin to produce the same product. For example, we have seen that Brazil is not the only coffee-growing nation in Latin America. Moreover, it is now grown in some African countries as well. Cocoa is another such product. Ecuador once had a monopoly on this source of chocolate, but now must compete with Brazil, Nigeria, and Ghana.

Changes in Land Ownership

Despite the money that the plantation crops may bring into a country, most subsistence farmers and peasant agricultural workers remain poor. Many of the plots they till are too small or have such poor soil that they are unproductive. It is estimated that approximately 10 percent of all Latin Americans own about 90 percent of the land. Having some of the best crop and cattle-raising lands, they are among the wealthiest people in the region.

Land reform, a way in which the large estates could be broken up and land redistributed more equally, might reduce the poverty. A major difficulty is that the people who control the government and decide what laws to pass tend to be members of the landowning aristocracy. Many of them would be unwilling to pass laws that would end their privileged position in society.

Several nations undertake land reform programs. It has been suggested that the governments should buy the estates from the hacendados and distribute the land among the poor. Some nations have tried to do this. Others have attempted to bring about agrarian reforms in other ways.

Mexico was the first Latin American nation to introduce land reforms in the years following the revolution of 1910. Hacendados were allowed to keep small land holdings, but the rest was transferred to rural communities called *ejidos* (ay-*he'*dohss). Today about half of Mexico's farm lands are controlled by ejidos. Peasants are allowed to use the land, but ownership is retained by the community.

In the 1950s and 1960s several nations acted to break up large estates. Venezuela began a well-planned program of land reform in 1958. Since then millions of acres have been redistributed. Fidel Castro, following the Communist model, organized most of Cuba's large estates into collective and state farms. Military governments in Peru and Bolivia have enacted agrarian reform laws. Under President Eduardo Frei (*fray'* e), who held office from 1964 to 1970, land reform was begun in Chile. The pace was accelerated by Allende, the president until 1973. Since 1973 a repressive military junta has ruled Chile and many reform plans were suspended.

The task ahead. Dividing up the land is not enough. Farmers must be given an opportunity to learn better ways of farming and proper care of the land. They must obtain loans at low interest rates so that they can buy better tools, seed, and fertilizers. They must have transportation to get their products to the market. Unless these improvements are also made, division of the land into small plots may mean less production, rather than more.

Reviewing Your Reading

1. How did the Indians farm their land?
2. How do most farmers earn their living today?
3. Describe the hacienda.
4. Name some Latin American plantation crops and explain the importance of plantation agriculture.
5. Why is one-product agriculture risky?
6. Describe efforts made toward land reform.

Industry

For many centuries the land was exploited for its minerals, which were often sent elsewhere to be refined and made into usable items. Like plantation crops, some nations have relied very heavily on the revenues from the sale of these minerals. In the early 1980s a worldwide recession led to a drop in demand for these minerals and severe economic problems for the exporting nations.

LATIN AMERICA: MINERALS

- 🅱 Bauxite
- Coal
- 🅲 Copper
- Gold
- Iron
- 🅻 Lead
- Oil
- 🆂 Silver
- 🆃 Tin
- 🆉 Zinc

Foreign investment aided industrial development. Since the early nineteenth century, foreigners have made investments in various Latin American nations. During the second half of the nineteenth century, Britain became involved in the economic development of Argentina. The British wanted to exchange their manufactured goods for Argentine food and raw materials. Since lack of transportation was a major problem, the British constructed most of the Argentine railroads between 1857 and 1912. Grain, sugar, beef, and other products could then be transported to ships. These developments added much to Argentine prosperity and economic stability.

In the twentieth century, United States corporations became major investors, especially in oil and mining. In 1970 United States firms had approximately $12 billion invested in Latin America, or about half as much as in Canada or Europe. North American investors helped create oil industries in Venezuela and Mexico. Oil companies in the United States lost their properties in Mexico in the 1930s as a result of a nationalization program. In 1976 the Venezuelan government nationalized its oil industry but compensated United States companies for their losses.

All over Latin America a sense of nationalism is one the rise. With increased nationalism has come a desire to eliminate foreign influences. In a few countries – notably Cuba, Mexico, Bolivia, Peru, and Chile – the government has taken over certain businesses owned by United States firms.

When Fidel Castro came to power in 1959, all United States properties in Cuba, valued at $1.4 billion, were seized without compensation. In all, more than $3 billion worth of properties have been seized since 1959. Fear of seizure has decreased the number of foreign investors. But many Latin American leaders feel that, under proper controls, foreign investments are still needed.

Bolivia and Chile rely on their mineral exports for revenue. Almost 70 percent of Bolivian exports are minerals, and another 20 percent of export income comes from natural gas and oil. Bolivia is the world's second-largest producer of tin. Zinc, silver, and tungsten are also exported. Because tin can be produced more cheaply elsewhere, prices for Bolivian tin are low. A heavy dependence on tin sales contributes to Bolivia's serious economic difficulties. The drop in the price of oil in the early 1980s also hurt Bolivia.

Chile depends on exports of minerals for revenue almost as much as does Bolivia, despite a better developed economy. The Atacama Desert of northern Chile is the world's greatest source of natural nitrates for fertilizer. Until synthetic nitrates were developed, Chile shipped great quantities of the fertilizer to Europe and the United States. Nitrates are still important today, but copper is the major mineral export.

Chile is currently the world's largest exporter of copper. All of the Chilean copper mines are now controlled by the government. Formerly many mines were operated by United States companies such as the Anaconda Company and the Kennecott Copper Corporation. However, Chilean president Allende expropriated the remaining United States controlled copper mines in September 1971.

The mining town of Sewell, Chile, clings to this Andean mountainside at an elevation of 8,000 feet. Below the town lies El Teniente, *the world's largest underground copper mine.*

The Orinoco Llanos (*yah'nohss*), a plain lying between the Orinoco River and the Andes Mountains, is a region of recent agricultural development. Despite the severe problems of flooding in the rainy season and drought the rest of the year, an important cattle industry is growing. Dams to control flooding and irrigation facilities to relieve the droughts are encouraging development of cattle farms.

Mexico's prospects for prosperity get a jolt. Some years ago Mexico found major new oil reserves. The country's economic picture brightened in the 1970s as the price of oil soared in world markets. The big boost in income led Mexico to undertake major development programs. In the early 1980s, however, Mexican dreams of a bright economic future began to dim. The price of oil stopped rising – and even dropped a bit. Inflation remained high, and the nation had an enormous foreign debt. The country was on the brink of bankruptcy when the United States, its major trading partner, offered to help return Mexico to a more sound financial basis. Prospects for economic progress remained unclear.

Brazilian rubber boom. Brazil experienced a short-lived era of prosperity with rubber production. The industrial development of Europe and the United States in the late nineteenth century created a growing demand for rubber. Between 1900 and 1912 the Amazon valley supplied the rest of the world with natural rubber. Unfortunately for Brazil, an Englishman took some rubber tree seeds to Europe. They were later used to create the rubber plantations of Malaya and Ceylon. With cheap labor in Asia, these plantations soon captured the world markets. A period of spectacular prosperity along the Amazon came to a sudden end. The rubber boom demonstrates the danger of basing an economy on a single product.

This pattern is changing somewhat. In mining areas Brazilian engineers are seeking a variety of minerals which might be mined. To further expand their economies, many nations are also developing the means to process their raw materials instead of simply exporting them.

Economic progress in Venezuela. Despite a high birth rate, Venezuela still has an abundance of land and other resources. After the ouster of the dictator Marcos Pérez Jiménez in 1958, large landholdings were broken up and other basic reforms enacted.

Oil has been the great resource of Venezuela. While the industry was largely developed by foreign interests, mainly from the United States, Venezuela succeeded in getting a generous share of the profits. With wealth from oil great new industrial development took place. By 1972 the value of industrial production exceeded that of oil. Then, as in Mexico, soaring oil prices brought even greater hope for economic progress. But when oil prices leveled off in the early 1980s, the optimism was dampened. Still, Venezuela continued to rank among the top ten countries in oil production.

About one half of Venezuela is in the Guiana Highlands, south of the Orinoco River, a region which is becoming an important industrial area because of its rich iron ore and bauxite deposits.

Despite impressive economic progress, poverty and illiteracy are still widespread, and the rate of economic development barely keeps up with population growth. Industrialization is attracting people to the cities, relieving population pressures in rural areas. But jobs are often scarce in the cities, especially in Caracas.

Thousands of oil derricks extend for 65 miles along the shores of Lake Maracaibo, the center of Venezuela's petroleum industry and one of the richest oil-producing regions in South America.

Challenges to Economic Progress

Industrial development lags almost everywhere in Latin America. There are a number of reasons for this.

Industrial investment is limited. Many landholders are reluctant to invest their money in factories, transportation, and other industrial enterprises. Land holding is more attractive to them than the ownership of industry. Wealthy people desiring to make investments usually put their money into North American or European corporations. This lack of interest in developing home industries has been a major handicap.

The instability of governments discourages investments. Dictators who do not expect to be in power very long may only be interested in a personal fortune. They may not give attention to developing transportation facilities and other improvements necessary for modern industries. Wealthy people hesitate to invest their money when political conditions are unstable.

Tax reforms are needed. If a government is to construct schools, build highways, and do many other things to improve the economy, it must have money. The fairest way to collect the necessary funds is to tax according to ability to pay. The wealthiest people in Latin America often evade taxes, however. Aware of this problem, almost all Latin American nations are striving for tax reforms.

Rapid population growth counteracts economic progress. Although still high, Latin America's population growth rate is slowly declining. In 1984 the annual rate of growth for all Latin America was 2.4 percent. If that rate continues, the present population of about 400 million will double to 800 million in 30 years. In Mexico and Central America, where growth rates are 2.8 percent the population would double in only 25 years.

Demographers insist that unless the rate of population growth is reduced sharply in the near future, all other programs of economic development will be defeated. They urge a massive effort to narrow the gap between birth rates and death rates.

The greatest increase in Latin America's population has occurred since 1945. Great improvements in sanitation and the introduction of vaccines and drugs like penicillin reduced the mortality rates of infants and children in a dramatic way. Earlier, less than half of the children born reached adolescence. In the mid-1980s, 39 percent of Latin America's population was under fifteen years of age.

For generations the Catholic religion taught the people that the children were a gift from God and that a fortunate family received many. A popular saying in Latin America is: "He who does not receive children from God, receives nephews from the Devil." But it would be a mistake to attribute Latin America's population problem solely to the teachings of the Catholic Church. Predominantly Catholic nations like Italy, France, and Austria have very low birth rates. As long as children are seen as a source of security and care in old age, parents will want many children. As urban life develops, and government provides more fully for the needs of people, reliance on children for security will decline. Uruguay has the lowest birth rate in Latin America. It is also the most urbanized nation with the best developed welfare services.

Looking ahead. Latin Americans are recognizing the population crisis they face. Programs of family planning have increased, and the rate of growth has begun to decrease. As awareness of the consequences of a population explosion spreads, planners hope the downward trend will continue.

Reviewing Your Reading

1. What has the traditional source of industry been? How is it changing?
2. Why was the Brazilian rubber boom short-lived?
3. How have the Venezuelans been developing their resources?
4. Why has Latin American industrial development been slow?
5. What are some of the population problems facing Latin America?

CHAPTER REVIEW

Recalling Names and Places

ayllu	ejido	hacienda
campesino	hacendado	nationalization

Understanding This Chapter

1. The Incas had shown how the rugged terrain of Peru could be made agriculturally productive. Why did the Spaniards fail to learn form their example?
2. What economic measures can a nation take to reduce the risks of relying on one product like coffee or sugar?
3. Land reform usually means breaking up the large estates and redistributing the land among the poor. What is the rationale for such an action? Give arguments pro and con.
4. Can a nation benefit from foreign investment? What are the dangers?
5. Why should we try to help Mexico out of its financial problems at the cost of millions of dollars? Why not just let them "sink or swim?"

Chapter 50

Latin American Political Systems

Political parties developed soon after the wars of independence ended in 1825. Two issues divided people into separate political camps: (1) whether the governments should be central (unitary) or federal, and (2) what the proper relationship between church and state should be. Liberal and conservative parties emerged in most of the new republics. Generally, the liberals favored the separation of church and state and a federal system of government. The conservative parties wanted the traditional powers and privileges of the Church continued and favored strong centralized governments.

These parties have survived in some of the Latin American countries. In the conflict over the role of the Church, the liberal view prevailed in most places. Although influential, the Catholic Church is no longer the powerful institution it was in colonial times. The conservative view on government succeeded in most countries. Federal types of government exist only in a few countries. Even in these countries, provincial governments have little power compared to states in the United States.

In recent years other issues have caused polticial unrest and conflict in Latin America. One issue is land reform. Another, often linked closely to the breakup and redistrubution of big estates, is socialism versus private enterprise. Citizens supporting socialist or Communist programs are known as leftists. Those wanting to keep things the way they are or introduce change more slowly are often called conservatives or rightists. The struggle between these groups, particularly in Central America, has often been violent. It has brought political instability throughout the region.

New Political Parties Emerge

In the twentieth century new political parties reflect a changing society. Increasing literacy, spreading urban areas, expanding industries, and growing labor unions have been factors in their creation. Minority groups, like the Indians, are demanding greater representation.

Parties are more oriented to needs of common people than in the past. Thus "personalist" parties, organized around the ambitions of a caudillo, are less common today. Francois Duvalier in Haiti organized such a party, as did Rafael Trujillo (true-*he'*yoh) in the Dominican Republic, and Marcos Pérez Jiménez in Venezuela. However, most Latin American strong men try to identify themselves with some popular cause, such as agrarian reform, the labor movement, or Indian welfare.

LATIN AMERICA: POLITICAL

⊛ National capital

Despite social changes, continuance of widespread illiteracy and apathy permit military juntas and caudillos to govern many of the nations of Latin America. Some of the leaders of new political movements hope that they may change these conditions eventually.

The APRA in Peru. The Mexican Revolution of 1910 was the first movement to show concern for the welfare of Indians. These events inspired Victor Raúl Haya de la Torre in 1924 to form a political party in Peru called the *Alianza Popular Revolucionaria Americana* (APRA). He called for better education and agricultural assistance for Indians and other poor people and the return of Indian lands.

The APRA movement alarmed the wealthy landowners and the caudillos who represented them. For much of his life Haya de la Torre was either in exile or in prison. When he finally won an election in 1962, the army seized power and prevented Haya de la Torre from forming a government. Nevertheless, the support APRA received indicated that reform parties throughout Latin America might soon become more numerous.

Argentina under Perón. The rise of Juan Domingo Perón to power in Argentina from 1945 to 1955 illustrates how Latin American strong-man politics are changing. Like his predecessor, Perón was an army officer; however, he sought the support of the laboring class rather than the wealthy landowners.

Perón and his actress wife, Eva Duarte, made a popular team. They pushed through many laws to aid the urban laborers – better wages, stronger unions, and greater social security benefits – and worked on programs of aid to the poor and the sick. Following Eva's death in 1952, Perón's influence declined. His program's drove the nation close to bankruptcy, and he had abused civil rights. He was ousted from office in 1955 and spent eighteen years in exile, chiefly in Spain.

During Perón's exile, Argentina had a succession of military and civilian regimes. Perón was allowed to return in 1972. He and his new wife Isabel won

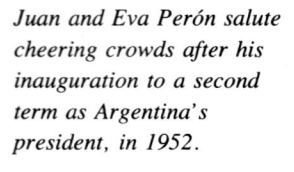

Juan and Eva Perón salute cheering crowds after his inauguration to a second term as Argentina's president, in 1952.

election as President and Vice-President in a landslide victory. He died nine months after taking office, and Isabel became President. A military group ousted her in 1976.

The election of President Raúl Alfonsín in December 1983 restored civilian government to Argentina. He responded to the popular demand that those responsible for the kidnapping and murder of more than 9500 people during the military rule be punished.

Although there was an attempt to restore human rights in Argentina, such was not yet the case in Chile in 1985. Despite citizen protests and demonstrations, a brutal military dictatorship led by General Augusto Pinochet continued. Thousands of citizens suffered torture, imprisonment, and internal exile.

Castro in Cuba. In 1959 Fidel Castro replaced Fulgencio Batista as his country's leader. In 1961 he began to transform Cuba into a Marxist state. His political movement officially became the Communist Party of Cuba. To keep this first Communist government in the Western Hemisphere afloat, the Soviet Union supported Castro with aid and loans of around $1 million a day. The poor have benefited from Castro's rule and great progress has been made in the elimination of illiteracy. Still, a completely successful economy has not been achieved. The country remains dependent on the Soviet Union for economic aid.

Major political parties. Today some of the political parties in Latin America are modeled after similar groups in Europe. This is true of the Christian Democrats, socialists, and Communists. Organized on European models, they have not always been closely in tune with Latin American problems.

Fidel Castro led the revolution that took over Cuba in 1959 and eventually made it a Communist country. Castro's Cuba has given aid to Marxist and other left-wing political and military groups throughout Latin America. Here he is greeted in Santiago by Salvador Allende, Socialist president of Chile from 1970 to 1973.

Voters in El Salvador, the most densely populated country in Latin America, elected a new moderate government in 1984, rejecting the candidates of the right-wing military parties. Leftist guerrillas and their supporters boycotted the elections, and forces on the left and the right continued to fight against each other and against the government.

The Christian Democrats are more independent of their European models than the Communists and socialists. They have supported reforms that would improve the lot of the common people and are often backed by the liberal priests of the Catholic Church. Because their methods and demands have been moderate, the Christian Democrats have not satisfied all who demand reforms. Some young priests have preferred to support the Communists and have even joined guerrilla movements to fight for change.

Although the presence of the socialist parties is not new, they are frequently less strongly established than some other political parties. Often they seem too radical for conservative voters and too conservative for radicals. As a consequence the socialist parties are small, often collaborating with other political groups. Their political philosophy is similar to socialists elsewhere. They recommend a gradual shift of economic institutions to governmental control.

The Communists have goals similar to the socialists; however, they want governmental controls to come quickly through revolution. The Soviets have supported Communist movements in Latin America. Soviet Communist leaders regard the creation of a Communist regime in Cuba as a major success.

A leftist movement with strong Communist support, the Sandinistas, took control of Nicaragua in 1979 after a bloody civil war. In neighboring El Salvador, the most densely populated nation in Central America, leftist rebels tried in the mid-1980s to topple a popularly elected moderate regime. This Salvandoran government also had to struggle with right-wing forces who wanted to suppress many democratic reforms along with the rebellion.

The rise of National Revolutionary parties. Of major importance has been the development of National Revolutionary parties in most Latin American countries. These groups are not of foreign origin nor are they controlled by Moscow or Peking as are many Communist parties. They are native organizations concerned with local problems.

Members of the National Revolutionary parties take their inspiration from the Mexican Revolution and advocate many of the same changes. Generally they urge a breakup of haciendas, the enactment of agricultural reforms, and broad economic development along modern lines. They are opposed to caudillo rule, desiring more democratic government.

In the opinion of many authorities, the best hope for the region lies with these revolutionary parties. They are trying to bring progressive reforms – democratic government, education, economic prosperity, and equality of opportunity for minority groups. In some places, like Venezuela, dictators suppressing these parties have been aided by North American interests. Such assistance has aroused much hostility toward the United States.

International Relations

When the United Nations was formed in 1945 the Latin Americans became enthusiastic supporters of the new international organization. They worked actively in its formation and soon held important positions in it. Like members of other smaller nations in the world, the Latin Americans feel that a strong United Nations protects them and provides a world forum for discussion of problems.

Latin Americans also feel a strong bond with citizens of developing countries of Africa and Asia. In the General Assembly of the United Nations their representatives often support each other in voting, and they hope to create a "third world" as an alternative to domination by the United States or the Soviet Union. Their cooperation is somewhat limited by the fact that most of the nations in this group are economic rivals. They produce many of the same tropical products.

Relations within Latin America. When the Latin American colonies became independent nations, definite boundaries had to be set. As long as they were colonies, these matters were less important. Furthermore the populations along the borderlands were usually very sparse. As time went on these questions had to be settled and sometimes there was conflict.

Because of common language and history most Latin American conflicts have not been severe. However, some boundary disputes have led to war. A major conflict was the War of the Pacific (1879–1883), which was a struggle for control of the Atacama Desert region. Chile had been actively exploiting the mineral resources of this area, divided between Chile, Peru, and Bolivia. Peru and Bolivia formed an alliance to oppose Chilean expansion of operations in their territories. War broke out, and the Chileans were victorious. Chile gained territory rich in nitrate deposits, and Bolivia lost its outlet to the sea when its Pacific shoreline was annexed by Chile.

A later Bolivian effort to gain access to the Atlantic by way of the Rio de La Plata led to war with Paraguay in the 1930s. This was a long and bitter war fought over some worthless borderlands between Paraguay and Bolivia. Bolivia's desire for access to the sea and the belief by some that there was oil in this region, called the Chaco, were the causes of this conflict. Bolivia was defeated again.

In the 1970s boundary disputes troubled several Latin American nations. Ecuador was especially bitter over past seizures of lands by Brazil, Colombia, and Peru. A four-day border war was fought between El Salvador and Honduras in July 1969.

Conflict between Central American neighbors distrubed that region in the early 1980s. The government of El Salvador charged the Sandinistas in Nicaragua with supporting Salvandoran leftist guerrillas. Nicaragua claimed that Honduras, with United States support, was harboring rebel forces seeking to overthrow the Sandinistas. Another sore point in some countries was the influx of refugees from areas of conflict, such as El Salvador and Nicaragua. Cuban aid to leftist forces in Central America and elsewhere was another part of the problem.

Cultural bonds with Europe are strong. Spain did not accept the independence of its colonies graciously. For a long time Spain refused to recognize the new Latin American nations and even launched an attack on Peru in 1864 in hopes of regaining control. Only after the Spanish-American War of 1898 did relations become more cordial.

Little bitterness developed between Brazil and Portugal because separation was achieved without major conflict. Today Brazil is the larger and wealthier nation, and relations are very friendly. Portuguese can migrate freely to Brazil, where they are welcomed warmly.

France was the intellectual center for Latin Americans for a long time. The leaders of independence movements, like Bolívar and San Martín, were inspired both by the American Revolution and by the eighteenth century French philosophers. French culture is much admired, and the study of French has been part of the education of the upper classes. Imitation of French artistic and literary styles is now less common as new writers and artists emphasize native themes.

Growing contacts with the Soviet Union. Communist parties have been established in a number of Latin American countries. The first one was founded in Argentina in 1918. However, they usually were small and ineffective. These early Communist parties had close ties with the Soviet Union and had little freedom to adapt their methods to local conditions due to the rigid controls imposed by the Soviet leader Joseph Stalin.

Today the Soviet Union is more skillful in its dealings with Latin America. It has tended to support leftist groups favoring land reform, a popular issue in Latin America. While the amount of trade is still not large, it is growing. Most of the trade of the Soviet Union and its satellites has been with Cuba, Argentina, Uruguay, and Brazil. After President Allende came to power, Soviet-Chilean relations gained new importance. Experienced Soviet diplomats were sent to Chile in 1971. President Allende also invited Soviet technologists to explore for oil. But his ouster in 1973 ended Soviet influence there.

Relations with the United States

The United States expressed sympathy for the cause of the Spanish colonies during their wars of independence. Further support was given in 1823 by the Monroe Doctrine, which opposed any restoration of Spanish rule in the Americas. Latin Americans were grateful for this support.

Friendly feelings declined a generation later when the United States expanded its territories at the expense of Mexico. As a result of a war in 1848 almost one half of Mexico's territory was annexed. This Mexican Cession, which included land from Texas to California, produced long-lasting feelings of resentment in Mexico.

Efforts at hemispheric cooperation. In the 1880s the United States helped create an organization to develop cooperation among the various countries on matters of importance to all of them. This organization, the Pan-American Union, later became part of the Organization of American States (OAS).

Manifest Destiny

Despite the Mexican Cession, many citizens of the United States were still dissatisfied. They believed in "Manifest Destiny," a doctrine which held that the United States had a God-given mission and duty to expand the nation's boundaries over North America as far as possible. Many declared that this expansion should extend west to the Pacific, north into Canada, and south to the Caribbean Islands, Mexico, and Central America.

Some individual Americans were prepared to fulfill the mission of Manifest Destiny. One William Walker organized a group of forty-five men and tried to seize Lower California from Mexico in 1853 but was defeated by Mexican forces. Two years later he went to Nicaragua, joined a rebel army, and made himself president of the country. His plan was to take over all of Central America. While trying to invade Honduras, however, Walker was captured. He was executed in 1860.

Manifest Destiny alone was not the only reason the United States was interested in Latin America. The Industrial Revolution created a need for expanded markets. Moreover, many North Americans believed that the reported Spanish mistreatment of Cubans was a just cause for the Spanish-American War of 1898. Following the opening of the Panama Canal in 1915, the United States played a greater role in the region, often interfering in the political and economic affairs of various nations. Such intervention was not welcome.

In 1933 a new President, Franklin D. Roosevelt, shifted United States policy from domination to cooperation. Relations with Latin America improved greatly. To a large extent Roosevelt's Good Neighbor Policy has been continued to the present time.

These Bolivian schoolchildren hold notebooks they received through the Alliance for Progress. In its first two years alone, the program distributed 1.5 million schoolbooks, provided food for a quarter of Latin America's schoolchildren, and built 17,000 new schoolrooms.

The United States was mainly interested in expanding trade, while the Latin Americans were more concerned with political questions, such as the right of the United States to intervene in the affairs of other states. Only after the Franklin Roosevelt administration, when the United States gave up this right, did members of the Pan-American Union begin to cooperate more successfully.

In spite of the greater equality now existing in the relations between the United States and Latin America, difficult problems remain. These are due partly to cultural differences between them as well as disagreements over representation in the decision-making boards of the OAS. The Latin Americans want the United States to have the voting power of just one member, the equal of El Salvador, for example. On the other hand, they expect the United States to bear major financial burdens – both because the United States is by far the wealthiest member and because the OAS is a vital link in the United States system of defense alliances. Members must decide how to give the United States the proper powers of decision and yet avoid the domination that Latin Americans resent.

The Alliance for Progress raised high hopes. Latin American nations received far less aid from the United States after World War II than was given to Europe. They felt neglected and resentful. In 1961 President John Kennedy announced an Alliance for Progress for which the United States pledged to donate $20 billion over a period of ten years. This aid had to be matched by major social reforms by the Latin American countries. Land and tax reforms were required. A total sum of $80 billion was also to be contributed by the Latin American governments over the ten-year period.

This ambitious program raised high hopes which have not been entirely realized. Latin American reforms were made, but they represent less than half of what was promised. After contributing funds for six years, the United States Congress cut its contributions sharply in 1968. This was a major setback for the program.

Looking ahead. Both Latin Americans and North Americans would like to see improved relations among the countries of the Western Hemisphere. Before relations can improve, many political observers suggest that some changes in United States attitudes are necessary. Many feel that in the past the United States has supported dictators or military juntas for the sake of trade advantages or out of fear of a Communist takeover. The United States has at times supported regimes whose violations of human rights were well known to the people of those nations. More important than profits from trade is a more stable and prosperous Latin America. Many Latin American experts believe that the United States should encourage democratic political and economic programs in Latin America and be prepared to offer assistance to those countries which ask for it. A stronger Latin America would benefit Latin America and the United States alike.

In the 1980s the United States was trying to stop the spread of communism in Central America. The government of El Salvador received aid to fight rebels who were supported by Cuba and the Soviet Union. The Reagan administration wanted to help rebels who were trying to oust the left-wing government in Nicaragua. This involvement in Central American politics helped to rekindle old worries about "Yankee imperialism" throughout Latin America.

CHAPTER REVIEW

Recalling Names and Places

Fidel Castro	Liberals	Sandinistas
Christian Democrats	Manifest Destiny	Spanish-American War
Conservatives	Juan Perón	socialists

593

Understanding This Chapter

1. What were the main differences between Liberal and Conservative parties?
2. How did the APRA differ from earlier political parties?
3. Why can Juan Domingo Perón be called the worker's caudillo? Why was he unable to stay in power?
4. How has Cuba changed under Fidel Castro?
5. Name and describe the major political parties often found in Latin American countries today.
6. Characterize the relationships Latin American nations have usually had with each other.
7. How have relations between Latin American countries and the Soviet Union changed?
8. Describe past and present relationships between the United States and Latin America. What was the purpose of the Alliance for Progress?

Chapter 51

Cultural Contributions of Latin America

The Indian civilizations of the Americas inspired early achievements in the arts and sciences. The arrival of the Spanish and Portuguese added new elements to the native art forms, and the blacks brought the richness of their African heritage to the Americas. This blend of the native American, European, and African traditions is apparent today in much of the region's outstanding art and literature.

Scientific Achievements

Latin America does not have a strong tradition of interest in science and mathematics as do some other cultural areas, for example, the Middle East. Although Spain shared in the Muslim civilization, the Christian conquest weakened the scientific tradition. The Church was sometimes suspicious of science, fearing that it might weaken the faith of people. Colonial Latin America was effectively isolated for centuries from the scientific thought of Europe and North America.

The needs of modern industry and technology have aroused more interest in science. However, most Latin American countries are handicapped in pursuing scientific studies, which can be enormously expensive. In 1947 an Argentine physiologist, Bernardo Houssay, won the Nobel Prize for medicine. He did outstanding work on the circulatory system and glands of the human body.

When North Americans think of research on causes of yellow fever, they generally give full credit to Walter Reed of the United States. Few realize that his success depended on the research of a Cuban scientist, Carlos Finlay. It was Finlay who had earlier proved that yellow fever virus was carried by a mosquito. A few years later Finlay did basic research on the problem of malaria.

Latin America Has a Strong Intellectual Tradition

During the colonial period Latin America was as isolated from European philosophy as from science. The ideas of British and French philosophers of the seventeenth and eighteenth centuries worried the Spanish rulers. Critical attitudes toward kings and notions about the rights of the common people were considered dangerous and had to be kept out. After independence, Latin American philosophers studied and imitated European thinkers.

Latin America has produced some brilliant and original philosophers. Any nation would take pride in thinkers like Francisco Romero (1891–1962), Argentina's great philosopher, or a man of such varied talents as Jóse Vasconcelos (vahss-kohn-*say*'lohss, 1881–1959) of Mexico.

Sarmiento, a fighter for education. An educational philosopher and one of the most remarkable men of Latin America was Domingo Faustino Sarmiento (1811–1883) of Argentina. He was a fearless critic of Argentine dictators and had to flee into exile a number of times. He founded newspapers and magazines, translated books, and traveled in Europe and the United States. He became the president of Argentina in 1868 and held office until 1874. Despite these many activities, he found time to write fifty-two books.

Sarmiento was so arrogant and egotistical that many people could not tolerate him. On the other hand he was brilliant and dedicated to education, a subject about which he wrote much. He greatly admired the United States and became a close friend of Horace Mann, the great North American educator. Above all he believed that education for the people was the duty of the state. Sarmiento's influence helped Argentina become one of the most literate countries of Latin America.

Intellectuals are concerned with current problems. Intellectuals in Latin America are called *pensadores* (thinkers). In Spanish the word implies a good deal more than it does in English. It is a word which carries great respect and honor. Generally intellectuals are esteemed more highly in Latin America than in the United States.

In recent years Latin American thinkers have become more nationalistic. Many have become active in politics in an effort to apply their theories to practical matters. Because of the great admiration for intellectuals, it is not difficult for them to get elected to political office. Sarmiento, for example, was elected president of Argentina mainly because he was considered a learned man.

Mexico City and Buenos Aires are the world's largest publishing centers of books in Spanish, and they print an enormous number of works each year. All literate Latin Americans are familiar with the books of such North American authors as William Faulkner, Ernest Hemingway, Sinclair Lewis, and Mark Twain. The average educated person in the United States would be hard put to name even one Latin American writer.

Argentine poet, essayist, and fantasist Jorge Luis Borges (1899–   ) is one of Latin America's most important literary figures. He continued to write and speak even after he had been blind for several decades.

Development of Literature

The earliest Latin American writings were the diaries and reports of the conquerors. Hernán Cortés, for example, wrote a series of letters to Charles V, king of Spain. In them, he described his experiences in Mexico. These letters are fascinating reading for the history student. The great defender of the Indians, Father Bartolomé de Las Casas, wrote a *General History of the Indies*. It belongs among the more notable of the early writings.

Later in the sixteenth century Alonso de Ercilla y Zúñiga (1533–1594) wrote a book that has been referred to as the greatest epic poem of Latin America. Called *La Araucana*, it describes the enormous courage and skill of the Araucanian Indians of Chile in resisting the Spanish invaders.

During the colonial period writers were carefully censored for any liberal ideas they might express. This close supervision tended to reduce writing to trivial topics. In the turbulent first decades of the nineteenth century most political leaders were quick to imprison or exile any writer who dared to criticize their governments. There were many courageous writers but, like Sarmiento, they often spent years in exile.

The Modernist movement in the arts. Beginning around 1885 a new style of expression emerged in the arts called *modernismo,* the Modernist movement. It began with poetry and then spread to the other arts. Instead of pale imitations of European styles, a distinctive Latin American mode of expression developed. In Brazil modernist writers turned to their country's native culture for literary sources. Writers borrowed words and expressions from the Indian and African cultures of Brazil. In Spanish-speaking Latin America, writers were anti-Spanish, but they turned toward France rather than native Indian or black cultures for inspiration. The outstanding modernist poet was Rubén Darío (1867–1917) of Nicaragua. He wrote very colorful and exotic poems.

In the 1920s and 1930s Spanish American novels continued to reflect the concern of the modernists with native American Indian culture. One of the outstanding novelists of social protest who also captures the mysticism of the Indians in his writings is Miguel Angel Asturias (1899–). This Guatemalan novelist and poet won the Nobel Prize in 1967. He is best known for his novel *Men of Maize.* Several of his books, *The President, The Green Pope,* and *The Mulatto and Mister Fly* have been translated into English. The Peruvian José Maria Arguedas, whose native tongue is the Quechua language, writes stories of the sierra Indian. In the works of two modern Mexican writers, Carlos Fuentes and Juan Ruflo, the reader can also see the influence of Indian mythology and symbolism.

Modern literature is varied. In the twentieth century there has been an enormous outpouring of literature in Latin America, some of it of outstanding quality. Poetry is a favorite form of expression. Two Chilean poets have won the Nobel Prize for Literature. Gabriela Mistral (1889–1957), prize winner in 1945, became well known for her sympathetic verses on children, the poor, and the downtrodden. Her major works are *Desolacion, Tala, Ternura,* and *Lagar.*

Pablo Neruda (1904–1973) won the Nobel Prize in 1971. As is typical of much of Latin American literature, his writings reflected a concern for the common people and their problems. Many anthologies of his work are available in English. Among the most important English translations is Neruda's major work, *The Heights of Macchu Picchu.*

A more recent Nobel Prize winner (1982) is Colombian novelist Gabriel García Marquez. His major works include *Autumn of the Patriarch*, a study of a nameless aging military dictator, and *One Hundred Years of Solitude*, an account of the rise and decline of a family in an imaginary Colombian village.

Prose writing is also often involved with social issues that beset life in Latin America. One of the greatest writers of prose is generally considered to be José Enrique Rodó (1871–1917) of Uruguay, who wrote much on the nature of morality, a subject that seems to attract the interest of many Latin Americans. Writers of fiction are especially concerned with social problems, such as the evils of slums and the problems of youth.

Brazilian writers reflect their country's concerns. To a large extent what has been said of Spanish-language literature applies equally to Brazilian literature. Yet Brazil has certain unique aspects to its culture – the large African element in its population, the recent practice of slavery, and the vastness of the territory resulting in many regional contrasts. These differences have given rise to a distinctive literature.

Colombian novelist Gabriel García Marquez won the Nobel Prize for literature in 1982.

> **A Tale of the Andes**
>
> *Lives of the common people are often hard. Their songs and stories are sad because tragedy is a frequent experience.* In *the Peruvian writer Ciro Alegria's novel,* The Hungry Dogs, *a young sheep herder tells a shepherd girl a legendary tale of the mountains. It is a typical Andean tale:*
>
> They say there was once a priest who had fallen in love with a girl, but as he was a priest the girl didn't love him. And one day all of a sudden the girl died. Then the priest, because he loved her so much, went and dug up her body and took the long bone of her leg and made himself a flute, and there beside her body he played this *yaravi* [a mountain song] on the flute day and night. And between his love and this sad music, he lost his mind. And the people who lived near by, who heard this *yaravi* day and night, went to see why he played this sad song so much, and they found him sitting beside the dead body of the girl, which was all rotted, crying and playing the flute. They spoke to him, but he did not answer or stop his playing. You see, he was mad. And he died playing this music. . . . Maybe that's why the dogs howl. Maybe the soul of the priest comes to listen to his music and then the dogs howl, for they say they do that when they see the souls of the dead.
>
> German Arciniegas (ed.), *The Green Continent* (New York: Alfred A. Knopf, Inc., 1944), pp. 48–49.

An interesting study, often called the finest example of Brazilian prose, has been translated into English as *Rebellion in the Backlands*. Written by Euclydes da Cunha (*coon'*yuh, 1866–1909), it describes the brutal suppression by the government of a religious community in the interior of northern Brazil. It reads like dramatic fiction, yet is a description of an actual happening.

One of Latin America's most eminent sociologists is Gilberto Freyre (*fray'* re, 1900–). After receiving his advanced education in the United States, he returned to his native Brazil where he wrote a series of fascinating studies. Three of them, translated into English as *The Masters and the Slaves, The Mansion and the Shanties,* and *Order and Progress* are among the most interesting studies of race relations written in the countries of the Western Hemisphere.

Latin American Creativity in Music

The different racial and cultural groups that have come together in Latin America have contributed to an unusually rich production of music. Europeans, Indians, and Africans have contributed their distinctive musical instruments, rhythms, and melodies. An interesting example is the development of a dance in Cuba called the *habañera*. It had its earliest beginnings in a French style of dance which was introduced to Cuba. There it underwent a good deal of change. From Cuba it spread to South America and eventually reached Argentina. There it was transformed still further to become the world-famous tango. The habañera attracted the French composer Georges Bizet, who included this dance in his popular opera *Carmen*. Most people today associate the habañera with this opera and probably believe it is a Spanish dance.

The African love of the dance has resulted in the development of a great variety of popular dances. Cuba, the West Indian islands, and Brazil – countries with large black populations – have originated a great number of popular dances. Some of the better known are the samba and maxixe from Brazil, the rumba, conga, and mambo from Cuba, the plena from Puerto Rico, and the merengue from the Dominican Republic. The complex rhythms and joyous moods of these dances appeal to people everywhere.

Creation of serious music is a recent development. The earliest Latin American to receive world-wide renown in music was the Brazilian composer Carlos Gomes (*go'*mace, 1836–1896). He wrote nine operas in all, but is best known for *Il Guarany*, which tells the story of the Guarani Indians. Although the opera is not often performed outside of Brazil, the overture is still very popular.

Other internationally known composers include Heitor Villa-Lobos (1887–1959) of Brazil, and Carlos Chávez (1899–1978) of Mexico. Villa-Lobos was a prolific composer, writing more than 700 works, both vocal and instrumental.

"The Pinzonin Family," by the modern Colombian artist Fernando Botero.

He was strongly influenced by Brazilian folk tunes and rhythms and often used Indian, Brazilian, and popular melodies in his work. One of his best known works, *Bachianas Brasileiras,* is based on Brazilian themes. Chávez was active both as a composer and symphony conductor. He wrote symphonies, ballets, and concertos.

Art and Architecture

In the twentieth century, Latin American art and architecture developed a new independence of expression. Earlier imitations of European styles gave way to distinctive forms, influenced by Indian culture and Latin American experiences. The willingness of its artists to experiment with new forms of expression gives Latin American art a fresh and exciting quality.

The Mexican muralists. Inspired by revolutionary ideals and a rich heritage of Indian arts, Mexico produced a trio of great artists. In the 1920s and 1930s Diego Rivera, José Clemente Orozco (oh-*rohss*'koh), and David Alfaro Siqueiros created impressive mural paintings. They used Indian themes which became famous throughout the world.

Painters today are developing new styles, many of them highly individualistic. Two Mexican painters, Rufino Tamayo and Carlos Mérida, are less nationalistic than Rivera and his associates. They express personal feelings, often in very abstract forms.

Although Mexico has dominated Latin American painting, artists of note have appeared elsewhere. Roberto Matta Echauren and Enrique Castro Cid of Chile and Alejandro Obregón of Colombia have received international recognition.

"The Coming of Quetzalcoatl" is part of a larger fresco by Jose Clemente Orozco. The fresco traces Aztec culture from its beginnings to the arrival of the Europeans. In the top left corner is Quetzalcoatl, the Great White Father of Aztec legend. Surrounded by earlier Indian deities, he rises above the pyramids of Teotihuacán, which are dedicated to his worship.

One of the striking modern buildings in Brasília, Brazil's capital city. The entire city was built at once, on a completely undeveloped site. It was completed in 1960.

Like some of the modern writers, many of these younger artists consider themselves internationalists and do not want to be identified with a particular country.

Brazilian architecture. Brazil is without doubt the leader in the development of original design and planning in architecture. In Mexico, Colombia, and Venezuela excellent work has been done in designing university buildings and housing projects. However, the Brazilians have demonstrated a degree of imagination and daring that is unique. The great opportunity for Brazilian architects came when the government decided to move the capital from Rio de Janeiro to a location 600 miles inland to encourage development of the back country. In 1960 the new capital city of Brasília was inaugurated.

Brasília has been built on an empty plain where no town existed before. It is a completely planned city in every detail. The plan was drawn up by Lucio Costa, and the buildings were designed by Oscar Niemeyer. Both men are Brazil's most distinguished architects. The city is a spectacular example of planning and architecture. Many consider it one of the great artistic creations of all time.

CHAPTER REVIEW

Recalling Names and Places

Brasília	modernismo	Diego Rivera
Rubén Darío	Oscar Niemeyer	José Rodó
Carlos Finlay	pensadores	Domingo Sarmiento
Gilberto Freyre		Heitor Villa-Lobos

Understanding This Chapter

1. Name some scientific fields to which Latin Americans have contributed.
2. What role have intellectuals (*pensadores*) played in Latin American history?
3. Trace the development of Latin American literature.
4. How has Latin American music been influenced by its diverse peoples?
5. Describe the characteristics of modern art and architecture in this region.

Atlas

WORLD: CLIMATE REGIONS

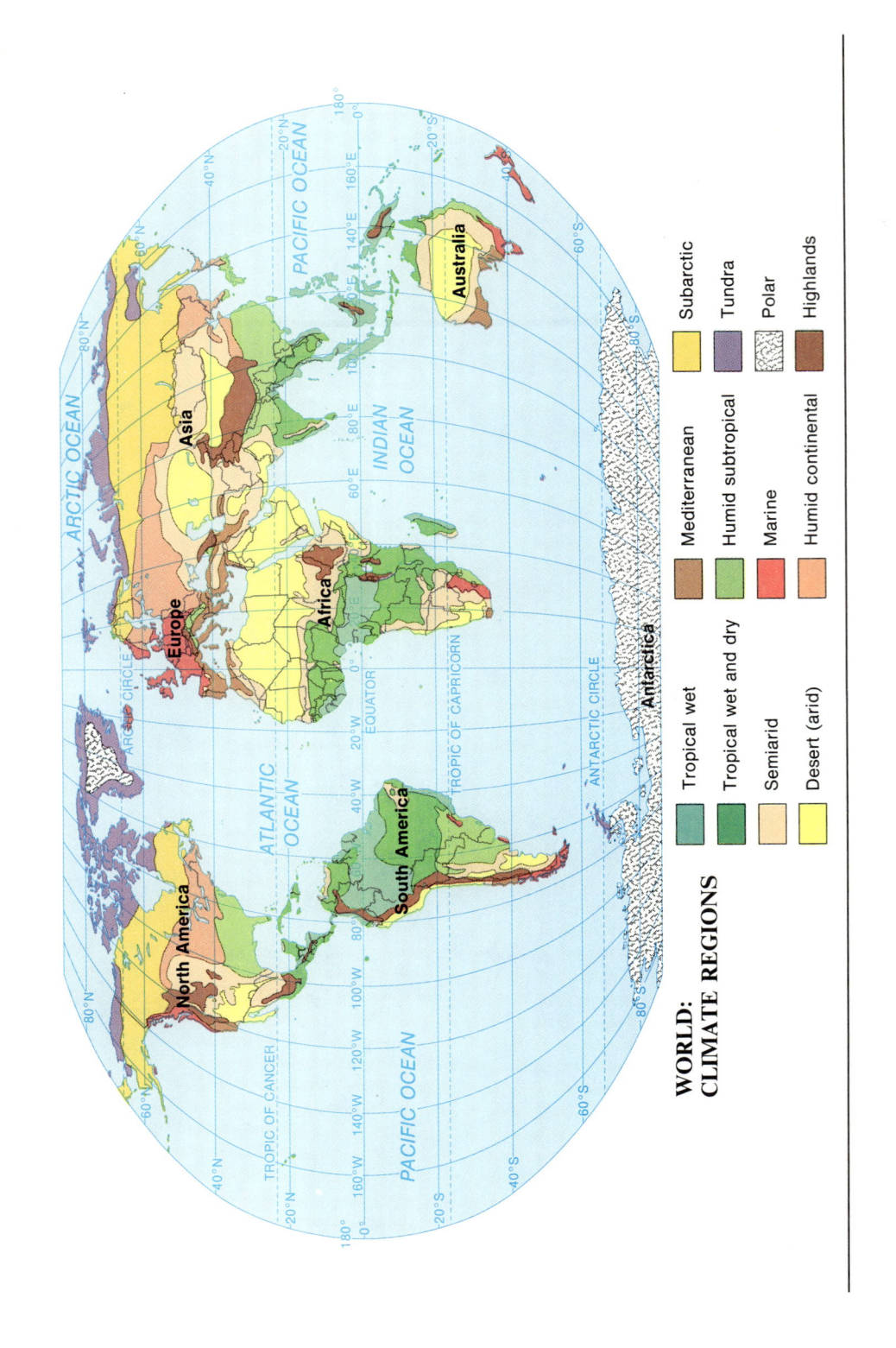

604

WORLD: AVERAGE YEARLY PRECIPITATION

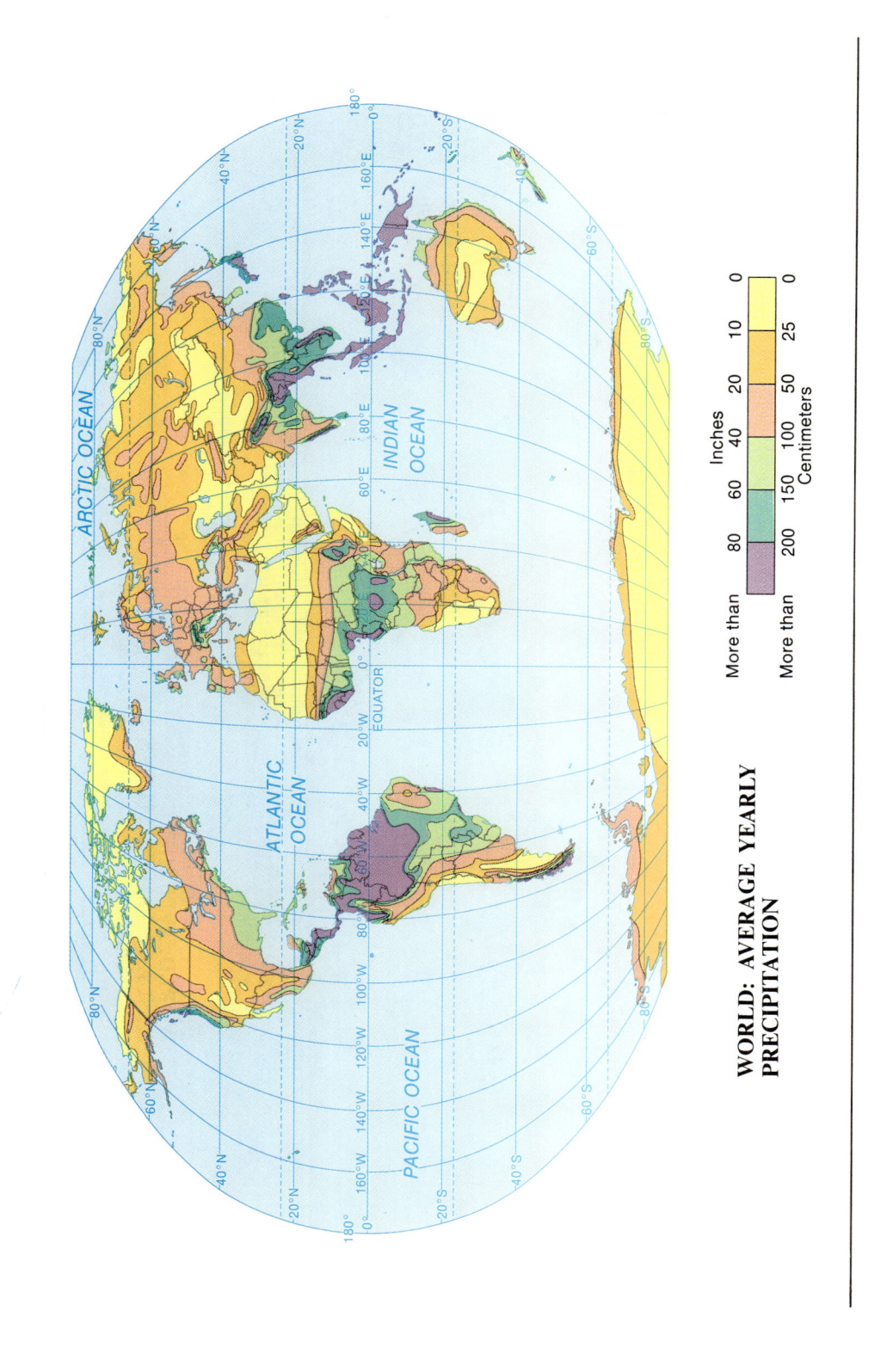

WORLD: AVERAGE JANUARY TEMPERATURES

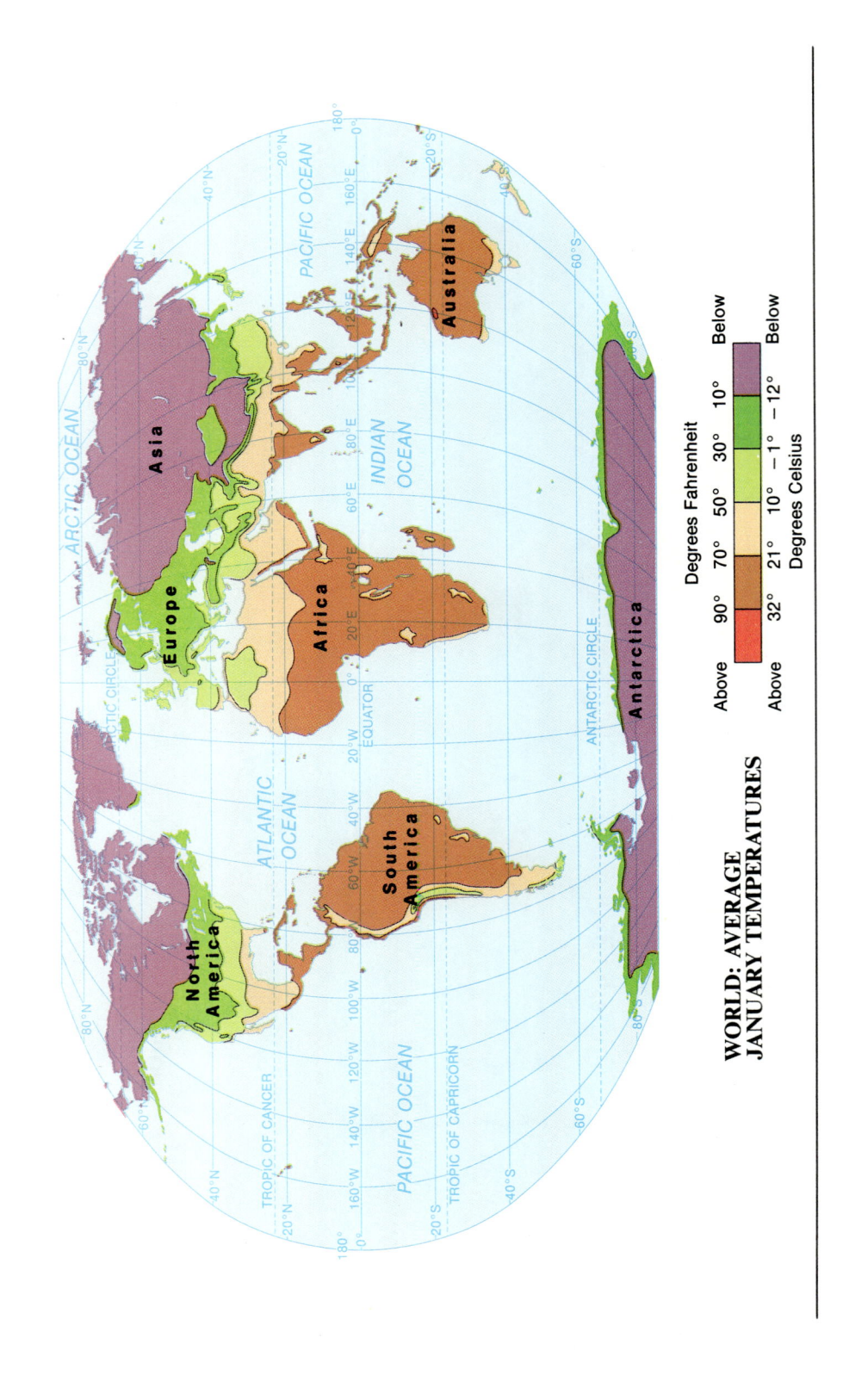

WORLD: AVERAGE JULY TEMPERATURES

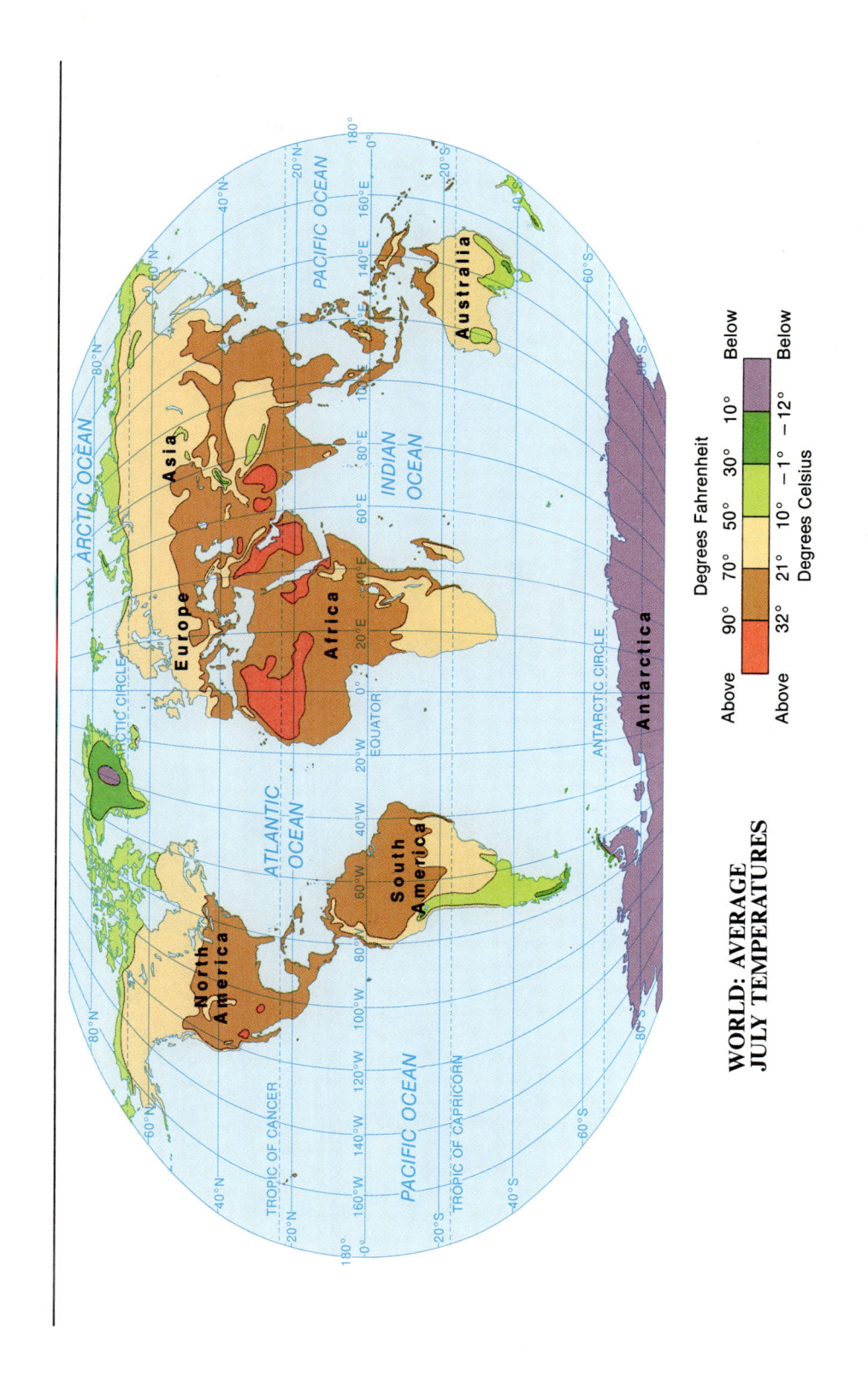

WORLD: LANDFORMS

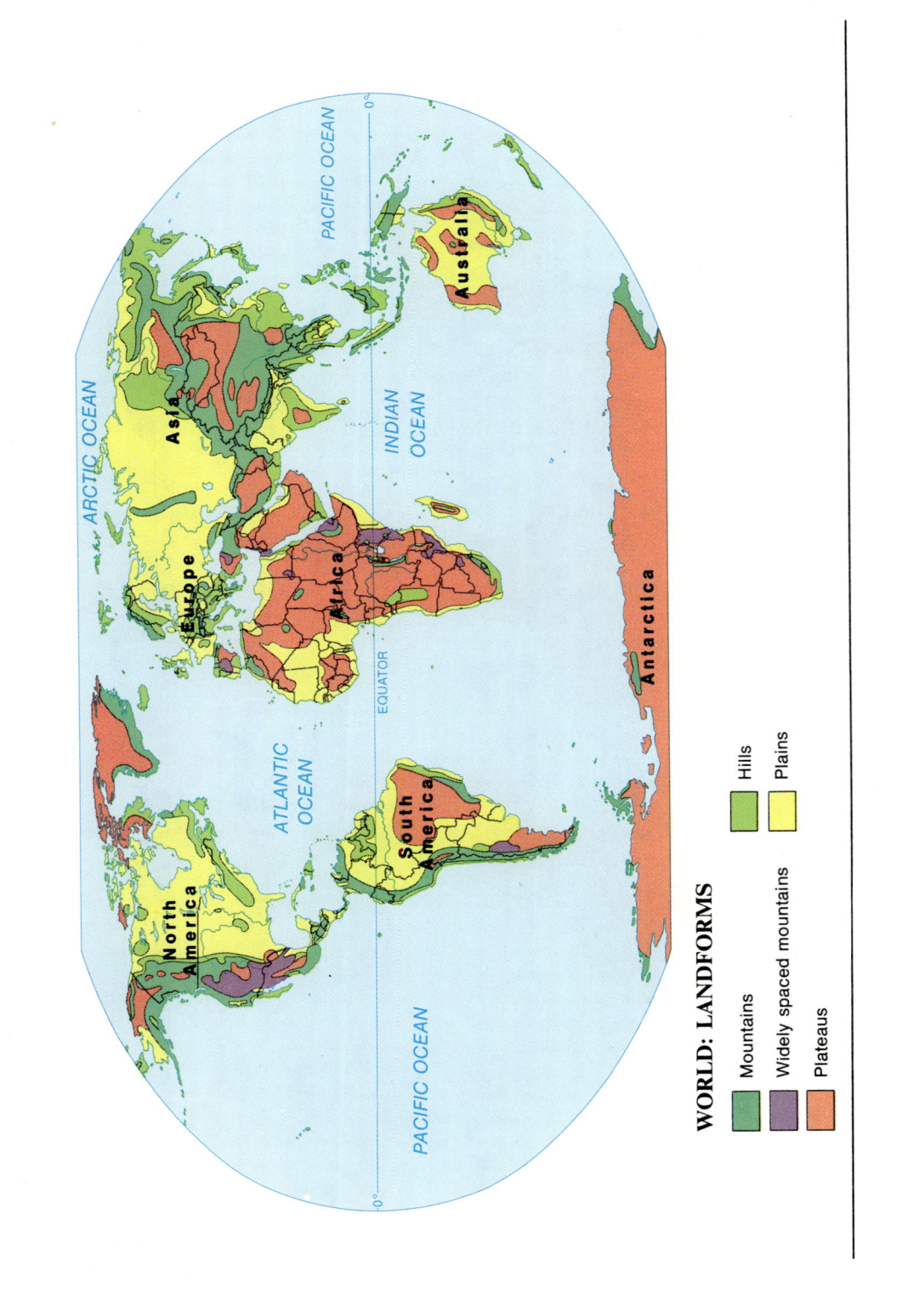

WORLD: LAND USE

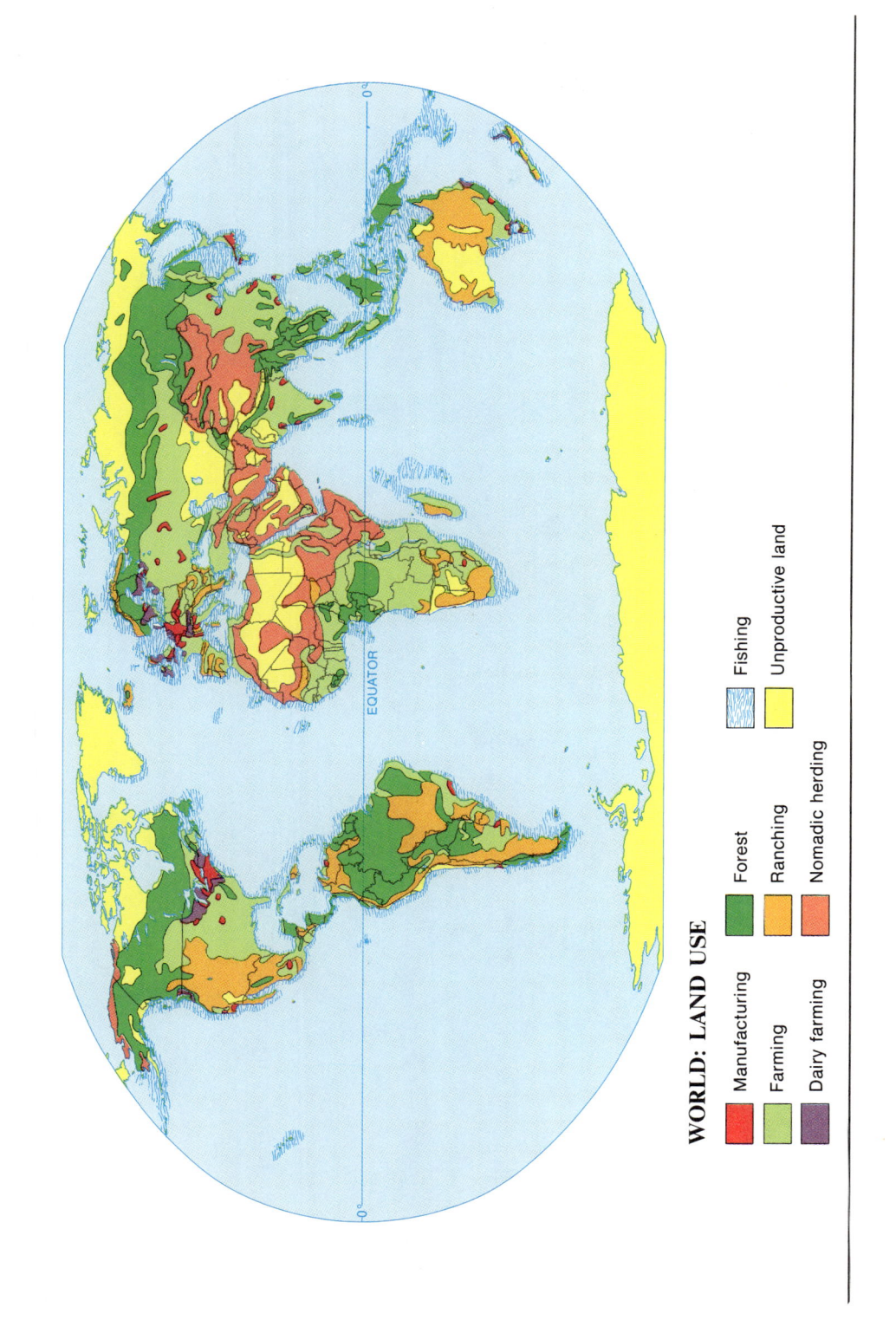

■ Manufacturing	■ Forest	■ Fishing	
■ Farming	■ Ranching	■ Unproductive land	
■ Dairy farming	■ Nomadic herding		

WORLD: POPULATION DENSITY

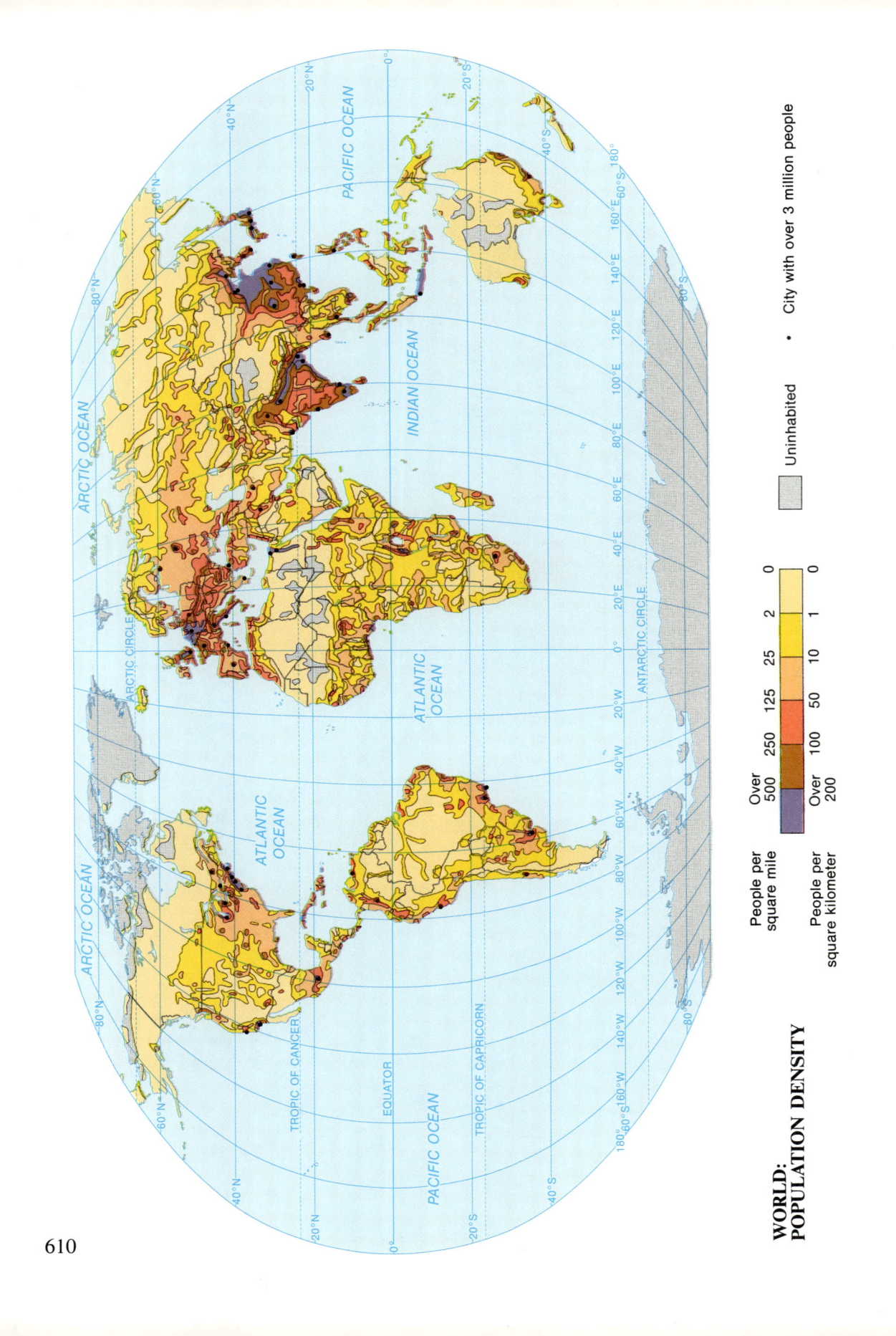

610

WORLD: NATURAL VEGETATION

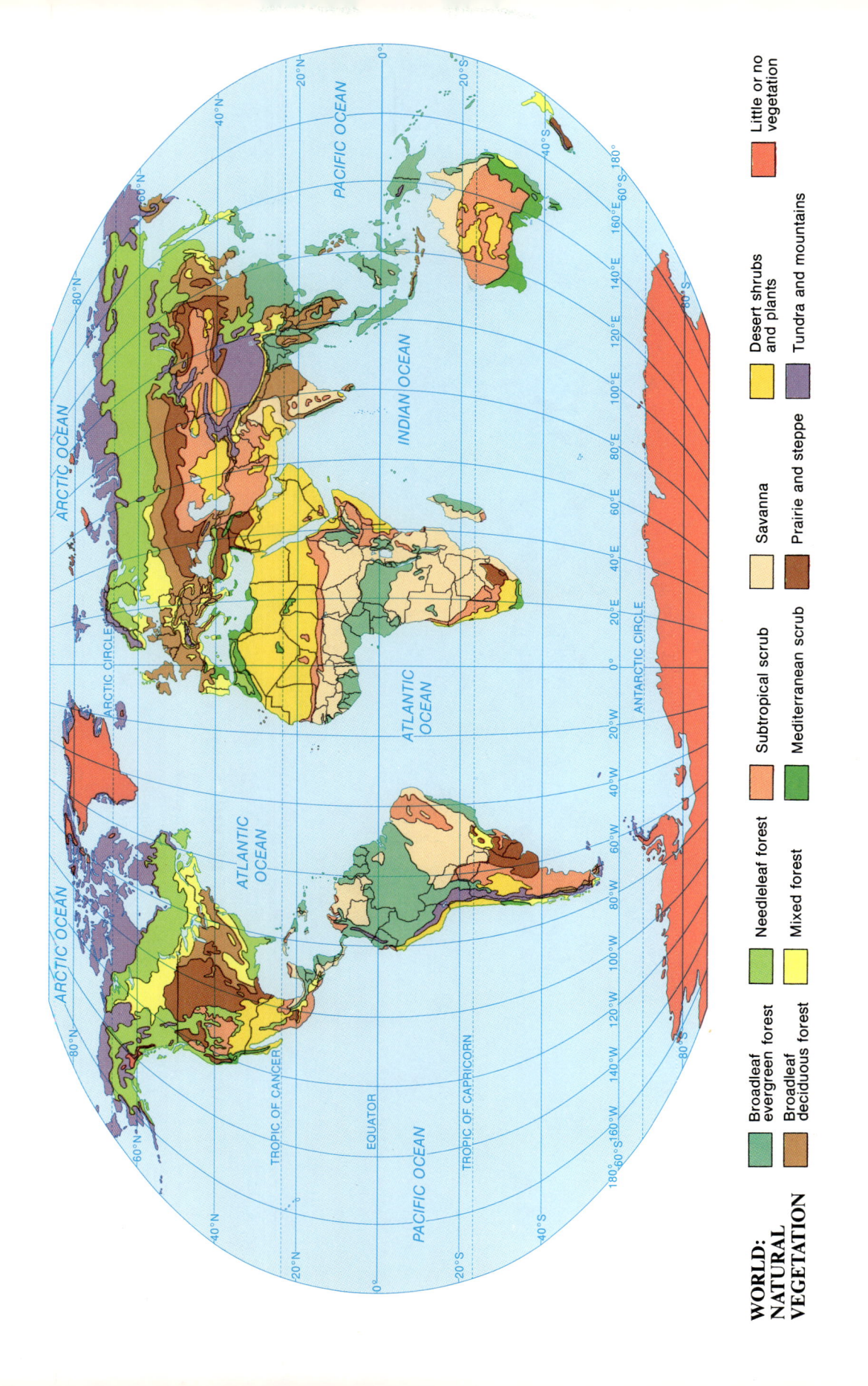

WORLD: FOOD STAPLE PRODUCTION

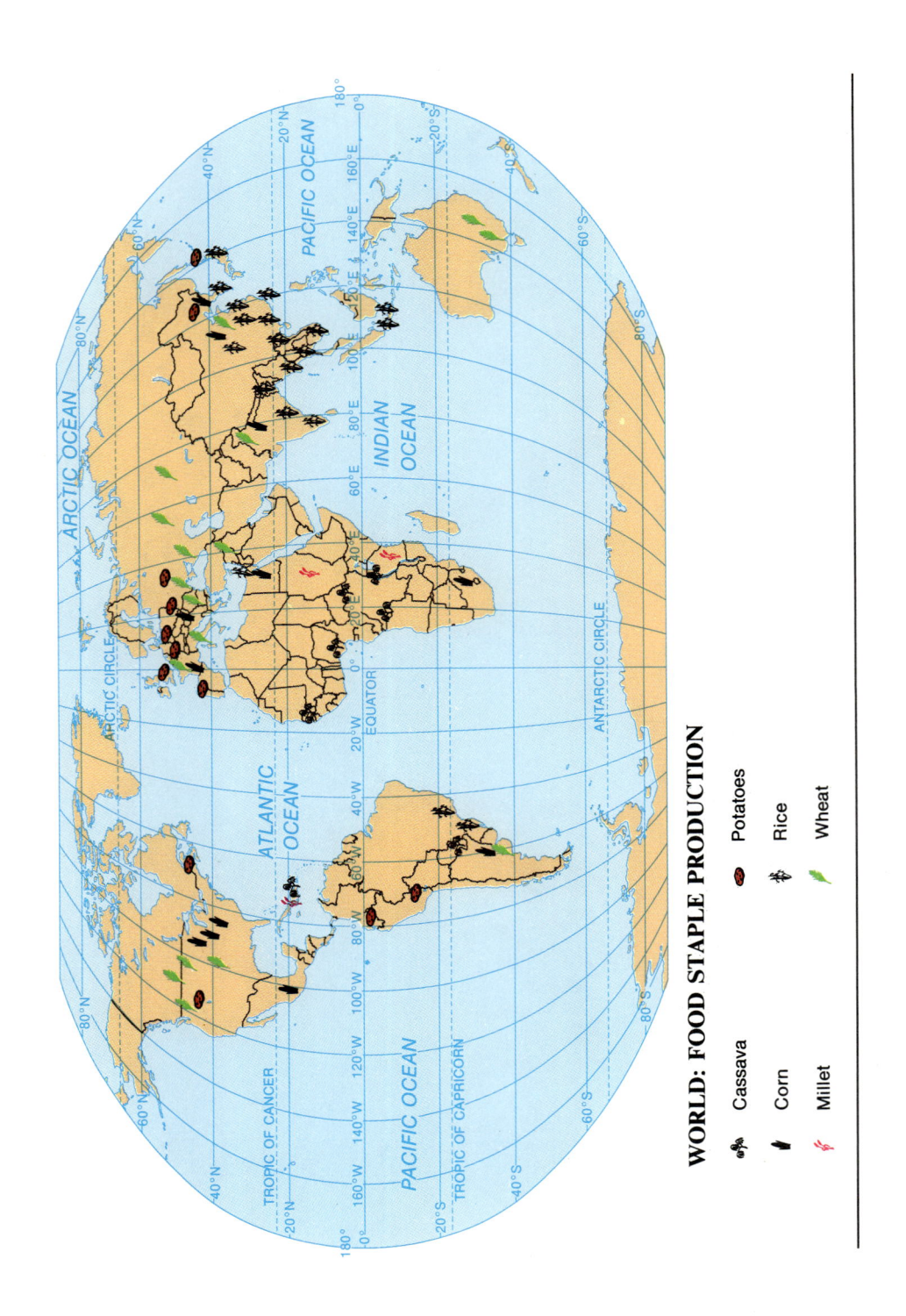

- Cassava
- Corn
- Millet
- Potatoes
- Rice
- Wheat

WORLD: ANIMAL RESOURCES

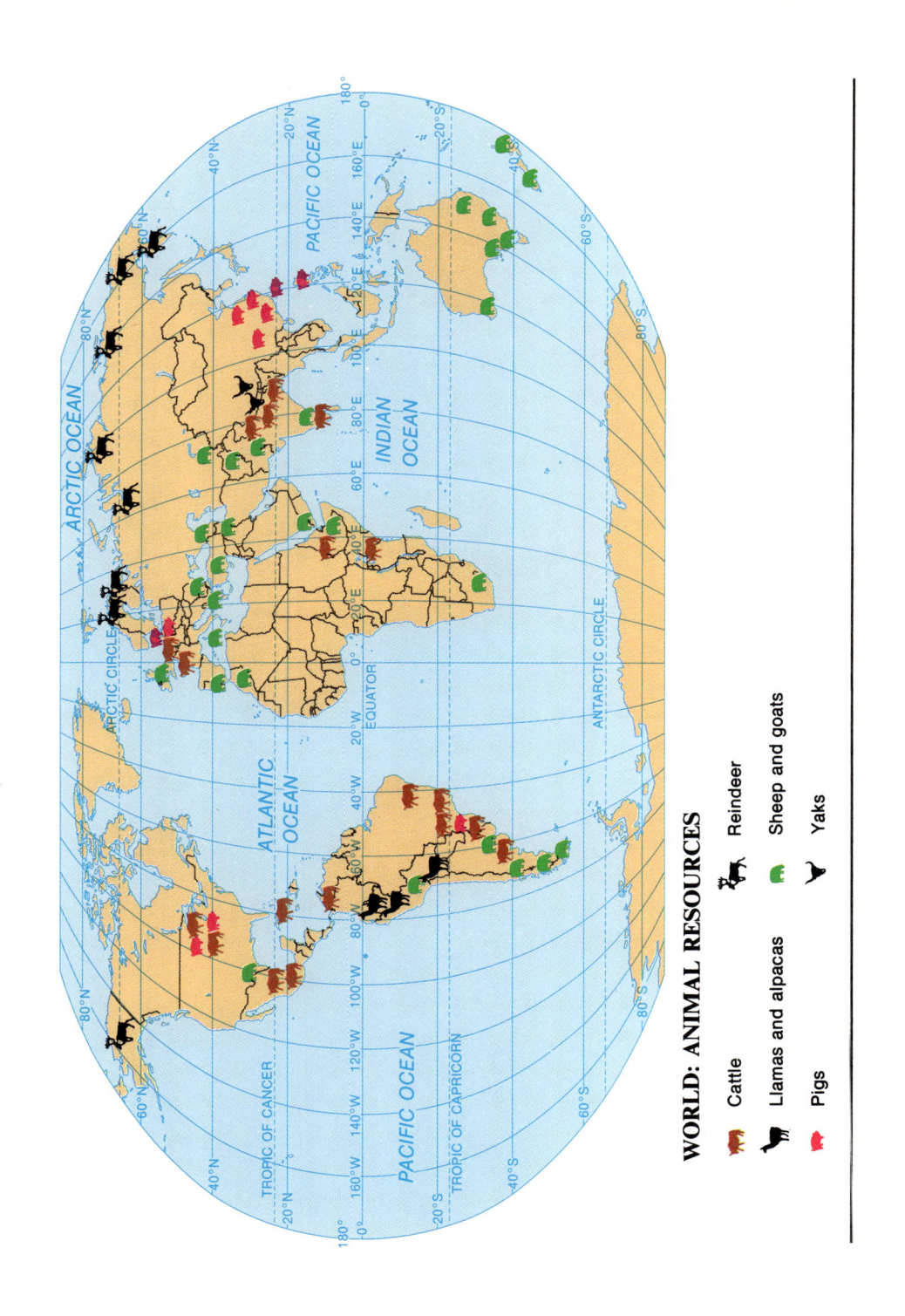

613

WORLD: GROSS NATIONAL PRODUCT

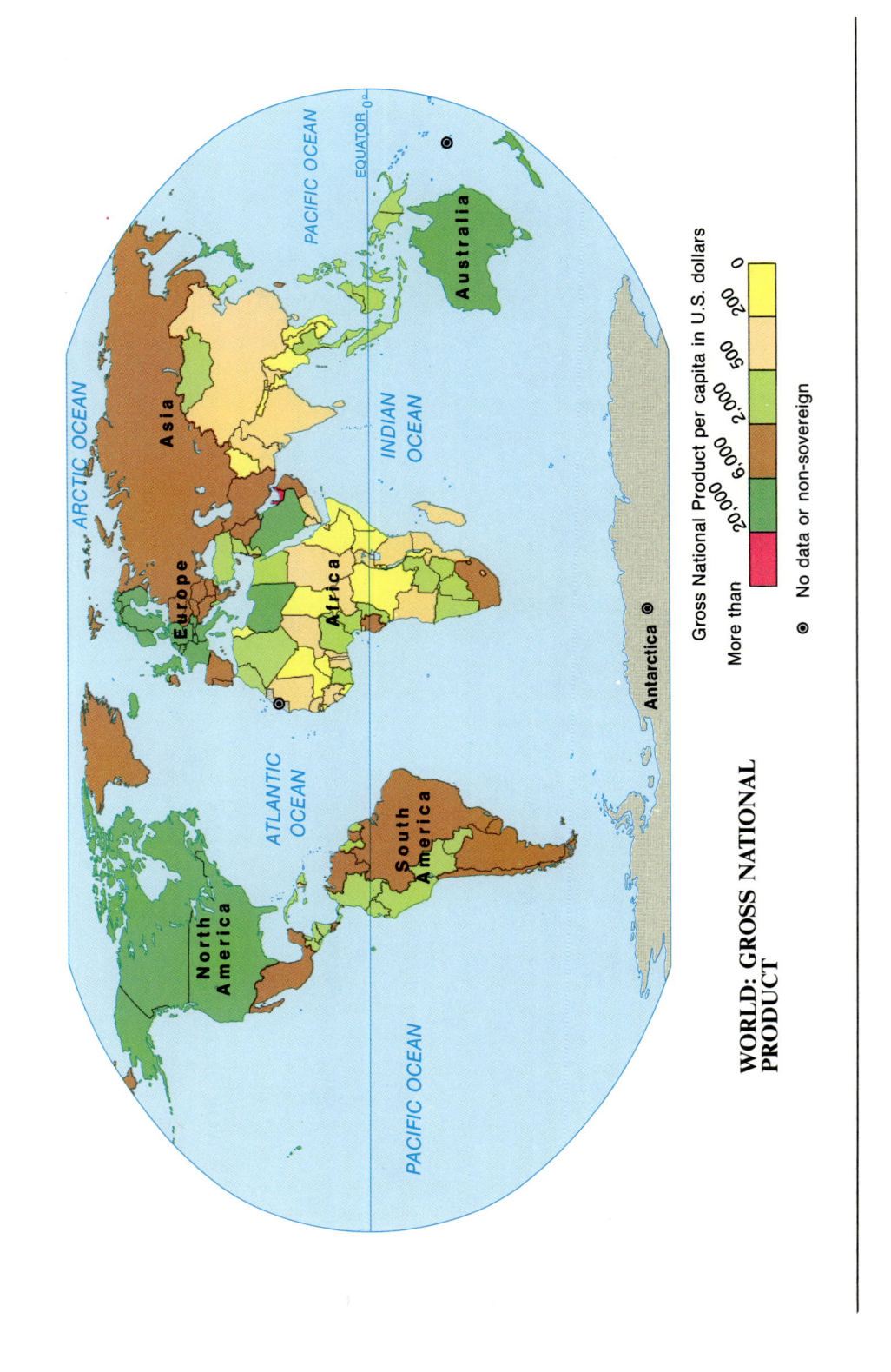

Gross National Product per capita in U.S. dollars: 0, 200, 500, 2,000, 6,000, 20,000, More than

No data or non-sovereign

614

Index

Index

See also the List of Maps following the Table of Contents

Abbasids, 52, 56
Abdallah, King of Transjordan, 61, 90
Abdul Hamid, 57
Abrahams, Peter, 177
Abu Bakr, 49
acculturation, 19
Achebe, Chinua, 149, 180
Adana, Turkey, 39
Adrianople, Treaty of, 469
Affonso I, King of Kongo, 131-132
Afghanistan, 34, 37, 48, 513
    See also Middle East
Africa, 107-184
    ancient kingdoms, 122-129
    Asians in, 162-163
    and China, 320
    climate, 110-113
    colonies in, 136-138, 164-168
    cultural contributions, 176-184
    and development of culture, 11-12
    economic activities, 155-163
    geography, 110-119
    history, 120-139
    languages, 116-118
    Latin America and, 568
    peoples, 116-117
    political activities, 164-174
    social institutions, 140-154
    Soviet Union and, 514
    See also names of individual countries
Africanus, Leo, 125
Afrikaaners, 136
    See also apartheid; Boers; South African Republic
Afrikaans, 118
Afro-Asian languages, 118
age set (age group), 142
agriculture
    Africa, 155-160
    "bush-fallow," 155
    China, 289, 306-310
    India, 216, 230-234
    Japan, 370-371
    Latin America, 572-577
    Middle East, 40, 63, 66, 75-81
    origins of, 13-14

plantation, single-crop, 79-80, 404, 428-430, 574-577
slash-and-burn, shifting, 428
Southeast Asia, 404, 426-432
Soviet Union, 487-494
Agricultural Revolution, 13-14
Aguinaldo, Emilio, 414
ahimsa, 201
Ajanta caves, 250
Akbar, Emperor, 200
Akira, Kurosawa, 389
Alaska, 470
Alegría, Ciro, 598
Alexander I, Tsar of Russia, 466
Alexander II (Tsar Liberator), 468
Alexander III, Tsar of Russia, 464
Alexander the Great, 45, 196-197
Alexandria, 66
Alfonsín, Raúl, 587
Algeria, 105, 122, 168
    See also Africa
Ali, Muhammad's son-in-law, 49, 52, 72
Alianza Popular Revolucionaria Americana (APRA), 586
Allende Gossens, Salvador, 513, 555, 572, 577, 579, 590-591
Alliance for Progress, 593
Alliance Party of Malaysia, 439-440
Almohad, 54
Almoravids, 53-54, 123
Altai Mountains, 260
Amazon River, 532
Amida Buddha, 363-365
Amin, Idi, 163, 172
Amistad Mutiny, 134
Amritsar Massacre, 210
Amu Darya, river, 37
Amur River, 260, 469, 512
Analects of Confucius, 295
Anand, Mulk Raj, 254
Ananda temple, 443
Anatolia, 36-37, 45, 48, 54, 58, 88
    See also Middle East
ancestor veneration, 298, 303
ancestor worship, 151
Anderson, Hans Christian, 253
Andes, mountains, 530-532
Andropov, Yuri, 477

Angkor, Cambodia, 401
Angkor Thom temple, 444
Angkor Wat temple, 443
Angola, 114, 127, 514
    See also Africa
animals and animal husbandry
    Africa, 13, 112, 120, 151, 155-157
    China, 261
    Latin America, 572
    Middle East, 13, 76-78
    origins of, 13
    Southeast Asia, 13, 428
    Soviet Union, 493
animism
    Africa, 150
    Japan, 362
    Latin America, 568
    Southeast Asia, 422
Ankara, Turkey, 39
Anna, Tsarina of Russia, 465
anthropologists, cultural, 4
Antofagasta, Chile, 536
apartheid, 136, 172-174
Aquino, Benigno, 440-441
Arab empire, ancient, 50-53
Arab League, 89
Arab Socialism, 89-91
Arabian Nights, 102
Arabian Peninsula, 34-36, 40, 66
Arabic numerals, 98, 255-256
Arabs, 36-37, 50-53, 89-94, 121, 322
    See also Muslim
Aral Sea, 453
Arbenz Guzman, Jacobo, 576
archipelago definition, 395
Argentina, 528, 531, 552-556, 586-587, 595
    See also Latin America
Arguedas, José María, 597
Armas, Carlos Castillo, 576
Armenia and Armenians, 37, 42, 91
    See also Middle East
art and architecture
    Africa, 181-183
    China, 324-330
    India, 249-253
    Japan, 382-386
    Latin America, 538, 600-602

617

art and architecture — *continued*
    Middle East, 103-106
    Paleolithic, 13
    Southeast Asia, 443-445
    Soviet Union, 522
Aruba, 529
    See also Latin America
Aryans, 195-196
Ashanti, 143-145
Ashanti Union of Akan States, 128
Ashoka, Emperor, 198
Asia, Southeast. *See* Southeast Asia
Asia Minor. *See* Anatolia
Askia Muhammad (Askia the Great), 126-127
Asturias, Miguel Angel, 597
Aswan Dam, 80
Atacama Desert (Chile), 579
Atahualpa, 544
Atlas Mountains, 36, 39, 64
autocracy, 461, 467-469
Axum, 129
ayllus, 573
Aztecs, 541-542

B
a'ath Party, 92
Baha'i faith, 91
Baganda tribes, 129, 151
Baghdad, 35, 52-53, 66
Bahrein, 40
    See also Middle East
Balfour Declaration, 60
bamboo, 398
Bangkok, Thailand, 394-397
Bangladesh, 246-247, 513
Barbados, 529
    See also Latin America
barter, 27, 152
Barumbu, Zaire, 114
Basho, Matsuo, 387
Batista, Fulgencio, 513, 587
Batlle y Ordóñez, José, 555
Batu Khan, 459
Baykal, Lake, 450, 454
bedouin, 64-67
Beijing (Peking). *See* China
Beirut, Lebanon, 66, 94
Bengal, India, 203-204
Ben-Gurion, David, 94
Benin, 127-128, 182
    See also Africa
Berbers, 40, 48, 58, 122
    See also Almohad
Berlin-to-Baghdad Railway, 59
Bhagavad Gita, 253
Biafra, 140, 166

Bihzad, 106
Bizet, Georges, 598-599
black priest, 478-479
Blacks, 557
    See also Africa, peoples
Blue Mosque, 103
Boers, 134-136
Bogotá, Colombia, 532-533
Bolívar, Simón, 548-550, 558
Bolivia, 528, 556, 578-579, 589-590
    See also Latin America
Bolsheviks, 471-472
Bombay, India, 193
Bonaparte, Joseph, 548
Bonaparte, Napoleon, 58, 466, 548
Borobudur monument, 444-445
Borodin, Aleksandr, 523
Boxer Rebellion, 280-281
boyars, 462
Brahma, 222-224
Brahman, 222-223
Brahmaputra River, 188, 191
Brahmin, 215, 225-226
Brahmo Samaj, 207
Brasilia, Brazil, 602
Brazil, 528-531, 548-549, 552, 554-555, 580, 597-602
    See also Latin America
Brest-Litovsk, Treaty of, 472
Brezhnev, Leonid, 476-477
bride wealth, 68, 145-146
Britain and the British
    in Africa, 135-138, 159
    in China, 320
    in India, 202-212, 225-227, 230-232, 240-241
    in Middle East, 58-62
    in Southeast Asia, 405-407
Brunei, 387, 394
    See also Southeast Asia
Buddha, 224-225, 443-444
Buddhism
    China, 296-298, 302, 324, 328
    India, 198, 224-225, 249-250
    Japan, 338, 361-365, 383
    Mahayana, 225, 296, 363
    Southeast Asia, 403, 406, 419, 422-423, 443-445
    Theravada, 225, 422, 444
Buenos Aires, Argentina, 532
Buganda, 129
Bulganin, Nikolai, 475-476
Burma, 275, 294, 406-408
    See also Southeast Asia
Burundi, 172
    See also Africa
Byelorussians, White or Great Russians, 455
Byzantine empire, 47-48, 50, 54

C
adres, 317
Cairo, Egypt, 56, 66
Calcutta, India, 193, 194
caliphate, 50-52
calligraphy
    China, 328
    Middle East, 105
Cambodia, 392, 394-395, 401, 409-411, 435-436, 446
    Kampuchea, 436-438
    See also Southeast Asia
campesinos, 572
Cape Town, South Africa, 112
capitalism, defined, 503
Caribbean islands, 530-532
Casablanca, 66
cash crops, defined, 159
    See also crops
Caspian Sea, 35, 39, 75
caste system, 28, 215-217, 225-226
    See also stratification, social
Castro, Fidel, 513, 555, 577, 579, 587
Catherine I, Tsarina of Russia, 465
Catherine the Great (Catherine II), Tsarina of Russia, 465
Catholic Church and Catholics
    Africa, 170-171
    China, 273-274, 279
    Latin America 546-547, 567-571, 584
    Southeast Asia, 405, 408
    Soviet Union, 509
    See also Christianity
Caucasus Mountains, 455
Caucasus region, 455, 469
caudillo, 550-551, 584-586
Central Committee (U.S.S.R.), 503
Central Committee of National Party Congress (China), 316
Chad, 172
    See also Africa
Chad, Lake, 115, 126
Chamanand, Kriangsak, 439
Chan, Ts'ao, 328
Chand, Prem, 254
Chandragupta I, 197
Chang (Yangtze) River, 266
change, social and cultural, 16-20
    See also land reform; reform
Charles V, King of Spain, 596
Chávez, Carlos, 599
Chekhov, Anton, 518
Chernenko, Konstantin, 477
Chiang Kai-shek, 283-287
Chichen Itza, Mexico, 539
Chikamatsu Monzaemon, 389
Chile, 528, 531, 536, 552, 572, 578-580, 587-590

See also Latin America
China, 257-330
    Africa and, 174
    agricultural regions, 306
    Britain and, 320
    climate, 260-262
    cultural contributions, 321-330
    economic activities, 306-313
    geography, 260-267
    history, 268-288
    India and, 248-249
    Japan and, 282, 285, 319, 344, 380
    Nan Chao and, 401-402
    North, 261-267, 306
    political activities, 314-320
    social institutions, 289-305
    Russia, Soviet Union, and, 279-280, 319, 469-470, 512-513
    South, 260-267, 306
    Southeast Asia and, 417
    United States and, 280, 318
Chinese Communists, 283-288
Chingis Khan (Genghis Khan), 56
cholo, 560-561
Christian Democrats, 587-588
Christianity
    Africa, 150, 152-153
    China, 273-274, 277, 279, 302
    India, 205
    Japan, 340
    Latin America, 568-571
    Middle East, 40, 47-50, 59
    Southeast Asia, 423-424
    Soviet Union, 457-459, 509
    See also Catholic Church; Copts; Lutheran Church; Russian Orthodox Church
Chulalongkorn, King of Thailand, 408
Chongqing, China, 266
Cid, Enrique Castro, 600
Cinque, 134
civil disobedience, and Gandhi, 210-212
civil service, 294, 324
Cixi (Tsu-hsi), Empress Dowager, 278-280
clans, 28-29, 141, 294, 330
class system, 28-29
climate
    Africa, 110-113
    China, 260-264
    India, 189-191
    Japan, 334-335
    Latin America, 533-536
    Middle East, 37-40
    Southeast Asia, 396-397
    Soviet Union, 450-454
Clive, Robert, 203-204
coffee-growing, 576
collectives, 492-493, 577

Colombia, 528, 531, 533
    See also Latin America
colonialism. *See* foreign activities and influence; *names of colonizing countries*
communes, 308-310, 427, 486
Communism, 488-489
Communist Party
    China, 316-317, 326
    Latin America, 587-589
    Southeast Asia, 409, 415, 418-419
    Soviet Union, 503-510
Community Development Program (India), 233
compadres, 565-566
Confucianism
    China, 268-271, 295-296, 301, 303, 327-328
    Southeast Asia, 419
Confucius, 268-271, 293, 295-296
Congo, People's Republic of, 127, 170-171
    See also Africa
Congo River, 115, 137
Conservatives (Latin America), 584
Constantine, Emperor, 47
Constantinople, 47, 55-57
cooperative farms, 233, 308
Copts
    Africa, 129-130, 152
    Middle East, 40, 50, 91
Cortés, Hernán, 542, 545, 596
Costa, Lucio, 601
Costa Rica, 528, 531, 551
    See also Latin America
Council of Ministers, Soviet, 504
cousins, 22
    parallel, 22, 68
criollos, 560
crops
    Africa, 155-160
    China, 260-265, 306-310
    India, 232-234
    Japan, 371
    Latin America, 546-547, 574-576
    Middle East, 75-79
    Southeast Asia, 428-432
    Soviet Union, 452-454, 493-494
Crusades, 54-55
Cuba, 134, 174, 513, 528, 531, 555-556, 572, 578, 587
    See also Latin America
Cui, Cesar, 523
cultural contributions
    Africa, 176-184
    China, 312-330
    India, 249-256
    Japan, 382-389
    Latin America, 595-602

    Middle East, 97-106
    Southeast Asia, 443-446
    Soviet Union, 515-525
culture, 2-30
    changes in, 16-20
    defined, 2-7
    evolution of, 11-15
    norms and laws of, 5-7
    patterns of, 8
    uniformities of, 21
Cunha, Euclydes da, 598
Curaçao, 529
    See also Latin America
Cyril, 457-458
Czechoslovakia, 511
    See also Soviet Union

Daimyo, 339-342
Damascus, Syria, 66
dance
    Southeast Asia, 446
    Soviet Union, 523-525
Dandi Salt March, 212
Darío, Rubén, 597
debt serfdom, 462
Deccan Plateau, 188-189
Decembrists, 466-467
deforestation
    Africa, 160
    Latin America, 534
    Middle East, 78
democracies
    Africa, 168-170
    Japan, 376-379
    Middle East, 92-94
    Southeast Asia, 439-442
Dewey, Commodore George, 414
dharma, 216, 223
Dhugasvili, Joseph. *See* Stalin
Diamond Sutra, 321
Dias, Bartholomew, 131, 202
diaspora, and Jews, 44
Díaz, Porfirio, 551, 553-554
dictatorship, 170-171, 408, 435, 550-553
Diem, Ngo Dinh, 411-412
Diet (Japan), 366-378
Dinesen, Isak, 156
Diop, Birago, 180
Diop, David, 180
divine kingship, 121
divorce. *See* marriage customs
diwan, 194
Dnieper River, 454
Dokuchayev, Vasily, 515
Dome of the Rock, Jerusalem, 103
Dominican Republic, 528, 531
    See also Latin America

Domostroy, 477, 481
Don River, 454
Dostoevski, Fëdor, 202-203
Dupleix, Joseph, 202-203
Dutch, 134-136, 359, 404, 428, 528-529
Dutch East India Company, 403-404
dynasties
    Gupta (India), 198-199
    Han (China), 270-271
    Mamluk (Middle East), 56
    Maurya (India), 197-198
    Meiji (Japan), 343, 354-356, 376-377
    Ming (China), 325
    Qin (Ch'in) (China), 270
    Qing (Ch'ing) (China), 272-273, 276-278
    Shang (China), 268, 324
    Sui (China), 271
    Sung (China), 325
    Tang (T'ang) (China), 271-272, 324
    Xia (China), 268
    Zhou (Chou) (China), 268-270, 324

Echauren, Roberto Matta, 600
ecological problems
    population, 75, 81, 146, 150, 217, 289-300, 582
    soil, 75-78, 155, 159, 306, 427-428, 494, 536
    water, 75, 191, 261, 451, 535
economic activities
    Africa, 155-163
    China, 306-313
    and culture, 27
    development of, 25
    India, 230-239
    Japan, 368-375
    Latin America, 572-582
    Middle East, 75-86
    Southeast Asia, 426-434
    Soviet Union, 491-502
Ecuador, 528, 531, 533
    See also Latin America
education
    Africa, 146, 153
    China, 294, 301-303
    India, 225-228
    Japan, 357-361
    Latin America, 566
    learning, and culture, 4
    Middle East, 68-69, 82
    Southeast Asia, 419-424
    Soviet Union, 484-485
Egypt, 13-14, 36, 43, 45, 53, 59, 78-83, 89-92, 513
    See also Middle East

Eisenhower, Dwight, 379
Eisenstein, Sergei M., 521
ejidos, 577
Elburz Mountains, 36
Elizabeth, Tsarina of Russia, 465
Ellora temple, 250-251
El Salvador, 528, 589-590
    See also Latin America
employment
    in Japan, 372-373
    in Soviet Union, 498-501
encomienda system, 544
Equator, Kenya, 114
Ercilla y Zúñiga, Alonzo de, 596
Estenssoro, Victor Paz, 556
etatism (Turkey), 82
Ethiopia, 114, 129-130, 514
    See also Africa
ethnocentrism, 9
European influence. *See* foreign activities and influence
evolution
    biological, 11-15
    cultural, 16-19

Faisal, King of Iraq, 61
Faisal, King of Saudi Arabia, 91
Falkland Islands (Islas Malvinas), 554
family
    Africa, 124, 141-146
    authority, 23-24
    China, 291-294, 298-301
    democratic, 24
    extended, 22-23, 68, 144-149, 480, 486-488, 565
    India, 217-220
    Japan, 350-356
    joint, 23, 144, 217-218, 291, 417-419
    Latin America, 562-566
    matriarchal, 23, 142-143
    Middle East, 67-68
    nuclear, 22, 68, 298-299, 356, 417-419, 487, 563-565
    patriarchal, 23, 67-68, 141, 144, 480-481, 565
    patrilineal, 22, 144
    patrilocal, 144, 292
    Southeast Asia, 417-419
    Soviet Union, 480-482, 485-488
    structure and organization, 21-24
Famine Code of 1883, 230
Farouk, King of Egypt, 91
al Fazari, 121
fellahin, 63, 80

Ferdinand VII, King of Spain, 548
Fertile Crescent, 34-37
fetish, 151-152
feudalism, 339
Fez, Morocco, 66
filial piety (China), 292-293
Finland, 461
Finlay, Carlos, 595
Firdawsi, 101
fire, use of, 11
fish and fishing
    Africa, 115, 158-159
    Japan, 335-336
Fitzgerald, Edward, 102
Five-year plans
    Chinese, 311-312
    Indian, 235
    Soviet, 492-493, 495-497
folkways, defined, 5
foreign activities and influence in
    Africa, 130-139, 164-168
    China, 273-287
    India, 202-207, 236, 240-241
    Japan, 340,
    Latin America, 544-548,
    Middle East, 54-62
    Southeast Asia, 403-413
    Soviet Union, 470, 474-475
foreign relations of
    Africa, 174
    China, 318-320
    India, 246-248
    Japan, 379-381
    Latin America, 589-593
    Middle East, 95
    Southeast Asia, 411-413
    Soviet Union, 476-477, 510-514
forest products, 159, 398, 430-432, 534
forests, tropical rain, 112, 397, 534
Four Modernizations (China), 312
Four Noble Truths, 224-225
France and the French
    in Africa, 168-171
    in China, 279
    in India, 202-203
    in Latin America, 528-529
    in Middle East, 58-61
    in Russia, 465-466
    in Southeast Asia, 408-409
Francis Ferdinand, Archduke of Austria, 471
Frei, Eduardo, 577
French Guiana, 527
    See also Latin America
Freyre, Gilberto, 598
Fuentes, Carlos, 597
Fuji, Mount, 335
Fujiwara family, 339
Fyodor, Tsar of Russia, 463

Gagarin, Yuri, 516
Gama, Vasco da, 131, 202
Gandhi, Indira, 213, 243-244
Gandhi, Mohandas, 210-212, 217
Ganges River, 188-192
Gempaku, Sugita, 359
geography
    Africa, 110-115
    China, 260-267
    and culture, 29-30
    India, 188-192
    influencing culture,
    Japan, 334-337
    Latin America, 530-536
    Middle East, 34-40
    Southeast Asia, 394-399
    Soviet Union, 450-456
    See also Physical maps
Germany
    and Africa, 137-138
    and Middle East, 59
Ghana, 122-123, 165
    See also Africa
Ghats, mountains, 188-189
Gilels, Emil, 523
Glinka, Konstantin, 515
Glinka, Mikhail, 523
Goa, India, 202
Gobi Desert, 260, 261
Gogol, Nikolai, 517
Golkar Party (Indonesia), 442
Gomes, Carlos, 599
Gómez, Juan Vicente, 552
Gorbachev, Mikhail, 477
government
    Africa, 168-171
    China, 316-317
    development of, 24-25
    India, 240-248
    Japan, 376-379
    Latin America, 584-584
    Middle East, 90-95
    Southeast Asia, 435-442
    Soviet Union, 503-510
Gowon, Major General Yakubu, 166
"Great Leap Forward" (China), 312
Great Mosque, Damascus, 103
Great Purge, 473-474
Great Rift Valley, 114
Great Wall of China, 260
Greeks
    and India, 196-197
    and Middle East, 42
Green Revolution, 233-234, 430
Greenberg, Joseph, 118
gross national product, defined, 169
Guadeloupe, 529
    See also Latin America

Guangxu (Kuang Hsu), 279
Guatemala, 528
    See also Latin America
gun (arquebus) 127
Guyana, 529, 570
    See also Latin America

Hacienda system, 574
haiku, 386
Haiti, 528, 531, 584
    See also Latin America
Harappa, Pakistan, 15, 195
Harappan civilization, 195-196
harijans, 217
Harris, Joel Chandler, 177
Harun al-Rashid, 102
Hassan, King of Morocco, 91
Haya de la Torre, Victor Raul, 586
Helmand River, 37
Herzl, Theodore, 61
Heyerdahl, Thor, 537
Hidalgo y Costilla, Father Miguel, 548
Hideyoshi, 339
hijra, 50
Himalayan Mountains, 260
Hindu Kush Mountains, 37
Hinduism
    Africa, 150
    India, 193, 200-201, 207-248, 250-256
Hirobumi, Ito, 376
Hiroshige, 385
history
    Africa, 120-139
    China, 268-288
    India, 195-214
    Japan, 338-347
    Latin America, 537-557
    Middle East, 43-62
    Southeast Asia, 400-416
    Soviet Union, 457-477
Hitler, Adolph, 474-475
Ho Chi Minh, 409
Ho Chi Minh City, Vietnam, 397
Hokkaido island, Japan, 334
Hokusai, 385
Homo habilis, 11
Homo sapiens, 11-12
Honduras, 528, 531
    See also Latin America
Honen, 363
Hong Kong, 276, 320
Hong Xiuchuan (Hung Hsiu-ch'uan), 277
Honshu island, Japan, 334
Houphouet-Boigny, Felix, 169-170
Houssay, Bernardo, 595
Huai River, 260

Huang (Yellow) River, 265-266
Huayna, 544
Huks (Philippines), 415
Hulagu, 56
Husein, ibn-Ali, 59
Hussein, King of Jordan, 90
hydroelectric power, 113, 115, 161, 355

Ibadan, Nigeria, 112
Ibn Battuta, 99, 121, 124
Ibn Ishaq, 49
Ibn Sa'ud, King of Saudi Arabia, 60, 91
Ibn Sena (Avicenna), 99
Ife, Nigeria, 181-183
illiteracy
    Africa, 146
    China, 292,302
    India, 243
    Japan, 357
    Latin America, 548, 557, 566, 586
    Middle East, 69, 82
    Southeast Asia, 420-421
    Soviet Union, 484
Imperial Rule Assistance Association (IRAA), 346
imports, 159,
    See also trade
Incas, 542-544
independence movements
    Africa, 167-168
    India, 207-214
    Latin America, 548-557
India, 185-256
    Bangladesh and, 246-248, 513
    climate, 189-191
    cultural contributions, 249-256
    economic activities, 230-238
    geography, 188-193
    history, 195-214
    Kashmir and, 246
    languages, 244-245
    political activities, 240-248
    social institutions, 215-228
    Southeast Asia and, 417
    Soviet Union and, 512-513
Indian Congress Party, 243
Indian National Congress, 209
Indians of Latin America, 538-547, 560-561, 566, 572-573
Indochina, French, 408-409
    See also Southeast Asia
Indo-Gangetic Plain, 188
Indonesia, 84, 394-395, 403-404, 414, 441-442, 444-445
    See also Southeast Asia

621

Indus River, 15, 37, 184, 192
Industrial Revolution, 15, 30
industry
    Africa, 160-161
    China, 310-313
    India, 235-237
    Japan, 336-337, 369-375
    Latin America, 577-582
    Middle East, 82-85
    Southeast Asia, 432-434
    Soviet Union, 491-492, 495-502
inheritance rules, 26-27, 80
initiation rites
    Africa, 141-142
    Southeast Asia,
institutions, social. *See* social institutions
invention, and culture, 16
Iran, 34, 39, 45, 48, 66, 83-84, 89, 91
    See also Middle East
Iraq, 34, 48, 82-84, 89-92
    See also Middle East
Ironsi, General, 166
Irrawaddy River, 394
Isfahan, Iran, 66
Islam, Muslim
    Africa, 123-124, 150, 143
    India, 200-201, 212-213, 252-253
    Latin America, 570
    Middle East, 16, 40-41, 48-58, 67-70, 87, 91
    "Pillars of," 70-72
    Southeast Asia, 403, 423,
    Soviet Union, 455, 507
Isma'il, 58-59
Israel, 35, 60, 89-95, 174, 504, 513
    See also Middle East
Istambul, 47, 57, 66
    See also Constantinople
Italy
    and Brazil, 552
    and Middle East, 59
Iturbide, Augustín de, 548
Ivan the Great (Ivan III), Tsar of Russia, 461-462
Ivan the Terrible (Ivan IV), Tsar of Russia, 462-463
Ivory Coast, 169-170
    See also Africa

Jahan, Shah, 252-253
Jagannath Car Festival, 223
Jakarta, Indonesia, 404
Jamaica, 529
    See also Latin America
Jamshedpur, India, 235
Japan
    Burma and, 406
    China and, 285, 319
    climate, 334-337
    cultural contributions, 382-389
    economic activities, 368-375
    expansion, 343
    geography, 334-337
    history, 338-347
    Indochina and, 409
    political activities, 376-381
    religions, 361-366
    social institutions, 349-361
Java, Indonesia, 404, 444
Java Man (Pithecanthropus erectus), 11
Jayavarman II, 401
Jerusalem, Israel, 35, 55
Jews
    Latin America, 570
    Middle East, 40, 43-44, 50, 59-62
    Soviet Union, 499, 508-510
jihad, 50
Jiménez, Marcos Péres, 553
Joao VI, King of Portugal, 549
Jodo (Pure Land Sect), 363-365
Johnson, Andrew, 470
Johnson, Lyndon, 412
Johnston, Eric, 76
Jordan, 34, 90
    See also Middle East
Juárez, Benito, 551
Judar, 127
jungle, definition, 112
Junichiro, Tanizaki, 387-388
juntas, 548

Kaaba, 48-49, 72
kabuki, 389
Kakuei, Tanaka, 380
Kalahari, 13, 110, 112
Kalidasa, 254
Kamakura, Japan, 339
kami, 362
Kang Yuwei, 279
Kangxi (K'ang-hsi), Emperor, 273
Kanto, Japan, 335-336
Kariba, Lake, 115
Karli temple, 249-250
karma, 223, 423
Kashmir, 246
Kaunda, Kenneth, 177
Kazakhs, 506-507
Kemal Atatürk, Mustafa, 57-59, 69, 82, 88, 92-93
Kennedy, John F., 593
Kenya, 11, 114, 140, 169
Kenya, Mount, 114
Kenyatta, Jomo, 169, 177
Khadija, 48-49
Khajuraho temple, 251
Khalid, King of Saudi Arabia, 91
Khmer empire, 443-444
Khmer Republic, 436
Khoisan languages, 118
Khrushchev, Nikita, 319, 509
al-Khwarizmi, Muhammad ibn-Musa, 98
Kiev, U.S.S.R., 457-459
Kilimanjaro, Mount, 114
Kim Van Kieu, 446
King, Martin Luther, 211
Kinki, Japan, 336
kinsman, kinship system, 22
Kirov, Sergei, 473
Kita-Kyushu, Japan, 336
Kittikachorn, Premier Thanom, 439
knowledge, influencing culture, 30
    See also science and mathematics
koan, 365
Kobe, Japan, 336
Kogan, Leonid, 523
kolkhozi, 493
Kongo, kingdom of, 131-132
Koran, 49-50, 67, 70-72, 100
Korea, 338, 343-344
koseki, 350-351, 354
Kosygin, Aleksei, 476
Krakatoa, 396
Kruger, Paul, 135
Kshatriya, 215-215, 225-226
Kuomintang, 281-284
Kurds, 40, 64, 91
Kuwait, 84
    See also Middle East
Kyoto, Japan, 336
Kyushu, Japan, 334, 336

Labor, 26
    See also economic activities; employment
lacquerware, sculpture, 325-326
Lafontaine, Jean de, 253
La Guma, Alex, 177
land. *See* agriculture; crops
land reforms
    China, 284-285, 308
    India, 233-234
    Japan, 233
    Latin America, 576-577, 584
    Middle East, 63, 79-80
language
    Africa, 118
    Afro-Asian, 118
    China, 262, 302, 329
    evolution of, 12, 24
    India, 244-245
    Japan, 338, 359, 386
    Latin America, 528, 566
    Middle East, 40, 100
    Southeast Asia, 392, 397

Soviet Union, 455, 458, 465, 484
    universality of, 21
Lao She, 328-329
Lao Tsu, 270, 296, 438
    Way and Its Power (Tao Te Ching), 296
Laos, 392, 394, 437-438
    See also Southeast Asia
Las Casas, Father Bartolome de, 596
Latin America, 527-602
    and agricultural revolution, 13
    climate, 533-536
    countries of, 528-529
    cultural contributions, 595-602
    economic activities, 572-582
    geography, 530-533
    history, 537-557
    political activities, 584-593
    social institutions, 558-561
    Soviet Union and 513
Latvia, 509
    See also Soviet Union
laws, defined, 5
leaching, 112
Leakey family, 11
Lebanon, 91-93
    See also Middle East
Legalism, 270
Lena River, 453-454
Lenin (Vladimir Ulyanov), 471-473, 492
Leopold, King of Belgium, 136-137
Lermantov, Michael, 520
Lesotho, 168
    See also Africa
Lesseps, Ferdinand de, 58
Liberals (Latin America), 584
liberation theology (Latin America), 571
Lima, Peru, 544, 566
Lin Biao, 315, 317
Lin Zexu (Lin Tse-hsu), 276
Linton, Ralph, 18
literature
    Africa, 176-180
    China, 327-329
    India, 253-255
    Japan, 387-389
    Latin America, 596-598
    Middle East, 100-102
    oral tradition, 176-177
    Southeast Asia, 445-446
    Soviet Union, 517-522
Lithuania, 509
    See also Soviet Union
Liu Shaoqi, 314
Livingston, David, 129
Lobachevski, Nikolai Ivanovich, 515
Lok Sabha, 242-243
Lomonosov, Mikhail Vasilievich, 515
Lon Nol, General, 435-436
Long March, 283-284

Louis IX, King of France, 55
Lu Xun (Lu Hsun), 328
Luo tribe, 140
Lutheran church, in Latin America, 570
Luthuli, Albert, 177
Lye, Camara, 180

M
Macartney, Lord, 275
Macaulay, Thomas B., 226
Madagascar, 112
    See also Africa
madrasah, 69
Madurai temple, 251
Magdelena River, 533
Magellan, Ferdinand, 404
Magsaysay, Ramon, 416
Mahabharata, 222, 253, 444
Malacca, 202
Malawi, Lake, 114
Malaya, 402-403, 405, 413-414
    See also Southeast Asia
Malaysia, 394, 397, 413-414, 439-440
    See also Southeast Aisa
Malenkov, Georgi, 475
Mali, empire of, 123-125
Mamluks, 56
Manchuria, 261-265, 285, 319
Manchurian incident, 285, 345
Manchus, 272-282
Mandingoes, 123
    See also Mali, empire of
Manifest Destiny, 591
Manila, Philippines, 397
Mansur, Caliph, 52
al Mansur, Ruler of Morocco, 127
Manuel I, King of Portugal, 132
Mao Zedong (Mao Tse-tsung), 283–284, 214–320
Maoism, 301-304
Maracaibo, Lake, 533
Marco Polo Bridge, 345
Marcos, Ferdinand, 440–441
"marginal man," 149
Marquez, Gabriel Garcïa, 597
Marrakesh, 54
marriage customs
    Africa, 145-146
    China, 292, 298-299
    India, 218-220
    Japan, 352-356
    Latin America, 563
    Middle East, 67-68
    Southeast Asia, 417-419
    Soviet Union, 480-481, 485-486
Marshall Plan, 510-511
Martinique, 529
    See also Latin America

Marx, Karl, 467, 488, 503, 555
Marxism-Leninism, 302, 474
Massemba-Delbat, Alphonse, 171
Mau-Mau, 141
Maurya, Ashoka, 198
Maurya, Chandragupta, 197
Maurya empire, 197-198
May Fourth incident, 282
Mayas, 538-540
Mboya, Tom, 140
Mecca, 48, 66
medicine man, 151-152
Medina, 50, 66
Mediterranean climate, 39, 112
Meiji
    government, 376-377
    Restoration, 343, 354
Meir, Golda, 82
Mekong River, 394
Mencius, 268-270
Mendeleev, Dmitri, 515
Merida, Carlos, 600
Mesopotamia (Iraq), 13-14, 34, 45
mestizos, 528, 560-563
Methodius, 457-458
Mexican Revolution, 553-554
Mexico, 84, 528, 531, 541-542, 562, 566, 577-580, 591, 600-601
    See also Latin America; Mexican Revolution
Mexico City, 542, 545, 566
miai, 352
Middle East, 31-106
    and agricultural and urban revolution, 13-14
    ancient Arab empire, 40-42, 48-54
    climate, 37-40
    cultural contributions, 97-106
    economic activities, 75-85
    geography, 34-37
    history, 43-62
    peoples, 40-42
    political activities, 87-95
    social institutions, 63-74
    Soviet Union and, 513
    See also names of countries
"Middle Kingdom," 298
migrations, prehistoric, 537
Miller, Wright, 483
mineral resources
    Africa, 114, 122, 156, 160-161
    China, 313
    India, 193, 195, 235
    Japan, 337
    Latin America, 545, 556, 568, 577-580
    Middle East, 83-85, 95
    Southeast Asia, 397, 404, 433
    Soviet Union, 495, 508
Ming ceramics, 324-325

minorities. *See* racism, racial discrimination
mir, 482
Mistral, Gabriela, 597
Mobutu, Joseph D. (Mobutu Sese Seko), 168
modernismo, 597
Mohenjo Daro, Pakistan, 15, 195-196
Moiseyev, Igor, 523
monarchies
    African, 164, 168-169
    Arab, 90-91
    constitutional, 90-91
    Indian, 240
    See also name of monarchy
Mongkut, King of Thailand, 408
Mongolia, 261-264
Mongols, 50, 272, 339, 400-401, 459-461, 508
monogamy, 23
monotheism, 44, 49, 568
Monroe Doctrine, 591
monsoons, 198-190, 397
Montevideo, Uruguay, 532
mores, defined, 5
Morocco, 66, 82, 91, 122
Moscovy, 461
Moscow, U.S.S.R., 460-461, 466, 475
motion pictures
    China, 329-220
    India, 255
    Japan, 389
    Soviet Union, 521
Mozambique, 114
    See also Africa
Mphahlele, Ezekiel, 177
Mubarak, Hosni, 89
mudras, 249
Mugabe, Robert, 174
Mughal empire, 200-201
Muhammad, 40, 48-50
    See also Islam, Muslim
Muhammad Ali, 59
mulattoes, 560
Murdock, George, 21
Musa, Mansa, 124-125
music
    Africa, 183-184
    China, 329-330
    Latin America, 598-600
    Soviet Union, 523
Muslim League, 209, 212
Muslims. *See* Islam, Muslim
Mussorgski, Modest, 523

Nagoya, Japan, 336
Nan Chao, 401-402
Nanjing, China, 266

Nanjing, Treaty of, 276-287
Napoleon Bonaparte, 548
Nara, Japan, 336, 338
Nara Buddhism, 363
Nasser, Gamal Abdel, 80, 83, 91-92
Nat worship, 422
National People's Congress, 317
National Revolutionary parties (Latin America), 589
nationalism
    Africa, 166-167
    India, 207-212
    Japan, 338-347
    Latin America, 550-557, 578
    Middle East, 59-60, 87-94
    Southeast Asia, 406-407, 413-416
    Soviet Union (non-Russian), 506-508
Nationalist Party (China), 281-287
nationalization, 83-84, 573, 578
Ne Win, General, 435
Neanderthal Man, 11
needs, basic, 21-30
negritude, 166, 180
Nehru, Jawaharlal, 213
Nemuro, Japan, 335
Neolithic revolution, 13
Nerchinsk, Treaty of, 469
Neruda, Pablo, 597
New Delhi, India, 191, 242-243
New Economic Policy (NEP), 492
Ngouabi, Marien, 172
Nicaragua, 528, 531, 556, 589-590
    See also Latin America
Nicholas I (Iron Tsar), 467-468
Nicholas II, Tsar of Russia, 468-469
Niemeyer, Oscar, 601
Niger River, 114-115
Niger-Congo languages, 118
Nigeria, 84, 112, 140, 164-166, 172, 181-183
    See also Africa
Nigerian Civil War, 166
Nile River, 13-14, 36, 43, 114
    See also Egypt
Nilo-Saharan languages, 118
Nilotics, 115
Nixon, Richard, 318
no play, 388-389
Noble Eightfold Path, 225
Nobunaga, 339
nomads, 63-64
nonviolence, 210-212
North Africa, 36, 58-59, 112-113
    See also Africa; Middle East
Nyerere, Julius K., 163

Oases, 36, 65-66
Ob-Irtysh rivers, 454

Obregón, Alejandro, 600
Odessa, U.S.S.R., 453
O'Higgins, Bernardo, 548
oil. *See* mineral resources
Oistrakh, David, 523
Ojukwu, General Odumegwu, 166
Okinawa, 379
Oleg, 457
oligarchy, 376, 550
Oman, 40
Omar Khayyam, 102
OPEC, 84
Open Door Policy (China), 280
Opium War, 276
oral tradition
    Africa, 176-177
    Soviet Union, 517
Orange Free State, 135-136
    See also Africa
Organization of African Unity (OAU), 130, 167
Organization of American States (OAS), 591
Orinoco River, 532-533
Orozoco, Jose Clemente, 600
Osaka, Japan, 336
Osei Tutu, 128
Ottoman empire, 43, 56-58
Oymyakon, Siberia, 450-452

Pa Chin, 328
Padang, Indonesia, 397
Pagan empire, 400-401, 443
Pahlevi, Shah Mohammed Reza, 83, 91
Pakistan, 195-196, 246-247
Paleolithic (Old Stone) Age, 12-13
Palestine, 35, 60-62, 91, 94-95
Palestine Liberation Organization (PLO), 94
Pallava kingdom, 199
Pamir Mountains, 260
pampas, 532, 535
Pan-Africanism, 167
Panama, 528
    See also Latin America
Pan-American Union, 591
Pan-Arabism, 88-90
Panchatantra, 253
panchayat, 216
Pan-Turkism, 88
Paraguay, 527
    See also Latin America
Pasternak, Boris, 520
pastoralists, 63
Patagonia, 535-536
Pathet Lao, 438
Paul I, Tsar of Russia, 466
Peace Preservation Law (Japan), 377

Pearl Harbor, 346
"pebble tools," 13
Pedro I, Emperor of Brazil, 548-549
Pedro II, Emperor of Brazil, 549
Peking. *See* Beijing
Peking, Treaty of, 469
Peking Man, 11
peninsulares (Latin America), 558
pensadores (Latin America), 596
peoples
    Africa, 116-118
    Baltic, 507
    India, 195-204
    Latin America, 558-562
    Middle East, 40-42
    Southeast Asia, 397, 409
    Soviet Union, 454-456
People's Liberation Army (China), 317
permafrost, 451-452
Perón, Eva Duarte, 586
Perón, Isabel, 586-587
Perón, Juan Domingo, 554, 586-587
Perry, Matthew, 341
Peru, 528, 531, 542-544, 578
    See also Latin America
Persian empire, 45-47
Persians, 37
Peter III, Tsar of Russia, 465
Peter the Great, Tsar of Russia, 464-465
Philippines, 394-395, 404-405, 414-416
    See also Southeast Asia
Phnom Penh, Cambodia, 397
physical maps
    Africa, 111
    China, 261
    India, 189
    Japan, 355
    Latin America, 531
    Middle East, 37
    Southeast Asia, 395
    Soviet Union, 451
Picasso, Pablo, 183
"Pillars of Islam," 70-72
Pinochet, Augusto, 587
Pizarro, Francisco, 544-545
Pizzaro, Gonzalo, 558
Poland, 465, 475, 511
Politburo
    China, 316-317
    U.S.S.R., 503-504
political activities
    Africa, 164-174
    China, 314-320
    and culture, 24-28
    India, 207-213, 240-248
    Japan, 376-381
    Latin America, 584-593
    Middle East, 87-95
    Southeast Asia, 435-442

    Soviet Union, 503-514
    universal, 21
political maps
    Africa, 165
    China, 318
    India, 241
    Japan, 335
    Latin America, 585
    Middle East, 88
    Southeast Asia, 436
    Soviet Union, 451
    world, 6-7
polyandry, 23
polygamy, 23, 67, 145, 418
population. *See* peoples
population problem
    Africa, 150
    China, 300
    India, 238
    Latin America, 517, 582
    Middle East, 36, 81
porcelain, 16, 324-325
Portugal and the Portuguese
    in Africa, 131-132
    in China, 273
    in India, 202
    in Latin America, 547-549
    in Southeast Asia, 403-404
Presidium (Soviet), 504
primogeniture, 27
property
    private, 27
    tribal, 140-141
puberty rites, 141-142, 146, 151
Puerto Rico, 529
    See also Latin America
Punjab, India, 192
purdah, 218
Puri, India, 223
Pushkin, Alexander, 517
Pygmies, 117

Qatar, 40, 84
    See also Middle East
Quianlong (Ch'ien-lung), Emperor, 273
Quito, Ecuador, 532-533
Quotations of Chairman Mao, 303-304
Quraysh tribe, 48

Racial discrimination and racism
    Africa, 135-138, 171-174, 177
    Japan, 363
    Latin America, 558-561
    Middle East, 91
    origins of, 10
    Southeast Asia, 417, 442
    Soviet Union, 506-510

Rajya Sabha, 243
Ramadan, 72
Ramayana, 222, 253, 445
Rao, Raja, 254
Rasputin, 469
Ray, Satyajit, 255
al-Razi (Rhazes), 99
Red River (Southeast Asia), 388, 402
Reds (Russians), 472
reform, agricultural. *See* land reform
reform, social and economic
    U.S. Occupation in Japan, 377-379
    Chiang Kai-Shek's attempts at,
        284-285
    in India, 204-205, 217, 219-220,
        233, 238
    Manchus' attempts at, 277-279
    in Turkey (Middle East), 69-70
religion
    Africa, 129-131, 141, 150-154
    China, 262, 295-298, 303
    India, 195-201, 212-213, 221-225,
        246-247, 249-256
    Japan, 361-366
    Latin America, 567-571
    Middle East, 40-57, 63-74, 97,
        100, 103, 105
    Paleolithic, 13
    Southeast Asia, 422-424
    Soviet Union, 452, 455, 483-484,
        488-489, 507-510
    See also names of religions
religious discrimination and persecution
    See also racism
    China, 297, 303-305
    Soviet Union, 488-489, 507-510
republics
    African, 168-170
    Latin American, 548-556
revitalization, cultural, 19
Rhodes, Cecil, 135
Rhodesia, 119
    See also Zimbabwe
ribats, 47
Richard II, King of England, 55
Richter, Sviatoslav, 523
Rimski-Korsakov, Nicholas, 523
Rio de la Plata, 533
Rivera, Diego, 600-601
Rizal, Jose, 414
Rodó, José Enrique, 597
Romanov, Michael, Tsar of Russia, 463
Romero, Francisco, 595
Romero, Oscar, 570-571
Roosevelt, Franklin D., 593
Roosevelt, Theodore, 344
Rosas, Manuel, 552
Rostropovich, Mstislav, 523
Rowlatt Acts, 210
Roxas, Manuel, 415

625

Roy, Ram Mohun, 207, 226
Rub'al Khali (Empty Quarter), 39
rubber making, 430
Ruflo, Juan, 597
Rurik, 457
Russia. *See* Soviet Union
Russian Orthodox Church, 458-459, 461, 479-480, 488-489, 509
Russian Revolution, 471-474
Russo-Japanese War, 343-344, 464

Saigon. *See* Ho Chi Minh City
Sahara, 34, 36, 64, 120, 122
Sakhalin Island, 344
Saladin, 55
Salween River, 394
samurai, 339-341, 349
sankin-kotai system, 341
San Martín, José de, 548, 590
Santa Anna, Antonio López de, 550-551
Santo Domingo, Dominican Republic, 528
See also Latin America
Sarmiento, Domingo Faustino, 552
Sassanian empire, 48, 50
Sassou-Ngnessou, Denis, 171
sati, 205, 218
satori, 365, 387
satyagraha, 210-212
Sa'ud. *See* Ibn Saud, King of Saudi Arabia.
Saudi Arabia, 36, 40, 59-60, 90-91
See also Africa
savannah region, 112, 534-535
Sayyid Ahmad Khan, 209
science and mathematics
  China, 321-324
  India, 86, 255-256
  Latin America, 538, 595
  Middle East, 97-100
  Soviet Union, 515-517
Selassie, Haile, Emperor of Ethiopia, 130
Selim I, Sultan, 57
Seljuks, 41-42
Senghor, Leopold Sedar, 166, 180
sepoys, 203
  mutiny of, 205-206
seppuku, 342
serfdom, 462, 466
Shah-nameh, 101
Shanghai, China, 266
sheikh, 66-67
shelter, 26-27
Shi'a, 72
Shiite Muslims, 41, 52, 72
Shikibu, Murasaki, 387
Shikoku, Japan, 334-335

Shinto, 338-339, 362, 366
Shiva, 222, 251
shogun, 339-341
Sholokov, Mikhail, 519
Shonagon, Sei, 387
Shudra, 215-216
Shwe Dagon temple, 443
Sian, China, 261
Siberia, 450, 496
Siddartha Gautama. *See* Buddha
Sierre Leone, 114
  See also Africa
Sihanouk, Norodom, 411
Sinai desert, 81
Singapore, 394
Singh, Khushwant, 255
Sino-Japanese War, First, 279-280
Sino-Japanese War, Second, 345-346
Sino-Soviet Treaty, 319-320
Siqueiros, Alfaro, 600-601
slavery and slave trade 108, 122, 128, 132-134, 142, 205, 576
social institutions
  Africa, 140-154
  China, 289-305
  and culture, 21-24
  India, 215-228
  Japan, 349-361
  Latin America, 558-566
  Middle East, 63-74
  Southeast Asia, 417-422
  Soviet Union, 478-490
socialism
  Africa, 170-171, 174
  Latin America, 572, 584; *see also* Chile; Cuba
  Middle East, (defined) 83, 90-91
  Soviet Union, 484-488
society, defined, 2
Soka Gakkai, 366
Solomon, King of the Jews, 44
Solzhenitsyn, Alexander, 520
Songhai empire, 125-127
South Africa, 111
  See also Africa
Southeast Asia, 391-446
  and agricultural revolution, 13
  climate, 396-397
  cultural contributions, 443-446
  economic activities, 426-434
  geography, 394-395
  history, 400-416
  Japan and, 380-381
  peoples, 387, 409
  political activities, 435-442
  social institutions, 417-425
Soviet Union, 447-526
  Africa and, 174
  China and, 279-280, 285-286, 312, 319-320, 513
  Cuba and, 587; *see also* Cuba

  climate, 450-454
  cultural contributions, 515-526
  economic activities, 491-502
  Ethiopia and, 130
  expansion of Russia, 469-470
  foreign affairs, 510-514
  geography, 450-454
  history, 457-477
  India and, 248, 513
  Japan and, 343-344, 380
  Latin America and, 553-557, 590-593
  peoples, 454-456
  political activities, 503-510
  social institutions, 478-490
sovkhoz, 494
Soyinka, Wole, 180
Spain and the Spanish
  and Arabs, 40, 53-54
  Latin America, 544-547, 590
  Southeast Asia, 404-405
Spanish-American War, 414
Srivijaya, 403
Stakhanov, Alexei, 490
Stalin, Joseph (Joseph Dhugasvili), 473-475, 496, 507, 519, 522
Stalingrad, U.S.S.R., 475
Standing Committee (China), 317
Stanley, Henry, 137
status, social. *See* stratification, social
steppes, 453
Strategic Arms Limitation Treaty (SALT), 512
stratification, social
  Africa, 142-144
  China, 289-291, 298-301
  and culture, 28-30
  India, 215-217
  Japan, 349-350
  Latin America, 558-562
  Middle East, 64-67
  Soviet Union, 478-480, 484
stupa, 249-250
subsistance farming, 427-428, 574
Sudan, 172
  See also Africa
Suez Canal, 58, 62, 85, 95
Suharto, General, 441-442
Sukarno, Achmed, 414, 441
Suleiman, 57, 103
Suleymaniya Mosque, 103
sultan, 56
Sun Goddess, 338, 362
Sun Yat-sen, 281-284
  Three Principles of the People, 281
Sunnah, 72
Sunni Ali, 126
Sunni Muslims, 41, 72
Supreme Soviet, 504-505
Surinam, 529
  See also Latin America

sutras, 225, 354
   Lotus Sutra, 363, 366
Swahili, 118
swaraj, 210
Swaziland, 168
   See also Africa
Syria, 35, 66, 84, 92
Syrian Desert, 34

Taft, William Howard, 415
taiga, 452
Taiping Rebellion, 277
Taiwan, 280, 286, 318-319,
Taj Mahal, 252-253
Tale of the Genji (scroll), 384
Tamayo, Rufino, 600
Tamerlane, 56
Tannenbaum, Frank, 568
Tanzania, 11, 114, 169,
   See also Africa
Taoism, 268-270, 296, 303
Tassili n' Ahaggar, 120
Tatars, 459-461, 525
Tchaikowsky, Peter, 523
tea ceremony, 384-385
Tehran, Iran, 66
Tendai sect, 363
Tenochtitlan, 542
Thailand, 394, 401-402, 408, 419, 421, 439
   See also Southeast Asia
thought reform (China), 304-305
thugi, 205
Tibet, 262-265
Tigris and Euphrates Rivers, 34-36, 43
Timbuktu, Mali, 126
Timor, 404
Titicaca, Lake, 533
Titov, Gherman, 516
Tokugawa, Ieyasu, 339-341
Tokyo, Japan, 336-337, 340
Tolstoy, Leo, 517
Tonkin, Gulf of, 412
torana, 249
totems, 141
trade, 27-28
   See also economic activity; foreign affairs
transportation
   Africa, 162
   China, 265-267
   India, 193, 205, 231
   Japan, 335
   Latin America, 542
   Middle East, 75
   Southeast Asia, 399
   Soviet Union, 454, 498
Transjordan, 60-62
   See also Jordan

Transvaal, 135
   See also Africa
treaties. *See names of treaties*
tribalism, 171-172
tribes
   Baganda (Africa), 129, 151
   bedouin (Middle East), 64-67
   Berbers (Middle East), 40, 54, 64
   Bunyoro (Africa), 143, 145
   Bushmen (Africa), 116-118
   Hottentots (Africa), 116-118
   Ibo (Africa), 140, 164, 166
   Khmer (Southeast Asia), 401
   Kikuyu (Africa), 140, 141, 151
   Luo (Africa), 140
   Pygmies (Africa), 116-118
   Quraysh (Middle East), 48-50
   Swazi (Africa), 143-144
   Turkoman (Middle East), 64
   Zulus (Africa), 135
tributary (tribute) system, 273-276
Trinidad and Tobago, 529
   See also Latin America
Trotsky, Leon, 472-473
Trujillo, Rafael, 584
Tianshan Mountains, 260
Tu Fu, 327-328
Tuaregs, 64
tundra, 451-452
Tunisia, 112
   See also Africa
Turgenev, Ivan, 517
Turkey, 34, 36-37, 56-58, 69-70, 91-94
   See also Middle East
Turks, 41-42
Tutola, Amos, 180
Twenty-four Paragons of Filial Piety, 292

Uaupes, Brazil, 535
Uganda, 163
   See also Africa
Ukraine, U.S.S.R., 507
Ulyanov, Vladamov. *See* Lenin
Umar, 49
Umayyads, 52
underground system (Soviet Union), 499-500, 522
Union of Soviet Socialist Republics (U.S.S.R.). *See* Soviet Union
United Arab Republic (U.A.R.), 92
United Nations Environment Program
   Africa and, 160
United States of America
   Africa and, 172-174
   China and, 280, 318-319
   India and, 248
   Japan and, 341-342, 370, 379-380

   Latin America and, 578-579, 591-593
   Middle East and, 94
   Southeast Asia and, 412-414, 436
   Soviet Union and, 510-512
untouchables (harijans), 217
Upanishads, 221-222
Ural Mountains, 453
urban revolution, 14-15
Uruguay, 528, 555
   See also Latin America
Utamaro, 385
Uxmal, 539

Vaishya, 215-216, 225-226
varna, 206-208
Vasconcelos, José, 595
Vedas, 221
vegetation, world map, 611
   See also Climate; geography
Venezuela, 528, 531, 552, 578, 580
   See also Latin America
viceroyalties, 545
Victoria, Queen of England, 206-207
Victoria Falls, Lake, 115
Viet Cong (National Front for Liberation of South Vietnam), 411
Viet Minh (Vietnam Independence League), 409-410
Vietnam, 279, 318, 392, 402, 408-412, 418-419, 437-438, 445-446
   See also Southeast Asia
Vikings, 457
Villa-Lobos, Heitor, 599-600
Vishnu, 221-222, 443
Vladimir I, Ruler of Kiev, 458
Vladivostok, U.S.S.R., 469
Volga River, 454, 461
voodoo, 568

Wadis, 32
War of the Pacific, 589-590
white priests, 474-475
Whites (Russians), 473
women's roles and rights
   Africa, 124, 144-146, 150
   China, 291-292, 298-300, 313
   India, 218-220
   Japan, 351-359
   Latin America, 562-566
   Middle East, 67-70, 91
   Southeast Asia, 417-419
   Soviet Union, 480, 485-486
World War I, 59-60, 210, 344, 471-473
World War II, 285-286, 311, 346-347, 369, 406, 474-475
Wu Ch'eng-en, 328

X

Xi River, 260-261, 267
Xinjiang (Sinkiang), 261, 512

Y

Yakutsk, U.S.S.R., 456
Yamato clan, 338-339
Ya'qubi, 52
Yasunari, Kawabata, 387-388
Yenisei River 453
Yermak, 469
Yezhov, Nicholas, 474
Yokohama, Japan, 336
Youlou, Fulbert, President of Congo, 171
Young Communist League (China), 317
Young Pioneers (China), 317
Yuan Shih-kai, General, 282
Yucatan, 539
  See also Latin America; Mexico
Yugoslavia, 511
  See also Soviet Union

Z

Zagros Mountains, 36
zaibatsu, 368, 371
Zaire, 112, 114-115
  See also Africa
Zambezi River, 114–115
Zambia, 114–115
  See also Africa
zamindar, 205
Zanzibar, 137
Zen Buddhism, 365, 383
Zhejiang, China, 265
Zhou Enlai (Chou En-lai), 317
Zimbabwe, 114-115, 128-129, 174
  See also Africa
Zionism, 60
Zorastrian Religion, 48

Acknowledgments

Maps

The maps used in this book were adapted from Ginn Social Studies, copyright © 1986, except the map on page 17, which was drawn by Norman C. Adams.

Pictures

Page
- iii *Title Page:* The Oriental Institute of Chicago/Rosenthal Art Slides
- 1 *Unit Opening Photographs:* (full page) Art Resource, NY; (inset) The Oriental Institute of Chicago/Rosenthal Art Slides
- 3 (top left) Paul Conklin; (left) Alan Band Associates; (right) S. Kessler/STOCK, Boston
- 9 American Museum of Natural History, New York
- 12 D. Cooper/Anthro-Photo
- 14 (both) The University Museum, University of Pennsylvania
- 17 United Nations
- 23 Peter Menzel/STOCK, Boston
- 25 Tass from Sovfoto
- 27 Paul Conklin
- 29 (left) P. Wolf/Alpha; (right) United Nations/ILO
- 31 *Unit Opening Photographs:* (full page) Abu-Lughod/Anthro-Photo; (inset) C. K. Walter/The Picture Cube
- 38 (left) Owen Franken/STOCK, Boston; (right) Pix, Inc.
- 41 N. Keddie/Anthro-Photo
- 44 Courtesy of the Metropolitan Museum of Art, Rogers Fund, 1916
- 46 Art Resource, NY
- 47 Alan Band Associates
- 51 Seattle Art Museum
- 55 Biblioteca Nacional, Madrid
- 58 Keystone Press Agency
- 60 Zionist Archives and Library
- 61 Zionist Archives and Library
- 64 DeWys, Inc. (Englebert)
- 65 (left) Chris Walter/Anthro-Photo; (top right) M. Tyler/Anthro-Photo; (bottom right) Borys Malkin/Anthro-Photo
- 69 Owen Franken/STOCK, Boston
- 71 Courtesy of Arthur T. Gregorian
- 73 Art Resource, NY
- 74 A. Dejean/Sygma
- 77 (top) Middle East Features/Black Star; (bottom) Erich Hartmann/Magnum
- 78 Art Resource, NY
- 80 (top) Art Resource, NY; (bottom) Jacques Pavlovsky/Sygma
- 81 DeWys, Inc.
- 85 Standard Oil Company of New Jersey
- 90 AP/Wide World Photos
- 91 AP/Wide World Photos
- 92 James Nachtwey/Black Star
- 94 (top) Keystone Press Agency; (bottom) Art Resource, NY
- 95 P. Manoukian/Sygma
- 98 GAC Photo Archives

629

Page	Credit
100	Library of Congress
103	Hans Parzelt, Munich
104	Art Resource, NY
105	Courtesy of the Metropolitan Museum of Art, bequest of Edward C. Moore, 1891
107	*Unit Opening Photographs:* (full page) Heisey/Alpha; (inset) Marc and Evelyne Bernheim/Woodfin Camp Associates
113	Rilling/Anthro-Photo
115	Heisey/Alpha
116	Shostak/Anthro-Photo
121	(top) Mme. Irene Lhote; (bottom) Eliot Elisofon
125	British Museum
128	Kofod/FPG
130	Keystone Press Agency
131	The Newberry Library, Chicago
134	New Haven Colony Historical Society
136	Historical Pictures Service
138	American Museum of Natural History
141	(both) Owen Franken/STOCK, Boston
143	Ruth MacDonald
146	B. Campbell/Sygma
147	Paul Conklin
148	Marc and Evelyne Bernheim/Woodfin Camp Associates
152	D. Henrioud/WHO
153	Owen Franken/STOCK, Boston
158	(top left) Devore/Anthro-Photo; (bottom left; right) Baldwin/Anthro-Photo
161	Keystone Press Agency
167	B. Campbell/Sygma
169	(top) Keystone Press Agency; (bottom) A. Dejean/Sygma
170	Marc and Evelyne Bernheim/Woodfin Camp Associates
171	United Nations
172	Tannenbaum/Sygma
173	AP/Wide World Photos
177	Afro Audio-Visual
178	(left) Eliot Elisofon; (right) Museum of Primitive Art, NY
179	(left) Museum of Primitive Art, NY; (right) Segy Gallery for African Art
180	AP/Wide World Photos
181	Peter Dublin
182	(all) Marc and Evelyne Bernheim/Woodfin Camp Associates
183	T. Vacca/Anthro-Photo
185	*Unit Opening Photographs:* (both) Art Resource, NY
190	Bettmann Archive
192	Agency for International Development
196	(left) Rapho Guillumette; (top right) Department of Archaeology, Government of Pakistan; (bottom right) Museum of Fine Arts, Boston
199	GAC Photo Archives
201	Fogg Art Museum, Harvard University
203	GAC Photo Archives
206	Culver Pictures
209	Historical Pictures Service
211	UPI/Bettmann Archive
213	AP/Wide World Photos
215	(left) Cary Wolinsky/STOCK, Boston; (right) Doranne Jacobson/Art Resource, NY
218	Cary Wolinsky/STOCK, Boston
219	Doranne Jacobson/Art Resource, NY
221	(top) Burt Glinn/Magnum; (bottom) Umberto La Paglia
222	(all) Museum of Fine Arts, Boston
223	Doranne Jacobson/Art Resource, NY
224	Bettmann Archive
227	Cary Wolinsky/STOCK, Boston
231	United Nations
234	(both) CARE

236	(left) Cary Wolinsky/STOCK, Boston; (right) Jehangir Gazdar/Woodfin Camp Associates
237	A. Nogues/Sygma
242	AP/Wide World Photos
244	Raghu Rai/Magnum
245	Raghu Rai/Magnum
247	Alastair Matheson/UNICEF
250	(top) Museum of Fine Arts, Boston; (bottom) Art Resource, NY
251	Federico Borromeo/Art Resource, NY
252	Marilyn Silverstone/Magnum
254	Museum of Fine Arts, Boston
255	(top) AP/Wide World Photos; (bottom) Raghu Rai/Magnum
257	*Unit Opening Photographs:* (full page) S. Van Etten/The Picture Cube; (inset) Gwendolyn Stewart
263	Alan Band Associates
264	(top) Michal Heron; (bottom) Eastfoto
265	Alan Band Associates
266	Eastfoto
269	Museum of Fine Arts, Boston
271	Marc Riboud/Magnum
274	National Palace Museum, Taipei
275	Peabody Museum, Salem/Mark Sexton
278	Brown Brothers
280	US Signal Corps/National Archives
281	UPI/Bettmann Archive
283	(top) AP/Wide World Photos; (bottom) UPI/Bettmann Archive
284	Eastfoto
287	Henri Cartier-Bresson/Magnum
290	Bettmann Archive
291	Museum of Fine Arts, Boston
292	(both) Scott Stamp & Coin Company
293	(both) Scott Stamp & Coin Company
295	Museum of Fine Arts, Boston
297	Bettmann Archive
300	Eastfoto
303	Eastfoto
307	(top) Eastfoto; (bottom) S-E. Hedin/carl e. östman
309	Alan Band Associates
311	Eastfoto
315	Eastfoto
316	Henri Bureau/Magnum
317	Arthur Grace/Sygma
319	AP/Wide World Photos
322	The Granger Collection
323	Marc Riboud/Magnum
324	Museum of Fine Arts, Boston
325	Rene Burri/Magnum
326	(left) The Smithsonian Institution, Freer Gallery of Art, Washington DC; (right) Robert S. Crandall, from The Granger Collection
327	Robert S. Crandall, from The Granger Collection
328	Gwendolyn Stewart
330	Marc Riboud/Magnum
331	*Unit Opening Photographs:* (both) James H. Simon/The Picture Cube
336	Umberto La Paglia
340	The Smithsonian Institution, Freer Gallery of Art, Washington
342	(left) U.S. Bureau of Ships; (right) Collection of the Chrysler Museum of Norfolk, Virginia
343	Library of Congress
345	Historical Pictures Service
347	UPI/Bettmann Archive
349	Library of Congress
352	(all) Peter Dublin
353	Alan Band Associates

631

355	Marilyn Silverstone/Magnum
358	Japan Information Center, Consulate General of Japan
360	Richard Kaivar/Magnum
362	Umberto La Paglia
364	(both) Rene Burri/Magnum
369	Victor Minca/Art Resource, NY
370	Rene Burri/Magnum
378	Japan Information Center, Consulate General of Japan
379	Richard Kaivar/Magnum
381	AP/Wide World Photos
382	Japan Information Center, Consulate General of Japan
383	Museum of Fine Arts, Boston
384	Henri Cartier-Bresson/Magnum
386	J. Cannon/carl e. östmann
387	Orion Press
388	Peter Dublin
391	*Unit Opening Photographs:* (full page) Joel Halpern/Anthro-Photo; (inset) David Agee/Anthro-Photo
396	Bettmann Archive
398	Umberto La Paglia
399	Theodore Pikora
400	Bradley Smith/Gemini Smith
403	British Museum
405	Matthew Naythons/STOCK, Boston
406	Bettmann Archive
409	Alan Band Associates
410	Robert Capa/Magnum
412	Rene Burri/Magnum
414	Fred Mayer/Magnum
415	Culver Pictures
416	Alan Band Associates
418	Alan Band Associates
419	DeWys, Inc. (Englebert)
420	Theodore Pikora
423	Umberto La Paglia
424	John Launois/Black Star
426	Wolfe Worldwide
429	P. J. Griffiths/Magnum
431	(both) Werner Bischof/Magnum
432	Anna Riwkin/carl e. östmann
437	Burk Uzzle/Magnum
438	Jean-Claude Labbe/Gamma
440	Matsumoto/Sygma
444	Marc Riboud/Magnum
445	DeWys, Inc. (Englebert)
447	*Unit Opening Photographs:* (full page) Tass from Sovfoto; (inset) S. Van Etten
452	Sovfoto
454	(left) Erich Lessing/Magnum; (right) Tass from Sovfoto
455	Tass from Sovfoto
458	Sovfoto
460	(top) Art Resource NY; (bottom) Gwendolyn Stewart
463	Gwendolyn Stewart
464	Tass from Sovfoto
465	Tass from Sovfoto
467	Tass from Sovfoto
468	Bettmann Archive
470	Library of Congress
472	Sovfoto
474	AP/Wide World Photos
476	Eastfoto
477	Tass from Sovfoto

479	Anna Cross/Sovfoto
482	Novosti from Sovfoto
485	Sovfoto
487	Gwendolyn Stewart
489	Tass from Sovfoto
490	S. Zal/Sygma
493	Art Resource, NY
497	Marc Riboud/Magnum
500	Fabian/Sygma
501	Esko Newhill
506	(left) Alan Band Associates; (all others) Sovfoto
508	S-E. Hedin/carl e. östman
509	Tass from Sovfoto
511	Tass from Sovfoto
513	Novosti from Sovfoto
516	Esko Newhill
517	(both) Sovfoto
518	Sovfoto
520	AP/Wide World Photos
521	Sovfoto
523	Sovfoto
524	Sovfoto
527	*Unit Opening Photographs:* (full page) Ulrike Welsch; (inset) Steve Maines/STOCK, Boston
530	Ulrike Welsch
533	Martin Rogers/STOCK, Boston
539	Art Resource, NY
540	Art Resource, NY
541	Eric Simmons/STOCK, Boston
542	Borys Malkin/Anthro-Photo
546	The Museum of Mankind
547	Historical Pictures Service
548	(all) Culver Pictures
551	(top) Bettmann Archive; (bottom) GAC Photo Archives
554	Culver Pictures
555	Peter L. Gould
556	Patrick Chauvel/Sygma
560	Edward Grazda/Magnum
561	Ellis Herwig/STOCK, Boston
562	Frank Wing/STOCK, Boston
564	(all) Ulrike Welsch
567	Batya Weinbaum
569	Peter Menzel/STOCK, Boston
570	NCPhoto
573	Ira Kirschenbaum/STOCK, Boston
575	(top) Weldon King/FPG; (all others) Wil Wilkins/Alpha
579	UPI/Bettmann Archive
581	D. Goldberg/Sygma
586	AP/Wide World Photos
587	AP/Wide World Photos
588	C. Urraca/Sygma
592	AP/Wide World Photos
596	AP/Wide World Photos
597	Susan Meiselas/Magnum
599	Nancy Sayles Day Collection of Modern Latin American Art, Museum of Art, Rhode Island School of Design
600	By permission of the Trustees of Dartmouth College
601	Rene Burri/Magnum